ROAD ATLAS

2023 BRITAIN & IRELAND

CW00821967

www.philips-maps.co.uk

First published in 2009 as
Complete Road Atlas Britain and Ireland by Philip's,
a division of Octopus Publishing Group Ltd
www.octopusbooks.co.uk
Carmelite House, 50 Victoria Embankment
London EC4Y 0DZ
An Hachette UK Company
www.hachette.co.uk
Fourteenth edition 2022
First impression 2022

ISBN 978-1-84907-609-8 spiral-bound
ISBN 978-1-84907-608-1 perfect-bound

Cartography by Philip's
Copyright © 2022 Philip's

This product includes mapping data licensed from Ordnance Survey®, with the permission of the Controller of Her Majesty's Stationery Office. © Crown copyright 2022. All rights reserved. Licence number 100011710.

The map of Ireland on pages XVI–XVII is based upon the Crown Copyright and is reproduced with the permission of Land & Property Services under delegated authority from the Controller of Her Majesty's Stationery Office, © Crown Copyright and database right 2022, PMLPA number 100503, and on Ordnance Survey Ireland by permission of the Government © Ordnance Survey Ireland / Government of Ireland Permit number 9257.

Information for National Parks, Areas of Outstanding Natural Beauty, National Trails and Country Parks in Wales supplied by the Countryside Council for Wales.

Information for National Parks, Areas of Outstanding Natural Beauty, National Trails and Country Parks in England supplied by Natural England. Data for Regional Parks, Long Distance Footpaths and Country Parks in Scotland provided by Scottish Natural Heritage.

Gaelic name forms used in the Western Isles provided by Comhairle nan Eilean.

Data for the National Nature Reserves in England provided by Natural England. Data for the National Nature Reserves in Wales provided by Countryside Council for Wales. Darparwyd data'n ymwneud â Gwarchodfeydd Natur Cenedlaethol Cymru gan Gyngor Cefn Gwlad Cymru.

Information on the location of National Nature Reserves in Scotland was provided by Scottish Natural Heritage.

Data for National Scenic Areas in Scotland provided by the Scottish Executive Office. Crown copyright material is reproduced with the permission of the Controller of HMSO and the Queen's Printer for Scotland. Licence number C02W0003960.

Printed in China

*Data from Nielsen Total Consumer Market 2021 weeks 1-52

CONTENTS

II Key to map symbols

III Smart motorways and motorway service areas

IV Restricted motorway junctions

VI Route planning maps

XVI Road map of Ireland

XVIII Tourism and transport

XX Distances and journey times

1 Key to road map pages

2 Road maps of Britain

161 Urban approach maps

161 Bristol *approaches*
162 Birmingham *approaches*
164 Cardiff *approaches*
165 Edinburgh *approaches*
166 Glasgow *approaches*

167 Leeds *approaches*
168 London *approaches*
172 Liverpool *approaches*
173 Manchester *approaches*
174 Newcastle *approaches*

175 Town plans

175 Aberdeen, Ayr, Bath
176 Birmingham, Blackpool, Bournemouth
177 Bradford, Brighton, Bristol
178 Bury St Edmunds, Cambridge, Canterbury, Cardiff
179 Carlisle, Chelmsford, Cheltenham, Chester
180 Chichester, Colchester, Coventry, Derby
181 Dorchester, Dumfries, Dundee, Durham
182 Edinburgh, Exeter, Gloucester
183 Glasgow, Grimsby, Harrogate
184 Hull, Inverness, Ipswich, Kendal
185 King's Lynn, Lancaster, Leeds
186 London
188 Leicester, Lincoln, Liverpool
189 Llandudno, Llanelli, Luton, Macclesfield

190 Manchester, Maidstone, Merthyr Tydfil
191 Middlesbrough, Milton Keynes, Newcastle, Newport
192 Newquay, Northampton, Norwich, Nottingham
193 Oxford, Perth, Peterborough, Plymouth
194 Poole, Portsmouth, Preston, Reading
195 St Andrews, Salisbury, Scarborough, Shrewsbury,
196 Sheffield, Stoke-on-Trent (Hanley), Southampton
197 Southend, Stirling, Stratford-upon-Avon, Sunderland
198 Swansea, Swindon, Taunton, Telford
199 Torquay, Truro, Winchester, Windsor
200 Wolverhampton, Worcester, Wrexham, York

201 Index to town plans

213 Index to road maps of Britain

Inside back cover:
County and unitary authority boundaries

Road map symbols

M3	Motorway, toll motorway
5 8	Motorway junction – full, restricted access
S S	Motorway service area – full, restricted access
	Motorway under construction
A303	Primary route – dual, single carriageway
S	Service area, roundabout, multi-level junction
4 5	Numbered junction – full, restricted access
	Primary route under construction
	Narrow primary route
Newbury	Primary destination
A303	A road – dual, single carriageway
	A road under construction, narrow A road
B3089	B road – dual, single carriageway
	B road under construction, narrow B road
	Minor road – over 4 metres, under 4 metres wide
	Minor road with restricted access
2	Distance in miles
TOLL	Toll, steep gradient – arrow points downhill
	Tunnel
	National trail – England and Wales
	Long distance footpath – Scotland
	Railway with station
	Level crossing, tunnel
	Preserved railway with station
	National boundary
	County / unitary authority boundary
	Car ferry, catamaran
	Passenger ferry, catamaran
	Hovercraft
CALAIS	Ferry destination
Ferry	Car ferry – river crossing
	Principal airport, other airport
	National park, Area of Outstanding Natural Beauty – England and Wales National Scenic Area – Scotland Forest park / regional park / national forest
	Beach
	Linear antiquity
	Roman road
1643	Hillfort, battlefield – with date
261	Viewpoint, nature reserve, spot height – in metres
	Golf course, youth hostel, sporting venue
	Camp site, caravan site, camping and caravan site
P&R	Shopping village, park and ride
29	Adjoining page number – road maps

Approach map symbols

M6	Motorway
	Toll motorway
6 5	Motorway junction – full, restricted access
S	Service area
	Under construction
A6	Primary route – dual, single carriageway
S	Service area
	Multi-level junction
	roundabout
	Under construction
A195	A road – dual, single carriageway
B1288	B road – dual, single carriageway
	Minor road – dual, single carriageway
	Ring road
3	Distance in miles
	Congestion charge area
COSELEY	Railway with station
LOXDALE	Tramway with station
M	Underground or metro station

Town plan symbols

	Motorway
	Primary route – dual, single carriageway
	A road – dual, single carriageway
	B road – dual, single carriageway
	Minor through road
	One-way street
	Pedestrian roads
	Shopping streets
	Railway with station
City Hall	Tramway with station

	Bus or railway station building
	Shopping precinct or retail park
	Park
	Building of public interest
	Theatre, cinema
P	Parking, shopmobility
Bank	Underground station
West St	Metro station
H	Hospital, Police station
PO	Post office

Tourist information

Abbey, cathedral or priory	Farm park	Race course
Ancient monument	Garden	Roman antiquity
Aquarium	Historic ship	Safari park
Art gallery	House	Theme park
Bird collection or aviary	House and garden	Tourist information
Castle	Motor racing circuit	Zoo
Church	Museum	Other place of interest
Country park England and Wales Scotland	Picnic area	
	Preserved railway	

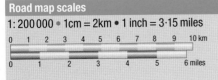

Road map scales
1 : 200 000 • 1cm = 2km • 1 inch = 3·15 miles

0 1 2 3 4 5 6 7 8 9 10 km

0 1 2 3 4 5 6 miles

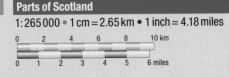

Parts of Scotland
1 : 265 000 • 1cm = 2.65 km • 1 inch = 4.18 miles

0 2 4 6 8 10 km

0 1 2 3 4 5 6 miles

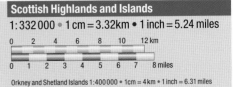

Scottish Highlands and Islands
1 : 332 000 • 1cm = 3.32km • 1 inch = 5.24 miles

0 2 4 6 8 10 12 km

0 1 2 3 4 5 6 7 8 miles

Orkney and Shetland Islands 1 : 400 000 • 1cm = 4 km • 1 inch = 6.31 miles

Smart motorways and motorway service areas

Smart motorways

M1

J6a–J10	Controlled, 4-lane
J10–J13	Dynamic hard shoulder
J16–J13	All lane running ⚠
J19–J16	All lane running
J23a–J24	Controlled, 4-lane
J24–J25	All lane running
J25–J28	Controlled, 4-lane
J28–J31	All lane running
J31–J32	Controlled, 4-lane
J32–J35a	All lane running
J39–J42	All lane running

M3

J2–J4a	All lane running
J9–J14	All lane running (planned)

M4

J3–J12	All lane running ⚠

M4–M5 interchange

M4 J20 / M5 J15
Dynamic hard shoulder*

M5

J4a–J6	All lane running

M6

J2–J4	All lane running
J4–J5	Dynamic hard shoulder
J5–J8	Dynamic hard shoulder
J8–J10a	Dynamic hard shoulder
J10a–J11a	Controlled, 3-lane
J11a–J13	All lane running
J13–J15	All lane running ⚠
J16–J19	All lane running

M20

J3–J5	All lane running
J5–J7	Controlled, 4-lane

M23

J8–J10	All lane running

M25

J2–J3	Controlled, 4-lane
J5–J6	All lane running
J6–J7	Controlled, 4-lane
J7–J11	Controlled, 4-lane
J11–J14	Controlled, 5-lane
J12–J14	Controlled, 4-lane
J14–J15	Controlled, 6-lane
J15–J23	Controlled, 4-lane
J23–J27	All lane running
J27–J30	Controlled, 4-lane

M27

J4–J11	All lane running ⚠

M40–M42 interchange

M42 J3a	All lane running ⚠

M42

J3a–J7	Dynamic hard shoulder
J7–J9	Controlled, 4-lane

M56

J6–J8	All lane running ⚠

M60

J8–J12	Controlled, 3-lane
J12–J17	Controlled, 4-lane

M62

J10–J12	All lane running
J18–J20	All lane running
J20–J25	All lane running (planned)
J25–J26	All lane running
J25–J30	Dynamic hard shoulder
J28–J29	Controlled, 4-lane

⚠ Undergoing conversion to smart motorway
*Scheme full name: *M4 Junctions 19–20 M5 Junctions 16–17*

Information for smart motorways supplied by National Highways

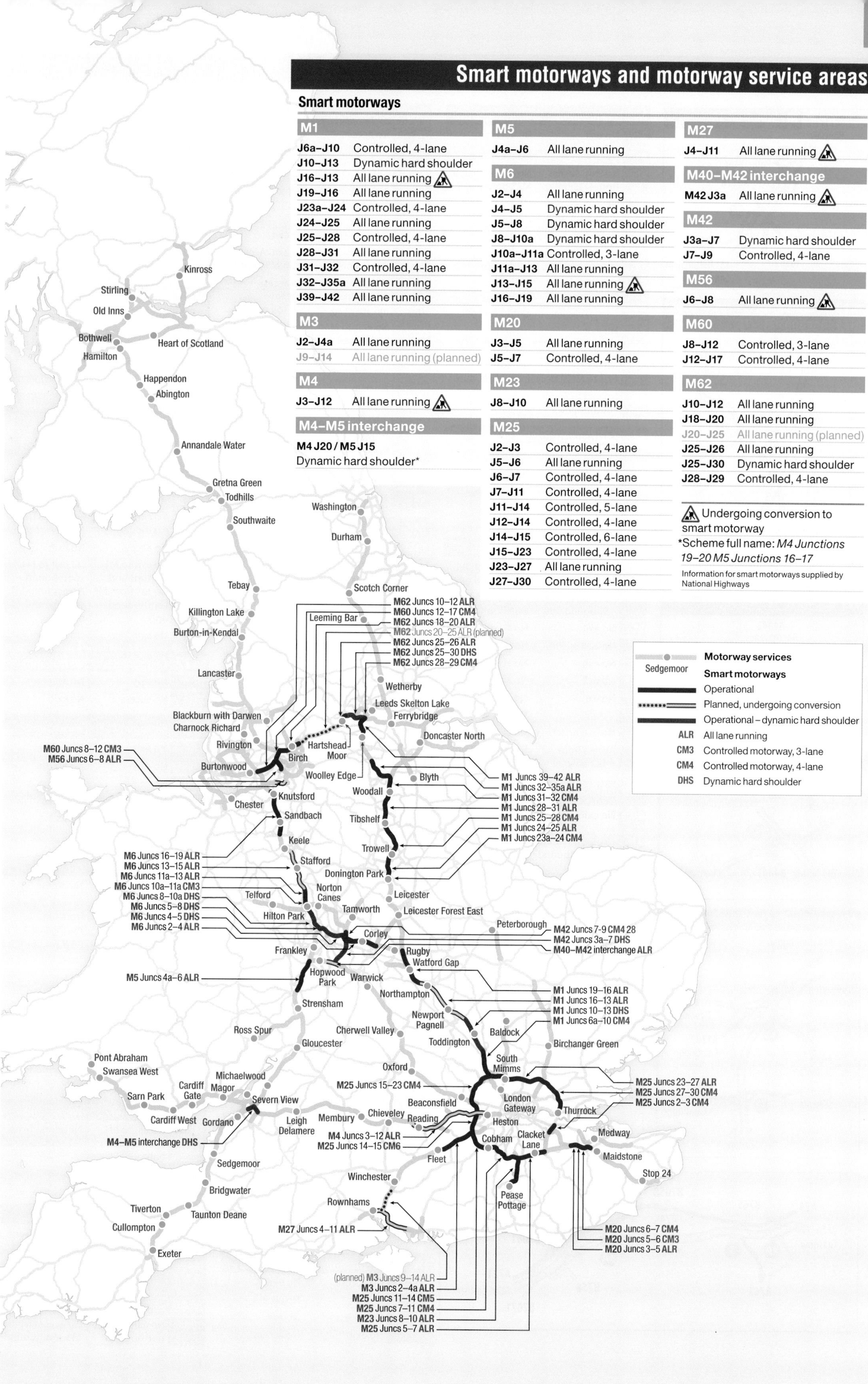

Legend

● Sedgemoor		Motorway services
		Smart motorways
▬▬▬		Operational
┅┅┅		Planned, undergoing conversion
▬▬▬		Operational – dynamic hard shoulder
ALR		All lane running
CM3		Controlled motorway, 3-lane
CM4		Controlled motorway, 4-lane
DHS		Dynamic hard shoulder

Map labels

Kinross
Stirling
Old Inns
Bothwell
Hamilton
Heart of Scotland
Happendon
Abington
Annandale Water
Gretna Green
Todhills
Southwaite
Washington
Durham
Tebay
Killington Lake
Burton-in-Kendal
Lancaster
Scotch Corner
Leeming Bar
Wetherby
Leeds Skelton Lake
Ferrybridge
Doncaster North
Blackburn with Darwen
Charnock Richard
Rivington
Hartshead Moor
Birch
Burtonwood
Woolley Edge
Blyth
Woodall
Knutsford
Chester
Sandbach
Tibshelf
Keele
Trowell
Stafford
Donington Park
Norton Canes
Telford
Leicester
Hilton Park
Tamworth
Leicester Forest East
Corley
Peterborough
Frankley
Rugby
Watford Gap
Hopwood Park
Warwick
Northampton
Strensham
Newport Pagnell
Ross Spur
Cherwell Valley
Baldock
Gloucester
Toddington
Birchanger Green
Pont Abraham
Oxford
South Mimms
Swansea West
Michaelwood
Sarn Park
Cardiff Gate
Magor
Severn View
London Gateway
Thurrock
Cardiff West
Gordano
Leigh Delamere
Membury
Chieveley
Beaconsfield
Reading
Heston
Cobham
Clacket Lane
Medway
Sedgemoor
Fleet
Maidstone
Stop 24
Bridgwater
Winchester
Tiverton
Taunton Deane
Rownhams
Pease Pottage
Cullompton
Exeter

Map annotations

M62 Juncs 10–12 ALR
M60 Juncs 12–17 CM4
M62 Juncs 18–20 ALR
M62 Juncs 20–25 ALR (planned)
M62 Juncs 25–26 ALR
M62 Juncs 25–30 DHS
M62 Juncs 28–29 CM4

M60 Juncs 8–12 CM3
M56 Juncs 6–8 ALR

M1 Juncs 39–42 ALR
M1 Juncs 32–35a ALR
M1 Juncs 31–32 CM4
M1 Juncs 28–31 ALR
M1 Juncs 25–28 CM4
M1 Juncs 24–25 ALR
M1 Juncs 23a–24 CM4

M6 Juncs 16–19 ALR
M6 Juncs 13–15 ALR
M6 Juncs 11a–13 ALR
M6 Juncs 10a–11a CM3
M6 Juncs 8–10a DHS
M6 Juncs 5–8 DHS
M6 Juncs 4–5 DHS
M6 Juncs 2–4 ALR

M5 Juncs 4a–6 ALR

M42 Juncs 7–9 CM4 28
M42 Juncs 3a–7 DHS
M40–M42 interchange ALR

M1 Juncs 19–16 ALR
M1 Juncs 16–13 ALR
M1 Juncs 10–13 DHS
M1 Juncs 6a–10 CM4

M25 Juncs 15–23 CM4
M25 Juncs 23–27 ALR
M25 Juncs 27–30 CM4
M25 Juncs 2–3 CM4

M4–M5 interchange DHS
M4 Juncs 3–12 ALR
M25 Juncs 14–15 CM6

M27 Juncs 4–11 ALR

M20 Juncs 6–7 CM4
M20 Juncs 5–6 CM3
M20 Juncs 3–5 ALR

(planned) M3 Juncs 9–14 ALR
M3 Juncs 2–4a ALR
M25 Juncs 11–14 CM5
M25 Juncs 7–11 CM4
M23 Juncs 8–10 ALR
M25 Juncs 5–7 ALR

Restricted motorway junctions

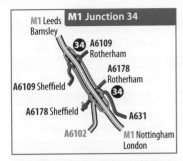

M1 Junction 34

M1 Leeds Barnsley
A6109 Rotherham
A6178 Rotherham
A6109 Sheffield
A6178 Sheffield
A631
A6102
M1 Nottingham London

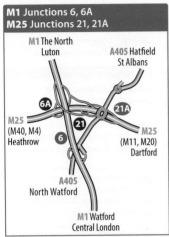

M1 Junctions 6, 6A
M25 Junctions 21, 21A

M1 The North Luton
A405 Hatfield St Albans
M25 (M40, M4) Heathrow
M25 (M11, M20) Dartford
A405 North Watford
M1 Watford Central London

M4 Junctions 25, 25A, 26

A4042 Abergavenny Cwmbran
A4051 Cwmbran
B4596 Caerleon
A4042
A4051 Newport
B4596 Chepstow London
M4 Cardiff

M5 Junction 11A

A417 Gloucester
M5 Cheltenham (A40)
M5 Bristol
B4641
A417 Cirencester

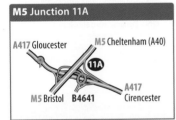

M11 Junctions 13, 14

A14 Huntingdon
A1307 Dry Drayton Oakington
A14 Newmarket
A1307 Cambridge
A428 St Neots
A1303 St Neots
A1303 Cambridge
M11 London

M8 Junctions 8, 9 · M73 Junctions 1, 2

M73 Stirling
M8 Glasgow
A89 Coatbridge
A8 M8 Edinburgh
B7058
A74
M73
A74
B7001
A721
M74 Carlisle
B765
A74
M74 Glasgow
A763
B758
B7071

M1	Northbound	Southbound
2	No exit	No access
4	No exit	No access
6A	No exit. Access from M25 only	No access. Exit to M25 only
7	No exit. Access from A414 only	No access. Exit to A414 only
17	No access. Exit to M45 only	No exit. Access from M45 only
19	No exit to A14	No access from A14
21A	No access	No exit
23A		Exit to A42 only
24A	No exit	No access
35A	No access	No exit
43	No access. Exit to M621 only	No exit. Access from M621 only
48	No exit to A1(M) southbound	

M3	Eastbound	Westbound
8	No exit	No access
10	No access	No exit
13	No access to M27 eastbound	
14	No exit	No access

M4	Eastbound	Westbound
1	Exit to A4 eastbound only	Access from A4 westbound only
2	Access from A4 eastbound only	Access to A4 westbound only
21	No exit	No access
23	No access	No exit
25	No exit	No access
25A	No access	No exit
29	No exit	No access
38		No access
39	No exit or access	No exit
42	Access from A483 only	Exit to A483 only

M5	Northbound	Southbound
10	No exit	No access
11A	No access from A417 eastbound	No exit to A417 westbound

M6	Northbound	Southbound
3A	No access.	No exit. Access from M6 eastbound only
4A	No exit. Access from M42 southbound only	No access. Exit to M42 only
5	No access	No exit
10A	No access. Exit to M54 only	No exit. Access from M54 only
11A	No exit. Access from M6 Toll only	No access. Exit to M6 Toll only
20	No exit to M56 eastbound	No access from M56 westbound
20A	No exit	No access
24	No exit	No access
25	No access	No exit
30	No exit. Access from M61 northbound only	No access. Exit to M61 southbound only
31A	No access	No exit
45	No access	No exit

M6 Toll	Northbound	Southbound
T1		No exit
T2	No exit, no access	No access
T5	No exit	No access
T7	No access	No exit
T8	No access	No exit

M8	Eastbound	Westbound
6	No exit	No access
6A	No access	No exit
7	No Access	No exit
7A	No exit. Access from A725 northbound only	No access. Exit to A725 southbound only
8	No exit to M73 northbound	No access from M73 southbound
9	No access	No exit
13	No exit southbound	Access from M73 southbound only
14	No access	No exit
16	No exit	No access
17	No exit	
18		No exit
19	No exit to A814 eastbound	No access from A814 westbound
20	No exit	No access
21	No access from M74	No exit
22	No exit. Access from M77 only	No access. Exit to M77 only
23	No exit	No access
25	Exit to A739 northbound only. Access from A739 southbound only	
25A	No exit	No access
28	No exit	No access
28A	No exit	No access
29A	No exit	No access

M9	Eastbound	Westbound
2	No access	No exit
3	No exit	No access
6	No access	No exit
8	No exit	No access

M11	Northbound	Southbound
4	No exit	No access
5	No access	No exit
8A	No access	No exit
9	No access	No exit
13	No access	No exit
14	No exit to A428 westbound	No exit. Access from A14 westbound only

M20	Eastbound	Westbound
2	No access	No exit
3	No exit. Access from M26 eastbound only	No access. Exit to M26 westbound only
10	No access	No exit
11A	No access	No exit

M23	Northbound	Southbound
7	No exit to A23 southbound	No access from A23 northbound
10A	No exit	No access

M25	Clockwise	Anticlockwise
5	No exit to M26 eastbound	No access from M26 westbound
19	No access	No exit
21	No exit to M1 southbound. Access from M1 southbound only	No exit to M1 southbound. Access from M1 southbound only
31	No exit	No access

M27	Eastbound	Westbound
10	No exit	No access
12	No access	No exit

M40	Eastbound	Westbound
3	No exit	No access
7	No exit	No access
8	No exit	No access
13	No exit	No access
14	No access	No exit
16	No access	No exit

M42	Northbound	Southbound
1	No exit	No access
7	No access Exit to M6 northbound only	No exit. Access from M6 northbound only
7A	No access. Exit to M6 southbound only	No exit
8	No exit. Access from M6 southbound only	Exit to M6 northbound only. Access from M6 southbound only

M45	Eastbound	Westbound
M1 J17	Access to M1 southbound only	No access from M1 southbound
With A45	No access	No exit

M48	Eastbound	Westbound
M4 J21	No exit to M4 westbound	No access from M4 eastbound
M4 J23	No access from M4 westbound	No exit to M4 eastbound

M49	Southbound	Northbound
18A	No exit to M5 northbound	No access from M5 southbound

M53	Northbound	Southbound
11	Exit to M56 eastbound only. Access from M56 westbound only	Exit to M56 eastbnd only. Access from M56 westbound only

M56	Eastbound	Westbound
2	No exit	No access
3	No access	No exit
4	No exit	No access
7		No access
8	No exit or access	No access
9	No access from M6 northbound	No access to M6 southbound
15	No exit to M53	No access from M53 northbound

M57	Northbound	Southbound
3	No exit	No access
5	No exit	No access

M60	Clockwise	Anticlockwise
2	No exit	
3	No exit to A34 northbound	No exit to A34 northbound
4	No access from M56	No exit to M56
5	No exit to A5103 southbound	No exit to A5103 northbound
14	No exit	No access
16	No exit	No access
20	No access	No exit
22		No access
25	No access	
26		No exit or access
27	No exit	No access

M61	Northbound	Southbound
2	No access from A580 eastbound	No exit to A580 westbound
3	No access from A580 eastbound. No access from A666 southbound	No exit to A580 westbound
M6 J30	No exit to M6 southbound	No access from M6 northbound

M62	Eastbound	Westbound
23	No access	No exit

M65	Eastbound	Westbound
9	No access	No exit
11	No exit	No access

M66	Northbound	Southbound
1	No access	No exit

M67	Eastbound	Westbound
1A	No access	No exit
2	No exit	No access

M69	Northbound	Southbound
2	No exit	No access

M73	Northbound	Southbound
2	No access from M8 eastbound	No exit to M8 westbound

M74	Northbound	Southbound
3	No access	No access
3A	No exit	No access
7	No exit	No access
9	No exit or access	No access
10		No exit
11	No exit	No access
12	No access	No exit

M77	Northbound	Southbound
4	No exit	No access
6	No exit	No access
7	No exit	
8	No access	No access

M80	Northbound	Southbound
4A	No access	No exit
6A	No exit	No access
8	Exit to M876 northbound only. No access	Access from M876 southbound only. No exit

M90	Northbound	Southbound
1	Access from A90 northbound only	No access. Exit to A90 southbound only
2A	No access	No exit
7	No exit	No access
8	No access	No access
10	No access from A912	No exit to A912

M180	Eastbound	Westbound
1	No access	No exit

M621	Eastbound	Westbound
2A	No exit	No access
4	No exit	
5	No access	No exit
6	No access	No exit

M876	Northbound	Southbound
2	No access	No exit

A1(M)	Northbound	Southbound
2	No access	No exit
3		No access
5	No exit	No exit, no access
14	No exit	No access
40	No access	No access
43	No exit. Access from M1 only	No access. Exit to M1 only
57	No access	No exit
65	No access	No exit

A3(M)	Northbound	Southbound
1	No exit	No access
4	No access	No exit

A38(M) with Victoria Rd, (Park Circus) Birmingham	
Northbound	No exit
Southbound	No access

A48(M)	Northbound	Southbound
M4 Junc 29	Exit to M4 eastbound only	Access from M4 westbound only
29A	Access from A48 eastbound only	Exit to A48 westbound only

A57(M)	Eastbound	Westbound
With A5103	No access	No exit
With A34	No access	No exit

A58(M)	Southbound
With Park Lane and Westgate, Leeds	No access

A64(M)	Eastbound	Westbound
With A58 Clay Pit Lane, Leeds	No access from A58	No exit to A58

A74(M)	Northbound	Southbound
18	No access	No exit
22		No exit to A75

A194(M)	Northbound	Southbound
A1(M) J65 Gateshead Western Bypass	Access from A1(M) northbound only	Exit to A1(M) southbound only

M3 Junctions 13, 14
M27 Junction 4

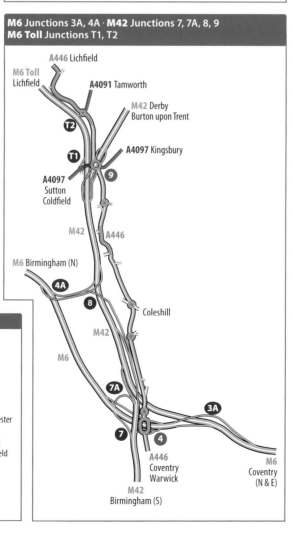

M6 Junctions 3A, 4A · M42 Junctions 7, 7A, 8, 9
M6 Toll Junctions T1, T2

M6 Junction 20 · M56 Junction 9

M62 Junctions 32A, 33 · A1(M) Junctions 40, 41

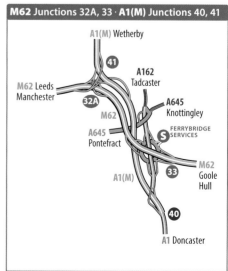

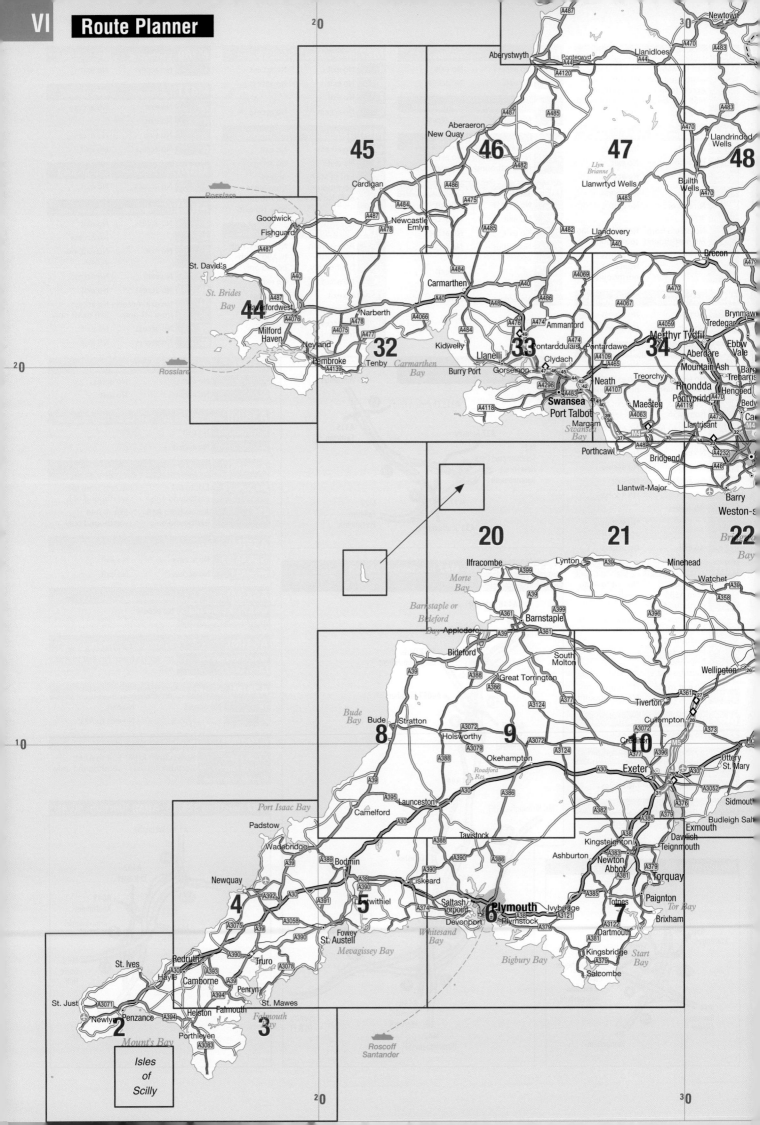

45

46

47

48

Aberystwyth

Llanidloes

Aberaeron
New Quay

Cardigan

Newcastle
Emlyn

Carmarthen

Llandovery

Llandrindod
Wells

Llanwrtyd Wells

Builth
Wells

Brecon

Goodwick
Fishguard

St. David's

St. Brides Bay

44

Haverfordwest

Narberth

Milford Haven

Neyland

Pembroke

32

Tenby

Carmarthen Bay

Kidwelly

Llanelli

Burry Port

33

Ammanford

Pontardawe
Pontardulais
Clydach

Gorseinon

Neath

Swansea
Port Talbot

Margam

Swansea Bay

Porthcawl

34

Merthyr Tydfil

Aberdare
Mountain Ash

Rhondda

Pontypridd

Maesteg

Llantrisant

Bridgend

Brynmawr
Tredegar

Ebbw Vale
Trenarris

Hengoed

Llantwit-Major

Barry
Weston-s

20

Ilfracombe

Lynton

Minehead

Morte Bay

Watchet

Barnstaple

21

Appledore

Bideford

South Molton

Barnstaple or Bideford Bay

Great Torrington

Tiverton

Cullompton

Wellington

8

Bude

Stratton

Bude Bay

Holsworthy

9

Okehampton

Roadford Res.

Crediton

10

Ottery St. Mary

Exeter

Sidmouth

Camelford

Launceston

Tavistock

Budleigh Salt

Exmouth

Port Isaac Bay

Padstow

Wadebridge

Bodmin

Liskeard

Saltash
Torpoint

Kingsteignton

Ashburton

Newton Abbot

Dawlish
Teignmouth

Torquay

Paignton

Tor Bay

Brixham

Newquay

4

Redruth

St. Ives
Hayle

Camborne

Penryn

5

Lostwithiel

Fowey
St. Austell

Mevagissey Bay

Devonport

6
Plymouth
Plymstock

Ivybridge

7

Totnes

Dartmouth

Kingsbridge

Start Bay

Salcombe

Bigbury Bay

Whitesand Bay

Truro

St. Mawes

Falmouth Bay

St. Just

Newlyn
Penzance

Helston

Falmouth

Porthleven

2

Mount's Bay

3

Isles of Scilly

Roscoff
Santander

Rosslare

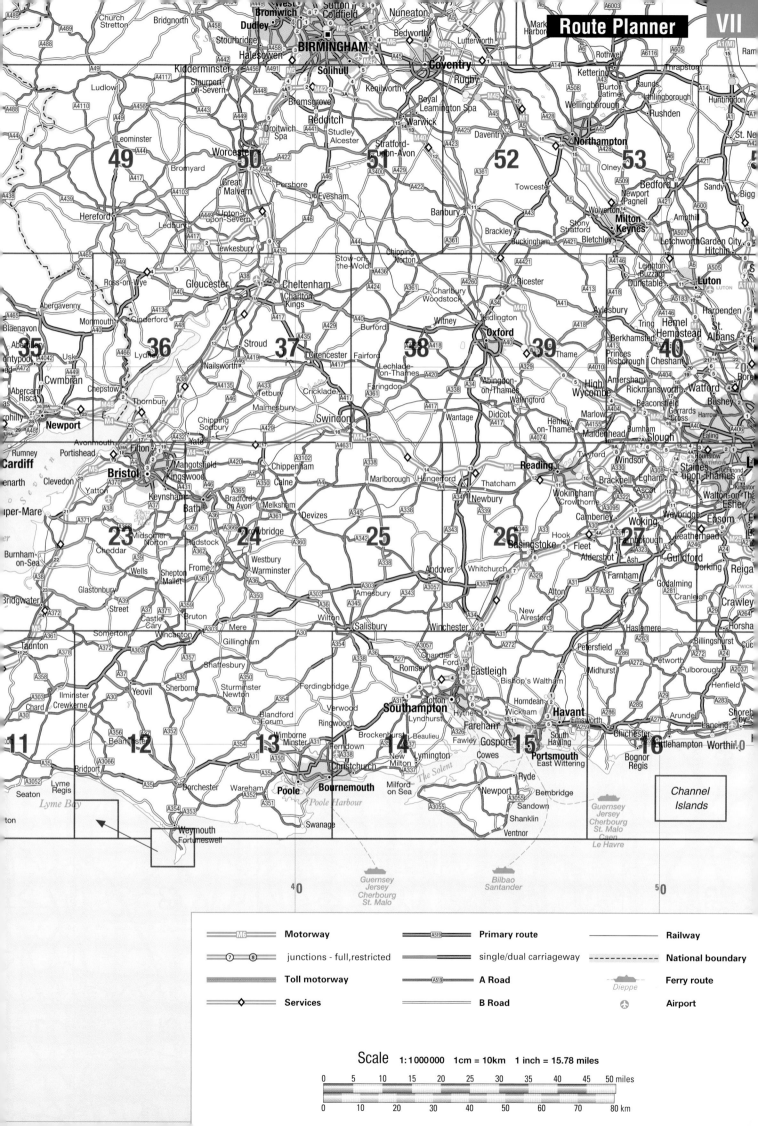

Channel Islands

Scale 1:1 000 000   1cm = 10km   1 inch = 15.78 miles

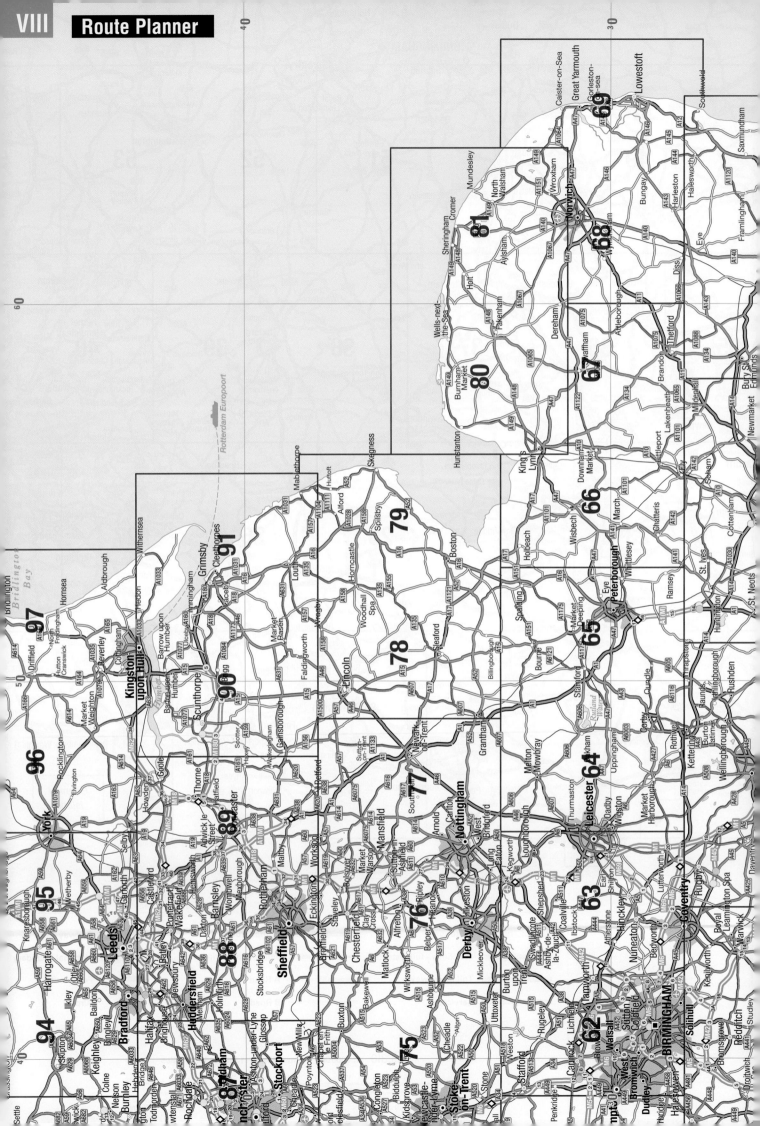

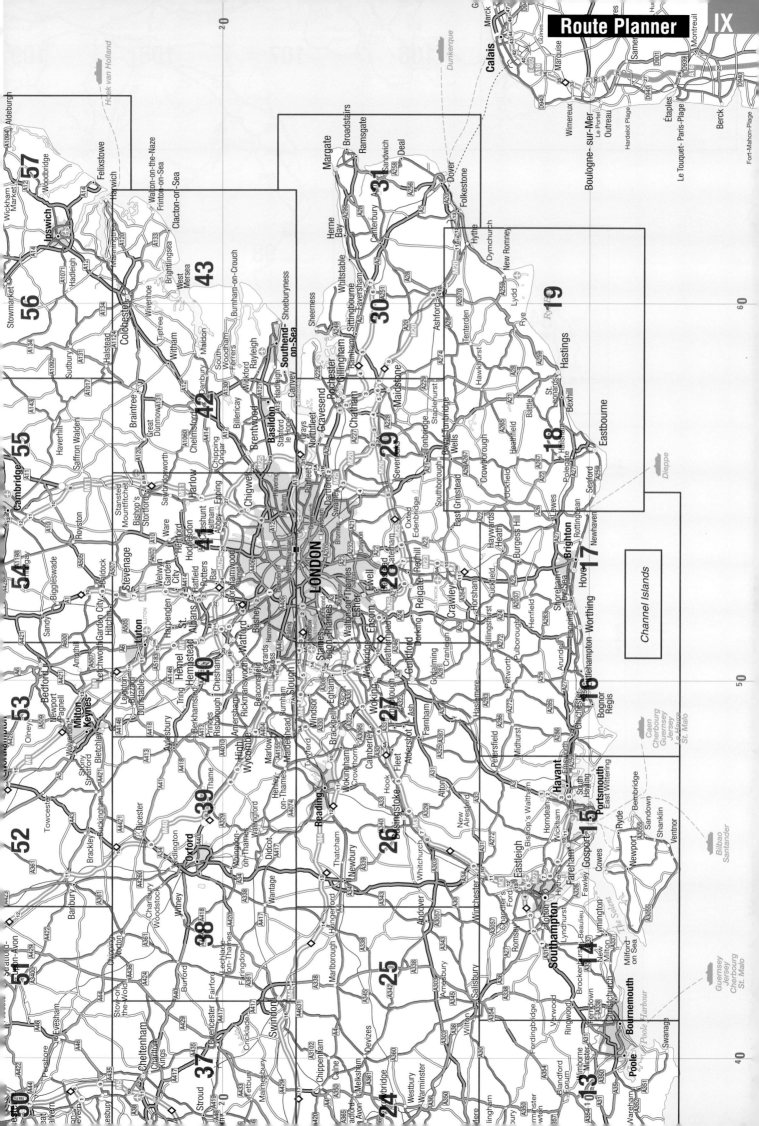

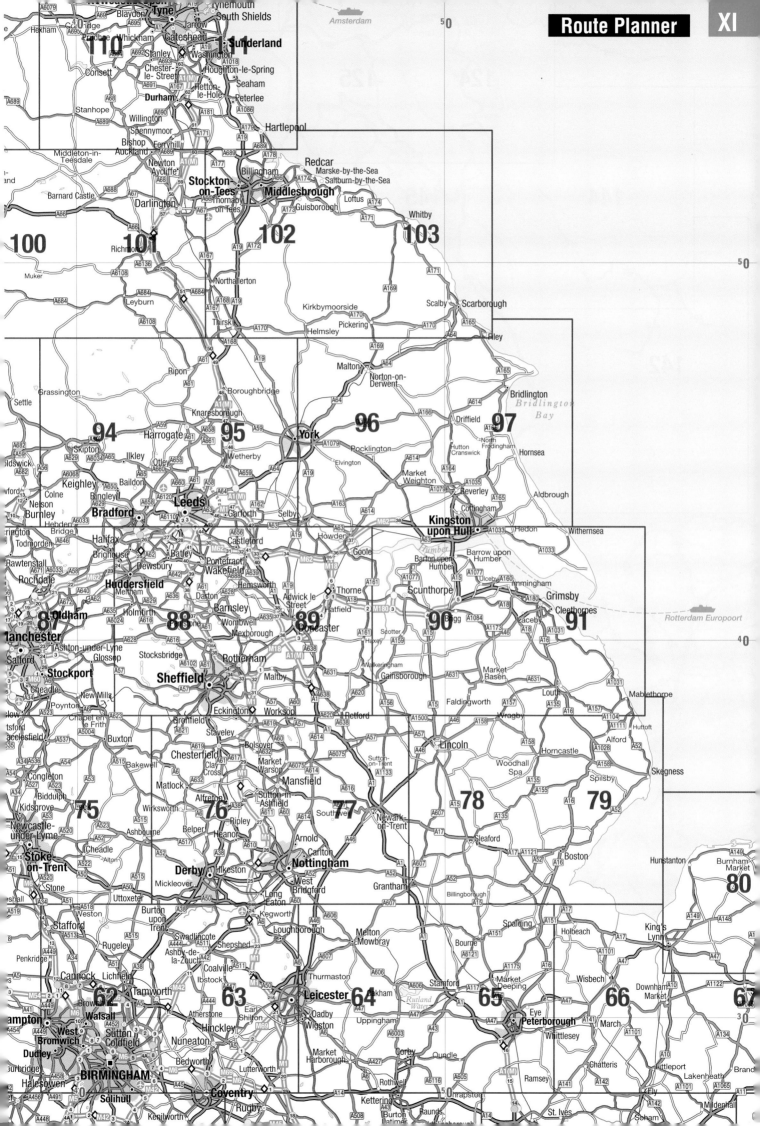

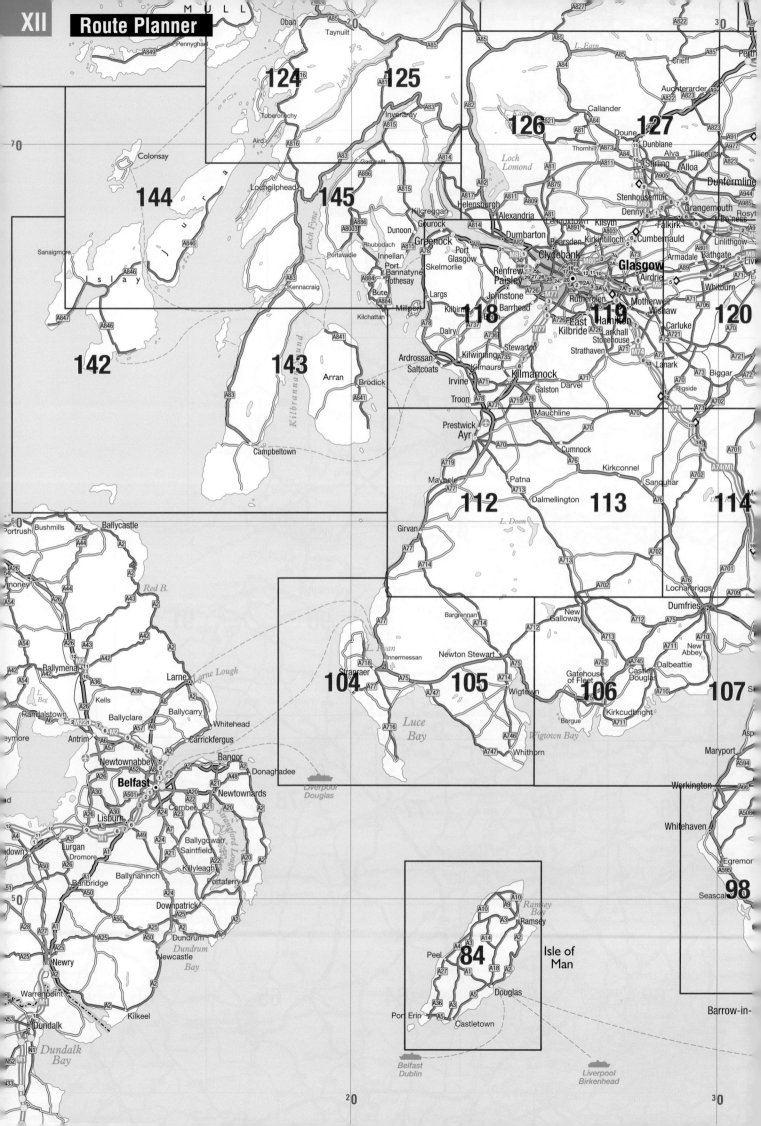

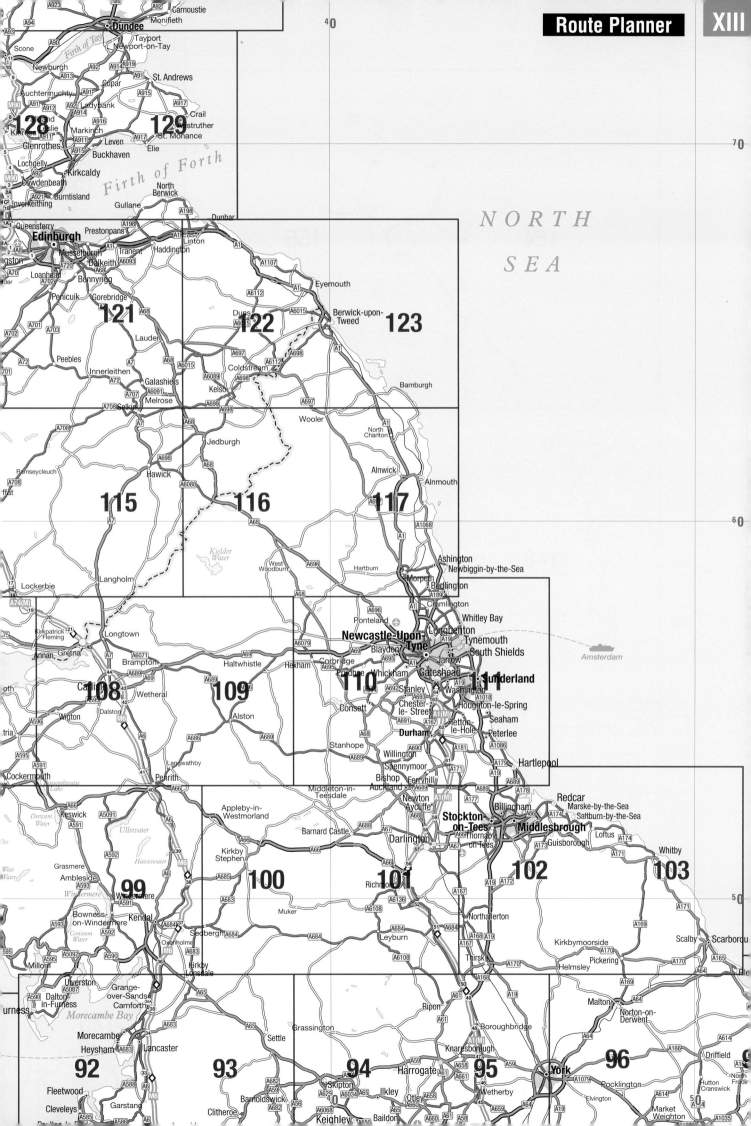

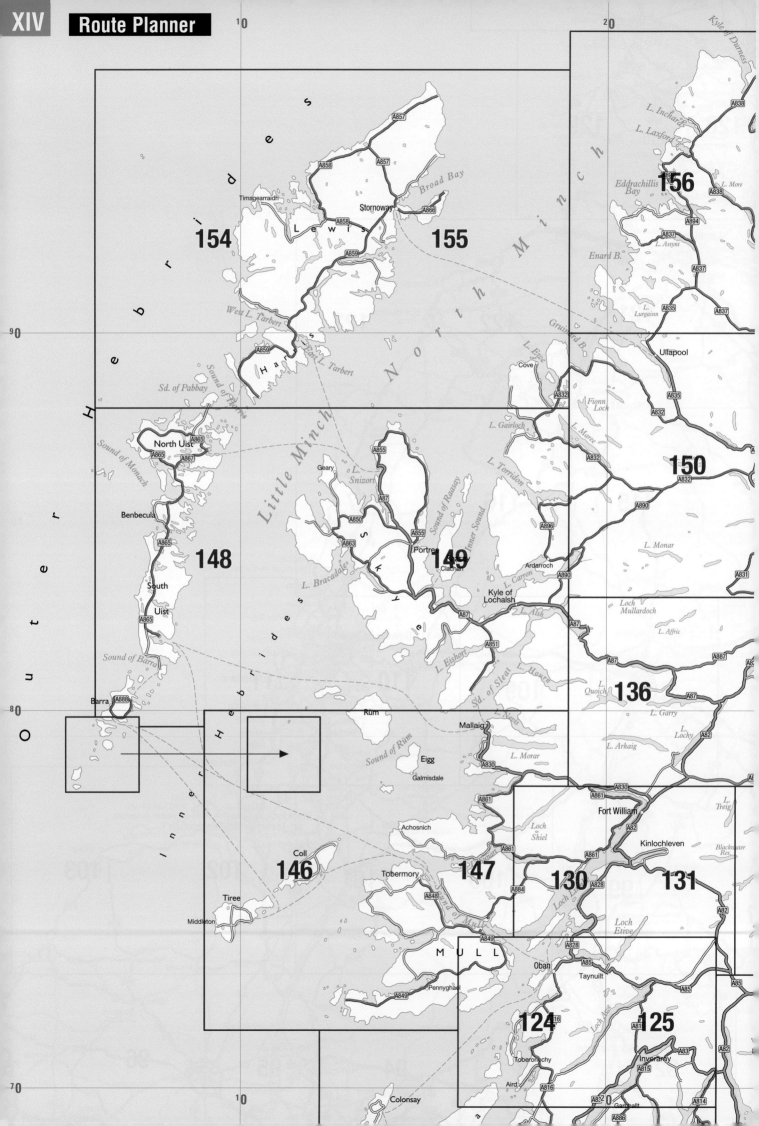

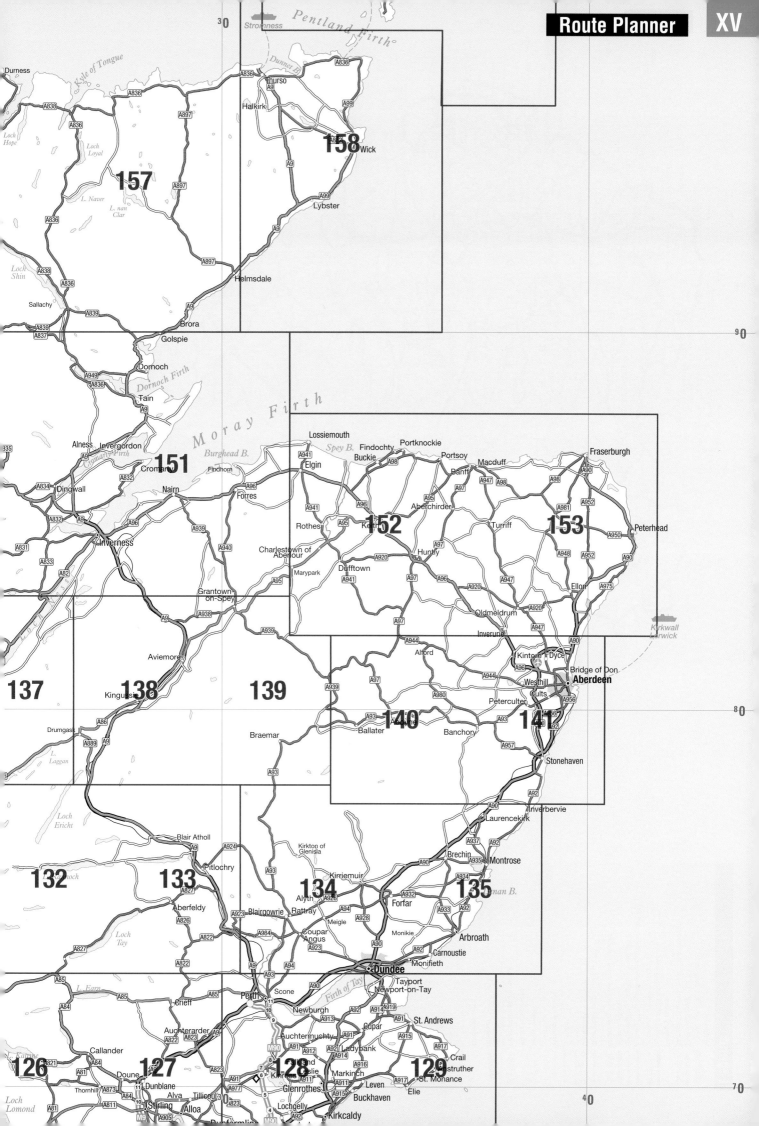

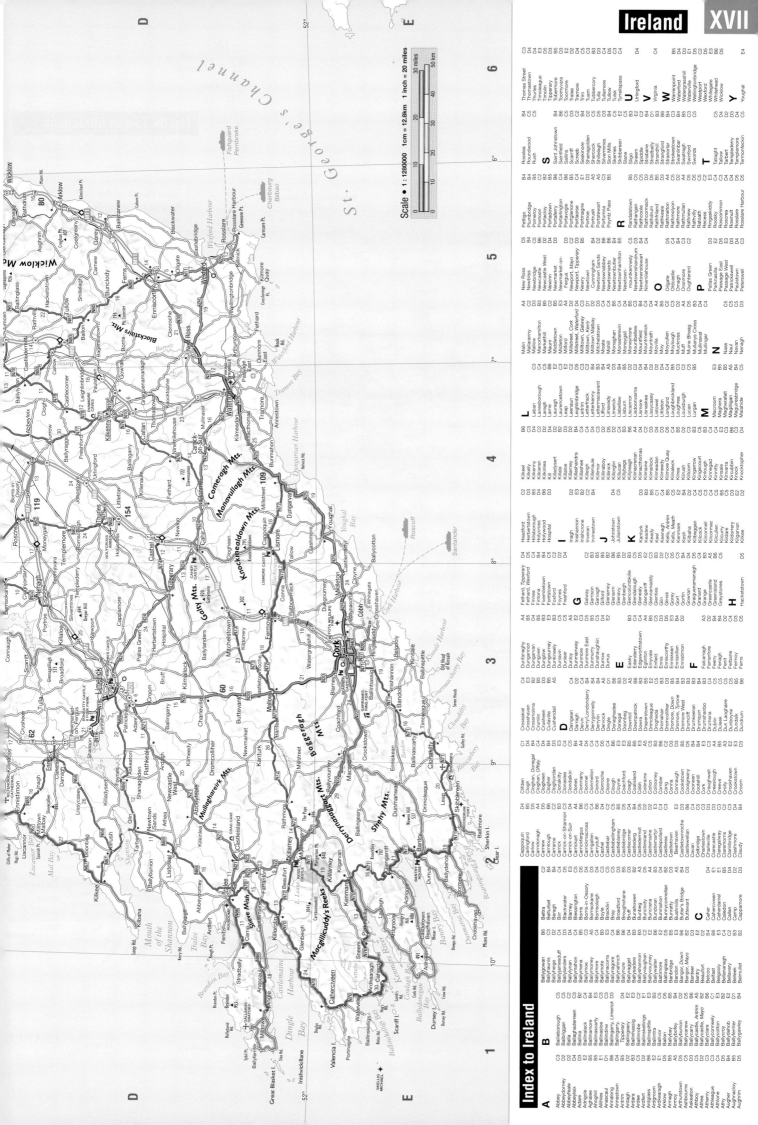

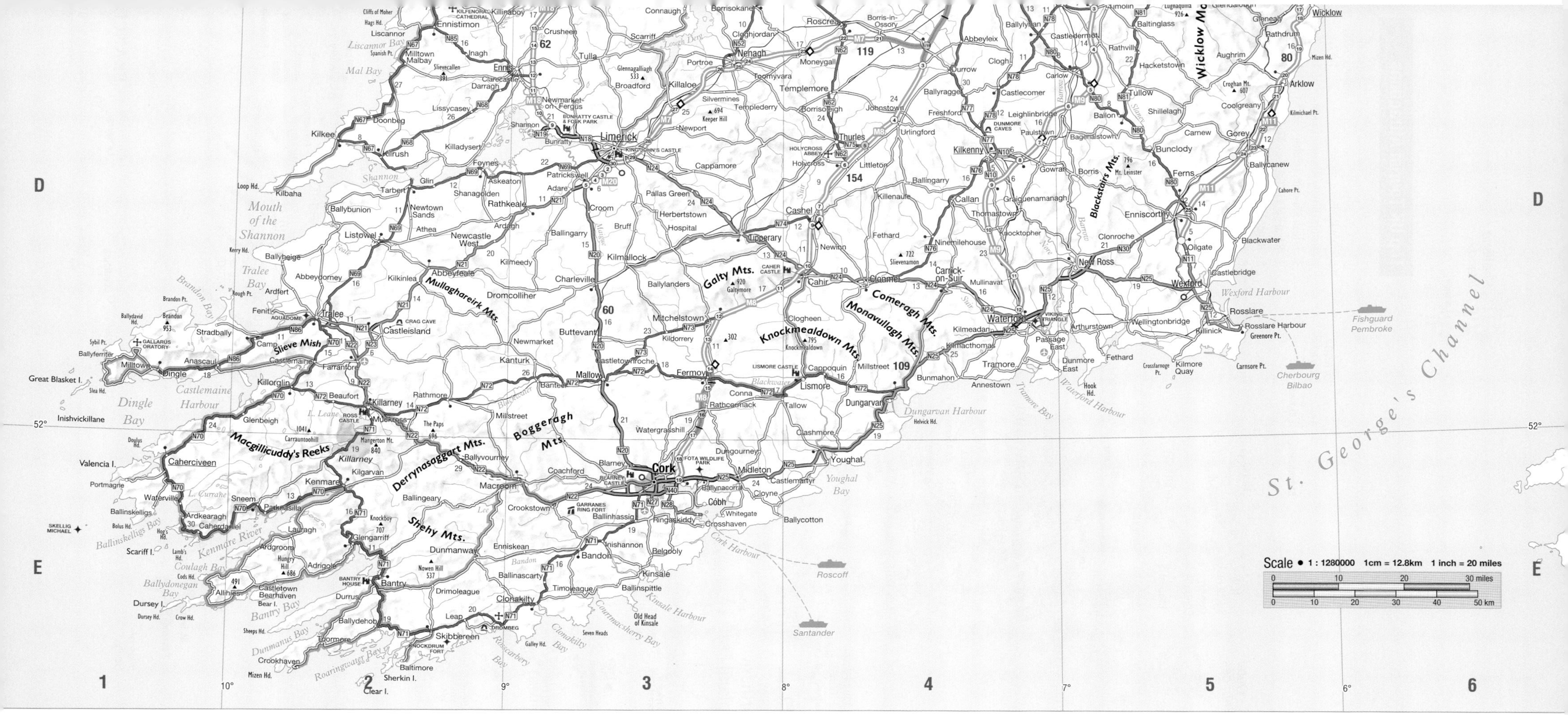
D
E
1
2
3
4
5
6
10°
9°
8°
7°
6°
52°
Scale • 1 : 1280000 1cm = 12.8km 1 inch = 20 miles
0 10 20 30 miles
0 10 20 30 40 50 km
St. George's Channel
Wicklow Mts.
Blackstairs Mts.
Galty Mts.
Comeragh Mts.
Monavullagh Mts.
Knockmealdown Mts.
Boggeragh Mts.
Mullaghareirk Mts.
Slieve Mish
Macgillicuddy's Reeks
Derrynasaggart Mts.
Shehy Mts.
Mouth of the Shannon
Tralee Bay
Dingle Bay
Castlemaine Harbour
Kenmare River
Bantry Bay
Dunmanus Bay
Roaringwater Bay
Courtmacsherry Bay
Kinsale Harbour
Cork Harbour
Youghal Bay
Dungarvan Harbour
Tramore Bay
Waterford Harbour
Wexford Harbour
Fishguard
Pembroke
Cherbourg
Bilbao
Roscoff
Santander
Limerick
Cork
Waterford
Wexford
Kilkenny
Tralee
Killarney
Clonmel
Thurles
Ennis
Wicklow
Arklow
Rosslare Harbour
Great Blasket I.
Valencia I.
Clear I.
Sherkin I.
Mizen Hd.
Old Head of Kinsale

Index to Ireland

Tourism

Tourism symbols

▨	National Park
▨	Area of Outstanding Natural Beauty
▨	National Scenic Area
▨	Built-up area
—	Long distance footpath
●	Town of tourist interest
◆	Other tourist attraction
○	Other town

Top Ireland Tourist Attractions

		Visitors in millions (2019)
1.	Guinness Storehouse, Dublin	1.7
2.	Cliffs of Moher Visitor Experience, Clare	1.6
3.	Dublin Zoo, Dublin	1.3
4.	The Book of Kells, Dublin	1.1
5.	Castletown House Parklands, Kildare	1.0
6.	Kilkenny Castle Parklands, Kilkenny	0.9
7.	National Gallery of Ireland, Dublin	0.8
8.	Glendalough Monument & Site, Wicklow	0.7
9.	Tayto Park, Meath	0.7
10.	National Botanic Gardens, Dublin	0.7

Top UK Tourist Attractions

		Visitors in millions (2020)
1.	Tate Modern, London	1.4
2.	Natural History Museum, London	1.3
3.	British Museum, London	1.3
4.	Royal Botanic Gardens, Kew	1.2
5.	National Gallery, London	1.2
6.	Chester Zoo	1.2
7.	RHS Garden Wisley	1.0
8.	Victoria & Albert Museum, London	0.9
9.	Science Museum, London	0.9
10.	Somerset House, London	0.7
11.	Southbank Centre, London	0.7
12.	Horniman Museum and Gardens, London	0.6
13.	ZSL Whipsnade Zoo	0.5
14.	Longleat	0.5
15.	Westonbirt, The National Arboretum	0.5
16.	Attingham Park	0.5
17.	Royal Botanic Garden, Edinburgh	0.5
18.	ZSL London Zoo	0.5
19.	Tower of London	0.4
20.	National Museum of Scotland, Edinburgh	0.4

Transport symbols

———	Motorway
———	Other important road
———	Main railway
———	Main ferry route
- - -	Channel Tunnel
✈	Main airport
⛴	Main ferry port
○	Other town

Top UK Ferry ports

		International passengers in thousands (2020)
1.	Dover	4,376
2.	Holyhead	808
3.	Portsmouth	469
4.	Harwich	347
5.	Hull	227
6.	Newhaven	133
7.	Tyne	115
8.	Pembroke Dock	93
9.	Immingham	83
10.	Plymouth	78

Top UK Airports

		International passengers in millions (2020)
1.	London Heathrow	22.1
2.	London Gatwick	10.2
3.	London Stansted	7.5
4.	Manchester	7.0
5.	London Luton	5.6
6.	Edinburgh	3.5
7.	Birmingham	2.9
8.	Bristol	2.2
9.	Glasgow	1.9
10.	Belfast International	1.7
11.	Liverpool John Lennon	1.3
12.	Newcastle	1.1
13.	Aberdeen	1.0
14.	London City	0.9
15.	East Midlands	0.9
16.	Leeds Bradford	0.8
17.	George Best Belfast City	0.5
18.	Southend	0.4
19.	Doncaster Sheffield	0.3
20.	Southampton	0.3

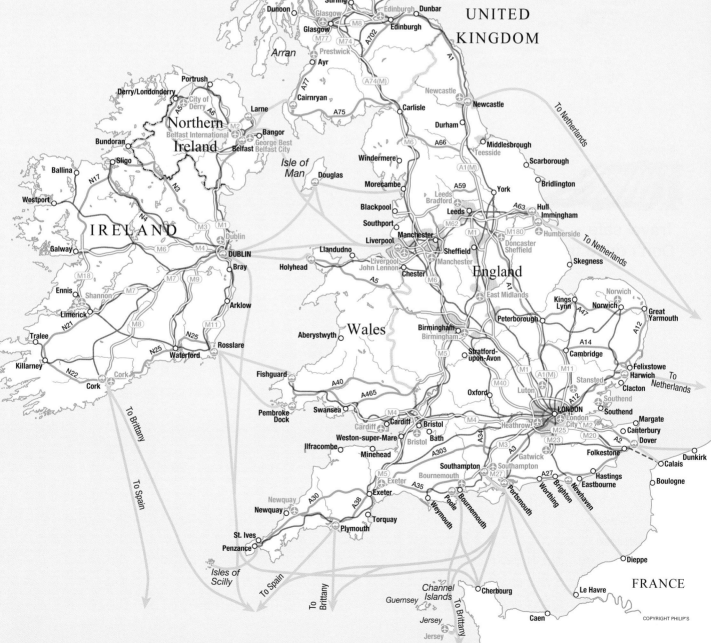

COPYRIGHT PHILIP'S

Distance table

How to use this table

Distances are shown in miles and kilometres with estimated journey times in hours and minutes.

For example: the distance between Dover and Fishguard is 331 miles or 533 kilometres with an estimated journey time of 6 hours, 20 minutes.

Estimated driving times are based on an average speed of 60mph on Motorways and 40mph on other roads. Drivers should allow extra time when driving at peak periods or through areas likely to be congested.

Supporting

THINK!

Travel safe –
Don't drive tired

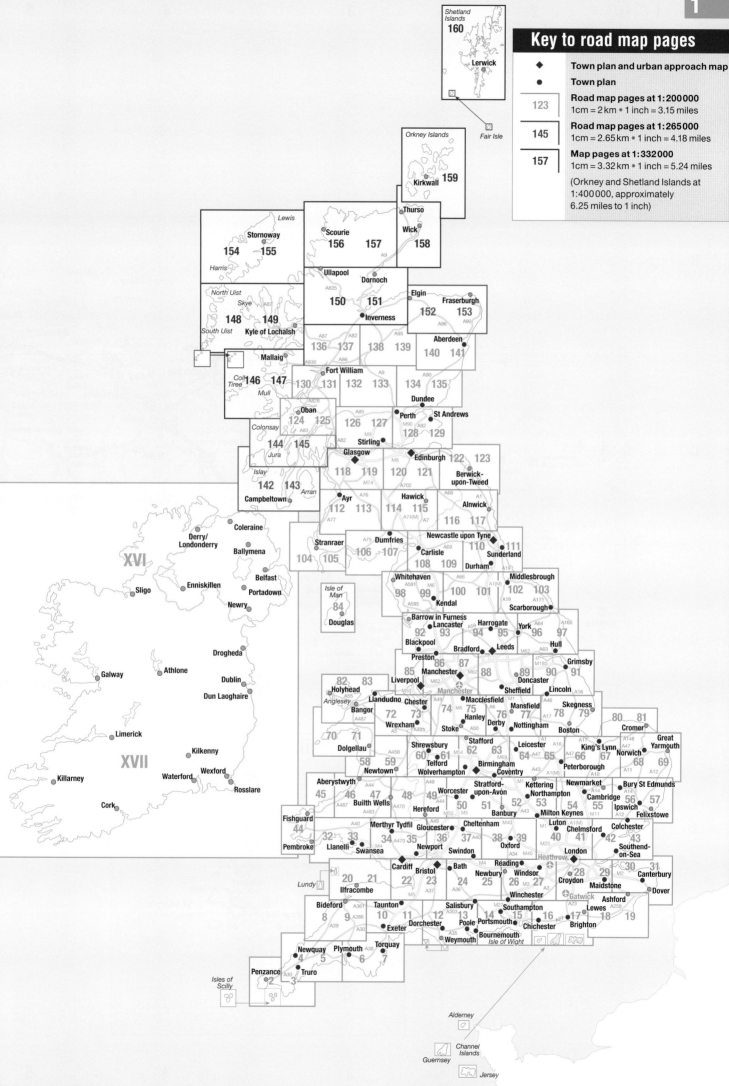

Key to road map pages

◆ Town plan and urban approach map

● Town plan

123	**Road map pages at 1:200000** 1cm = 2 km • 1 inch = 3.15 miles
145	**Road map pages at 1:265000** 1cm = 2.65 km • 1 inch = 4.18 miles
157	**Map pages at 1:332000** 1cm = 3.32 km • 1 inch = 5.24 miles

(Orkney and Shetland Islands at 1:400000, approximately 6.25 miles to 1 inch)

Shetland Islands **160**
Lerwick

Fair Isle

Orkney Islands
Kirkwall **159**
Thurso

Lewis
Stornoway
154 **155**
Harris

Scourie
156 **157** Wick
A9 **158**

Ullapool
Dornoch
A835
150 **151**
Inverness

Elgin
Fraserburgh
152 **153**
A96 A90
Aberdeen

North Uist
Skye A87
148 **149**
South Uist Kyle of Lochalsh

A87 A82 A95
136 **137** **138** **139**
A86
A90
140 **141**

Mallaig
A830
146 **147** **130** **131** **132** **133** **134** **135**
Coll Fort William A9
Tiree
Mull
A828
Oban **124** **125** **126** **127** Perth St Andrews
A85 Dundee
Colonsay M90 A92
128 **129**
M9
A83 Stirling
144 **145** A82
Jura **118** **119** **120** **121**
Glasgow Edinburgh **122** **123**
Islay M8
142 **143** M74 A702 Berwick-
Arran upon-Tweed
Campbeltown M74
A76 A68 A1
Ayr Hawick Alnwick
112 **113** **114** **115**
A77 A74(M) A7 **116** **117**

Coleraine
Derry/ Ballymena
Londonderry Stranraer Dumfries Newcastle upon Tyne
104 **105** **106** **107** **110** **111**
Sligo Enniskillen Belfast Carlisle Sunderland
Portadown A69
Newry A591 Durham A19
108 **109**
XVI Whitehaven Middlesbrough
Isle of A1(M)
Man A66 **102** **103**
98 **99** **100** **101**
84 A595 Kendal A171
Scarborough
Douglas
Barrow in Furness Harrogate
Lancaster A59 York A64 A165
Drogheda **92** **93** **94** **95** **96** **97**
Athlone Blackpool Bradford Leeds
Galway Preston M62 A63 Hull
Dublin **85** **86** **87** **88** M180 **90** **91**
Dun Laoghaire Liverpool M62 Grimsby
82 **83** Manchester Doncaster
Holyhead M61 **89**
Anglesey M53 Sheffield Lincoln
Limerick A55 Llandudno Chester Macclesfield A46
Bangor **72** **73** **74** **75** **76** Mansfield A16 Skegness
Kilkenny A487 Wrexham M6 A6 **77** **78** **79**
XVII A5 Stoke Hanley Derby
70 **71** Nottingham Boston **80** **81**
Killarney Dolgellau A483 A50 A1 Cromer
Stafford M1 A17 King's Lynn A148 Great
Waterford Wexford Shrewsbury **62** **63** Leicester A16 **66** **67** Norwich Yarmouth
Aberystwyth **58** **59** **60** **61** M54 **64** **65** Peterborough **68** **69**
Rosslare Telford M69 A43 A1(M) A10 A12
Cork Newtown Birmingham A47 Newmarket
Wolverhampton Coventry Northampton Cambridge Bury St Edmunds
45 **46** **47** **48** **49** Worcester Stratford- Kettering **54** **55** **56** **57**
A44 upon-Avon **53** A14 Ipswich
A487 Builth Wells A470 Hereford **50** **51** **52** Milton Keynes M11 A12 Felixstowe
Fishguard Merthyr Tydfil A49 Banbury Luton Chelmsford Colchester
44 Gloucester A1(M)
32 **33** **34** **35** **36** **37** **38** **39** **40** **41** **42** **43**
Pembroke Llanelli Newport Cheltenham Oxford M25 London Southend-
Swansea A470 Swindon A40 Croydon on-Sea
M4 A34 M40 Heathrow Canterbury
Cardiff Bristol Bath Reading Windsor **28** **29** **30** **31**
20 **21** **22** **23** **24** **25** **26** **27** Maidstone
Lundy Ilfracombe Newbury Gatwick Dover
M5 Winchester A23
Bideford A36 M2 Ashford
A361 Taunton Salisbury Southampton Lewes
8 **9** **10** **11** **12** **13** **14** **15** **16** **17** **18** **19**
A39 A386 Dorchester Portsmouth Chichester Brighton
Exeter Poole
A30 Weymouth Bournemouth
Newquay Plymouth Torquay Isle of Wight
4 **5** **6** **7**
Penzance Truro
Isles of **2** **3**
Scilly

Alderney

Channel Islands
Guernsey Jersey

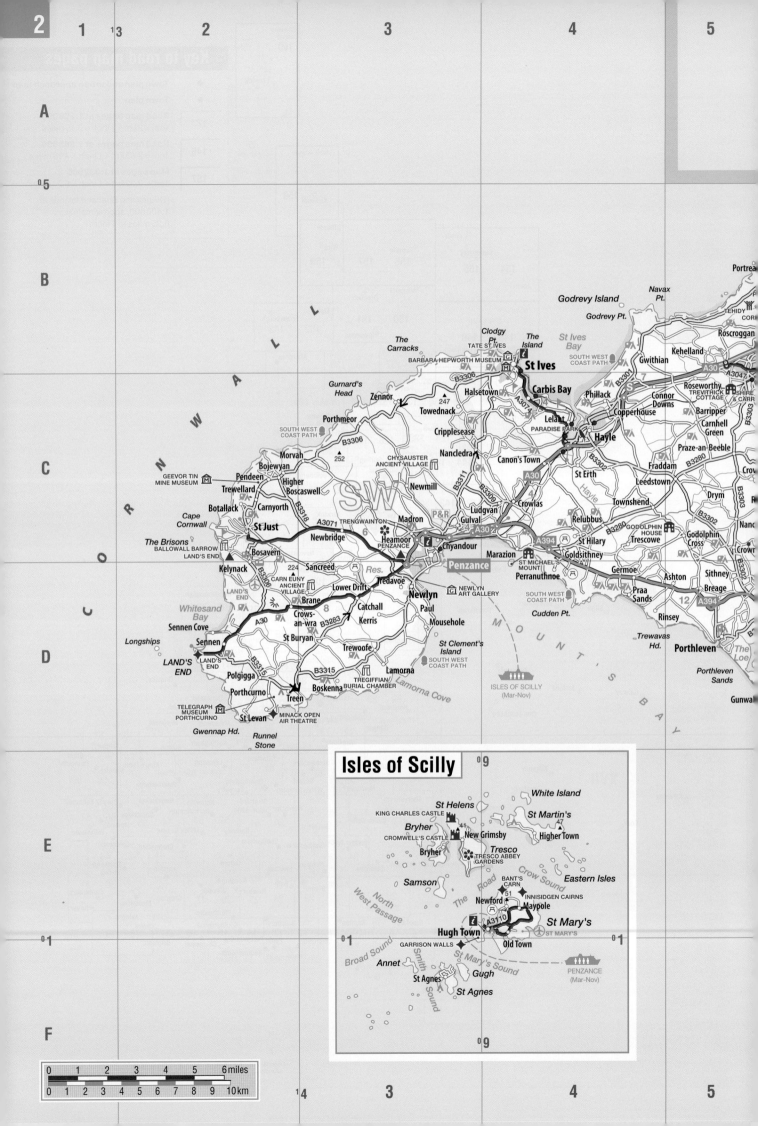

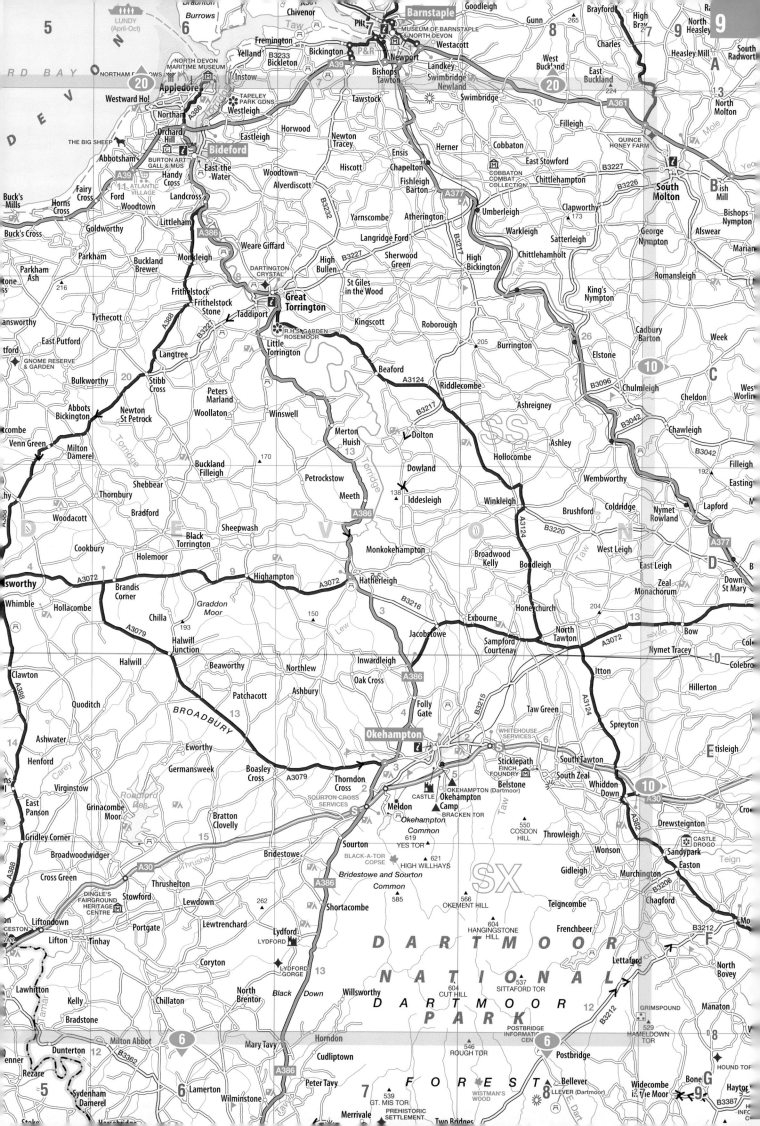

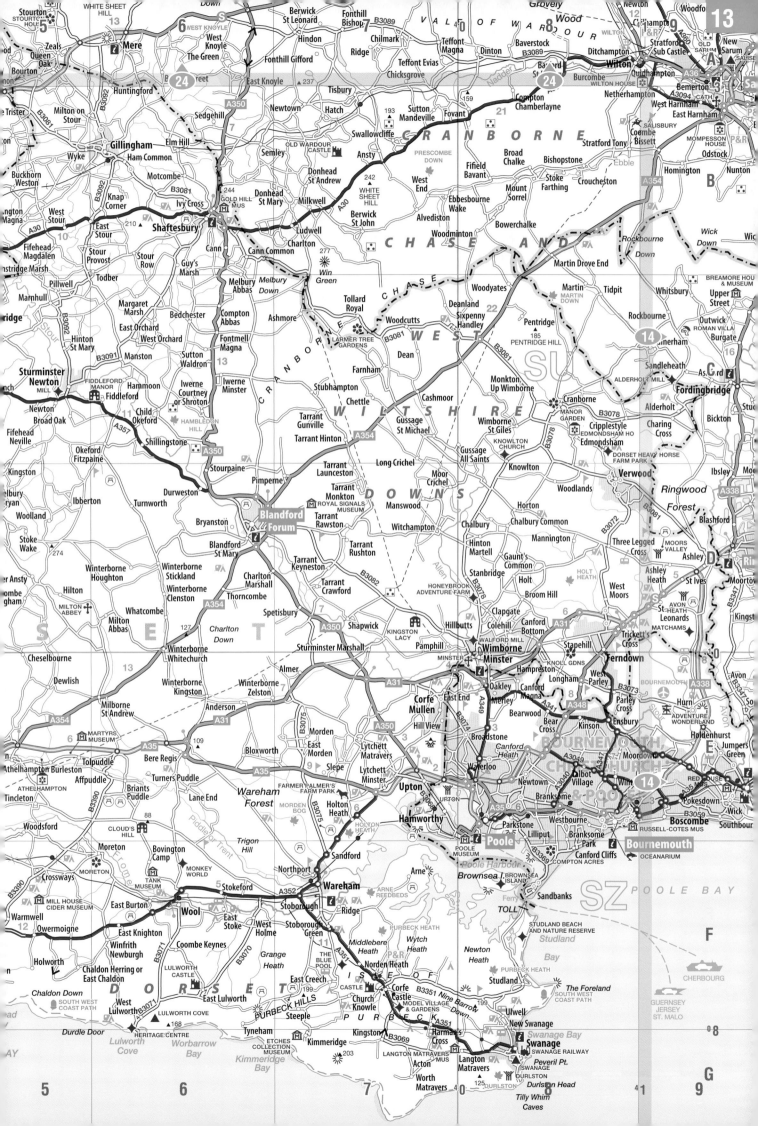

1 2 3 2 3 Trwyn Port Eynon 4 5

GOWER
Port Eynon
Port Eynon Bay
Bae Port Eynon

A

18

B

North West
Point
North East
Point

LUNDY MARINE
NATURE RESERVE

LUNDY

142

South West
Point

Surf
Point

ILFRACOMBE
BIDEFORD
(April-Oct)

1 5
2 2

C

2 1
1 4

D

SS

N
O
R
T
H

D
E
V
O
N

LUNDY
(April-Oct)

HELE CORN MILL
Rillage Pt.
Combe Martin
Bay
Trentishoe

Ilfracombe
ILFRACOMBE
MUSEUM
WATERMOUTH CASTLE
Hele
Girt Down
349
Heale

Bull Pt.
206
Lee
Whitestone
Slade
Berrynarbor
Sterridge
Combe
Martin
WILDLIFE & DINOSAUR PARK
Kentisbury

Rockham Bay

E

Morte Point
Mortehoe

Woolacombe
MORTE
BAY

B3343
Trimstone
269
A3123
Berry Down
Cross
Patchole
Kentisbury
Ford

Cheglinch
Berry
Down
EXMOO
ZO

210
Dean
West
Down
Bittadon
East Down

Woolacombe Sand
SOUTH WEST
COAST PATH
North
Buckland
Churchill
Arlington
ARLINGTON
COURT

Baggy Pt.
Pickwell
Putsborough
Nethercott
Halsinger
Milltown
Muddiford
Loxhore
Knightaco

Georgeham
Croyde Bay
Croyde
Darracott
Knowle
Marwood
Guineaford
198
Shirwell
Br
Fle

B3231 158 Lobb
14
Pippacott
MARWOOD
HILL GARDENS
Kingsheanton
BROOMHILL
Shirwell
Cross
Stoke
Rivers

Saunton
Braunton
Heanton
Punchardon
Prixford
Yeo

ELLIOT GALLERY
Saunton
Sands
Wrafton
TOLL
Ashford
Burridge
Goodleigh
Gunn

F

Braunton
Burrows
Chivenor
A361
Pilton
Barnstaple
MUSEUM OF BARNSTAPLE
& NORTH DEVON
Westacott

Taw
Fremington
Yelland
Bickington
Newport
Landkey
Swimbridge
Newland

LUNDY
(April-Oct)
Bickleton
A39
P&R
Bishops
Tawton

BIDEFORD BAY
NORTH DEVON
MARITIME MUSEUM
NORTHAM BURROWS
Instow
9
Swimbridge

13
9

Appledore
Westleigh
TAPELEY
PARK GDNS

Westward Ho!
Northam
A386
Westleigh
Horwood
Newton
Tracey
Ensis
Herner
Col ton

Titchbe
THE BIG SHEEP
Orchard
Hill
3
Bideford
4
5
Abbotsham
BURTON ART
GALL & MUS
Handy
East-the-
-Water
Woodtown
Hiscott
Chapelton
East St
CLOVELLY VILLAGE
A39
COBBATON
COMBAT

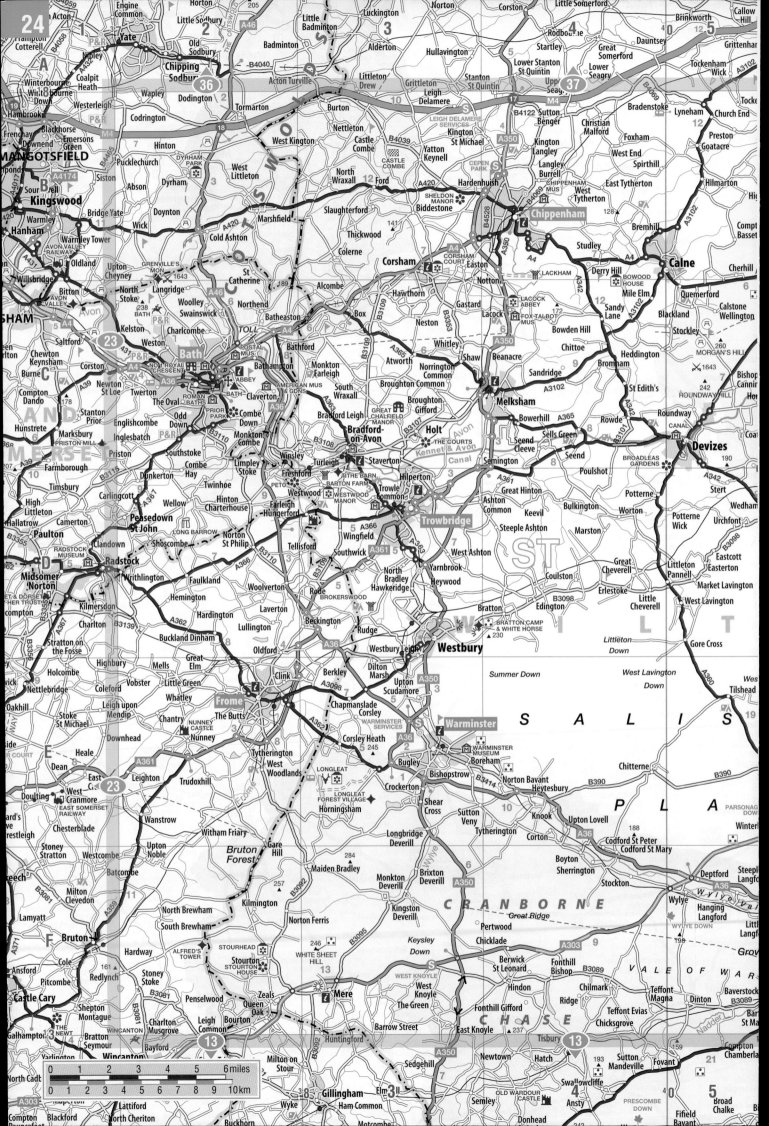

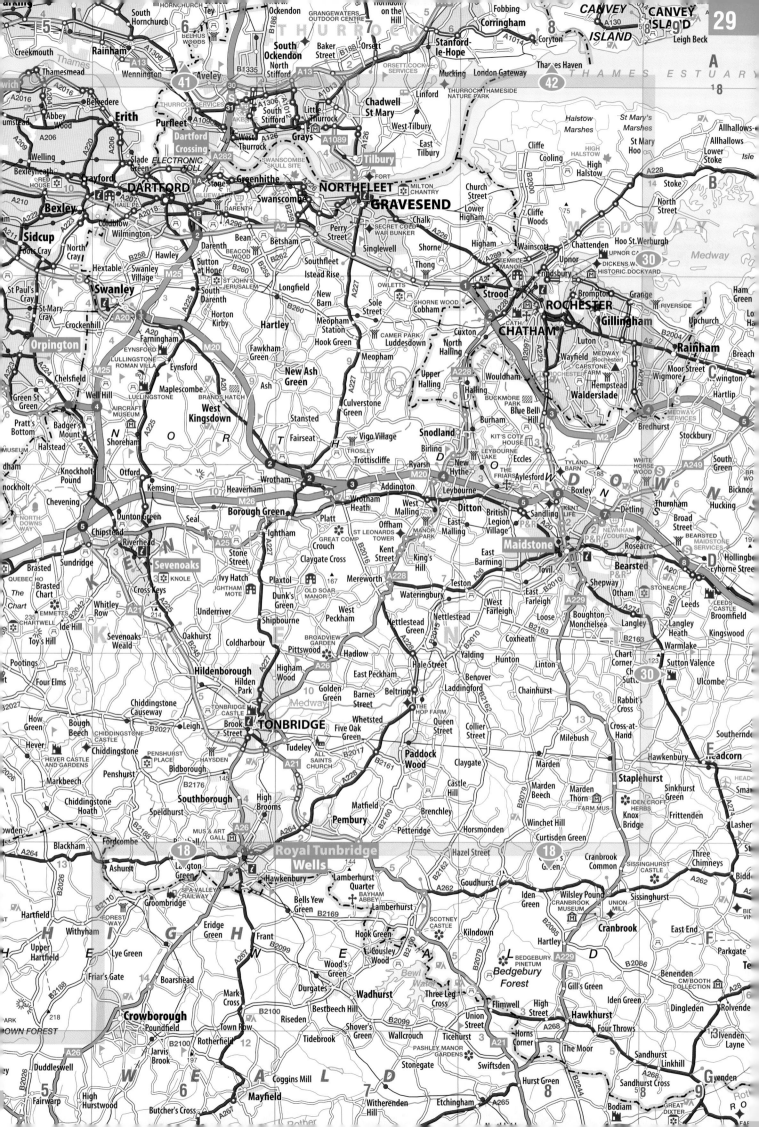

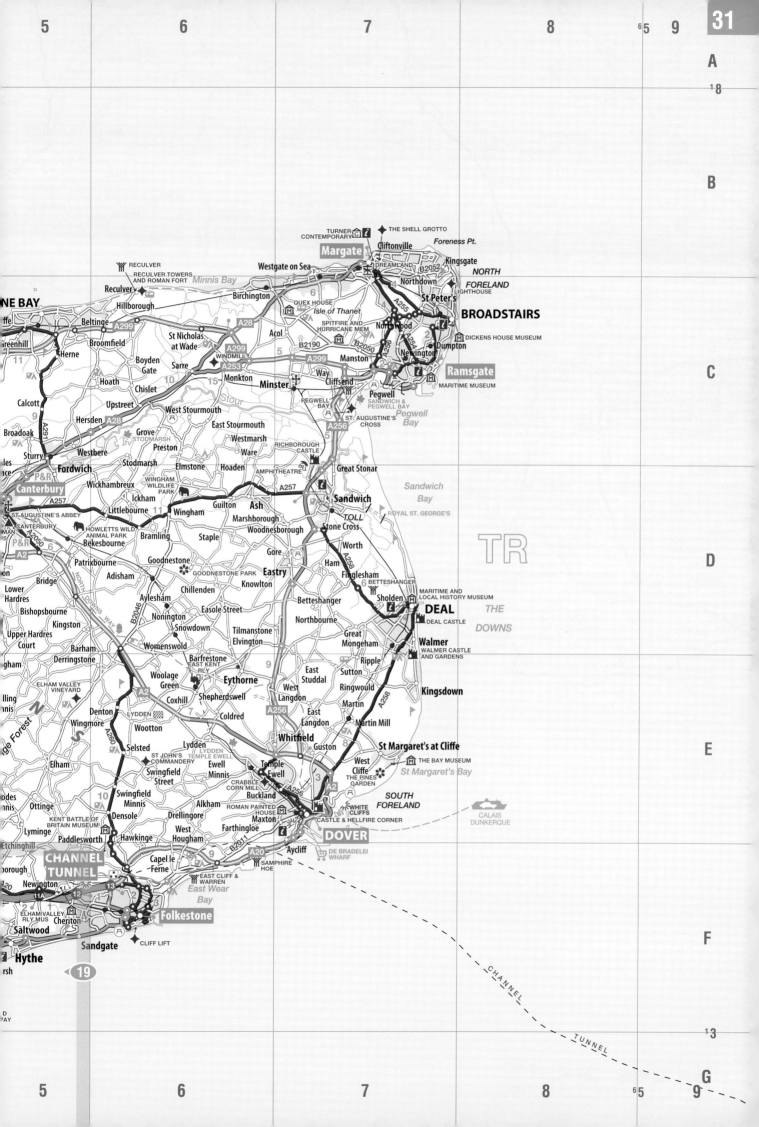

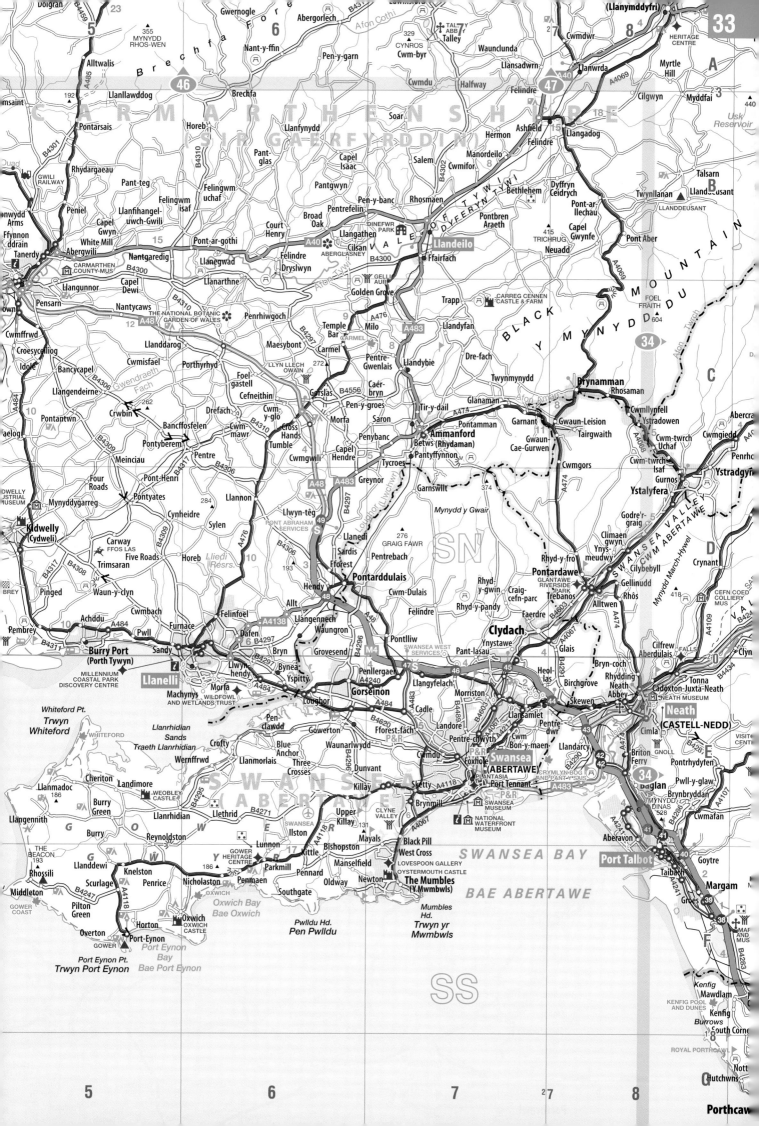

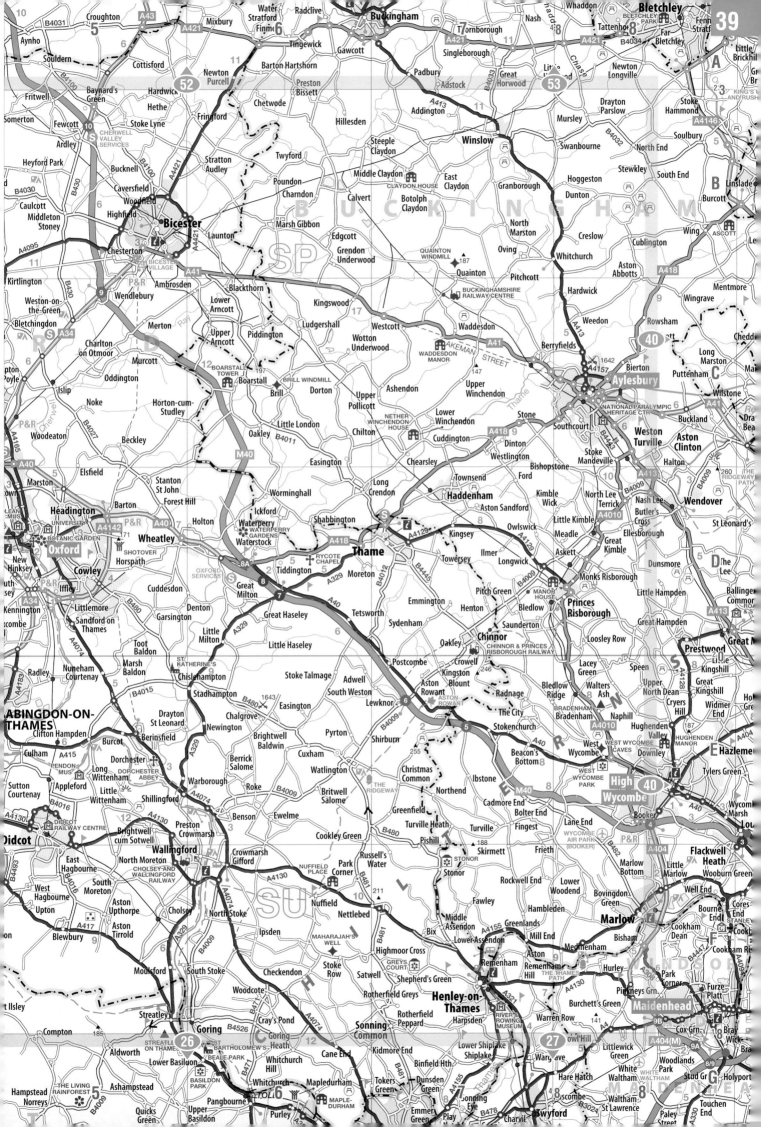

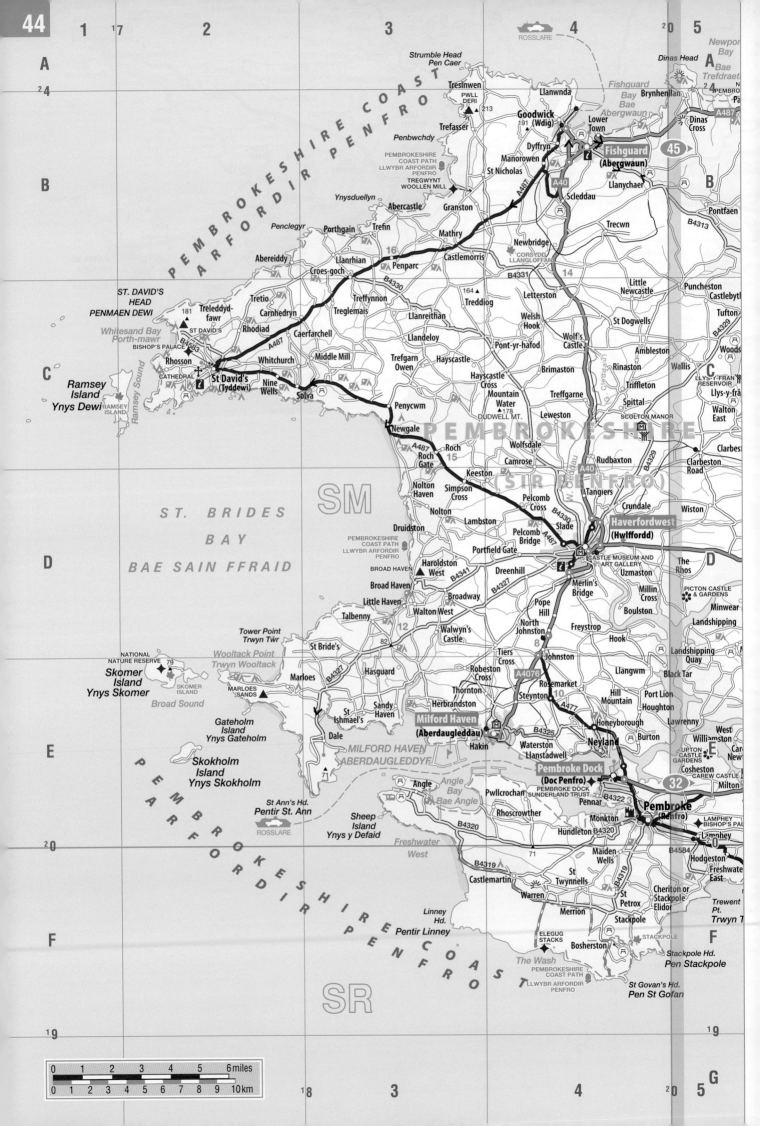

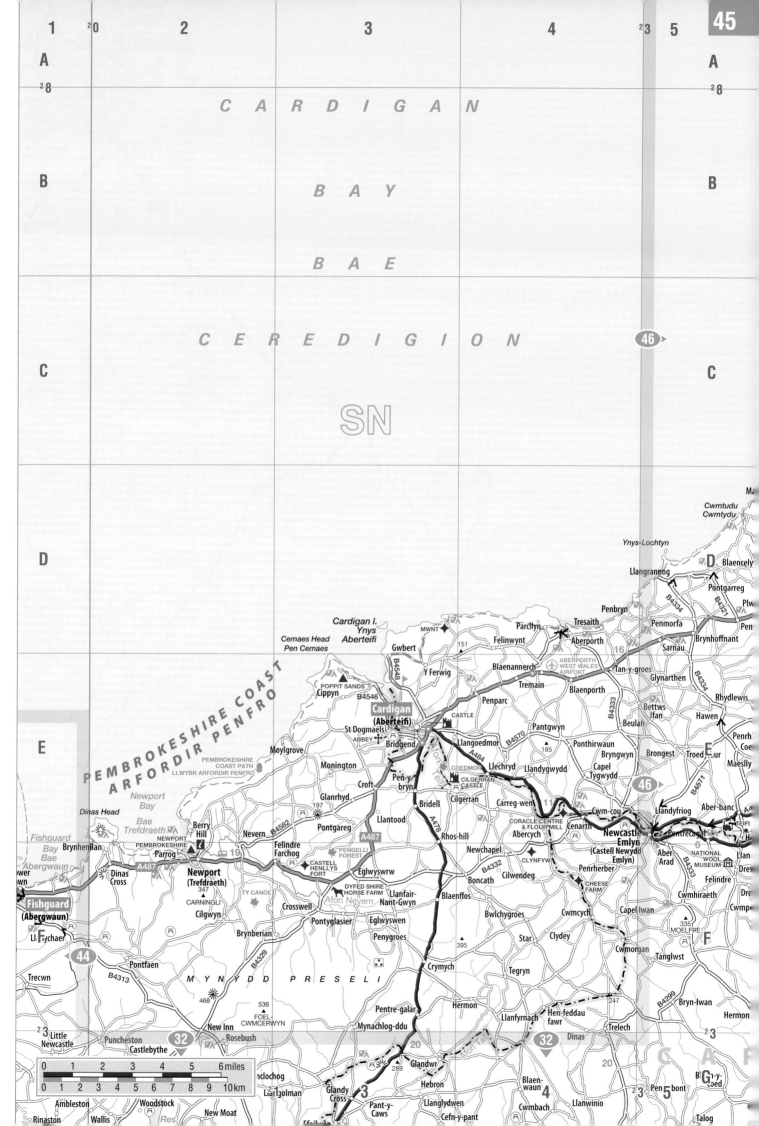

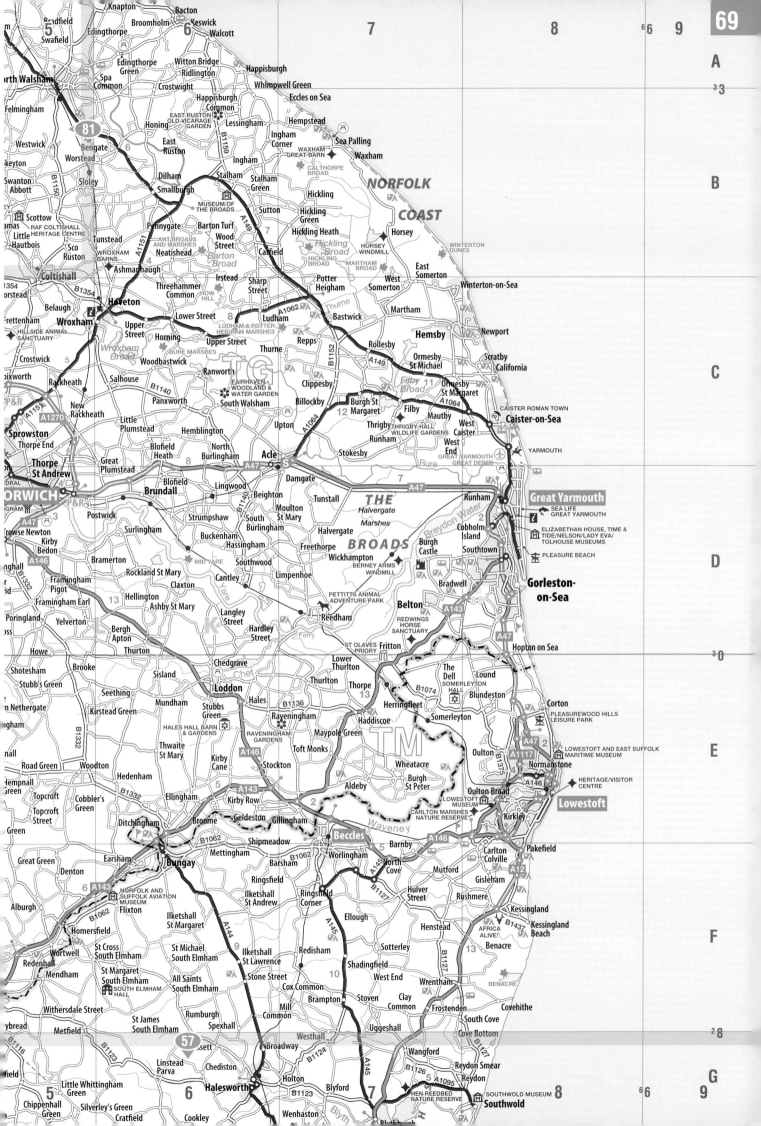

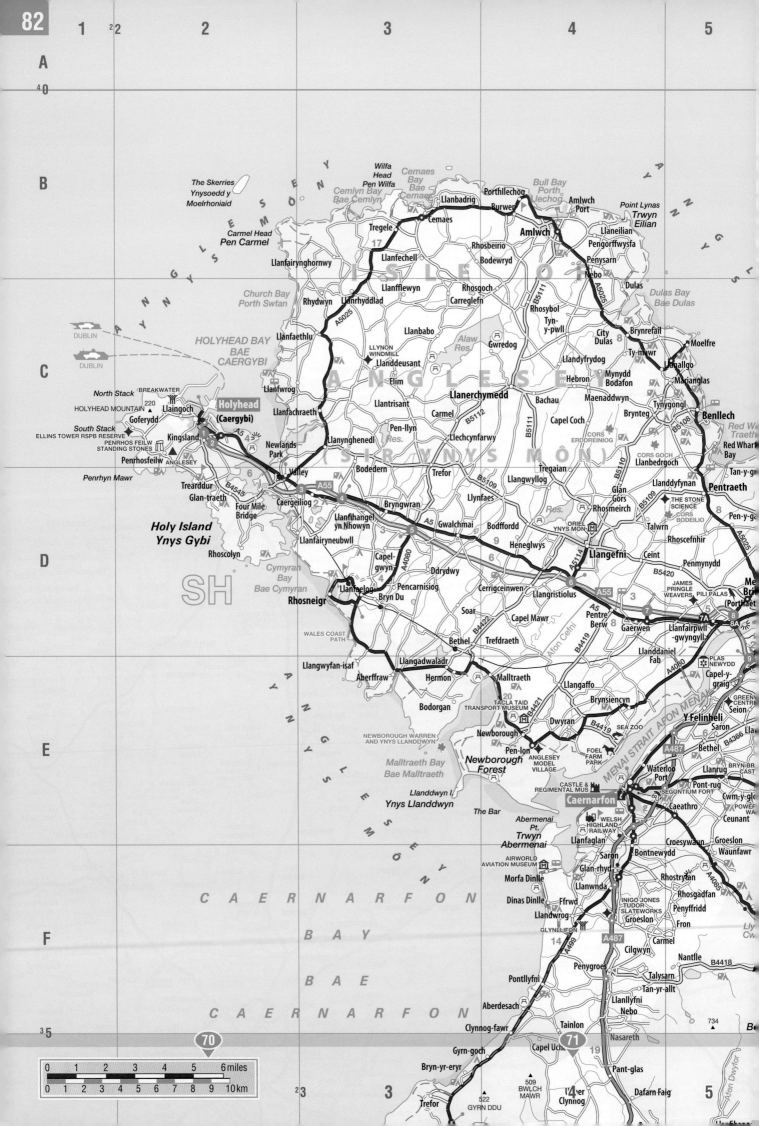

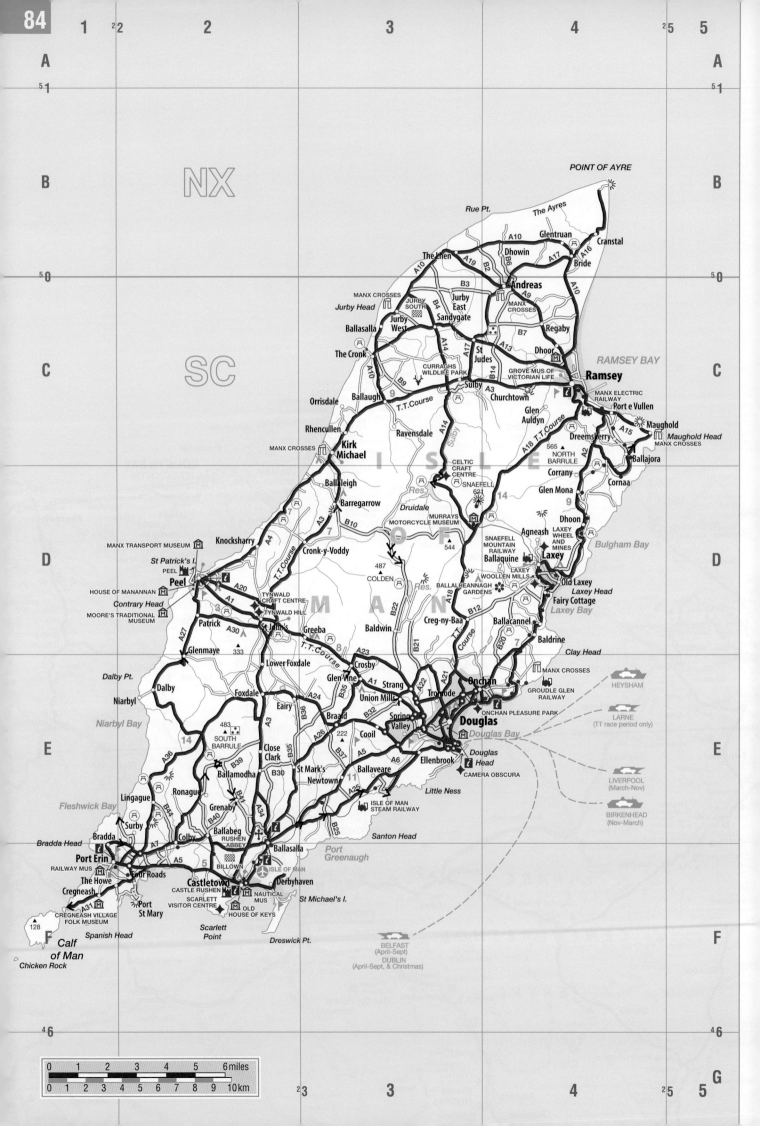

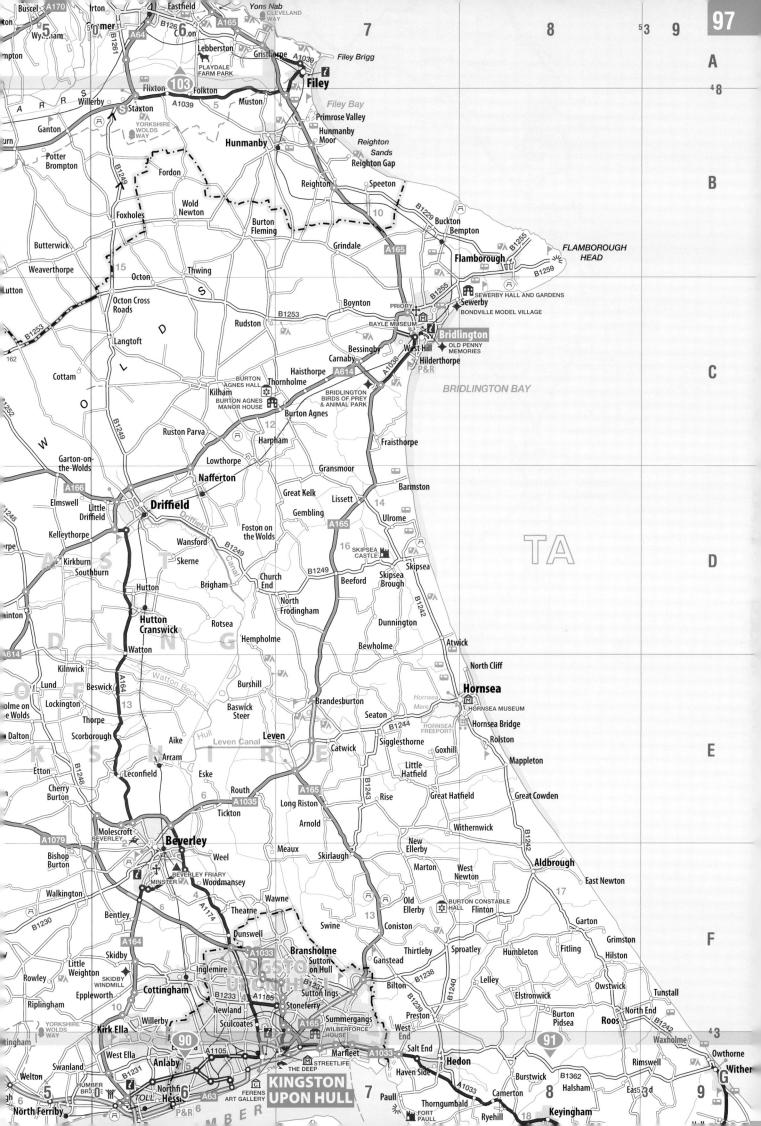

1   18   2   3   20   4   5

A

58

B

BELFAST

LARNE

Milleur Pt.

Corsewall Pt.

Barnhills

North Cairn

South Cairn   B738   Corsewall
                Loch
Dounan Bay   Connell   Kirkcolm

Mains of Airies   Ervie

                Low
                Salchrie   The Wig

C

Knocknain   Leswalt   LOCH RYAN

Slouchnawen   B738   B7043
Bay   Craigencross

                    A718

                Glenstockadale

Broadsea Bay   T   H   E   R   Stranraer

Knockglass   CASTLE OF
            ST JOHN
            VISITOR
            CENTRE
        STRANRAER
        MUSEUM

Black Hd.   B738

Dunskey Ho.   A77   182   Lochans

D   5

            Portpatrick   Awhirk

                8   Stoneykirk

Port of Spittal Bay   B7042

Cairngarroch   KIRKMADRINE
            STONES   Sandhead

Cairngarroch Bay   Sandhead Bay

    Money Hd.

                Clachanmore

Hole Stone Bay   Ardwell
                Ardwell   Chapel Rossan
                Mains
E
    Ardwell Pt.   Logan   10
                Mains
                            Balgowan Pt.
                LOGAN
                BOTANIC
    Mull of Logan   GARDEN
            LOGAN FISH POND
            MARINE LIFE CENTRE
Port Nessock or Port Logan Bay

            Port Logan
54
    Cairnywellan Hd.   B7065   A716

    Clanyard Bay

    Low Clanyard
                        Drumm
Laggantalluch Hd.   Kirkmaiden
            164
F   Damnaglaur   B7041

    Crammag Hd.

                Cairngaan
19   3   20   4   5

Port Kemin

CARLETON
STLE

112   Colmonell

B734 265   Knockdolian

            Heronsford
            Glen Tig

Ballantrae   Balkiss

Ballantrae Bay

Downan Pt.   Auchencrosh

                439
                BENERAIRD

            Mark   257
17   Glen App

                    Main Water of L

            Cairnryan   Penwhirn
                        Res.

                    Braid Fell

        A77

            Innermessan   Auchmant

                    Black Loch
                    CASTLE KENNEDY
                    GARDENS
        A751   White Loch
            Aird   Castle Kennedy
                        H
                    Soulseat   IGL
                    Loch   GA
                A75

                Mark

        B7077   6

                    Torrs War
            5   B7084   6

        A716

0   1   2   3   4   5   6miles
0 1 2 3 4 5 6 7 8 9 10km

A
B
C
D
E
F
G

5   6   7   8   9

BLYTH

117

Bedlington
Station
East
Sleekburn
Cowpen
Cambois
West Sleekburn
Gate

East
Hartford
New
Delaval
Bebside
A189
A192
A1061
Shankhouse
Seaton
New
Hartley
Seaton Sluice
Seaton Delaval Hall
Hartley
ST MARY'S LIGHTHOUSE
St Mary's or Bait I.
England Coast Path

Cramlington
Seaton
Delaval
Holywell
East
Cramlington
Seghill
Annitsford
Burradon
Backworth
Larsdon
WHITLEY BAY
Camperdown
Killingworth
Monkseaton
Shiremoor
Longbenton
Marden
Cullercoats
BLUE REEF AQUARIUM
TYNEMOUTH
CASTLE & PRIORY
STEPHENSON
RAILWAY MUSEUM
Tynemouth
North
Shields
ARBEIA ROMAN FORT AND MUSEUM
THE
RISING SUN
Willington
WALLSEND
South Shields
SOUTH SHIELDS MUSEUM
Heaton
Tyne Tunnel
Westoe
THE LEAS AND
MARSDEN ROCK
Marsden Bay
Byker
Jarrow
SEGEDUNUM
FORT
JARROW HALL
ST PAUL'S
MONASTERY
Harton
Marsden
CASTLE KEEP
Gateshead
Walker
Hedworth
SOUTER
LIGHTHOUSE
Hebburn
Whiteleas
Cleadon
Whitburn Colliery
INTERNATIONAL
STADIUM
Pelaw
Boldon
Colliery
Felling
Carr Hill
Boldon
Whitburn
FULWELL WINDMILL
Downhill
Fulwell
Low Fell
Hylton
Castle
Southwick
Roker
Wrekenton
Springwell
Usworth
Castletown
Monkwearmouth
NATIONAL GLASS CENTRE
ST PETER'S CHURCH
STATION
MUS
Blackfell
OLD
HALL
South
Hylton
Pallion
SUNDERLAND MINSTER
WASHINGTON
Birtley
WASHINGTON
SERVICES
Lambton
THE WILDFOWL &
WETLANDS TRUST
PENSHAW MON
Pennywell
High
Barnes
Sunderland
Ouston
Fatfield
Hendon
Rickleton
Penshaw
East
Herrington
New
Silksworth
**Shiney
Row**
New
Herrington
Newbottle
Doxford
Park
Tunstall
Ryhope
RYHOPE ENGINES MUS
Bournmoor
DOWN AT
THE FARM
Burdon
Northlea
Fence
Houses
Seaton
**HOUGHTON-LE-
SPRING**
West
Lea
SEAHAM
Chester
Moor
Great
Lumley
Colliery
Row
East
Rainton
Dalton-le-
Dale
Plawsworth
West
Rainton
**Hetton-le-
Hole**
Cold
Hesledon
Kimblesworth
Leamside
Murton
DALTON PARK
Hawthorn
Pity Me
FINCHALE
PRIORY
Low
Moorsley
Easington Lane
South Hetton
Beacon Pt.
Framwellgate
Moor
Pittington
Easington Colliery
Carrville
Littletown
Haswell
Easington
Sherburn
Sherburn Hill
Haswell Plough
DURHAM
CITY
DURHAM CATH
Shotton
Colliery
Horden
DURHAM UNIV
ORIENTAL MUS
Ludworth
PETERLEE
Shincliffe
Old
Cassop
Shadforth
CASTLE
EDEN DENE
Shotton
Blackhall Colliery
Bowburn
Old
Quarrington
Thornley
**Wheatley
Hill**
Castle Eden
Blackhall Rocks
DURHAM
SERVICES
CASSOP
VALE
High Hesleden
Croxdale
Hett
Quarrington
Hill
Wingate
Deaf Hill
Hesleden
DURHAM COAST
Kelloe
Station
Town
Hart Station
Cornforth
Trimdon
Grange
Hutton
Henry
Sheraton
Hart
ST HILDA'S PARISH CHURCH
THE NATIONAL MUS OF THE ROYAL NAVY
Ferryhill
Trimdon
Trimdon
Colliery
High Throston
Hartlepool Bay
Ferryhill
Station
Fishburn
Elwick
West
Park
SUMMERHILL
Hartlepool
Mainsforth
Bishop
Middleham
Butterwick
Dalton
Piercy
Rift
House
Chilton
Chilton
Lane
Seaton Carew
Leasingthorne
101
Sedgefield
102
Tees Bay
Rushyford
Old Eldon
Bradbury
Greatham
Graythorp
**NEWTON
AYCLIFFE**
Middridge
Mordon
Wynyard
Village
Newton Bewley
Wolviston
TEESMOUTH
Salt Scar
REDCAR

AMSTERDAM

NZ

HARTLEPOOL

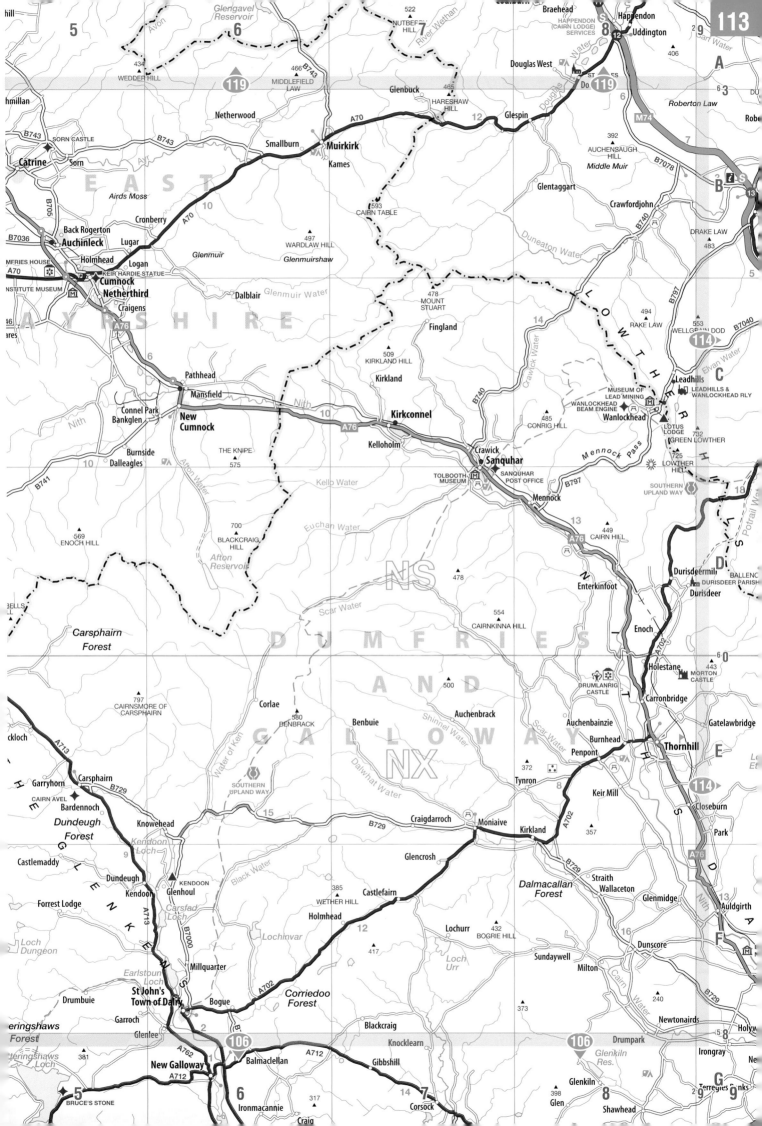

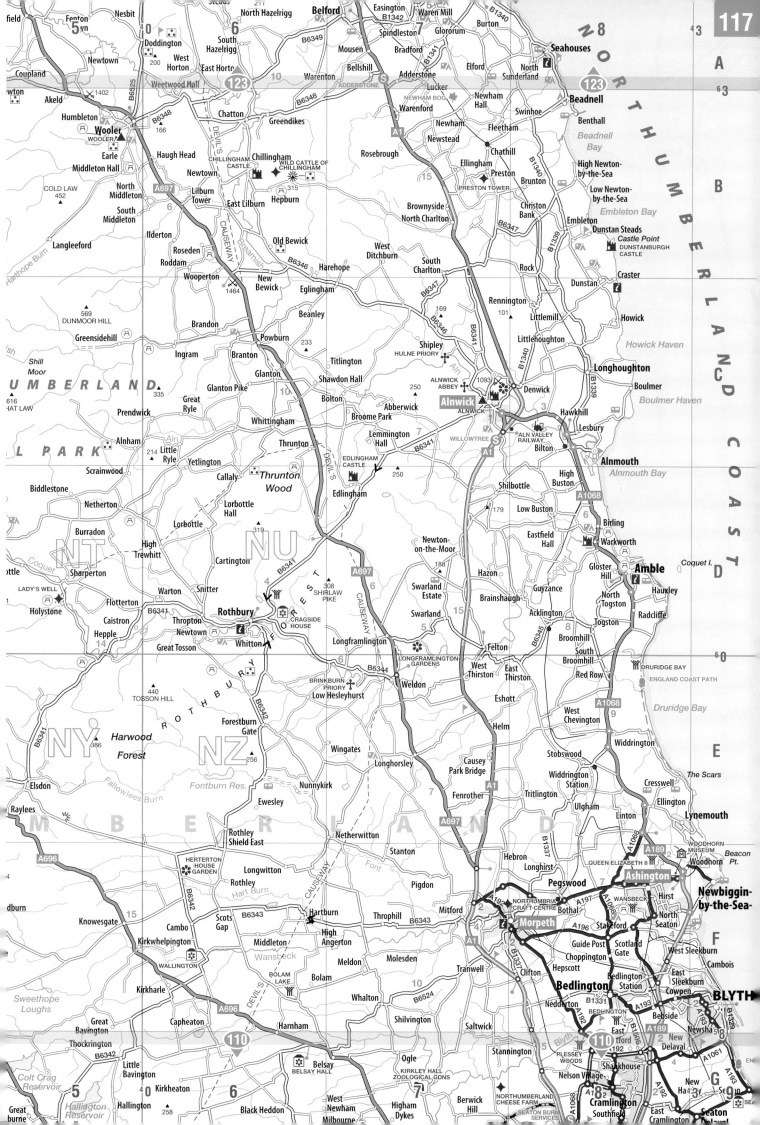

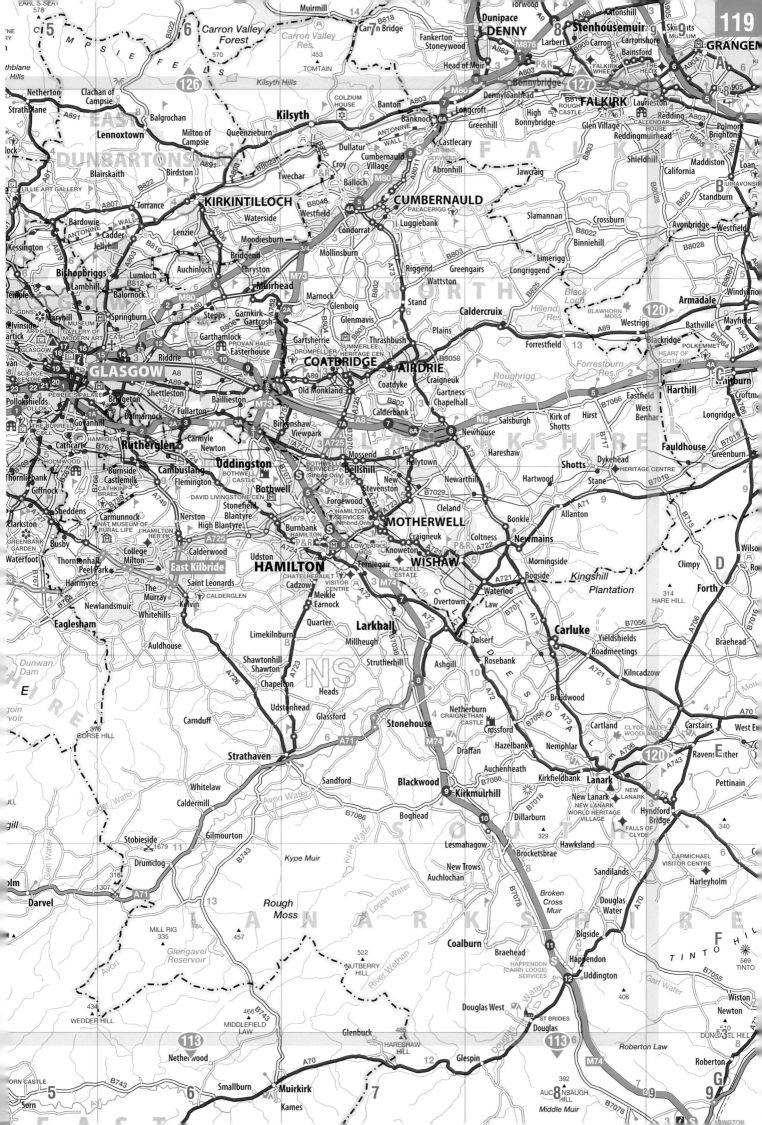

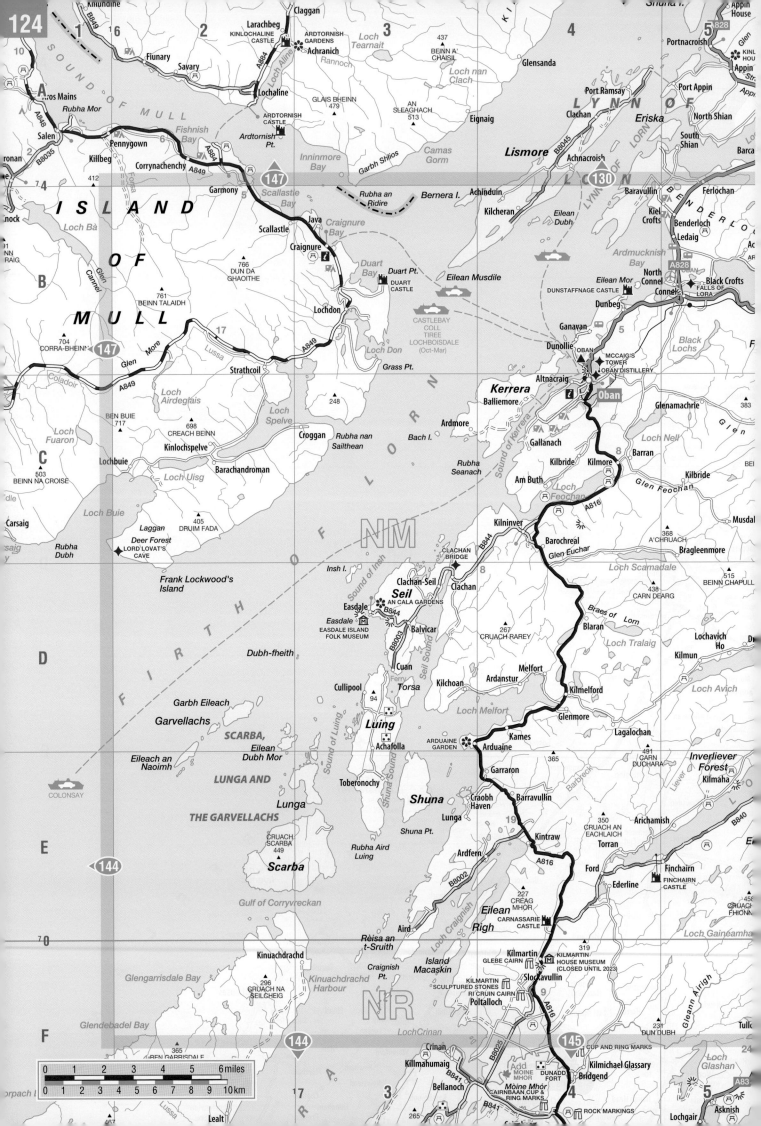

A

ARM

14   1   19

Gleann Udalain

Allt-nan-sugh   Sallachy
A87
8   3

uchertyre

Nostie
Ardelve   A87
Dornie   Bundalloch   Camas-luinie

Glas
Eilean   Eilean Donan
Castle   634

Totaig   Keppoch

B

Letterfearn   Inverinate   SGURR AN AIRGID
841

Keppoch   Dorusduain

BEINN A'CHUIRN   Ruarach
603

Morvich
RATAGAN   Carn-gorm
Ratagan   Ault a'chruinn

C

ACKS

ENELG BROCHS

Balvraid   779

e Bhig

BEINN NAN
CAORACH
774   Glenshiel Forest   1010
THE SADDLE

Arnisdale

Glen Arnisdale
Corran   918

D

NOYDART   DRUIM FADA
713

894

LUINNE BHEINN
939   Glen Barrisdale

Barrisdale
Bay

E

946
LL BUIDHE
859   147   Glen Dessarry

usrory   1040
SGURR NA
CICHE   858

nlochmorar

Oban   829
882   CARN MOR   Glen Pean
718
AN STAC

F

Kinlochbeoraid   965
SGURR NAN
COIREACHAN   963
SGURR THUILM

NM

796
SGURR
AN UTHA   STATION
MUSEUM   Wauchan

14
7   8   Glenfinnan   GLENFINNAN
MONUMENT   130

0   1   2   3   4   5   6 miles
0   1   2   3   4   5   6   7   8   9   10km

SGUMAN
COINNTICH
879   150

Carnach   Allt na Doire Garbhe

Loch na
Leitreach   FALLS OF GLOMACH

Loch nan
Eun   Glen Elchaig   Elchaig

SGURR NAN
CEATHREAMHNAN
1151

Loch a'Bhealaich

BEINN FADA
OR BEN ATTOW
1032   Glen Gniomhaidh

KINTAIL

Kintail Forest

1067
FIVE SISTERS

1027

1719
31

SGURR AN
LOCHAIN
1004   Cluanie Inn

Cluanie Forest

Kinlochhourn Forest   879
BUIDHE BHEINN   906
SGURR
THIONAIL

Kinloch Hourn   Glen Quoich

1027
SGURR
A'MHAORAICH

1035
GLEOURAICH

LOCH QUOICH

Abhainn Chosaidh

919
GAIRICH

1003
SGURR MOR   Glen Kingie

Kingie

656
MEALL BLAIR

880   Loch
SGURR   Blàir
MHURLAGAIN
Murlaggan

Strathan   LOCH

987
GAOR BHEINN

Gleann Camgharaidh

Glen Dubh Lighe

South
Garvan   Duisky   Blaich
A861   A830

Killilan Forest

AO ACH BUIDHE
899

West
Benula
Forest   Gleann Sithidh   Gleann A'Choilich

East Benula Forest   150

1005

1086
AN RIABHACHAN

SGURR NA
LAPAICH

1069   1111
TOM A
CHOINICH

1183
CARN EIGE

888
AONACH SHASUINN

979
CISTE DHUBH

1120
A'CHRALAIG

1109
SGURR NAN
CONBHAIREAN

Ceannacroc Forest

Loch Mullardoch   Glen Cannich

1053
TOLL
CREAGACH

Gleann nam Fiadh

GLEN
AFFRIC

Affric Lodge

Glen Affric

GLEN AFFRIC   Loch
Affric

Affric

GLEN AFFRIC   Glenaffric   Forest

706
CARN A
CHAOCHAIN

NH

Ceannacroc Lodge
A887

Lundie

LOCH CLUANIE

Cluanie
Lodge   A87   5

HIGH

Bunloinn Forest

Loch Loyne

Loyne

1021
AONACH
AIR CHRITH

Glen
Loyne   Garry

Kingie   Aultnaslat   Inchlaggan
Kingie   Tomdoun
Glen   Garry

540
Glenquoich Forest

556
GLAS BHEINN

804
GEAL CHARN

NN

Lochy Forest

Inver Mallie

Glen   Mallie

Mallie

Clan Cameron Museum
796
BEINN BHAN

Gairlochy

Strone

Glen Loy
Forest   Muirshearlich

Kinlocheil   Fassfern   A830
11   TREASURES OF
THE EARTH

NEPTUNE'S
STAIRCASE
LOCKS   B8004   TOR CA

Corpach   Banavie
Caol

Mullardoch House   5
Liatri

Glencannich For

Fa

LO

539   Guisachan

Allt Garbh   Allt Riabhach

Doe

Tomchra

L   A887   G

Bun Loyne

901
BEINN   788
Beinneun   MEALL
Forest

A87   13
Ardochy   LOCH G
House
Greenfield

LOCH

901
BEN TEE

Glengarry Forest

935
SRON A'CHOIRE
GHAIRBH

Clunes Forest

Achnasaul   B8005
Clunes
Achnacarry   Bunarkaig   A82

Stronaba

6
COI
CEIRSL

COMMANDO MEMORIAL

Kilmonivaig   Spean
Bridge
Inv

GREAT
GLEN WAY   Brackletter   Highbridge

Glen   Loy   131   A82   7

Strone   Gloy

131   Killiechonate

Leanachan Forest

Lochy

NEVIS RANGE
MOUNTAIN EXPERIENCE

11   Achaphubuil   INVERLOCHY
CASTLE   Lochyside
3   20   To   ndy
A861   149

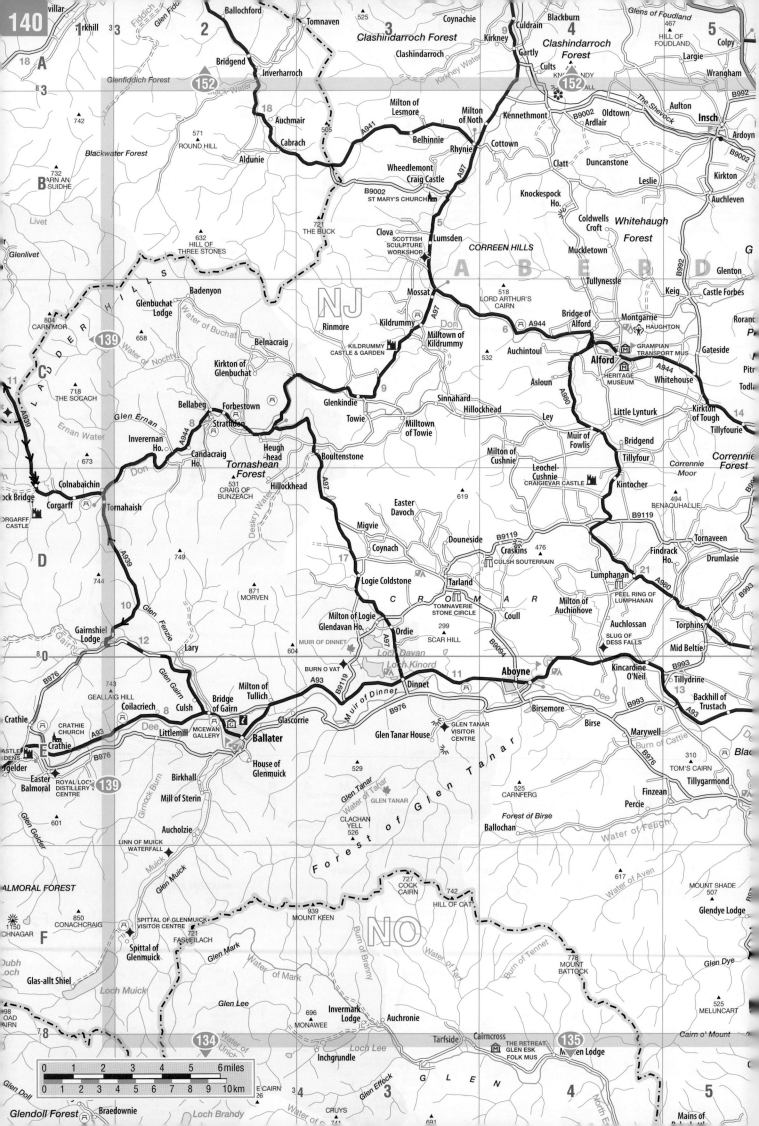

NF

NL

NF

Canna
Garrisdale Pt.
A'Chill
Sanday
Canna Harbour
Sound of Canna
Rubha Shamhnan Insir
Kilmory
Kilmory Glen
MALLAIG
(Sun only)
Guirdil Bay
Rubha na Roinne
A'Bhrideanach
Kinloch Glen
Loch Scresort
571 ORVAL
R Ú M
Schooner Pt.
KINLOCH CASTLE
Rubha Port na Caranean
Harris
Glen Harris
812 ASKIVAL
781 AINSHVAL
Rubha Sgorr an t-Snidhe
Rubha nam Meirleach
Bay of Laig
Cleadale
Rubha an Fhasaidh
Eigg
Kildro
393 AN SGURR
Galmisda
Eile
Eilean nan Each
Muck
137
Port Mor

Bhatarsaigh (Vatersay)
Uidh
Bagh Bhatarsaigh
Bhatarsaigh
148
Caolas Shanndraigh
Flodaigh (Flodday)
207
Sanndraigh (Sandray)
Lingeigh (Lingay)
Greanamul
Caolas Phabaigh
Theisgeir (Heiskers)
171
Pabaidh (Pabbay)
Caolas Mhiui Laigh
273
Miùgh Laigh (Mingulay)
Bearnaraigh (Berneray)
Caolas Bhearnaraigh
Barra Hd.

THE SMALL ISLES

SOUND OF RÙM

SOUND OF EIGG

Oigh-sgeir

CASTLEBAY LOCHBOISDALE (Oct - Mar)

Sanna Point
Sanna Bay
Sanna
Portuairk
Achnaha
Point of Ardnamurchan
ARDNAMURCHAN LIGHTHOUSE
Achosnich
An Acairseid
Ormsaigmore
Ormsaigbeg
Kilcho
Kilchoan Bay

Cairns of Coll
Rubha Mor
Eilean Mor
Sorisdale
Bousd
Cliad Bay
Arnabost
Gallanach
Grishipoll
Ardmore Bay
Ardmore Pt.
Ballyhaugh
Loch Cliad
73
COLL
Quinish Pt.
Glengorm Castle
MULL MUSEUM
104
Arinagour
Caliach Pt.
Quinish
Mishnish
S'AIRDE-BEINN
Tobermory
Hogh Bay
Arileod
Totronald
Acha
Eilean Ornsay
Rubha an Aird
Sunipol
292
MULL THEATRE
Feall Bay
Breachacha Castle
Friesland
Loch Eatharna
Calgary Bay
Mornish
Penmore Mill
Dervaig
Achnadrish
THE OLD BYRE HERITAGE CENTRE
Crossapol Bay
Soa
Loch Breachacha
Calgary
SPB
Calgary Pt.
Gunna
Treshnish Pt.
Ensay
342 CARN MOR
Achnacraig
Haunn
Kilninian
Achleck
TIREE
Vaul Bay
Caolas
Rubha Dubh
Rubh a'Chaoil
Burg
Fanmore
390
Hough Skerries
Balephetrish Bay
Vaul
Salum
Ruaig
Treshnish Isles
LOCH TUATH
Ballygown
EAS FORS WATERFALL
424 BEINN NA DROma
Balevullin
Kenovay
Gott Bay
Fladda
Oskamull
R. Chraiginis
Soa
Lagganulva
Kilkenneth
Scarinish
Heanish
Eilean Dioghlum
Lunga
Bearnus
313
Ulva
Killie
Middleton
Moss
Heylipol
TIREE
Rubha Traigh an Duin
Gometra
Ulva House
Port Mor
Crossapol
Hynish Bay
Bac Mor
Eorsa
Loch a'Phuill
Barrapol
Balemartine
141
Mannal
Little Colonsay
INCH KENNETH CHAPEL
LOCH NA KEAL
Rinn Thorbhais
Balephull
Staffa
STAFFA
Inch Kenneth
I S L E O F
Balephuil Bay
Hynish
FINGAL'S CAVE
17
De
Port Snoig
Balnahard
MACKINNON'S CAVE
561
Erisgeir
THE BURG
519
Glen Seilisdeir
BEINN NA SREINE
ARDMEANACH
Kilfin Bay
MACLEAN'S CROSS
Eilean Annraidh
Rubha nan Cearc
100
IONA ABBEY AND CATHEDRAL
ST COLUMBA EXHIBITION & WELCOME CENTRE
Kintra
LOCH SCRIDAIN
Torran
IONA HERITAGE CENTRE
Baile Mor
Aridhglas
Iona
Stac an Aoineidh
Fidden
Fionnphort
A849
Eorabus
Tiraghoil
Lee
18
Bunessan
376 CRUACHAN MIN
Erraid
Soa I.
Loch Assapol
ROSS OF MULL
Uisken
Scoor
Eilean a'Chalmain
Ardalanish
Ardchiavaig
125
Rubha nam Braithrean
Rubh Ardalanish
144
Torran Rocks
Malcolm's P

148
149

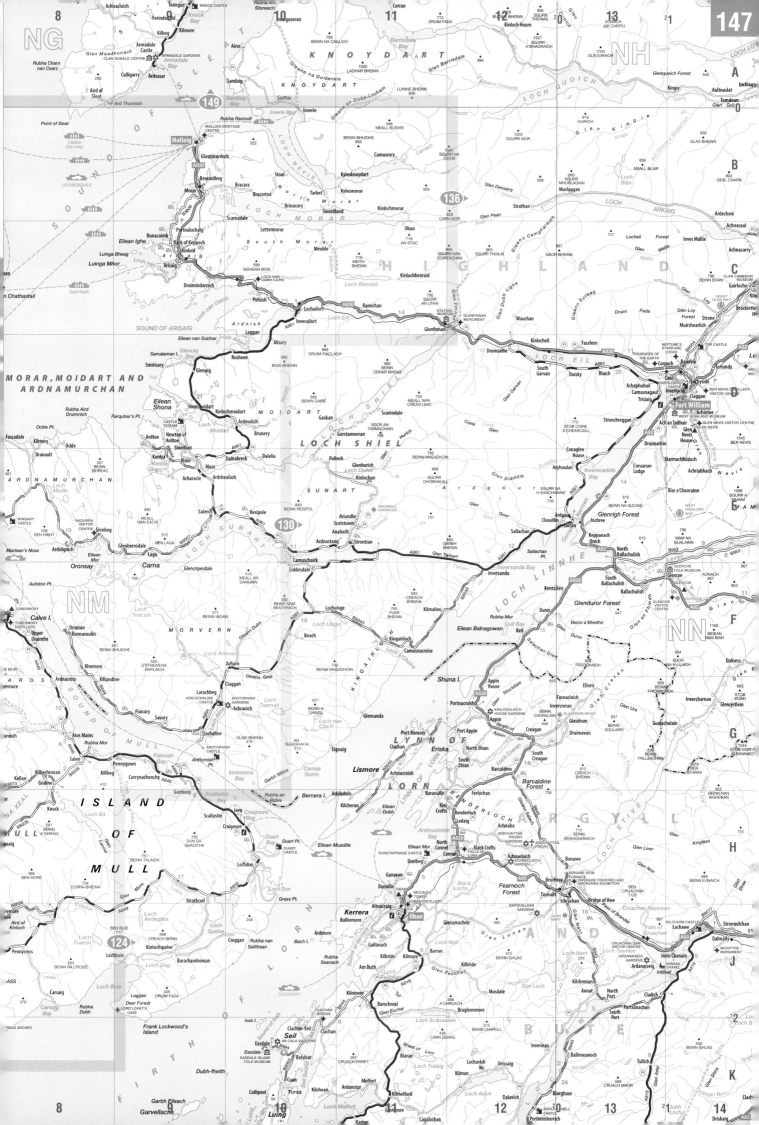

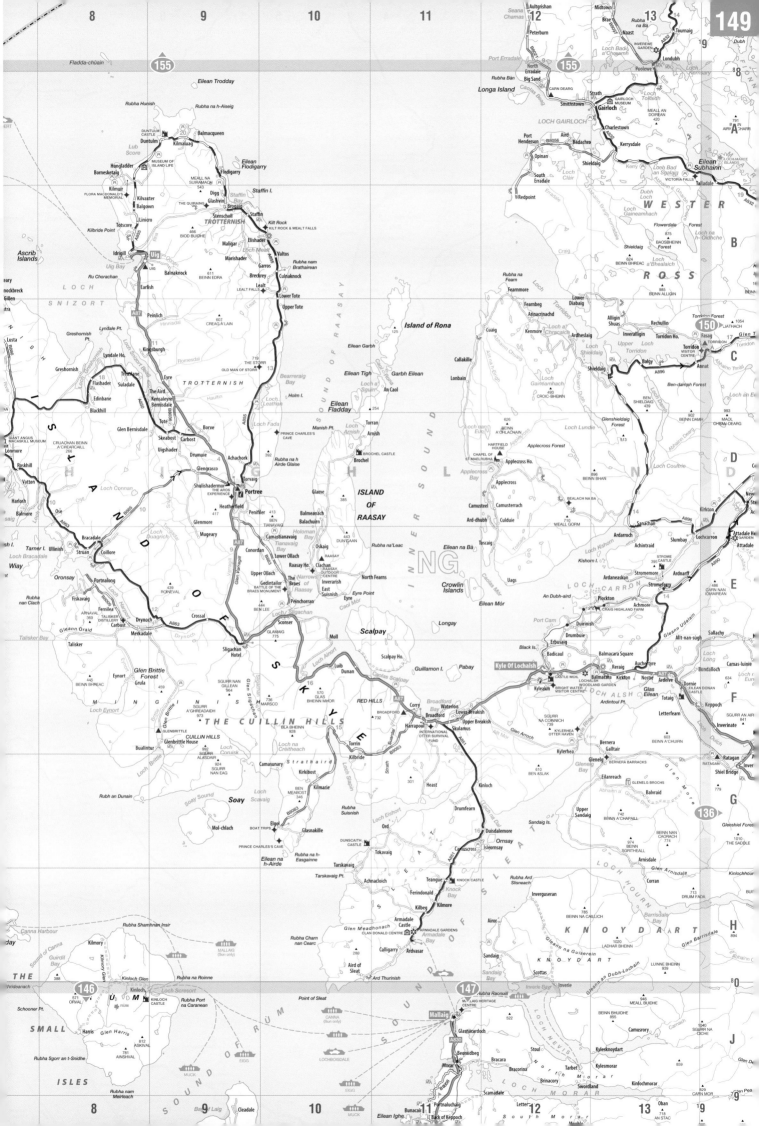

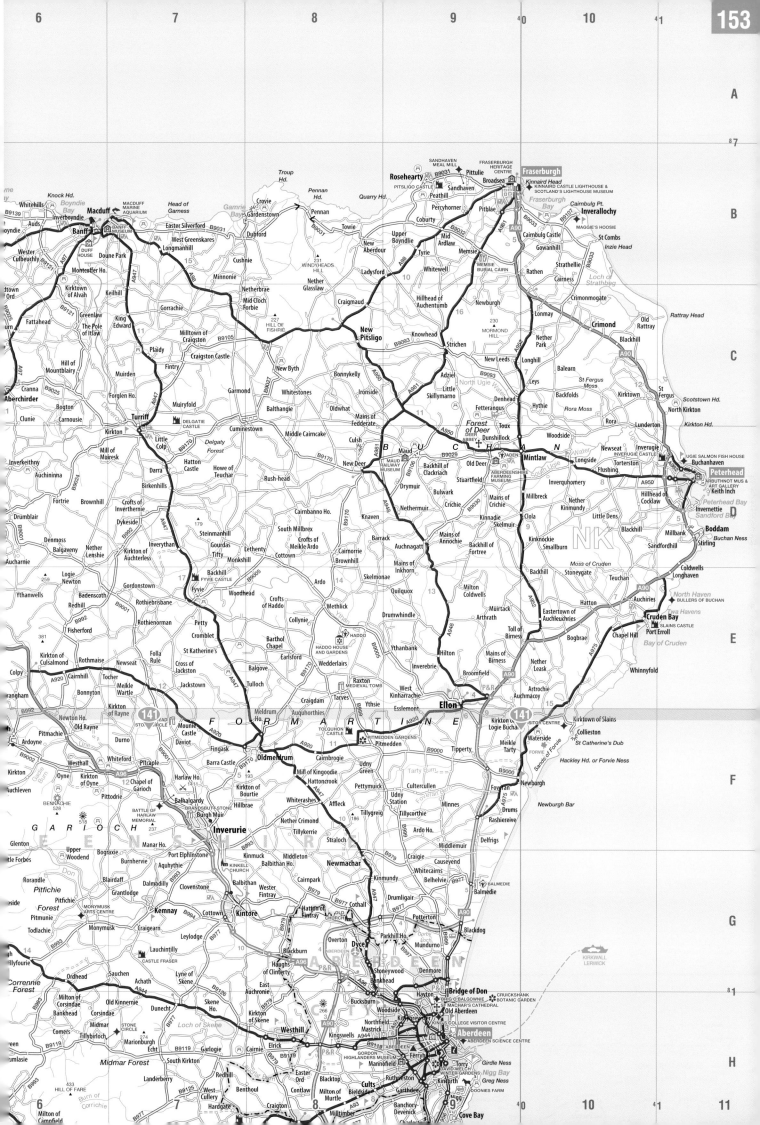

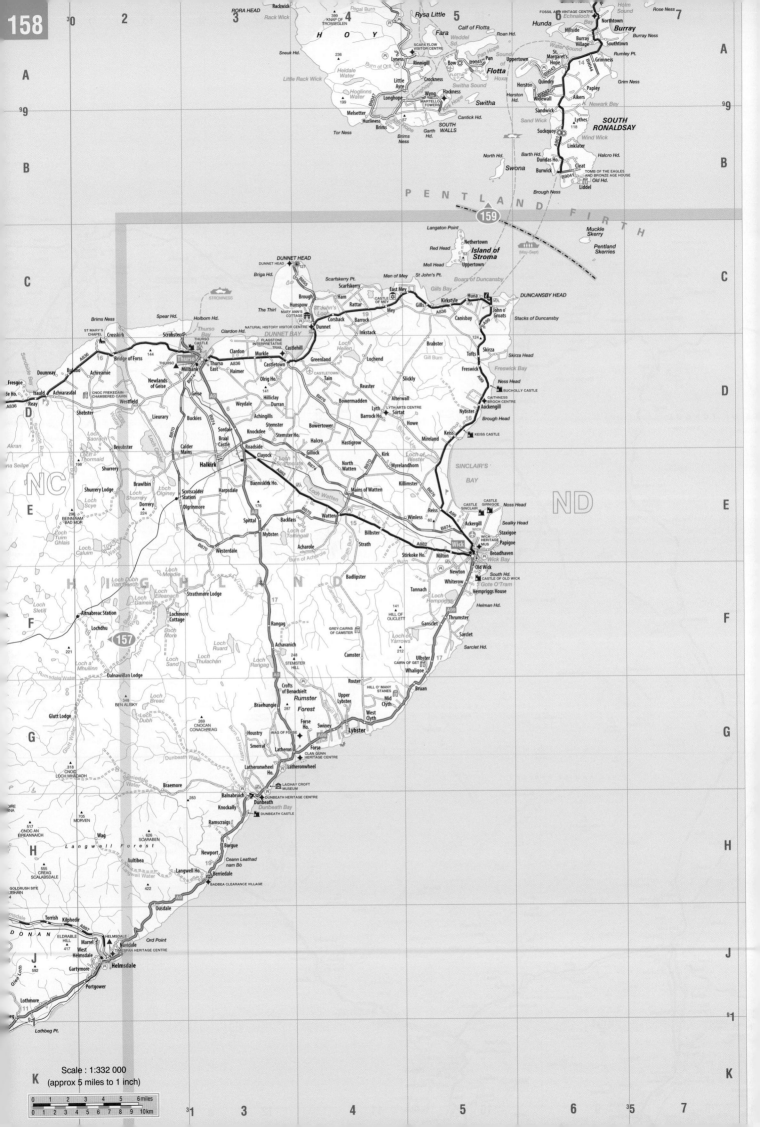

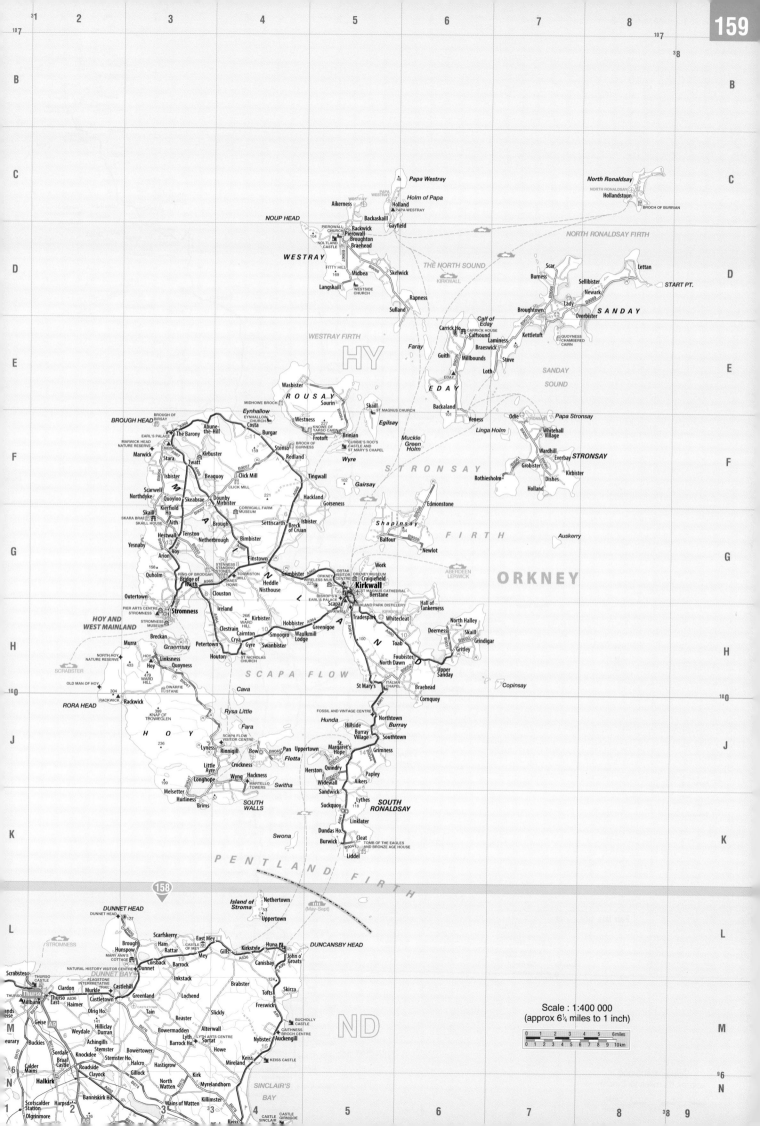

Scale : 1:400 000
(approx 6¼ miles to 1 inch)

0 1 2 3 4 5 6miles
0 1 2 3 4 5 6 7 8 9 10km

Cardiff approaches

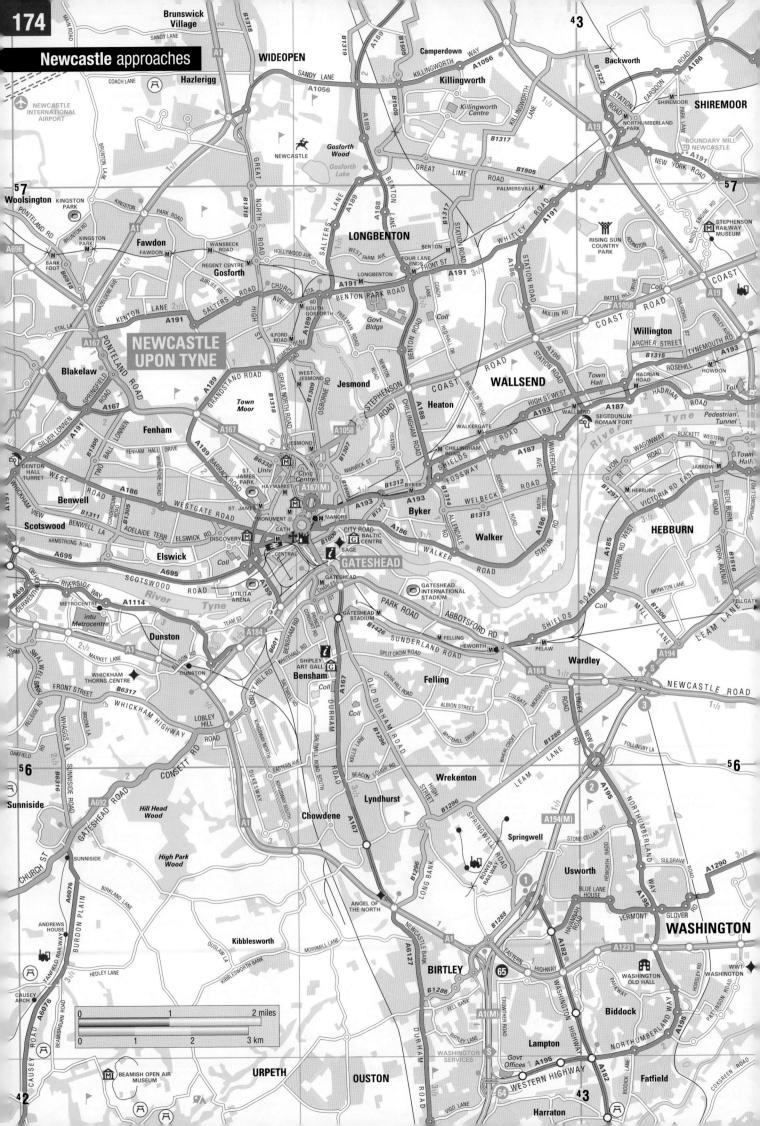

Town plan symbols

Motorway

Primary route – dual, single carriageway

A road – dual, single carriageway

B road – dual, single carriageway

Minor through road

One-way street

Pedestrian roads

Shopping streets

Railway with station

Tramway with station

Underground or Metro station

[H] Hospital

[P] Parking

Police

[PO] Post Office

Shopmobility

▲ Youth hostel

Bus or railway station building

Shopping precinct or retail park

Park

Congestion charge zone

✝ Abbey or cathedral

Ancient monument

Aquarium

Art gallery

Bird collection or aviary

Building of interest

Castle

Church of interest

Cinema

Garden

Historic ship

House

House and garden

Museum

Preserved railway

Roman antiquity

Safari park

Theatre

Tourist information

Zoo

✦ Other place of interest

Aberdeen

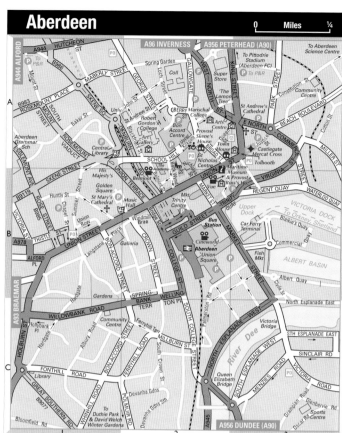

Ayr

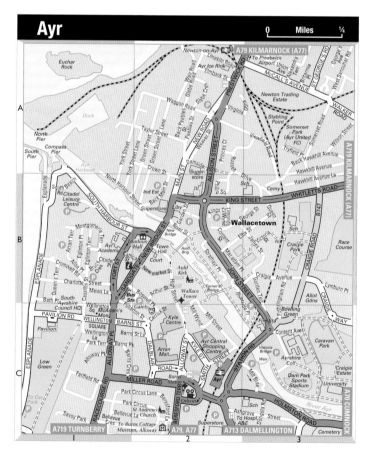

Bath

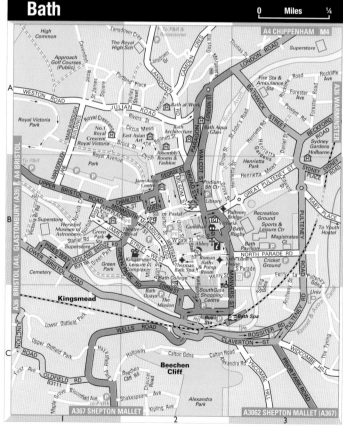

Birmingham

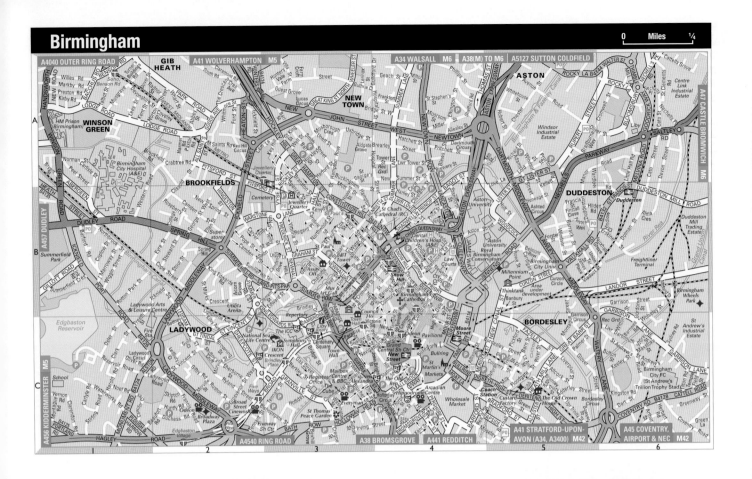

Blackpool

Bournemouth

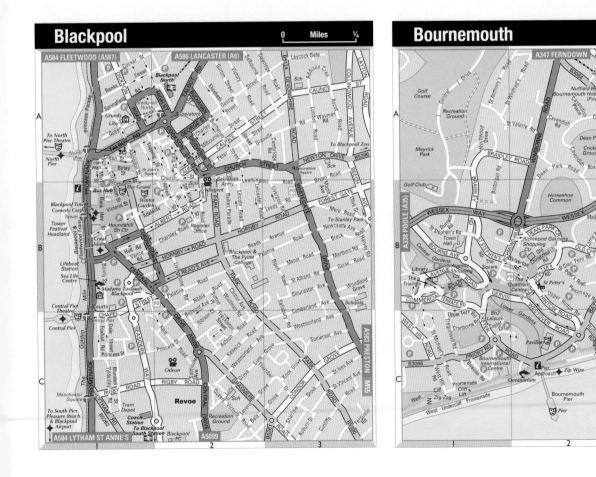

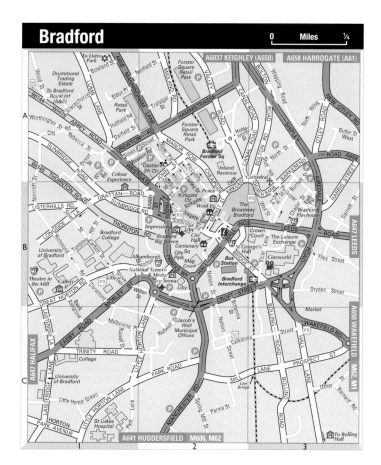

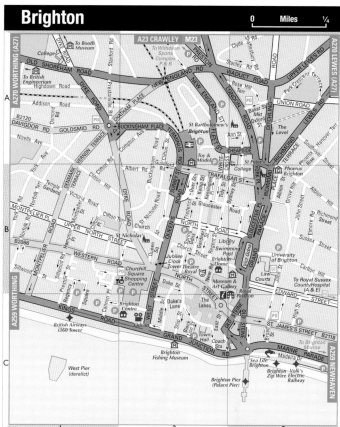

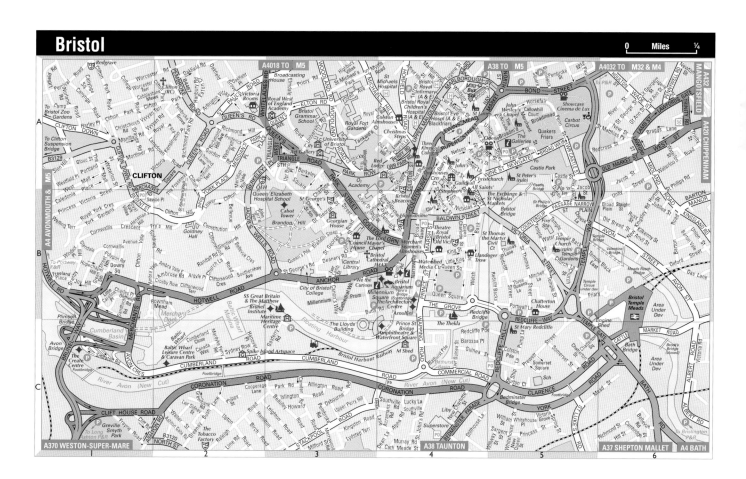

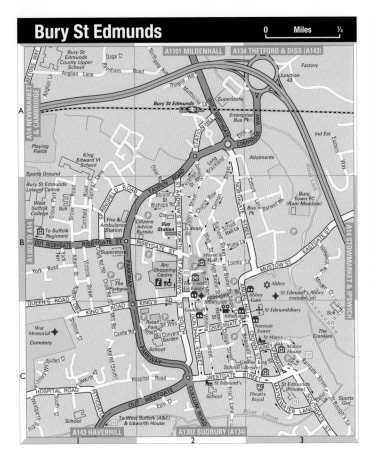

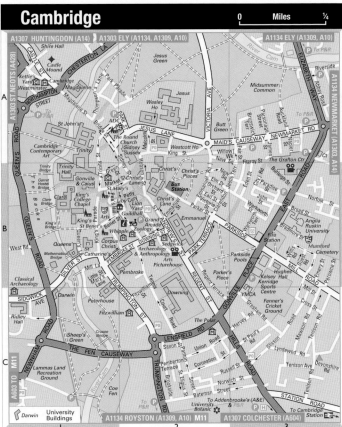

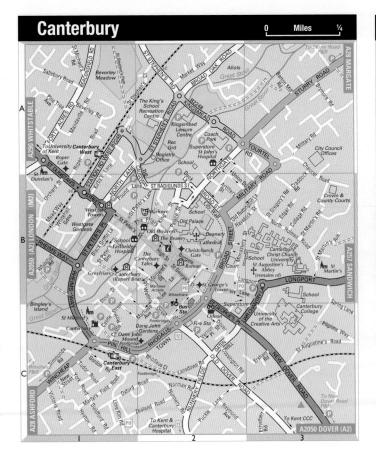

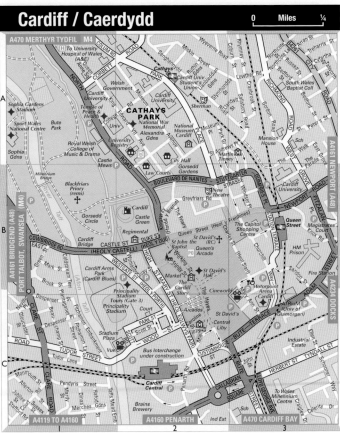

Carlisle

0   Miles   ¼

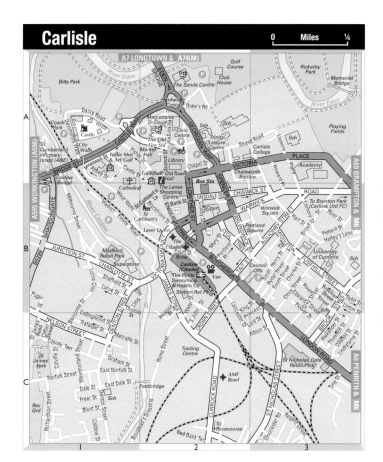

Chelmsford

0   Miles   ¼

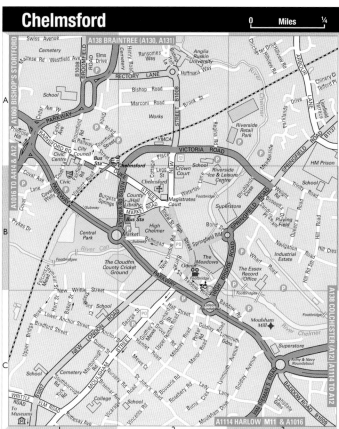

Cheltenham

0   Miles   ¼

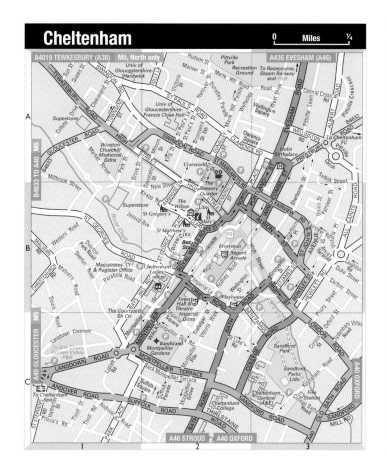

Chester

0   Miles   ¼

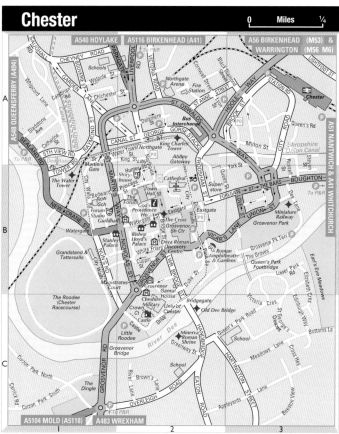

Chichester

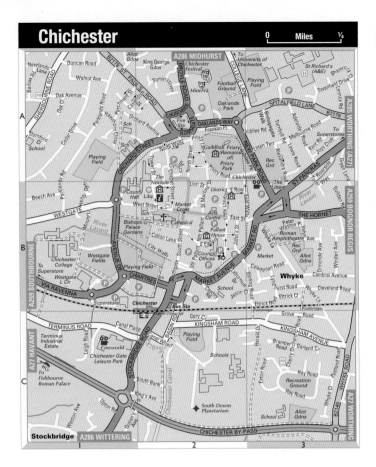

Colchester

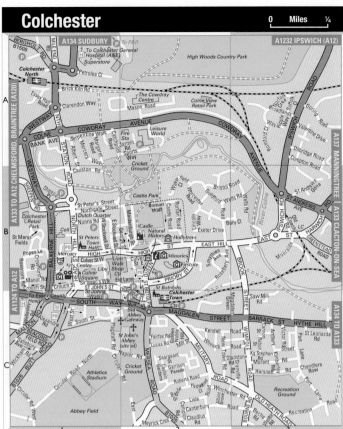

Coventry

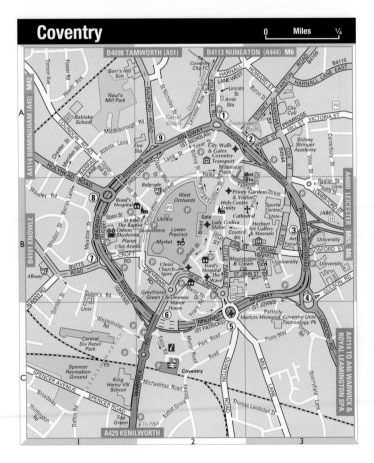

Derby

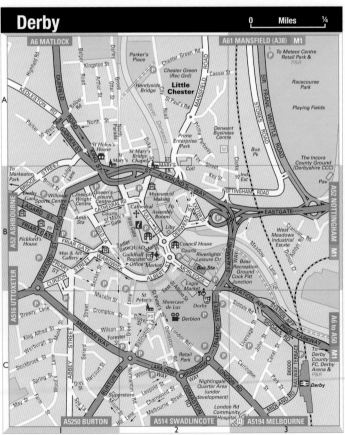

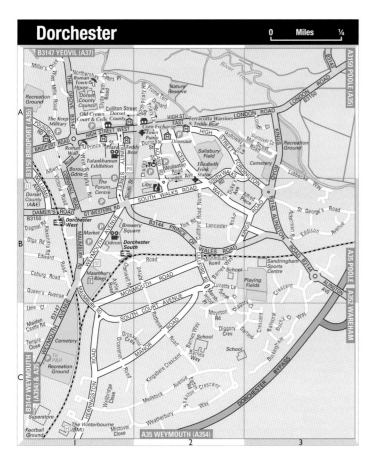

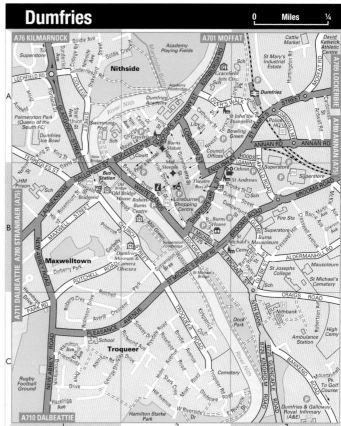

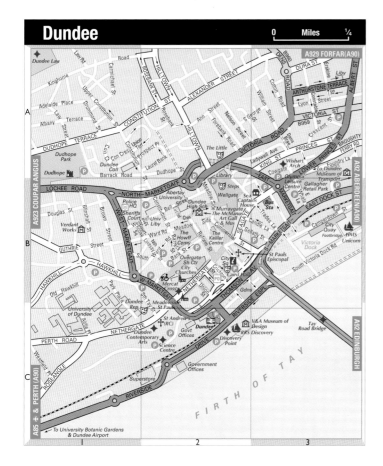

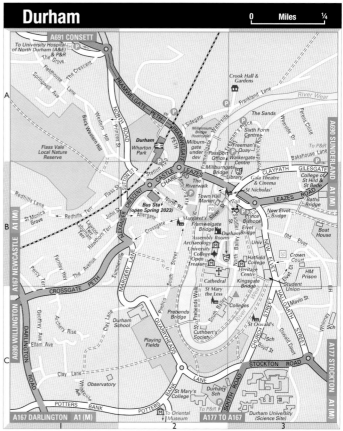

Edinburgh

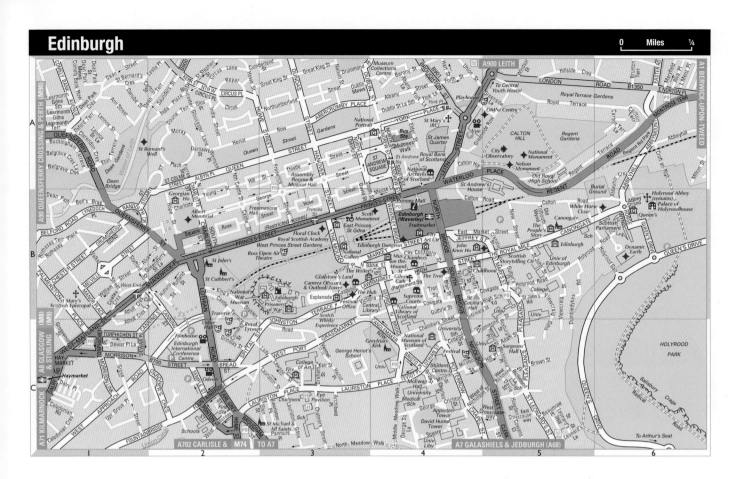

Exeter

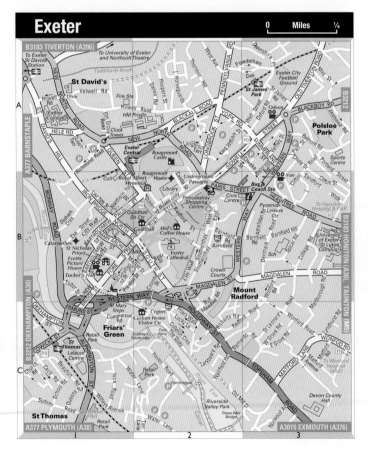

Gloucester

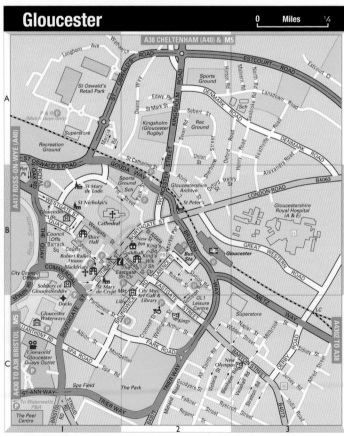

Glasgow

0 — Miles — ¼

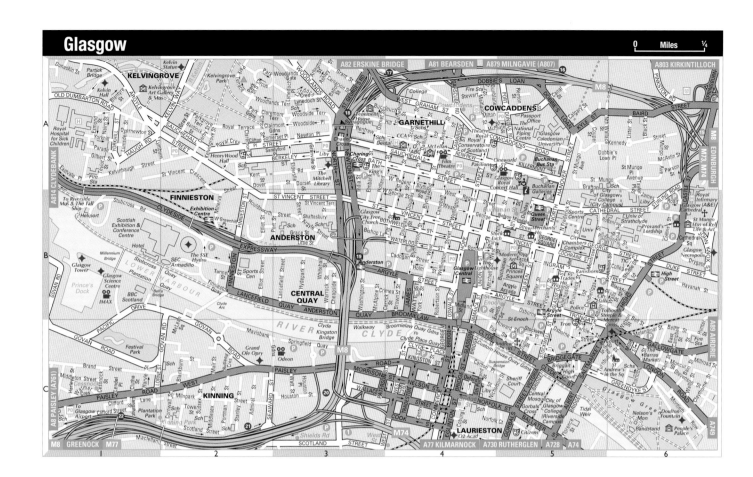

Grimsby

0 — Miles — ¼

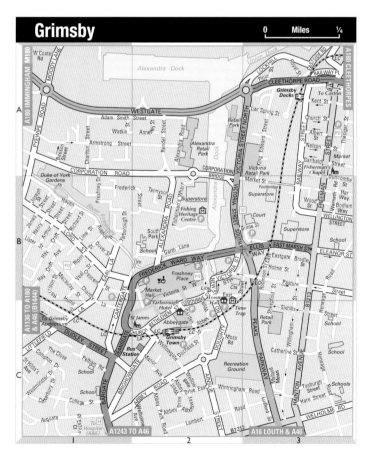

Harrogate

0 — Miles — ¼

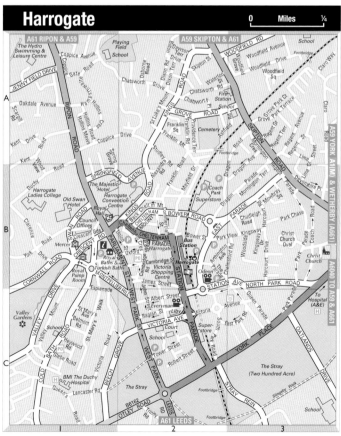

Hull

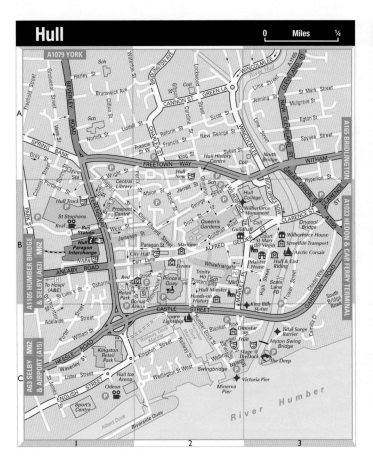

Inverness

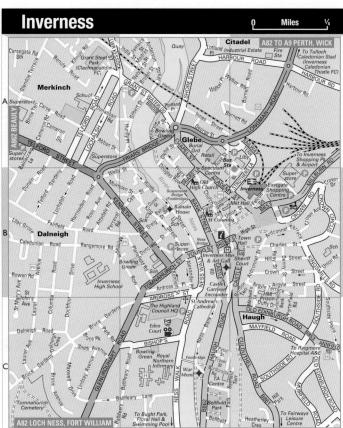

Ipswich

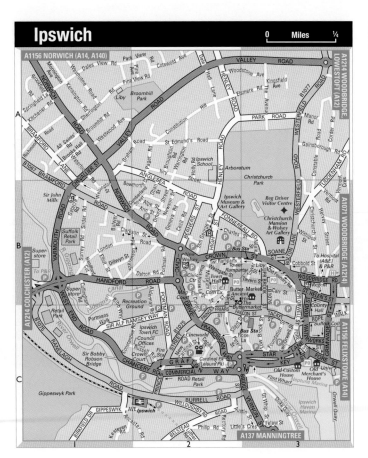

Kendal

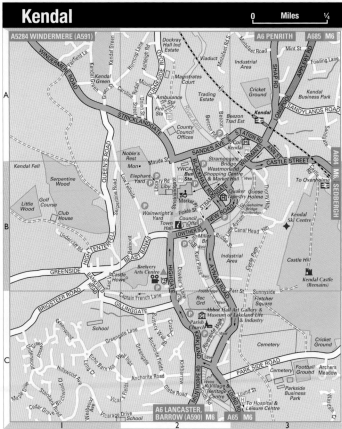

King's Lynn

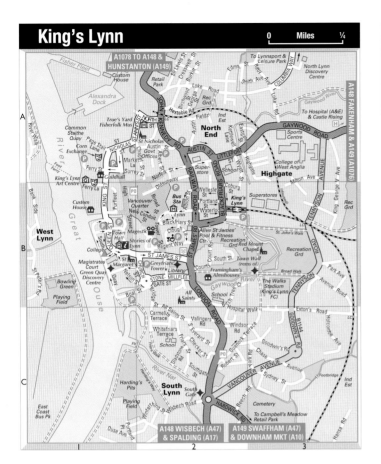

Lancaster

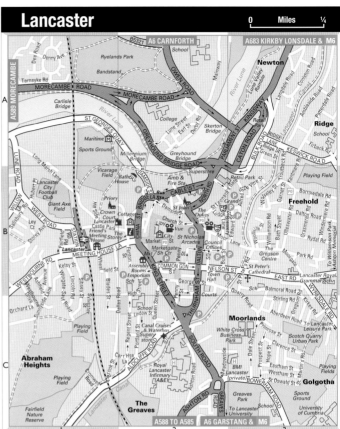

Leeds

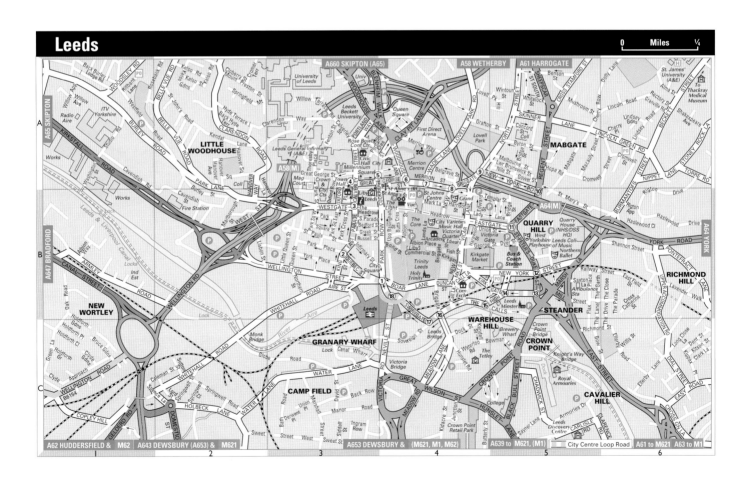

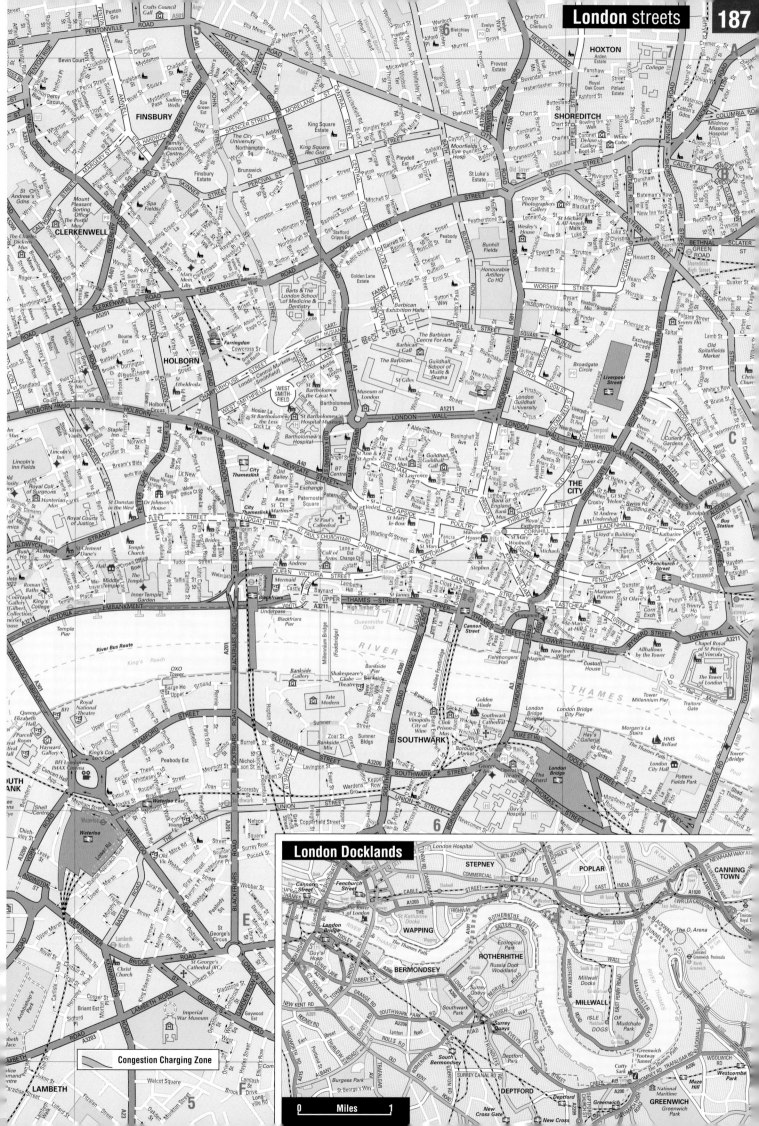

London Docklands

Congestion Charging Zone

Miles
0   1

Leicester

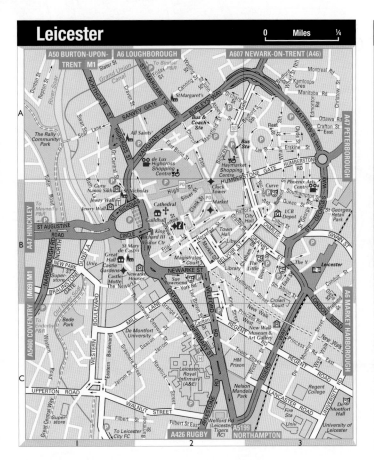

Lincoln

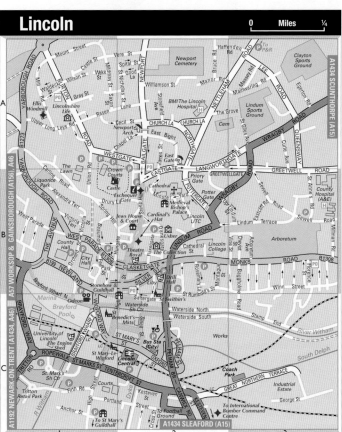

Liverpool

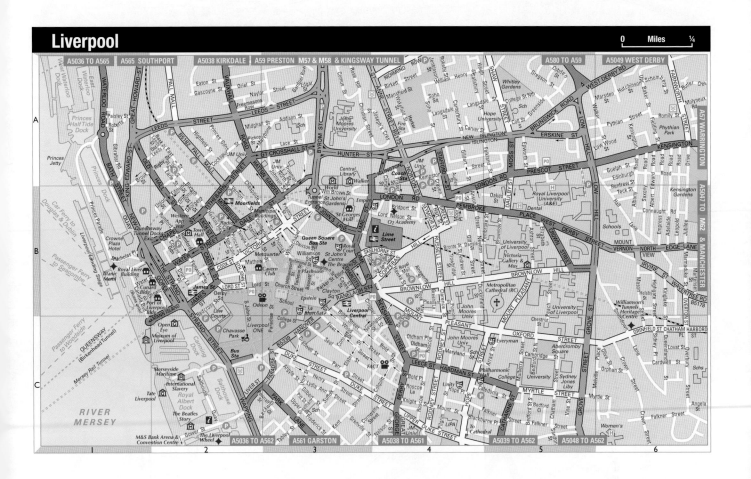

Llandudno
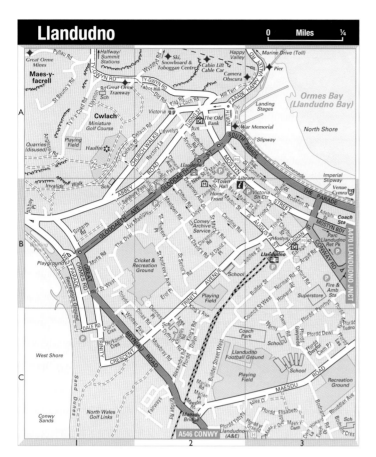

Llanelli
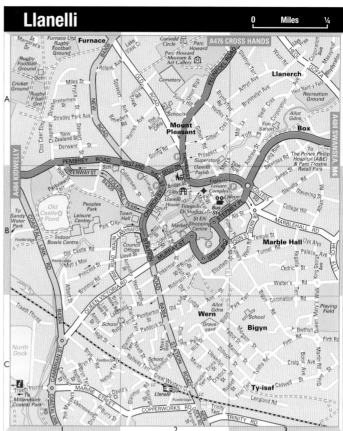

Luton
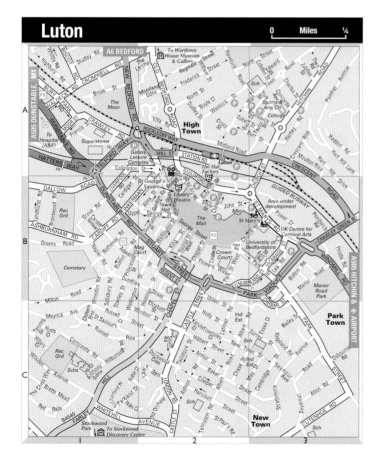

Macclesfield
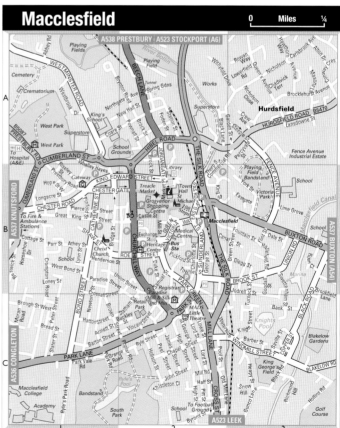

Manchester

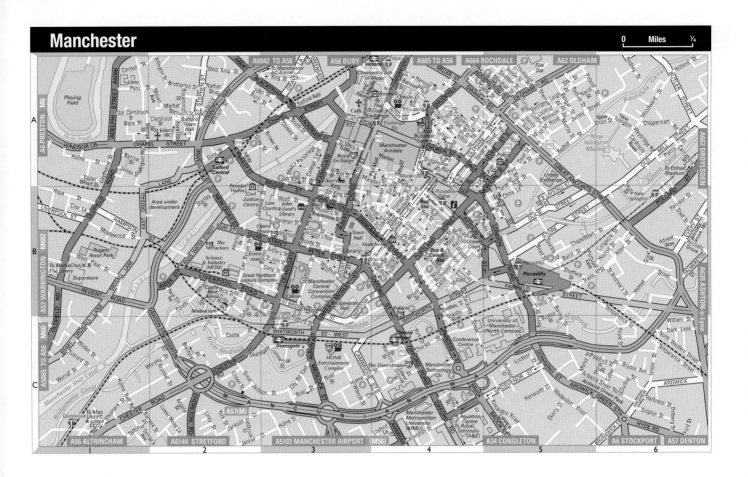

Maidstone

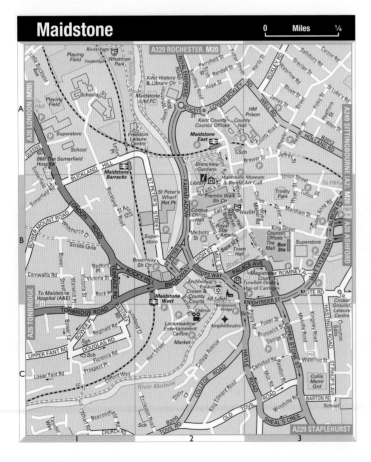

Merthyr Tydfil / Merthyr Tudful

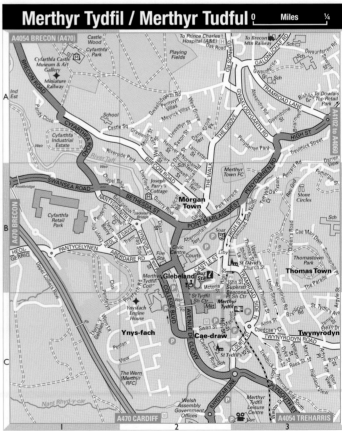

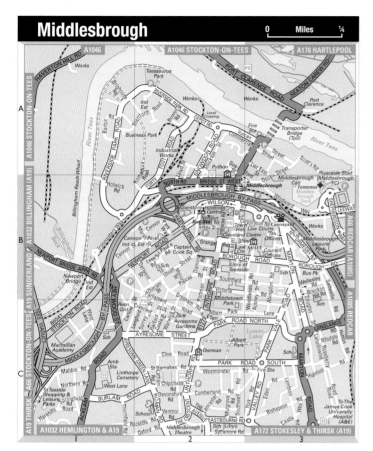

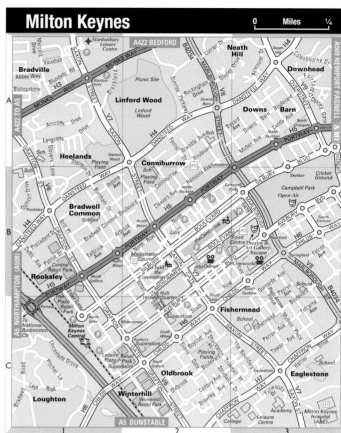

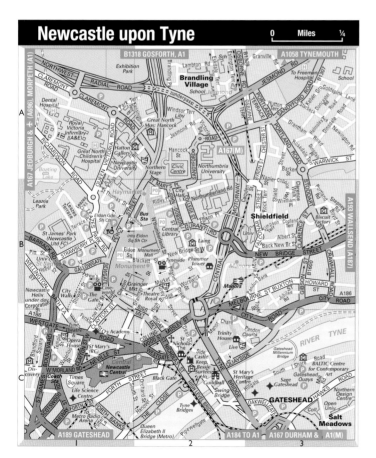

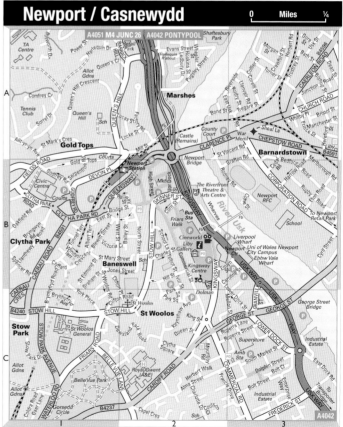

Newquay

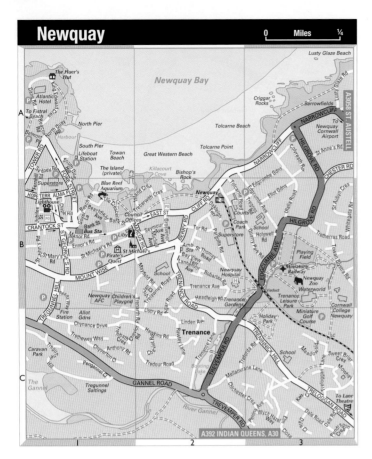

Northampton

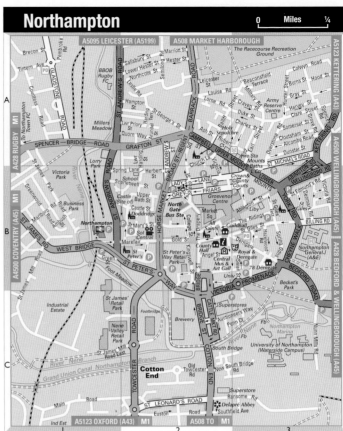

Norwich

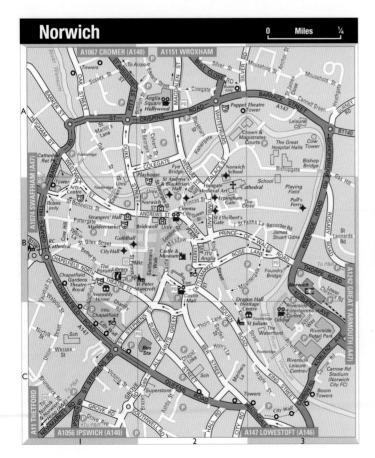

Nottingham

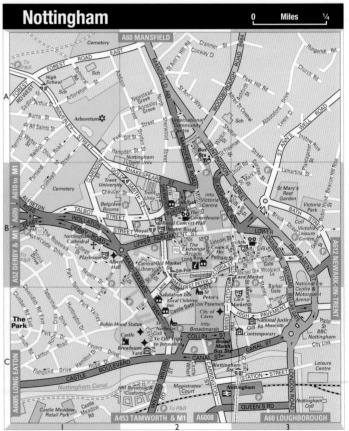

Oxford

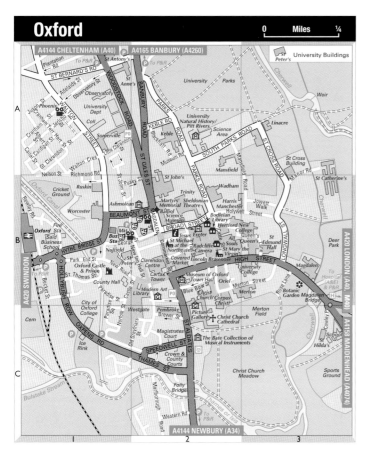

Perth

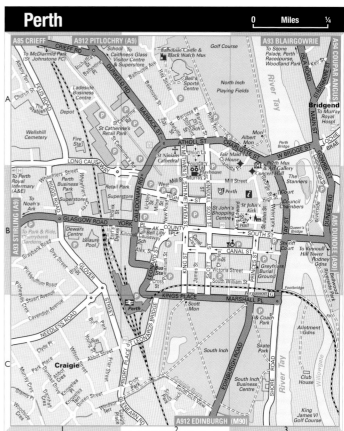

Peterborough

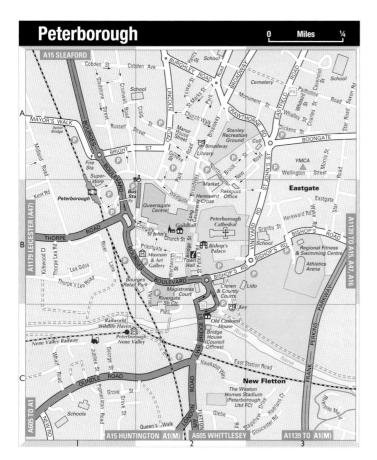

Plymouth

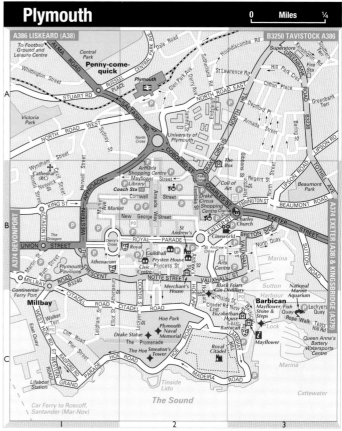

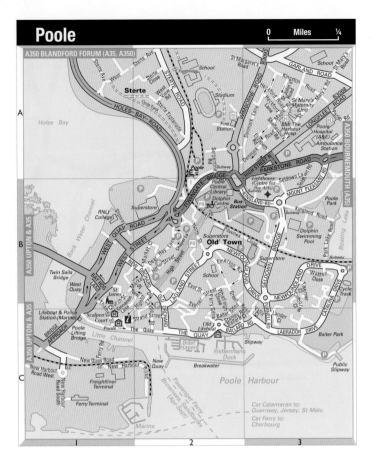

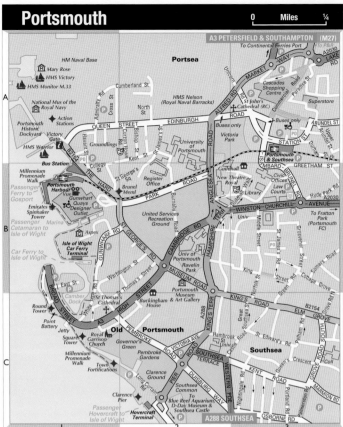

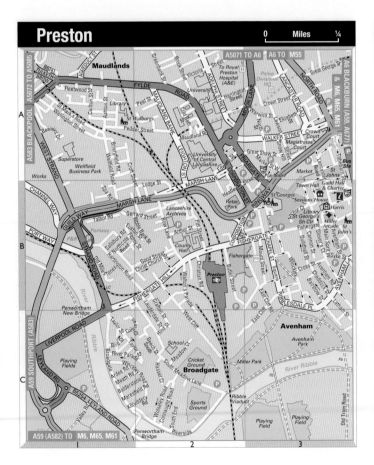

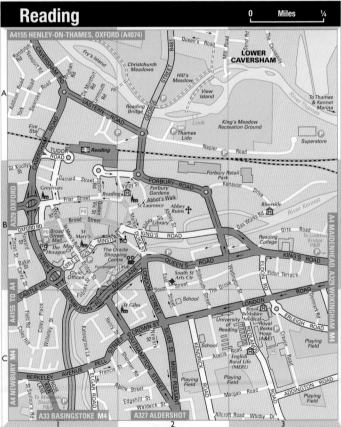

St Andrews

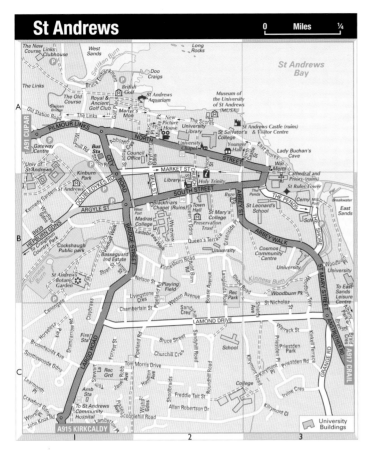

Salisbury

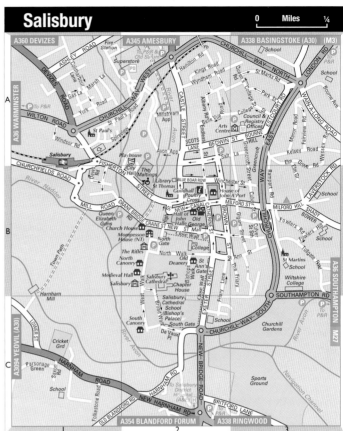

Scarborough

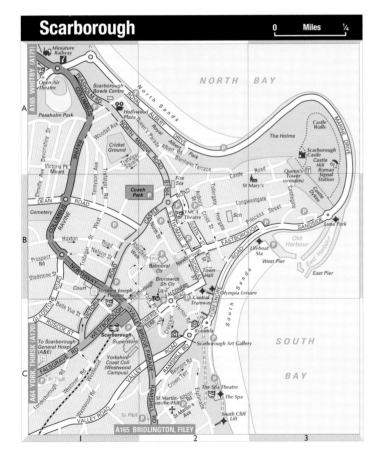

Shrewsbury

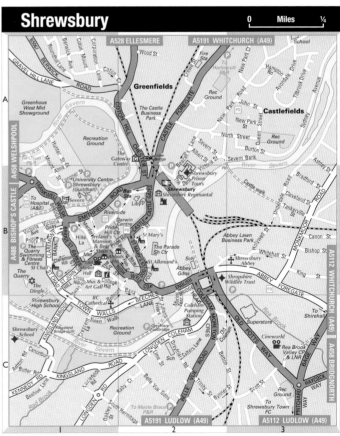

Sheffield

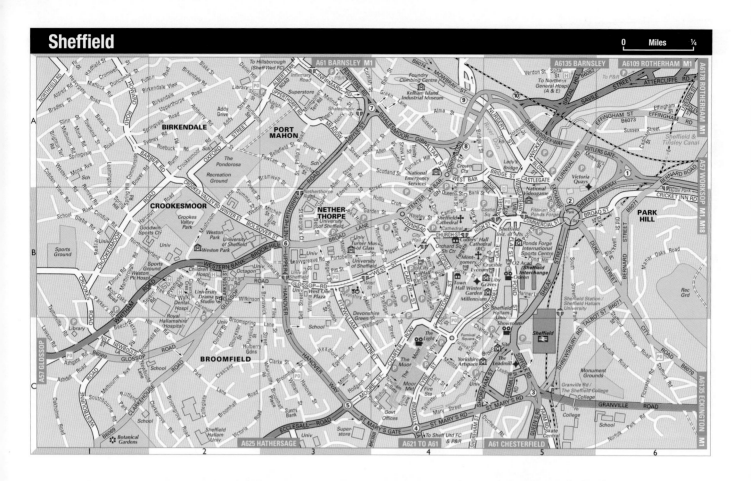

Stoke-on-Trent (Hanley)

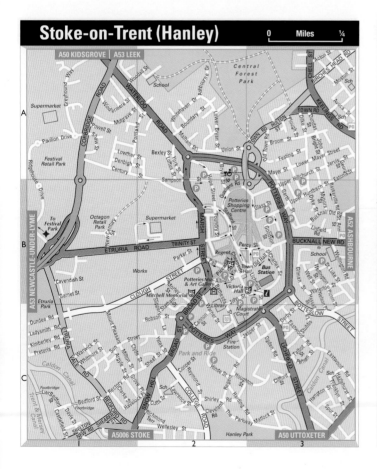

Southampton

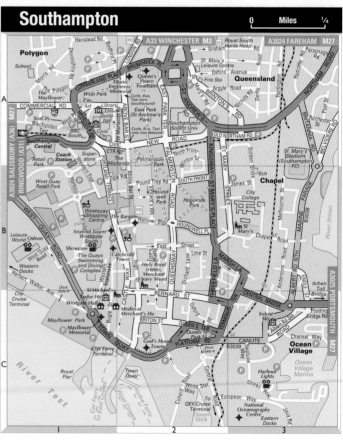

Southend-on-Sea

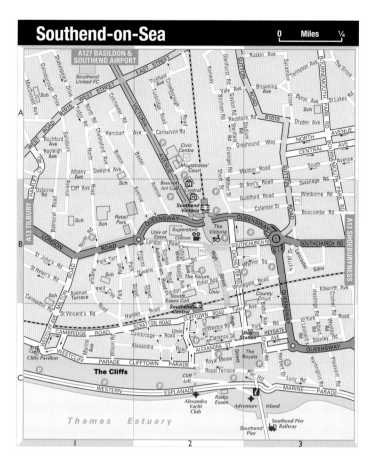

Stirling

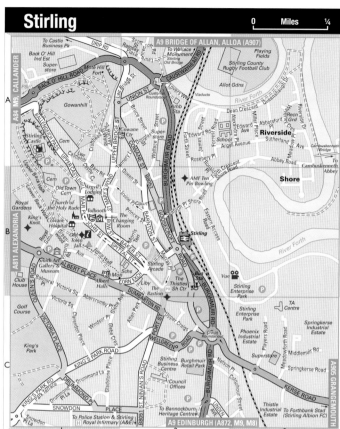

Stratford-upon-Avon

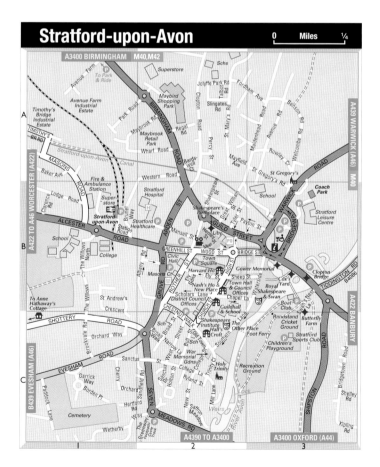

Sunderland

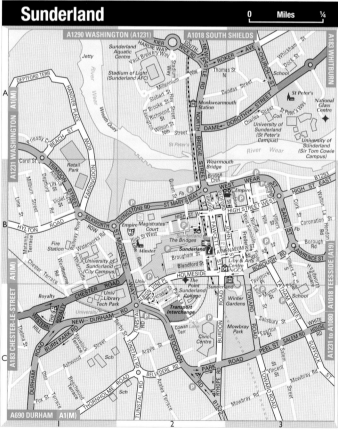

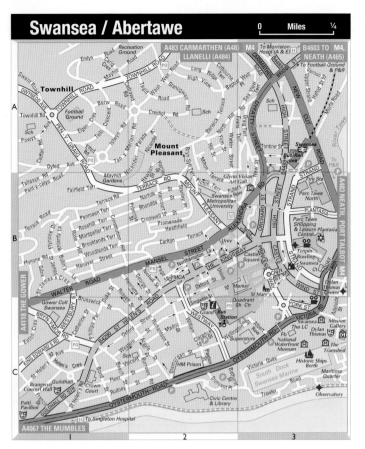

Swansea / Abertawe

0 — Miles — ¼

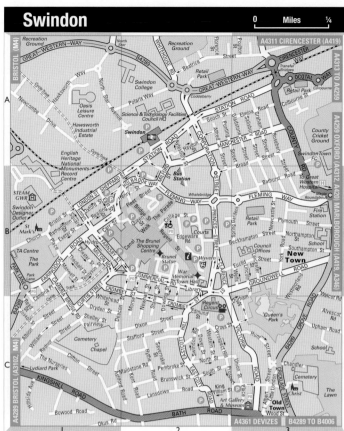

Swindon

0 — Miles — ¼

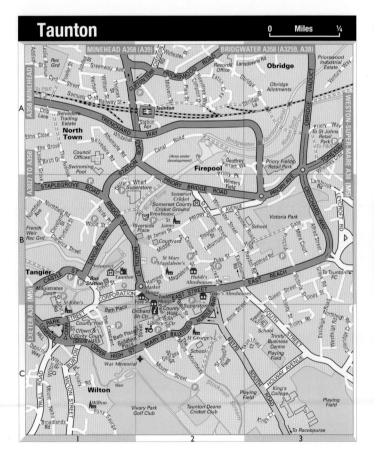

Taunton

0 — Miles — ¼

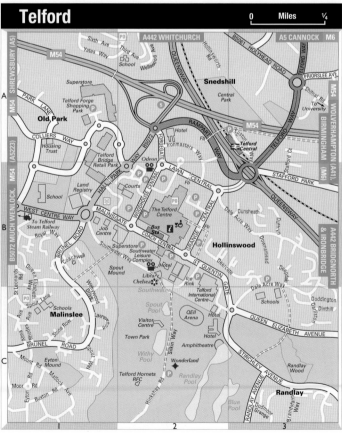

Telford

0 — Miles — ¼

Torquay
0   Miles   ¼

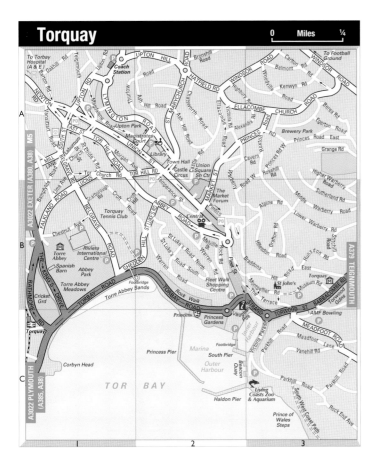

Truro
0   Miles   ¼

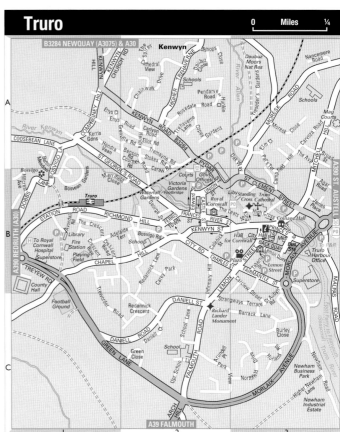

Winchester
0   Miles   ¼

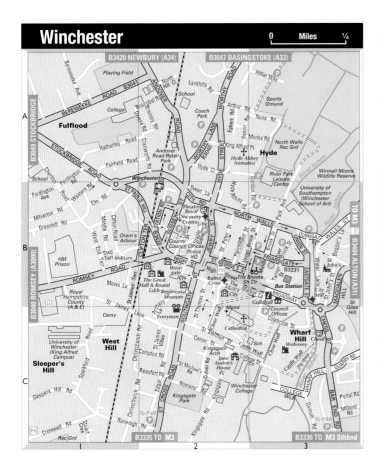

Windsor
0   Miles   ¼

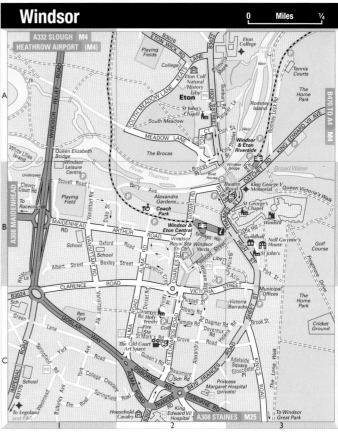

Wolverhampton

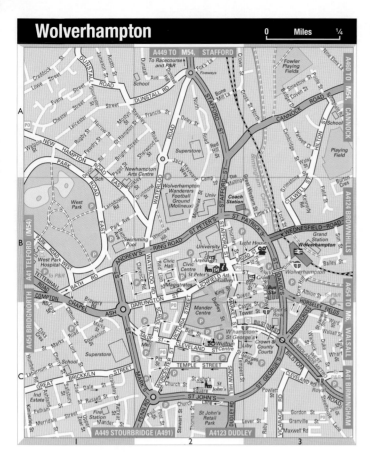

Worcester

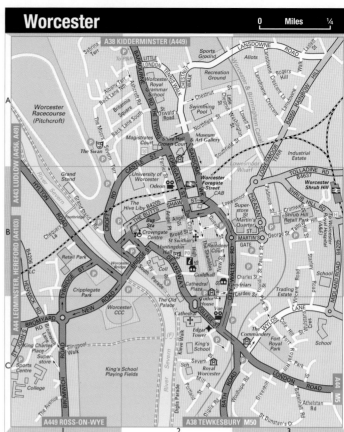

Wrexham / Wrecsam

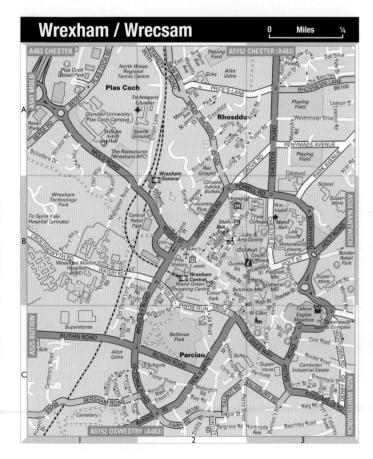

York

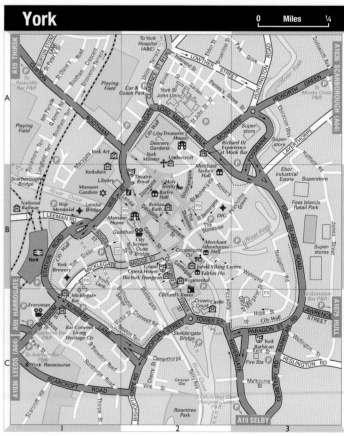

Town plan indexes

202 Brighton • Bristol • Bury St Edmunds • Cambridge • Canterbury • Cardiff • Carlisle

Rebecca St A1
Richmond Rd B1
Russell St C1
St George's Hall B2
St Lukes Hospital C1
Shipley Airedale Rd A3/B3
Shopmobility A2
Simes St A1
Smith St B2
Spring Mill St C2
Stott Hill A3
Sunbridge Rd A1/B1/B2
Theatre in the Mill B1
Thornton Rd A1/B1
Trafalgar St A2
Trinity Rd C1
Tumbling Hill St B1
Tyrrel St B2
Univ of Bradford B1/C1
Usher St C3
Valley Rd A2
Vicar La B3
Wakefield Rd C3
Wapping Rd A3
Well St B3
Westgate A1
White Abbey Rd A1
Wigan Rd A1
Wilton St B1
Wood St A1
Wool Exchange B2
Worthington St A1

Brighton 177

Addison Rd A1
Albert Rd B2
Albion Hill B3
Albion St B3
Ann St A3
Baker St A3
Black Lion St C2
Brighton A2
Brighton Centre C2
Brighton Fishing Museum C2
Brighton Pier (Palace Pier) C3
Brighton Zip Wire C3
British Airways i360Tower C1
Broad St C3
Buckingham Place A2
Buckingham Rd B2
Cannon Place C1
Carlton Hill B3
Chatham Place A1
Cheapside A3
Church St B2
Churchill Square Shopping Centre B2
Clifton Hill B1
Clifton Place B1
Clifton Rd B1
Clifton St A2
Clifton Terr B1
Clyde Rd A3
Coach Station C3
Compton Ave A2
Davigdor Rd A1
Denmark Terr B1
Ditchling Rd A3
Dome B2
Duke St B2
Duke's La C2
Dyke Rd A1/B2
East St C2
Edward St B3
Elmore Rd B3
Fleet St A2
Frederick St B2
Gardner St B2
Gloucester Place B3
Gloucester Rd B2
Goldsmid Rd A1
Grand Junction Rd C2
Grand Pde B3
Grove Hill B3
Guildford St A2
Hampton Place B1
Hanover Terr A3
High St C3
Highdown Rd A1
Information Ctr C2
John St B3
Jubilee Clock Tower B2
Kemp St B2
Kensington Place B2
Kings Rd C1
Lanes,The C2
Law Courts B3
Lewes Rd A3
Library B2
London Rd A3
Madeira Dr C3
Marine Pde C3
Middle St C2
Montpelier Place B1
Montpelier Rd B1
Montpelier St B1
Mus & Art Gallery B3
New England Rd A2
New England St A2
New Rd B2
Nizells Ave A1
Norfolk Rd B1
Norfolk Terr B1
North Rd B2
North St B2
Odeon C2
Old Shoreham Rd A1
Old Steine C3
Osmond Rd A1
Over St B2
Oxford St A3
Park Crescent Terr A3
Phoenix Brighton B3
Phoenix Rise A3
Police Station B3
Post Office A1/A3/C3
Preston Rd A2
Preston St B1
Prestonville Rd A1
Queen's Rd B2
Queen Sq B2
Regency Sq C1
Regent St B2
Richmond Place B3
Richmond St B3
Richmond Terr A3
Rose Hill Terr A3
Royal Pavilion B2
St Bartholomew's A3
St James's St C3
St Nicholas Rd B2
St Nicholas' B2
St Peter's A3
Sea Life Brighton C3
Shaftesbury Rd A3
Ship St C2
Sillwood Rd B1
Sillwood St B1
Southover St A3
Spring Gdns B2
Stanford Rd A1
Stanley Rd A3
Surrey St B2
Sussex St B3
Swimming Pool B3
Sydney St B3
Temple Gdns B1
Terminus Rd A2
Theatre Royal B2
Tidy St B2
Town Hall C2
Toy & Model Mus A2
Trafalgar St B2
Union Rd A3
Univ of Brighton B3
Upper Lewes Rd A3
Upper North St B1
Viaduct Rd A3
Victoria Gdns B3
Victoria Rd B1
Volk's Electric Railway C3
West Pier (derelict) C1
West St C2
Western Rd B1
Whitecross St B2
YHA C3
London B1
York Place B3
York Rd B1

Bristol 177

Acramans Rd C4
Albert Rd C6
Alfred Hill A4
All Saint's St A4
All Saints' B4
Allington Rd C3
Alpha Rd C4
Ambra Vale B1
Ambra Vale East B2
Ambrose Rd B2
Amphitheatre & Waterfront Sq C4
Anchor Rd B3
Anvil St B6
Arcade,The A5
Architecture Centre,The B4
Argyle Place B2
Arlington Villas A2
Arnolfini B4
Art Gallery A3
Ashton Gate Rd C2
Ashton Rd C1
Avon Bridge C1
Avon Cres C1
Avon St B6
Baldwin St B4
Baltic Wharf C2
Baltic Wharf Leisure Centre & Caravan Park C2
Baltic Wharf Marina C2
Barossa Place C4
Barton Manor B6
Barton Rd B6
Barton Vale B6
Bath Rd C6
Bathurst Basin C4
Bathurst Parade C4
Beauley Rd C3
Bedminster Bridge C5
Bedminster Parade C4
Bellevue B2
Bellevue Cres B2
Bellevue Rd C6
Berkeley Place A2
Berkeley Sq A3
Birch Rd C2
Blackfriars A4
Bond St A5
Braggs La A6
Brandon Hill B3
Brandon Steep B3
Bristol Aquarium B4
Bristol Beacon B4
Bristol Bridge B5
Bristol Cath (CE) B3
Bristol Eye Hospital (A&E) A4
Bristol Grammar School A3
Bristol Harbour Railway C3
Bristol Royal Children's Hosp A4
Bristol Royal Infirmary (A&E) A4
Bristol Temple Meads Station B6
Broad Plain B6
Broad Quay B4
Broad St A4
Broad Weir A5
Broadcasting Ho A3
Broadmead A5
Brunel Institute B3
Brunel Way C1
Brunswick Sq A5
Burton Close C5
Bus Station A4
Butts Rd B3
Cabot Circus A5
Cabot Tower B3
Caledonia Place B1
Callowhill Ct A5
Cambridge St C6
Camden Rd C3
Camp Rd A1
Canada Way C2
Cannon St A4
Canon's Way B3
Cantock's Close A3
Canynge Rd A1
Canynge Sq A1
Castle Park A5
Castle St A5
Cathedral Walk B3
Catherine Meade St C4
Cattle Market Rd C6
Central Library B3
Charles Place B1
Charlotte St B3
Charlotte St South B3
Chatterton Ho B5
Chatterton Sq C5
Chatterton St C5
Cheese La B5
Christchurch A4
Christchurch Rd A1
Christmas Steps A4
Church La B2/B5
Church St B5
City Museum A3
City of Bristol Coll B3
Civil and Family Justice Centre B5
Clare St B4
Clarence Rd C5
Cliff Rd C1
Cliff House Rd C1
Clifton Cath (RC) A2
Clifton Down A1
Clifton Down Rd A1
Clifton Hill B2
Clifton Park A1/A2
Clifton Park Rd A1
Clifton Rd A2
Clifton Vale B1
Cliftonwood Cres B2
Cliftonwood Rd B2
Cliftonwood Terr B2
Cobblestone Mews A1
College Green B3
College Rd A1
College St B3
Colston Almshouses A4
Colston Ave B4
Colston Parade C5
Colston St A4
Commercial Rd C4
Constitution Hill B2
Cooperage La C2
Corn St B4
Cornwallis Ave B1
Cornwallis Cres B1
Coronation Rd C2/C4
Council House B3
Counterslip B5
Create Ctr,The C1
Crosby Row B2
Crown Court A4
Culver St B3
Cumberland Basin C1
Cumberland Close C2
Cumberland Rd C2/C3
Dean La C4
Deanery Rd B3
Denmark St B4
Dowry Sq B1
Eaton Cres A2
Elmdale Rd A3
Elton Rd A3
Eugene St A4/A6
Exchange and St Nicholas' Mkts, The B4
Fairfax St A4
Fire Station A5
Floating Harbour C3
Fosseway,The A2
Foster Almshouses A4
Frayne Rd C1
Frederick Place A2
Freeland Place B1
Friary B5
Frogmore St B3
Fry's Hill B2
Galleries shopping centre,The A5
Gas La B6
Gasferry Rd C3
Georgian House B3
Glendale B1
Glentworth Rd B2
Gloucester St A1
Goldney Hall B2
Goldney Rd B1
Gordon Rd A2
Granby Hill B1
Grange Rd A1
Great Ann St A6
Great George Rd B3
Great George St A6/B3
Green St North B1
Green St South B1
Greenay Bush La C2
Greenbank Rd C2
Greville Smyth Park C1
Grove,The B4
Guildhall A4
Guinea St C4
Hamilton Rd C3
Hanbury Rd A2
Hanover Place C2
Harley Place A1
Haymarket A5
Hensman's Hill B1
High St B4
Highbury Villas A3
Hill St B3
Hill St C6
Hippodrome B4
Hopechapel Hill B1
Horfield Rd A4
Horsefair,The A5
Horton St B6
Host St A4
Hotwell Rd B1/B2
Houlton St A6
Howard Rd C3
IMAX Cinema B4
Information Ctr B4
Islington Rd C3
Jacob St A5/A6
Jacob's Wells Rd B2
John Carr's Terr B2
John Wesley's Chapel A5
Joy Hill B1
Jubilee St B6
Kensington Place A2
Kilkenny St B6
King St B4
Kingsland Rd B6
Kingston Rd C3
Lamb St A6
Lansdown Rd A2
Lawford St A6
Lawfords Gate A6
Leighton Rd C3
Lewins Mead A4
Lime Rd C2
Litfield Rd A1
Little Ann St A6
Little Caroline Pl B1
Little George St A6
Little King St B4
Llandoger Trow B4
Lloyds' Building, The C3
Lodge St A4
Lord Mayor's Chapel,The B4
Lower Castle St A5
Lower Church La A4
Lower Clifton Hill B2
Lower Guinea St C4
Lower Lamb St B3
Lower Maudlin St A4
Lower Park Rd A4
Lower Sidney St C2
Lucky La C4
Lydstep Terr C3
M Shed C4
Magistrates' Court A4
Manilla Rd A1
Mardyke Ferry Rd C2
Maritime Heritage Centre B3
Marlborough Hill A4
Marlborough St A4
Marsh St B4
Mead St C5
Merchant Dock B2
Merchant Seamen's Almshouses B4
Merchant St A5
Merchants Rd A1
Merchants Rd C1
Meridian Place A2
Meridian Vale A2
Merrywood Rd C3
Midland Rd A6
Milford St C3
Millennium Prom B3
Millennium Sq B3
Mitchell La B5
Mortimer Rd A1
Murray Rd C4
Myrtle Rd A3
Narrow Plain B5
Narrow Quay B4
Nelson St A4
New Charlotte St C4
New Kingsley Rd B6
New Queen St C5
New St A6
Newgate A5
Newton St A6
Norland Rd A1
North St C2
O2 Academy B3
Oakfield Grove A2
Oakfield Place A2
Oakfield Rd A2
Old Bread St B6
Old Market St A6
Old Park Hill A4
Oldfield Rd B1
Orchard Ave B4
Orchard La B4
Orchard St B4
Osbourne Rd C3
Oxford St B6
Park Place A2
Park Rd C3
Park Row A3
Park St A3
Passage St B5
Pembroke Grove A2
Pembroke Rd A2
Pembroke Rd C3
Pembroke St A5
Penn St A5
Pennywell Rd A6
Percival Rd A1
Pero's Bridge B4
Perry Rd A4
Phipps St C2
Pip 'n' Jay B5
Plimsoll Bridge B1
Police Sta A6
Polygon Rd B1
Portland St A1
Portwall La B5
Post Office A1/A3/A5/B1/B4/C4/C5
Prewett St C5
Prince St B4
Prince St Bridge C4
Princess St C5
Princess Victoria St B1
Priory Rd A3
Pump La C5
QEH Theatre A2
Quakers Friars A5
Quay St A4
Queen Charlotte St B4
Queen Elizabeth Hospital School B2
Queen Sq B4
Queen St A5
Queen's Ave A3
Queen's Parade B3
Queen's Rd A2/A3
Raleigh Rd C2
Randall Rd B2
Red Lodge A4
Redcliffe Backs B5
Redcliffe Bridge B4
Redcliffe Hill C5
Redcliffe Parade C4
Redcliffe St B5
Redcliffe Way B5
Redcross St A6
Redgrave Theatre A1
Regent St B1
Richmond Hill A2
Richmond Hill Ave A2
Richmond La A2
Richmond Park Rd A2
Richmond St C6
Richmond Terr A2
River St A6
Rownham Mead B2
Royal Fort Rd A3
Royal Park A2
Royal West of England Academy A3
Royal York Cres B1
Royal York Villas B1
Rupert St A4
Russ St B6
St Andrew's Walk B2
St George's B3
St George's Rd B3
St James A4
St John's A4
St John's Rd C4
St Luke's Rd C5
St Mary Redcliffe C5
St Matthias Park A6
St Michael's Hill A3
St Michael's Hospital A3
St Michael's Park A3
St Nicholas St B4
St Paul St A5
St Paul's Rd A2
St Peter's (ruin) A5
St Philip's Bridge B5
St Philips Rd A6
St Stephen's B4
St Stephen's St B4
St Thomas St B5
St Thomas the Martyr B5
Sandford Rd B1
Sargent St C5
Saville Place B1
Ship La C5
Shopmobility A5
Showcase Cinema de Lux A5
Silver St A4
Sion Hill A1
Small St A4
Smeaton Rd C1
Somerset Sq C5
Somerset St C5
Southernhay Ave B2
Southville Rd C4
Spike Island Artspace C2
Spring St C5
Superstore C4
SS Great Britain and the Matthew B2
Stackpool Rd C3
Staight St B6
Stillhouse La C4
Sydney Row C2
Tankard's Close A3
Temple Back B5
Temple Back East B5
Temple Bridge B5
Temple Church B5
Temple Circus B5
Temple Gate C5
Temple St B5
Temple Way B5
Terrell St A4
Theatre Royal (Bristol Old Vic) B4
Thekla B4
Thomas La B5
Three Kings of Cologne A4
Three Queens La B5
Tobacco Factory, The C2
Tower Hill B5
Tower La A4
Trenchard St A4
Triangle South A3
Triangle West A3
Trinity Rd A6
Trinity St A6
Tyndall Ave A3
Union St A5
Union St B6
Unity St A6
Unity St B3
University of Bristol A3
University Rd A3
Upper Byron Place A3
Upper Maudlin St A4
Upper Perry Hill C3
Upton Rd C2
Valentine Bridge B6
Victoria Grove C5
Victoria Rd C6
Victoria Rooms A2
Victoria Sq A2
Victoria St B5
Vyvyan Rd A1
Vyvyan Terr A1
Wade St A6
Walter St C2
Wapping Rd C4
Water La B5
Waterloo Rd A6
Waterloo St A1
Waterloo St A6
Watershed Media Centre B4
We the Curious B3
Welling Terr B1
Welsh Back B4
West Mall A1
West St A6
Westfield Place A1
Wetherell Place A2
Whitehouse Place C5
Whitehouse St C5
Whiteladies Rd A2
Whitson St A4
William St C5
Willway St C5
Windsor Place B1
Wine St A4
Woodland Rd A3
Woodland Rise A3
Worcester Rd A1
Worcester Terr A1
YHA B4
York Gdns B1
York Place A2
York Rd C5

Bury St Edmunds 178

Abbey Gardens B3
Abbey Gate B3
Abbeygate B2
Abbeygate St B2
Albert Cres B1
Albert St B1
Angel Hill B2
Angel La B2
Anglian Lane A1
Arc Shopping Ctr B2
Athenaeum C2
Baker's La C3
Barwell Rd B3
Beetons Way A1
Bishops Rd B2
Bloomfield St B2
Bridewell La C2
Bullen Close C1
Bury St Edmunds Station A2
Bury St Edmunds County Upper School A1
Bury St Edmunds Leisure Centre B1
Bury Town FC (Ram Meadow) B3
Bus Station B2
Business Park B3
Butter Mkt B2
Cannon St B2
Castle Rd C1
Cemetery C1
Chalk Rd (N) B1
Chalk Rd (S) B1
Church Row B2
Churchgate St C2
Citizens Advice Bureau B2
College St C2
Compiegne Way A3
Corn Exchange, The B2
Cornfield Rd B1
Cotton Lane B3
Courts B2
Covent Garden C2
Crown St C3
Cullum Rd C2
Eastern Way A3
Eastgate St B3
Enterprise Business Park A2
Etna Rd A2
Eyre Close C2
Fire & Ambulance Station B1
Friar's Lane C2
Gage Close A1
Garland St B2
Greene King Brewery C3
Grove Park B1
Grove Rd B1
Guildhall C2
Guildhall St C2
Hatter St C2
High Baxter St B2
Honey Hill C3
Hospital Rd C1/C2
Ickworth Dr C1
Industrial Estate A3
Information Ctr B2
Ipswich St A2
King Edward VI School A1
King's Rd C1/B2
Library B2
Long Brackland A2
Looms La B2
Lwr Baxter St B2
Malthouse La A2
Manor House C3
Maynewater La C3
Mill Rd C1
Mill Rd (South) C1
Minden Close B3
Moyse's Hall B2
Mustow St B3
Norman Tower C3
Northgate Ave A2
Northgate St B2
Osier Rd A2
Out Northgate A2
Out Risbygate B1
Out Westgate C2
Parkway B1/C2
Parkway,The B1
Peckham St B2
Petticoat La C1
Phoenix Day Hospital C1
Pinners Way C1
Police Station C3
Post Office B2
Pump La B2
Queen's Rd B1
Raingate St C3
Raynham Rd A1
Retail Park C1
Risbygate St B1/B2
Robert Boby Way C2
St Andrew's St North B2
St Andrew's St South B2
St Botolph's La C3
St Edmund's C2
St Edmund's Abbey (Remains) B3
St Edmunds Hospital (Private) C3
St Edmundsbury C3
St John's St B2
St Marys C3
School Hall La B2
Shillitoe Close C1
South Close C1
Southgate St C3
Sparhawk St C3
Spring Lane B1
Springfield Rd B1
Station Hill A2
Swan La C3
Tayfen Rd B2
Theatre Royal C3
Thingoe Hill A2
Victoria St B1
Vinefields,The B3
War Memorial C1
Well St B2
West Suffolk Coll B1
Westgarth Gdns C1
Westgate St C2
Whiting St C2
York Rd B1
York Terr B1

Cambridge 178

Abbey Rd A3
ADC A2
Anglia Ruskin Univ B3
Archaeology & Anthropology B2
Arts Picturehouse B2
Arts Theatre B1
Auckland Rd A3
Backs,The B1
Bateman St C2
Benet St B1
Bradmore St B3
Bridge St A1
Broad St B3
Brookside C2
Brunswick Terr A3
Burleigh St B3
Bus Station B2
Butt Green A2
Cambridge Contemporary Art Gallery B1
Castle Mound A1
Castle St A1
Cemetery B3
Chesterton La A1
Christ's (Coll) B2
Christ's Lane B2
Christ's Pieces B2
City Rd B3
Clare Bridge B1
Clare (Coll) B1
Clarendon St C2
Coe Fen C2
Coronation St C2
Corpus Christi (Coll) B1
Court A3
Cross St C3
Crusoe Bridge C1
Darwin (Coll) C1
Devonshire Rd C3
Downing (Coll) C2
Downing St B2
Earl St B2
East Rd B3
Eden St B3
Elizabeth Way A3
Elm St B2
Emery St B3
Emmanuel (Coll) B2
Emmanuel Rd B2
Emmanuel St B2
Fair St A3
Fen Causeway,The C1
Fenner's Cricket Gd C3
Fire Station B3
Fitzroy St A3
Fitzwilliam Mus C2
Fitzwilliam St C2
Garrett Hostel Bridge B1
Glisson Rd C3
Gonville & Caius (Coll) B1
Gonville Place C2
Grafton Centre,The A3
Grand Arcade B2
Green St B1
Gresham Rd C3
Guest Rd B3
Guildhall B2
Harvey Rd C3
Hills Rd C3
Hobson St B2
Hughes Hall (Coll) B3
Information Ctr B2
James St A3
Jesus (Coll) A2
Jesus Green A2
Jesus La A2
Jesus Terr B3
John St B3
Kelsey Kerridge Sports Centre B3
Kettle's Yard A1
King's Bridge B1
King St A2
King's (Coll) B1
King's College Chapel B1
King's Parade B1
Lammas Land Recreation Gd C1
Lensfield Rd C2
Library B2
Lion Yard B2
Little St Mary's La B1
Lyndewod Rd C3
Magdalene (Coll) A1
Magdalene St A1
Maid's Causeway A3
Malcolm St A2
Market St B1
Mathematical Bridge B1
Mawson Rd C3
Midsummer Comm A3
Mill La B1
Mill Rd B3
Mill St C3
Mumford B3
Museum of Cambridge A1
Museum of Classical Archaeology C1
Napier St A3
New Square A2
Newmarket Rd A3
Newnham Rd C1
Norfolk St B3
Northampton St A1
Norwich St C2
Orchard St B2
Panton St C2
Paradise St B3
Park Parade A1
Park St A2
Park Terr B2
Parker St B2
Parker's Piece B2
Parkside B3
Parkside Pools B3
Parsonage St A3
Pea's Hill B1
Pemberton Terr C2
Pembroke (Coll) B2
Pembroke St B1
Perowne St B3
Peterhouse (Coll) C1
Petty Cury B2
Polar Mus,The C2
Police Station B3
Post Office A3/B2/C1/C2/C3
Queen's La B1
Queen's Rd B1
Queens' (Coll) B1
Regent St B2
Regent Terr B2
Ridley Hall (Coll) C1
Riverside A3
Round Church, The A1
Russell St C2
St Andrew's St B2
St Benet's B1
St Catharine's (Coll) B1
St Eligius St C2
St John's (Coll) A1
St Mary's B1
St Paul's Rd C3
Saxon St C2
Sedgwick Mus B2
Sheep's Green C1
Shire Hall A1
Sidgwick Ave C1
Sidney St A2
Sidney Sussex (Coll) A2
Silver St B1
Station Rd C3
Tenison Ave C3
Tenison Rd C3
Tennis Court Rd B2
Thompson's La A1
Trinity (Coll) A1
Trinity Bridge B1
Trinity Hall (Coll) B1
Trinity St B1
Trumpington Rd C2
Trumpington St B1
Union Rd C2
University Botanic Gardens C2
Victoria Ave A2
Victoria St B2
Warkworth St B3
Warkworth Terr B3
Wesley House (Coll) A2
West Rd B1
Westcott Ho (Coll) A2
Westminster (Coll) A1
Whipple B2
Willis Rd B3
Willow Walk A2
YMCA C3
Zoology B2

Canterbury 178

Artillery St B2
Barton Mill Rd A3
Beaconsfield Rd A1
Beaney,The B2
Beverley Meadow A1
Beverley Rd A1
Bingley's Island B1
Black Griffin La B1
Broad Oak Rd A2
Broad St B2
Brymore Rd A3
Burgate B2
Bus Station C2
Canterbury Castle C1
Canterbury Christ Church University B3
Canterbury College C3
Canterbury East C1
Canterbury Tales, The B2
Canterbury West A1
Castle Row C1
Castle St C1
Cathedral B2
Causeway,The A2
Chaucer Rd A3
Christchurch Gate B2
City Council Offices A3
City Wall B2
Coach park A2
College Rd B3
Cossington Rd C2
Court B2
Craddock Rd A3
Crown & County Courts B3
Dane John Gdns C2
Dane John Mound C1
Deanery B2
Dover St C2
Duck La B2
Eastbridge Hosp B1
Edgar Rd B3
Ersham Rd C3
Ethelbert Rd C3
Fire Station C2
Forty Acres Rd A1
Friars,The B2
Gordon Rd C1
Greyfriars B1
Guildford Rd C1
Havelock St B2
Heaton Rd C1
High St B2
Information Centre A2/B2
Ivy La B2
New St C1
King St B2
King's School B2/B3
King's School Recreation Ctr,The A2
Kingsmead Leisure Centre A2
Kingsmead Rd A2
Kirby's La B1
Lansdown Rd C2
Lime Kiln Rd C1
Longport B3
Lower Chantry La C3
Mandeville Rd A1
Market Way A2
Marlowe Arcade B2
Marlowe Ave C2
Marlowe Theatre B2
Martyrs Field Rd C1
Mead Way B1
Military Rd B2
Monastery St B2
Museum of Canterbury (Rupert Bear Museum) B1
New Dover Rd C3
New St C1
Norman Rd C2
North Holmes Rd B3
North La B1
Northgate A2
Nunnery Fields C2
Nunnery Rd C2
Oaten Hill C2
Odeon Cinema C2
Old Dover Rd C2
Old Palace B2
Old Ruttington La B2
Old Weavers B2
Orchard St B1
Oxford Rd C1
Palace St B2
Pilgrims Way C3
Pin Hill C1
Pine Tree Ave A1
Police Station C2
Post Office B2, C1, C2
Pound La B1
Puckle La C2
Raymond Ave C2
Recreation Ground A2
Registry Office A2
Rheims Way B1
Rhodaus Close C2
Rhodaus Town C2
Roman Museum B2
Roper Gateway A1
Roper Rd A1
Rose La B2
Shopmobility B2
St Augustine's Abbey (remains) B3
St Augustine's Rd C3
St Dunstan's A1
St Dunstan's St A1
St George's Place C2
St George's St B2
St George's Tower B2
St Gregory's Rd B3
St John's Hosp A2
St Margaret's St B2
St Martin's B3
St Martin's Ave B3
St Martin's Rd B3
St Michael's Rd A1
St Mildred's C1
St Peter's Grove B1
St Peter's La B2
St Peter's Place B1
St Peter's St B1
St Radigunds St B2
St Stephen's Ct A1
St Stephen's Path A1
St Stephen's Rd A2
Salisbury Rd A1
Simmonds Rd C1
Spring La C3
Station Rd West B1
Stour St B1
Sturry Rd A3
Tourtel Rd A3
Tudor Rd C1
Union St B2
University for the Creative Arts C3
Vernon Place C2
Victoria Rd C1
Watling St B2
Westgate Gdns B1
Westgate Towers B1
Whitefriars B2
Whitehall Gdns B1
Whitehall Rd B1
Wincheap C1
York Rd C1
Zealand Rd C2

Cardiff
Caerdydd 178

Adam St B3
Alexandra Gdns A2
Allerton St C1
Arran St A3
ATRiuM (University of Glamorgan) C3
Beauchamp St C1
Bedford St A3
Blackfriars Priory (rems) B1
Bvd De Nantes B2
Brains Brewery C2
Brook St B1
Bute Park A1
Bute St C2
Bute Terr C3
Callaghan Sq C2/C3
Capitol Shopping Centre,The B3
Cardiff Arms Park (Cardiff Blues) B1
Cardiff Bridge B1
Cardiff Castle B2
Cardiff Central Station C2
Cardiff Story,The B2
Cardiff Univ A1/A2/B3
Cardiff University Student's Union A2
Caroline St C2
Castle Green B2
Castle Mews A1
Castle St (Heol y Castell) B1
Cathays Station A2
Celerity Drive C3
Central Library C2
Charles St (Heol Siarl) B3
Churchill Way B3
City Hall A2
City Rd A3
Clare Rd C1
Clare St C1
Coburn St A3
Coldstream Terr B1
College Rd A1
Colum Rd A1
Court C2
Court Rd C1
Craiglee Drive C3
Cranbrook St A3
Customhouse St C2
Cyfartha St A3
David's B2/C2
Despenser Place C1
Despenser St C1
Dinas St C1
Duke St (Heol y Dug) B2
Dumfries Place B3
East Grove A3
Ellen St C3
Fire Station B3
Fitzalan Place B3
Fitzhamon Emb C1
Fitzhamon La C1
Friary,The B2
g39 B2
Gloucester St C1
Glynrhondda St A2
Gordon Rd A3
Gorsedd Gdns B2
Green St B1
Greyfriars Rd B2
Hafod St C1
Hayes,The B2
Herbert St C3
High St B2
HM Prison B3
Industrial Estate C3
John St C3
Jubilee St C1
King Edward VII Ave A1
Kingsway (Ffordd y Brenin) B2
Knox Rd B3
Law Courts B2
Llanbleddian Gdns A2
Llantwit St A2
Lloyd George Ave C3
Lower Cathedral Rd B1
Lowther Rd A3
Magistrates Court B3
Mansion House A3
Mardy St C1
Mark St B1
Market B2
Mary Ann St C3
Merches Gdns C1
Mill La C2
Millennium Bridge B1
Miskin St A2
Monmouth St C1
Motorpoint Arena Cardiff C3
Museum Ave A2
Museum Place A2
National Museum Cardiff A2
National War Memorial A2
Neville Place C1
New Theatre B2
Newport Rd B3
Northcote La A3
Northcote St A3
Parade,The A3
Park Grove A4
Park Place A2
Park St C2
Penarth Rd C2
Pendyris St C1
Plantaganet St C1
Post Office B2
Principality Stadium C1
Principality Stadium Tours (Gate 3) B2
Quay St B2
Queen's Arcade B2
Queen Anne Sq A1
Queen St (Heol y Frenhines) B2
Queen St Station B3
Regimental Museums B2
Rhymney St A3
Richmond Rd A3
Royal Welsh College of Music and Drama A1
Russell St A3
Ruthin Gdns A2
St Andrews Place A2
St David's B2
St David's Hall B2
St John the Baptist B2
St Mary St (Heol Eglwys Fair) B2
St Peter's St A3
Salisbury Rd A3
Sandon St B3
Schooner Way C3
Scott Rd C2
Scott St C2
Senghennydd Rd A2
Sherman Theatre A2
Sophia Gardens A1
Sophia Gardens Stadium A1
South Wales Baptist College A3
Sport Wales National Ctr A1
Stafford Rd C1
Stadium Plaza C1
Station Terr B3
Stuttgarter Strasse B2
Sussex St C1
Taffs Mead Emb C1
Talworth St A3
Temple of Peace & Health A1
Treharris St A3
Trinity St B2
Tudor La C1
Tudor St C1
Tyndall St C3
Vue C2
Walk,The A3
Welsh Government A1
West Grove A3
Westgate St (Heol y Porth) B2
Windsor Place B3
Womanby St B2
Wood St C2
Working St B2
Wyeverne Rd A2

Carlisle 179

Abbey St A1
Aglionby St B3
Albion St C3
Alexander St C3
AMF Bowl C2
Annetwell St A1
Bank St B2
Bitts Park A1
Blackfriars St B2
Blencome St C1
Blunt St C1
Botchergate B2
Boustead's Grassing C2
Bowman St B3
Bridge St A1
Broad St B3
Brook St C3
Brunswick St B2
Bus Station B2
Caldew Bridge A1
Caldew St C1
Carlisle (Citadel) Station B2
Carlisle College A2
Castle A1
Castle St A1
Castle Way A1
Cathedral A1
Cecil St B2
Chapel St A2
Charles St B3
Charlotte St B1
Chatsworth Square A2
Chiswick St B2
Citadel,The B2
City Walls A1
Civic Centre A2
Clifton St C1
Close St B3
Collingwood St C1

Colville St C1
Colville Terr C1
Council Offices B3
Court B2
Court St Brow B2
Crosby St B2
Crown St C2
Currock Rd C2
Dacre Rd A1
Dale St C1
Denton St C1
Devonshire Walk A1
Duke's Rd A2
East Dale St C1
East Norfolk St C1
Eden Bridge A2
Edward St B3
Elm St B1
English St B2
Fire Station A2
Fisher St A1
Flower St B3
Freer St C1
Fusehill St B3
Georgian Way A2
Gloucester Rd C3
Golf Course A2
Graham St C1
Grey St B3
Guildhall Mus A2
Halfey's La B3
Hardwicke Circus A2
Hart St B3
Hewson St C2
Howard Place A3
Howe St B3
Information Ctr A2
James St B2
Junction St B1
King St B2
Lancaster St B2
Lanes Shopping Centre, The B2
Laser Quest B2
Library A2
Lime St B1
Lindisfarne St C3
Linton St B3
Lismore Place A3
Lismore St B3
London Rd C3
Lonsdale Rd B2
Lord St C3
Lorne Cres B1
Lorne St B1
Lowther St B2
Madford Retail Pk B1
Magistrates' Ct A2
Market Hall A2
Mary St B2
Memorial Bridge A3
Metcalfe St C1
Milbourne St B1
Myddleton St B3
Nelson St C1
Norfolk St C1
Old Fire Sta, The A2
Old Town Hall A2
Oswald St C3
Peter St A2
Petteril St B3
Pools B2
Portland Place B2
Portland Sq B2
Post Office A2/B2/C1/C3
Princess St C2
Pugin St B1
Red Bank Terr C2
Regent St C3
Richardson St C1
Rickerby Park A3
Rickergate A2
River St B3
Rome St C2
Rydal St B3
St Cuthbert's B2
St Cuthbert's La B2
St James' Park C1
St James' Rd C1
St Nicholas Gate Retail Park C3
St Nicholas St C3
Sands Centre, The A2
Scotch St A2
Shaddongate B1
Sheffield St B1
Shopmobility A2
South Henry St B3
South John St C2
South St B3
Spencer St B2
Station Retail Park B2
Strand Rd A2
Superstore B1
Sybil St B3
Tait St B2
Thomas St B1
Thomson St C3
Trafalgar St C1
Trinity Leisure Ctr A2
Tullie Museum & Art Gallery A1
Tyne St C3
Univ of Cumbria B3
Viaduct Estate Rd B1
Victoria Place A2
Victoria Viaduct B2
Vue B2
Warwick Rd B2
Warwick Sq B3
Water St B2
West Walls B1
Westmorland St C1

Chelmsford 179

Anchor St C1
Anglia Ruskin Univ A2
Arbour La A3
Baddow Rd B2/C3
Baker St C1
Barrack Sq B2
Bellmead B2
Bishop Hall La A2
Bishop Rd A2
Bond St B2
Boswells Dr B3
Bouverie Rd C2
Bradford St C1
Braemar Ave C1
Brook St A2
Broomfield Rd A1
Burgess Springs B3
Burns Cres C2
Bus Station B1/B2
Cedar Ave A1
Cedar Ave West A1
Cemetery A1
Cemetery A2
Cemetery C1
Central Park B1
Chelmsford B2
Chelmsford A1
Chichester Dr A3
Chinery Close A3
City Council A1
Civic Centre A1
Civic Theatre B1
Cloudfm County Cricket Gd, The B2
College C1
Cottage Place A2
County Hall B2
Coval Ave B1
Coval La B1
Coval Wells B1
Crown Court B2
Duke St B2
Elm Rd C1
Elms Dr A1
Essex Record Office, The B3
Fairfield Rd B1
Falcons Mead B1
George St C2
Glebe Rd A1
Godfrey's Mews C2
Goldlay Ave C3
Goldlay Rd C2
Grove Rd C2
Hall St C2
Hamlet Rd C2
Hart St C1
Henry Rd A2
High Bridge Rd B2
High Chelmer Shopping Centre B2
High St B2
Hill Cres B3
Hill Rd B3
Hill Rd Sth B3
Hillview Rd A3
HM Prison A3
Hoffmans Way A2
Hospital B2
Lady La C2
Langdale Gdns C3
Legg St B2
Library B2
Lionfield Terr A3
Lower Anchor St C1
Lynmouth Ave C2
Lynmouth Gdns C3
Magistrates Court B2
Maltese Rd A1
Manor Rd C2
Marconi Rd A2
Market B2
Market Rd B2
Marlborough Rd C1
Meadows Shopping Centre, The B2
Meadowside A3
Mews Ct C2
Mildmay Rd C2
Moulsham Dr C2
Moulsham Mill C3
Moulsham St C1/C2
Navigation Rd B3
New London Rd B2/C1
New St A2/B2
New Writtle St C1
Nursery Rd C2
Orchard St C2
Odeon B2
Parker Rd C2
Parklands Dr A3
Parkway A1/B1/B2
Police Station A2
Post Office B2/C2
Primrose Hill A1
Prykes Dr B1
Queen St C1
Queen's Rd B3
Railway St A1
Rainsford Rd A1
Ransomes Way A2
Rectory La A2
Regina Rd A2
Riverside Ice & Leisure Centre B2
Riverside Retail Pk A3
Rosebery Rd C2
Rothesay Ave C1
St John's Rd C2
Sandringham Pl B3
Seymour St B1
Shopmobility B2
Shrublands Close B3
Southborough Rd C1
Springfield Rd A3/B2/B3
Stapleford Close C1
Superstore B2/C3
Swiss Ave A1
Telford Place A3
Tindal St B2
Townfield St A1
Trinity Rd B3
University B1
Upper Bridge Rd C1
Upper Roman Rd C2
Van Dieman's Rd C3
Viaduct Rd B1
Vicarage Rd C1
Victoria Rd A2
Victoria Rd South B2
Vincents Rd C2
Waterloo La B2
Weight Rd B3
Westfield Ave A1
Wharf Rd B3
Writtle Rd C1
YMCA A2
York Rd C1

Cheltenham 179

Albert Rd A3
Albion St B3
All Saints Rd B3
Ambrose St B2
Andover Rd C1
Back Montpellier Terr C2
Bandstand C2
Bath Pde B2
Bath Rd C2
Bays Hill Rd C1
Bennington St B2
Berkeley St B3
Brewery Quarter, The A2
Brunswick St South A2
Bus Station B2
Carlton St B3
Central Cross Road A3
Cheltenham Coll C2
Cheltenham FC A3
Cheltenham General (A&E) C3
Cheltenham Ladies' College B2
Christchurch Rd B1
Cineworld A2
Clarence Rd A2
Clarence Sq A2
Clarence St B2
Cleeveland St A1
College Baths Road C3
College Rd C2
Colletts Dr A1
Corpus St C3
Devonshire St A2
Douro Rd B1
Duke St B3
Dunalley Pde A2
Dunalley St A2
Everyman B2
Evesham Rd A3
Fairview Rd B3
Fairview St B3
Fire Station C3
Folly La A2
Gloucester Rd A1
Grosvenor St B3
Grove St A1
Hanover St A2
Hatherley St C1
Henrietta St A2
Hewlett Rd B3
High St B2/B3
Holst Birthplace Museum A3
Hudson St A2
Imperial Gdns C2
Imperial La B2
Imperial Sq C2
Information Ctr B2
Keynsham Rd C3
King St A2
Knapp Rd B2
Lansdown Cres C1
Lansdown Rd C1
Leighton Rd B3
Library B2
London Rd C3
Lypiatt Rd C1
Magistrates' Court & Register Office B1
Malvern Rd B1
Manser St A2
Market St A1
Marle Hill Pde A2
Marle Hill Rd A2
Millbrook St A1
Milsom St A2
Montpellier Gdns C2
Montpellier Grove C2
Montpellier Pde C2
Montpellier Spa Rd C2
Montpellier St C1
Montpellier Terr C2
Montpellier Walk C2
New St B2
North Place B2
Old Bath Rd C3
Oriel Rd B2
Overton Park Rd B1
Overton Rd B1
Oxford St C3
Parabola Rd B1
Park Place C1
Park St A1
Pittville Circus A3
Pittville Crescent A3
Pittville Lawn A3
Pittville Park A2
Playhouse B2
Portland St B3
Prestbury Rd A3
Prince's Rd C1
Priory St B3
Promenade B2
Queen St A1
Recreation Ground A2
Regent Arcade B2
Regent St B2
Rodney Rd B2
Royal Cres B2
Royal Well Place B2
Royal Wells Rd B2
St George's Place B2
St Georges Rd B1
St Gregory's B2
St James St B3
St John's Ave B3
St Luke's Rd C2
St Margarets Rd A2
St Mary's B2
St Matthew's B2
St Paul's La A2
St Paul's Rd A2
St Paul's St A2
St Stephen's Rd C1
Sandford Parks Lido C3
Sandford Mill Road C3
Sandford Park C3
Sandford Rd C2
Selkirk St A3
Sherborne Place B3
Sherborne St B3
Suffolk Pde C2
Suffolk Rd C1
Suffolk Sq C1
Sun St A1
Swindon Rd B2
Sydenham Villas Rd C3
Tewkesbury Rd A1
The Courtyard B1
Thirlstaine Rd C2
Tivoli Rd C1
Tivoli St C1
Town Hall & Theatre B2
Townsend St A1
Trafalgar St C2
Union St B3
University of Gloucestershire (Francis Close Hall) A2
University of Gloucestershire (Hardwick) A1
Victoria Place B3
Victoria St A2
Vittoria Walk C2
Wellesley Rd A2
Wellington Rd A3
Wellington Sq A3
Wellington St B2
West Drive A3
Western Rd B1
Wilson, The B2
Winchcombe St B3
Winston Churchill Meml Gardens A1

Chester 179

Abbey Gateway A2
Appleyards La C3
Bars, The B3
Bedward Row B1
Beeston View C3
Bishop Lloyd's Palace B2
Black Diamond St A2
Bottoms La C3
Boughton B3
Bouverie St A1
Bus Interchange A2
Bridge St B2
Bridgegate C2
Brook St A3
Brown's La C2
Cambrian Rd A1
Canal St A2
Carrick Rd C1
Castle C2
Castle Dr C2
Cathedral B2
Catherine St A1
Cheshire Military Museum C2
Chester A3
Cheyney Rd A1
Chichester St A1
City Rd A3
City Walls B1/B2
City Walls Rd B1
Cornwall St A2
Cross Hey C3
Cross, The B2
Crown Ct C2
Cuppin St B2
Curzon Park North C1
Curzon Park South C1
Dee Basin A1
Dee La B3
Delamere St A2
Deva Roman Discovery Ctr B2
Dingle, The C1
Duke St B2
Eastgate B2
Eastgate St B2
Eaton Rd C2
Edinburgh Way C3
Elizabeth Cres B3
Fire Station A2
Foregate St B2
Forum Studio B2
Forum, The B2
Frodsham St B2
Gamul House B2
Garden La A1
George St A2
Gladstone Ave A1
God's Providence House B2
Gorse Stacks A2
Greenway St C2
Grosvenor Bridge C1
Grosvenor Mus B2
Grosvenor Park B3
Grosvenor Park Terr C1
Grosvenor Shopping Ctr B2
Grosvenor St B2
Groves Rd B3
Groves, The B3
Guildhall Mus B1
Handbridge C2
Hartington St C3
Hoole Way A2
Hunter St B2
Information Ctr B2
King Charles' Tower A2
King St A2
Library B2
Lightfoot St A3
Little Roodee C2
Liverpool Rd A2
Love St B3
Lower Bridge St B2
Lower Park Rd B3
Lyon St A2
Magistrates Court B2
Meadows La C3
Meadows, The B3
Milton St A3
Minerva Roman Shrine C2
Miniature Railway B3
New Crane St B1
Nicholas St B2
Northgate A2
Northgate Arena A2
Northgate St A2
Nun's Rd B1
Old Dee Bridge C2
Overleigh Rd C2
Park St B2
Police Station B2
Post Office A2/A3
Princess St B2
Queen St B2
Queen's Park Rd C3
Queen's Rd A3
Race Course B1
Raymond St A1
River La C2
Roman Amphitheatre & Gardens B2
Roodee (Chester Racecourse), The B1
Russell St A3
St Anne St A2
St George's Cres C3
St Martin's Gate A1
St Martin's Way B1
St Oswalds Way A2
Saughall Rd A1
Sealand Rd A1
South View Rd A1
Stanley Palace B1
Station Rd A3
Steven St A3
Storyhouse B2
Superstore B2
Tower Rd B1
Town Hall B2
Union St B3
Univ of Chester C2
Vicar's La B2
Victoria Cres C3
Victoria Rd A2
Walpole St A1
Water Tower St A1
Water Tower, The B1
Watergate B1
Watergate St B2
Whipcord La A1
White Friars B2
York St B3

Chichester 180

Adelaide Rd A3
Alexandra Rd A3
Arts Centre B2
Ave de Chartres B1/B2
Barlow Rd A1
Basin Rd C2
Beech Ave B1
Bishops Palace Gardens B2
Bishopsgate Walk A3
Bramber Rd C3
Broyle Rd A2
Bus Station B2
Caledonian Rd B3
Cambrai Ave B3
Canal Place C1
Canal Wharf C2
Canon La B2
Cathedral B2
Cavendish St A1
Cawley Rd B2
Cedar Dr A1
Chapel St A2
Cherry Orchard Rd C3
Chichester B2
Chichester By-Pass C2/C3
Chichester Coll B1
Chichester Cinema B3
Chichester Festival A2
Chichester Gate Leisure Pk C1
Churchside A2
Cineworld B1
City Walls B2
Cleveland Rd B3
College La A2
Cory Close C2
Council Offices B2
County Hall B2
District B2
Duncan Rd A1
Durnford Close A1
East Pallant B2
East Row B2
East St B2
East Walls B3
Eastland Rd C3
Ettrick Close B3
Ettrick Rd B3
Exton Rd C3
Fire Station A2
Football Ground A2
Franklin Place A2
Friary (Rems of) A2
Garland Close C3
Green La A3
Grove Rd C3
Guilden Rd B3
Guildhall A2
Hawthorn Close A1
Hay Rd C3
Henty Gdns B1
Herald Dr C3
Hornet, The B3
Information Ctr B2
John's St B2
Joys Croft A3
Jubilee Pk A3
Jubilee Rd A3
Juxon Close B1
Kent Rd A3
King George Gdns A2
King's Ave C2
Kingsham Ave C3
Kingsham Rd C2
Laburnum Grove B2
Leigh Rd C1
Lennox Rd A3
Lewis Rd A3
Library B2
Lion St B2
Litten Terr A3
Litten, The A3
Little London B2
Lyndhurst Rd B3
Market B3
Market Ave B2
Market Cross B2
Market Rd B3
Melbourne Rd A3
Minerva B2
Mount La B1
New Park Rd A3
Newlands La A1
North Pallant B2
North St A2
North Walls A2
Northgate A2
Novium, The B2
Oak Ave A1
Oak Close A1
Oaklands Park A2
Oaklands Way A2
Orchard Ave A1
Orchard St A1
Ormonde Ave B3
Pallant House B2
Parchment St A1
Parklands Rd A1/B1
Peter Weston Place B3
Police Station C2
Post Office A1/B2/C3
Priory La A2
Priory Park A2
Priory Rd A2
Queen's Ave C1
Riverside A3
Roman Amphitheatre B3
St Cyriacs A2
St Martins' St B2
St Pancras A3
St Paul's Rd A2
St Richard's Hospital (A&E) A3
Shamrock Close A3
Sherbourne Rd A1
Somerstown A2
South Bank C2
South Downs Planetarium C2
South Pallant B2
South St B2
Southgate B2
Spitalfield La A3
Stirling Rd B3
Stockbridge Rd C1/C2
Swanfield Dr A3
Terminus Ind Est C1
Tower St A2
Tozer Way A3
Turnbull Rd A3
Upton Rd C1
Velyn Ave B3
Via Ravenna B1
Walnut Ave A1
West St B2
Westgate B1
Westgate Fields B1
Westgate Leisure Centre B1
Weston Ave C1
Whyke Close C3
Whyke La B3
Whyke Rd C3
Winden Ave B3

Colchester 180

Abbey Gateway C2
Albert St A1
Albion Grove C2
Alexandra Rd C1
Artillery St C3
Arts Centre B1
Balkerne Hill B1
Barrack St C3
Beaconsfield Rd C1
Beche Rd C3
Bergholt Rd A1
Bourne Rd C3
Brick Kiln Rd A1
Brigade Grove C2
Bristol Rd B2
Broadlands Way A3
Brook St B3
Bury Close B2
Bus Sta B2
Butt Rd C1
Campion Rd C2
Cannon St C3
Canterbury Rd C2
Captain Gardens C2
Castle B2
Castle Park B2
Castle Rd B2
Catchpool Rd A1
Causton Rd B1
Chandlers Row C3
Circular Rd East C2
Circular Rd North C1
Circular Rd West C1
Clarendon Way A1
Claudius Rd C2
Colchester A1
Colchester Camp Abbey Field C1
Colchester Retail Pk B1
Colchester Town C2
Colne Bank Ave A1
Colne View Retail Pk A2
Compton Rd A3
Cowdray Ave A1/A2
Cowdray Ctr, The A2
Crouch St B1
Crowhurst Rd B1
Culver Square Shopping Centre B1
Culver St East B2
Culver St West B1
Dilbridge Rd A3
East Hill B2
East St B3
East Stockwell St B1
Eld La B1
Essex Hall Rd A1
Exeter Dr B2
Fairfax Rd C2
Fire Station A2
Firstsite B2
Flagstaff Rd C1
Garrison Parade C2
George St B2
Gladstone Rd C2
Golden Noble Hill C2
Goring Rd A3
Granville Rd C3
Greenstead Rd B3
Guildford Rd B2
Harsnett Rd C3
Harwich Rd B3
Head St B1
High St B1/B2
High Woods Country Park A2
Hollytrees B2
Hyderabad Close C2
Hythe Hill C3
Information Ctr B2
Jarmin Rd A2
Kendall Rd C2
Kimberley Rd C3
King Stephen Rd C3
Leisure World A2
Library B1
Lincoln Way B2
Lion Walk Shopping Centre B1
Lisle Rd C2
Lucas Rd C2
Magdalen Green C3
Magdalen St C2
Maidenburgh St B2
Maldon Rd C1
Manor Rd B1
Margaret Rd A1
Mason Rd A2
Mercers Way A1
Mercury B1
Mersea Rd C2
Meyrick Cres C2
Mile End Rd A1
Military Rd C2
Mill St C2
Minories B2
Moorside B3
Morant Rd C3
Napier Rd C2
Natural History B2
New Town Rd C2
Norfolk Cres A3
North Hill B1
North Station Rd A1
Northgate St B1
Nunns Rd B1
Odeon B1
Old Coach Rd B3
Old Heath Rd C3
Osborne St B2
Petrolea Close A1
Police Station C1
Popes La B1
Port La C3
Post Office B2/C1
Priory St B2
Queen St B2
Rawstorn Rd B1
Rebon St C3
Recreation Rd C3
Ripple Way A3
Roberts Rd C2
Roman Rd B2
Roman Wall B2
Romford Close A3
Rosebery Ave B2
St Andrews Ave B3
St Andrews Gdns B3
St Botolph St B2
St Botolphs B2
St John's Abbey (site of) C2
St John's St B1
St Johns Walk Shopping Centre B1
St Leonards Rd C3
St Marys Fields B1
St Peter's St B1
St Peters B1
Salisbury Ave C1
Saw Mill Rd C3
Sergeant St C2
Serpentine Walk A1
Sheepen Place B1
Sheepen Rd B1
Sir Isaac's Walk B1
Smythies Ave B2
South St C1
South Way C1
Sports Way A2
Suffolk Close A3
Superstore A1
Town Hall B1
Valentine Dr A3
Victor Rd C3
Wakefield Close B2
Wellesley Rd C1
Wells Rd B2/B3
West St C1
West Stockwell St B1
Weston Rd C3
Westway A1
Wickham Rd C1
Wimpole Rd C3
Winchester Rd C2
Winnock Rd C2
Worcester Rd B2

Coventry 180

Abbots La A1
Albany A1
Albany Rd B1
Alma St B3
Ambulance Sta A2
Art Faculty B3
Asthill Grove C2
Bablake School A1
Barras La A1/B1
Barr's Hill School A1
Belgrade B2
Bishop St A2
Bond's Hospital B1
Broad Gate B2
Broadway C1
Burges, The B2
Bus Station A3
Butts Radial B1
Byron St A3
Canterbury St A3
Cathedral B3
Central Six Retail Park C1
Chester St A1
Cheylesmore Manor House B2
Christ Church Spire B2
City Coll A3
City Walls & Gates A2
Corporation St B2
Council House B2
Coundon Rd A1
Coventry Station C2
Coventry Transport Museum A2
Coventry University Technology Park C3
Cox St A3
Croft Rd B1
Dalton Rd C1
Deasy Rd C3
Earl St B2
Eaton Rd C2
Fairfax St B2
Fire Sta A2
Foleshill Rd A2
Ford's Hospital B2
Fowler Rd A1
Friars Rd C2
Gordon St C1
Gosford St B3
Greyfriars Green B2
Greyfriars Rd B2
Gulson Rd B3
Hales St A2
Harnall Lane East A3
Harnall Lane West A2
Herbert Art Gallery & Museum B3
Hertford St B2
Hewitt Ave A1
High St B2
Hill St B1
Holy Trinity B2
Holyhead Rd A1
Howard St A3
Huntingdon Rd C1
Information Ctr C2
Jordan Well B3
King Henry VIII School C1
Lady Godiva Statue B2
Lamb St A2
Leicester Row A2
Library B2
Lincoln St A2
Little Park St B2
London Rd C3
Lower Ford St B3
Lower Precinct Shopping Centre B2
Magistrates & Crown Courts B2
Manor House Drive B2
Manor Rd C2
Market B2
Martyrs Meml C2
Meadow St B1
Meriden St A1
Michaelmas Rd C2
Middleborough Rd A1
Mile La C3
Millennium Place A2
Much Park St B3
Naul's Mill Park A1
New Union B2
Odeon B1
Park Rd C2
Parkside C3
Planet Ice Arena B1
Post Office A3,B2
Primrose Hill St A3
Priory Gardens & Visitor Centre B2
Priory St B3
Puma Way C3
Quarryfield La C3
Queen's Rd B2
Quinton Rd C2
Radford Rd A2
Raglan St B3
Ringway (Hill Cross) A1
Ringway (Queens) B1
Ringway (Rudge) B1
Ringway (St Johns) B3
Ringway (St Nicholas) A2
Ringway (St Patricks) C2
Ringway (Swanswell) A2
Ringway (Whitefriars) B3
St John St B2
St John the Baptist B2
St Nicholas St A2
Sidney Stringer Academy A3
Skydome B1
Spencer Ave C1
Spencer Rec Gnd C1
Spencer Rd C1
Spon St B1
Sports Centre B3
Stoney Rd C2
Stoney Stanton Rd A3
Superstore B2
Swanswell Pool A3
Thomas Landsdail St C2
Tomson Ave A1
Top Green C1
Tower St A2
Trinity St B2
University B3
Univ Sports Ctr B3
Upper Hill St A1
Upper Well St A2
Victoria St A3
Vine St A3
Wave, The B2
Warwick Rd C2
Waveley Rd B1
West Orchards Shopping Ctr B2
Westminster Rd C1
White St A3
Windsor St B1

Derby 180

Abbey St C1
Agard St B1
Albert St B2
Albion St B2
Ambulance Station B1
Arthur St A1
Ashlyn Rd B3
Assembly Rooms B2
Babington La C2
Bass Recreation Gd B3
Becket St B1
Belper Rd A1
Bold La B1
Bradshaw Way C2
Bradshaw Way Retail Park C2
Bridge St B1
Brook St B1
Burton Rd C1
Bus Station B2
Business Park A3
Caesar St A2
Canal St C3
Carrington St C3
Cathedral B2
Cathedral Rd B1
Charnwood St C2
Chester Green Rd A2
City Rd A2
Clarke St A3
Cock Pitt Junction B3
Council House B2
Courts B1
Cranmer Rd B3
Crompton St C1
Crown & County Courts B2
Curzon St B1
Darley Grove A1
Derbion C2
Derby C3
Derby C2
Derby Gaol B2
Derwent Bsns Ctr A2
Derwent St B2
Drewry La C1
Duffield Rd A1
Duke St A2
Dunton Close B3
Eagle Market C2
East St B2
Eastgate B3
Exeter St B2
Farm St C1
Ford St B1
Forester St C1
Fox St A2
Friar Gate B1
Friary St B1
Full St B2
Garden St A1
Gerard St C1
Gower St C2
Green La C2
Grey St C1
Guildhall B2
Handyside Bridge A2
Harcourt St C1
Highfield Rd A1
Hill La C2
Incora County Ground (Derbyshire CCC), The B3
Information Ctr B2
Iron Gate B2
John St C3
Joseph Wright Ctr B1
Kedleston Rd A1
Key St B2
King Alfred St C1
King St A1
Kingston St A1
Lara Croft Way C2
Leopold St C2
Liversage St C3
Lodge La B1
London Rd C2
London Rd Community Hospital C2
Macklin St C1
Mansfield Rd A2
Market B2
Market Place B2
May St C1
Meadow La B3
Melbourne St C2
Mercian Way C1
Midland Rd C3
Monk St C1
Morledge B2
Mount St C1
Mus & Art Gallery B1
Mus of Making B2
North Parade A1
North St A1
Nottingham Rd B3
Osmaston Rd C2
Otter St A1
Park St C3
Parker St A1
Pickford's House B1
Police Station A2, B2
Post Office A1/A2/B1/C2/C3
Pride Parkway C3
Prime Enterprise Pk A2
Prime Parkway A2
QUAD B2
Queens Leisure Ctr B1
Racecourse Park A3
Railway Terr C3
Register Office B2
Riverlights Leisure Centre B2
Sadler Gate B1
St Alkmund's Way B1/B2
St Helens House A1
St Mary's A1
St Mary's Bridge A2
St Mary's Bridge Chapel A2
St Mary's Gate B1
St Paul's Rd A2
St Peter's C2
St Peter's St C2
Showcase De Lux C2
Siddals Rd C3
Sir Frank Whittle Rd A3
Spa La C1
Spring St C1
Stafford St B1
Station Approach C3
Stockbrook St C1
Stores Rd A3
Traffic St C2
Wardwick B1
Werburgh St C1
West Ave A1
West Meadows Industrial Estate B3
Wharf Rd A2
Wilmot St C2
Wilson St C1
Wood's La C1

Dorchester 181

Ackerman Rd B3
Acland Rd A2
Albert Rd A1
Alexandra Rd B1
Alfred Place B3
Alfred Rd B2
Alington Ave C3
Alington Rd B3
Ashley Rd B1
Balmoral Cres C3
Barnes Way B2/C2
Borough Gdns A1
Brewery Sq B1
Bridport Rd A1
Buckingham Way C3
Caters Place A1
Cemetery A3/C1
Charles St A2
Coburg Rd B1
Colliton St A1
Cornwall Rd A1
Cromwell Rd B1
Culliford Rd B2
Culliford Rd North B2
Dagmar Rd B1
Damer's Rd B1
Diggory Cres C2
Dinosaur Mus A2
Dorchester Bypass C2
Dorchester South Station B1
Dorchester West Station B1
Dorset County (A&E) B1
Dorset County Council Offices A1
Dorset County Museum A1
Duchy Close C3
Duke's Ave B2
Durngate St A2
Durnover Court A3
Eddison Ave B3
Edward Rd B1
Egdon Rd C2
Elizabeth Frink Statue B2
Farfrae Cres B2
Forum Centre, The B1
Friary Hill A2
Friary Lane A2
Frome Terr A2
Garland Cres C3
Glyde Path Rd A1
Grosvenor Cres C1
Grosvenor Rd C1
Grove, The A1
Gt Western Rd B1
Herrington Rd C1
High St East A2
High St Fordington A2
High Street West A1
Holloway Rd A2
Icen Way A2
Information Ctr B2
Keep Military Museum, The A1
Kings Rd A3/B3
Kingsbere Cres C2
Lancaster Rd B2
Library B1
Lime Close C1
Linden Ave B2
London Close A3
London Rd A2/A3
Lubbecke Way A3
Lucetta La B2
Maiden Castle Rd C1
Manor Rd C2
Market B1
Marshwood Place B2
Maumbury Rd B1
Maumbury Rings B1
Mellstock Ave C2
Mill St A3
Miller's Close A1
Mistover Close C1
Monmouth Rd B1/B2
Moynton Rd C2
Nature Reserve A2
North Sq A2
Northernhay A1
Odeon B1
Old Crown Court & Cells A1
Olga Rd B1
Orchard St A2
Plaza A1
Police Station B1
Post Office B1
Pound Lane A2
Poundbury Rd A1
Prince of Wales Rd B2
Prince's St A1
Queen's Ave B1
Roman Town Ho A1
Roman Wall A1
Rothesay Rd C2
St George's Rd B3
Salisbury Field A2
Sandringham Sports Centre B3
Shaston Cres C2
Smokey Hole La B3
South Court Ave C1
South St B1
South Walks Rd B2
Superstore C3
Teddy Bear Mus A1
Temple Close C1
Terracotta Warriors & Teddy Bear Mus A2
Town Hall A2
Town Pump A2
Trinity St A1
Tutankhamun Ex B1
Victoria Rd B1
Weatherbury Way C2
Wellbridge Close C1
West Mills Rd A1
West Walks Rd A1
Weymouth Ave C1
Williams Ave B1
Winterbourne (BMI) C1
Wollaston Rd A2
York Rd B2

Dumfries 181

Academy St A2
Aldermanhill Rd B3
Ambulance Station C3
Annan Rd A3
Ardwall Rd A3
Ashfield Dr A1
Atkinson Rd C1
Averill Cres C1
Balliol Ave C1
Bank St B2
Bankend Rd C3
Barn Slaps B3
Barrie Ave B3
Beech Ave A1
Bowling Green A3
Brewery St B2
Bridgend Theatre B1
Brodie Ave C2
Brooke St B2
Broomlands Dr C1
Brooms Rd B3
Buccleuch St A2
Burns House B2
Burns Mausoleum B3
Burns St B2
Burns Statue A2
Bus Station B1
Cardoness St A3
Castle St A2
Catherine St A2
Cattle Market A3
Cemetery B3
Cemetery C2
Church Cres A2
Church St B2
College Rd A1
College St A1
Corbelly Hill B1
Corberry Park B1
Cornwall Mt A3
Council Offices A2
Court A2
Craigs Rd C3
Cresswell Ave B3
Cresswell Hill B3
Cumberland St B3
David Keswick Athletic Centre A3
David St B1
Dock Park C3
Dockhead B2
Dumfries A3
Dumfries Academy A2
Dumfries Ice Bowl A1
Dumfries Museum & Camera Obscura B2

204 Dundee • Durham • Edinburgh • Exeter • Glasgow • Gloucester

Dumfries & Galloway Royal Infirmary (A&E) C3
East Riverside Dr C3
Edinburgh Rd A2
English St B2
Fire Station B3
Friar's Vennel A2
Galloway St B1
George Douglas Dr C1
George St A2
Gladstone Rd C2
Glasgow St A1
Glebe St B3
Glencaple Rd C3
Goldie Ave A1
Goldie Cres A1
Golf Course C3
Gracefield Arts Centre A2
Greyfriars A2
Grierson Ave B3
Hamilton Ave C1
Hamilton Starke Pk C2
Hazelrigg Ave C1
Henry St B3
Hermitage Dr C1
High Cemetery C3
High St A2
Hill Ave C2
Hill St B1
HM Prison B1
Holm Ave C2
Hoods Loaning A3
Howgate St B1
Huntingdon Rd A3
Information Ctr B2
Irish St B2
Irving St A2
King St A1
Kingholm Rd C3
Kirkpatrick Ct C2
Laurieknowe B1
Leafield Rd B3
Library A2
Lochfield Rd A1
Loreburn Pk A3
Loreburn St A2
Loreburne Shopping Centre B2
Lover's Walk A2
Martin Ave B3
Mausoleum B3
Maxwell St B1
McKie Ave B3
Mews La A2
Mid Steeple B2
Mill Green B2
Mill Rd B1
Moat Rd C2
Moffat Rd A3
Mountainhall Pk C3
Nelson St B1
New Abbey Rd B1/C1
New Bridge B1
Newall Terr A2
Nith Ave A2
Nith Bank C3
Nithbank Hosp C3
Nithside Ave A1
Odeon B2
Old Bridge B1
Old Bridge Ho B1
Palmerston Pk (Queen of the South FC) A1
Park Rd C1
Pleasance Ave C1
Police HQ A3
Police Sta A2/A3
Portland Dr A1
Post Office B1/B2/B3
Priestlands Dr C1
Primrose St B1
Queen St B3
Queensberry St A2
Rae St A2
Richmond Ave C2
Robert Burns Ctr B2
Roberts Cres C1
Robertson Ave C3
Robinson Dr C1
Rosefield Rd C2
Rosemount St B1
Rotchell Park C1
Rotchell Rd B1
Rugby Football Gd C1
Ryedale Rd C2
St Andrews B2
St John the Evangelist A2
St Josephs College B3
St Mary's Ind Est A3
St Mary's St A3
St Michael St B2
St Michael's B2
St Michael's Bridge B2
St Michael's Bridge Rd B2
St Michael's Cemetery B3
Shakespeare St B2
Solway Dr C2
Stakeford St A1
Stark Cres C2
Station Rd A3
Steel Ave A1
Sunderries Ave A1
Sunderries Rd A1
Superstore B3
Suspension Brae B2
Swimming Pool A1
Terregles St B1
Theatre Royal B2
Troqueer Rd C2
Union St A1
Wallace St B3
Welldale B2
West Riverside Dr C2
White Sands B2

Dundee 181

Abertay University B2
Adelaide Place A1
Airlie Place C1
Albany Terr A1
Albert St A3
Alexander St A2
Ann St A2
Arthurstone Terr A3
Bank St B2
Barrack Rd A1
Barrack St B2
Bell St B2
Blinshall St B1
Broughty Ferry Rd A3
Brown St B1
Bus Station B3
Caird Hall B2
Camperdown St B3
Candle La B3
Carmichael St A1
City Churches B2
City Quay B3
City Square B2
Commercial St B2
Constable St A3
Constitution Cres A1
Constitution Ct A1
Constitution St A1/B2
Cotton Rd A3
Courthouse Sq B1
Cowgate A3
Crescent St A3
Crichton St B2
Dens Brae A3
Dens Rd A3
Discovery Point C2
Douglas St B1
Drummond St A1
Dudhope Castle A1
Dudhope St A2
Dudhope Terr A1
Dundee C2
Dundee Contemporary Arts C2
Dundee High School B2
Dundee Law A1
Dundee Rep C2
Dunhope Park A1
Dura St A3
East Dock St B3
East Marketgait B3
East Whale La B3
Erskine St A3
Euclid Cres B2
Forebank Rd A2
Foundry La A3
Gallagher Retail Pk B3
Gellatly St B3
Government Offices C2
Guthrie St B1
Hawkhill B1
Hilltown A2
HMS Unicorn B3
Howff Cemetery, The B2
Information Ctr B2
Keiller Shopping Ctr B2
Keiller Ctr, The B2
King St A3
Kinghorne Rd A1
Ladywell Ave A3
Laurel Bank A2
Law Rd A1
Law St A1
Library A2/A3
Library and Steps Theatre A2
Little Theatre, The A2
Lochee Rd B1
Lower Princes St A3
Lyon St A3
McManus Art Gallery & Museum, The B2
Meadow Side B2
Meadowside St Pauls B2
Mercat Cross B2
Murraygate B2
Nelson St A2
Nethergate B2/C1
North Lindsay St B2
North Marketgait B2
Old Hawkhill B1
Olympia Leisure Ctr B3
Overgate Shopping Centre B2
Park Place B1
Perth Rd C1
Police Station B1
Post Office B2
Princes St A3
Prospect Place A2
Reform St B2
Riverside Dr C2
Riverside Esplanade C2
Roseangle C1
Rosebank St A2
RRS Discovery C2
St Andrew's C2
St Pauls Episcopal B3
Science Centre C2
Seagate B2
Sheriffs Court B1
Shopmobility B2
South George St A2
South Marketgait B3
South Tay St B2
South Victoria Dock Road B3
South Ward Rd B2
Tay Road Bridge C3
Thomson Ave B2
Trades La B3
Union St B2
Union Terr A1
University Library B2
Univ of Dundee B1
Upper Constitution St A1
Verdant Works B1
V&A Museum of Design C2
Victoria Dock B3
Victoria Rd A2
Victoria St A3
Ward Rd B1
Wellgate B2
West Bell St B1
West Marketgait B1/B2
Westfield Place C1
William St A3
Wishart Arch A3

Durham 181

Alexander Cres B2
Allergate B2
Archery Rise C1
Assembly Rooms B2
Avenue, The B1
Back Western Hill A1
Bakehouse La A3
Baths B3
Baths Bridge B3
Boat House B3
Bowling A2
Boyd St C3
Bus Station B2
Castle Chare B2
Cathedral B2
Church St C3
Clay La C1
Claypath B3
College of St Hild & St Bede B3
County Hospital B1
Crescent, The A1
Crook Hall & Gardens A3
Crossgate B2
Crossgate Peth C1
Crown Court B3
Darlington Rd C1
Durham A2
Durham Castle B2
Durham School C2
Durham University (Science Site) C3
Ellam Ave C1
Elvet Bridge B3
Elvet Court B3
Farnley Hey B1
Ferens Close A3
Fieldhouse La A1
Flass St B1
Flass Vale Local Nature reserve A1
Framwelgate Bridge B2
Framwelgate A2
Framwelgate Peth A2
Framwelgate Waterside A2
Frankland La A3
Freeman's Place A3
Freeman's Quay Leisure Centre A3
Gala Theatre & Cinema B3
Geoffrey Ave C1
Gilesgate B3
Grey College C3
Grove, The A1
Hallgarth St C3
Hatfield College B3
Hawthorn Terr B1
Heritage Centre B3
HM Prison B3
John St B1
Kingsgate Bridge B3
Laburnum Terr B1
Lawson Terr B1
Leazes Rd B2/B3
Library B2
Margery La B2
Market B2
Mavin St C3
Millburngate B2
Millburngate Bridge B2
Millennium Bridge (foot/cycle) A2
Mountjoy Research Centre C3
Museum of Archaeology B2
New Elvet B3
New Elvet Bridge B3
North Bailey B3
North End A1
Observatory C1
Old Elvet B3
Open Treasure B2
Oriental Mus C2
Oswald Court C3
Passport Office A2
Percy Terr B1
Pimlico C2
Police Station B3
Post Office A1/B2
Potters Bank C1/C2
Prebends Bridge C2
Prebends Walk C2
Prince Bishops Shopping Centre B3
Princes St A1
Providence Row A3
Quarryheads La C2
Redhills La B1
Redhills Terr B1
Riverwalk, The B2
Saddler St B3
St Cuthbert's Society C2
St Margaret's B2
St Mary the Less C2
St Mary's College C2
St Monica Grove B1
St Nicholas' B3
St Oswald's C3
Sands, The A3
Shopmobility B3
Sidegate A2
Silver St B2
Sixth Form College A3
South Bailey C2
South Rd C3
South St B2
Springwell Ave A1
Station Approach B2
Stockton Rd C3
Student Union B3
Summerville B1
Sutton St B2
Town Hall B2
Univ Arts Block B3
University Coll B2
Walkergate Centre A3
Wearside Dr A3
Western Hill A1
Wharton Park A2
Whinney Hill C3
Whitehouse Ave C1
YHA C3

Edinburgh 182

Abbey Strand B6
Abbeyhill B6
Abbeyhill Cres B6
Abbeymount A6
Abercromby Place A3
Adam St C5
Albany La A4
Albany St A4
Albert Memorial B2
Albyn Place A2
Alva Place A6
Alva St B1
Ann St A1
Appleton Tower C4
Archibald Place C3
Assembly Rooms & Musical Hall A3
Atholl Crescent B1
Atholl Crescent La C1
Bank St B4
Barony St A4
Beaumont Place C5
Belford Rd B1
Belgrave Cres A1
Belgrave Cres La A1
Bell's Brae B1
Blackfriars St B4
Blair St B4
Bread St C2
Bristo Place C4
Bristo St C4
Brougham St C2
Broughton St A4
Brown St C5
Brunton Terr A6
Buckingham Terr A1
Burial Ground A6
Bus Station A4
Caledonian Cres C1
Caledonian Rd C1
Calton Hill A4
Calton Hill A5
Calton Rd B4
Camera Obscura & Outlook Tower B3
Candlemaker Row C4
Canning St B2
Canongate B5
Canongate B5
Carlton St A1
Carlton Terr A6
Carlton Terrace La A6
Castle St B2
Castle Terr B2
Castlehill B3
Central Library B4
Chalmers Hosp C3
Chalmers St C3
Chambers St C4
Chapel St C4
Charles St C4
Charlotte Sq B2
Chester St B1
Circus La A2
Circus Place A2
City Art Centre B4
City Chambers B4
City Observatory A5
Clarendon Cres A1
Clerk St C5
Coates Cres B1
Cockburn St B4
College of Art C3
Comely Bank Ave A1
Comely Bank Row A1
Cornwall St C2
Cowans Close C5
Cowgate B4
Cranston St B5
Crichton St C4
Croft-An-Righ A6
Cumberland St A2
Dalry Place C1
Dalry Rd C1
Danube St A1
Darnaway St A2
David Hume Tower C4
Davie St C5
Dean Bridge A1
Dean Gdns A1
Dean Park Cres A1
Dean Park Mews A1
Dean Park St A1
Dean Path B1
Dean St A1
Dean Terr A1
Dewar Place C1
Dewar Place La C1
Doune Terr A2
Drummond Place A3
Drummond St C5
Drumsheugh Gdns B1
Dublin Mews A3
Dublin St A4
Dublin St La South A4
Dumbiedykes Rd B5
Dundas St A3
Dynamic Earth B6
Earl Grey St C2
East Crosscauseway C5
East Market St B4
East Norton Place A6
East Princes St Gdns B3
Easter Rd A6
Edinburgh (Waverley) B4
Edinburgh Castle B3
Edinburgh Dungeon B4
Edinburgh Int Conference Ctr C2
Elder St A4
Esplanade B3
Eton Terr A1
Eye Pavilion C3
Festival Office B3
Festival Theatre Edinburgh C4
Filmhouse C2
Fire Station C2
Floral Clock B3
Forres St A2
Forth St A4
Fountainbridge C2
Frederick St A3
Freemasons' Hall B3
Fruitmarket B4
Gardner's Cres C2
George Heriot's School C3
George IV Bridge B4
George Sq C4
George Sq La C4
George St B3
Georgian House B2
Gladstone's Land B3
Glen St C3
Gloucester La A2
Gloucester Place A2
Gloucester St A2
Graham St C3
Grassmarket C3
Great King St A3
Great Stuart B1
Greenside La A5
Greenside Row A5
Greyfriars Kirk C4
Grindlay St C2
Grosvenor St C1
Grove St C1
Gullan's Close B5
Guthrie St B4
Hanover St A3
Hart St A4
Haymarket C1
Haymarket Sta C1
Heriot Place C3
Heriot Row A2
High School Yard B5
High St B4
Hill Place C5
Hill St A2
Hillside Cres A5
Holyrood Abbey (Remains) A6
Holyrood Gait B6
Holyrood Park C6
Holyrood Rd B5
Home St C2
Hope St B2
Horse Wynd B6
Howden St C5
Howe St A2
Hub, The B3
India Place A2
India St A2
Infirmary St B4
Information Ctr B4
Jeffrey St B4
John Knox House B4
Johnston Terr C3
Keir St C3
Kerr St A2
King's Stables Rd B2
Lady Lawson St C3
Lauriston Gdns C3
Lauriston Park C3
Lauriston Place C3
Lauriston St C3
Lawnmarket B3
Learmonth Gdns A1
Learmonth Terr A1
Leith St A4
Lennox St A1
Lennox St La A1
Leslie Place A2
London Rd A5
Lothian Rd B2
Lothian St C4
Lower Menz Place A6
Lynedoch Place B1
Manor Place B1
Market St B4
Marshall St C4
Maryfield A6
McEwan Hall C4
Medical School C4
Melville St B1
Meuse La B4
Middle Meadow Walk C4
Milton St A6
Montrose Terr A6
Moray Place A2
Morrison Link C1
Morrison St C1
Mound Place B3
Mound, The B3
Multrees Walk A4
Mus Collections Ctr A4
Museum of Childhood B5
Museum of Edinburgh B5
Museum of Fire C3
Museum on the Mound B4
National Archives of Scotland A4
National Museum of Scotland C4
National Gallery B3
National Library of Scotland B4
National Monument A5
National Portrait Gallery B4
National War Museum B3
Nelson Monument A5
Nelson St A3
New St B5
Nicolson Sq C4
Nicolson St C4
Niddry St B4
North Bank St B3
North Bridge B4
North Castle St A2
North Charlotte St A2
North Meadow Walk C3
North St Andrew St A4
North St David St A3
North West Circus Place A2
Northumberland St A3
Odeon C2
Old Royal High School A5
Old Tolbooth Wynd B5
OMNi Centre A4
Oxford Terr A1
Palace of Holyroodhouse B6
Palmerston Place B1
Panmure Place C3
Parliament Sq B4
People's Story, The B5
Playhouse Theatre A4
Pleasance C5
Police Station C2
Ponton St C2
Post Office A3/B4/B5/C1/C2/C4
Potterrow C4
Princes Mall B4
Princes St B3
Princes St B3
Prisoners of War B3
Queen's Gallery B6
Queen St A2
Queen Street Gdns A3
Queen's Dr B6/C6
Queensferry Rd A1
Queensferry St B1
Queensferry St La B2
Radical Rd C6
Randolph Cres B1
Regent Gdns A5
Regent Rd B5
Regent Rd Park A6
Regent Terr A5
Richmond La C5
Richmond Place C5
Rose St B2
Ross Open Air Theatre B3
Rothesay Place B1
Rothesay Terr B1
Roxburgh Place C5
Roxburgh St C5
Royal Bank of Scotland A4
Royal Circus A2
Royal Lyceum C2
Royal Mile, The B5
Royal Scottish Academy B3
Royal Terr A5
Royal Terrace Gdns A5
Rutland Sq B2
Rutland St B2
St Andrew Sq A4
St Andrew Sq A4
St Andrew's House A4
St Bernard's Cres A1
St Bernard's Well A1
St Cecilia's Hall B4
St Colme St A2
St Cuthbert's B2
St Giles' B4
St James Quarter Shopping Centre A4
St John St B5
St John's B2
St John's Hill B5
St Leonard's Hill C5
St Leonard's La C5
St Leonard's St C5
St Mary's A4
St Mary's Scottish Episcopal B1
St Mary's St B5
St Michael & All Saints C3
St Stephen St A2
Salisbury Crags C6
Saunders St A2
Scotch Whisky Experience B3
Scott Monument B4
Scottish Parliament B6
Scottish Storytelling Centre B5
Semple St C2
Shandwick Place B2
South Bridge B4
South Charlotte St B2
South College St C4
South Learmonth Gdns A1
South St Andrew St A4
South St David St A3
Spittal St C2
Stafford St B1
Student Centre C4
Surgeons' Hall C5
Supreme Courts B4
Teviot Place C4
Thistle St A3
Torphichen Place C1
Torphichen St C1
Traverse Theatre B2
Tron Sq B4
Tron, The B4
Union St A4
University C4
University Library C4
Univ of Edinburgh B5
Upper Grove Place C1
Usher Hall C2
Vennel C3
Victoria St B3
Viewcraig Gdns B5
Viewcraig St B5
Vue A4
Walker St B1
Waterloo Place A4
Waverley Bridge B4
Wemyss Place A2
West Approach Rd C1
West Crosscauseway C5
West End B1
West Maitland St C1
West of Nicholson St C4
West Port C3
West Princes Street Gdns B3
West Richmond St C5
West Tollcross C2
White Horse Close B5
William St B1
Windsor St A5
Writer's Museum, The B4
York La A4
York Place A4
York Place A4
Young St B2

Exeter 182

Alphington St C1
Athelstan Rd B3
Barnardo Rd C3
Barnfield Hill B3
Barnfield Rd B2/B3
Barnfield Theatre B2
Bartholomew St East B1
Bartholomew St West B1
Bear St B2
Beaufort Rd C1
Bedford St B2
Belgrave Rd A3
Belmont Rd A3
Blackall Rd A2
Blackboy Rd A3
Bonhay Rd B1
Bull Meadow Rd C2
Bus & Coach Sta B3
Castle St B2
Catacombes C1
Cecil Rd C1
Cheeke St A3
Church Rd C1
Chute St A3
City Wall B1/B2
Civic Centre B2
Clifton Rd B3
Clifton St B3
Clock Tower A1
College Rd B3
Colleton Cres C2
Commercial Rd C1
Coombe St B2
Cowick St C1
Crown Courts B2
Custom House Visitor Centre C2
Cygnet Theatre C2
Danes' Rd A2
Denmark Rd B3
Devon County Hall C3
Devonshire Place A3
Dinham Cres B1
East Grove Rd C3
Edmund St C1
Elm Grove Rd A1
Exe St B1
Exeter Cathedral B2
Exeter Central Station A1
Exeter City Football Ground A3
Exeter College A1
Exeter Picture Ho B1
Fire Station A1
Fore St B1
Friars Walk C2
Guildhall B2
Guildhall Shopping Centre B2
Haven Rd C2
Heavitree Rd B3
Hele Rd A1
High St B2
HM Prison A2
Holloway St C2
Hoopern St A2
Horseguards A2
Howell Rd A1
Information Ctr B3
Iron Bridge B1
Isca Rd C1
Jesmond Rd A3
King St B1
King William St A2
Larkbeare Rd C2
Leisure Centre C1
Library B2
Longbrook St A2
Longbrook Terr A2
Lower North St B1
Lucky La C2
Lyndhurst Rd C3
Magdalen Rd B3
Magdalen St B2
Market B2
Market St B2
Marlborough Rd C3
Mary Arches St B1
Matford Ave C3
Matford La C3
Matford Rd C3
May St A3
Mol's Coffee Ho B2
New Bridge St B1
New North Rd A1/A2
North St B1
Northernhay St B1
Norwood Ave C3
Odeon A3
Okehampton St C1
Old Mill Close C2
Old Tiverton Rd A3
Oxford Rd A3
Paris St B2
Parr St A3
Paul St B1
Pennsylvania Rd A2
Portland Street A3
Post Office A3/B2/C1
Powderham Cres A3
Preston St B1
Princesshay Shopping Centre B2
Pyramids Leisure Centre B3
Quay, The C2
Queen St A1
Queen's Terr A1
Queens Rd C1
Radford Rd C2
Richmond Rd A1
Roberts Rd C2
Rougemont Castle A2
Rougemont Ho B2
Royal Albert Memorial Museum B2
St David's Hill A1
St James' Pk Sta A3
St James' Rd A3
St Leonard's Rd C3
St Mary Steps C1
St Nicholas Priory B1
St Thomas Sta C1
Sandford Walk B3
School Rd C1
Sidwell St A2
Smythen St B1
South St B2
Southernhay East B2
Southernhay West B2
Spicer Rd B3
Sports Centre A3
Summerland St A3
Sydney Rd C1
Tan La C2
Thornton Hill A2
Topsham Rd C3
Tucker's Hall B1
Tudor St B1
Underground Passages B2
University of Exeter (St Luke's Campus) B3
Velwell Rd A1
Verney St A3
Vue B3
Water La C1/C2
Weirfield Rd C2
Well St A3
West Ave A2
West Grove Rd C3
Western Way A3/B1/B2
Willeys Ave C1
Wonford Rd B3/C3
York Rd A2

Glasgow 183

Admiral St C2
Albert Bridge C5
Albion St B5
Anderston B2
Anderston Quay B3
Argyle Arcade B5
Argyle St A1/A2/B3/B4/B5
Argyle Street B5
Arlington St A3
Arts Centre B3
Ashley St A3
Bain St C6
Baird St A6
Baliol St A3
Ballater St C5
Barras (Mkt), The C6
Bath St A3
BBC Scotland B1
Bell St C6
Bell's Bridge B1
Bentinck St A2
Berkeley St A3
Bishop La B3
Black St A6
Blackburn St C2
Blackfriars St B6
Blantyre St A1
Blythswood Sq A4
Blythswood St B4
Bothwell St B4
Brand St C1
Breadalbane St A2
Bridge St C4
Bridge St C4
Bridgegate C5
Briggait C5
Broomielaw B4
Broomielaw Quay Gdns B3
Brown St B4
Brunswick St B5
Buccleuch St A3
Buchanan Bus Sta A5
Buchanan Galleries A5
Buchanan St B5
Buchanan St B5
Cadogan St B4
Caledonian Univ A5
Calgary St A5
Cambridge St A4
Canal St A5
Candleriggs B5
Carlton Place C4
Carnarvon St A3
Carrick St B4
Castle St B6
Cathedral Sq B6
Cathedral St B5
Central Mosque C5
Centre for Contemporary Arts A4
Centre St C4
Cessnock C1
Cessnock St C1
Charing Cross A3
Charlotte St C6
Cheapside St B3
Cineworld A5
Citizens' Theatre C5
City Chambers Complex B5
City Halls B5
City of Glasgow Coll (City Campus) B5
City of Glasgow Coll (Riverside Campus) C5
Clairmont Gdns A2
Claremont St A2
Claremont Terr A2
Claythorne St C6
Cleveland St A3
Clifford La C1
Clifford St C1
Clifton Place A2
Clifton St A2
Clutha St C1
Clyde Arc B2
Clyde Place C4
Clyde Place Quay C4
Clyde St C5
Clyde Walkway C3
Clydeside Expressway B2
Coburg St C4
Cochrane St B5
College St B6
Collins St B6
Commerce St C4
Cook St C4
Cornwall St C2
Couper St A5
Cowcaddens A4
Cowcaddens Rd A4
Crimea St B3
Custom House Quay Gdns C4
Dalhousie St A4
Dental Hospital A4
Derby St A2
Dobbie's Loan A4/A5
Dobbie's Loan Pl A5
Dorset St A3
Douglas St B4
Doulton Fountain C6
Dover St A2
Drury St B4
Drygate B6
Duke St B6
Dunaskin St A1
Dunblane St A4
Dundas St B5
Dunlop St C5
East Campbell St C6
Eastvale Place A1
Eglinton St C4
Elderslie St A3
Elliot St B2
Elmbank St A3
Esmond St A1
Exhibition Ctr B2
Festival Park C1
Film Theatre A4
Finnieston Quay B2
Finnieston St B2
Fire Station C6
Florence St C5
Fox St C5
Gallowgate C6
Garnet St A3
Garnethill St A4
Garscube Rd A4
George Sq B5
George St B5
George V Bridge C4
Gilbert St A1
Glasgow Bridge C4
Glasgow Cath B6
Glasgow Central B4
Glasgow City Free Church B4
Glasgow Green C6
Glasgow Necropolis B6
Glasgow Royal Concert Hall A5
Glasgow Science Centre B1
Glasgow Tower B1
Glassford St B5
Glebe St A6
Gorbals Cross C5
Gorbals St C5
Gordon St B4
Govan Rd B1/C1/C2
Grace St B3
Grafton Place A5
Grand Ole Opry C2
Grant St A3
Granville St A3
Gray St A2
Greendyke St C6
Grey Eagle St B7
Harley St C1
Harvie St C1
Haugh Rd A1
Havanah St B6
Heliport B1
Henry Wood Hall A2
High Court C5
High St B6
High Street B6
Hill St A3
Holland St A3
Holm St B4
Hope St A5
Houldsworth St B2
Houston Place C3
Houston St C3
Howard St C5
Hunter St C6
Hutcheson St B5
Hydepark St B3
Imax Cinema B1
India St A3
Information Ctr B5
Ingram St B5
Jamaica St B4
James Watt St B4
John Knox St B6
John St B5
Kelvin Hall A1
Kelvin Statue A2
Kelvin Way A2
Kelvingrove Art Gallery & Mus A1
Kelvingrove Park A2
Kelvingrove St A2
Kelvinhaugh St A1
Kennedy St A6
Kent Rd A2
Killermont St A5
King St B5
King's, The A3
Kingston Bridge C3
Kingston St C4
Kinning Park C2
Kyle St A5
Lancefield Quay B2
Lancefield St B3
Langshot St C1
Lendel Place C1
Lighthouse, The B4
Lister St A6
Little St B3
London Rd C6
Lorne St C1
Lower Harbour B1
Lumsden St A1
Lymburn St A1
Lyndoch Cres A3
Lynedoch Place A3
Lynedoch St A3
Maclellan St C1
Mair St C2
Maitland St A4
Mansell St C7
Mavisbank Gdns C2
Mcalpine St B3
Mcaslin St A6
McLean Sq C2
McLellan Gallery A4
McPhater St A4
Merchants' Ho B5
Middlesex St C2
Middleton St C1
Midland St B4
Miller St B5
Millennium Bridge B1
Millroad St C6
Milnpark St C2
Milton St A4
Minerva St B2
Mitchell St West B4
Mitchell Liby, The A3
Modern Art Gallery B5
Moir St C6
Molendinar St C6
Moncur St C6
Montieth Row C6
Montrose St B5
Morrison St C3
Nairn St A1
National Piping Centre, The A5
Nelson Mandela Sq B5
Nelson St C4
Nelson's Monument C6
Newton Place A3
Newton St A3
Nicholson St C4
Nile St B5
Norfolk Court C4
Norfolk St C4
North Frederick St B5
North Hanover St B5
North Portland St B6
North St A3
North Wallace St A5
O2 ABC A3
O2 Academy C4
Odeon C3
Old Dumbarton Rd A1
Osborne St B5/C5
Oswald St B4
Overnewton St A1
Oxford St C4
Pacific Dr B1
Paisley Rd C3
Paisley Rd West C1
Park Circus A2
Park Gdns A2
Park St South A2
Park Terr A2
Parkgrove Terr A2
Parnie St C5
Parson St A6
Partick Bridge A1
Passport Office A5
Pavilion Theatre A4
Pembroke St A3
People's Palace C6
Pitt St A4/B4
Plantation Park C1
Plantation Quay B1
Police Mus B5
Police Station A4/A6
Port Dundas Rd A5
Port St A2
Portman St C2
Prince's Dock B1
Princes Sq B5
Provand's Lordship B6
Queen St B5
Queen Street B5
Ramshorn B5
Renfrew St A3/A4
Renton St A5
Richmond St B5
Robertson St B4
Rose St A4
Rottenrow B5
Royal Concert Hall A5
Royal Conservatoire of Scotland A4
Royal Cres A2
Royal Exchange Sq B5
Royal Highland Fusiliers Mus A3
West Glasgow Ambulatory Care A1
Royal Infirmary B6
Royal Terr A2
Rutland Cres C2
St Andrew's in the Square C6
St Andrew's (RC) C5
St Andrew's St C5
St Enoch B5
St Enoch Shopping Centre B5
St Enoch Sq B4
St George's Rd A3
St James Rd B6
St Kent St C6
St Mungo Ave A5/A6
St Mungo Museum of Religious Life & Art B6
St Mungo Place A6
St Vincent Cres A2
St Vincent Place B5
St Vincent St B3/B4
St Vincent Terr B3
Saltmarket C5
Sandyford Place A3
Sauchiehall St A2/A4
SEC Armadillo B2
School of Art A4
Sclater St B7
Scotland St C2
Scott St A4
Scottish Exhibition & Conference Ctr B1
Seaward St C2
Shaftesbury St B3
Sheriff Court C5
Shields Rd C3
Shopmobility A5
Shuttle St B6
Somerset Place A2
South Portland St C4
Springburn Rd A6
Springfield Quay C3
SSE Hydro The B2
Stanley St C2
Stevenson St C6
Stewart St A4
Stirling Rd B6
Stobcross Quay B1
Stobcross Rd B1
Stock Exchange B5
Stockwell Place C5
Stockwell St B5
Stow College A4
Sussex St C2
Synagogue A3
Taylor Place A6
Tenement House A3
Teviot St A1
Theatre Royal A4
Tolbooth Steeple & Mercat Cross C6
Tower St C2
Trades House B5
Tradeston St C4
Transport Mus A1
Tron C5
Trongate B5
Tunnel St B2
Turnbull St C5
Union St B4
Univ of Strathclyde B6
Victoria Bridge C5
Virginia St B5
Wallace St C3
Walls St B6
Walmer Cres C1
Warrock St B3
Washington St B3
Waterloo St B4
Watson St B6
Watt St C3
Wellington St B4
West Campbell St B4
West George St B4
West Graham St A4
West Greenhill Pl B2
West Regent St B4
West Regent St B4
West St C4
West St C4
Whitehall St B3
Wilkes St C7
Wilson St B5
Woodlands Gate A3
Woodlands Terr A2
Woodside Place A3
Woodside Terr A3
York St B4
Yorkhill Pde A1
Yorkhill St A1

Gloucester 182

Albion St C1
Alexandra Rd B3
Alfred St C3
All Saints Rd C2
Alvin St B2
Arthur St C2
Barrack Square B1

Grimsby • Harrogate • Hull • Inverness • Ipswich • Kendal • King's Lynn • Lancaster 205

Barton St C2
Blackfriars ✝ B1
Blenheim Rd C2
Bristol Rd C1
Brunswick Rd C2
Bruton Way B2
Bus Station B2
Cineworld C1
City Council Offices B1
City Mus, Art Gallery & Library B2
Clarence St B2
Commercial Rd B1
Council Offices B1
Courts B1
Cromwell St C2
Deans Way A2
Denmark Rd A3
Derby Rd C3
Docks ✦ C1
Eastgate St B2
Eastgate, The B1
Edwy Pde A2
Estcourt Close A3
Estcourt Rd A3
Falkner St C2
GL1 Leisure Centre C2
Gloucester Cath ✝ B1
Gloucester Life B1
Gloucester Quays Outlet C1
Gloucester Sta ≥ B2
Gloucester Waterways C1
Gloucestershire Archive B2
Gloucestershire Royal Hospital (A&E) H B3
Goodyere St C2
Gouda Way A1
Great Western Rd B3
Guildhall B2
Heathville Rd A3
Henry Rd B3
Henry St B2
Hinton Rd A2
India Rd C3
Information Ctr B1
Jersey Rd C3
King's C2
King's Walk Shopping Centre B2
Kingsholm (Gloucester Rugby) A2
Kingsholm Rd A2
Lansdown Rd A3
Library C2
Llanthony Rd C1
London Rd B3
Longhorn Ave A1
Longsmith St B1
Malvern Rd A3
Market B2
Market Parade B2
Mercia Rd A1
Metz Way C3
Midland Rd C2
Millbrook St C3
Montpellier C1
Napier St C3
Nettleton Rd C2
New Inn B2
New Olympus C3
North Rd A3
Northgate St B2
Oxford Rd A2
Oxford St B2
Park & Ride Gloucester A1
Park Rd C2
Park St B2
Park, The C2
Parliament St C1
Peel Centre, The C1
Pitt St B1
Police Station C3
Post Office B2
Quay St B1
Quay, The B1
Recreation Gd A1/A2
Regent St C2
Robert Raikes Ho B1
Royal Oak Rd B1
Russell St B2
Ryecroft St C2
St Aldate St B2
St Ann Way C1
St Catherine St A2
St Mark St A2
St Mary de Crypt B1
St Mary de Lode B1
St Nicholas's B1
St Oswald's Rd A1
St Oswald's Retail Park A1
St Peter's B2
Seabroke Rd A3
Sebert St A2
Severn Rd C1
Sherborne St B2
Shire Hall B1
Sidney St C3
Soldiers of Gloucestershire B1
Southgate St B1/C1
Spa Field C1
Spa Rd C1
Sports Ground A2/B2
Station Rd B2
Stratton Rd C3
Stroud Rd C1
Superstore A1
Swan Rd A2
Trier Way C1/C2
Union St A2
Vauxhall Rd C3
Victoria St C2
Walham Lane A1
Wellington St C2
Westgate Retail Pk B1
Westgate St B1
Widden St C2
Worcester St B2

Grimsby 183

Abbey Drive East C2
Abbey Drive West C2
Abbey Park Rd C2
Abbey Rd C2
Abbey Walk C2
Abbeygate Shopping Centre C2
Abbotsway C2
Adam Smith St A1/A2
Ainslie St C2
Albert St A3
Alexandra Dock A2/B2
Alexandra Rd A2/B2
Alexandra Retail Pk A2
Annesley St A2
Armstrong St A1
Arthur St B1
Augusta St C1
Bargate C1
Beeson St A1
Bethlehem St C2
Bodiam Way B3
Bradley St B3
Brighowgate C1/C2
Bus Station C2
Canterbury Dr C1
Cartergate B1/C1
Catherine St C3
Chantry La B1
Charlton St A1
Church La C2
Church St A3
Cleethorpe Rd A3
Close, The C1
College St C1
Compton Dr C1
Corporation Bridge A2
Corporation Rd A1
Court B2/B3
Crescent St B1
Deansgate C1
Doughty Rd C2
Dover St B1
Duchess St C2
Dudley St C1
Duke of York Gdns B1
Duncombe St B3
Earl La B1
East Marsh St B3
East St B2
Eastgate B3
Eastside Rd A3
Eaton Ct C1
Eleanor St B3
Ellis Way B3
Fisherman's Chapel A3
Fisherman's Wharf B2
Fishing Heritage Centre B2
Flour Sq A3
Frederick St B1
Frederick Ward Way B2
Freeman St A3/B3
Freshney Dr B1
Freshney Place B2
Garden St C2
Garibaldi St A3
Garth La B2
Grime St B3
Grimsby Docks Station ≥ A3
Grimsby Town Station ≥ C2
Hainton Ave C3
Har Way B3
Hare St C3
Harrison St B1
Haven Ave B1
Hay Croft Ave B1
Hay Croft St B1
Heneage Rd B3/C3
Henry St B1
Holme St B3
Hume St C1
James St B1
Joseph St B1
Kent St A3
King Edward St A3
Lambert Rd C2
Library B2
Lime St B1
Lister St B1
Littlefield La C1
Lockhill A3
Lord St B1
Lower Spring St A3
Ludford St C3
Macaulay St B1
Mallard Mews C3
Manor Ave C2
Market A3
Market Hall B2
Market St B3
Moody Lane A3
Moss Rd C2
Nelson St A3
New St B2
Osbourne St B2
Pasture St B3
Peaks Parkway C3
Pelham Rd C1
Police Station B3
Post Office B1/B2
Pyewipe Rd A1
Railway Place A3
Railway St A3
Recreation Ground C2
Rendel St A2
Retail Park A2/B3
Richard St B1
Ripon St B1
Robinson St East B3
Royal St A3
St Hilda's Ave C1
St James C2
Sheepfold St B3/C3
Shopmobility B2
Sixhills St C3
South Park B2
Superstore B3/B2
Tasburgh St C3
Tennyson St B2
Thesiger St A3
Time Trap C2
Town Hall B2
Veal St B1
Victoria Retail Park A3
Victoria St North A2
Victoria St South B2
Victoria St West B2
Watkin St A1
Welholme Ave C2
Welholme Rd C3
Wellington St B3
Wellowgate C2
Werneth Rd B3
West Coates Rd A1
Westgate A2
Westminster Dr C1
Willingham St C3
Wintringham Rd C2
Wood St B3
Yarborough Dr B1
Yarborough Hotel C2

Harrogate 183

Albert St C2
Alexandra Rd B2
Arthington Ave B2
Ashfield Rd A2
Back Cheltenham Mount B2
Beech Grove C1
Belmont Rd C1
Bilton Dr A2
BMI The Duchy Hospital H C1
Bower Rd B2
Bower St B2
Bus Station B2
Cambridge Rd B2
Cambridge St B2
Cemetery A2
Chatsworth Grove A2
Chatsworth Place A2
Chatsworth Rd A2
Chelmsford Rd B3
Cheltenham Cres B2
Cheltenham Mt B2
Cheltenham Pde B2
Christ Church B3
Christ Church Oval B3
Chudleigh Rd B3
Clarence Dr B1
Claro Rd A3
Claro Way A3
Coach Park B2
Coach Rd B3
Cold Bath Rd C1
Commercial St B2
Coppice Ave A1
Coppice Dr A1
Coppice Gate A1
Cornwall Rd B1
Council Offices B1
Crescent Gdns B1
Crescent Rd B1
Dawson Terr A2
Devonshire Place B3
Dixon Rd A2
Dixon Terr A2
Dragon Ave B3
Dragon Parade B2
Dragon Rd B2
Duchy Rd B1
East Parade B2
East Park Rd C3
Esplanade B1
Everyman C2
Fire Station A2
Franklin Mount A2
Franklin Rd B2
Franklin Square A2
Glebe Rd C1
Grove Park Ct A3
Grove Park Terr A3
Grove Rd A2
Hampsthwaite Rd A1
Harcourt Dr B3
Harcourt Rd B3
Harrogate ≥ B2
Harrogate Convention Centre B1
Harrogate Justice Ctr (Magistrates' and County Courts) C2
Harrogate Ladies College B1
Harrogate Theatre B2
Heywood Rd C1
Hollins Cres A1
Hollins Mews A1
Hollins Rd A1
Hydro Leisure Centre, The A1
Information Ctr B1
James St B2
Jenny Field Dr A1
John St B2
Kent Dr A1
Kent Rd A1
Kings Rd A2
Kingsway B3
Kingsway Dr B3
Lancaster Rd C1
Leeds Rd C2
Lime Grove B3
Lime St A3
Mayfield Grove B2
Mercer B1
Montpellier Hill B1
Mornington Cres A3
Mornington Terr B3
Mowbray Sq B3
North Park Rd B3
Oakdale Ave A1
Oatlands Dr C3
Odeon B2
Osborne Rd A2
Otley Rd C2
Oxford St B2
Parade, The B2
Park Chase B3
Park Parade B3
Park View B2
Parliament St B1
Police Station B3
Post Office B2/C1
Providence Terr A2
Queen Parade C3
Queen's Rd C1
Raglan St C2
Regent Ave A3
Regent Grove A3
Regent Parade A3
Regent St A3
Regent Terr A3
Ripon Rd A1
Robert St C2
Royal Baths & Turkish Baths B1
Royal Pump Room B1
St Luke's Mount A2
St Mary's Ave C1
St Mary's Walk C1
Scargill Rd A1
Skipton Rd A3
Skipton St A2
Slingsby Walk C3
South Park Rd C2
Spring Grove A1
Springfield Ave B1
Station Ave B2
Station Parade B2
Stray Rein C3
Stray, The C2/C3
Studley Rd A2
Superstore B2/C1
Swan Rd B1
Tower St C2
Trinity Rd C2
Union St B2
Valley Dr C1
Valley Gardens C1
Valley Mount C1
Victoria Ave C2
Victoria Rd C1
Victoria Shopping Centre B2
Waterloo St A2
West Park C2
West Park St C2
Wood View A1
Woodfield Ave A3
Woodfield Dr A3
Woodfield Grove A3
Woodfield Rd A3
Woodfield Square A3
Woodside B3
York Place C3
York Rd B1

Hull 184

Adelaide St C1
Albert Dock C1
Albion St B2
Alfred Gelder St B2
Anlaby Rd B1
Arctic Corsair ✦ B3
Beverley Rd A1
Blanket Row C2
Bond St B2
Bonus Arena B2
Bridlington Ave A2
Brook St B1
Brunswick Ave A1
Bus Station B1
Camilla Close C3
Cannon St A2
Caroline St A2
Carr La B2
Castle St C2
Central Library B1
Charles St A2
Citadel Way B3
Clarence St B3
Cleveland St A3
Clifton St A1
Colonial St B1
Court B2
Deep, The C3
Dinostar C2
Dock Office Row B3
Dock St B2
Drypool Bridge B3
Egton St A3
English St C1
Ferens Gallery B2
Ferensway B1
Fire Sta A1
Francis St A2
Francis St West A2
Freehold St A1
Freetown Way A2
FrüitTheatre C2
Garrison Rd B3
George St B2
Gibson St A2
Great Thornton St B1
Great Union St A3
Green La A2
Grey St A1
Grimston St B2
Grosvenor St A1
Guildhall B2
Guildhall Rd B2
Hands-on History B2
Harley St A1
Hessle Rd C1
High St B3
Hull Minster B2
Hull Paragon Interchange Sta ≥ B1
Hull & East Riding Museum B3
Hull Ice Arena C1
Hull City Hall B2
Hull College B3
Hull History Centre A2
Hull New Theatre A2
Hull Truck Theatre B1
Humber Dock Marina C2
Humber Dock St C2
Humber St C2
Hyperion St A3
Information Ctr B2
Jameson St B1
Jarratt St B2
Jenning St A3
King Billy Statue ✦ C2
King Edward St B2
King St A2
Kingston Retail Pk C1
Kingston St C2
Liddell St A1
Lime St A3
Lister St C1
Lockwood St A2
Maister House B3
Maritime Mus B2
Market B2
Market Place C2
Minerva Pier C2
Mulgrave St A3
Myton Swing Bridge C3
Myton St B1
NAPA (Northern Acad of Performing Arts) B1
Nelson St C2
New Cleveland St A3
New George St A2
Norfolk St A1
North Bridge A3
North St B1
Odeon C1
Old Harbour C3
Osborne St B1
Paragon St B2
Park St B1
Percy St A2
Pier St C2
Police Station B1
Porter St C1
Portland St B1
Post Office B1/B2
Posterngate C2
Prince's Quay B2
Prospect Centre B1
Prospect St B1
Queen's Gdns B2
Railway Dock Marina C2
Railway St C2
Real B1
Red Gallery B1
Reform St A2
Retail Park B1
Riverside Quay C2
Roper St B2
St James St C1
St Luke's St B1
St Mark St A3
St Mary the Virgin B3
St Stephens Shopping Centre B1
Scale La Footbridge B3
Scott St A2
South Bridge Rd B3
Sport's Centre C1
Spring Bank A1
Spring St B1
Spurn Lightship C2
Spyvee St A3
Stage @The Dock C3
southwater B3
Sykes St A2
Tidal Surge Barrier ✦ C3
Tower St B3
Trinity House B2
Vane St A1
Victoria Pier ✦ C2
Waterhouse La B2
Waterloo St A1
Waverley St C1
Wellington St C2
Wellington St West C2
West St B1
Whitefriargate B2
Wilberforce Dr B2
Wilberforce Ho B3
Wilberforce Monument ✦ B3
William St C1
Wincolmlee A3
Witham A3
Wright St A1

Inverness 184

Abban St A1
Academy St B2
Alexander Place B2
Anderson St A2
Annfield Rd C3
Ardconnel St B3
Ardconnel Terr B3
Ardross Place B2
Ardross St B2
Argyle St B3
Argyle Terr B3
Attadale Rd B1
Ballifeary La C2
Ballifeary Rd C1/C2
Balnacraig La A1
Balnain House ✦ B2
Balnain St B2
Bank St B2
Bellfield Park C2
Bellfield Terr C3
Benula Rd A1
Birnie Terr A1
Bishop's Rd C2
Bowling Green C2
Bridge St B2
Brown St A2
Bruce Ave C1
Bruce Gdns C1
Bruce Pk C1
Burial Ground A2
Burnett Rd A3
Bus Station B3
Caledonian Rd B1
Cameron Rd A1
Cameron Sq A1
Carse Rd A1
Carsegate Rd Sth A1
Castle Garrison Encounter ✦ B2
Castle Rd B2
Castle St B3
Celt St B2
Chapel St A2
Charles St B3
Church St B2
Columba Rd B1/C1
Crown Ave B3
Crown Circus B3
Crown Dr B3
Crown Rd B3
Crown St B3
Culduthel Rd C3
Dalneigh Cres C1
Dalneigh Rd C1
Denny St B3
Dochfour Dr B1/C1
Douglas Row B2
Duffy Dr C3
Dunabban Rd A1
Dunain Rd B1
Duncraig St B2
Eastgate Shopping Centre B3
Eden Court C2
Fairfield Rd B1
Falcon Sq B3
Fire Station A3
Fraser St B2
Fraser St C2
Friars' Bridge A2
Friars' La B2
Friars' St A2
George St A2
Gilbert St A2
Glebe St A2
Glendoe Terr A1
Glenurquhart Rd C1
Gordon Terr B3
Gordonville Rd C2
Grant St A2
Grant Street Park (Clachnacuddin FC) A1
Greig St B2
Harbour Rd A3
Harrowden Rd B1
Haugh Rd C2
Heatherley Cres C3
High St B3
Highland Council HQ, The C2
Hill Park C3
Hill St B3
HM Prison B3
Huntly Place A2
Huntly St B2
India St A2
Industrial Estate A3
Information Ctr B2
Innes St A2
Inverness ≥ B3
Inverness High Sch B1
Inverness Museum & Art Gallery B2
Jamaica St A2
Kenneth St B2
Kilmuir Rd A1
King St B2
Kingsmills Rd B3
Laurel Ave B1/C1
Library A3
Lilac Grove B1
Lindsay Ave C1
Lochalsh Rd A1/B1
Longman Rd A3
Lotland Place A2
Lower Kessock St A1
Madras St A2
Maxwell Dr C1
Mayfield Rd C3
Millburn Rd B3
Mitchell's La C3
Montague Row B2
Muirfield Rd C3
Muirtown St B1
Nelson St A2
Ness Bank C2
Ness Bridge B2
Ness Walk B2/C2
Old Edinburgh Rd C3
Old High Church B2
Park Rd C1
Paton St C2
Perceval Rd B1
Planefield Rd B2
Police Station A3
Porterfield Bank C3
Porterfield Rd C3
Portland Place A2
Post Office A2/B1/B2
Queen St B2
Queensgate B2
Railway Terr A3
Rangemore Rd B1
Reay St B3
Riverside St A2
Rose St A2
Ross Ave B1
Rowan Rd B1
Royal Northern Infirmary H C2
St Andrew's Cath ✝ C2
St Columba B2
St John's Ave C1
St Mary's Ave C1
Sheriff Court B3
Shore St A2
Smith Ave C1
Southside Place C3
Southside Rd C3
Spectrum Centre B2
Strothers La B3
Superstore A1/B2
TA Centre C2
Telford Gdns B1
Telford Rd A1
Telford St A1
Tomnahurich Cemetery C1
Tomnahurich St B2
Town Hall B3
Union Rd B3
Union St B3
Victorian Market B3
Walker Place A2
Walker Rd A3
War Memorial ✦ C2
Waterloo Bridge A2
Wells St B1
Young St B2

Ipswich 184

Alderman Rd B2
All Saints' Rd A1
Alpe St B2
Ancaster Rd C1
Ancient House B3
Anglesea Rd B2
Ann St B2
Arboretum A2
Austin St C2
Avenue, The A3
Belstead Rd C2
Berners St B2
Bibb Way B1
Birkfield Dr C1
Black Horse La B2
Bolton La B3
Bond St C3
Bowthorpe Close B2
Bramford La A1
Bramford Rd A1
Bridge St C2
Brookfield Rd A1
Brooks Hall Rd A1
Broomhill A2
Broomhill Park A2
Broomhill Rd A1
Broughton Rd A2
Bulwer Rd B1
Burrell Rd C2
Bus Station B2
Butter Market B2
Buttermarket Shopping Ctr, The B3
Cardinal Park Leisure Park C2
Carr St B3
Cecil Rd B2
Cecilia St C2
Chancery Rd C2
Charles St B2
Chevallier St A1
Christchurch Mansion & Wolsey Art Gallery B3
Christchurch Park A3
Christchurch St B3
Cineworld C2
Civic Centre B2
Civic Dr B2
Clarkson St B1
Cobbold St B3
Commercial Rd C2
Constable Rd A3
Constantine Rd C1
Constitution Hill A2
Corder Rd A3
Corn Exchange B2
Cotswold Ave A2
Council Offices C2
County Hall B3
Crown Court C2
Crown St B2
Cullingham Rd B1
Cumberland St B2
Curriers La B2
Dale Hall La A2
Dales View Rd A1
Dalton Rd B2
Dillwyn St B1
Elliot St B1
Elm St B2
Elsmere Rd A3
Falcon St C2
Felaw St C3
Fire Station C2
Flint Wharf C3
Fonnereau Rd B2
Fore St C3
Foundation St C3
Franciscan Way C2
Friars St C2
Gainsborough Rd A3
Gatacre Rd B1
Geneva Rd B2
Gippeswyk Ave C1
Gippeswyk Park C1
Grafton Way C2
Graham Rd A1
Great Whip St C3
Grimwade St C3
Handford Cut B1
Handford Rd B1
Henley Rd A2
Hervey St B3
High St B2
Holly Rd A2
Ipswich Haven Marina ✦ C3
Ipswich Museum & Art Gallery B2
Ipswich School A2
Ipswich Station ≥ C2
Ipswich Town FC (Portman Road) C2
Ivry St A2
Kensington Rd A1
Kesteven Rd C1
Key St C3
Kingsfield Ave A3
Kitchener Rd A1
Library A1
Little's Cres C2
London Rd B1
Low Brook St C3
Lower Orwell St C3
Luther Rd C2
Magistrates Court B2
Manor Rd A3
Mornington Ave A1
Museum St B2
Neale St B3
New Cardinal St C2
New Cut East C3
New Wolsey C2
Newson St B2
Norwich Rd A1/B1
Oban St B2
Old Custom Ho C3
Old Foundry Rd B3
Old Merchant's House C3
Orford St B2
Paget Rd A2
Park Rd A3
Park View Rd A2
Peter's St C2
Philip Rd C2
Pine Ave A2
Pine View Rd A2
Police Station B2
Portman Rd B2
Portmans Walk C1
Post Office B2
Princes St C2
Prospect St B1
Queen St B2
Ranelagh Rd C1
Recreation Ground B1
Rectory Rd C2
Regent Theatre B3
Reg Driver Visitor Centre ✦ B3
Retail Park C1
Retail Park C2
Richmond Rd A1
Rope Walk C3
Rose La C2
Russell Rd C2
St Edmund's Rd A2
St George's St B2
St Helen's St B3
Sherrington Rd A1
Shopmobility B2
Silent St C2
Sir Alf Ramsey Way C1
Sir Bobby Robson Bridge C2
Sirdar Rd B1
Sir John Mills Theatre B1
Soane St B3
Springfield La A1
Star La C3
Stevenson Rd B1
Stoke Quay C3
Suffolk College C3
Suffolk Retail Park B1
Superstore B1
Surrey Rd B1
Tacket St C3
Tavern St B3
Tower Ramparts B2
Tower Ramparts Shopping Centre B2
Tower St B3
Town Hall B2
Tuddenham Rd A3
University C3
Upper Brook St B3
Upper Orwell St B3
Valley Rd A2
Vermont Cres B3
Vermont Rd B3
Vernon St C3
Warrington Rd A2
Waterloo Rd A1
Waterworks St C3
Wellington St B1
West End Rd B1
Westerfield Rd A3
Westgate St B2
Westholme Rd A1
Westwood Ave A1
Willoughby Rd C2
Withipoll St B3
Woodbridge Rd B3
Woodstone Ave A3
Yarmouth Rd B1

Kendal 184

Abbot Hall Art Gallery & Mus of Lakeland Life & Industry C2
Ambulance Station A2
Anchorite Fields C2
Anchorite Rd C2
Ann St A3
Appleby Rd A3
Archers Meadow C3
Ashleigh Rd A2
Aynam Rd B2
Bankfield Rd B1
Beast Banks B2
Beezon Fields A2
Beezon Rd A2
Beezon Trad Est A3
Belmont B2
Birchwood Close C1
Blackhall Rd B2
Brewery Arts Centre B2
Bridge St B2
Brigsteer Rd C1
Burneside Rd A2
Bus Station B2
Buttery Well Rd C2
Canal Head North B3
Captain French La C2
Caroline St A2
Castle Hill B3
Castle Howe B2
Castle Rd B3
Castle St A3/B3
Cedar Grove C1
Council Offices B2
County Council Offices A2
Cricket Ground A3
Cricket Ground C3
Cross La C2
Dockray Hall Industrial Estate A2
Dowker's La B2
East View B1
Echo Barn Hill C1
Elephant Yard B2
Fairfield La A1
Finkle St B2
Fire Station A2
Fletcher Square C3
Football Ground C3
Fowling La A3
Gillinggate C2
Glebe Rd C2
Golf Course B1
Goose Holme B3
Gooseholme Bridge B3
Green St A1
Greengate C2
Greengate La C1/C2
Greenside B1
Greenwood C1
Gulfs Rd B2
High Tenterfell B1
Highgate B2
Hillswood Ave C1
Horncop La A2
Information Ctr B2
Kendal A3
Kendal Business Park A3
Kendal Castle (Remains) B3
Kendal Fell B1
Kendal Green A1
Kendal Ski Ctr ✦ B3
Kendal Station ≥ A3
Kent Place B2
Kirkbarrow C2
Kirkland C2
Library B2
Library Rd B2
Little Aynam B3
Little Wood B1
Long Close C1
Longpool A3
Lound Rd C3
Lound St C3
Low Fellside B2
Lowther St B2
Magistrates Court A2
Maple Dr C1
Market Place B2
Maude St B2
Miller Bridge B2
Milnthorpe Rd C2
Mint St A3
Mintsfeet Rd A2
Mintsfeet Rd South A2
New Rd B2
Noble's Rest B2
Parish Church C2
Park Side Rd C3
Parkside Business Park C3
Parr St B3
Police Station A2
Post Office A3/B2
Quaker Tapestry ✦ B2
Queen's Rd B1
Riverside Walk C2
Rydal Mount A2
Sandes Ave A2
Sandgate A3
Sandylands Rd A3
Serpentine Rd B1
Serpentine Wood B1
Shap Rd A3
South Rd C2
Stainbank Rd C1
Station Rd A3
Stramongate B2
Stramongate Bridge B2
Stricklandgate A2/B2
Sunnyside C3
Thorny Hills B3
Town Hall B2
Undercliff Rd B1
Underwood C1
Union St A2
Vicar's Fields C2
Vicarage Dr C1/C2
Wainwright's Yard B2
Wasdale Close C3
Well Ings C2
Westmorland Shopping Centre & Market Hall B2
Westwood Ave C1
Wildman St A3
Windermere Rd A1
YHA B2
YWCA B2

King's Lynn 185

Albert St A2
Albion St B2
Alive St James' Swimming Pool B2
All Saints B2
All Saints St B2
Austin Fields A2
Austin St A2
Avenue Rd B3
Bank Side B1
Beech Rd C2
Birch Tree Close B2
Birchwood St A2
Blackfriars Rd B2
Blackfriars St B2
Boal St B1
Bridge St B2
Broad St B2
Broad Walk B3
Burkitt St A2
Bus Station A2
Carmelite Terr C2
Chapel St A2
Chase Ave C3
Checker St C2
Church St B2
Clough La B2
Coburg St B2
Coll of West Anglia A3
Columbia Way A3
Comm Staithe Quay A1
Corn Exchange A1
County Court Rd B2
Cresswell St A2
Custom House A1
East Coast Business Park C1
Eastgate St A2
Edma St A2
Exton's Rd C3
Ferry La B1
Ferry St A1
Framingham's Almshouses B2
Friars St C2
Friars Walk C2
Gaywood Rd A3
George St A2
Gladstone Rd C2
Goodwin's Rd C3
Green Quay Discovery Centre ✦ B1
Greyfriars' Tower ✦ B2
Guanock Terr C2
Guildhall A1
Hansa Rd C3
Harding's Way C2
Hardwick Rd C2
Hextable Rd A2
High St B1
Holcombe Ave C3
Hospital Walk C2
Information Ctr A1
John Kennedy Rd A2
Kettlewell Lane A2
King George V Ave B3
King St B1
King's Lynn Art Centre A1
King's Lynn Sta ≥ B2
Library B2
Littleport St A2
Loke Rd A2
London Rd B2
Lynn Museum B2
Magistrates Court B1
Majestic B2
Market La A1
Millfleet B2
Milton Ave A3
Nar Valley Walk C2
Nelson St B1
New Conduit St B2
Norfolk St A2
North Lynn Discovery Centre ✦ A3
North St A2
Oldsunway B2
Ouse Ave C1
Page Stair Lane A1
Park Ave B3
Police Station B2
Portland Place C1
Portland St B2
Purfleet B1
Queen St B1
Raby Ave A3
Railway Rd A2
Red Mount Chapel B3
Regent Way B2
River Walk A1
Robert St C2
Shopmobility B2
St Ann's St A1
St James St B2
St James' Rd B2
St John's Walk B3
St Margaret's B1
St Nicholas A2
St Nicholas St A1
St Peter's Rd B1
Sir Lewis St A2
Smith Ave A3
South Everard St C2
South Gate ✦ C2
South Quay B1
South St B2
Southgate St C2
Stonegate St B2
Stories of Lynn B1
Surrey St A1
Sydney St C3
Tennyson Ave B3
Tennyson Rd B3
The Walks Stadium (King's Lynn FC) B3
Tower St B2
Town Hall B1
Town Wall (Remains) ✦ B3
True's Yard Fisherfolk Museum A2
Valingers Rd C2
Vancouver Ave C2
Vancouver Quarter B2
Waterloo St B2
Wellesley St B2
Whitefriars Terrace C2
Windsor Rd C2
Winfarthing St C2
Wisbech Road C2
Wyatt St A2
York Rd C3

Lancaster 185

Aberdeen Rd C3
Aldcliffe Rd C2
Alfred St B3
Ambleside Rd A3
Ambulance & Fire Station B2
Ashfield Ave B1
Ashton Rd C2
Assembly Rooms Emporium B2
Balmoral Rd B3
Bath House B2
Bath St B3
Blades St B1
BMI Lancaster (private) H C2
Borrowdale Rd B3
Bowerham Rd C3
Brewery La B2
Bridge La B2
Brook St C1
Bulk Rd A3
Bulk St B2
Bus Station B2
Cable St B2
Canal Cruises & Waterbus ✦ C2
Carlisle Bridge A1
Carr House La C2
Castle B1
Castle Park B1
Caton Rd A3
China St B2
Church St B2
City Museum B2
Clarence St C3
Common Gdn St B2
Coniston Rd A3
Cottage Museum B2
Council Offices B2
Courts B2
Cromwell Rd C1
Crown Court B1
Dale St C3
Dallas Rd B1/C1
Dalton Rd B3
Dalton Sq B2
Damside St B2
De Vitre St B3
Dee Rd A1
Denny Ave A1
Derby Rd A2
Dukes, The B2
Earl St A2
East Rd B3
Eastham St C3
Edward St B3
Fairfield Nature Reserve C1
Fairfield Rd B1
Fenton St B2
Firbank Rd A3
Friend's Meeting House B1
Garnet St B3
George St B2
Giant Axe Field B1
Grand B2
Grasmere Rd B3
Greaves Park C3
Greaves Rd C2
Green St A3
Gregson Ctr, The B3
Gregson Rd C3
Greyhound Bridge A2
Greyhound Bridge Rd A2
High St B2
Hill Side B1
Hope St C3
Hubert Place B1
Information Ctr B2
Kelsy St B1
Kentmere Rd B3
Keswick Road A3
King St B2
Kingsway A3
Kirkes Rd C3
Lancaster City Football Club B1
Lancaster Royal Grammar School B3
Lancaster Sta ≥ B1
Langdale Rd A3
Ley Ct B1
Library B2
Lincoln Rd B1
Lindow St C2
Lodge St B2
Long Marsh La B1
Lune Rd A1
Lune St A2
Lune Valley Ramble A3
Mainway A2
Maritime Mus A1
Marketgate Shopping Centre B2
Market St B2
Meadowside C2
Meeting House La B1
Millennium Bridge A2
Moor La B2
Moorgate B3
Morecambe Rd A1/A2
Nelson St B2
North Rd B2
Orchard La C1
Owen Rd A2
Park Rd B3
Parliament St A3
Patterdale Rd A3
Penny St B2
Police Station B2
Portland St C2
Post Office B2/B3
Primrose St C3
Priory B1
Prospect St C3
Quarry Rd B3
Queen St C2
Regent St C2
Ridge La A3
Ridge St A3
Royal Lancaster Infirmary (A&E) H C2
Rydal Rd B3
Ryelands Park A1
St Georges Quay A1
St John's B2
St Leonard's Gate B2
St Martin's Rd C3
St Nicholas Arcades Shopping Centre B2
St Oswald St C3
St Peter's ✝ B3

206 Leeds • Leicester • Lincoln • Liverpool • Llandudno • Llanelli

St Peter's Rd B3
Salisbury Rd B1
Scotch Quarry Urban Park C3
Sibsey St B1
Skerton Bridge A2
South Rd C2
Station Rd B1
Stirling Rd C3
Storey Ave B1
Sunnyside La C1
Sylvester St C1
Tarnsyke Rd A1
Thurnham St C2
Town Hall B2
Troutbeck Rd B3
Ulleswater Rd B3
Univ of Cumbria C3
Vicarage Field B1
Vue B2
West Rd B1
Westbourne Dr C1
Westbourne Rd B1
Westham St C3
Wheatfield St B1
White Cross Business Park C2
Williamson Rd B3
Willow La B1
Windermere Rd B3
Wingate-Saul Rd B1
Wolseley St B3
Woodville St B3
Wyresdale Rd C3

Leeds 185

Aire St B3
Albion Place B4
Albion St B4
Albion Way B1
Alma St A6
Ambulance Sta B5
Arcades B4
Armley Rd B1
Armories Dr C5
Back Burley Lodge Rd A1
Back Hyde Terr A2
Back Row C3
Bath Rd C3
Beckett St A6
Bedford St B3
Belgrave St A4
Belle Vue Rd A2
Benson St A5
Black Bull St C5
Blenheim Walk A3
Boar La B4
Bond St B4
Bow St C5
Bowman La C4
Brewery C4
Brewery Wharf C5
Bridge St A5/B5
Briggate B4
Bruce Gdns C1
Burley Rd A1
Burley St B1
Burmantofs St B6
Bus & Coach Sta B5
Butterly St C4
Butts Cres B4
Byron St A5
Call La B4
Calls,The B5
Calverley St A3/B3
Canal St B1
Canal Wharf C3
Carlisle Rd C5
Cavendish Rd A1
Cavendish St A2
Chadwick St C5
Cherry Place A6
Cherry Row A5
City Museum A4
City Varieties Music Hall B4
City Sq B3
Civic Hall A3
Clarence Road C5
Clarendon Rd A2
Clarendon Way A3
Clark La C6
Clay Pit La A4
Cloberry St A2
Close,The B6
Clyde Approach C1
Clyde Gdns C1
Coleman St C2
Commercial St B4
Concord St A5
Cookridge St A4
Copley Hill C1
Core,The B4
Corn Exchange B4
Cromer Terr A2
Cromwell St A5
Cross Catherine St B6
Cross Green La C6
Cross Stamford St A5
Crown & County Courts A3
Crown Point Bridge C5
Crown Point Rd C4
Crown Point Retail Park C4
David St C3
Dent St C6
Derwent Place C3
Dial St C6
Dock St C4
Dolly La A6
Domestic St C2
Drive,The B6
Duke St B5
Duncan St B4
Dyer St B5
East Field St B6
East Pde B3
East St C5
Eastgate B5
Easy Rd C6
Edward St B4
Ellerby La C6
Ellerby Rd C6
Fenton St A3
Fire Station B2
First Direct Arena A4
Fish St B4
Flax Place B5
Garth,The B5
Gelderd Rd C1
George St B4
Globe Rd C2
Gower St A5
Grafton St A4
Grand Theatre B4
Granville Rd A6
Great George St A3
Great Wilson St C4
Greek St B3
Green La C1
Hanover Ave A2
Hanover La A2
Hanover Sq A2
Hanover Way A2
Harewood St B4
Harrison St B4
Haslewood Close B6
Haslewood Drive B6
Headrow,The B3/B4
High Court B5
Holbeck La C2
Holdforth Close C1
Holdforth Gardens B1
Holdforth Grove C1
Holdforth Place C1
Holy Trinity B4
Hope Rd A5
Hunslet La C4
Hunslet Rd C4
Hyde Terr A2
Infirmary St B3
Information Ctr B3
Ingram Row C3
ITV Yorkshire A1
Junction St C4
Kelso Gdns A2
Kelso Rd A2
Kelso St A2
Kendal La A2
Kendell St C4
Kidacre St C4
King Edward St B4
King St B3
Kippax Place C6
Kirkgate B4
Kirkgate Market B4
Kirkstall Rd A1
Kitson St C6
Knight's Way Bridge C5
Lady La B4
Lands La B4
Lane,The B5
Lavender Walk B6
Leeds Art Gallery B3
Leeds Beckett Univ A3
Leeds Bridge C4
Leeds Coll of Music B5
Leeds Discovery Centre C5
Leeds General Infirmary (A&E) A3
Leeds Minster B5
Leeds Station B3
Library B3/B4
Light,The B4
Lincoln Green Rd A6
Lincoln Rd A6
Lindsey Gdns A6
Lindsey Rd A6
Lisbon St B3
Little Queen St B3
Long Close La C6
Lord St C2
Lovell Park A4
Lovell Park Hill A4
Lovell Park Rd A4
Lower Brunswick St A5
Mabgate A5
Macauly St A5
Magistrates Court A3
Manor Rd C3
Mark La B4
Marlborough St B2
Marsh La B5
Marshall St C3
Meadow La C4
Meadow Rd C4
Melbourne St A5
Merrion Centre A4
Merrion St A4
Merrion Way A4
Mill St B5
Millennium Sq A3
Monk Bridge C2
Mount Preston St A2
Mushroom St A5
Neville St C4
New Briggate A4/B4
New Market St B4
New York Rd A5
New York St B5
Nile St A5
Nippet La A6
North St A4
Northern Ballet B5
Northern St B3
Oak Rd B1
Oxford Place B3
Oxford Row A3
Parade,The B6
Park Cross St B3
Park La A2
Park Place B3
Park Row B4
Park Sq B3
Park Sq East B3
Park Sq West B3
Park St B3
Police Station B5
Pontefract La B6
Portland Cres A3
Portland Way A3
Post Office B4/B5
Quarry House (NHS/DSS HQ) B5
Quebec St B3
Queen St B3
Radio Aire A1
Railway St B5
Rectory St A6
Regent St A5
Richmond St C5
Rigton Approach B6
Rigton Dr B6
Rillbank La A1
Rosebank Rd A1
Rose Bowl Conference Centre A3
Royal Armouries C5
Russell St B3
St Anne's Cathedral (RC) A4
St Anne's St B4
St James' Hosp A6
St John's Rd A2
St Johns Centre B4
St Mary's St B5
St Pauls St B3
Saxton La B5
Sayner La C5
Shakespeare Ave A6
Shannon St B6
Sheepscar St South A5
Siddall St C3
Skinner La A5
South Pde B3
Sovereign St C4
Spence La C2
Springfield Mount A2
Springwell Ct C2
Springwell Rd C2
Springwell St C2
Stoney Rock La A6
Studio Rd A1
Sutton St C2
Sweet St C3
Sweet St West C3
Swinegate B4
Templar St B5
Tetley,The C4
Thoresby Place A3
Torre Rd A6
Town Hall A3
Trinity Leeds B4
Union Place C3
Union St B5
University of Leeds A3
Upper Accommodation Rd B6
Upper Basinghall St B4
Vicar La B4
Victoria Bridge C4
Victoria Gate B4
Victoria Quarter B4
Victoria Rd C4
Vue B4
Wade La A4
Washington St A1
Water La C3
Waterloo Rd C4
Wellington Rd B2/C1
Wellington St B3
West St B2
West Yorkshire Playhouse B5
Westfield Rd A1
Westgate B3
Whitehall Rd B3/C2
Whitelock St A5
Willis St C6
Willow Approach A1
Willow Ave A1
Willow Terrace Rd A3
Wintoun St A5
Woodhouse La A3/A4
Woodsley Rd A1
York Place B3
York Rd B6

Leicester 188

Abbey St A2
All Saints' A1
Aylestone Rd C2
Bath La A1
Bede Park C1
Bedford St A3
Bedford St South A3
Belgrave Gate A2
Belvoir St B2
Braunstone Gate B1
Burleys Way A2
Burnmoor St C2
Bus & Coach Sta A2
Canning St A2
Carlton St C2
Castle Motte B1
Castle Gardens B1
Cathedral B2
Charles St B3
Chatham St B2
Christow St A3
Church Gate A2
City Hall B3
Clank St B2
Clock Tower B2
Clyde St A3
Colton St B3
Conduit St B3
Crafton St East A3
Craven St A1
Crown Courts B3
Curve B3
De Lux B2
De Montfort Hall C3
De Montfort St C3
De Montfort Univ C1
Deacon St C2
Dover St B3
Duns La B1
Dunton St A1
East St B3
East Bond Street A2
Eastern Boulevard C1
Edmonton Rd A3
Erskine St A3
Filbert St C1
Filbert St East C2
Fire Station C3
Fleet St A3
Friar La B2
Friday St A2
Gateway St C2
Gateway,The C2
Glebe St B3
Granby St B3
Grange La C2
Grasmere St C1
Great Central St A1
Great Hall B1
Guildhall B2
Guru Nanak Sikh Museum B1
Halford St B2
Havelock St C2
Haymarket Shopping Centre A2
High St A2
Highcross Shopping Centre A2
Highcross St A1
HM Prison C2
Horsefair St B2
Humberstone Gate B2
Humberstone Rd A3
Infirmary St C2
Information Ctr B2
Jarrom St C2
Jewry Wall B1
Kamloops Cres A3
King Richard III Visitor Centre B2
King St B2
Lancaster Rd C3
LCB Depot B3
Lee St A3
Leicester Royal Infirmary (A&E) C2
Leicester Station B3
Library B2
London Rd C3
Lower Brown St B2
Magistrates' Court B2
Manitoba Rd A3
Mansfield St A2
Market B2
Market St B2
Mill La C2
Montreal Rd A3
Narborough Rd North B1
Nelson Mandela Pk C2
New Park St B1
New St B2
New Walk C3
New Walk Museum & Art Gallery C3
Newarke Houses B2
Newarke St B2
Newarke,The B1
Northgate St A1
Orchard St A2
Ottawa Rd A3
Oxford St C2
Phoenix Arts Ctr B3
Police Station A3
Post Office B2
Prebend St C3
Princess Rd East C3
Princess Rd West C3
Queen St B3
Rally Com Park,The A2
Regent College C3
Regent Rd C2/C3
Repton St A1
Rutland St B3
St Augustine Rd B1
St Georges Retail Pk B3
St George St B3
St Georges Way B3
St John St A2
St Margaret's A2
St Margaret's Way A2
St Martins B2
St Mary de Castro B1
St Matthew's Way A3
St Nicholas B1
St Nicholas Circle B1
Sanvey Gate A2
Silver St B2
Slater St A1
Soar La A1
South Albion St B3
Southampton St B3
Sue Townsend Theatre B2
Swain St B3
Swan St A1
Tigers Way C3
Tower St C3
Town Hall B2
Tudor Rd B1
Univ of Leicester C3
University Rd C3
Upperton Rd C1
Vaughan Way A2
Walnut St C2
Watling St A2
Welford Rd B2
Welford Rd (Leicester Tigers RC) C2
Wellington St B2
West St C3
West Walk C3
Western Boulevard C1
Western Rd C1
Wharf St North A3
Wharf St South A3
Y Theatre,The B3
Yeoman St B3
York Rd B2

Lincoln 188

Alexandra Terr B1
Anchor St C1
Arboretum B3
Arboretum Ave B3
Avenue,The B1
Baggholme Rd B3
Bailgate A2
Beaumont Fee B1
BMI The Lincoln Hospital A2
Brayford Way C1
Brayford Wharf East C1
Brayford Wharf North B1
Bruce Rd A2
Burton Rd A1
Bus Station (City) C2
Canwick Rd C2
Cardinal's Hat B2
Carline Rd B1
Castle B1
Castle St A1
Cathedral B2
Cathedral St B2
Cecil St A2
Chapel La A2
Cheviot St B3
Church La A2
City Hall B1
Clasketgate B2
Clayton Sports Gd A3
Coach Park C2
Collection,The B2
County Hospital (A&E) B3
County Hall B1
Courts C1
Cross St C2
Crown Courts B1
Curle Ave A3
Danesgate B2
Drill Hall B2
Drury La B1
East Bight A2
East Gate A2
Eastcliff Rd B3
Eastgate B2
Egerton Rd A3
Ellis Windmill A1
Engine Shed,The C1
Exchequer Gate B2
Firth Rd C1
Flaxengate B2
Florence St B3
George St C3
Good La A2
Gray St A1
Great Northern Terr C3
Greetwell Rd B3
Greetwellgate B3
Grove,The A3
Haffenden Rd A2
High St B2/C1
Hungate B2
James St A2
Jews House & Ct B2
Kesteven St C2
Langworthgate A2
Lawn,The B1
Lee Rd A3
Library B2
Lincoln Central Station C2
Lincoln College B2
Lincolnshire Life A1
Lincoln Univ Technical College (UTC) B2
Lindum Rd B2
Lindum Sports Gd A3
Lindum Terr B3
Liquorice Park B1
Mainwaring Rd A3
Manor Rd A2
Market C2
Massey Rd A3
Medieval Bishop's Palace B2
Mildmay St A1
Mill Rd A1
Millman Rd B3
Minster Yard B2
Monks Rd B3
Montague St B2
Mount St A1
Nettleham Rd A2
Newland B1
Newport A2
Newport Arch A2
Newport Cemetery A2
Northgate A2
Odeon C1
Orchard St B1
Oxford St C2
Park St B1
Pelham Bridge C2
Pelham St C2
Portland St C2
Post Office A1/B2/B3
Potter Gate B2
Priory Gate B2
Queensway A3
Rasen La A1
Ropewalk C1
Rosemary La B2
St Anne's Rd B3
St Benedict's C1
St Giles Ave A3
St Mark's Shopping Centre C1
St Marks St C1
St Mary-le-Wigford C1
St Mary's St C2
St Nicholas St A2
St Rumbold's St B2
St Swithin's B2
Saltergate C1
Saxon St A1
Sewell Rd B3
Silver St B2
Sincil St C2
Spital St A2
Spring Hill B1
Stamp End C3
Steep Hill B2
Stonebow & Guildhall C2
Stonefield Ave A2
Tentercroft St C1
Theatre Royal B2
Tritton Rd C1
Tritton Retail Park C1
Union Rd B1
Univ of Lincoln C1
Upper Lindum St B3
Upper Long Leys Rd A1
Usher B2
Vere St A2
Victoria St B1
Victoria Terr B1
Vine St B3
Wake St A1
Waldeck St A1
Waterside North C2
Waterside Shopping Centre C2
Waterside South C2
West Pde B1
Westgate A2
Wigford Way C1
Williamson St A2
Wilson St A1
Winn St B3
Wragby Rd A3
Yarborough Rd A1

Liverpool 188

Abercromby Sq C5
Addison St A3
Adelaide Rd B6
Ainsworth St B4
Albany Rd B6
Albert Edward Rd B6
Angela St C6
Anson St B4
Argyle St C3
Arrad St C4
Ashton St B5
Audley St A4
Back Leeds St A2
Basnett St B3
Bath St A1
Beacon,The B3
Beatles Story, The C2
Beckwith St C3
Bedford Close C5
Bedford St North C5
Bedford St South C5
Benson St C4
Berry St C4
Birkett St A4
Bixteth St B2
Blackburne Place C4
Bluecoat B3
Bold Place C4
Bold St C4
Bolton St B3
Bridport St B4
Bronte St B4
Brook St A1
Brownlow Hill B4/B5
Brownlow St B5
Brunswick Rd A5
Brunswick St B1
Bus Station C2
Butler Cres A6
Byrom St A3
Caledonia St C4
Cambridge St C5
Camden St A4
Canada Blvd B1
Canning Dock C2
Canterbury St A4
Cardwell St C6
Carver St A4
Cases St B3
Castle St B2
Catherine St C5
Cavern Club B3
Central Library A3
Chapel St B2
Charlotte St B3
Chatham Place C6
Chatham St C5
Cheapside B2
Chavasse Park C2
Chestnut St C5
Christian St A3
Church St B3
Clarence St B4
Clayton Square Shopping Centre B3
Coach Station A4
Cobden St A5
Cockspur St A2
College St C3
College St North A5
College St South A5
Colquitt St C4
Comus St A3
Concert St C3
Connaught Rd B6
Cook St B2
Copperas Hill B4
Cornwallis St C3
Covent Garden B2
Craven St A4
Cropper St B3
Crown St B5/C6
Cumberland St B2
Cunard Building B1
Dale St B2
Dansie St B4
Daulby St B5
Dawson St B3
Dental Hospital B5
Derby Sq B2
Drury La B2
Duckinfield St B4
Duke St C3
Earle St A2
East St A2
Eaton St A2
Edgar St A3
Edge La B6
Edinburgh Rd A6
Edmund St B2
Elizabeth St B5
Elliot St B3
Empire Theatre B4
Empress Rd B6
Epstein Theatre B3
Epworth St A5
Erskine St A5
Everyman Theatre C5
Exchange St East B2
FACT C4
Falkland St A5
Falkner St C5/C6
Farnworth St A6
Fenwick St B2
Fielding St A6
Fire Sta A4
Fleet St C3
Fraser St A4
Freemasons Row A2
Gardner Row A3
Gascoyne St A2
George St B2
Gibraltar Road A1
Gilbert St C3
Gildart St A4
Gill St B4
Goree B2
Gower St C2
Gradwell St C3
Great Crosshall St A3
Great George St C4
Great Howard St A1
Great Newton St B4
Greek St B4
Green La B4
Greenside A5
Greetham St C3
Gregson St A5
Grenville St C3
Grinfield St C6
Grove St C5
Guelph St A6
Hackins Hey B2
Haigh St A4
Hall La B6
Hanover St B3
Harbord St C6
Hardman St C4
Harker St A4
Hart St B4
Hatton Garden A2
Hawke St B4
Helsby St B6
Henry St C3
Highfield St A2
Highgate St B6
Hilbre St B4
Hope Place C4
Hope St C4
Hope University A5
Houghton St B3
Hunter St A3
Hutchinson St A6
Information Ctr B4/C2
Institute for the Performing Arts C4
Int Slavery Mus C2
Irvine St B6
Irwell St B2
Islington A4
James St B2
James St Station B2
Jenkinson St A4
John Moores Univ A2/A3/A4/B4/C4
Johnson St A3
Jubilee Drive B6
Kempston St A4
Kensington A6
Kensington Gdns B6
Kensington St A6
Kent St C3
King Edward St A1
Kinglake St B6
Knight St C4
Lace St A3
Langsdale St A4
Law Courts C2
Leece St C4
Leeds St A2
Leopold Rd B6
Lime St B3
Lime St Station B4
Liver St C2
Liverpool Central Station B3
Liverpool Landing Stage B1
Liverpool Institute for Performing Arts (LIPA) C4
Liverpool ONE C2
Liverpool Wheel, The C2
London Rd A4/B4
Lord Nelson St B4
Lord St B2
Lovat St C6
Low Hill A5
Low Wood St A6
Lydia Ann St C3
M&S Bank Arena C2
Mansfield St A4
Marmaduke St B6
Marsden St A6
Martensen St B6
Marybone A3
Maryland St C4
Mason St B6
Mathew St B2
May St B4
Melville Place C6
Merseyside Maritime Museum C2
Metquarter B3
Metropolitan Cathedral (RC) B5
Midghall St A2
Molyneux Rd A6
Moor Place B4
Moorfields B2
Moorfields Sta B2
Moss St A5
Mount Pleasant B4/B5
Mount St C4
Mount Vernon B6
Mulberry St C5
Municipal Buildings B2
Mus of Liverpool C2
Myrtle St C5
Naylor St A2
Nelson St C4
New Islington A4
New Quay B1
Newington St C3
North John St B2
North St A3
North View B6
Norton St A4
O2 Academy B4
Oakes St B5
Odeon B2
Old Hall St A1
Old Leeds St A2
Oldham Place C4
Oldham St C4
Olive St C6
Open Eye Gallery C2
Oriel St A2
Ormond St B2
Orphan St C6
Overbury St C6
Overton St B6
Oxford St C5
Paisley St A1
Pall Mall A2
Paradise St C3
Park La C3
Parker St B3
Parr St C3
Peach St B5
Pembroke Place B4
Pembroke St B5
Philharmonic Hall C5
Phythian Park A6
Pickop St A2
Pilgrim St C4
Pitt St C3
Playhouse Theatre B3
Pleasant St B4
Police HQ C2
Police Sta A4/A6/B4
Pomona St B4
Port of Liverpool Building B2
Post Office A2/A4/A5/B2/B3/B4/C4
Pownall St C2
Prescot St A5
Preston St B3
Princes Dock A1
Princes Gdns A2
Princes Jetty A1
Princes Pde B1
Princes St B2
Pythian St A6
Queen Sq Bus Sta B3
Queensland St C6
Queensway Tunnel (Docks exit) B1
Queensway Tunnel (Entrance) B3
Radio City B2
Ranelagh St B3
Redcross St B2
Renfrew St B6
Renshaw St B4
Richmond Row A4
Richmond St B3
Rigby St A2
Roberts St A1
Rock St B4
Rodney St C4
Rokeby St A4
Romily St A6
Roscoe La C4
Roscoe St C4
Rose Hill A3
Royal Albert Dock C2
Royal Court Theatre B3
Royal Liver Building B1
Royal Liverpool Hospital (A&E) B5
Royal Mail St B4
Rumford Place B2
Rumford St B2
Russell St B4
St Andrew St B4
St Anne St A4
St Georges Hall B3
St John's Centre B3
St John's Gdns B3
St John's La B3
St Joseph's Cres A4
St Minishull St B5
St Nicholas Place B1
St Paul's Sq A2
Salisbury St A4
Salthouse Dock C2
Salthouse Quay C2
Sandon St C5
Saxony Rd B6
Schomberg St A6
School La B2
Seel St C3
Seymour St B4
Shaw St A5
Shopmobility C2
Sidney Place C6
Sir Thomas St B3
Skelhorne St B4
Slater St C3
Smithdown La B6
Soho Sq A4
Soho St A4
South John St B2
Springfield A4
Stafford St A4
Standish St A3
Stanley St B2
Strand St C2
Strand,The B2
Suffolk St C3
Sydney Jones Liby C5
Tabley St C3
Tarleton St B3
Tate Liverpool Gallery C2
Teck St B6
Temple St B2
Titanic Memorial B1
Tithebarn St B2
Town Hall B2
Trowbridge St B4
Trueman St A3
Union St B2
Unity Theatre C4
University C5
Univ of Liverpool B5
Upper Baker St A6
Upper Duke St C4
Upper Frederick St C3
Vauxhall Rd A2
Vernon St B2
Victoria Gallery & Museum B5
Victoria St B2
Vine St C5
Wakefield St A4
Walker Art Gallery A3
Walker St A6
Wapping C2
Water St B1/B2
Waterloo Rd A1
Wavertree Rd B6
West Derby Rd A6
West Derby St B5
Western Approaches War Museum B2
Whitechapel B3
Whitley Gdns A5
William Brown St B3
William Henry St A4
Williamson Sq B3
Williamson St B3
Williamson's Tunnels Heritage Centre C6
Women's Hosp C6
Wood St B3
World Museum, Liverpool A3
York St C3

Llandudno 189

Abbey Place B1
Abbey Rd B1
Adelphi St B3
Alexandra Rd C2
Anglesey Rd A1
Argyll Rd B3
Arvon Ave A2
Atlee Close C3
Augusta St B3
Back Madoc St B2
Bodafon St B3
Bodhyfryd Rd A2
Bodnant Cres C3
Bodnant Rd C3
Bridge Rd C2
Bryniau Rd C1
Builder St B3
Builder St West C2
Cabin Lift Cable Car A2
Camera Obscura A3
Caroline Rd B2
Chapel St A2
Charlton St B3
Church Cres C1
Church Walks A2
Claremont Rd B2
Clement Ave A2
Clifton Rd B2
Clonmel St B3
Coach Station B3
Conway Rd B3
Conwy Archive Service B2
Council St West C3
Cricket and Rec Gd B2
Cwlach Rd A2
Cwlach St A1
Cwm Howard La C3
Cwm Place C3
Cwm Rd C3
Dale Rd C1
Deganwy Ave B2
Denness Place C2
Dinas Rd C2
Dolydd B1
Erol Place B2
Ewloe Dr C3
Fairways C2
Ffordd Dewi C3
Ffordd Dulyn C2
Ffordd Dwyfor C3
Ffordd Elisabeth C3
Ffordd Gwynedd C3
Ffordd Las C3
Ffordd Morfa C3
Ffordd Penrhyn C3
Ffordd Tudno C3
Ffordd yr Orsedd C3
Ffordd Ysbyty C2
Fire & Ambulance Station B3
Garage St B3
George St A2
Gloddaeth Ave B1
Gloddaeth St B2
Gogarth Rd B1
Great Orme Mines A1
Great Ormes Rd B1
Great Orme Tramway A2
Happy Valley A2
Happy Valley Rd A3
Haulfre Gardens A1
Herkomer Cres C1
Hill Terr A2
Home Front Mus B2
Hospice B1
Howard Rd B3
Information Ctr B2
Invalids' Walk B1
James St B2
Jubilee St B3
King's Ave C2
King's Rd C2
Knowles Rd C2
Lees Rd C2
Library B2
Llandudno A2
Llandudno (A&E) C2
Llandudno Sta B3
Llandudno Football Ground C2
Llewelyn Ave A2
Lloyd St B2
Lloyd St West B1
Llwynon Rd A1
Llys Maelgwn B1
Madoc St B2
Maelgwn Rd B2
Maes-y-Cwm C3
Maes-y-Orsedd C3
Maesdu Bridge C2
Maesdu Rd C2/C3
Marian Place C2
Marian Rd C2
Marine Drive (Toll) A3
Market St A2
Miniature Golf Course A1
Morfa Rd B1
Mostyn B3
Mostyn Broadway B3
Mostyn St B3
Mowbray Rd C2
New St A2
Norman Rd B3
North Parade A2
North Wales Golf Links C1
Old Bank,The A2
Old Rd A2
Oval,The B1
Oxford Rd B3
Parade,The B3
Parc Llandudno Retail Park B3
Pier A3
Plas Rd A2
Police Station B3
Post Office A2/B3
Promenade A3
Pyllau Rd A1
Rectory La A2
Rhuddlan Ave C3
St Andrew's Ave B2
St Andrew's Place B2
St Beuno's Rd A1
St David's Place B2
St David's Rd B2
St George's Place A3
St Mary's Rd B2
St Seriol's Rd B2
Salisbury Pass B1
Salisbury Rd B2
Somerset St B3
South Parade A2
Stephen St B3
Tabor Hill A2
Town Hall B2
Trinity Ave B1
Trinity Cres C1
Trinity Sq B3
Tudno St A2
Ty-Coch Rd A2
Ty-Gwyn Rd A1/A2
Ty'n-y-Coed Rd A1
Vaughan St B3
Victoria Shopping Centre B3
Victoria A2
War Memorial A2
Werny Wylan C3
West Parade B1
Whiston Pass A2
Winllan Ave C2
Wyddfyd Rd A2
York Rd A2

Llanelli 189

Alban Rd B3
Albert St B1
Als St B3
Amos St C1
Andrew St A3
Ann St C2
Annesley St B2
Arfryn Ave A3
Avenue Cilfig,The A2
Belvedere Rd A1
Bigyn Park Terr C3
Bigyn Rd C3
Bond Ave C3
Brettenham St A1
Bridge St B2
Bryn Place C1
Bryn Rd C1
Bryn Terr C1
Bryn-More Rd C1
Brynhyfryd Rd A2
Brynmelyn Ave A3
Brynmor Rd B1
Burry St C1
Bus Station B2
Caersalem Terr C2
Cambrian St C1
Caswell St C3
Cedric St B3
Cemetery A2
Chapman St A1
Charles Terr C2
Church St B2
Clos Caer Elms A1
Clos Sant Paul C2
Coastal Link Rd B1/C1
Coldstream St B2
Coleshill Terr B1
College Hill B3
College Sq B3
Copperworks Rd C2
Coronation Rd C3
Corporation Ave A3
Council Offices B2
Court B2
Cowell St B2
Cradock St C2
Craig Ave C3
Cricket Ground A1
Derwent St A1
Dillwyn St C2
Druce St C1
Eastgate Leisure Complex B2
Elizabeth St B2
Emma St C2
Erw Rd B1
Felinfoel Rd A2
Fire Station A3
Firth Rd C3
Fron Terr C3
Furnace United Rugby Football Ground A1
Gelli-On B2
George St C2
Gilbert Cres A2
Gilbert Rd A2
Glanmor Rd C2
Glanmor Terr C2
Glasfryn Terr A3
Glenalla Rd B3
Glevering St B3
Goring Rd A2
Gorsedd Circle A2
Grant St C3
Graveyard C2
Great Western Close C2
Greenway St B1
Hall St B2
Harries Ave A2
Hedley Terr A2
Heol Elli B3
Heol Goffa A3
Heol Nant-y-Felin A3
Heol Siloh B2
Hick St C2
High St C1
Indoor Bowls Ctr B1
Inkerman St B2
Island Place B2
James St B3
John St B2
King George Ave B3
Lake View Close A2
Lakefield Place C1
Lakefield Rd C1
Langland Rd C3
Leisure Centre B1
Library B2
Llanelli House B2
Llanelli Parish Church B2
Llanelli Station C2
Llewellyn St C2
Lliedi Cres A3
Lloyd St B2
Llys Alys B3
Llys Fran A3
Llysnewedd C1
Long Row A3
Maes Gors C2
Maesyrhaf A3
Mansel St C3
Marblehall Rd B3
Marborough Rd A
Margam St C
Marged St C
Marine St C
Mariners,The C
Market B
Market St B
Marsh St C
Martin Rd C
Miles St A
Mill La A3/B
Mincing La B
Murray St B
Myn y Mor B
Nathan St C
Nelson Terr C
Nevill St C
New Dock Rd C
New Rd A
New Zealand St A
Odeon B
Old Lodge C
Old Rd A
Paddock St C
Palace Ave B
Parc Howard A
Parc Howard Museum & Art Gallery A
Park Cres B
Park St B
Parkview Terr B
Pemberton St C
Pembrey Rd A
Peoples Park B
Police Station B
Post Office B2/C
Pottery Place B
Pottery St B
Princess St B
Prospect Place A
Pryce St A
Queen Mary's Walk C
Queen Victoria Rd C
Raby St B
Railway Terr C
Ralph St B
Ralph Terr C
Regalia Terr B
Rhydyrafon A
Richard St B
Robinson St B
Roland Ave A
Russell St C
St David's Close C
St Elli Shopping Ctr B
St Margaret's Dr A
Spowart Ave A
Station Rd B2/C
Stepney Place B
Stepney St B
Stewart St A
Stradey Park Ave A

London • Luton • Macclesfield • Maidstone 207

Sunny Hill A2
Superstore A2
Swansea Rd A3
Talbot St C3
Temple St B3
Thomas St A2
Tinopolos TV
Studios ✦ B2
Toft Place A3
Town Hall B2
Traeth Ffordd C1
Trinity Rd C3
Trinity Terr C2
Tunnel Rd B3
Tyisha Rd C3
Union Blgs A2
Upper Robinson St B2
Vauxhall Rd B3
Walter's Rd B3
Waun Lanyrafon B2
Waun Rd A3
Wern Rd B3
West End A2
Y Bwthyn C3
Zion Row B3

London 186
bbey Orchard St E3
bchurch La D6
bingdon St E4
chilles Way D2
cton St B4
ddington St E4
ir St D3
lbany St B2
lbemarle St D3
lbert Embankment F4
ldenham St A3
ldersgate St C6
ldford St D2
ldgate ⊖ C7
ldgate High St C7
ldwych C4
llsop Place B1
mwell St B5
ngel ⊖ A5
ppold St C7
rgyle Sq B4
rgyle St B4
rgyll St C3
rnold Circus B7
rtillery La C7
rtillery Row E3
ssociation of
Photographers
Gallery 🏛 B6
aker St ⊖ B1
aker St B1
aldwin's Gdns C5
altic St B6
ank ⊖ C6
ank Museum 🏛 C6
ank of England C6
ankside D6
ankside Gallery 🏛 D5
anner St B6
arbican ⇌⊖ C6
arbican Centre
for Arts,The C6
arbican Gallery 🏛 C6
asil St E1
astwick St B6
ateman's Row B7
ath St B6
ayley St C3
aylis Rd E5
eak St D3
edford Row C4
edford Sq C3
edford St D4
edford Way B3
eech St C6
elgrave Place E2
elgrave Sq E2
ell La C7
elvedere Rd E4
erkeley Sq D2
erkeley St D2
ernard St B4
erners Place C3
erners St C3
erwick St C3
ethnal Green Rd B7
evenden St B6
evis Marks C7
FI (British Film
nstitute) 🎥 D4
FI London IMAX
inema 🎥 D5
dborough St B4
nney St C2
rdcage Walk E3
shopsgate C7
ackfriars ⇌ D5
ackfriars Bridge D5
ackfriars Passage D5
ackfriars Rd E5
andford St C1
omfield St C6
oomsbury St C3
oomsbury Way C4
olton St D2
ond St ⊖ C2
orough High St E6
oswell St C4
ow St C4
owling Green La B5
rad St D5
ressenden Place E3
rewer St D3
rick St D2
ridge St E4
ritannia Walk B6
ritish Film
nstitute (BFI) 🎥 D4
ritish Library 🏛 B3
ritish Museum 🏛 C4
ritton St B5
road Sanctuary E3
roadway E3
rook Dr F5
rook St D2
runswick Place B6
runswick Shopping
entre,The B4
runswick Sq B4
rushfield St C7
ruton St D2
ryanston St C1
T Centre C6
uckingham Gate E3
uckingham
alace 🏛 E3
uckingham Palace
d F2
unhill Row B6
Byward St D7
Cabinet War Rooms &
Churchill Mus 🏛 E3
Cadogan La E2
Cadogan Place E1
Cadogan Sq F1
Caledonian Rd A4
Calshot St A4
Calthorpe St B4
Calvert Ave B7
Cambridge Circus C3
Camomile St C7
Cannon St D6
Cannon St ⇌⊖ D6
Capel Manor Coll B2
Carey St C4
Carlisle La E4
Carlisle Place E3
Carlton House Terr D3
Carmelite St D5
Carnaby St C3
Carter La C5
Carthusian St C6
Cartwright Gdns B4
Castle Baynard St D5
Cavendish Place C2
Cavendish Sq C2
Caxton Hall E3
Caxton St E3
Central St B6
Chalton St B3
Chancery Lane ⊖ C5
Chapel St E2
Charing Cross ⇌⊖ D4
Charing Cross Rd C3
Charles Dickens
Museum,The B4
Charles II St D3
Charles Sq B6
Charles St D2
Charlotte Rd B7
Charlotte St C3
Chart St B6
Charterhouse Sq C5
Charterhouse St C5
Cheapside C6
Chenies St C3
Chesham St E2
Chester Sq F2
Chesterfield Hill D2
Chiltern St C2
Chiswell St C6
City Garden Row A5
City Rd B6
City Thameslink ⇌ C5
City University,The B5
Claremont Sq A5
Clarges St D2
Clerkenwell Close B5
Clerkenwell Green B5
Clerkenwell Rd B5
Cleveland St C3
Clifford St D3
Clink Prison Mus 🏛 D6
Clock Museum 🏛 C6
Club Row B7
Cockspur St D3
Coleman St C6
Columbia Rd B7
Commercial St C7
Compton St B5
Conduit St D2
Constitution Hill E2
Copperfield St E5
Coptic St C4
Cornhill C6
Cornwall Rd D5
Coronet St B7
Courtauld
Gallery 🏛 D4
Covent Garden ⊖ D4
Covent Garden ✦ D4
Cowcross St C5
Cowper St B6
Cranbourn St D3
Craven St D4
Crawford St C1
Creechurch La C7
Cremer St A7
Cromer St B4
Cumberland Gate D1
Cumberland Terr A2
Curtain Rd B7
Curzon St D2
Cut,The E5
D'arblay St C3
Davies St C2
Dean St C3
Deluxe Gallery 🏛 B7
Denmark St C3
Dering St C2
Devonshire St C2
Diana, Princess of
Wales Meml Walk E3
Dingley Rd B6
Dorset St C1
Doughty St B4
Dover St D2
Downing St E4
Druid St E7
Drummond St B3
Drury La C4
Drysdale St B7
Duchess St C2
Dufferin St B6
Duke of Wellington
Place E2
Duke St C2
Duke St D3
Duke St Hill D6
Duke's Place C7
Duncannon St D4
East Rd B6
Eastcastle St C3
Eastcheap D7
Eastman Dental
Hospital 🏥 B4
Eaton Place E2
Eaton Sq E2
Eccleston St E2
Edgware Rd C1
Eldon St C6
Embankment ⊖ D4
Endell St C4
Endsleigh Place B3
Euston ⇌⊖ B3
Euston Rd B3
Euston Square ⊖ B3
Evelina Children's
Hospital E4
Eversholt St A3
Exmouth Market B5
Fann St B6
Farringdon ⇌⊖ C5
Farringdon Rd C5
Farringdon St C5
Featherstone St B6
Fenchurch St D7
Fenchurch St ⇌ D7
Fetter La C5
Finsbury Circus C6
Finsbury Pavement C6
Finsbury Sq B6
Fitzalan St F5
Fitzmaurice Place D2
Fleet St C5
Floral St D4
Florence Nightingale
Museum 🏛 E4
Folgate St C7
Foot Hospital 🏥 B3
Fore St C6
Foster La C6
Foundling Museum,
The 🏛 B4
Francis St F3
Frazier St E5
Freemason's Hall C4
Friday St C6
Gainsford St E7
Garden Row E5
Gee St B6
George St C2
Gerrard St D3
Giltspur St C5
Glasshouse St D3
Gloucester Place C1
Golden Hinde ⛵ D6
Golden La B6
Golden Sq D3
Goodge St ⊖ C3
Goodge St C3
Gordon Sq B3
Goswell Rd B5
Gough St B4
Goulston St C7
Gower St B3
Gracechurch St D6
Grafton Way B3
Gray's Inn Rd B4
Great College St E4
Great Cumberland
Place C1
Great Eastern St B7
Great Guildford St D6
Great Marlborough
St C3
Great Ormond St B4
Great Ormond St
Children's Hosp 🏥 B4
Great Percy St B4
Great Peter St E3
Great Portland St ⊖ B2
Great Portland St C2
Great Queen St C4
Great Russell St C3
Great Scotland Yd D4
Great Smith St E3
Great Suffolk St D5
Great Titchfield St C3
Great Tower St D7
Great Windmill St D3
Greek St C3
Green Park ⊖ D3
Green St D2
Greencoat Place F3
Gresham St C6
Greville St B4/C5
Greycoat Hosp Sch E3
Greycoat Place E3
Grosvenor Cres E2
Grosvenor Gdns E2
Grosvenor Place E2
Grosvenor Sq D2
Grosvenor St D2
Guards Museum
and Chapel 🏛 E3
Guildhall
Art Gallery 🏛 C6
Guilford St B4
Guy's Hospital 🏥 D6
Haberdasher St B6
Hackney Rd B7
Half Moon St D2
Halkin St E2
Hall St B5
Hallam St C2
Hampstead Rd B3
Hanover Sq C2
Hans Cres E1
Hanway St C3
Hardwick St B5
Harley St C2
Harrison St B4
Hastings St B4
Hatfields D5
Hay's Galleria D7
Hay's Mews D2
Hayles St F5
Haymarket D3
Hayward Gallery 🏛 D4
Helmet Row B6
Herbrand St B4
Hercules Rd E4
Hertford St D2
High Holborn C4
Hill St D2
HMS Belfast ⛵ D7
Hobart Place E2
Holborn ⊖ C4
Holborn C5
Holborn Viaduct C5
Holland St D5
Holmes Mus 🏛 B1
Holywell La B7
Horse Guards' Rd D3
Houndsditch C7
Houses of
Parliament 🏛 E4
Howland St C3
Hoxton Sq B7
Hoxton St B7
Hunter St B4
Hunterian Mus 🏛 C4
Hyde Park D1
Hyde Park Cnr ⊖ E2
Imperial
War Museum 🏛 E5
Inner Circle B2
Ironmonger Row B6
James St C2
James St D4
Jermyn St D3
Jockey's Fields C4
John Carpenter St D5
John St B4
Judd St B4
Kennington Rd E5
King Charles St E4
King St D3
King St D4
King William St C6
King's Coll London D5
King's Cross ⇌ A4
King's Cross Rd B4
King's Cross St
Pancras ⊖ A4
King's Rd E2
Kingsland Rd B7
Kingsley St C3
Kingsway C4
Kinnerton St E2
Knightsbridge ⊖ E1
Lamb St C7
Lamb's Conduit St C4
Lambeth Bridge F4
Lambeth High St F4
Lambeth North ⊖ E5
Lambeth Palace 🏛 E4
Lambeth Palace Rd E4
Lambeth Rd E5
Lambeth Walk F4
Lancaster Place D4
Langham Place C2
Leadenhall St C7
Leake St E4
Leather La C5
Leicester Sq ⊖ D3
Leicester St D3
Leonard St B6
Lever St B6
Lexington St D3
Lidlington Place A3
Lime St D7
Lincoln's Inn Fields C4
Lindsey St C5
Lisle St D3
Liverpool St C7
Liverpool St ⇌⊖ C7
Lloyd Baker St B5
Lloyd Sq B5
Lombard St C6
London
Aquarium 🐟 E4
London Bridge
⇌⊖ D6
London Bridge
Hospital 🏥 D6
London City Hall 🏛 D7
London Dungeon,
The 🏛 E4
London Guildhall
University C6
London Rd E5
London Transport
Museum 🏛 D4
London Wall C6
London Eye ✦ E4
Long Acre D4
Long La C5
Longford St B2
Lower Belgrave St E2
Lower Grosvenor Pl E2
Lower Marsh E5
Lower Thames St D6
Lowndes St E2
Ludgate Circus C5
Ludgate Hill C5
Luxborough St C2
Lyall St E2
Macclesfield Rd B6
Madame Tussaud's
✦ B2
Maddox St D2
Malet St C3
Mall,The E3
Manchester Sq C2
Manchester St C2
Mandeville Place C2
Mansell St D7
Mansion House 🏛 C6
Mansion House ⊖ D6
Maple St C3
Marble Arch ⊖ C1
Marble Arch D1
Marchmont St B4
Margaret St C3
Margery St B5
Mark La D7
Marlborough Rd D3
Marshall St C3
Marsham St E3
Marylebone High St C2
Marylebone La C2
Marylebone Rd B2
Marylebone St C2
Mecklenburgh Sq B4
Middle Temple La C5
Middlesex St
(Petticoat La) C7
Midland Rd A3
Minories C7
Monck St E3
Monmouth St C4
Montagu Place C1
Montagu Sq C1
Montagu St C4
Montague Place C3
Monument ⊖ D6
Monument St D6
Monument,The ✦ D6
Moor La C6
Moorfields C6
Moorfields Eye
Hospital 🏥 B6
Moorgate C6
Moorgate ⇌⊖ C6
Moreland St B5
Morley St E5
Mortimer St C3
Mount Pleasant B5
Mount St D2
Murray Grove A6
Museum of Garden
History 🏛 E4
Mus of London 🏛 C6
Museum St C4
Myddelton Sq B5
Myddelton St B5
National Gallery 🏛 D3
National Hospital 🏥 B4
National Portrait
Gallery 🏛 D3
Neal St C4
Nelson's Column ✦ D4
New Bond St C2/D2
New Bridge St C5
New Cavendish St C2
New Change C6
New Fetter La C5
New Inn Yard B7
New North Rd A6
New Oxford St C3
New Scotland Yard E3
New Sq C4
Newgate St C5
Newton St C4
Nile St B6
Noble St C6
Noel St C3
North Audley St D2
North Cres C3
North Row D2
Northampton Sq B5
Northington St B4
Northumberland
Ave D4
Norton Folgate C7
Nottingham Place C2
Obstetric Hosp 🏥 B3
Old Bailey C5
Old Broad St C6
Old Compton St C3
Old County Hall E4
Old Gloucester St C4
Old King Edward St C6
Old Nichol St B7
Old Paradise St F4
Old Spitalfields Mkt C7
Old St B6
Old St ⇌⊖ B6
Old Vic 🎭 E5
Open Air Theatre 🎭 B2
Operating Theatre
Museum 🏛 D6
Orange St D3
Orchard St C2
Ossulston St A3
Outer Circle B1
Oxford Circus ⊖ C3
Oxford St C2/C3
Paddington St C2
Palace St E3
Pall Mall D3
Pall Mall East D3
Pancras Rd A4
Panton St D3
Paris Gdn D5
Park Cres B2
Park La D2
Park Rd B1
Park St D2
Park St D6
Parker St C4
Parliament Sq E4
Parliament St E4
Paternoster Sq C5
Paul St B6
Pear Tree St B5
Penton Rise B4
Penton St A5
Pentonville Rd A4/A5
Percival St B5
Petticoat La
(Middlesex St) C7
Petty France E3
Phoenix Place B4
Phoenix Rd A3
Photo Gallery 🏛 D3
Piccadilly D2
Piccadilly Circus ⊖ D3
Pitfield St B7
Pollock's
Toy Museum 🏛 C3
Polygon Rd A3
Pont St E1
Portland Place C2
Portman Mews C2
Portman Sq C2
Portman St C1
Portugal St C4
Postal Museum,
The B4
Poultry C6
Primrose St C7
Princes St C6
Procter St C4
Provost St B6
Quaker St B7
Queen Anne St C2
Queen Elizabeth
Hall 🎭 D4
Queen Sq B4
Queen St D6
Queen Street Place D6
Queen Victoria St D5
Queens Gallery 🏛 E3
Radnor St B6
Rathbone Place C3
Rawstorne St B5
Red Lion Sq C4
Red Lion St C4
Redchurch St B7
Redcross Way D6
Regency St F3
Regent Sq B4
Regent St C3
Regent's Park B2
Richmond Terr E4
Ridgmount St C3
Rivington St B7
Robert St B2
Rochester Row F3
Ropemaker St C6
Rosebery Ave B5
Roupell St D5
Royal Academy
of Arts 🏛 D3
Royal Academy of
Dramatic Art
(RADA) B3
Royal Acad of Music B2
Royal Artillery
Memorial ✦ E2
Royal College of
Nursing C2
Royal College of
Surgeons C4
Royal Festival Hall
🎭 D4
Royal London Hospital
for Integrated
Medicine C4
Royal National
Theatre 🎭 D5
Royal National
Throat, Nose and
Ear Hospital 🏥 B4
Royal Opera Ho 🎭 D4
Russell Sq B3
Russell Square ⊖ B4
Sackville St D3
Sadlers Wells 🎭 B5
Saffron Hill C5
St Alban's St D3
St Andrew St C5
St Bartholomew's
Hospital 🏥 C5
St Botolph St C7
St Bride St C5
St George's Circus E5
St George's Rd E5
St Giles High St C3
St James's Pal 🏛 D3
St James's Park ⊖ E3
St James's St D3
St John St B5
St Margaret St E4
St Mark's Hosp 🏥 B5
St Martin's La D4
St Martin's Le
Grand C6
St Mary Axe C7
St Pancras
International ⇌ A4
St Paul's ⊖ C6
St Paul's Cath ✝ C6
St Paul's
Churchyard C5
St Peter's Hosp 🏥 D4
St Thomas St D6
St Thomas' Hosp 🏥 E4
Savile Row D3
Savoy Place D4
Savoy St D4
School of Hygiene &
Tropical Medicine C3
Scrutton St B7
Sekforde St B5
Serpentine Rd D1
Seven Dials C4
Seward St B5
Seymour St C1
Shad Thames D7
Shaftesbury Ave D3
Shakespeare's Globe
Theatre 🎭 D6
Shepherd Market D2
Sherwood St D3
Shoe La C5
Shoreditch High St B7
Shoreditch High St
⊖ B7
Shorts Gdns C4
Shrek's
Adventure ✦ E4
Sidmouth St B4
Silk St C6
Sir John Soane's
Museum 🏛 C4
Skinner St B5
Sloane St E1
Snow Hill C5
Soho Sq C3
Somerset House 🏛 D4
South Audley St D2
South Carriage Dr E1
South Molton St C2
South Place C6
South St D2
Southampton Row C4
Southampton St D4
Southwark ⊖ D5
Southwark Bridge D6
Southwark Bridge
Rd D6
Southwark Cath ✝ D6
Southwark St D6
Speakers' Corner D1
Spencer St B5
Spital Sq C7
Stamford St D5
Stanhope St B3
Stephenson Way B3
Stock Exchange C5
Stoney St D6
Strand C5
Stratton St D2
Sumner St D5
Sutton's Way B6
Swanfield St B7
Swinton St B4
Tabernacle St B6
Tate Modern 🏛 D6
Tavistock Place B4
Tavistock Sq B3
Tea & Coffee
Museum 🏛 D6
Temple ⊖ D5
Temple Ave D5
Temple Place D4
Terminus Place E2
Thayer St C2
Theobald's Rd C4
Thorney St F4
Threadneedle St C6
Throgmorton St C6
Tonbridge St B4
Tooley St D7
Torrington Place B3
Tothill St E3
Tottenham Court Rd B3
Tottenham Ct Rd ⊖ C3
Tottenham St C3
Tower Bridge ✦ D7
Tower Bridge App D7
Tower Bridge Rd E7
Tower Hill D7
Tower Hill ⊖ D7
Tower of London,
The 🏛 D7
Toynbee St C7
Trafalgar Square D3
Trinity Sq D7
Trocadero Centre D3
Tudor St D5
Turnmill St C5
Ufford St E5
Union St D5
Univ Coll Hosp 🏥 B3
University College
London (UCL) B3
Univ of London C3
Univ of Westminster C2
University St B3
Upper Belgrave St E2
Upper Berkeley St C1
Upper Brook St D2
Upper Grosvenor St D2
Upper Ground D5
Upper Montague St C1
Upper St Martin's
La D4
Upper Thames St D6
Upper Wimpole St C2
Upper Woburn Pl B3
Vere St C2
Vernon Place C4
Vestry St B6
Victoria ⇌⊖ E2
Victoria Emb D4
Victoria Place
Shopping Centre F2
Victoria St E3
Villiers St D4
Vincent Sq F3
Vinopolis
City of Wine 🏛 D6
Virginia Rd B7
Wakley St B5
Walbrook C6
Wallace
Collection 🏛 C2
Wardour St C3/D3
Warner St B5
Warren St ⊖ B3
Warren St B3
Waterloo ⇌⊖ E5
Waterloo Bridge D4
Waterloo East ⇌ D5
Waterloo Rd E5
Watling St C6
Webber St E5
Welbeck St C2
Wellington Arch ✦ E2
Wellington Mus 🏛 E2
Wells St C3
Wenlock St A6
Wentworth St C7
West Smithfield C5
West Sq E5
Westminster ⊖ E4
Westminster
Abbey ✝ E4
Westminster Bridge E4
Westminster Bridge
Rd E5
Westminster
Cathedral (RC) ✝ E3
Westminster City
Hall E3
Westminster Hall
🏛 E4
Weymouth St C2
Wharf Rd A6
Wharton St B4
Whitcomb St D3
White Cube 🏛 B7
White Lion Hill D5
White Lion St A5
Whitecross St B6
Whitefriars St C5
Whitehall D4
Whitehall Place D4
Wigmore Hall C2
Wigmore St C2
William IV St D4
Wilmington Sq B5
Wilson St C6
Wilton Cres E2
Wimpole St C2
Windmill Walk D5
Woburn Place B4
Woburn Sq B3
Women's Hosp 🏥 C3
Wood St C6
Woodbridge St B5
Wootton St D5
Wormwood St C7
Worship St B6
Wren St B4
Wynyatt St B5
Young Vic 🎭 E5
York Rd E4
York St C1
York Terrace East B2
York Terrace West B2
York Way A4

Luton 189
Adelaide St B1
Albert Rd C2
Alma St B2
Alton Rd C3
Anthony Gdns C3
Arthur St C2
Ashburnham Rd B1
Ashton Rd C2
Back St A2
Bailey St C3
Baker St C2
Biscot Rd A1
Bolton Rd B3
Boyle Close A2
Brantwood Rd B1
Bretts Mead C1
Bridge St B2
Brook St A1
Brunswick St A3
Burr St A3
Bury Park Rd A1
Bute St B2
Buxton Rd B2
Cambridge St C3
Cardiff Grove B1
Cardiff Rd B1
Cardigan St A2
Castle St B2/C2
Chapel St C2
Charles St A3
Chase St C2
Cheapside B2
Chequer St C3
Chiltern Rise C1
Church St B2/B3
Cinema 🎥 A2
Cobden St A3
College A3
Collingdon St A1
Concorde Ave A3
Corncastle Rd C1
Cowper St C2
Crawley Green Rd B3
Crawley Rd A1
Crescent Rd A3
Crescent Rise A3
Cromwell Rd A1
Cross St A2
Cross Way,The C1
Crown Court B2
Cumberland St B2
Cutenhoe Rd C3
Dallow Rd B1
Downs Rd B1
Dudley St A2
Duke St A2
Dumfries St B1
Dunstable Place B2
Dunstable Rd A1/B1
Edward St A3
Elizabeth St C2
Essex Close C3
Farley Hill C1
Flowers Way B2
Francis St A1
Frederick St A2
Galaxy Leisure
Complex A2
George St B2
George St West B2
Gordon St B2
Grove Rd B1
Guildford St A2
Haddon Rd A3
Harcourt St C2
Hart Hill Drive A3
Hart Hill Lane A3
Hartley Rd A3
Hastings St B2
Hat Factory,The 🎭 B2
Hatters Way A1
Havelock Rd A2
Hibbert St C2
High Town Rd A3
Highbury Rd A1
Hightown Community
Sports & Arts Ctr A3
Hillary Cres C1
Hillborough Rd C1
Hitchin Rd A3
Holly St C2
Holm C1
Hucklesby Way A2
Hunts Close C1
Inkerman St A2
John St B2
Jubilee St A3
Kelvin Close C2
King St B2
Kingsland Rd C3
Larches,The A2
Latimer Rd C2
Lawn Gdns C2
Lea Rd B3
Library B2
Library Rd B2
Library Theatre 🎭 B2
Liverpool Rd B1
London Rd C2
Luton Station ⇌ A2
Lyndhurst Rd B1
Magistrates Court B2
Mall,The B2
Manchester St B2
Manor Rd B3
Manor Road Park B3
May St C3
Meyrick Ave C1
Midland Rd A2
Mill St A2
Milton Rd B1
Moor St A1
Moor,The A1
Moorland Gdns A2
Moulton Rise A3
Napier Rd B1
New Bedford Rd A1
New Town St C2
North St A3
Old Bedford Rd A2
Old Orchard C2
Osbourne Rd C3
Oxen Rd A3
Park Sq B2
Park St B3/C3
Park St West B2
Park Viaduct B3
Parkland Drive C1
Police Station 🏢 B1
Pomfret Ave A3
Pondwicks Rd B3
Post Office 📮 A1/B2
Power Court B3
Princess St B1
Red Rails C1
Regent St B2
Reginald St A2
Rothesay Rd B1
Russell Rise C1
Russell St C1
Ruthin Close C1
St Ann's Rd B3
St George's Square B2
St Mary's ⛪ B3
St Marys Rd B3
St Paul's Rd C2
St Saviour's Cres C1
Salisbury Rd B1
Seymour Ave C3
Seymour Rd C3
Silver St B2
South Rd C2
Stanley St B1
Station Rd A2
Stockwood Cres C2
Stockwood Park C1
Strathmore Ave C2
Stuart St B2
Studley Rd A1
Surrey St C3
Sutherland Place C1
Tavistock St C2
Taylor St A3
Telford Way A1
Tennyson Rd C2
Tenzing Grove C1
Thistle Rd B3
Town Hall B2
Townsley Close C2
UK Centre for
Carnival Arts ✦ B3
Union St B2
University of
Bedfordshire B3
Upper George St B2
Vicarage St B3
Villa Rd A2
Waldeck Rd A1
Wardown House
Museum & Gallery
🏛 A2
Wellington St B1/B2
Wenlock St A2
Whitby Rd A1
Whitehill Ave C1
William St A2
Wilsden Ave C1
Windmill Rd B3
Windsor St C2
Winsdon Rd B1
York St A3

Macclesfield 189
108 Steps B2
Abbey Rd A1
Alton Dr A3
Armett St C1
Athey St B1
Bank St C3
Barber St C3
Barton St C1
Beech La A2
Beswick St B1
Black La A2
Black Rd C3
Blakelow Gardens C3
Blakelow Rd C3
Bond St B1/C1
Bread St C1
Bridge St B1
Brock St A2
Brocklehurst Ave A3
Brook St B3
Brookfield La B3
Brough St West C1
Brown St C1
Brynton Rd A2
Buckley St C2
Bus Station B2
Buxton Rd B3
Byrons St C2
Canal St B3
Carlsbrook Ave A3
Castle St B2
Catherine St B1
Cemetery A1
Chadwick Terr A3
Chapel St C2
Charlotte St B2
Chester Rd B1
Chestergate B1
Christ Church ⛪ B1
Churchill Way B2
Coare St A1
Commercial Rd B2
Conway Cres A3
Copper St C3
Cottage St B1
Crematorium A1
Crew Ave A3
Crompton Rd B1/C1
Cross St C2
Crossall St C1
Cumberland St A1/B1
Dale St B3
Duke St B2
Eastgate B3
Exchange St B2
Fence Ave B3
Fence Ave Ind Est A3
Flint St B3
Foden St A2
Fountain St B3
Garden St A3
Gas Rd B2
Gateway Gallery ✦ B1
George St B2
Glegg St B3
Golf Course C3
Goodall St B3
Grange Rd C1
Great King St B1
Green St B3
Grosvenor
Shopping Centre B2
Gunco La C3
Half St C2
Hallefield Rd B3
Hatton St C1
Hawthorn Way A3
Heapy St C3
Henderson St B1
Heritage Centre 🏛 B2
Hibel Rd A2
High St C2
Hobson St C2
Hollins Rd C3
Hope St West B1
Horseshoe Dr B1
Hurdsfield Rd A3
Information Ctr ℹ B2
James St C2
Jodrell St B3
John St C2
Jordangate A2
King Edward St B2
King George's Field C3
King St B2
King's School A1
Knight Pool C3
Knight St C3
Lansdowne St A3
Library B2
Lime Grove B3
Loney St B1
Longacre St B1
Lord St C2
Lowe St C2
Lowerfield Rd A3
Lyon St B1
Macclesfield Coll C1
Macclesfield Sta ⇌ B2
MADS Little
Theatre 🎭 C2
Marina B3
Market B2
Market Place B2
Masons La A3
Mill La C2
Mill Rd C2
Mill St B2
Moran Rd C1
New Hall St A2
Newton St C1
Nicholson Ave A3
Nicholson Close A3
Northgate Ave A2
Old Mill La C2
Paradise Mill 🏛 C2
Paradise St B1
Park Green B2
Park La C1
Park Rd C1
Park St C2
Park Vale Rd C1
Parr St B1
Peel St C3
Percyvale St A3
Peter St C1
Pickford St B2
Pierce St B1
Pinfold St B1
Pitt St C2
Police Station 🏢 B2
Pool St C2
Poplar Rd C2
Post Office 📮 B2
Pownall St A2
Prestbury Rd A1/B1
Queen Victoria St B2
Queen's Ave A3
Registrar B2
Retail Park C2
Richmond Hill C3
Riseley St B1
Roan Ct B3
Roe St B2
Rowan Way A3
Ryle St C2
Ryle's Park Rd C1
St George's St C2
St Michael's ⛪ B2
Samuel St B2
Saville St C3
Shaw St B1
Silk Rd,The A2/B2
Slater St C1
Snow Hill C3
South Park C1
Spring Gdns A2
Statham St C2
Station St A2
Steeple St A3
Sunderland St B2
Superstore A1/A2/C2
Swettenham St B3
Thistleton Close C2
Thorp St B2
Town Hall B2
Townley St B2
Treacle Market ✦ B2
Turnock St C3
Union Rd B3
Union St B2
Victoria Park B3
Vincent St C2
Waters Green B2
Waterside C2
West Bond St B1
West Park A1
West Park Mus 🏛 A1
Westbrook Dr A1
Westminster Rd A1
Whalley Hayes B1
Windmill St C3
Withyfold Dr A2
York St B3

Maidstone 190
Albion Place B3
All Saints ⛪ B2
Allen St A3
Amphitheatre ✦ C2
Archbishop's Palace
🏛 B2
Bank St B2
Barker Rd C2
Barton Rd C3
Beaconsfield Rd C1
Bedford Place B1
Bishops Way B2
Bluett St A3
BMI The Somerfield
Hospital 🏥 A1
Bower La C1
Bower Mount Rd B1
Bower Place C1
Bower St B1
Boxley Rd A3
Brenchley Gardens A2
Brewer St A3
Broadway B2
Broadway
Shopping Centre B2
Brunswick St C3
Buckland Hill A1
Buckland Rd B1
Bus Station B3
Campbell Rd C3
Church Rd C1
Church St B3
Cinema 🎥 C2
Clifford Way C1/C2
College Ave C2
College Rd C2
Collis Meml Gdn C3
Cornwallis Rd B1
Corpus Christi Hall B2
Council Offices B3
County Hall A2
County Rd A3
Crompton Gdns C3
Crown & County
Courts B2
Curzon Rd A3
Dixon Close C2
Douglas Rd C1
Earl St B2
Eccleston Rd C2
Fairmeadow B2
Fisher St A2
Florence Rd C1
Foley St A3
Foster St C3
Freedom Leisure
Centre A1/A2
Fremlin Walk
Shopping Centre B2
Gabriel's Hill B3
George St C3
Grecian St A3
Hardy St A3
Hart St C2
Hastings Rd C3
Hayle Rd C3
Hazlitt 🎭 B2
Heathorn St A3
Hedley St A3
High St B2
HM Prison A3
Holland Rd A3
Hope St A2
Information Ctr ℹ B2
James St A3
James Whatman
Way A2
Jeffrey St A3
Kent County Council
Offices A2
Kent History &
Library Centre A2
King Edward Rd C2
King St B3
Kingsley Rd C3
Knightrider St B3
Launder Way C1
Lesley Place A1
Library B2
Little Buckland Ave A1
Lockmeadow
Leisure Complex C2
London Rd B1
Lower Boxley Rd A2
Lower Fant Rd C1
Magistrates Court B3
Maidstone Barracks
Station ⇌ A1
Maidstone East
Station ⇌ A2
Maidstone Museum &
Bentlif Art Gall 🏛 B2
Maidstone Utd FC B2
Maidstone West
Station ⇌ B2
Mall,The C3
Market C2
Market Buildings B2
Marsham St B3
Medway St B2
Melville Rd C3
Mill St B2
Millennium Bridge C2
Mote Rd B3
Muir Rd C3
Old Tovil Rd C2
Palace Ave B3
Perryfield St A2
Police Station 🏢 B3
Post Office 📮 B2/C3
Priory Rd C3

Prospect Place C1
Pudding La B2
Queen Anne Rd B3
Queens Rd A1
Randall St A2
Rawdon Rd C3
Reginald Rd C1
Riverstage A1
Rock Place B1
Rocky Hill B1
Romney Place B3
Rose Yard B2
Rowland Close C1
Royal Engineers' Rd A2
Royal Star Arcade B2
St Annes Ct B1
St Faith's St B2
St Luke's Rd A3
St Peter St B2
St Peter's Bridge B2
St Peter's Wharf Retail Park B2
St Philip's Ave C3
Salisbury Rd A3
Sandling Rd A2
Scott St A2
Scrubs La B1
Sheal's Cres C3
Somerfield La B1
Somerfield Rd B1
Staceys St A2
Station Rd A2
Superstore A1/B2/B3
Terrace Rd B1
Tonbridge Rd C1
Tovil Rd C2
Town Hall B2
Trinity Park B3
Tufton St B3
Tyrwhitt-Drake Mus of Carriages B2
Union St B3
Upper Fant Rd C1
Upper Stone St C3
Victoria St B1
Warwick Place B1
Wat Tyler Way B3
Waterloo St C3
Waterlow Rd A3
Week St B2
Well Rd A3
Westree Rd C1
Wharf Rd C1
Whatman Park A1
Wheeler St A3
Whitchurch Close B1
Woodville Rd C3
Wyatt St B3
Wyke Manor Rd B3

Manchester 190

Adair St B6
Addington St A5
Adelphi St A1
Advent Way B6
Albert Sq B3
Albion St C3
Ancoats Grove B6
Ancoats Grove North B6
Angela St C2
Aquatics Centre C4
Ardwick Green North C5
Ardwick Green Pk C5
Ardwick Green South C5
Arlington St A2
Artillery St B3
Arundel St C2
Atherton St B2
Atkinson St B3
Aytoun St B4
Back Piccadilly A4
Baird St B5
Balloon St A4
Bank Place A1
Baring St B5
Barrack St C1
Barrow St A1
Bendix St A5
Bengal St A5
Berry St C5
Blackfriars Rd A3
Blackfriars St A3
Blantyre St C2
Bloom St B4
Blossom St A5
Boad St B5
Bombay St B4
Booth St A3
Booth St B4
Bootle St B3
Brazennose St B3
Brewer St A5
Bridge St A3
Bridgewater Hall B3
Bridgewater Place A4
Bridgewater St B2
Brook St C4
Brotherton Dr A2
Brown St A3
Brown St B4
Brunswick St C6
Brydon Ave C6
Buddhist Centre A4
Bury St A2
Bus & Coach Sta B4
Bus Station B4
Butler St A6
Buxton St C5
Byrom St B3
Cable St A5
Cambridge St C3/C4
Camp St B3
Canal St B4
Cannon St A1
Cardroom Rd A6
Carruthers St A6
Castle St C2
Castlefield Arena B2
Cateaton St A3
Cathedral † A3
Cathedral St A3
Cavendish St C4
Chapel St A1/A3
Chapeltown St B5
Charles St C4
Charlotte St B4
Chatham St B4
Chepstow St B3
Chester Rd C1/C2
Chester St C4
Chetham's School of Music A3
China La B5
Chippenham Rd A6
Chorlton Rd C2
Chorlton St B4
Church St A2
Church St A4
City Park A4
City Rd East C3
Civil Justice Centre B2
Cleminson St A2
Clowes St A3
College Land A3
Collier St B2
Commercial St C3
Conference Centre C4
Cooper St B4
Copperas St A4
Corn Exchange, The A4
Cornbrook C1
Cornell St A5
Corporation St A4
Cotter St C6
Cotton St A5
Cow La B1
Cross St B3
Crown Court B4
Crown St C2
Dalberg St C6
Dale St A4/B5
Dancehouse, The C4
Dantzic St A4
Dark La C6
Dawson St C2
Dean St A5
Deansgate A3/B3/C2
Deansgate Castlefield C3
Deansgate Sta C3
Dolphin St C6
Downing St C5
Ducie St B5
Duke Place B2
Duke St B2
Durling St C6
East Ordsall La A2/B1
Edge St A4
Egerton St C2
Ellesmere St C1
Everard St C1
Everyman B2
Every St B6
Exchange Sq A4
Factory, The B2
Fairfield St B5
Faulkner St B4
Fennel St A3
Fire Sta B5
Ford St A2
Ford St C6
Fountain St B4
Frederick St A2
Gartside St B2
Gaythorne St A1
George Leigh St A5
George St B4
Gore St A2
Goulden St A5
Granby Row B4
Gravel La A3
Great St B6
Great Ancoats St A5
Great Bridgewater St B3
Great George St A1
Great Jackson St C2
Great Marlborough St C4
Great Northern Leisure Complex B3
Greengate A3
Grosvenor St C5
Gun St A5
Hall St B3
Hampson St B1
Hanover St A4
Hanworth Close C5
Hardman St B3
Harkness St C6
Harrison St B5
Hart St B4
Helmet St B6
Henry St A5
Heyrod St B6
High St A4
Higher Ardwick C6
Hilton St A4/A5
Holland St A6
HOME Entertainment Complex C3
Hood St A5
Hope St B1
Hope St B4
Houldsworth St A5
Hoyle St C6
Hulme Hall Rd C1
Hulme St A1
Hulme St C3
Hyde Rd C6
Islington Way A1
Information Ctr B4
Irwell St A2
Jackson Cres C2
Jackson's Row B3
James St A1
Jenner Close C2
Jersey St A5
John Dalton St B3
John Ryland's Library B3
John St A4
Kennedy St B3
Kincardine Rd C5
King St A3
King St West A3
Law Courts B3
Laystall St B5
Lever St A5
Library B3
Linby St C2
Little Lever St A4
Liverpool Rd B2
Liverpool St B1
Lloyd St B3
Lockton Close C5
London Rd B5
Long Millgate A3
Longacre St B6
Loom St A5
Lower Byrom St B2
Lower Mosley St B3
Lower Moss La C2
Lower Ormond St C4
Loxford La C4
Luna St A5
Major St B4
Mamucium B2
Manchester Arndale A4
Manchester Art Gallery B4
Manchester Central Convention Complex B3
Manchester Metropolitan Univ (MMU) B4/C4
Manchester Piccadilly Station B5
Manchester Technology Ctr C4
Mancunian Way C3
Manor St C5
Marble St A4
Market St A2
Market St A4
Market St A4
Marsden St A3
Marshall St A5
Mayan Ave A2
Medlock St C3
Middlewood St B1
Miller St A4
Minshull St B4
Mosley St A4
Mount St B3
Mulberry St B3
Murray St A5
Museum of Science & Industry (MOSI) B2
Nathan Dr A2
National Football Museum A4
Naval St A5
New Bailey St A2
New Elm Rd B2
New Islington A6
New Islington Station B6
New Quay St B2
New Union St A6
Newton St A5
Nicholas St B4
North Western St C6
Oak St A4
Odeon A4/B3
Old Mill St B6
Oldfield Rd A1/C1
Oldham Rd A5
Oldham St A4
Opera House B3
Ordsall La C1
Oxford Rd C4
Oxford Rd C4
Oxford St B4
Paddock St C6
Palace Theatre B4
Pall Mall A3
Palmerston St B6
Parker St B4
Peak St B5
Penfield Close C5
Peoples' History Museum B2
Peru St A1
Peter St B3
Piccadilly A4
Piccadilly B5
Piccadilly Gdns A4
Piercy St A6
Poland St A5
Police Museum A5
Police Station B3/B5
Pollard St B6
Port St A5
Portland St B4
Portugal St East B5
Post Office A2/A4/A5/B3/B4/C4
Potato Wharf B2
Princess St B3/C4
Quay St A2
Quay St B2
Queen St B3
Radium St A5
Redhill St A5
Regent Retail Park B1
Regent Rd B1
Rice St B2
Richmond St B4
River St C3
Roby St B5
Rodney St A6
Rosamond St A2
Royal Exchange A3
Sackville St B4
St Andrew's St B6
St Ann St A3
St Ann's A3
St George's Ave C1
St James St B4
St John St B3
St John's Cathedral (RC) † A2
St Mary's B3
St Mary's Gate A3
St Mary's Parsonage A3
St Peter's Sq B3
St Stephen St A2
Salford Approach A3
Salford Central A2
Sheffield St B5
Sherratt St A5
Shopmobility A4
Shudehill A4
Shudehill A4
Sidney St C4
Silk St A5
Silver St B4
Skerry Close C5
Snell St B6
South King St B3
Sparkle St B5
Spear St A4
Spring Gdns A4
Stanley St B2
Store St B5
Superstore B1
Swan St A4
Tariff St B5
Tatton St C1
Temperance St B6/C6
Thirsk St C6
Thomas St A4
Thompson St A5
Tib La B3
Tib St A4
Town Hall (Manchester) B3
Town Hall (Salford) A2
Trafford St C3
Travis St B5
Trinity Way A2
Turner St A4
Union St C6
Univ of Manchester (North Campus) C5
Univ of Salford A1
Upper Brook St C5
Upper Cleminson St A1
Upper Wharf St A1
Urban Exchange A5
Vesta St B6
Victoria A4
Victoria Station A4
Wadesdon Rd C5
Water St B2
Watson St B3
West Fleet St B1
West King St A2
West Mosley St B4
Weybridge Rd A6
Whitworth St B4
Whitworth St West C3
William St A2
William St C6
Wilmott St C3
Windmill St B3
Windsor Cres A1
Withy Grove A4
Woden St C1
Wood St B3
Woodward St A6
Worrall St C1
Worsley St C2
York St B4
York St C2
York St C4

Merthyr Tydfil
Merthyr Tudful 190

Aberdare Rd B2
Abermorlais Terr B2
Alexandra Rd A3
Alma St C3
Arfryn Place C3
Argyle St C3
Avenue De Clichy C2
Beacons Place Shopping Centre C2
Bethesda St B2
Bishops Grove A3
Brecon Rd A1/B2
Briarmead A3
Bryn St C3
Bryntirion Rd B3/C3
Bus Station B2
Cae Mari Dwn B3
Caedraw Rd C2
Castle Sq A1
Castle St B2
Chapel C2
Chapel Bank B1
Church St B3
Civic Centre B2
Clos Penderyn B1
Coedcae'r Ct C3
College Boulevard C2
County and Crown Courts B2
Court St C3
Cromwell St B2
Cyfarthfa Castle, Mus and Art Gallery A1
Cyfarthfa Ind Est A1
Cyfarthfa Park A1
Cyfarthfa Retail Pk B1
Cyfarthfa Rd A1
Dane St A2
Dane Terr A2
Danyparc B3
Darren View A3
Dixon St B2
Dyke St C3
Dynevor St B2
Elwyn Dr C2
Fire Station B2
Fothergill St B3
Galonuchaf Rd A3
Garth St B2
Georgetown B2
Grawen Terr A2
Grove Pk A2
Grove, The A2
Gurnos Rd A2
Gwaelodygarth Rd A2/A3
Gwaunfarren Grove A3
Gwaunfarren Rd A3
Gwendoline St A3
Hampton St C3
Hanover St A2
Heol S O Davies B1
Heol-Gerrig B1
High St A3/B2/B3/C2
Highland View C3
Howell Close B1
Information Ctr B2
Jackson's Bridge B2
James St C3
John St B3
Joseph Parry's Cottage B2
Lancaster St A2
Library B2
Llewellyn St A2
Llwyfen St B2
Llwyn Berry B1
Llwyn Dic Penderyn B1
Llwyn-y-Gelynen C1
Lower Thomas St B3
Market C2
Mary St C3
Masonic St C2
Merthyr Tydfil Coll B2
Merthyr Town FC B3
Merthyr Tydfil Leisure Centre C3
Merthyr Tydfil Sta C3
Meyrick Villas A2
Miniature Railway A1
Mount St A2
Nantygwenith St B1
Norman Terr B2
Oak Rd A2
Old Cemetery B3
Pandy Close A1
Pantycelynen B1
Parade, The B3
Park Terr B2
Penlan View C2
Penry St B2
Pentwyn Villas A2
Penyard Rd B3
Penydarren Park A3
Penydarren Rd B3
Plymouth St C3
Police Station C2
Pont Marlais West B2
Post Office B2
Quarry Row B2
Queen's Rd B3
Rees St C3
Rhydycar Link C2
Riverside Park A1
St David's B3
St Tydfil's C2
St Tydfil's Ave C3
St Tydfil's Square Shopping Centre C2
Saxon St A2
School of Nursing A2
Seward St A3
Shiloh La B3
Stone Circles B3
Stuart St A2
Summerhill Place B3
Superstore B3
Swan St C2
Swansea Rd B1
Taff Glen View C3
Taff Vale Ct B3
Theatre Soar B2
Thomastown Park B3
Tramroad La A3
Tramroad Side B2
Tramroad Side North B3
Tramroad Side South C3
Trevithick Gdns C3
Trevithick St A3
Tudor Terr B2
Twynyrodyn Rd C3
Union St B3
Upper Colliers Row B1
Upper Thomas St B3
Victoria St B2
Vue C3
Vulcan Rd B2
Walk, The B2
Warlow St C3
Well St A2
Welsh Assembly Government Offices C2
Wern La C1
Wern, The (Merthyr RFC) C2
West Grove A2
William St C3
Yew St C3
Ynysfach Engine House C2
Ynysfach Rd C2

Middlesbrough 191

Abingdon Rd C3
Acklam Rd C1
Albert Park C2
Albert Rd B2
Albert Terr C2
Ambulance Station C1
Aubrey St C3
Avenue, The C2
Ayresome Gdns C2
Ayresome Green La C1
Ayresome St C2
Barton Rd A1
Bilsdale Rd C3
Bishopton Rd C3
Borough Rd B2/B3
Bowes Rd A2
Breckon Hill Rd B3
Bridge St West B2
Brighouse Rd A1
Burlam Rd C1
Bus Station B2
Cannon Park B1
Cannon Park Way B2
Cannon St B1
Captain Cook Sq B2
Carlow St C1
Castle Way C3
Chipchase Rd C2
Cineworld B3
Cleveland Centre B2
Clive Rd C2
Commercial St A2
Corporation Rd B2
Costa St C2
Council Offices B3
Crescent Rd C2
Crescent, The C2
Cumberland Rd C2
Depot Rd A2
Derwent St B2
Devonshire Rd C2
Diamond Rd B2
Dock St B3
Dorman Mus C2
Douglas St B3
Eastbourne Rd C2
Eden Rd C3
Fire Sta A3
Forty Foot Rd A2
Gilkes St B2
Gosford St A2
Grange Rd B2
Gresham Rd B2
Harehills Rd C1
Harford St C2
Hartington Rd B2
Haverton Hill Rd A1
Hey Wood St B1
Highfield Rd C3
Hillstreet Centre B2
Holwick Rd B1
Hutton Rd C3
Ironmasters Way B1
Lambton Rd C3
Lancaster Rd C2
Lansdowne Rd C3
Latham Rd C2
Law Courts B2/B3
Lees Rd B2
Leeway B3
Library B2/C2
Linthorpe Cemetery C1
Linthorpe Rd B2
Lloyd St B2
Longford St C2
Longlands Rd C3
Lower East St A3
Lower Lake C3
Macmillan Acad C1
Maldon Rd C1
Manor St B2
Marsh St B2
Marton Rd B3
Middlesbrough By-Pass B2/C1
Middlesbrough Coll B3
Middlesbrough Dock B3
Middlesbrough Leisure Park B3
Middlesbrough Station B2
Middletown Park C2
MIMA B3
Mulgrave Rd C2
Newport Bridge B1
Newport Bridge Approach Rd B1
Newport Rd B2
North Ormesby Rd B3
North Rd B2
Northern Rd C1
Outram St B2
Oxford Rd C2
Park La C2
Park Rd North C2
Park Rd South C2
Park Vale Rd C3
Parliament Rd B1
Police Station A2
Port Clarence Rd A3
Portman St B2
Post Office B3/C1/C2
Princes Rd B2
Python A2
Riverside Park Rd A1
Riverside Stadium (Middlesbrough FC) B3
Rockliffe Rd C2
Romaldkirk Rd B1
Roman Rd C2
Roseberry Rd C3
St Barnabas' Rd C2
St Paul's Rd B2
Saltwells Rd B3
Scott's Rd A3
Seaton Carew Rd A3
Shepherdson Way B3
Shopmobility B2
Snowdon Rd A2
South West Ironmasters Park B1
Southfield Rd B2
Southwell Rd C2
Springfield Rd C1
Startforth Rd A2
Stockton Rd C1
Stockton St A2
Superstore B2
Surrey St C2
Sycamore Rd C2
Tax Offices B3
Tees Viaduct C1
Teessaurus Park A2
Teesside Tertiary College C3
Temenos B3
Thornfield Rd C1
Town Hall B2
Transporter Bridge (Toll) A3
Union St B2
Univ of Teesside B2
Upper Lake C2
Valley Rd C3
Ventnor Rd C2
Victoria Rd B2
Vulcan St A2
Warwick St C2
Wellesley Rd B3
West La C1
West Lane Hosp C1
Westminster Rd C2
Wilson St B2
Windward Way B3
Woodlands Rd B2
York Rd C3

Milton Keynes 191

Abbey Way A1
Arbrook Ave B1
Armourer Dr A3
Arncliffe Dr A1
Avebury C2
Avebury Blvd C2
Bankfield B3
Bayard Ave A2
Belvedere A2
Bishopstone A1
Blundells Rd A1
Boundary, The C3
Boycott Ave C2
Bradwell Common Boulevard B1
Bradwell Rd C1
Bramble Ave A2
Brearley Ave C2
Breckland A1
Brill Place B1
Burnham Dr B1
Campbell Park B3
Cantle Ave A3
Central Retail Park C1
Century Ave C2
Chaffron Way C3
Childs Way C1
Christ the Cornerstone B2
Cineworld B2
Civic Offices B2
Cleavers Ave B2
Colesbourne Dr A3
Conniburrow Blvd B2
Currier Dr A2
Dansteed Way A2/A3/B1
Deltic Ave B1
Downs Barn A2
Downs Barn Blvd A3
Eaglestone C3
Eelbrook Ave B1
Elder Gate B1
Evans Gate C2
Fairford Cres A3
Falcon Ave B3
Fennel Dr A2
Fishermead Blvd C3
Food Centre B3
Fulwoods Dr C3
Glazier Dr A2
Glovers La A1
Grafton Gate C1
Grafton St A1/C2
Gurnards Ave B3
Harrier Dr C3
The Hub Leisure Quarter B2/C2
Ibstone Ave B1
intu Milton Keynes B2
Langcliffe Dr A1
Leisure Centre C3
Leisure Plaza C1
Leys Rd C1
Library B2
Linceslade Grove C1
Linford Wood A2
Magistrates Court B2
Marlborough Gate B3
Marlborough St A2/B3
Mercers Dr A1
Midsummer C2
Midsummer Blvd B2
Milton Keynes Central C1
Milton Keynes Hospital (A&E) C3
Monks Way A1
Mullen Ave A3
Mullion Place C3
Neath Hill A3
North Elder C1
North Grafton B1
North Overgate A3
North Row B2
North Saxon B2
North Secklow B2
North Skeldon A3
North Witan B1
Oakley Gdns A3
Odeon B2
Oldbrook Blvd C2
Open-Air Theatre B3
Overgate A3
Overstreet A3
Patriot Dr B1
Pencarrow Place B3
Penryn Ave B3
Perran Ave C3
Pitcher La C1
Place Retail Pk, The C1
Police Station B2
Portway B2
Post Office A2/B2/B3
Precedent Dr B1
Quinton Dr B1
Ramsons Ave B2
Retail Park C2
Rockingham Dr A2
Rooksley B1
Saxon Gate B2
Saxon St A1/C3
Secklow Gate B2
Shackleton Place C2
Shopmobility B2
Silbury Blvd B2
Skeldon A3
South Enmore B3
South Grafton C2
South Row C2
South Saxon C2
South Secklow B3
South Witan C2
Springfield B3
Stainton Dr A1/B1
Stanton Wood A1
Stantonbury A1
Stantonbury Leisure Centre A1
Strudwick Dr C2
Sunrise Parkway A2
Superstore C1/C2
Theatre & Art Gallery B3
theCentre:mk B2
Tolcarne Ave C3
Towan Ave C3
Trueman Place C2
Vauxhall A1
Winterhill Retail Park C2
Witan Gate B2
Xscape B3

Newcastle upon Tyne 191

Albert St B3
Argyle St B3
Back New Bridge St B3
BALTIC Centre for Contemporary Art C3
Barker St A3
Barrack Rd B1
Bath La B1
Bessie Surtees House C2
Bigg Market C2
Biscuit Factory B3
Black Gate C2
Blackett St B2
Blandford Sq C1
Boating Lake A1
Boyd St B3
Brandling Park A2
Bus Station B2
Buxton St B3
Byron St A3
Camden St B2
Castle Keep C2
Central C1
Central Library B2
Central Motorway B2
Chester St A3
Cineworld B1
City Hall B2
City Rd B3/C3
City Walls C1
Civic Centre A2
Claremont Rd A1
Clarence St B3
Clarence Walk B3
Clayton St C1/B1
Clayton St West C1
Close, The C2
Coach Station C1
College St B2
Collingwood St C2
Copland Terr B3
Coppice Way B3
Corporation St B1
Courts C3
Crawhall Rd B3
Dean St C2
Dental Hospital A1
Dinsdale Place A3
Dinsdale Rd A3
Discovery C1
Doncaster Rd A3
Durant Rd B2
Eldon Sq B1
Ellison Place B2
Eskdale Terr A2
Eslington Terr A1
Exhibition Park A1
Falconar St B3
Fenkle St C1
Forth Banks C1
Forth St C1
Gallowgate B1
Gate, The B1
Gateshead Millennium Bridge C3
Gateshead Quays C3
Gibson St B3
Goldspink La A3
Grainger Market B2
Grainger St B2
Grantham Rd A3
Granville Rd A3
Great North Children's Hospital A1
Great North Mus:Hancock A2
Grey St B2
Groat Market C2
Guildhall C2
Hancock St A2
Hanover St C2
Hatton Gallery A1
Hawks Rd C3
Haymarket B2
Heber St B1
Helmsley Rd A3
High Bridge B2
High Level Bridge C2
Hillgate C3
Howard St B3
Hutton Terr A3
intu Eldon Square Shopping Centre B2
Jesmond A2
Jesmond Rd A2/A3
John Dobson St B2
Jubilee Rd B3
Kelvin Grove A3
Kensington Terr A2
Laing Gallery B2
Lambton Rd A2
Leazes Cres B1
Leazes La B1
Leazes Park B1
Leazes Park Rd B1
Leazes Terr B1
Library A2
Life Science Ctr C1
Live C2
Low Friar St C1
Manor Chare C2
Manors B2
Manors Station B2
Market St B2
Melbourne St B2
Mill Rd C3
Monument B2
Monument Mall Shopping Centre B2
Morpeth St A2
Mosley St C2
Napier St A3
New Bridge St West B2/B3
Newcastle Central Station C1
Newcastle Univ A1
Newgate St B1
Newington Rd A3
Northern Design Ctr C3
Northern Stage Theatre A2
Northumberland Rd B2
Northumberland St B2
Northumbria Univ A2
Northwest Radial Rd A1
O2 Academy C1
Oakwellgate C3
Open Univ C3
Orchard St C2
Osborne Rd A2
Osborne Terr A3
Pandon C3
Pandon Bank B3
Park Terr A1
Percy St B1
Pilgrim St B2
Pipewellgate C2
Pitt St B1
Plummer Tower A2
Police Station C1
Portland Rd A3/B3
Portland Terr A3
Post Office B1/B2
Pottery La C1
Prudhoe Place B1
Prudhoe St B1
Quayside C2
Queen Elizabeth II Bridge C2
Queen Victoria Rd A1
Richardson Rd A1
Ridley Place B2
Rock Terr B3
Rosedale Terr A3
Royal Victoria Infirmary A1
Sage Gateshead C3
St Andrew's St B1
St James B1
St James' Blvd C1
St James' Park (Newcastle Utd FC) B1
St Mary's Heritage Centre C3
St Mary's (RC) † C1
St Mary's Place B2
St Nicholas † C2
St Nicholas St C2
St Thomas' St B1
Sandyford Rd A2/A3
Shield St B3
Shieldfield B3
Shopmobility B1
Side, The C2
Simpson Terr B3
South Shore Rd C3
South St C1
Starbeck Ave A3
Stepney Rd B3
Stoddart St B3
Stowell St B1
Strawberry Place B1
Swing Bridge C2
Temple St C1
Terrace Place B1
Theatre Royal B2
Times Sq C1
Tower St B3
Trinity House C2
Tyne Bridge C2
Tyne Bridges C2
Tyne Theatre & Opera House C1
Tyneside B2
Victoria Square A2
Warwick St A3
Waterloo St C1
Wellington St B1
Westgate Rd C1/C2
Windsor Terr A2
Worswick St B2
Wretham Place B3

Newport
Casnewydd 191

Albert Terr B1
Allt-yr-Yn Ave A1
Alma St C2
Ambulance Station C3
Bailey St B2
Barrack Hill A2
Bath St A3
Bedford Rd B3
Belle Vue La C1
Belle Vue Park C1
Bishop St A3
Blewitt St B1
Bolt Close C3
Bolt St C3
Bond St A2
Bosworth Dr A1
Bridge St B1
Bristol St A3
Bryngwyn Rd B1
Brynhyfryd Ave C1
Brynhyfryd Rd C1
Bus Station B2
Caerau Cres C1
Caerau Rd B1
Caerleon Rd A3
Capel Cres C2
Cardiff Rd C2
Caroline St B3
Castle (Remains) A2
Cedar Rd B3
Charles St B2
Charlotte Dr C2
Chepstow Rd A3
Church Rd A3
Cineworld B2
Civic Centre B1
Clarence Place A2
Clifton Place B1
Clifton Rd C1
Clyffard Cres B1
Clytha Park Rd B1
Clytha Sq C2
Coldra Rd C1
Collier St A3
Colne St B3
Comfrey Close A1
Commercial Rd C3
Commercial St B2
Corelli St A3
Corn St B2
Corporation Rd B3
Coulson Close C2
County Court A2
Courts A1
Courts B1
Crawford St A3
Cyril St B3
Dean St A3
Devon Place B1
Dewsland Park Rd C2
Dolman B2
Dolphin St C3
East Dock Rd C3
East St B1
East Usk Rd A3
Ebbw Vale Wharf B3
Emlyn St B2
Enterprise Way C3
Eton Rd B3
Evans St A2
Factory Rd A2
Fields Rd B1
Francis Dr C2
Frederick St C3
Friars Rd C1
Friars Walk B2
Gaer La C1
George St C3
George St Bridge C3
Godfrey Rd B1
Gold Tops B1
Gore St A3
Gorsedd Circle C1
Grafton Rd A3
Graham St B1
Granville St C3
Harlequin Dr A1
Harrow Rd B3
Herbert Rd A3
Herbert Walk C2
Hereford St A3
High St B2
Hill St B2
Hoskins St A2
Information Ctr B2
Ivor St B2
Jones St B1
Junction Rd A3
Keynshaw Ave C2
King St C2
Kingsway B2
Kingsway Centre B2
Ledbury Dr A2
Library A3
Library, Museum & Art Gallery B2
Liverpool Wharf B3
Llanthewy Rd B1
Llanvair Rd A3
Locke St A2
Lower Dock St C3
Lucas St A2
Manchester St A3
Market B2
Marlborough Rd B3
Mellon St C3
Mill St A2
Morgan St A3
Mountjoy Rd C2
Newport Bridge A2
Newport Ctr B2
Newport RFC B3
Newport Station B2
North St B2
Oakfield Rd B1
Park Sq C2
Police Sta A3/C2
Post Office B2/C3
Power St A1
Prince St A3
Pugsley St A2
Queen St C2
Queen's Close A1
Queen's Hill A1
Queen's Hill Cres A1
Queensway B2
Railway St B
Riverfront Theatre & Arts Centre, The B
Riverside A
Rodney Rd B
Royal Gwent (A&E) C
Rudry St A
Rugby Rd B
Ruperra La C
Ruperra St C
St Edmund St B
St Mark's Cres A
St Mary St B
St Vincent Rd A
St Woolos † C
St Woolos General (no A&E) C
St Woolos Rd B
School La B
Serpentine Rd B
Shaftesbury Park A
Sheaf La A
Skinner St B
Sorrel Dr A
South Market St C
Spencer Rd B
Stow Hill B2/C1/C2
Stow Park Ave C
Stow Park Dr C
TA Centre A
Talbot St B
Tennis Club A
Tregare St A
Trostrey St A
Tunnel Terr B
Turner St A
Univ of Wales Newport City Campus B
Upper Dock St B
Usk St A
Usk Way B3/C
Victoria Cres B
War Memorial A
Waterloo Rd C
West St B
Wharves B
Wheeler St A
Whitby Place A
Windsor Terr B
York Place C

Newquay 19

Agar Rd
Alma Place
Ambulance Station
Anthony Rd
Atlantic Hotel
Bank St
Barrowfields
Bay View Terr
Beach Rd
Beachfield Ave
Beacon Rd
Belmont Place
Berry Rd
Blue Reef Aquarium
Boating Lake
Bus Station
Chapel Hill
Chester Rd
Cheviot Rd C1/
Chichester Cres
Chynance Dr
Chyverton Close
Cliff Rd
Coach Park
Colvreath Rd
Cornwall College Newquay
Council Ofices
Crantock St
Crescent, The
Criggar Rocks
Dale Close
Dale Rd
Dane Rd
East St
Edgcumbe Ave
Edgcumbe Gdns
Eliot Gdns
Elm Close
Ennor's Rd
Fernhill Rd
Fire Station
Fore St
Gannel Rd
Golf Driving Range
Gover La
Great Western Beach
Grosvenor Ave
Harbour
Hawkins Rd
Headleigh Rd
Hilgrove Rd A3/
Holywell Rd
Hope Terr
Huer's Hut, The
Information Ctr
Island Cres
Jubilee St
Kew Close
Killacourt Cove
King Edward Cres
Lanhenvor Ave
Library
Lifeboat Station
Lighthouse
Linden Ave
Listry Rd
Lusty Glaze Beach
Lusty Glaze Rd
Manor Rd
Marcus Hill
Mayfield Rd
Meadowside
Mellanvrane La
Michell Ave
Miniature Golf Course
Miniature Railway ✦
Mount Wise
Mowhay Close
Narrowcliff
Newquay
Newquay Hosp
Newquay Town Football Ground
Newquay Zoo
North Pier
North Quay Hill
Oakleigh Terr
Pargolla Rd

Pendragon Cres . . C3
Pengannel Close . C1
Penina Ave C2
Pirate's Quest . . . B1
Police Station &
Courts B2
Post Office . . . B1/B2
Quarry Park Rd . . C3
Rawley La C1
Reeds Way B1
Robartes Rd C2
St Anne's Rd A3
St George's Rd . . B1
St John's Rd B1
St Mary's Rd B1
St Michael's B1
St Michael's Rd . . C3
St Thomas' Rd . . . B2
Seymour Ave . . . B2
South Pier A1
South Quay Hill . A1
Superstore C3
Sweet Briar Cres . C3
Sydney Rd A1
Tolcarne Beach . . A2
Tolcarne Point . . B2
Tolcarne Rd B2
Tor Rd B1
Towan Beach . . . A1
Towan Blystra Rd . B3
Tower Rd A2
Trebarwith Cres . B2
Tredour Rd C2
Treforda Rd C3
Tregoss Rd B3
Tregunnel Hill . B1/C1
Tregunnel Saltings . C1
Trelawney Rd . . . C3
Treloggan La . . . C3
Treloggan Rd . . . C3
Trembath Cres . . C1
Trenance B2
Trenance Gardens . B2
Trenance La B2
Trenance Leisure Pk B3
Trenance Rd B2
Trenarth Rd B2
Treninnick Hill . . C3
Tretherras Rd . . . B3
Trethewey Way . . C1
Trevemper Rd . . . C2
Jlalia Rd A2
Vivian Close B2
Waterworld B2
Whitegate Rd . . . B3
Wych Hazel Way . . C1

Northampton 192
8 Derngate B3
Abington Sq B2
Abington St B2
Ailcombe St A3
All Saints's B2
Ambush St B1
Angel St B2
Army Reserve Ctr . A3
Arundel St A2
Ash St A2
Auctioneers Way . C2
Bailiff St A2
Barrack Rd A2
BOB Rugby FC . . A1
Beaconsfield Terr . A3
Becket's Park . . . C3
Bedford Rd B3
Billing Rd B3
Brecon St B1
Brewery C2
Bridge St B2
Broad St A2
Burns St A3
Bus Station B2
Campbell St A2
Castle (Site of) . . B2
Castle St B2
Castle Market Rd . C2
Central Museum &
Art Gallery B2
Charles St B3
Cheyne Walk . . . B3
Church La A2
Clare St A2
Cloutsham St . . . A3
College St B2
Colwyn Rd A3
Cotton End C2
Countess Rd . . . A1
County Hall B2
Court C2
Craven St A3
Crown & County
Courts B2
Denmark Rd B3
Derngate B3
Doddridge
Church B2
Drapery,The B2
Duke St A3
Dunster St A3
Earl St A3
Euston Rd C2
Fire Station B2
Foot Meadow . . . B2
Gladstone Rd . . . A1
Gold St B2
Grafton St A2
Gray St A2
Green St B1
Greenwood Rd . . C1
Greyfriars B2
Grosvenor Centre . B2
Grove Rd A2
Guildhall B2
Hampton St A3
Harding Terr A1
Hazelwood Rd . . . B2
Hervey St A2
Holy Sepulchre . . A2
Hood St A3
Horse Market . . . B2
Hunter St A3
Information Ctr . . B2
Kettering Rd A3
Kingswell St B2
Lady's La B2
Leicester St A2
Leslie Rd A1
Library B2
Lorne Rd A2
Lorry Park A1
Louise Rd A1
Lower Harding St . A2
Lower Hester St . . A2

Lower Mounts . . . B3
Lower Priory St . . A2
Main Rd C1
Marefair B2
Market Sq B2
Marlboro St B1
Marriott St A2
Millers Meadow . . C1
Military Rd B3
Mounts Baths
Leisure Centre . . B2
NeneValley
Retail Park C1
New South Bridge
Rd C2
Northampton General
Hospital (A&E) . . B3
Northampton
Marina C2
Northampton Sta . B1
Northcote St A2
Nunn Mills Rd . . . C3
OldTowcester Rd . C2
Overstone Rd . . . A3
Pembroke Rd . . . A1
Penn Court C1
Police Station . . . B1
Post Office . . . A1/B3
Quorn Way A2
Ransome Rd C3
Regent Sq A2
Ridings,The B3
Robert St A2
Royal & Derngate
Theatres B3
St Andrew's Rd . . B1
St Andrew's St . . A2
St Edmund's Rd . . B3
St George's St . . . B2
St Giles B3
St Giles St B3
St Giles'Terr . . . B3
St James Park Rd . B1
St James Retail Pk . C1
St James'Mill Rd . B1
St James'Mill Rd
East C1
St Leonard's Rd . . C2
St Mary's St B2
St Michael's Rd . . A3
St Peter's Way
Shopping Precinct B2
St Peter's Way . . B2
Salisbury St A2
Scarletwell St . . . B2
Semilong Rd A2
Sheep St B2
Sol Central
(Leisure Centre) . B2
Somerset St A3
South Bridge . . . C2
Southfield Ave . . C2
Spencer Bridge Rd. A1
Spencer Rd A2
Spring Gdns B3
Spring La B2
Superstore B3
Swan St B2
Tintern Ave A2
Towcester Rd . . . C2
Univ of Northampton
(Waterside
Campus) C3
Upper Bath St . . . B2
Upper Mounts . . . A2
Victoria Park . . . B2
Victoria Promenade B2
Victoria Rd B3
Victoria St A2
Wellingborough Rd B2
West Bridge B2
York Rd B3

Norwich 192
Albion Way C3
All Saints Green . . C2
Anchor St A3
Anglia Sq A2
Argyle St C3
Arts Centre B1
Ashby St C2
Assembly House . B1
Bank Plain B2
Barker St A1
Barn Rd B1
Barrack St A3
Ber St C2
Bethel St B1
Bishop Bridge . . . B3
Bishopbridge Rd . A3
Bishopgate B2
Blackfriars St . . . A2
Botolph St A2
Bracondale C3
Brazen Gate C2
Bridewell Mus . . B2
Brunswick Rd . . . C1
Bull Close Rd . . . A2
Bus Station C2
Calvert St A2
Cannell Green . . . A3
Carrow Rd C3
Castle & Mus . . . B2
Castle Mall B2
Castle Meadow . . B2
Cathedral † B2
Cath Retail Park . . A1
Cattlemarket St . . B2
Chantry Rd C1
Chapel Loke C2
Chapelfield East . . C1
Chapelfield Gdns . C1
Chapelfield North . C1
Chapelfield Rd . . C1
Cinema City B2
City Hall B1
City Rd C2
City Wall C1/C3
Close,The B2/B3
Colegate A2
Coslany St B1
Cow Hill B1
CowTower A3
Cowgate A2
Crown & Magistrates'
Courts B1
Dragon Hall Heritage
Centre C3
Duke St B1
Edward St A2
Elm Hill B2
Erpingham Gate . B2
Fishergate A2

Forum,The B1
Foundry Bridge . . B3
Fye Bridge A2
Garden St C2
Gas Hill B3
Gentlemans Walk . B1
Grapes Hill B1
Great Hospital
Halls,The A3
Grove Ave C1
Grove Rd C1
Guildhall B1
Gurney Rd A3
Hall Rd C2
Heathgate A3
Heigham St A1
Hollywood B2
Horn's La C2
Hungate Medieval
Art B2
Information Ctr . . B1
intu Chapelfield . . C1
Ipswich Rd C1
ITV Anglia C1
James Stuart Gdns . B3
King St B2
King St C3
Koblenz Ave C3
Leisure Centre . . B1
Library B1
London St B2
Lower Clarence Rd . B3
Maddermarket . . B1
Magdalen St A2
Mariners La C2
Market B1
Market Ave B2
Mountergate B3
Mousehold St . . . A3
Newmarket Rd . . C1
Norfolk St C1
Norwich City FC . . C3
Norwich Gallery . B2
Norwich School . B2
Norwich Station . B3
Oak St A1
Odeon C2
Palace St B2
Pitt St A1
Playhouse B2
Police Station . . . B1
Post Office
. . . A2/B2/B3/C1
Pottergate B1
Prince of Wales Rd . B2
Princes St B2
Pull's Ferry B3
PuppetTheatre . . A2
Queen St B2
Queens Rd C2
Recorder Rd B3
Riverside
Entertainment Ctr C3
Riverside Leisure
Centre C3
Riverside Rd B3
Riverside Retail Pk. C3
Rosary Rd B3
Rose La B2
Rouen Rd B2
St Andrews St . . . B2
St Augustines St . . A1
St Benedicts St . . B1
St Crispins Road . . A1
St Ethelbert's Gate
. . . . B2
St Faiths La B2
St Georges St . . . A2
St Giles St B1
St James Close . . A3
St Julians St C2
St Leonards Rd . . B3
St Martin's La . . . A1
St Peter Mancroft . B1
St Peters St B1
St Stephens Rd . . C1
St Stephens St . . . C1
Shopmobility . . . C1
Silver Rd A3
Silver St A2
Southwell Rd . . . C2
St. Andrew's &
Blackfriars' Hall . B2
Strangers' Hall . . B1
Superstore C2
Surrey St C2
Sussex St A1
Theatre Royal . . . B1
Thorn La B2
Thorpe Rd B3
Tombland B2
Union St C1
Vauxhall St B1
Victoria St C1
Vue B2
Walpole St B1
Waterfront,The . . C3
Wensum St A2
Wessex St C2
Westwick St B1
Wherry Rd C3
Whitefriars A2
Willow La B1

Nottingham 192
Abbotsford Dr . . . A3
Addison St A1
Albert Hall B1
Alfred St Central . . A3
Alfreton Rd B1
All Saints St A1
Annesley Grove . . A2
Arboretum A1
Arboretum St . . . A1
Arthur St A1
ArtsTheatre B3
Ashforth St A2
Balmoral Rd A1
Barker Gate B3
Bath St B3
BBC Nottingham . B3
Beacon Hill Rise . . B3
Belgrave Rooms . . B1
Bellar Gate B3
Belward St B3
Brewhouse Yard . C1
Broad Marsh Bus
Station C2
Broad St B3
Brook St B3
Burns St A1
Burton St B2
Bus Station C2
Canal St C2
Carlton St B3

Carrington St . . . C2
Castle C1
Castle Boulevard . C1
Castle Gate C2
Castle Meadow Rd . C1
Castle Meadow
Retail Park C1
Castle Rd C1
Castle Wharf . . . C2
Cavendish Rd East . C1
Cemetery A1/B1
Chaucer St B2
Cheapside B2
Church Rd A3
City Link C3
City of Caves . . . C2
Clarendon St . . . B1
Cliff Rd C3
Clumber Rd East . . C1
Clumber St B2
College St B1
Collin St C2
Contemporary . . C2
Conway Close . . . A3
Cornerhouse,
The B2
Council House . . B2
Cranbrook St . . . B3
Cranmer St A2
Cromwell St B1
Curzon St B3
Derby Rd B1
Dryden St A2
Exchange Ctr,The . B2
Fishpond Dr C1
Fletcher Gate . . . B3
Forest Rd East . . A1
Forest Rd West . . A1
Friar La C2
Gedling Grove . . A1
Gedling St B3
George St B3
Gill St A2
Glasshouse St . . . B2
Goldsmith St . . . B2
Goose Gate B3
Great Freeman St . A2
Guildhall B2
Hamilton Dr C1
Hampden St A1
Heathcote St . . . B3
High Pavement . . C3
High School A1
HM Revenue &
Customs C2
Holles Cres A1
Hope Dr C1
Hungerhill Rd . . . A3
Huntingdon Dr . . C1
Huntingdon St . . A2
Information Ctr . . B2
Instow Rise A3
International
Community Ctr . . A2
intu Broadmarsh . . C2
intuVictoria Centre B2
Kent St B3
King St B2
Lace Market C3
Lace MktTheatre . B3
Lamartine St . . . B3
Leisure Ctr C3
Lenton Rd C1
Lewis Close A3
Lincoln St B2
London Rd C3
Long Row B2
Low Pavement . . C2
Lower Parliament
St B3
Magistrates' Court . C2
Maid Marian Way . C2
Mansfield Rd . . A2/B2
Middle Hill C2
Milton St B2
Mount St C2
National Ice Centre &
Motorpoint Arena . C3
National Justice
Museum C3
Newcastle Dr . . . C1
Newstead Grove . A1
North Sherwood St A2
Nottingham Arena . C3
Nottingham
Cathedral † . . . B1
Nottingham Coll. . C2
Nottingham
Station C2
NottinghamTrent
University . . . A2/B2
Old Mkt Square . B2
Oliver St A1
Park Dr C1
Park Row B1
ParkTerr C1
ParkValley C1
Park,The C1
Peas Hill Rd A2
Peel St A1
Pelham St B2
Peveril Dr C1
Plantagenet St . . A3
Playhouse
Theatre B1
Plumptre St C3
Police Sta . . . B1/B2
Poplar St C3
Portland Rd B1
Post Office
. . . . A2/B2
Queen's Rd C2
Raleigh St A1
Regent St B1
Rick St B3
Robin Hood St . . B3
Robin Hood
Statue C2
Ropewalk,The . . . B1
Royal Centre . . . B2
Royal Children Inn
. . . . C1
Royal Concert Hall
. . . . B2
St Ann's Hill Rd . . A2
St Ann's Way . . . A2
St Ann's Well Rd . A3
St James' St B2
St Mark's St A3
St Mary's Rest Gdn A3
St Mary's Gate . . B3
St Nicholas C2
St Peter's B2
St Peter's Gate . . B2
Salutation Inn . . . C2
Shakespeare St . . B2
Shelton St A2
Shopmobility . . . B2

South Parade . . . B2
South Rd C1
South Sherwood St . B2
Station Street . . . C2
Stoney St B3
Talbot St B1
Tattershall Dr . . . C1
Tennis St B3
Tennyson St A1
Theatre Royal . . . B2
Trent St C3
Trent University . A1
Union Rd A3
Upper Parliament
St B2
Victoria Leisure Ctr B3
Victoria Park . . . B3
Victoria St B2
Walter St A1
Warser Gate B3
Watkin St A2
Waverley St A1
Wheeler Gate . . . B2
Wilford Rd C2
Wilford St C2
Wollaton St B1
Woodborough Rd . A3
Woolpack La B3
Ye OldTrip to
Jerusalem C1
York St A2

Oxford 193
Adelaide St A1
Albert St A1
All Souls (Coll) . . B2
Ashmolean Mus . B1
Balliol (Coll) B2
Banbury Rd A1
Bate Collection of
Musical Instruments
. . . . C2
Beaumont St . . . B1
Becket St B1
Blackhall Rd . . . A2
Blue Boar St . . . B2
Bodleian Library . B2
Botanic Garden . B3
Brasenose (Coll) . . B2
Brewer St C2
Broad St B2
Burton-Taylor
Theatre B2
Bus Station B1
Canal St A1
Cardigan St A1
CarfaxTower . . . B2
Castle B1
Castle St B1
Catte St B2
Cemetery C1
Christ Church (Coll) B2
Christ Church
Cathedral † . . . C2
Christ Church
Meadow C2
City of Oxford Coll . C1
Clarendon Centre . B2
Cornmarket St . . B2
Corpus Christi
(Coll) B2
County Hall B1
Covered Market . . B2
Cowley Place . . . C3
Cranham St A1
CranhamTerr . . . A1
Cricket Ground . . C1
Crown & County
Courts B3
Deer Park B3
Exeter (Coll) B2
Fire Sta A1
Folly Bridge C2
George St B1
Great Clarendon St A1
Harris Manchester
(Coll) B2
Hart St A1
Hertford (Coll) . . B2
High St B2
Hollybush Row . . B1
Holywell St B2
Hythe Bridge St . . B1
Ice Rink A1
Information Ctr . . B2
Jericho St A1
Jesus (Coll) B2
Jowett Walk B3
Juxon St A1
Keble (Coll) A2
Keble Rd A2
Library A2
Linacre (Coll) . . . A3
Lincoln (Coll) . . . B2
Little Clarendon St . A1
Longwall St B3
Magdalen (Coll) . . B3
Magdalen Bridge . B3
Magdalen St B2
Magistrate's Court . C2
Manor Rd B3
Mansfield (Coll) . . A2
Mansfield Rd . . . B3
Market B2
Marlborough Rd . . C2
Martyrs' Meml . . B2
Merton (Coll) . . . B2
Merton Field . . . C2
Merton St B2
Museum of
Modern Art . . . B2
Mus of Oxford . . B2
Museum Rd A2
New College (Coll) B2
New Inn Hall St . . B2
New Rd B1
NewTheatre . . . B2
Nuffield (Coll) . . . B1
Observatory A1
Observatory St . . A1
Odeon B1/B2
Old Fire Station . B1
Old Greyfriars St . C2
Oriel (Coll) B2
Oxford Castle &
Prison B1
Oxford University
Research Centres . A1
Oxpens Rd C1
Paradise Sq C1
Paradise St B1
Park End St B1
Parks Rd A2/B2
Pembroke (Coll) . . C2

Phoenix A1
Picture Gallery . . C2
Plantation Rd . . . A1
Playhouse B2
Police Station . . . B2
Post Office . . . A1/B2
Pusey St B1
Queen's (Coll) . . . B3
Queen's La B2
Radcliffe Camera
. . . . B2
Rewley Rd B1
Richmond Rd . . . A1
Rose La B3
Ruskin (Coll) . . . B1
Said Bsns School . A1
St Aldates C2
St Anne's (Coll) . . A1
St Antony's (Coll) . A1
St Bernard's Rd . . A1
St Catherine's (Coll) B3
St Cross Building . B3
St Cross Rd B3
St Edmund Hall
(Coll) B3
St Giles St A2
St Hilda's (Coll) . . C3
St John St B1
St John's (Coll) . . B2
St John's St A2
St Mary the Virgin
. . . . B2
St Michael at the
Northgate B2
St Peter's (Coll) . . B1
StThomas St . . . B1
Science Area . . . A2
Science Museum . B2
Sheldonian
Theatre B2
Somerville (Coll) . A1
South Parks Rd . . A2
Speedwell St . . . C2
Sports Ground . . C3
Thames St C1
Town Hall B2
Trinity (Coll) B2
Turl St B2
Univ Coll (Coll) . . B2
Univ Natural History
Museum & Pitt Rivers
Museum A2
University Parks . . A2
Wadham (Coll) . . B2
Walton Cres A1
Walton St A1
Western Rd C2
Westgate C2
Woodstock Rd . . A1
Worcester (Coll) . . B1

Perth 193
AK Bell Library . . B1
Abbot Cres C1
Abbot St C1
Albany Terr A1
Albert Monument . A3
Alexandra St . . . B2
Atholl St A2
Balhousie Ave . . . A2
Balhousie Castle &
Black Watch
Museum A2
Balhousie St A2
Ballantine Place . . A1
Barossa Place . . . A2
Barossa St A2
Barrack St A2
Bell's Sports Ctr . . A2
Bellwood C3
Blair St B1
Burgh Ave C2
Bus Station B2
Caledonian Rd . . B1
Canal Cres B1
Canal St B2
Cavendish Ave . . C1
Charles St B2
Charlotte Place . . A2
Charlotte St A2
Church St A1
City Hall B2
Club House B2
Clyde Place C1
Coach Park B2
Commercial St . . B2
Concert Hall . . . B2
Council Chambers . B2
County Place . . . B1
Court B2
Craigie Place . . . C2
Crieff Rd A1
Croft Park B1
Cross St B2
Darnhall Cres . . . C1
Darnhall Dr C1
Dewars Centre . . B1
Dundee Rd B3
Dunkeld Rd A1
Earl's Dykes B1
Edinburgh Rd . . . C2
Eastgate B2
East Station Road . B2
Fergusson B2
Feus Rd A1
Fire Station A1
Foundary La B1
Friar St B1
George St B2
Glamis Place . . . C1
Glasgow Rd B1
Glenearn Rd C2
Glover St B1/C1
Golf Course A3
Gowrie St A3
Gray St A3
Graybank Rd . . . B1
Greyfriars Burial Gd B3
Hay St A2
High St B2/B3
Inchaffray St . . . A1
Ind/Retail Park . . A1
Information Ctr . . B2
Isla Rd A3
James St B3
Kenmore St A1
King Edward St . . B2
King James VI
Golf Course . . . A3
Kings Place C2
Kinnoull Causeway B1
Kinnoull St B2
Knowelea Place . . C1
KnoweleaTerr . . . C1
Leisure Pool C2
Leonard St B2

Lickley St A3
Lochie Brae A3
Long Causeway . . A1
Low St A1
Main St A1
Marshall Place . . C2
Melville St A2
Mill St B2
Milne St B2
Murray Cres C1
Murray St B2
Needless Rd C1
New Rd B1
North Inch A2
North Methven St . A2
Park Place C1
Perth B1
Perth Bridge A3
Perth Business Pk . A1
Perth Museum &
Art Gallery B2
Perth Station . . . B2
Pickletullum Rd . . C1
Pitheavlis Cres . . . C1
Playhouse B1
Police Station . B2/C2
Pomarium St . . . B1
Princes St B2
Priory Place C2
Queen St C1
Queen's Bridge . . B3
Queen's (Coll) . . . B3
Riggs Rd B1
Riverside A3
Riverside Park . . . A3
Rodney Gdns . . . C3
RoseTerr A2
St Catherine's
Rd A1/A2
St Catherine's
Retail Park A1
St John St B2
St John's Kirk . . . B2
St John's Shopping
Centre B2
St Leonards Bridge B2
St Ninians Cath † . A2
Scott Monument . A3
Scott St B2
Sheriff Court . . . B2
Shore Rd C3
Skate Park A3
South Inch C2
South Inch Bsns Ctr C2
South Inch Park . . C2
South InchView . . C2
South Methven St . B2
South St B2
South William St . B2
Stables,The A1
Stanners,The . . . A3
Stormont St A2
Strathmore St . . . A3
Stuart Ave C1
Superstore . . . B1/B2
Tay St B3
Union La A2
Victoria St B2
Watergate B2
Wellshill Cemetery A1
West Bridge St . . A3
West Mill St B1
Whitefriars Cres . . A1
Whitefriars St . . . A1
Wilson St B1
WindsorTerr C1
Woodside Cres . . C1
York Place B1
Young St C1

Peterborough 193
Athletics Arena . . A3
Bishop's Palace . . B2
Bishop's Rd . . B2/B3
Boongate B3
Bourges Boulevard A1
Bourges Retail
Park B1/B2
Bridge House
(Council Offices) . C2
Bridge St B2
Bright St A2
Broadway A2
Broadway A2
Brook St A2
Burghley Rd A3
Bus Station A2
Cavendish St . . . A3
Charles St A2
Church St B2
Church Walk . . . A2
Cobden Ave A3
Cobden St A3
Cowgate B2
Craig St A2
Crawthorne Rd . . A2
Cromwell Rd . . . A2
Dickens St A2
Eastfield Rd A3
Eastgate B3
East Station Road . B2
Fire Station A1
Fletton Ave C2
Frank Perkins
Parkway C3
Geneva St A2
George St A2
Gladstone St . . . A1
Glebe Rd C2
Gloucester Rd . . . C1
Granby St B3
Grove St C1
Guildhall B2
Hadrians Ct C3
Hankey St A2
Henry St A1
Hereward Cross
(shopping) B2
Hereward Rd . . . B3
Information Ctr . . B2
Jubilee St C1
Kent Rd A1
KeyTheatre C2
Kirkwood Close . . A1
Lea Gdns B1
Library B2
Lincoln Rd A1
London Rd C2
Long Causeway . . B2
Lower Bridge St . . C2
Magistrates Court . C2
Manor House St . . A2
Mayor's Walk . . . A1
Midland Rd B1
Monument St . . . A2
Morris St A2

Mus & Art Gallery . B2
NeneValley
Railway C1
New Rd A2
New Rd B1
Northminster . . . A2
Old Customs Ho . C2
Oundle Rd C1
Padholme Rd . . . A3
Palmerston Rd . . C1
Park Rd A1
Passport Office . . A2
Peterborough
Cathedral † . . . B2
Peterborough
NeneValley . . . B2
Peterborough
Station B1
Police Station . . . A2
Post Office . . . A3/B2
Priestgate B2
Queen's Walk . . . C2
Queensgate Centre B2
Railworld Wildlife
Haven C1
Regional Fitness &
Swimming Centre A3
River La B2
Rivergate
Shopping Centre . B2
Riverside Mead . . C3
Russell St A1
St John's St B2
St John's St A3
St Marks St A2
St Peter's Rd . . . B2
Saxon Rd A3
Spital Bridge . . . A1
Stagshaw Dr . . . C3
Star Rd A3
Superstore B1
Thorpe Lea Rd . . B1
Thorpe Rd B1
Thorpe's Lea Rd . . B1
TowerSt A2
Town Hall B2
Viersen Platz . . . B2
Vineyard Rd B3
Wake Rd B3
Wellington St . . . A3
Wentworth St . . . B2
Westgate A2
Weston Homes
Stadium
(Peterborough
United FC)The . . C2
Whalley St A3
Wharf Rd A1
Whitsed St A3
YMCA A3

Plymouth 193
Alma Rd A1
Anstis St B1
Armada Shopping
Centre B2
Armada St A2
Armada Way . . . B2
Arts Centre B2
Athenaeum C2
Athenaeum St . . . C2
Barbican C3
Barbican C3
Baring St A3
Bath St C1
Beaumont Park . . B3
Beaumont Rd . . . B3
Black Friars
Gin Distillery . . C2
Box,The A2
Breton Side B3
Coach Sta B2
Castle St C3
Catalina Dr A3
Chapel La C3
Church St B1
Cinnamon La . . . C3
Citadel Rd C2
Citadel Rd East . . C2
Civic Centre B2
Cliff Rd C2
Clifton Place . . . A3
Cobourg St A2
College of Art . . . A2
Continental Ferry
Port A1
Cornwall St B2
Crescent,The . . . C2
Dale Rd A2
Deptford Place . . A3
Derry Ave A2
Derry's Cross . . . B2
Drake Circus . . . B2
Drake Circus
Shopping Centre . B2
Drake Statue . . . C2
Eastlake St B2
Ebrington St . . . B3
Elizabethan Ho . . C3
Elliot St C2
Endsleigh Place . . A2
Exeter St B3
Fire Station B3
Fish Quay C3
Gibbons St A3
Glen Park Ave . . . A2
Grand Parade . . . C2
Great Western Rd . C1
Greenbank Rd . . . A3
GreenbankTerr . . A3
Guildhall B2
Hampton St B3
Harwell St B1
Hill Park Cres . . . A3
Hoe Approach . . . C2
Hoe Rd C2
Hoe,The C2
Hoegate St C3
Houndiscombe Rd . A2
Information Ctr . . C3
James St A2
Kensington Rd . . A3
King St B1
Lambhay Hill . . . C3
Leigham St C1
Library A2
Lipson Rd . . . A3/B3
Lockyer St C2
Lockyers Quay . . C3
Madeira Rd C2
Marina C3
Market B1

Market Ave B1
Martin St B1
Mayflower St . . . B2
Mayflower Stone
& Steps C3
Mayflower C3
Merchant's Ho . . B2
Millbay Rd B1
National Marine
Aquarium C3
Neswick St B1
New George St . . B2
New St C3
North Cross A2
North Hill A3
North Quay B3
North Rd East . . . A2
North Rd West . . A1
North St A3
Notte St C2
Octagon,The . . . B1
Octagon St B1
Pennycomequick
. . . . A1
Pier St C1
Plymouth Naval
Memorial C2
Plymouth Pavilions B1
Plymouth Sta . . . A2
Police Station . . . B2
Post Office . . B2,C1,C2
Princess St B2
Promenade,The . . C2
Prysten House . . C3
Queen Anne's Battery
Watersports Ctr . . C3
Radford Rd C1
Regent St B3
Rope Walk C3
Royal Citadel . . . C3
Royal Pde B2
RoyalTheatre . . . B2
Russell St B2
St Andrew's B2
St Andrew's Cross
. . . . B2
St Andrew's St . . B2
St Lawrence Rd . . A2
Saltash Rd A2
Shopmobility . . . B2
Smeaton'sTower . C2
SouthernTerr . . . A3
Southside St C3
Stuart Rd A1
Sutherland Rd . . . A3
Sutton Rd B3
Sydney St A1
Teats Hill Rd . . . C3
Tothill Ave B3
Union St B1
Univ of Plymouth . A2
Vauxhall St . . . B2/B3
Victoria Park . . . A1
Walker Terr C1
West Hoe Rd . . . C1
Western Approach . B1
Whittington St . . A1
Wyndham St . . . B1

Poole 194
Ambulance Station A3
Baiater Gdns . . . C2
Baiter Park C3
Ballard Close . . . C2
Ballard Rd C2
Bay Hog La B1
BMIThe Harbour
Hospital C1
Bridge Approach . C1
Bus Station B2
Castle St B2
Catalina Dr C3
Chapel La B2
Church St C1
Cinnamon La . . . B1
Colborne Close . . B3
Dear Hay La B2
Denmark La A3
Denmark Rd A3
Dolphin Ctr B2
East St B2
Elizabeth Rd . . . A3
Emerson Rd B2
Ferry Rd C1
FerryTerminal . . . C1
Fire Station A2
Freightliner
Terminal A1
Furnell Rd B3
Garland Rd A3
Green Rd B2
Heckford La A3
Heckford Rd A3
High St B2
High St North . . . A3
Hill St B2
Holes Bay Rd . . . A1
Hospital (A&E) . . C1
Information Ctr . . C2
Kingland Rd B3
Kingston Rd A3
Labrador Dr C3
Lagland St B2
Lander Close . . . B3
Lighthouse, Poole
Ctr for the Arts . B3
Longfleet Rd . . . A3
Maple Rd A3
Market Close . . . B2
Market St B2
Mount Pleasant Rd B3
New Harbour Rd . . C1
New Harbour Rd
South C1
New Harbour Rd
West C1
New Orchard . . . B1
New Quay Rd . . . B1
New St B2
Newfoundland Dr . B2
North St B2
Old Lifeboat C1
Old Orchard B2
Parish Rd A3
Park Lake Rd . . . C2
Parkstone Rd . . . A3
Perry Gdns C2
Pitwines Close . . B2
Police Station . . . B3
Poole Central Liby B2
Poole Lifting Bridge C1
Poole Park B3
Poole Station . . . B2
Poole Museum . . C1
Post Office B2
Quay,The C2

RNLI College . . . C1
St John's Rd A3
St Margaret's Rd . A3
St Mary's
Maternity Unit . . A3
St Mary's Rd A3
Seldown Bridge . . B3
Seldown La B3
Seldown Rd B3
Serpentine Rd . . . A2
Scaplen's Court . . C1
Shaftesbury Rd . . A3
Skinner St B2
Slipway C1
Stanley Rd C2
Sterte Ave A2
Sterte Ave West . . A1
Sterte Close A2
Sterte Esplanade . A2
Sterte Rd A2
Strand St C2
Superstore B3
Swimming Pool . . B3
Taverner Close . . B3
Thames St C1
Towngate Bridge . B2
Twin Sails Bridge . A1
Vallis Close A3
Waldren Close . . B3
West Quay C1
West Quay Rd . . . B1
West St C1
WestView Rd . . . A2
Whatleigh Close . C2
Wimborne Rd . . . A3

Portsmouth 194
Action Stations . . C1
Admiralty Rd . . . A1
Alfred Rd A2
Anglesea Rd B2
Arundel St B3
Aspex C3
Bishop St A2
Broad St C1
Buckingham Ho . B2
Burnaby Rd B2
Bus Station B3
Camber Dock . . . C1
Cambridge Rd . . . B2
Car Ferry to Isle of
Wight C1
Cascades
Shopping Centre . A3
Castle Rd C2
Civic Offices B3
Clarence Pier . . . C1
College St B1
Commercial Rd . . A3
Cottage Grove . . C3
Cross St A1
Cumberland St . . A1
Duisburg Way . . . C1
Durham St A3
East St C1
Edinburgh Rd . . . B2
Elm Grove C3
Emirates Spinnaker
Tower B1
Governor's Grn . . C1
Great Southsea St . C2
Green Rd C3
Greetham St B3
Grosvenor St . . . C3
Groundlings A2
Grove Rd North . . C3
Grove Rd South . . C3
Guildhall B3
Guildhall Walk . . B3
Gunwharf Quays . C1
Designer Outlet . . B1
Gunwharf Rd . . . B1
Hambrook St . . . C2
HampshireTerr . . B2
Hanover St A1
Hard,The B1
High St C2
HM Naval Base . . A1
HMS Nelson (Royal
Naval Barracks) . A2
HMS Monitor
M.33 . . . . A1
HMSVictory A1
HMS Warrior . . . B1
Hovercraft
Terminal C2
Hyde Park Rd . . . B3
Information Ctr
. . . . A1/B3
Isambard Brunel Rd B3
Isle of Wight Car Ferry
Terminal C1
Kent Rd C2
Kent St A1
King St C2
King's Rd C2
King'sTerr C2
Lake Rd A3
Law Courts B3
Library B3
Long Curtain Rd . . C1
Marina A1
Market Way A3
Marmion Rd C3
Mary Rose A1
Middle St C3
Millennium
Promenade
Walk B1/C1
Museum Rd B2
National Museum of
the Royal Navy . . A1
Naval Rec Gd . . . C2
Nightingale Rd . . C2
Norfolk St C3
North St A2
Osborne Rd C3
Paradise St A3
Park Rd B2
Passenger Catamaran
to Isle of Wight . . B1
Passenger Ferry to
Gosport B1
Pelham Rd C3
Pembroke Gdns . . C2
Pier Rd C2
Point Battery . . . C1
Police Station . . . B3
Portsmouth &
Southsea Sta . . . B3
Portsmouth Harbour
Station B1
Portsmouth Historic
Dockyard A1
Portsmouth Museum
& Art Gallery . . . B2

210 Preston • Reading • St Andrews • Salisbury • Scarborough • Sheffield • Shrewsbury • Southampton

Post Office . . . A1/A2/A3/B3
Queen St . . . A1
Queen's Cres . . . C3
Ravelin Park . . . B2
Register Office . . . B2
Round Tower ✦ . . . C1
Royal Garrison Church . . . C1
St Edward's Rd . . . C3
St George's Rd . . . B2
St George's Sq . . . B1
St George's Way . . . B2
St James's Rd . . . B3
St James's St . . . A2
St John's Cathedral (RC) ✝ . . . A3
St Thomas's Cath ✝ . . . C1
St Thomas's St . . . B2
Shopmobility . . . A3/B1
Somers Rd . . . B3
Southsea Common . . . C2
Southsea Terr . . . C2
Square Tower ✦ . . . C1
Station St . . . A3
Town Fortifications ✦ . . . C1
Unicorn Rd . . . A2
United Services Recreation Ground . . . B2
University of Portsmouth . . . A2/B2
University of Portsmouth . . . B3
Upper Arundel St . . . A3
Victoria Ave . . . C2
Victoria Park . . . A2
Victory Gate . . . A1
Vue . . . B1
Warblington St . . . B1
Western Pde . . . C2
White Hart Rd . . . C1
Winston Churchill Ave . . . B3

Preston 194

Adelphi St . . . A2
Anchor Ct . . . B3
Aqueduct St . . . A1
Ardee Rd . . . C1
Arthur St . . . B2
Ashton St . . . A1
Avenham La . . . B3
Avenham Park . . . C3
Avenham Rd . . . B3
Avenham St . . . B3
Bairstow St . . . B3
Balderstone Rd . . . C1
Beamont Dr . . . A1
Beech St South . . . C2
Bird St . . . C1
Bow La . . . B2
Brieryfield Rd . . . A1
Broadgate . . . C1
Brook St . . . A2
Bus Station . . . A3
Butler St . . . B2
Cannon St . . . B3
Carlton St . . . A1
Chaddock St . . . B3
Channel Way . . . B1
Chapel St . . . B3
Christ Church St . . . B2
Christian Rd . . . B2
Cold Bath St . . . A2
Coleman Ct . . . C1
Connaught Rd . . . C2
Corporation St . . . A2/B2
County Hall . . . B2
Cricket Ground . . . C2
Croft St . . . A1
Cross St . . . B3
Crown Court . . . A3
Crown St . . . A3
East Cliff . . . C3
East Cliff Rd . . . B3
Edward St . . . A2
Elizabeth St . . . A3
Euston St . . . B1
Fishergate . . . B2/B3
Fishergate Hill . . . B2
Fishergate Shopping Centre . . . B2
Fitzroy St . . . B1
Fleetwood St . . . A1
Friargate . . . A3
Fylde Rd . . . A1/A2
Gerrard St . . . B2
Glover's Ct . . . B3
Good St . . . B2
Grafton St . . . B2
Great George St . . . A3
Great Shaw St . . . A3
Greenbank St . . . A2
Guild Way . . . B1
Guild Hall & Charter . . . B3
Guildhall St . . . B3
Harrington St . . . A2
Harris Museum . . . B3
Hartington Rd . . . B1
Hasset Close . . . C2
Heatley St . . . B2
Hind St . . . C2
Information Ctr . . . B3
Kilruddery Rd . . . C1
Lancashire Archives . . . B2
Lancaster Rd . . . A3/B3
Latham St . . . B3
Lauderdale St . . . C2
Lawson St . . . A3
Leighton St . . . A2
Leyland Rd . . . C1
Library . . . A1
Library . . . B3
Liverpool Rd . . . C1
Lodge St . . . B2
Lune St . . . B3
Magistrate's Court . . . A3
Main Sprit West . . . B3
Maresfield Rd . . . C1
Market St West . . . A3
Marsh La . . . B1/B2
Maudland Bank . . . A2
Maudland Rd . . . A2
Meadow Ct . . . C2
Meath Rd . . . C1
Miller Arcade ✦ . . . B3
Miller Park . . . C3
Moor La . . . A3
Mount St . . . B3
North Rd . . . A3
North St . . . A3
Northcote Rd . . . B1
Old Milestones . . . B1
Old Tram Rd . . . C3
Pedder St . . . A1/A2
Peel St . . . A2
Penwortham Bridge . . . C2
Penwortham New Bridge . . . C1
Pitt St . . . B2
Playhouse . . . A3
Police Station . . . A3
Portway . . . B1
Post Office . . . B3
Preston Station . . . B2
Retail Park . . . B2
Ribble Bank St . . . B2
Ribble Viaduct . . . C2
Ribblesdale Place . . . B3
Ringway . . . B3
River Parade . . . C1
Riverside . . . C2
St George's Shopping Centre . . . B3
St Georges . . . B3
St John's Minster . . . B3
St Johns Shopping Centre . . . A3
St Mark's Rd . . . A1
St Walburges . . . A1
Salisbury Rd . . . B1
Sessions House . . . B3
Snow Hill . . . A3
South End . . . C2
South Meadow La . . . C2
Spa Rd . . . B1
Sports Ground . . . C2
Strand Rd . . . B1
Syke St . . . B3
Talbot Rd . . . B1
Taylor St . . . C1
Tithebarn St . . . A3
Town Hall . . . B3
Tulketh Brow . . . A1
University of Central Lancashire . . . A2
Valley Rd . . . C1
Victoria St . . . A2
Walker St . . . A3
Walton's Parade . . . B2
Warwick St . . . A3
Wellfield Business Park . . . A1
Wellfield Rd . . . A1
Wellington St . . . A1
West Cliff . . . C2
West Strand . . . A1
Winckley Rd . . . C1
Winckley Square . . . B3
Wolseley Rd . . . C2

Reading 194

Abbey Ruins ✝ . . . B2
Abbey Sq . . . B2
Abbey St . . . B2
Abbot's Walk . . . B2
Acacia Rd . . . C2
Addington Rd . . . C3
Addison Rd . . . A1
Allcroft Rd . . . C3
Alpine St . . . C2
Baker St . . . B1
Berkeley Ave . . . C1
Bridge St . . . B1
Brigham Rd . . . A1
Broad St . . . B1
Broad Street Mall . . . B1
Carey St . . . B1
Castle Hill . . . C1
Castle St . . . B1
Causeway, The . . . A3
Caversham Rd . . . A1
Christchurch Meadows . . . A2
Civic Offices . . . B1
Coley Hill . . . C1
Coley Place . . . C1
Craven Rd . . . C3
Crown St . . . C2
De Montfort Rd . . . A1
Denmark Rd . . . C3
Duke St . . . B2
East St . . . B2
Edgehill St . . . C2
Eldon Rd . . . B3
Eldon Terr . . . B3
Elgar Rd . . . C1
Erleigh Rd . . . C3
Field Rd . . . C1
Fire Station . . . A1
Fobney St . . . B1
Forbury Gdns . . . B2
Forbury Rd . . . B2
Forbury Retail Park . . . B2
Francis St . . . C1
Friar St . . . B1
Garrard St . . . B1
Gas Works Rd . . . B3
George St . . . A2
Great Knollys St . . . B1
Greyfriars . . . B1
Grove, The . . . B2
Gun St . . . B1
Henry St . . . C1
Hexagon Theatre, The . . . B1
Hill's Meadow . . . A2
Howard St . . . B1
Inner Distribution Rd . . . B1
Katesgrove La . . . C1
Kenavon Dr . . . B2
Kendrick Rd . . . C2
King's Meadow Recreation Gd . . . A2
King's Rd . . . B2
Library . . . B2
London Rd . . . C3
London St . . . B2
Lynmouth Rd . . . A1
Magistrate's Court . . . B1
Market Place . . . B2
Mill La . . . B2
Mill Rd . . . A2
Minster St . . . B1
Morgan Rd . . . C3
Mount Pleasant . . . C2
Museum of English Rural Life (MERL) . . . C3
Napier Rd . . . A2
Newark St . . . C2
Newport Rd . . . A1
Oracle Shopping Centre, The . . . B1
Orts Rd . . . B3
Oxford Road . . . B1
Pell St . . . C1
Post Office . . . B1
Queen Victoria St . . . B1
Queen's Rd . . . A2
Queen's Rd . . . B2
Randolph Rd . . . A1
Reading Bridge . . . A2
Reading College . . . B3
Reading Station . . . A1
Redlands Rd . . . C3
Riverside Mus . . . B3
Rose Kiln La . . . C1
Royal Berkshire Medical Mus . . . C3
Royal Berks Hospital (A&E) . . . C3
St Giles . . . C2
St Laurence . . . B2
St Mary's . . . B1
St Mary's Butts . . . B1
St Saviour's Rd . . . C1
Send Rd . . . A3
Sherman Rd . . . C2
Sidmouth St . . . B2
Silver St . . . C2
South St . . . B2
South St Arts Ctr ✦ . . . B2
Southampton St . . . C2
Station Rd . . . B1
Superstore . . . A3
Swansea Rd . . . A1
Thames Lido . . . A2
Tudor Road . . . A1
Univ of Reading . . . C3
Valpy St . . . B2
Vastern Rd . . . A1
Vue . . . B2
Waldeck St . . . C2
Watlington St . . . B3
West St . . . B1
Whitby Dr . . . C3
Wolseley St . . . C1
York Rd . . . A1
Zinzan St . . . B1

St Andrews 195

Abbey St . . . B2
Abbey Walk . . . B3
Abbotsford Cres . . . A1
Albany Pk . . . C3
Allan Robertson Dr . . . C2
Ambulance Station . . . C1
Anstruther Rd . . . C3
Argyle St . . . B1
Auld Burn Rd . . . B2
Bassaguard Ind Est . . . B1
Bell St . . . B2
Blackfriars Chapel (Ruins) . . . B2
Boase Ave . . . B2
Braid Cres . . . C3
Brewster Place . . . C3
Bridge St . . . B1
British Golf Mus . . . A1
Broomfaulds Ave . . . C1
Bruce Embankment . . . A1
Bruce St . . . C2
Bus Station . . . A1
Byre Theatre . . . B2
Canongate . . . C1
Cathedral and Priory (Ruins) ✝ . . . B3
Cemetery . . . B1
Chamberlain St . . . C1
Church St . . . B2
Churchill Cres . . . C2
City Rd . . . A1
Claybraes . . . C1
Cockshaugh Public Park . . . B1
Cosmos Com Ctr . . . B3
Council Office . . . A2
Crawford Gdns . . . C1
Doubledykes Rd . . . B1
Drumcarrow Rd . . . C1
East Sands . . . B3
East Scores . . . A3
Fire Station . . . C1
Forrest St . . . C1
Fraser Ave . . . C1
Freddie Tait St . . . C2
Gateway Centre . . . A1
Glebe Rd . . . B2
Golf Place . . . A1
Grange Rd . . . C3
Greenside Place . . . B2
Greyfriars Gdns . . . A2
Hamilton Ave . . . C2
Hepburn Gdns . . . B1
Holy Trinity . . . B2
Horseleys Park . . . C1
Information Ctr . . . B2
Irvine Cres . . . C3
James Robb Ave . . . C1
James St . . . B1
John Knox Rd . . . C1
Kennedy Gdns . . . B1
Kilrymont Close . . . C3
Kilrymont Place . . . C3
Kilrymont Rd . . . C3
Kinburn Park . . . B1
Kinkell Terr . . . C3
Kinnesburn Rd . . . B2
Ladebraes Walk . . . B2
Lady Buchan's Cave . . . A3
Lamberton Place . . . C1
Lamond Dr . . . C2
Langlands Rd . . . B2
Largo Rd . . . C1
Learmonth Place . . . C1
Library . . . B2
Links Clubhouse . . . A1
Links, The . . . A1
Livingstone Cres . . . B2
Long Rocks . . . A2
Madras College . . . B2
Market St . . . A2
Martyr's Monument . . . A1
Murray Pk . . . A2
Murray Place . . . A2
Museum of the University of St Andrews (MUSA) ✦ . . . A2
Nelson St . . . B2
New Course, The . . . A1
New Picture Ho . . . A2
North Castle St . . . A3
North St . . . A2
Old Course, The . . . A1
Old Station Rd . . . A1
Pends, The . . . B3
Pilmour Links . . . A1
Pipeland Rd . . . B2/C2
Police Sta . . . A2/C1
Post Office . . . B2
Preservation Trust . . . B2
Priestden Park . . . C3
Priestden Place . . . C3
Priestden Rd . . . C3
Queen's Gdns . . . B2
Queen's Terr . . . B2
Roundhill Rd . . . C2
Royal & Ancient Golf Club . . . A1
St Andrews . . . B1
St Andrews Aquarium . . . A2
St Andrews Botanic Garden . . . B1
St Andrews Castle (Ruins) & Visitor Centre . . . A2
St Leonard's Sch . . . B3
St Mary St . . . B3
St Mary's College . . . B2
St Nicholas St . . . C3
St Rules Tower ✦ . . . B3
St Salvator's Coll . . . A2
Sandyhill Cres . . . C2
Sandyhill Rd . . . C2
Scooniehill Rd . . . C2
Scores, The . . . A2
Shields Ave . . . C3
Shoolbraids . . . C2
Shore, The . . . B3
Sloan St . . . B1
South St . . . B2
Spottiswoode Gdns . . . C1
Station Rd . . . A1
Swilcen Bridge . . . A1
Tom Morris Dr . . . C2
Tom Stewart La . . . C1
Town Hall . . . B2
Union St . . . A2
Univ Chapel . . . A2
University Library . . . A2
Univ of St Andrews . . . A1
Viaduct Walk . . . B1
War Memorial . . . A3
Wardlaw Gdns . . . B1
Warrack St . . . C3
Watson Ave . . . B2
West Port . . . B2
West Sands . . . A1
Westview . . . B2
Windmill Rd . . . A1
Winram Place . . . C1
Wishart Gdns . . . C2
Woodburn Pk . . . B3
Woodburn Place . . . B3
Woodburn Terr . . . B3
Younger Hall . . . A2

Salisbury 195

Albany Rd . . . A2
Arts Centre . . . A3
Ashley Rd . . . A1
Avon Approach . . . A2
Ayleswade Rd . . . C2
Bedwin St . . . A2
Belle Vue . . . A2
Bishops Walk . . . B2
Blue Boar Row . . . B2
Bourne Ave . . . A3
Bourne Hill . . . A3
Britford La . . . C2
Broad Walk . . . C2
Brown St . . . B2
Castle St . . . A2
Catherine St . . . B2
Chapter House . . . B2
Church House . . . B2
Churchfields Rd . . . B1
Churchill Gdns . . . C3
Churchill Way East . . . B3
Churchill Way North . . . A3
Churchill Way South . . . C2
Churchill Way West . . . A1
City Hall . . . B2
Close Wall . . . B2
Coldharbour La . . . A1
College St . . . A3
Council and Registry Offices . . . A3
Court . . . A1
Crane Bridge Rd . . . B2
Crane St . . . B2
Cricket Ground . . . C1
Culver St South . . . B3
De Vaux Place . . . C2
Devizes Rd . . . A1
Dews Rd . . . B1
Elm Grove . . . B3
Elm Grove Rd . . . A3
Endless St . . . A2
Estcourt Rd . . . A3
Exeter St . . . C2
Fairview Rd . . . A3
Fire Station . . . A1
Fisherton St . . . A1
Folkestone Rd . . . C1
Fowlers Hill . . . B3
Fowlers Rd . . . B3
Friary La . . . B2
Friary, The . . . B3
Gas La . . . A1
Gigant St . . . B3
Greencroft . . . B3
Greencroft St . . . A3
Guildhall . . . B2
Hall of John Halle . . . B2
Hamilton Rd . . . A2
Harnham Mill . . . B1
Harnham Rd . . . C1/C2
High St . . . B2
House of John A'Port . . . B2
Information Ctr . . . B2
Kelsey Rd . . . A3
King's Rd . . . A2
Laverstock Rd . . . B3
Library . . . B2
London Rd . . . A3
Lower St . . . C1
Maltings, The . . . B2
Manor Rd . . . A3
Marsh La . . . A1
Medieval Hall . . . B2
Milford Hill . . . B3
Milford St . . . B3
Mill Rd . . . B1
Mill Stream App . . . A2
Mompesson Ho . . . B2
New Bridge Rd . . . C2
New Canal . . . B2
New Harnham Rd . . . C2
New St . . . B2
North Canonry . . . B2
North Gate . . . B2
North Walk . . . B2
Old Blandford Rd . . . C1
Old Deanery . . . B2
Old George Hall . . . B2
Park St . . . A3
Parsonage Green . . . C1
Playhouse Theatre . . . A2
Police Station . . . A3
Post Office . . . A2/B2
Poultry Cross . . . B2
Queen Elizabeth Gdns . . . B1
Queen's Rd . . . A3
Rampart Rd . . . B3
Rifles, The . . . B2
St Ann St . . . B2
St Ann's Gate . . . B2
St Marks Rd . . . A3
St Martins . . . B3
St Paul's . . . A1
St Paul's Rd . . . A1
St Thomas . . . B2
Salisbury Cathedral ✝ . . . B2
Salisbury Cathedral School (Bishop's Palace) . . . C2
Salisbury Museum, The . . . B2
Salisbury Sta . . . A1
Salt La . . . A3
Saxon Rd . . . C1
Scots La . . . A2
Shady Bower . . . B3
Shopmobility . . . B2
South Canonry . . . C2
South Gate . . . C2
Southampton Rd . . . B2
Spire View . . . A1
Sports Ground . . . C3
Tollgate Rd . . . B3
Town Path . . . B1
Wain-a-Long Rd . . . A3
Wessex Rd . . . A3
West Walk . . . C2
Wilton Rd . . . A1
Wiltshire College . . . B3
Winchester St . . . B3
Windsor Rd . . . A1
Wyndham Rd . . . A2
YHA . . . B3
York Rd . . . A1

Scarborough 195

Aberdeen Walk . . . B2
Albert Rd . . . A2
Albion Rd . . . C2
Auborough St . . . B2
Balmoral Ctr . . . B2
Belle Vue St . . . C1
Belmont Rd . . . C2
Blenheim Terrace . . . A2
Brunswick Shopping Centre . . . B2
Castle Dykes . . . B3
Castle Hill . . . A3
Castle Rd . . . B2
Castle Walls . . . A3
Castlegate . . . B3
Cemetery . . . C1
Central Tramway ✦ . . . B2
Coach Park . . . B1
Columbus Ravine . . . A1
Court . . . B1
Crescent, The . . . C2
Cricket Ground . . . A1
Cross St . . . B2
Crown Terr . . . C2
Dean Rd . . . B1
Devonshire Dr . . . A1
East Harbour . . . B3
East Pier . . . B3
Eastborough . . . B2
Elmville Ave . . . B1
Esplanade . . . C2
Falconers Rd . . . B2
Falsgrave Rd . . . C1
Fire Station . . . B2
Foreshore Rd . . . B2
Friargate . . . B2
Gladstone Rd . . . B1
Gladstone St . . . B1
Hollywood Plaza . . . A1
Holms, The . . . A3
Hoxton Rd . . . B1
King St . . . B2
Library . . . B2
Lifeboat Station ✦ . . . B3
Londesborough Rd . . . C1
Longwestgate . . . B3
Marine Dr . . . A3
Luna Park . . . B3
Miniature Railway . . . A1
Nelson St . . . B1
Newborough . . . B2
Nicolas St . . . B2
North Marine Rd . . . A1
North St . . . B2
Northway . . . B1
Old Harbour . . . B3
Olympia Leisure ✦ . . . B2
Peasholm Park . . . A1
Peasholm Rd . . . A1
Police Station . . . B1
Post Office . . . B2
Princess St . . . B3
Prospect Rd . . . B1
Queen St . . . B2
Queen's Parade . . . A2
Queen's Tower (Remains) . . . A3
Ramshill Rd . . . C2
Roman Signal Sta . . . A3
Roscoe St . . . C1
Rotunda Mus . . . C2
Royal Albert Dr . . . A2
Royal Albert Park . . . A2
St Martin-on-the-Hill . . . C2
St Martin's Ave . . . C2
St Mary's . . . B3
St Thomas St . . . B2
Sandside . . . B3
Scarborough . . . C1
Scarborough Art Gallery . . . C2
Scarborough Bowls Centre . . . A1
Scarborough Castle . . . A3
Shopmobility . . . C2
Somerset Terr . . . C2
South Cliff Lift ✦ . . . C2
Spa Theatre, The . . . C2
Spa, The ✦ . . . C2
Stephen Joseph Theatre . . . C1
Tennyson Ave . . . B1
Tollergate . . . B2
Town Hall . . . B2
Trafalgar Rd . . . B1
Trafalgar Square . . . A1
Trafalgar St West . . . B1
Valley Bridge Par . . . C2
Valley Rd . . . C1
Vernon Rd . . . C2
Victoria Park Mount . . . A1
Victoria Rd . . . B1
West Pier . . . B3
Westborough . . . C1
Westover Rd . . . C1
Westwood . . . C1
Woodall Ave . . . A1
YMCA Theatre . . . B2
York Place . . . B2
Yorkshire Coast College (Westwood Campus) . . . C1

Sheffield 196

Addy Dr . . . A2
Addy St . . . A2
Adelphi St . . . A3
Albert Terrace Rd . . . A3
Albion St . . . A2
Aldred Rd . . . A1
Allen St . . . A4
Alma St . . . A4
Angel St . . . B5
Arundel Gate . . . B5
Arundel St . . . C4
Ashberry Rd . . . A2
Ashdell Rd . . . C1
Ashgate Rd . . . C1
Athletics Centre . . . B2
Attercliffe Rd . . . A6
Bailey St . . . B4
Ball St . . . A4
Balm Green . . . B4
Bank St . . . B4
Barber Rd . . . A2
Bard St . . . B5
Barker's Pool . . . B4
Bates St . . . A1
Beech Hill Rd . . . C1
Beet St . . . B3
Bellefield St . . . A3
Bernard Rd . . . A6
Bernard St . . . B6
Birkendale . . . A2
Birkendale Rd . . . A2
Birkendale View . . . A1
Bishop St . . . C4
Blackwell Place . . . B6
Blake St . . . A2
Blonk St . . . A5
Bolsover St . . . B2
Botanical Gdns . . . C1
Bower Rd . . . A1
Bradley St . . . A1
Bramall La . . . C4
Bramwell St . . . A3
Bridge St . . . A4/A5
Brighton Terrace Rd . . . A1
Broad La . . . B3
Broad St . . . B6
Brocco St . . . A3
Brook Hill . . . B3
Broomfield Rd . . . C1
Broomgrove Rd . . . C2
Broomhall Place . . . C3
Broomhall Rd . . . C2
Broomhall St . . . C3
Broomspring La . . . C2
Brown St . . . C5
Brunswick St . . . B3
Burgess St . . . B4
Burlington St . . . A2
Burns Rd . . . A2
Cadman St . . . A6
Cambridge St . . . B4
Campo La . . . B4
Carver St . . . B4
Castle Square . . . B5
Castlegate . . . A5
Cathedral . . . B4
Cathedral (RC) ✝ . . . B4
Cavendish St . . . B3
Charles St . . . C4
Charter Row . . . C4
Children's Hosp . . . B2
Church St . . . B4
City Hall . . . B4
City Hall . . . B4
City Rd . . . C6
Claremont Cres . . . B2
Claremont Place . . . B2
Clarke St . . . C3
Clarkegrove Rd . . . C2
Clarkehouse Rd . . . C1
Clarkson St . . . B2
Cobden View Rd . . . A1
Collegiate Cres . . . C2
Commercial St . . . B5
Commonside . . . A1
Conduit Rd . . . B1
Cornish St . . . A3
Corporation St . . . A4
Cricket Inn Rd . . . B6
Cromwell St . . . A1
Crookes Rd . . . B1
Crookes Valley Park . . . B2
Crookes Valley Rd . . . B2
Crookesmoor Rd . . . A2
Crown Court . . . A4
Crucible Theatre . . . B5
Cutlers' Hall . . . B4
Cutlers Gate . . . A6
Daniel Hill . . . A2
Dental Hospital . . . B2
Derek Dooley Way . . . A5
Devonshire Green . . . B3
Devonshire St . . . B3
Division St . . . B4
Dorset St . . . C2
Dover St . . . A3
Duchess Rd . . . C5
Duke St . . . B5
Duncombe St . . . A1
Durham Rd . . . B2
Earl St . . . C4
Earl Way . . . C4
Ecclesall Rd . . . C3
Edward St . . . B3
Effingham Rd . . . A6
Effingham St . . . A6
Egerton St . . . C3
Eldon St . . . B3
Elmore Rd . . . B1
Exchange St . . . B5
Eyre St . . . C4
Fargate . . . B4
Farm Rd . . . C5
Fawcett St . . . A3
Filey St . . . B3
Fir St . . . A1
Fire Station . . . C4
Fitzalan Square/ Ponds Forge . . . B5
Fitzwater Rd . . . C6
Fitzwilliam Gate . . . C4
Fitzwilliam St . . . B3
Flat St . . . B5
Foley St . . . A6
Foundry Climbing Centre . . . A4
Fulton Rd . . . A1
Furnace Hill . . . A4
Furnival Rd . . . A5
Furnival Sq . . . C4
Furnival St . . . C4
Garden St . . . B3
Gell St . . . B3
Gibraltar St . . . A4
Glebe Rd . . . B1
Glencoe Rd . . . C6
Glossop Rd . . . B2/B3/C1
Gloucester St . . . C2
Government Offices . . . C4
Granville Rd . . . C6
Granville Rd / The Sheffield Coll . . . B5
Graves Gallery . . . B5
Green La . . . A4
Hadfield St . . . A1
Hanover St . . . C3
Hanover Way . . . C3
Harcourt Rd . . . B1
Harmer La . . . B5
Havelock St . . . C2
Hawley St . . . B4
Haymarket . . . B5
Headford St . . . C3
Heavygate Rd . . . A1
Henry St . . . A3
High St . . . B4
Hodgson St . . . C3
Holberry Gdns . . . C2
Hollis Croft . . . B4
Holly St . . . B4
Hounsfield Rd . . . B3
Howard Rd . . . A1
Hoyle St . . . A3
Hyde Park . . . A6
Infirmary Rd . . . A3
Infirmary Rd . . . A3
Jericho St . . . A3
Johnson St . . . A5
Kelham Island Industrial Mus . . . A4
Lawson Rd . . . C1
Leadmill Rd . . . C5
Leadmill St . . . C5
Leadmill, The ✦ . . . C5
Leamington St . . . A1
Leavygreave Rd . . . B3
Lee Croft . . . B4
Leopold St . . . B4
Leveson St . . . A6
Library . . . A2/B5/C1
Light, The . . . C4
Lyceum Theatre . . . B5
Malinda St . . . A3
Maltravers St . . . A5
Manor Oaks Rd . . . B6
Mappin St . . . B3
Marlborough Rd . . . B1
Mary St . . . C4
Matilda St . . . C4
Matlock Rd . . . A1
Meadow St . . . A3
Melbourn Rd . . . A1
Melbourne Ave . . . C1
Millennium Galleries . . . B5
Milton St . . . C3
Mitchell St . . . B3
Mona Ave . . . A1
Mona Rd . . . A1
Montgomery Terrace Rd . . . A3
Montgomery Theatre . . . B4
Monument Grounds . . . C6
Moor Oaks Rd . . . B1
Moor, The . . . C4
Moor Market . . . C4
Moore St . . . C3
Mowbray St . . . A4
Mushroom La . . . B2
National Emergency Service . . . A4
National Videogame Museum . . . B5
Netherthorpe Rd . . . B3
Netherthorpe Rd . . . B3
Newbould La . . . C1
Nile St . . . C1
Norfolk Park Rd . . . C6
Norfolk Rd . . . C6
Norfolk St . . . B4
North Church St . . . B4
Northfield Rd . . . A1
Northumberland Rd . . . B1
Nursery St . . . A5
O2 Academy . . . B5
Oakholme Rd . . . C1
Octagon . . . B2
Odeon . . . B5
Old St . . . B6
Orchard Square Shopping Centre . . . B4
Oxford St . . . A2
Paradise St . . . B4
Park La . . . C2
Park Sq . . . B5
Parker's Rd . . . B1
Pearson Building (Univ) . . . C2
Penistone Rd . . . A3
Pinstone St . . . B4
Pitt St . . . B3
Police Station . . . B5
Pond Hill . . . B5
Pondorosa, The . . . A2
Pond St . . . B5
Ponds Forge International Sports Centre . . . B5
Portobello St . . . B3
Post Office . . . A2/B3/B5/C1/C3/C4/C6
Powell St . . . A2
Queen St . . . B4
Queen's Rd . . . C5
Ramsey Rd . . . B1
Red Hill . . . B3
Redcar Rd . . . B1
Regent St . . . B3
Rockingham St . . . B4
Roebuck Rd . . . A2
Royal Hallamshire Hospital . . . C2
Russell St . . . A4
Rutland Park . . . C1
St George's Close . . . B3
St Mary's Gate . . . C3
St Mary's Rd . . . C4/C5
St Philip's Rd . . . A3
Savile St . . . A5
School Rd . . . B1
Scotland St . . . A4
Severn Rd . . . B1
Shalesmoor . . . A4
Shalesmoor . . . A3
Sheaf St . . . B5
Sheffield Cath ✝ . . . B4
Sheffield Hallam University . . . B5
Sheffield Ice Sports Ctr – Skate Central . . . C5
Sheffield Institute of Arts . . . B5
Sheffield Interchange . . . B5
Sheffield Parkway . . . A6
Sheffield Station . . . C5
Sheffield Station/ Sheffield Hallam University . . . B5
Sheffield University . . . B2
Shepherd St . . . A3
Shipton St . . . A2
Shopmobility . . . B3
Shoreham St . . . C4
Showroom . . . C5
Shrewsbury Rd . . . C5
Sidney St . . . C4
Site Gallery . . . C5
Slinn St . . . A1
Smithfield . . . A4
Snig Hill . . . A5
Snow La . . . A4
Solly St . . . B3
South La . . . C4
South Street Park . . . B5
Southbourne Rd . . . C1
Spital Hill . . . A5
Spital St . . . A5
Spring Hill . . . B1
Spring Hill Rd . . . B1
Springvale Rd . . . A1
Stafford Rd . . . C6
Stafford St . . . B6
Suffolk Rd . . . C5
Summer St . . . B2
Sunny Bank . . . C3
Superstore . . . A3/C3
Surrey St . . . B4
Sussex St . . . A6
Sutton St . . . B3
Sydney Rd . . . A2
Sylvester St . . . C4
Talbot St . . . B5
Taptonville Rd . . . B1
Tenter St . . . B4
Town Hall . . . B4
Townend St . . . A1
Townhead St . . . B4
Trafalgar St . . . B4
Tree Root Walk . . . B2
Trinity St . . . A4
Trippet La . . . B4
Turner Museum of Glass . . . B3
Union St . . . B4
University Drama Studio . . . B2
Univ of Sheffield . . . B3
Upper Allen St . . . A3
Upper Hanover St . . . B3
Upperthorpe Rd . . . A2/A3
Verdon St . . . A5
Victoria Rd . . . C2
Victoria St . . . B3
Waingate . . . B5
Watery St . . . A3
Watson Rd . . . C1
Wellesley Rd . . . B2
Wellington St . . . C3
West Bar . . . A4
West Bar Green . . . A4
West One Plaza . . . B3
West St . . . B3
West St . . . B4
Westbourne Rd . . . C1
Western Bank . . . B2
Western Rd . . . A1
Weston Park . . . B2
Weston Park Hospital . . . B2
Weston Park Mus . . . B2
Weston St . . . B2
Wharncliffe Rd . . . C3
Whitham Rd . . . B1
Wicker . . . A5
Wilkinson St . . . B2
William St . . . C3
Winter Garden ✦ . . . B4
Winter St . . . B2
York St . . . B4
Yorkshire Artspace . . . C5
Young St . . . C4

Shrewsbury 195

Abbey Foregate . . . B3
Abbey Gardens . . . B2
Abbey Lawn Business Park . . . B3
Abbots House . . . B2
Albert St . . . A2
Alma St . . . B1
Ashley St . . . A3
Ashton Rd . . . C1
Avondale Dr . . . A3
Bage Way . . . C3
Barker St . . . B1
Beacall's La . . . A2
Beeches La . . . C2
Beehive La . . . C1
Belle Vue Gdns . . . C2
Belle Vue Rd . . . C2
Belmont Bank . . . C1
Berwick Ave . . . A1
Berwick Rd . . . A1
Betton St . . . C2
Bishop St . . . B3
Bradford St . . . B3
Bridge St . . . B1
Burton St . . . A3
Bus Station . . . B2
Butcher Row . . . B2
Butler Rd . . . C1
Bynner St . . . C2
Canon St . . . B3
Canonbury . . . C1
Castle Business Park, The . . . A2
Castle Foregate . . . A2
Castle Gates . . . B2
Castle Walk . . . B3
Castle St . . . B2
Cathedral (RC) ✝ . . . C1
Chester St . . . A2
Cineworld . . . C3
Claremont Bank . . . B1
Claremont Hill . . . B1
Cleveland St . . . B3
Coleham Head . . . B2
Coleham Pumping Station . . . C2
College Hill . . . B1
Corporation La . . . A1
Coton Cres . . . A1
Coton Hill . . . A2
Coton Mount . . . A1
Crescent La . . . C1
Crewe St . . . A2
Cross Hill . . . B1
Dana, The . . . B2
Darwin Centre . . . B2
Dingle, The . . . B1
Dogpole . . . B2
English Bridge . . . B2
Fish St . . . B2
Frankwell . . . B1
Gateway Ctr, The . . . A2
Gravel Hill La . . . A1
Greenhous West Mid Showground . . . A1
Greyfriars Rd . . . C2
Hampton Rd . . . A3
Haycock Way . . . C3
High St . . . B1
Hills La . . . B1
Holywell St . . . B3
Hunter St . . . A1
Information Ctr . . . B1
Ireland's Mansion & Bear Steps . . . B1
John St . . . A3
Kennedy Rd . . . C1
King St . . . B3
Kingsland Bridge . . . C1
Kingsland Bridge (toll) . . . C1
Kingsland Rd . . . C1
Library . . . B2
Lime St . . . C2
Longden Coleham . . . C2
Longden Rd . . . C1
Longner St . . . B1
Luciefelde Rd . . . C1
Mardol . . . B1
Marine Terr . . . C2
Market . . . B1
Monkmoor Rd . . . B3
Moreton Cres . . . C2
Mount St . . . A1
New Park Close . . . A3
New Park Rd . . . A2
New Park St . . . A3
North St . . . A2
Oakley St . . . C1
Old Coleham . . . C2
Old Market Hall . . . B1
Old Potts Way . . . C3
Parade Shopping Centre, The . . . B2
Police Station . . . B1
Post Office . . . B1/B2/B3
Pride Hill . . . B1
Pride Hill Centre . . . B1
Priory Rd . . . B1
Pritchard Way . . . C3
Quarry Swimming & Fitness Centre, The . . . B1
Queen St . . . A3
Raby Cres . . . C2
Rad Brook . . . C1
Rea Brook . . . C3
Rea Brook Valley Country Park & Local Nature Reserve . . . C3
Riverside . . . B1
Roundhill La . . . A1
St Alkmund's . . . B2
St Chad's . . . B1
St Chad's Terr . . . B1
St John's Hill . . . B1
St Julians Friars . . . C2
St Mary's . . . B2
St Mary's St . . . B2
Salters La . . . C2
Scott St . . . C3
Severn Theatre . . . B1
Severn Bank . . . A3
Severn St . . . A2
Shrewsbury . . . B2
Shrewsbury Abbey . . . B3
Shrewsbury High School . . . C1
Shrewsbury Mus & Art Gallery . . . B1
Shrewsbury Prison Tours ✦ . . . B2
Shrewsbury School ✦ . . . C1
Shropshire Regimental Museum . . . B2
Shropshire Wildlife Trust ✦ . . . B3
Smithfield Rd . . . B1
South Hermitage . . . C1
Square, The . . . B1
Superstore . . . C3
Swan Hill . . . B1
Sydney Ave . . . A3
Tankerville St . . . B3
Tilbrook Dr . . . A3
Town Walls . . . C1
Trinity St . . . C2
Underdale Rd . . . B3
University Centre Shrewsbury (Guildhall) . . . B1
Victoria Ave . . . B1
Victoria Quay . . . B1
Victoria St . . . B2
Welsh Bridge . . . B1
Whitehall St . . . B3
Wood St . . . A2
Wyle Cop . . . B2

Southampton 196

Above Bar St . . . A2
Albert Rd North . . . B3
Albert Rd South . . . C3
Andersons Rd . . . B3
Argyle Rd . . . A2
Arundel Tower ✦ . . . B1
Bargate, The ✦ . . . B2
BBC South . . . A1
Bedford Place . . . A1
Belvidere Rd . . . A3
Bernard St . . . C2
Blechynden Terr . . . A1
Brinton's Rd . . . A2
Britannia Rd . . . A3
Briton St . . . C2
Brunswick Place . . . A2
Bugle St . . . C1
Canute Rd . . . C3
Castle Way . . . C2
Catchcold Tower ✦ . . . B1
Central Bridge . . . C3
Central Rd . . . C2
Channel Way . . . C3
Chapel Rd . . . B3
City Art Gallery . . . A1
City College . . . B3
City Cruise Terminal . . . C1
Civic Centre . . . A1
Civic Centre Rd . . . A1
Coach Station . . . B1
Commercial Rd . . . A1
Cumberland Place . . . A1
Cunard Rd . . . C2
Derby Rd . . . A3
Devonshire Rd . . . A1
Dock Gate 4 . . . C2
Dock Gate 8 . . . B1
East Park (Andrew's Park) . . . A2
East Park Terr . . . A2
East St . . . B2
Endle St . . . B3
European Way . . . C2
Fire Station . . . A2
Floating Bridge Rd . . . C3
God's House Tower ✦ . . . C2
Golden Grove . . . A3
Graham Rd . . . A2
Guildhall . . . A1
Hanover Bldgs . . . B2
Harbour Lights . . . C3
Harbour Pde . . . B1
Hartington Rd . . . A3
Havelock Rd . . . A1
Henstead Rd . . . A1
Herbert Walker Ave . . . B1
High St . . . B2
Hoglands Park . . . B
Holy Rood (Rems), Merchant Navy Memorial . . . B
Houndwell Park . . . B
Houndwell Place . . . B
Hythe Ferry . . . C
Isle of Wight Ferry Terminal . . . C
James St . . . B
Kingsway . . . A
Leisure World . . . B
Library . . . A
Lime St . . . B
London Rd . . . A
Marine Pde . . . B
Marlands Shopping Centre, The . . . A
Marsh La . . . B
Mayflower Memorial ✦ . . . C
Mayflower Park . . . C
Mayflower Theatre, The . . . A
Medieval Merchant's House . . . C
Melbourne St . . . B
Morris Rd . . . A
National Oceanography Centre ✦ . . . C
Neptune Way . . . C
New Rd . . . A
Nichols Rd . . . A
North Front . . . A
Northam Rd . . . A
Ocean Dock . . . C
Ocean Village Marina . . . C
Ocean Way . . . C
Odeon . . . B
Ogle Rd . . . B
Old Northam Rd . . . A
Orchard La . . . B
Oxford Ave . . . A
Oxford St . . . C
Palmerston Park . . . A
Palmerston Rd . . . A
Parsonage Rd . . . A
Peel St . . . A
Platform Rd . . . C
Polygon, The . . . A
Portland Terr . . . B
Post Office . . . B
Pound Tree Rd . . . B
Quays Swimming & Diving Complex, The . . . B
Queen's Park . . . C
Queen's Peace Fountain ✦ . . . A
Queen's Terr . . . C
Queensway . . . B
Radcliffe Rd . . . A
Rochester St . . . A
Royal Pier . . . C
Royal South Hants Hospital . . . A
St Andrew's Rd . . . A
St Mary's . . . B
St Mary St . . . A
St Mary's Leisure Centre . . . A
St Mary's Place . . . B
St Mary's Rd . . . A
St Mary's Stadium (Southampton FC) . . . A
St Michael's . . . C
SeaCity Mus . . . A
Showcase Cinema de Lux . . . B
Solent Sky . . . C
South Front . . . B
Southampton Central Station . . . A
Southampton Solent University . . . A

Southend • Stirling • Stoke-on-Trent (Hanley) • Stratford-upon-Avon • Sunderland • Swansea • Swindon • Taunton • Telford 211

Terminus Terr C2
Threefield La B2
Titanic Engineers' Memorial ✦ A2
Town Quay C1
Town Walls B2
Tudor House C1
Vincent's Walk B2
Westgate Hall C1
West Marlands Rd A1
West Park A1
West Park Rd A1
West Quay Rd B1
West Quay Retail Park B1
Western Esplanade B1
Westquay Shopping Centre B1
Westquay South B1
White Star Way C2
Winton St A2

Southend-on-Sea 197

Adventure Island ✦ C3
Albany Ave A1
Albert Rd C3
Alexandra Rd C2
Alexandra St C2
Alexandra Yacht Club ✦ C2
Ashburnham Rd B2
Ave Rd B1
Avenue Terr B1
Balmoral Rd B1
Baltic Ave B3
Baxter Ave A2/B2
Beecroft Art Gallery B2
Bircham Rd A2
Boscombe Rd B3
Boston Ave A1/B2
Bournemouth Park Rd A3
Browning Ave A3
Bus Station C3
Byron Ave A3
Cambridge Rd C1/C2
Canewdon Rd B1
Carnarvon Rd A2
Central Ave A3
Central Museum B2
Chelmsford Ave A1
Chichester Rd B2
Church Rd C3
Civic Centre A2
Clarence Rd C2
Clarence St C2
Cliff Ave B1
Cliffs Pavilion C1
Clifftown Parade C2
Clifftown Rd C2
Colchester Rd A1
Coleman St B3
College Way B2
County Court B3
Cromer Rd B3
Crowborough Rd A2
Dryden Ave A3
East St A2
Elmer App B2
Elmer Ave B2
Forum, The B2
Gainsborough Dr A1
Gayton Rd A2
Glenhurst Rd A2
Gordon Place B2
Gordon Rd B2
Grainger Rd A2
Greyhound Way A3
Grove, The A3
Guildford Rd B3
Hamlet Ct Rd B1
Hamlet Rd C1
Harcourt Ave A1
Hartington Rd C3
Hastings Rd B3
Herbert Grove C3
Heygate Ave C3
High St B2/C2
Information Ctr C3
Kenway A2
Kilworth Ave B3
Lancaster Gdns B3
London Rd B1
Lucy Rd C3
MacDonald Ave A1
Magistrates' Court A2
Maldon Rd A2
Marine Ave C1
Marine Parade C3
Marine Rd C1
Milton Rd B1
Milton St B2
Napier Ave B2
North Ave A3
North Rd A1/B1
Odeon B2
Osborne Rd B1
Park Cres B1
Park Rd B1
Park St B1
Park Terr B1
Pier Hill C3
Pleasant Rd C3
Police Station A2
Post Office B2/B3
Princes St B2
Queens Rd B2
Queensway B2/B3/C3
Radio Essex C2
Rayleigh Ave A1
Redstock Rd A2
Rochford Ave A1
Royal Mews C2
Royal Terr C2
Royals Shopping Centre, The C3
Ruskin Ave A3
St Ann's Rd B3
St Helen's Rd B1
St John's Rd B1
St Leonard's Rd C3
St Lukes Rd A3
St Vincent's Rd C1
Salisbury Ave A1/B1
Scratton Rd C2
Shakespeare Dr A1
Shopmobility B2
Short St A2
South Ave A3
Southchurch Rd B3
Southend Central ⇌ B2
Southend Pier Railway C3
Southend United FC A1
Southend Victoria ⇌ B2
Stanfield Rd A2
Stanley Rd C3
Sutton Rd A3/B3
Swanage Rd B3
Sweyne Ave A1
Sycamore Grove A3
Tennyson Ave A3
Tickfield Ave A2
Tudor Rd A1
Tunbridge Rd A2
Tylers Ave B3
Tyrrel Dr B3
Univ of Essex B2/C2
Vale Ave A2
Victoria Ave A2
Victoria Shopping Centre, The B2
Warrior Sq B3
Wesley Rd C3
West Rd A1
West St A1
Westcliff Ave C1
Westcliff Parade C1
Western Esplanade C1
Weston Rd C2
Whitegate Rd B3
Wilson Rd C1
Wimborne Rd B3
York Rd C3

Stirling 197

Abbey Rd A3
Abbotsford Place A3
Abercromby Place C1
Albert Halls B1
Albert Place B1
Alexandra Place A3
Allan Park C2
Ambulance Station A2
AMF Ten Pin Bowling ✦ B2
Argyll Ave A3
Argyll's Lodging ✦ B1
Back O' Hill Ind Est A1
Back O' Hill Rd A1
Baker St B2
Ballengeich Pass A1
Balmoral Place B1
Barn Rd B1
Barnton St B2
Bastion, The ✦ C2
Bow St B1
Bruce St A2
Burghmuir Retail Park C2
Burghmuir Rd A2/B2/C2
Bus Station B2
Cambuskenneth Bridge A3
Castle Ct B1
Causewayhead Rd A2
Cemetery A1
Changing Room, The B1
Church of the Holy Rude B1
Clarendon Place C1
Club House B1
Colquhoun St C3
Corn Exchange B2
Council Offices C2
Court B2
Cowane Ctr A2
Cowane St A2
Cowane's Hosp B1
Crofthead Rd A1
Dean Cres A3
Douglas St A2
Drip Rd A1
Drummond La C1
Drummond Place C1
Drummond Place La C1
Dumbarton Rd C2
Eastern Access Rd B2
Edward Ave A3
Edward Rd A2
Forrest Rd A2
Fort A1
Forth Cres B2
Forth St A2
Gladstone Place C1
Glebe Ave C1
Glebe Cres C1
Golf Course C1
Goosecroft Rd B2
Gowanhill A1
Greenwood Ave B1
Harvey Wynd A1
Information Ctr B1
Irvine Place B2
James St A2
John St B1
Kerse Rd C3
King's Knot ✦ B1
King's Park C1
King's Park Rd C1
Laurencecroft Rd A2
Leisure Pool B2
Library B2
Linden Ave C2
Lovers Wk A2
Lower Back Walk B1
Lower Bridge St A2
Lower Castlehill A1
Mar Place B1
Meadow Place A3
Meadowforth Rd C3
Middlemuir Rd C3
Millar Place A3
Morris Terr B2
Mote Hill A1
Murray Place B2
Nelson Place C2
Old Town Cemetery B1
Old Town Jail ✦ B1
Park Terr C1
Phoenix Ind Est C3
Players Rd C3
Port St C2
Post Office B2
Princes St B2
Queen St B2
Queen's Rd B1
Queenshaugh Dr A3
Ramsay Place A2
Riverside Dr A3
Ronald Place A1
Rosebery Place A2
Royal Gardens B1
Royal Gardens B1
St Mary's Wynd B1
St Ninian's Rd C2
Scott St A2
Seaforth Place B2
Shore Rd B2
Smith Art Gallery & Museum B1
Snowdon Place C1
Snowdon Place La C1
Spittal St B2
Springkerse Ind Est C3
Springkerse Rd C3
Stirling Arcade B2
Stirling Business Centre C2
Stirling Castle A1
Stirling County Rugby Football Club A3
Stirling Enterprise Park B3
Stirling Old Bridge A2
Stirling Station ⇌ B2
Superstore A1/A2
Sutherland Ave A3
TA Centre C3
Tannery La A2
Thistle Ind Est C3
Thistles Shopping Centre, The B2
Tolbooth ✦ B1
Town Wall B1
Union St A2
Upper Back Walk B1
Upper Bridge St A1
Upper Castlehill B1
Upper Craigs C2
Victoria Place C1
Victoria Rd B1
Victoria Sq B1/C1
Vue B2
Wallace St A2
Waverley Cres A3
Wellgreen Rd C2
Windsor Place C1
YHA B1

Stoke-on-Trent (Hanley) 196

Acton St A3
Albion St B2
Argyle St C1
Ashbourne Grove A2
Avoca St A3
Baskerville Rd B3
Bedford Rd C1
Bedford St C1
Bethesda St B2
Bexley St A2
Birches Head Rd A3
Botteslow St C3
Boundary St A2
Broad St C2
Broom St A3
Bryan St A2
Bucknall New Rd B3
Bucknall Old Rd B3
Bus Station C3
Cannon St C2
Castlefield St C1
Cavendish St B1
Central Forest Park A2
Century Retail Park B1
Charles St B3
Cheapside B2
Chell St A3
Cinema A2
Clarke St C1
Cleveland Rd C2
Clifford St C3
Clough St B2
Clough St East B2
Clyde St C1
College Rd C2
Cooper St C2
Corbridge Rd A1
Cutts St C2
Davis St C1
Denbigh St A1
Derby St C2
Dilke St A3
Dudson Ctr, The A2
Dundas St A3
Dundee Rd C1
Dyke St B3
Eastwood Rd C3
Eaton St A3
Etruria Park B1
Etruria Rd B1
Etruria Vale Rd C1
Festing St A3
Festival Heights Retail Park A1
Festival Retail Park A1
Fire Station C2
Foundry St B2
Franklyn St C3
Garnet St B1
Garth St B3
George St A3
Gilman St B3
Glass St B3
Goodson St B3
Greyhound Way A1
Grove Place C1
Hampton St C3
Hanley Park C3
Hanley Park C2
Harding Rd C2
Hassall St B3
Havelock Place C1
Hazlehurst St C3
Hinde St C2
Hope St B2
Houghton St C2
Hulton St A3
Information Ctr B2
intu Potteries Shopping Centre B2
Jasper St C2
Jervis St A3
John Bright St A3
John St B2
Keelings Rd A3
Kimberley Rd C1
Ladysmith Rd C1
Lawrence St C2
Leek Rd C3
Library C2
Lichfield St C3
Linfield Rd B3
Loftus St A2
Lower Bedford St C1
Lower Bryan St A2
Lower Mayer St A3
Lowther St A1
Magistrates Court C2
Malham St A2
Marsh St B2
Matlock St C3
Mayer St A3
Milton St C1
Mitchell Arts Ctr B2
Moston St A3
Mount Pleasant C1
Mulgrave St A1
Mynors St B3
Nelson Place B3
New Century St B1
Octagon Retail Park B1
Ogden Rd C3
Old Hall St B3
Old Town Rd A3
Pall Mall B2
Palmerston St C3
Park and Ride C2
Parkway, The C2
Pavilion Dr A1
Pelham St C3
Percy St B2
Piccadilly B2
Picton St B3
Plough St A3
Police Station C2
Portland St A1
Post Office A3/B2
Potteries Museum & Art Gallery B2
Potteries Way C2
Powell St A1
Pretoria Rd C1
Quadrant Rd B2
Ranelagh St C2
Raymond St C2
Rectory Rd C1
Regent Rd C2
Regent Theatre B2
Richmond Terr C2
Ridgehouse Dr A1
Robson St C2
St Ann St B3
St Luke St B3
Sampson St B2
Shaw St A1
Sheaf St C2
Shearer St C1
Shelton New Rd C1
Shirley Rd C2
Slippery La B2
Shopmobility B3
Snow Hill C2
Spur St C3
Stafford St B2
Stubbs La C3
Sun St C1
Supermarket A1/B2
Superstore B2
Talbot St C3
Town Hall B2
Town Rd A3
Trinity St B2
Union St A2
Upper Hillchurch St A3
Upper Huntbach St B3
Victoria Hall B3
Warner St C2
Warwick St C1
Waterloo Rd A1
Waterloo St B3
Well St B3
Wellesley St C2
Wellington Rd B3
Wellington St B3
Whitehaven Dr A2
Whitmore St C1
Windermere St A1
Woodall St A1
Yates St C2
York St A2

Stratford-upon-Avon 197

Albany Rd B1
Alcester Rd B1
Ambulance Station B1
Arden St B1
Avenue Farm A1
Ave Farm Ind Est A1
Avenue Rd A3
Baker Ave A1
Bandstand C3
Benson Rd A3
Birmingham Rd A2
Boat Club B3
Borden Place C1
Bridge St B2
Bridgetown Rd C3
Bridgeway B3
Broad St C2
Broad Walk C2
Brookvale Rd C1
Brunel Way B1
Bull St C2
Butterfly Farm ✦ C3
Cemetery C1
Chapel La B2
Cherry Orchard C1
Chestnut Walk B2
Children's Playground C3
Church St C2
Civic Hall B2
Clarence Rd B1
Clopton Bridge ✦ B3
Clopton Rd A2
College B1
College La C2
College St C2
Com Sports Centre B1
Council Offices (District) B2
Courtyard, The C2
Cox's Yard ✦ B3
Cricket Ground C3
Ely Gdns B2
Ely St B2
Evesham Rd C1
Fire Station B1
Foot Ferry C3
Fordham Ave A2
Garrick Way C1
Gower Memorial ✦ B3
Great William St B2
Greenhill St B2
Greenway, The C2
Grove Rd B2
Guild St B2
Guildhall & School B2
Hall's Croft C2
Harvard House B2
Henley St B2
Hertford Rd C1
High St B2
Holton St C2
Holy Trinity C2
Information Ctr B3
Jolyffe Park Rd A2
Kipling Rd C3
Library B2
Lodge Rd B1
Maidenhead Rd A3
Mansell St B2
Masons Court B2
Masons Rd A1
Maybird Shopping Park A2
Maybrook Retail Park A2
Maybrook Rd A1
Mayfield Ave A2
Meer St B2
Mill La C2
Moat House Hotel B3
Narrow La C2
Nash's House & New Place B2
New St C2
Old Town C2
Orchard Way C1
Other Place, The C2
Paddock La C1
Park Rd A1
Payton St B2
Percy St A2
Police Station B2
Post Office B2
Recreation Ground C2
Regal Road A2
Rother St B2
Rowley Cres A3
Royal Shakespeare Theatre B3
Ryland St C2
Saffron Meadow C2
St Andrew's Cres B1
St Gregory's A3
St Gregory's Rd A3
St Mary's Rd A2
Sanctus Dr C2
Sanctus St C1
Sandfield Rd C2
Scholars La B2
Seven Meadows Rd C2
Shakespeare Inst C2
Shakespeare St B2
Shakespeare's Birthplace ✦ B2
Sheep St B2
Shelley Rd C3
Shipston Rd C3
Shottery Rd C1
Slingates Rd A2
Southern La C2
Station Rd B1
Stratford Healthcare B2
Stratford Hosp B2
Stratford Leisure Centre B3
Stratford Sports Club B1
Stratford-upon-Avon Station ⇌ B1
Swan Theatre B3
Swan's Nest La B3
Talbot Rd A2
Tiddington Rd B3
Timothy's Bridge Industrial Estate A1
Timothy's Bridge Rd A1
Town Hall & Council Offices B2
Town Sq B2
Trinity Close C2
Tyler St B2
War Memorial Gdns B3
Warwick Rd B3
Waterside B3
Welcombe Rd A3
West St C2
Western Rd A2
Wharf Rd A2
Willows North, The B1
Willows, The B1
Wood St B2

Sunderland 197

Albion Place C2
Alliance Place B1
Argyle St C2
Ashwood St C1
Athenaeum St B2
Azalea Terr C2
Beach St A1
Bedford St B2
Beechwood Terr C1
Belvedere Rd C2
Blandford St B2
Borough Rd B3
Bridge Cres B2
Bridge St B2
Bridges, The B2
Brooke St A2
Brougham St B2
Burdon Rd C2
Burn Park C1
Burn Park Rd C1
Burn Park Technology Park C1
Carol St B1
Charles St A3
Chester Rd C1
Chester Terr B1
Church St A3
Civic Centre C2
Cork St B3
Coronation St B3
Cowan Terr C2
Dame Dorothy St A2
Deptford Rd B1
Deptford Terr A1
Derby St C2
Derwent St C2
Dock St A3
Dundas St A2
Durham Rd C1
Easington St A2
Egerton St C3
Empire B2
Empire Theatre B2
Farringdon Row B1
Fawcett St B2
Fire Station B1
Fox St C1
Foyle St B3
Frederick St B3
Hanover Place A1
Havelock Terr C1
Hay St A2
Headworth Square B3
Hendon Rd B3
High St East B3
High St West B2/B3
Holmeside B2
Hylton Rd B1
Information Ctr B2
John St B3
Kier Hardie Way A2
Lambton St B3
Laura St C3
Lawrence St B3
Library & Arts Ctr B3
Lily St B1
Lime St B1
Livingstone Rd B2
Low Row B2
Magistrates' Court B2
Matamba Terr B1
Millburn St B1
Millennium Way A2
Minster B2
Monkwearmouth Sta Museum A2
Mowbray Park C3
Mowbray Rd C3
Murton St C3
National Glass Centre ✦ A3
New Durham Rd C1
Newcastle Rd A2
Nile St B3
Norfolk St B3
North Bridge St A2
Northern Gallery for Contemporary Art (NGCA) B3
Otto Terr C1
Park La C2
Park Lane C2
Park Rd C2
Paul's Rd B3
Peel St C3
Point, The ✦ B2
Police Station B2
Priestly Cres A1
Queen St B2
Railway Row B1
Retail Park B1
Richmond St A2
Roker Ave A2
Royalty Theatre C1
Royalty, The C1
Ryhope Rd C2
St Mary's Way B2
St Michael's Way B2
St Peter's A3
St Peter's A2
St Peter's Way A3
St Vincent St C3
Salem Rd C3
Salem St C3
Salisbury St C3
Sans St B3
Shopmobility B2
Silkworth Row B1
Southwick Rd A2
Stadium of Light (Sunderland AFC) A2
Stadium Way A2
Stobart St A2
Stockton Rd C2
Suffolk St C3
Sunderland B2
Sunderland Aquatic Centre A2
Sunderland College C2
Sunderland Museum B3
Sunderland St B3
Sunderland Sta ⇌ B2
Tatham St C3
Tavistock Place B3
Thelma St C1
Thomas St North A2
Thornholme Rd C1
Toward Rd C3
Transport Interchange C2
Trimdon St Way B1
Tunstall Rd C2
University C1
University Library C1
Univ of Sunderland (City Campus) B1
Univ of Sunderland (St Peter's Campus) A3
University of Sunderland (Sir Tom Cowie Campus) A3
Vaux Brewery Way A2
Villiers St B3
Villiers St South B3
Vine Place C2
Violet St B1
Walton La B3
Waterworks Rd B1
Wearmouth Bridge B2
West Sunniside B3
West Wear St B3
Westbourne Rd B1
Western Hill C1
Wharncliffe B1
Whickham St A3
White House Rd C3
Wilson St North A2
Winter Gdns C3
Wreath Quay A1

Swansea Abertawe 198

Adelaide St C3
Albert Row C3
Alexandra Rd B3
Argyle St C1
Baptist Well Place A2
Beach St C1
Belle Vue Way B3
Berw Rd A1
Berwick Terr A2
Bond St C1
Brangwyn Concert Hall C1
Bridge St A3
Brooklands Terr B1
Brunswick St C1
Bryn-Syfi Terr A2
Bryn-y-Mor Rd C1
Bullins La B1
Burrows Rd C1
Bus Station C2
Bus/Rail link A3
Cadfan Rd A1
Cadrawd Rd A1
Caer St B3
Carig Cres A1
Carlton Terr B2
Carmarthen Rd A3
Castle Square B3
Castle St B3
Catherine St C1
Cinema C3
Civic Ctr & Library C2
Clarence St C2
Colbourne Terr A2
Constitution Hill B1
Court B3
Creidiol Rd A2
Cromwell St B2
Crown Courts C1
Duke St B1
Dunvant Place C2
Dyfatty Park A3
Dyfatty St A3
Dyfed Ave A1
Dylan Thomas Centre ✦ B3
Dylan Thomas Theatre C3
Eaton Cres C1
Eigen Cres A1
Elfed Rd A1
Emlyn Rd A1
Evans Terr A3
Fairfield Terr B1
Ffynone Dr B1
Ffynone Rd B1
Fire Station B3
Firm St A2
Fleet St C1
Francis St C1
Fullers Row B2
George St B2
Glamorgan St C2
Glynn Vivian Art Gallery B3
Gower Coll Swansea C1
Graig Terr A3
Grand Theatre C2
Granogwen Rd A2
Guildhall C1
Guildhall Rd South C1
Gwent Rd A1
Gwynedd Ave A1
Hafod St A3
Hanover St B1
Harcourt St B2
Harries St A2
Heathfield B2
Henrietta St B2
Hewson St B2
High St A3/B3
High View A2
Hill St A2
Historic Ships Berth C3
HM Prison C2
Information Ctr C2
Islwyn Rd A1
King Edward's Rd C1
Kingsway, The B2
LC, The C3
Long Ridge A2
Madoc St C2
Mansel St B2
Maritime Quarter C3
Market B3
Mayhill Gdns B1
Mayhill Rd A1
Milton Terr A2
Mission Gallery C3
Montpelier Terr B1
Morfa Rd A3
Mount Pleasant B2
National Waterfront Museum C3
New Cut Rd A3
New St A3
Nicander Parade A2
Nicander Place A2
Nicholl St B2
Norfolk St B2
North Hill Rd A2
Northampton La B2
Observatory ✦ C3
Orchard St B3
Oxford St B2
Oystermouth Rd C1
Page St B2
Pant-y-Celyn Rd B1
Parc Tawe North B3
Parc Tawe Shopping & Leisure Centre B3
Patti Pavilion C1
Paxton St C2
Pen-y-Graig Rd A1
Penmaen Terr B1
Phillips Pde C1
Picton Terr B2
Plantasia B3
Plantasia B3
Police Station B2
Post Office A1/A2/C1/C2
Powys Ave A1
Primrose St B2
Princess Way B3
Promenade B2
Pryder Gdns A1
Quadrant Shopping Centre C2
Quay Park B3
Rhianfa La B1
Rhondda St B2
Richardson St C2
Rodney St C1
Rose Hill B1
Rosehill Terr B1
Russell St B1
St Helen's Ave C1
St Helen's Cres C1
St Helen's Rd C1
St James Gdns B1
St James's Cres B1
St Mary's B3
Sea View Terr A3
Singleton St C2
South Dock C3
Stanley Place B2
Strand B3
Swansea Castle B3
Swansea Metropolitan University B2
Swansea Mus C3
Swansea Station ⇌ A3
Taliesyn Rd B1
Tan y Marian Rd B1
Tegid Rd A2
Teilo Cres A1
Tenpin Bowling ✦ B3
Terrace Rd B1/B2
Tontine St A3
Townhill Rd A1
Tramshed, The C3
Trawler Rd C3
Union St B2
Upper Strand A3
Vernon St A3
Victoria Quay C3
Victoria Rd B3
Vincent St C1
Walter Rd B1
Watkin St A2
Waun-Wen Rd A2
Wellington St C2
Westbury St C1
Western St C1
Westway C2
William St C2
Wind St B3
Woodlands Terr B1
YMCA B2
York St C3

Swindon 198

Albert St C3
Albion St C1
Alfred St A2
Alvescot Rd C3
Art Gallery & Museum C3
Ashford Rd C1
Aylesbury St A2
Bath Rd C2
Bathampton St B1
Bathurst Rd B3
Beatrice St A2
Beckhampton St B3
Bowood Rd C1
Bristol St B1
Broad St A3
Brunel Shopping Centre, The B2
Brunel Statue B2
Brunswick St C2
Bus Station B2
Cambria Bridge Rd B1
Cambria Place B1
Canal Walk B2
Carr St B1
Cemetery C1/C3
Chandler Close C3
Chapel C1
Chester St B1
Christ Church C3
Church Place B1
Cirencester Way A3
Clarence St B2
Clifton St C1
Cockleberry ✦ A2
Colbourne ✦ A3
Colbourne St A3
College St B2
Commercial Rd B2
Corporation St A2
Council Offices B3
County Cricket Gd A3
County Rd A3
Courts B2
Cricklade Street C3
Crombey St B1/C2
Cross St C2
Curtis St B1
Deacon St C1
Designer Outlet (Great Western) B1
Dixon St C2
Dover St C2
Dowling St C2
Drove Rd C3
Dryden St C1
Durham St C3
East St B1
Eastcott Hill C2
Eastcott Rd C2
Edgeware Rd B2
Edmund St C2
Elmina Rd A3
Emlyn Square B1
English Heritage National Monuments Record Centre B1
Euclid St B3
Exeter St B1
Fairview C1
Faringdon Rd B1
Farnsby St B1
Fire Station C3
Fleet St B2
Fleming Way B2/B3
Florence St A2
Gladstone St A3
Gooch St A2
Graham St A3
Great Western Way A1/A2
Groundwell Rd B3
Hawksworth Way A1
Haydon St A2
Henry St B2
Hillside Ave C1
Holbrook Way B2
Hunt St C3
Hydro B1
Hythe Rd C2
Information Ctr B2
Joseph St C1
Kent Rd C2
King William St C2
Kingshill Rd C1
Lansdown Rd C2
Lawn, The C3
Leicester St B3
Library B2
Lincoln St B3
Little London C3
London St B1
Magic ✦ B3
Maidstone Rd C2
Manchester Rd A3
Maxwell St B1
Milford St B2
Milton Rd B1
Morse St C2
Newcastle St B3
Newcombe Drive A1
Hawsworth Ind Est A1
Newhall St C2
North St C2
North Star ✦ A1
North Star Ave A1
Northampton St B3
Nurseries, The C1
Oasis Leisure Ctr A1
Ocotal Way A3
Okus Rd C1
Old Town C3
Oxford St B1
Parade, The B2
Park Lane B1
Park Lane ✦ B1
Park, The B1
Pembroke St C2
Plymouth St B3
Polaris Way A2
Police Station B2
Ponting St A2
Post Office B1/B2/C3
Poulton St A3
Princes St B2
Prospect Hill C2
Prospect Place C2
Queen St B2
Queen's Park C3
Radnor St C1
Read St C1
Reading St B1
Regent Circus C2
Regent St B2
Retail Park A2/A3/B3
Rosebery St A3
St Mark's B1
Salisbury St A3
Savernake St C2
Science & Technology Facilities Council HQ A2
Shelley St C1
Sheppard St B1
Shopmobility B2
South St C2
Southampton St B3
Spring Gardens B3
Stafford Street C2
Stanier St C2
Station Road A2
STEAM GWR B1
Swindon College A2
Swindon Rd C2
Swindon Station ⇌ A2
Swindon Town Football Club A3
TA Centre B1
Tennyson St B1
Theobald St B1
Town Hall B2
Transfer Bridges ✦ A3
Union St C2
Upham Rd C3
Victoria Rd C3
Walcot Rd B3
War Memorial ✦ B2
Wells St B3
Western St C2
Westmorland Rd B3
Whalebridge ✦ B2
Whitehead St C1
Whitehouse Rd A2
William St C1
Wood St C3
Wyvern Theatre & Arts Centre B2
York Rd B3

Taunton 198

Addison Grove A1
Albemarle Rd A1
Alfred St B3
Alma St C2
Avenue, The A1
Bath Place C1
Belvedere Rd A1
Billet St B2
Billetfield C2
Birch Grove A1
Brewhouse Theatre B2
Bridge St B1
Bridgwater & Taunton Canal A2
Broadlands Rd C1
Burton Place C1
Bus Station B1
Canal Rd A2
Cann St C1
Canon St B2
Castle St B1
Cheddon Rd A2
Chip Lane A1
Clarence St B1
Cleveland St B1
Clifton Terr A2
Coleridge Cres C3
Compass Hill C1
Compton Close A2
Corporation St B1
Council Offices A1
County Walk Shopping Centre C2
Courtyard B2
Cranmer Rd B2
Crescent, The C1
Critchard Way B3
Cyril St A1
Deller's Wharf B1
Duke St B2
East Reach B3
East St B3
Eastbourne Rd B2
Eastleigh Rd C3
Eaton Cres A2
Elm Grove A1
Elms Close A1
Fons George C1
Fore St B2
Fowler St A1
French Weir Recreation Grd B1
Geoffrey Farrant Walk A2
Gray's Almshouses B2
Grays Rd B3
Greenway Ave A1
Guildford Place C1
Hammet St B2
Haydon Rd B3
Heavitree Way A2
Herbert St A1
High St C2
Holway Ave C3
Hugo St B3
Huish's Almshouses B2
Hurdle Way C2
Information Ctr C2
Jubilee St A1
King's College C3
Kings Close C3
Laburnum St B2
Lambrook Rd B3
Lansdowne Rd A3
Leslie Ave A1
Leycroft Rd B3
Library C2
Linden Grove A1
Magdalene St B2
Magistrates Court B1
Malvern Terr A2
Market House B2
Mary St C2
Middle St B2
Mitre Court B3
Mount Nebo C1
Mount St C2
Mount, The C2
Mountway C2
Museum of Somerset B1
North St B2
Northfield Ave B1
Northfield Rd B1
Northleigh Rd C3
Obridge Allotments A3
Obridge Lane A3
Obridge Rd A3
Obridge Viaduct A3
Orch Shopping Ctr C2
Osborne Way C1
Park St C1
Paul St C2
Plais St A2
Playing Field C3
Police Station C1
Portland St B1
Post Office B1/B2
Priorswood Ind Est A3
Priorswood Rd A2
Priory Ave B2
Priory Bridge Rd B2
Priory Fields Retail Park A3
Priory Park A2
Priory Way A3
Queen St B3
Railway St A1
Records Office A2
Recreation Grd A1
Riverside Place B2
St Augustine St B2
St George's C2
St Georges Sq C2
St James B2
St James St B2
St John's C1
St John's Rd B1
St Josephs Field C2
St Mary Magdalene's B2
Samuels Ct A1
Shire Hall & Law Courts C1
Somerset County Cricket Ground B2
Somerset County Hall C1
Somerset Cricket B2
South Rd C3
South St C3
Staplegrove Rd B1
Station Approach A2
Station Rd A1
Stephen St B2
Superstore C2
Swimming Pool A1
Tancred St B2
Tangier Way B1
Tauntfield Close C3
Taunton Castle B1
Taunton Dean Cricket Club C2
Taunton Station ⇌ A2
Thomas St A1
Toneway A3
Tower St B1
Trenchard Way A2
Trevor Smith Place C3
Trinity Business Centre C3
Trinity Rd C3
Trinity St B3
Trull Rd C1
Tudor House B2
Upper High St C1
Venture Way A3
Victoria Gate B3
Victoria Park B3
Victoria St B3
Viney St B3
Vivary Pk Golf Club C2
Vivary Rd C1
War Memorial ✦ C1
Wellesley St A2
Wheatley Cres A3
Whitehall A1
Wilfred Rd B3
William St A1
Wilton Church C1
Wilton Close C1
Wilton Grove C1
Wilton St C1
Winchester St B2
Winters Field B2
Wood St B1
Yarde Place B1

Telford 198

Alma Ave C1
Amphitheatre C2
Bowling Alley B2
Brandsfarm Way C3
Brunel Rd B1
Bus Station B2
Buxton Rd C1
Central Park A2
Chelsea Gardens B2
Coach Central B2
Coachwell Close B1
Colliers Way A1
Courts B2
Dale Acre Way B3
Darliston C3
Deepdale B3
Deercote B2
Dinthill C3
Doddington C3
Dodmoor Grange C3
Downemead B3
Duffryn B3
Dunsheath B3
Euston Way A3
Eyton Mound C1
Eyton Rd C1
Forgegate A2

212 Torquay • Truro • Winchester • Windsor • Wolverhampton • Worcester • Wrexham • York

Grange Central B2
Hall Park Way B1
Hinkshay Rd C2
Hollinsworth Rd A2
Holyhead Rd A3
Housing Trust A1
Ice Rink B2
Information Ctr B2
Ironmasters Way A2
Job Centre B1
Land Registry B1
Lawn Central B2
Lawnswood C1
Library B2
Malinsgate B1
Matlock Ave C1
Moor Rd C1
Mount Rd C1
Odeon B2
Park Lane A1
Police Station B1
Post Office A2/B2/C1
Priorslee Ave A3
Queen Elizabeth Ave C3
Queen Elizabeth Way B1
Queensway A2/B3
QEII Arena C2
Rampart Way A2
Randlay Ave C3
Randlay Wood C3
Rhodes Ave C1
Royal Way B1
St Leonards Rd B1
St Quentin Gate B2
Shifnal Rd A3
Silkin Way C2
Sixth Ave A1
Southwater Leisure Complex B2
Southwater Way B1
Spout Lane C1
Spout Mound B1
Spout Way C1
Stafford Court B3
Stafford Park B3
Stirchley Ave C3
Stone Row C1
Superstore B1
Telford Bridge Retail Park A1
Telford Central Station A3
Telford Centre, The B2
Telford Forge Shopping Park A1
Telford Hornets RFC C2
Telford Int Ctr C2
Telford Way A3
Third Ave A2
Town Park C2
Town Park Visitor Centre B2
Wellswood Ave A2
West Centre Way B1
Withywood Drive C1
Wonderland C2
Woodhouse Central B2
Yates Way A1

Torquay 199
Abbey Rd B2
Alexandra Rd A2
Alpine Rd B3
AMF Bowling C3
Ash Hill Rd A2
Babbacombe Rd B3
Bampfylde Rd B1
Barton Rd A1
Beacon Quay C2
Belgrave Rd A1/B1
Belmont Rd A3
Berea Rd A3
Braddons Hill Rd East B3
Brewery Park A3
Bronshill Rd A2
Carlton Rd A3
Castle Circus A2
Castle Rd A2
Cavern Rd A3
Central B2
Chatsworth Rd A2
Chestnut Ave B1
Church St A1
Coach Station A1
Corbyn Head C1
Croft Hill B1
Croft Rd B1
East St A1
Egerton Rd A3
Ellacombe Church Rd A3
Ellacombe Rd A2
Falkland Rd B1
Fleet St B2
Fleet Walk Shopping Centre B2
Grafton Rd B3
Grange Rd A3
Haldon Pier C2
Hatfield Rd A2
Highbury Rd A2
Higher Warberry Rd A3
Hillesdon Rd B3
Hoxton Rd A3
Hunsdon Rd B3
Information Ctr B2
Inner Harbour C3
Kenwyn Rd A3
King's Drive, The B1
Laburnum St A1
Law Courts A2
Library A2
Lime Ave B1
Living Coasts C3
Lower Warberry Rd B3
Lucius St B1
Lymington Rd A1
Magdalene Rd A1
Marina C2
Market Forum, The B2
Market St B2
Meadfoot Lane C3
Meadfoot Rd C3
Melville St B2
Middle Warberry Rd B3
Mill Lane A1
Montpellier Rd B3
Morgan Ave A1
Museum Rd B3
Newton Rd A1
Oakhill Rd A1
Outer Harbour C2
Parkhill Rd C3
Pimlico B2
Police Station A1
Post Office A1/B2
Prince of Wales Steps C3
Princes Rd A3
Princes Rd East A3
Princes Rd West A3
Princess Gdns C2
Princess Pier C2
Princess Theatre C2
Rathmore Rd B1
Recreation Grd B1
Riviera Int Ctr B1
Rock End Ave C3
Rock Rd B2
Rock Walk B2
Rosehill Rd A3
South West Coast Path C3
St Efride's Rd A1
St John's B3
St Luke's Rd B2
St Luke's Rd North B2
St Luke's Rd South B2
St Marychurch Rd A2
Scarborough Rd B1
Shedden Hill B2
South Pier C2
South St A1
Spanish Barn B1
Stitchill Rd B3
Strand B3
Sutherland Rd B3
Teignmouth Rd A1
Temperance St B2
Terrace, The B3
Thurlow Rd A1
Tor Bay B1
Tor Church Rd A1
Tor Hill Rd A1
Torbay Rd B2
Torquay Mus B3
Torquay Station C1
Torquay Tennis Club B1
Torre Abbey B1
Torre Abbey Meadows B1
Torre Abbey Sands B1
Torwood Gardens B3
Torwood St C3
Town Hall A2
Union Square Shopping Centre A2
Union St A1
Upton Hill A2
Upton Park A1
Upton Rd A1
Vanehill Rd C3
Vansittart Rd A1
Vaughan Parade C3
Victoria Parade C3
Victoria Rd A2
Warberry Rd West B2
Warren Rd B2
Windsor Rd A2/A3
Woodville Rd A3

Truro 199
Adelaide Ter B1
Agar Rd B3
Arch Hill C2
Arundell Place C2
Avenue, The A3
Avondale Rd B1
Back Quay B3
Barrack La C3
Barton Meadow A1
Benson Rd A2
Bishops Close A2
Bosvean Gdns B1
Bosvigo Gardens B1
Bosvigo La A1
Bosvigo Rd B2
Broad St A3
Burley Close C3
Bus Station B3
Calenick St B2
Campfield Hill B3
Carclew St B3
Carew Rd A2
Carey Park B2
Carlyon Rd A2
Carvoza Rd A3
Castle St B2
Cathedral View A2
Chainwalk Dr A2
Chapel Hill B1
Charles St B2
City Hall B3
City Rd B2
Coinage Hall B3
Comprigney Hill A1
Coosebean La A1
Copes Gdns A2
County Hall B1
Courtney Rd A2
Crescent Rd B1
Crescent Rise B1
Crescent, The B1
Daniell Court C2
Daniell Rd C2
Daniell St C2
Daubuz Close A2
Daubuz Moors Nature Reserve A3
Dobbs La B1
Edward St B2
Eliot Rd A2
Elm Court A3
Enys Close A1
Enys Rd A1
Fairmantle St B3
Falmouth Rd C2
Ferris Town B2
Fire Station B1
Frances St B2
George St B2
Green Close C2
Green La C1
Grenville Rd A2
Hall for Cornwall B3
Hendra Rd A2
Hendra Vean A1
High Cross B3
Higher Newham La C3
Higher Trehaverne A2
Hillcrest Ave B1
Hospital B2
Hunkin Close A2
Hurland Rd C3
Infirmary Hill B2
James Place B3
Kenwyn Church Rd A1
Kenwyn Hill A1
Kenwyn Rd A2
Kenwyn St B2
Kerris Gdns A1
King St B3
Leats, The B2
Lemon Quay B3
Lemon St Gallery B3
Library B1/B3
Malpas Rd B3
Magistrates Court A3
Market B3
Merrifield Close B1
Mitchell Hill A3
Moresk Close A3
Moresk Rd A3
Morlaix Ave C3
Nancemere Rd A3
Newham Business Park C3
Newham Ind Est C3
Newham Rd C3
Northfield Dr C3
Oak Way A3
Pal's Terr A3
Park View C2
Pendarves Rd A2
Plaza Cinema B3
Police Sta A2/B3
Post Office B3
Prince's St B3
Pydar St A2
Quay St B3
Redannick Cres C2
Redannick La B2
Richard Lander Monument C2
Richmond Hill B1
River St B2
Rosedale Rd A2
Royal Cornwall Museum B2
St Aubyn Rd C3
St Clement St B3
St George's Rd A1
Standing Cross B3
School La C2
Spires, The A2
Station Rd B1
Stokes Rd A2
Strangways Terr C3
Tabernacle St B3
Trehaverne La A2
Tremayne Rd A2
Treseder's Gdns A3
Treworder Rd B1
Treyew Rd B1
Truro Cathedral B3
Truro Harbour Office B3
Truro Station B3
Union St B3
Upper School La C2
Victoria Gdns B2
Waterfall Gdns B2

Winchester 199
Andover Rd A2
Andover Road Retail Park A2
Archery La C2
Arthur Rd A2
Bar End Rd C3
Beaufort Rd C2
Beggar's La B3
Bereweeke Ave A1
Bereweeke Rd A1
Boscobel Rd A2
Brassey Rd A2
Broadway B3
Brooks Shopping Centre, The B3
Bus Station B3
Butter Cross B2
Canon St C2
Castle Wall C2/C3
Cathedral C2
Cheriton Rd A1
Chesil St C3
Chesil Theatre C3
Christchurch Rd C1
City Mill B3
City Museum B2
City Rd B2
Clifton Rd B1
Clifton Terr B2
Close Wall C2/C3
Coach Park A2
Colebrook St C3
College St C2
College Walk C3
Compton Rd C2
Council Offices C3
County Council Offices B2
Cranworth Rd A2
Cromwell Rd C1
Culver Rd C2
Discovery Centre B2
Domum Rd C3
Durngate Place B3
Eastgate St B3
East Hill C3
Edgar Rd C2
Egbert Rd A2
Elm Rd B1
Everyman C2
Fairfield Rd A1
Fire Station B3
Fordington Ave B1
Fordington Rd A1
Friarsgate B3
Gordon Rd B3
Great Hall & Round Table, The B2
Greenhill Rd B1
Guildhall B3
Hatherley Rd A1
High St B2
Hillier Way A3
HM Prison B1
Hyde Abbey (Remains) A2
Hyde Abbey Rd B2
Hyde Close A2
Hyde St A2
Information Ctr B3
Jane Austen's House C2
Jewry St B2
King Alfred Place A2
Kingsgate Arch C2
Kingsgate Park C2
Kingsgate Rd C2
Kingsgate St C2
Lankhills Rd A2
Law Courts B2
Library B2
Lower Brook St B3
Magdalen Hill B3
Market La B2
Mews La B1
Middle Brook St B3
Middle Rd B1
Military Museums B2
Milland Rd C3
Milverton Rd B1
Monks Rd A3
North Hill Close A2
North Walls B2
North Walls Recreation Gnd A3
Nuns Rd A3
Oram's Arbour B1
Owens Rd A2
Parchment St B2
Park & Ride C3
Park Ave B3
Playing Field A1
Police HQ B1
Portal Rd C3
Post Office B2/C1
Ranelagh Rd C1
Regimental Museum B2
River Park Leisure Ctr B3
Romans' Rd C2
Romsey Rd B1
Royal Hampshire County Hospital (A&E) B1
St Cross Rd C2
St George's St B2
St Giles Hill C3
St James Villas C2
St James' La B1
St James' Terr B1
St John's B3
St John's St B3
St Michael's Rd C2
St Paul's Hill B1
St Peter St B2
St Swithun St C2
St Thomas St C2
Saxon Rd A2
School of Art B3
Sleepers Hill Rd C1
Southgate St B2
Sparkford Rd C1
Square, The B2
Staple Gdns B2
Station Rd B2
Step Terr B1
Stockbridge Rd A1
Stuart Cres C1
Sussex St B2
Swan Lane B2
Tanner St B3
Theatre Royal B2
Tower St B2
Union St B3
Univ of Southampton (Winchester School of Art) B3
University of Winchester (King Alfred Campus) C1
Upper Brook St B2
Wales St B3
Water Lane B3
Weirs, The C3
West End Terr B1
Western Rd B1
Westgate B2
Wharf Hill C3
Winchester Sta A2
Winnall Moors Wildlife Reserve A3
Wolvesey Castle C3
Worthy Lane A2
Worthy Rd A2

Windsor 199
Adelaide Sq C3
Albany Rd C2
Albert St B1
Alexandra Gdns B2
Alexandra Rd C2
Alma Rd B2
Arthur Rd B2
Bachelors Acre B3
Barry Ave B2
Beaumont Rd C2
Bexley St B1
Boat House B2
Brocas St B2
Brocas, The A2
Brook St C3
Bulkeley Ave C1
Castle Hill B3
Charles St B2
Claremont Rd C2
Clarence Cres B2
Clarence Rd B1
Clewer Court Rd B1
Coach Park B2
College Cres C1
Cricket Ground C3
Dagmar Rd C2
Datchet Rd B3
Devereux Rd C2
Dorset Rd C2
Duke St B1
Elm Rd C1
Eton College A3
Eton College Natural History Mus A2
Eton Ct A2
Eton Sq A2
Eton Wick Rd A2
Farm Yard B3
Fire Station C2
Frances Rd C2
Frogmore Dr B3
Gloucester Place C3
Goslar Way C1
Goswell Hill B2
Goswell Rd B2
Green La C1
Grove Rd C2
Guildhall B3
Helena Rd C2
Helston La B1
High St A2/B3
Holy Trinity C2
Home Park, The A3/C3
Household Cavalry C2
Imperial Rd C1
Information Ctr B2
Keats La A2
King Edward VII Ave A3
King Edward VII Hospital C2
King George V Memorial B3
King Stable St A2
King's Rd C3
Library A2/B2
Long Walk, The C3
Maidenhead Rd B1
Meadow La A2
Municipal Offices C3
Nell Gwynne's House B3
Osborne Rd C2
Oxford Rd B1
Park St B3
Peascod St B2
Police Station C2
Post Office A2/C1
Princess Margaret Hosp (private) C2
Old Court Art Space, The C2
Queen Elizabeth Bridge A1
Queen Victoria's Walk B3
Queen's Rd C2
River St B2
Romney Island A3
Romney Lock A3
Romney Lock Rd A3
Russell St C2
St George's Chapel B3
St John's B3
St John's Chapel A2
St Leonards Rd C2
St Mark's Rd C2
Sheet St C3
Shopmobility B2
South Meadow A2
South Meadow La A2
Springfield Rd C1
Stovell Rd B1
Sunbury Rd A2
Tangier La A2
Temple Rd C2
Thames St B3
Theatre Royal B3
Trinity Place C2
Vansittart Rd B1/C1
Victoria Barracks C2
Victoria St C2
Westmead C1
White Lilies Island A1
William St B2
Windsor & Eton Central B2
Windsor & Eton Riverside A3
Windsor Bridge B3
Windsor Castle B3
Windsor Leisure Ctr B1
Windsor Relief Rd A1
Windsor Royal Station Shopping Centre B2
Windsor Yards B2
York Ave C1
York Rd C1

Wolverhampton 200
Albion St B3
Arena B2
Art Gallery B2
Ashland St C1
Austin St A1
Badger Dr A3
Bailey St B3
Bath Ave B1
Bath Rd B1
Bell St C2
Berry St B3
Bilston Rd C3
Bilston St C3
Birmingham Canal A3
Bone Mill La A2
Brewery Rd B1
Bright St A1
Burton Cres B3
Bus Station B3
Cambridge St A3
Camp St B2
Cannock Rd A3
Castle St C2
Chapel Ash C1
Cherry St C1
Chester St A1
Church La C2
Church St C2
Civic Centre B2
Civic Hall B2
Clarence Rd B2
Cleveland St C2
Clifton St C1
Coach Station A2
Compton Rd B1
Corn Hill B3
Coven St A3
Craddock St A1
Cross St North A2
Crown & County Courts C3
Crown St A2
Culwell St B3
Dale St C1
Darlington St C1
Devon Rd A1
Drummond St B2
Dudley Rd C2
Dudley St B2
Duke St C3
Dunkley St B1
Dunstall Ave A2
Dunstall Hill A2
Dunstall Rd A1/A2
Evans St A1
Fawdry St A1
Field St B3
Fire Station C1
Fiveways A2
Fowler Playing Fields A3
Fox's La A2
Francis St A2
Fryer St B3
Gloucester St A1
Gordon St C3
Graiseley St C1
Grand B3
Grand Station B3
Granville St C3
Great Brickkiln St C1
Great Hampton St A1
Great Western St A2
Grimstone St B3
Harrow St A1
Hilton St A3
Hive Liby The B2
Horseley Fields C3
Humber Rd C1
Information Ctr B2
Jack Hayward Way A2
Jameson St A1
Jenner St C3
Kennedy Rd B3
Kimberley St C1
King St B2
Laburnum St C1
Lansdowne Rd B1
Leicester St A1
Lever St C3
Library C3
Lichfield St B2
Light House B3
Little's La B3
Lock St B3
Lord St C1
Lowe St A1
Maltings, The B2
Mander Centre C2
Mander St C1
Market C2
Market St B2
Maxwell Rd C3
Merridale St C1
Middlecross C3
Molineux St B2
Mostyn St A1
Newhampton Arts Centre B1
New Hampton Rd East A1
Nine Elms La A3
North Rd A2
Oaks Cres C1
Oxley St A2
Paget St A1
Park Ave B1
Park Road East A1
Park Road West B1
Paul St C2
Pelham St C1
Penn Rd C2
Piper's Row C3
Piper's Row C3
Pitt St C2
Police Station C3
Pool St C2
Poole St A3
Post Office A1/B2/B2/C2/C3
Powlett St C3
Queen St B2
Raby St C3
Railway Dr B3
Red Hill St B2
Red Lion St B2
Retreat St C1
Ring Rd B2
Royal, The C3
Rugby St A1
Russell St C1
St Andrew's B1
St David's B3
St George's C3
St George's Parade C2
St James St C3
St John's C2
St John's C2
St John's Retail Pk C2
St John's Square C2
St Mark's C1
St Marks Rd C1
St Marks St C1
St Patrick's B2
St Peter's B2
St Peter's B2
Salisbury St C1
Salop St C2
School St C2
Sherwood St A2
Smestow St A3
Snow Hill C2
Springfield Rd A3
Stafford St A2/B2
Staveley Rd A1
Steelhouse La C3
Stephenson St C1
Stewart St C2
Sun St B3
Tempest St C2
Temple St C2
Tettenhall Rd B1
Thomas St C2
Thornley St B2
Tower St C2
University B2
Upper Zoar St C1
Vicarage Rd C3
Victoria St C2
Walpole St A1
Walsall St C3
Ward St C3
Warwick St C3
Water St A3
Waterloo Rd B2
Wednesfield Rd B3
West Park (not A&E) B1
West Park Swimming Pool B1
Wharf St C3
Whitmore Hill B2
Wolverhampton B3
Wolverhampton B3
Wolverhampton St George's C2
Wolverhampton Wanderers Football Gnd (Molineux) B2
Worcester St C2
Wulfrun Centre C2
Yarwell Close A3
York St C3
Zoar St C1

Worcester 200
Albany Terr A1
Angel Place B2
Angel St B2
Ashcroft Rd A2
Athelstan Rd C3
Avenue, The C1
Back Lane North A1
Back Lane South A1
Barbourne Rd A2
Bath Rd C2
Battenhall Rd C3
Bridge St B2
Britannia Sq A1
Broad St B2
Bromwich La C1
Bromwich Rd C1
Bromyard Rd C1
Bus Station B2
Butts, The B2
Carden St B3
Castle St A2
Cathedral C2
Cathedral Plaza B2
Charles St B3
Chequers La B1
Chestnut St A2
Chestnut Walk A2
Citizens' Advice Bureau B2
City Walls Rd B2
Cole Hill C3
College St C2
Commandery, The C3
Cripplegate Park B1
Croft Rd B1
Cromwell St B3
Cross, The B2
Crowngate Ctr B2
Deansway B2
Diglis Pde C2
Diglis Rd C2
Edgar Tower C2
Farrier St A2
Foregate St B2
Fort Royal Hill C3
Fort Royal Park C3
Foundry St B3
Friar St C2
George St B3
Grand Stand Rd B1
Greenhill C3
Greyfriars B2
Guildhall B2
Henwick Rd B1
High St B2
Hill St B3
Hive, The B2
Huntingdon Hall B2
Hylton Rd B1
Information Ctr B2
King Charles Place Shopping Centre C1
King's School C2
King's School Playing Field C2
Kleve Walk C2
Lansdowne Cres A3
Lansdowne Rd A3
Lansdowne Walk A3
Laslett St A3
Little Chestnut St A2
Little London A2
London Rd C3
Lowell St A3
Lowesmoor B2
Lowesmoor Terrace A3
Lowesmoor Wharf A3
Magistrates Court A2
Midland Rd B3
Mill St C2
Moors Severn Terrace, The A1
Museum & Art Gallery A2
Museum of Royal Worcester C2
New Rd C1
New St B2
Northfield St A2
Odeon B2
Old Palace The C2
Padmore St B3
Park St C3
Pheasant St B3
Pitchcroft Racecourse A1
Police Station A2
Portland St C2
Post Office B2
Quay St B2
Queen St B2
Rainbow Hill A3
Recreation Ground A2
Reindeer Court B2
Rogers Hill A3
Sabrina Terr A1
St Dunstan's Cres C3
St John's C1
St Martin's Gate B3
St Martin's Quarter B3
St Oswald's Rd A2
St Paul's St B3
St Swithin's Church B2
St Wulstans Cres C3
Sansome Walk A2
Severn St C2
Shambles, The B2
Shaw St B2
Shire Hall Crown Court A2
Shrub Hill Rd B3
Shrub Hill Retail Pk B3
Slingpool Walk C1
South Parade B2
Southfield St A2
Sports Centre A3
Stanley Rd B3
Swan, The A1
Swimming Pool A2
Tallow Hill B3
Tennis Walk A2
Tolladine Rd B3
Tudor House B2
Tybridge St B1
Tything, The A2
Univ of Worcester B2
Vincent Rd B3
Vue C2
Washington St A3
Woolhope Rd C3
Worcester Bridge B2
Worcester County Cricket Club C1
Worcester Foregate Street B2
Worcester Shrub Hill B3
Worcester Royal Grammar School A2
Wylds La C3

Wrexham Wrecsam 200
Abbot St B2
Acton Rd A3
Albert St C3
Alexandra Rd C1
Aran Rd A3
Barnfield C3
Bath Rd C2
Beeches, The A3
Beechley Rd C3
Belgrave Rd C2
Belle Vue Park C2
Belle Vue Rd C2
Belvedere Dr A1
Bennion's Rd C3
Berse Rd A1
Bersham Rd C1
Birch St C3
Bodhyfryd B3
Border Retail Park B3
Bradley Rd C2
Bright St B1
Bron-y-Nant B1
Brook St C2
Bryn-y-Cabanau Rd C3
Bury St C1
Bus Station B2
Butchers Market B3
Caia Rd C3
Cambrian Ind Est C3
Caxton Place B2
Cemetery C1
Centenary Rd C1
Central Retail Park B2
Chapel St C2
Charles St B3
Chester Rd A3
Chester St B3
Cilcen Grove A3
Citizens Advice Bureau B2
Cobden Rd B1
Council Offices B3
County A2
Crescent Rd B3
Crispin La A2
Croesnewyth Rd B1
Cross St A2
Cunliffe St A2
Derby Rd C3
Dolydd Rd B1
Duke St B2
Eagles Meadow C3
Earle St C2
East Ave A2
Edward St C2
Egerton St B2
Empress Rd C1
Erddig Rd C2
Fairy Rd C2
Fire Station B2
Foster Rd A3
Foxwood Dr C1
Garden Rd A2
General Market B3
Gerald St B2
Gibson St C3
Glyndŵr University Plas Coch Campus A1
Greenbank St C3
Greenfield A2
Grosvenor Rd B2
Grove Park B3
Grove Park Rd B3
Grove Rd A3
Guildhall B2
Haig Rd C3
Hampden Rd C2
Hazel Grove A3
Henblas St B3
High St B3
Hightown Rd C3
Hill St B2
Holt Rd B3
Holt St B3
Hope St B2
Huntroyde Ave C3
Information Ctr B3
Island Green Shopping Centre B2
Jobcentre Plus B2
Jubilee Rd B2
King St B2
Kingsmills Rd C3
Lambpit St B3
Law Courts B3
Lawson Close A3
Lawson Rd A3
Lea Rd C2
Library & Arts Ctr B2
Lilac Way B1
Llys David Lord B1
Lorne St A2
Maesgwyn Rd B1
Maesydre Rd A3
Manley Rd B3
Market St B3
Mawddy Ave A2
Mayville Ave A2
Meml Gallery B2
Memorial Hall B3
Mold Rd A1
Mount St C3
Neville Cres A3
New Rd A2
North Wales Regional Tennis Centre A1
Oak Dr A3
Odeon B3
Park Ave A3
Park St A2
Peel St C1
Pen y Bryn C2
Pentre Felin C2
Penymaes Ave A3
Peoples Market B3
Percy St C2
Pines, The A3
Plas Coch Rd A1
Plas Coch Retail Pk A1
Police Station B3
Poplar Rd C2
Post Office A2/B3/C3
Powell Rd B3
Poyser St C2
Price's La A2
Primose Way B1
Princess St C1
Queen St B3
Queens Sq B2
Regent St B2
Rhosddu Rd A2/B2
Rhosnesni La A3
Rivulet Rd C3
Ruabon Rd C2
Ruthin Rd C1/C2
St Giles C3
St Giles Way C3
St James Ct A2
St Mary's B2
Salisbury Rd C3
Salop Rd C3
Sontley Rd C2
Spring Rd A2
Stanley St C3
Stansty Rd A2
Station Approach B2
Studio B2
Superstore B3/C1
Talbot Rd C2
Techniquest Glyndwr A2
Town Hill C2
Trevor St C2
Trinity St B2
Tuttle St C3
Vale Park A1
Vernon St B2
Vicarage Hill B2
Victoria Rd C2
Walnut St A2
War Memorial B3
Waterworld Leisure Centre B3
Watery Rd B1/B2
Wellington Rd C2
Westminster Dr A3
William Aston Hall A1
Windsor Rd A1
Wrecsam
Wrexham AFC A1
Wrexham Central B2
Wrexham General B2
Wrexham Maelor Hospital (A&E) B1
Wrexham Technology Park B1
Wynn Ave A2
Yale College B3
Yale Grove A3
Yorke St C3

York 200
Aldwark A2
Barbican Rd C3
Bar Convent Living Heritage Centre C1
Barley Hall B2
Bishopgate St C2
Bishopshill Senior C2
Bishopthorpe Rd C2
Blossom St C1
Bootham A1
Bootham Cres A1
Bootham Terr A1
Bridge St B2
Brook St A2
Brownlow St A2
Burton Stone La A1
Castle Museum C2
Castlegate B2
Cemetery Rd C3
Cherry St C2
City Screen B2
City Wall A2/B1/C3
Clarence St A2
Clementhorpe C2
Clifford St B2
Clifford's Tower B2
Clifton A1
Coach park A2
Coney St B2
Coppergate Ctr B2
Cromwell Rd C2
Crown Court C2
Davygate B2
Deanery Gdns A2
DIG B2
Dodsworth Ave A3
Eboracum Way A3
Ebor Industrial Est B3
Eldon St A2
Everyman C1
Fairfax House B2
Fire Station C3
Fishergate C3
Foss Islands Rd B3
Foss Islands Retail Park B3
Fossbank A3
Garden St A2
George St C3
Gillygate A2
Goodramgate B2
Grand Opera House B2
Grosvenor Terr A1
Guildhall B2
Hallfield Rd A3
Heslington Rd C3
Heworth Green A3
Holy Trinity B2
Hope St C3
Huntington Rd A3
Information Ctr B2
James St B3
Jorvik Viking Ctr B2
Kent St C3
Lawrence St C3
Layerthorpe A3
Leeman Rd B1
Lendal B2
Lendal Bridge B1
Library A2/B1
Longfield Terr A1
Lord Mayor's Walk A2
Lowther St A2
Mansion House B2
Margaret St C3
Marygate A1
Melbourne St C3
Merchant Adventurers' Hall B2
Merchant Taylors' Hall B2
Micklegate B1
Micklegate Bar C1
Monkgate A2
Moss St C1
Museum Gdns B1
Museum St B1
National Railway Museum B1
Navigation Rd B3
Newton Terr C2
North Pde A1
North St B2
Nunnery La C1
Nunthorpe Rd C1
Ouse Bridge B2
Paragon St C3
Park Grove A3
Park St C1
Parliament St B2
Peasholme Green B3
Penley's Grove St A2
Piccadilly B2
Police Station B2
Post Office B1/B2/C3
Priory St B1
Queen Anne's Rd A1
Regimental Mus B2
Richard III Experience at Monk Bar A2
Roman Bath B2
Rowntree Park C2
St Andrewgate B2
St Benedict Rd C1
St John St A2
St Olave's Rd A1
St Peter's Grove A1
St Saviourgate B2
Scarcroft Hill C1
Scarcroft Rd C1
Shambles, The B2
Shopmobility B2
Skeldergate C2
Skeldergate Bridge C2
Station Rd B1
Stonebow, The B2
Stonegate B2
Superstore A3
Sycamore Terrace A1
Terry Ave C2
Theatre Royal B2
Thorpe St C1
Toft Green B1
Tower St C2
Townend St A2
Treasurer's House A2
Trinity La B1
Undercroft Museum A2
Union Terrace A2
Victor St C2
Vine St C2
Walmgate B3
War Memorial B1
Wellington St C3
York Art Gallery A1
York Barbican C3
York Brewery B1
York Dungeon, The B2
York Minster A2
York St John University A2
York Station B1

Index

Abbreviations used in the index

Aberdeen	Aberdeen City
Aberds	Aberdeenshire
Ald	Alderney
Anglesey	Isle of Anglesey
Angus	Angus
Argyll	Argyll and Bute
Bath	Bath and North East Somerset
BCP	Bournemouth, Christchurch and Poole
Bedford	Bedford
Blackburn	Blackburn with Darwen
Blackpool	Blackpool
Bl Gwent	Blaenau Gwent
Borders	Scottish Borders
Brack	Bracknell
Bridgend	Bridgend
Brighton	City of Brighton and Hove
Bristol	City and County of Bristol
Bucks	Buckinghamshire
Caerph	Caerphilly
Cambs	Cambridgeshire
Cardiff	Cardiff
Carms	Carmarthenshire
C Beds	Central Bedfordshire
Ceredig	Ceredigion
Ches E	Cheshire East
Ches W	Cheshire West and Chester
Clack	Clackmannanshire
Conwy	Conwy
Corn	Cornwall
Cumb	Cumbria
Darl	Darlington
Denb	Denbighshire
Derby	City of Derby
Derbys	Derbyshire
Devon	Devon
Dorset	Dorset
Dumfries	Dumfries and Galloway
Dundee	Dundee City
Durham	Durham
E Ayrs	East Ayrshire
Edin	City of Edinburgh
E Dunb	East Dunbartonshire
E Loth	East Lothian
E Renf	East Renfrewshire
Essex	Essex
E Sus	East Sussex
E Yorks	East Riding of Yorkshire
Falk	Falkirk
Fife	Fife
Flint	Flintshire
Glasgow	City of Glasgow
Glos	Gloucestershire
Gtr Man	Greater Manchester
Guern	Guernsey
Gwyn	Gwynedd
Halton	Halton
Hants	Hampshire
Hereford	Herefordshire
Herts	Hertfordshire
Highld	Highland
Hrtlpl	Hartlepool
Hull	Hull
Invclyd	Inverclyde
IoM	Isle of Man
IoW	Isle of Wight
Jersey	Jersey
Kent	Kent
Lancs	Lancashire
Leicester	City of Leicester
Leics	Leicestershire
Lincs	Lincolnshire
London	Greater London
Luton	Luton
Mbro	Middlesbrough
Medway	Medway
Mers	Merseyside
Midloth	Midlothian
M Keynes	Milton Keynes
Mon	Monmouthshire
Moray	Moray
M Tydf	Merthyr Tydfil
N Ayrs	North Ayrshire
Neath	Neath Port Talbot
NE Lincs	North East Lincolnshire
Newport	City and County of Newport
N Lanark	North Lanarkshire
N Lincs	North Lincolnshire
N Nhants	North Northamptonshire
Norf	Norfolk
Northumb	Northumberland
Nottingham	City of Nottingham
Notts	Nottinghamshire
N Som	North Somerset
N Yorks	North Yorkshire
Orkney	Orkney
Oxon	Oxfordshire
Pboro	Peterborough
Pembs	Pembrokeshire
Perth	Perth and Kinross
Plym	Plymouth
Powys	Powys
Ptsmth	Portsmouth
Reading	Reading
Redcar	Redcar and Cleveland
Renfs	Renfrewshire
Rhondda	Rhondda Cynon Taff
Rutland	Rutland
S Ayrs	South Ayrshire
Scilly	Scilly
S Glos	South Gloucestershire
Shetland	Shetland
Shrops	Shropshire
S Lanark	South Lanarkshire
Slough	Slough
Som	Somerset
Soton	Southampton
Southend	Southend-on-Sea
Staffs	Staffordshire
Stirling	Stirling
Stockton	Stockton-on-Tees
Stoke	Stoke-on-Trent
Suff	Suffolk
Sur	Surrey
Swansea	Swansea
Swindon	Swindon
S Yorks	South Yorkshire
T&W	Tyne and Wear
Telford	Telford and Wrekin
Thurrock	Thurrock
Torbay	Torbay
Torf	Torfaen
V Glam	The Vale of Glamorgan
Warks	Warwickshire
Warr	Warrington
W Berks	West Berkshire
W Dunb	West Dunbartonshire
Wilts	Wiltshire
Windsor	Windsor and Maidenhead
W Isles	Western Isles
W Loth	West Lothian
W Mid	West Midlands
W Nhants	West Northamptonshire
Wokingham	Wokingham
Worcs	Worcestershire
Wrex	Wrexham
W Sus	West Sussex
W Yorks	West Yorkshire
York	City of York

How to use the index

Example

Trudoxhill Som **24** E2
- grid square
- page number
- county or unitary authority

A

Abbas Combe 12 B5
Abberley 50 C2
Abberton Essex . . 43 C6
  Worcs 50 D4
Abberwick 117 C7
Abbess Roding . . 42 C1
Abbey 11 C6
Abbey-cwm-hir . . 48 B2
Abbeydale 88 F4
Abbey Dore 49 F5
Abbey Field 43 B5
Abbey Hulton 75 E6
Abbey
  St Bathans 122 C3
Abbeystead 93 D5
Abbey Town 107 D8
Abbey Village . . . 86 B4
Abbey Wood 29 B5
Abbots Bickington . . 9 C5
Abbots Bromley . . 62 B4
Abbotsbury 12 F3
Abbotsham 9 B6
Abbotskerswell . . . 7 C6
Abbots Langley . . . 40 D3
Abbots Leigh 23 B7
Abbotsley 54 D3
Abbots Morton . . . 50 D5
Abbots Ripton . . . 54 B3
Abbots Salford . . . 51 E5
Abbotswood 14 B4
Abbotts Ann 25 E8
Abcott 49 B5
Abdon 61 F5
Aber 46 E3
Aberaeron 46 C3
Aberaman 34 D4
Aberangell 58 C5
Aber-Arad 46 F2
Aberarder 137 F7
Aberarder House . 138 E2
Aberarder Lodge . 137 F8
Abergargie 128 C3
Aberarth 46 C3
Aberavon 33 E8
Aber-banc 46 E2
Aberbeeg 35 D6
Abercanaid 34 D4
Abercarn 35 E6
Abercastle 44 B3
Abercegir 58 D5
Aberchirder 152 C6
Aber Cowarch . . . 59 C5
Abercraf 34 C2
Abercrombie 129 D7
Abercych 45 E4
Abercynafon 34 C4
Abercynon 34 E4
Aberdalgie 128 B2
Aberdâr
  = Aberdare 34 D3

Aberdare
  = Aberdâr 34 D3
Aberdaron 70 E2
Aberdaugleddau
  = Milford Haven . 44 E4
Aberdeen 141 D8
Aberdesach 82 F4
Aberdour 128 F3
Aberdovey 58 E3
Aberdulais 34 D1
Aberedw 48 E2
Abereiddy 44 B2
Abererch 70 D4
Aberfan 34 D4
Aberfeldy 133 E5
Aberffraw 82 E3
Aberffrwd 47 B5
Aberford 95 F7
Aberfoyle 126 D4
Abergavenny
  = Y Fenni 35 C6
Abergele 72 B3
Aber-Giâr 46 E4
Abergorlech 46 F4
Abergwaun
  = Fishguard 44 B4
Abergwesyn 47 D7
Abergwili 33 B5
Abergwynant 58 C3
Aber-gwynfi 34 E2
Abergwyngregyn . 83 D6
Abergynolwyn . . . 58 D3
Aber-Hirnant 72 F3
Aberhonddu
  = Brecon 34 B4
Aberhosan 58 E5
Aberkenfig 34 F2
Aberlady 129 F6
Aberlemno 135 D5
Aberllefenni 58 D4
Abermagwr 47 B5
Abermaw
  = Barmouth 58 C3
Abermeurig 46 D4
Abermule 59 E8
Abernaint 59 B8
Abernant 32 B4
Aber-nant 34 D4
Abernethy 128 C3
Abernyte 134 F2
Aberpennar
  = Mountain Ash . 34 E4
Aberporth 45 D4
Aber-Rhiwlech . . . 59 B6
Abersoch 70 E4
Abersychan 35 D6
Abertawe
  = Swansea 33 E7
Aberteifi
  = Cardigan 45 E3
Aberthin 22 B2
Abertillery
  = Abertyleri . . . 35 D6

Abertridwr Caerph. . 35 F5
  Powys 59 C7
Abertyleri
  = Abertillery . . . 35 D6
Abertysswg 35 D5
Aberuthven 127 C8
Aber-Village 35 B5
Aberyscir 34 B3
Aberystwyth 58 F2
Abhainn Suidhe . 154 G5
Abingdon-
  on-Thames 38 E4
Abinger Common . 28 E2
Abinger Hammer . 27 E8
Abington 114 B2
Abington Pigotts . 54 E4
Ab Kettleby 64 B4
Ab Lench 50 D5
Ablington Glos . . . 37 D8
  Wilts 25 E6
Abney 75 B8
Aboyne 140 E4
Abram 86 D4
Abriachan 151 H8
Abridge 41 E7
Abronhill 119 B7
Abson 24 B2
Abthorpe 52 E4
Abune-the-Hill . . 159 F3
Aby 79 B7
Acaster Malbis . . 95 E8
Acaster Selby . . . 95 E8
Accrington 87 B5
Acha 146 F4
Achabraid 145 E7
Achachork 149 D9
Achafolla 124 D3
Achagary 157 D10
Achahoish 144 F6
Achalader 133 E8
Achallader 131 E7
Acha Mor 155 E8
Achanalt 150 E5
Achanamara 144 E6
Achandunie 151 D9
Ach'an Todhair . . 130 B4
Achany 157 J8
Achaphubuil 130 B4
Acharacle 147 E9
Acharn Highld . . . 147 F10
  Perth 132 E4
Acharole 158 E4
Achath 141 C6
Achavanich 158 F3
Achavraat 151 G12
Achddu 33 D5
Achduart 156 J3
Achentoul 157 F11
Achfary 156 F5
Achgarve 155 H13
Achiemore Highld . 156 C6
  Highld 157 D11
A'Chill 148 H7

Achiltibuie 156 J3
Achina 157 C10
Achinduich 157 J8
Achindunie 124 B4
Achingills 158 D3
Achintee Highld . . 131 B5
  Highld 150 G2
Achintraid 149 E13
Achlean 138 E4
Achleck 146 G7
Achluachrach . . . 137 F5
Achlyness 156 D5
Achmelvich 156 G3
Achmore Highld . . 149 E13
  Stirling 132 F2
Achnaba Argyll . . 124 B5
  Argyll 145 E8
Achnabat 151 H8
Achnacarnin 156 F3
Achnacarry 136 F4
Achnacloich Argyll 125 B5
  Highld 149 H10
Achnaconeran . . . 137 C7
Achnacraig 146 G7
Achnacroish 130 E2
Achnadrish 146 F7
Achnafalnich 125 C8
Achnagarron 151 E9
Achnaha 146 E7
Achnahanat 151 B8
Achnahannet 139 B5
Achnairn 157 H8
Achnaluachrach . . 157 J9
Achnasaul 136 F4
Achnasheen 150 F4
Achosnich 146 E7
Achranich 147 G10
Achreamie 157 C13
Achriabhach 131 C5
Achriesgill 156 D5
Achrimsdale 157 J12
Achtoty 157 C9
Achurch 65 F7
Achuvoldrach . . . 157 D8
Achvaich 151 B10
Achvarasdal 157 C12
Ackergill 158 E5
Acklam Mbro . . . 102 C2
  N Yorks 96 C3
Ackleton 61 E7
Acklington 117 D8
Ackton 88 B5
Ackworth Moor
  Top 88 C5
Acle 69 C7
Acock's Green . . . 62 F5
Acol 31 C7
Acomb Northumb . 110 C2
  York 95 D8
Aconbury 49 F7
Acre 87 B5
Acrefair 73 E6
Acre Street 15 E8

Achitibuie 156 J3
Aberdeen . . . .

Acton Ches E . . . 74 D3
  Dorset 13 G7
  London 41 F5
  Shrops 60 F3
  Suff 56 E2
  Wrex 73 D7
Acton Beauchamp . 49 D8
Acton Bridge 74 B2
Acton Burnell 60 D5
Acton Green 49 D8
Acton Pigott 60 D5
Acton Round 61 E6
Acton Scott 60 F4
Acton Trussell . . . 62 C3
Acton Turville 37 F5
Adbaston 61 B7
Adber 12 B3
Adderley 74 E3
Adderstone 123 F7
Addiewell 120 C2
Addingham 94 E3
Addington Bucks . . 39 B7
  Kent 29 D7
  London 28 C4
Addinston 121 D8
Addiscombe 28 C4
Addlestone 27 C8
Addlethorpe 79 C8
Adel 95 F5
Adeney 61 C7
Adfa 59 D7
Adforton 49 B6
Adisham 31 D6
Adlestrop 38 B2
Adlingfleet 90 B2
Adlington 86 C4
Admaston Staffs . . 62 B4
  Telford 61 C6
Admington 51 E7
Adstock 52 F5
Adstone 52 D3
Adversane 16 B4
Advie 152 E1
Adwalton 88 B3
Adwell 39 E6
Adwick le Street . . 89 D6
Adwick upon
  Dearne 89 D5
Adziel 153 C9
Ae Village 114 F2
Affleck 141 B7
Affpuddle 13 E6
Affric Lodge 136 B4
Afon-wen 72 B5
Afton 14 F4
Agglethorpe 101 F5
Agneash 84 D4
Aigburth 85 F4
Aiginis 155 D9
Aike 97 E6
Aikerness 159 C5
Aikers 159 J5
Aiketgate 108 E4

Aikton 108 D2
Ailey 48 E5
Ailstone 51 D7
Ailsworth 65 E8
Ainderby
  Quernhow 102 F1
Ainderby Steeple . 101 E8
Aingers Green . . . 43 B7
Ainsdale 85 C4
Ainsdale-on-Sea . 85 C4
Ainstable 108 E5
Ainsworth 87 C5
Ainthorpe 103 D5
Aintree 85 E4
Aird Argyll 124 E3
  Dumfries 104 C4
  Highld 149 A12
  W Isles 155 D10
Aird a Mhachair . 148 D2
Aird a' Mhulaidh . 154 F6
Aird Asaig 154 G6
Aird Dhail 155 A9
Airdens 151 B9
Aird Mhidhinis . . 148 H2
Aird Mhighe . . . .
  W Isles 154 H6
  W Isles 154 J5
Aird Mhor 148 H2
Aird of Sleat . . . 149 H10
Airdrie 119 C7
Aird Thunga 155 D9
Airdtorrisdale . . . 157 C9
Aird Uig 154 D5
Airidh a Bhruaich 154 F7
Airieland 106 D4
Airmyn 89 B8
Airntully 133 F7
Airor 149 H12
Airth 127 F7
Airton 94 D2
Airyhassen 105 E7
Aisby Lincs 78 F3
  Lincs 90 E2
Aisgernis 148 F2
Aiskew 101 F7
Aislaby N Yorks . . 103 D6
  N Yorks 103 F5
  Stockton 102 C2
Aisthorpe 78 A2
Aith Orkney 159 G3
  Shetland 160 D8
  Shetland 160 H5
Aithsetter 160 K6
Aitkenhead 112 D3
Aitnoch 151 H12
Akeld 117 B5
Akeley 52 F5
Akenham 56 E5
Albaston 6 B2
Alberbury 60 C3
Albourne 17 C6
Albrighton Shrops . 60 C4
  Shrops 62 D2

Alburgh 69 F5
Albury Herts 41 B7
  Sur 27 E8
Albury End 41 B7
Alby Hill 81 D7
Alcaig 151 F8
Alcaston 60 F4
Alcester 51 D5
Alciston 18 E2
Alcombe Som . . . 21 E8
  Wilts 24 C3
Alconbury 54 B2
Alconbury Weald .
  Cambs 54 B3
Alconbury Weston . 54 B2
Aldbourne 25 B7
Aldbrough 97 F8
Aldbrough
  St John 101 C7
Aldbury 40 C2
Aldcliffe 92 C4
Aldclune 133 C6
Aldeburgh 57 D8
Aldeby 69 E7
Aldenham 40 E4
Alderbury 14 B2
Aldercar 76 E4
Alderford 68 C4
Alderholt 14 C2
Alderley 36 E4
Alderley Edge . . . 74 B5
Aldermaston 26 C3
Aldermaston
  Wharf 26 C4
Alderminster 51 E7
Alder's End 49 E8
Aldersey Green . . 73 D8
Aldershot 27 D6
Alderton Glos . . . 50 F5
  Shrops 60 B4
  Suff 57 E7
  Wilts 37 F5
  W Nhants 52 E5
Alderwasley 76 D3
Aldfield 95 C5
Aldford 73 D8
Aldham Essex . . . 43 B5
  Suff 56 E4
Aldie 151 C10
Aldingbourne . . . 16 D3
Aldingham 92 B2
Aldington Kent . . . 19 B7
  Worcs 51 E5
Aldington Frith . . . 19 B7
Aldochlay 126 E2
Aldreth 54 B5
Aldridge 62 D4
Aldringham 57 C8
Aldsworth 38 C1
Aldunie 140 B2

Aldwark Derbys . . 76 D2
  N Yorks 95 C7
Aldwick 16 E3
Aldwincle 65 F7
Aldworth 26 B3
Alexandria 118 B3
Alfardisworthy . . . 8 C4
Alfington 11 E6
Alfold 27 F8
Alfold Bars 27 F8
Alfold Crossways . 27 F8
Alford Aberds . . 140 C4
  Lincs 79 B7
  Som 23 F8
Alfreton 76 D4
Alfrick 50 D2
Alfrick Pound . . . 50 D2
Alfriston 18 E2
Algaltraig 145 F9
Algarkirk 79 F5
Alhampton 23 F8
Aline Lodge 154 F6
Alisary 147 D10
Alkborough 90 B2
Alkerton 51 E8
Alkham 31 E6
Alkington 74 F2
Alkmonton 75 F8
Alladale Lodge . . 150 C7
Allaleigh 7 D6
Allanaquoich . . . 139 E7
Allangrange
  Mains 151 F9
Allanton Borders . 122 D4
  N Lanark 119 D8
Allathasdal 148 H1
All Cannings 25 C5
Allendale Town . . 109 D8
Allenheads 109 E8
Allensford 110 D3
Allens Green 41 C7
Allensmore 49 F6
Allenton 76 F3
Aller 12 B2
Allerby 107 F7
Allerford 21 E8
Allerston 103 F6
Allerthorpe 96 E3
Allerton Mers . . . 86 F2
  W Yorks 94 F4
Allerton Bywater . 88 B5
Allerton
  Mauleverer . . . 95 D7
Allesley 63 F7
Allestree 76 F3
Allet 3 B6
Allexton 64 D5
Allgreave 75 C6
Allhallows 30 B2
Allhallows-on-Sea 30 B2
Alligin Shuas . . . 149 C13
Allimore Green . . 62 C2
Allington Lincs . . . 77 E8

Abb–Alt

Allington continued
  Wilts 25 C5
  Wilts 25 F7
Allithwaite 92 B3
Alloa 127 E7
Allonby 107 E7
Alloway 112 C3
All Saints
  South Elmham . 69 F6
All Stretton 60 E4
Allt 33 D6
Alltchaorunn . . . 131 D5
Alltforgan 59 B6
Alltmawr 48 E2
Alltnacaillich . . . 156 E7
Allt na h-Airbhe . 150 B4
Allt-nan-sùgh . . 136 B2
Alltsigh 137 C7
Alltwalis 46 F3
Alltwen 33 D8
Alltyblaca 46 E4
Allwood Green . . . 56 B4
Almeley 48 D5
Almer 13 E7
Almholme 89 D6
Almington 74 F4
Alminstone Cross . . 8 B5
Almondbank . . . 128 B2
Almondbury 88 C2
Almondsbury . . . 36 F3
Alne 95 C7
Alness 151 E9
Alnham 117 C5
Alnmouth 117 C8
Alnwick 117 C7
Alperton 40 F4
Alphamstone 56 F2
Alpheton 56 D2
Alphington 10 E4
Alport 76 C2
Alpraham 74 D2
Alresford 43 B6
Alrewas 63 C5
Alsager 74 D4
Alsagers Bank . . . 74 E5
Alsop en le Dale . . 75 D8
Alston Cumb . . . 109 E7
  Devon 11 D8
Alstone 50 F4
Alstonefield 75 D8
Alswear 10 B2
Altandhu 156 H2
Altanduin 157 G11
Altarnun 8 F4
Altass 156 J7
Alterwall 158 D4
Altham 93 F7
Althorne 43 E5
Althorpe 90 D2
Alticry 105 D6

Altnabreac Station....157 E13
Altnacealgach Hotel....156 H5
Altnacraig....124 C4
Altnafeadh....131 D6
Altnaharra....157 F8
Altofts....88 B4
Alton Derbys....76 C3
Hants....26 F5
Staffs....75 E7
Alton Pancras....12 D5
Alton Priors....25 C6
Altrincham....87 F5
Altrua....136 F5
Altskeith....126 D3
Altyre House....151 F13
Alva....127 E7
Alvanley....73 B8
Alvaston....76 F3
Alvechurch....50 B5
Alvecote....63 D6
Alvediston....13 B7
Alveley....61 F7
Alverdiscott....9 B7
Alverstoke....15 E2
Alverstone....15 F6
Alverton....77 E7
Alves....152 B1
Alvescot....38 D2
Alveston S Glos....36 F3
Warks....51 D7
Alvie....138 D4
Alvingham....91 E7
Alvington....36 D3
Alwalton....65 E8
Alweston....12 C4
Alwinton....116 D5
Alwoodley....95 E5
Alyth....134 E2
Amatnatua....150 B7
Am Baile....148 G2
Ambergate....76 D3
Amber Hill....78 E5
Amberley Glos....37 D5
W Sus....16 C4
Amble....117 D8
Amblecote....62 F2
Ambler Thorn....87 B8
Ambleside....99 D5
Ambleston....44 C5
Ambrosden....39 C6
Am Buth....124 C4
Amcotts....90 C2
Amersham....40 E2
Amesbury....25 E6
Amington....63 D6
Amisfield....114 F2
Amlwch....82 B4
Amlwch Port....82 B4
Ammanford
=Rhydaman....33 C7
Amod....143 E8
Amotherby....96 B3
Ampfield....14 B5
Ampleforth....95 B8
Ampney Crucis....37 D7
Ampney St Mary....37 D7
Ampney St Peter....37 D7
Amport....25 E7
Ampthill....53 F8
Ampton....56 B2
Amroth....32 D2
Amulree....133 F5
Anagach....139 B6
Anaheilt....130 C2
Anancaun....150 E3
An Caol....149 C11
Ancaster....78 E2
Anchor....59 F8
Anchorsholme....92 E3
An Cnoc....155 D9
Ancroft....123 E5
Ancrum....116 B2
Anderby....79 B8
Anderson....13 E6
Anderton....74 B3
Andover....25 E8
Andover Down....25 E8
Andoversford....37 C7
Andreas....84 C4
Anfield....85 E4
Angarrack....2 F4
Angersleigh....11 C6
Angle....44 E3
An Gleann Ur....155 D9
Angmering....16 D4
Angram N Yorks....95 E8
N Yorks....100 E3
Anie....126 C4
Ankerville....151 D11
Anlaby....90 B4
Anmer....80 E3
Anmore....15 C7
Annan....107 C8
Annat Argyll....125 C6
Highld....149 C13
Anna Valley....25 E8
Annbank....112 B4
Annesley....76 D5
Annesley Woodhouse....76 D4
Annfield Plain....110 D4
Annifirth....160 J3
Annitsford....111 B5
Annscroft....60 D4
Ansdell....85 B4
Ansford....23 F8
Ansley....63 E6
Anslow....63 B6
Anslow Gate....63 B5
Anstey Herts....54 F5
Leics....64 D2
Anstruther Easter....129 D7
Anstruther Wester....129 D7
Ansty Hants....26 E5
Warks....63 F7
Wilts....13 B7
W Sus....17 B6
Anthill Common....15 C7
Anthorn....107 D8
Antingham....81 D8
An t-Ob
=Leverburgh....154 J5
Anton's Gowt....79 E5
Antonshill....127 F7

Antony....5 D8
Anwick....78 D4
Anwoth....106 D2
Aoradh....142 B3
Apes Hall....67 E5
Apethorpe....65 E7
Apeton....62 C2
Apley....78 B4
Apperknowle....76 B3
Apperley....78 B4
Apperley Bridge....94 F4
Appersett....100 E3
Appin....130 E3
Appin House....130 E3
Appleby....90 C3
Appleby-in-Westmorland....100 B1
Appleby Magna....63 D7
Appleby Parva....63 D7
Applecross....149 D12
Applecross House....149 D12
Appledore Devon....11 C5
Devon....20 F3
Kent....19 C6
Appledore Heath....19 B6
Appleford....39 E5
Appleforth....114 F4
Appleshaw....25 E8
Applethwaite....98 B4
Appleton Halton....86 F3
Oxon....38 D4
Appleton-le-Moors....103 F5
Appleton-le-Street....96 B3
Appleton Roebuck....95 E8
Appleton Thorn....86 F4
Appleton Wiske....102 D1
Appletreehall....115 C8
Appletreewick....94 C3
Appley....11 B5
Appley Bridge....86 D3
Apse Heath....15 F6
Apsley End....54 F2
Apuldram....16 D2
Aquhythie....141 C6
Arabella....151 D11
Arbeadie....141 E5
Arberth
=Narberth....32 C2
Arbirlot....135 E6
Arboll....151 C11
Arborfield....27 C5
Arborfield Cross....27 C5
Arborfield Garrison....27 C5
Arbourthorne....88 F4
Arbroath....135 E6
Arbuthnott....135 B7
Archiestown....152 D2
Arclid....74 C4
Ardachu....157 J9
Ardalanish....146 K6
Ardanaiseig....125 C6
Ardaneaskan....149 E13
Ardanstur....124 D4
Ardargie House Hotel....128 C2
Ardarroch....149 E13
Ardbeg Argyll....142 D5
Argyll....145 E10
Ardcharnich....150 C4
Ardchiavaig....146 K6
Ardchullarie More....126 C4
Ardchyle....126 B4
Ard-dhubh....149 D12
Arddleen....60 C2
Ardechive....136 E4
Ardeley....41 B6
Ardelve....149 F13
Arden....126 F2
Ardens Grafton....51 D6
Ardentinny....145 E10
Ardentraive....145 F9
Ardeonaig....132 F3
Ardersier....151 F10
Ardessie....150 C3
Ardfern....124 E4
Ardgartan....125 E8
Ardgay....151 B8
Ardgour....130 C4
Ardheslaig....149 C12
Ardiecow....152 B5
Ardindrean....150 C4
Ardingly....17 B7
Ardington....38 F4
Ardlair....140 B4
Ardlamont House....145 G8
Ardleigh....43 B6
Ardler....134 E2
Ardley....39 B5
Ardlui....126 C2
Ardlussa....144 E5
Ardmair....150 B4
Ardmay....125 E8
Ardminish....143 D7
Ardmolich....147 D10
Ardmore Argyll....124 C3
Highld....151 C10
Highld....156 D5
Ardnacross....147 G8
Ardnadam....145 F10
Ardnagrask....151 G8
Ardnarff....149 E13
Ardnastang....130 C2
Ardnave....142 A3
Ardno....125 E7
Ardo....153 E8
Ardoch....133 F7
Ardochy House....136 D5
Ardo House....141 B8
Ardoyne....141 B5
Ardpatrick....144 G6
Ardpatrick House....144 H6
Ardpeaton....145 E11
Ardrishaig....145 E7
Ardross Fife....129 D7
Highld....151 D9
Ardrossan....118 E2
Ardshealach....147 E9
Ardsley....88 D4
Ardslignish....147 E8
Ardtalla....142 C5
Ardtalnaig....132 F4
Ardtoe....147 D9
Ardtrostan....127 B5

Arduaine....124 D3
Ardullie....151 E8
Ardvasar....149 H11
Ardvorlich....126 B5
Ardwell....104 E5
Ardwell Mains....104 E5
Ardwick....87 E6
Areley Kings....50 B3
Arford....27 F6
Argoed Caerph....35 E5
Powys....47 C8
Arichamish....124 E5
Arichastlich....125 B8
Aridhglas....146 J6
Arileod....146 F4
Arinacrinachd....149 C12
Arinagour....146 F5
Arion....159 G3
Arisaig....147 C9
Ariundle....130 C2
Arkendale....95 C6
Arkesden....55 F5
Arkholme....93 B5
Arkle Town....101 D5
Arkley....41 E5
Arksey....89 D6
Arkwright Town....76 B4
Arle....37 B6
Arlecdon....98 C2
Arlesey....54 F2
Arleston....61 C6
Arley....86 F4
Arlingham....36 C4
Arlington Devon....20 E5
E Sus....18 E2
Glos....37 D8
Armadale Highld....157 C10
W Loth....120 C2
Armadale Castle....149 H11
Armathwaite....108 E5
Arminghall....69 D5
Armitage....62 C4
Armley....95 F5
Armscote....51 E7
Armthorpe....89 D7
Arnabost....146 F5
Arncliffe....94 B2
Arncroach....129 D7
Arne....13 F7
Arnesby....64 E3
Arngask....128 C3
Arnisdale....149 G13
Arnish....149 D10
Arniston Engine....121 C6
Arnol....155 C8
Arnold E Yorks....97 E7
Notts....77 E5
Arnprior....126 E5
Arnside....92 B4
Aros Mains....147 G8
Arowry....73 F8
Arpafeelie....151 F9
Arrad Foot....99 F5
Arram....97 E6
Arrathorne....101 E7
Arreton....15 F6
Arrington....54 D4
Arrivain....125 B8
Arrochar....125 E8
Arrow....51 D5
Arthington....95 E5
Arthingworth....64 F4
Arthog....58 C3
Arthrath....153 E9
Arthurstone....134 E2
Artrochie....153 E10
Arundel....16 D4
Aryhoulan....130 C4
Asby....98 B2
Ascog....145 G10
Ascot....27 C7
Ascott....51 F8
Ascott-under-Wychwood....38 C3
Asenby....95 B6
Asfordby....64 C4
Asfordby Hill....64 C4
Asgarby Lincs....78 E4
Lincs....79 C6
Ash Kent....29 C6
Kent....31 D6
Som....12 B2
Sur....27 D6
Ashampstead....26 B3
Ashbocking....57 D5
Ashbourne....75 E8
Ashbrittle....11 B5
Ash Bullayne....10 D2
Ashburton....7 C5
Ashbury Devon....9 E7
Oxon....38 F2
Ashby....90 D3
Ashby by Partney....79 C7
Ashby cum Fenby....91 D6
Ashby de la Launde....78 D3
Ashby-de-la-Zouch....63 C7
Ashby Folville....64 C4
Ashby Magna....64 E2
Ashby Parva....64 F2
Ashby Puerorum....79 B6
Ashby St Ledgers....52 C3
Ashby St Mary....69 D6
Ashchurch....50 F4
Ashcombe....7 B7
Ashcott....23 F6
Ashdon....55 E6
Ashe....26 E3
Asheldham....43 D5
Ashen....55 E8
Ashendon....39 C7
Ashfield Carms....33 B7
Stirling....127 D6
Suff....57 C6
Ashfield Green....57 B6
Ashford Crossways 17 B6
Ashford Devon....20 F4
Hants....14 C2
Kent....30 E4
Sur....27 B8
Ashgill....119 E7

Ash Green....63 F7
Ashill Devon....11 C5
Norf....67 D8
Som....11 C8
Ashingdon....42 E4
Ashington Northumb....117 F8
Som....12 B3
W Sus....16 C5
Ashintully Castle....133 C8
Ashkirk....115 B7
Ashlett....15 D5
Ashleworth....37 B5
Ashley Cambs....55 C7
Ches E....87 F5
Devon....9 C8
Dorset....14 D2
Glos....37 E6
Hants....14 E3
Hants....25 F8
N Nhants....64 E4
Staffs....74 F4
Ashley Green....40 D2
Ashley Heath Dorset....14 D2
Staffs....74 F4
Ash Magna....74 F2
Ashmanhaugh....69 B6
Ashmansworth....26 D2
Ashmansworthy....8 C5
Ash Mill....10 B2
Ashmore....13 C7
Ashorne....51 D8
Ashover....76 C3
Ashow....51 B8
Ash Priors....11 B6
Ashprington....7 D6
Ash Street....56 E4
Ashtead....28 D2
Asthall....38 C2
Asthall Leigh....38 C3
Astley Shrops....60 C5
Warks....63 F7
Worcs....50 C2
Astley Abbotts....61 E7
Astley Bridge....86 C5
Astley Cross....50 C3
Astley Green....86 E5
Aston Ches E....74 E3
Ches W....74 B2
Derbys....88 F2
Hereford....49 B6
Herts....41 B5
Oxon....38 D3
Shrops....60 B5
Staffs....74 E4
S Yorks....89 F5
Telford....61 D6
W Mid....62 F4
Wokingham....39 F7
Aston Abbotts....39 B8
Aston Botterell....61 F6
Aston-by-Stone....75 F6
Aston Cantlow....51 D6
Aston Clinton....40 C1
Aston Crews....36 B3
Aston Cross....50 F4
Aston End....41 B5
Aston Eyre....61 E6
Aston Fields....50 C4
Aston Flamville....63 E8
Aston Ingham....36 B3
Aston juxta Mondrum....74 D3
Aston le Walls....52 D2
Aston Magna....51 F6
Aston Munslow....60 F5
Aston on Clun....60 F3
Aston-on-Trent....63 B8

Aston Rogers....60 D3
Aston Rowant....39 E7
Aston Sandford....39 D7
Aston Somerville....50 F5
Aston Subedge....51 E6
Aston Tirrold....39 F5
Aston Upthorpe....39 F5
Astrop....52 F3
Astwick....54 F3
Astwood M Keynes....53 E7
Worcs....50 D3
Astwood Bank....50 C5
Aswarby....78 F3
Aswardby....79 B6
Atcham....60 D5
Atch Lench....50 D5
Athelhampton....13 E5
Athelington....57 B6
Athelney....11 B8
Athelstaneford....121 B8
Atherington....9 B7
Atherstone....63 E7
Atherstone on Stour....51 D7
Atherton....86 D4
Atley Hill....101 D7
Atlow....76 E2
Attadale....150 H2
Attadale House....150 H2
Attenborough....76 F5
Atterby....90 E3
Attercliffe....88 F4
Attleborough Norf....68 E3
Warks....63 E7
Attlebridge....68 C4
Atwick....97 D7
Atworth....24 C3
Aubourn....78 C2
Auchagallon....143 E9
Auchallater....139 F7
Aucharnie....153 D6
Auchattie....141 E5
Auchavan....134 C1
Auchbreck....139 B8
Auchenback....118 D5
Auchenbainzie....113 E8
Auchenblae....135 B7
Auchenbrack....113 E7
Auchenbreck....145 E9
Auchencairn Dumfries....106 D4
Dumfries....114 F2
N Ayrs....143 F11
Auchencrosh....104 B5
Auchencrow....122 C4
Auchendinny....121 C5
Auchengray....120 D2
Auchenhalrig....152 B3
Auchenheath....119 E8
Auchenlochan....145 F8
Auchenmalg....105 D6
Auchensoul....112 E2
Auchentiber....118 E3
Auchertyre....149 F13
Auchgourish....138 C5
Auchincarroch....126 F3
Auchindrain....125 E6
Auchindrean....150 C4
Auchininna....153 D6
Auchinleck....113 B5
Auchinloch....119 B6
Auchinroath....152 C2
Auchintoul....140 C4
Auchiries....153 E10
Auchlee....141 E7
Auchleven....140 B5
Auchlochan....119 F8
Auchlossan....140 D4
Auchlunies....141 E7
Auchlyne....126 B4
Auchmacoy....153 E9
Auchmair....140 B2
Auchmantle....105 C5
Auchmillan....112 B5
Auchmithie....135 E6
Auchmuirbridge....128 D4
Auchmull....135 B5
Auchnacree....134 C4
Auchnagallin....151 H13
Auchnagatt....153 D9
Auchnaha....145 E8
Auchnashelloch....127 C6
Aucholzie....140 E2
Auchrannie....134 D2
Auchroisk....139 B6
Auchronie....140 F3
Auchterarder....127 C8
Auchteraw....137 D6
Auchterderran....128 E4
Auchterhouse....134 F3
Auchtermuchty....128 C4
Auchterneed....150 F7
Auchtertool....128 E4
Auchtertyre....152 C1
Auchtubh....126 B4
Auckengill....158 D5
Auckley....89 D7
Audenshaw....87 E7
Audlem....74 E3
Audley....74 D4
Audley End....56 F6
Auds....153 B6
Aughton E Yorks....96 F3
Lancs....85 D4
Lancs....93 C5
S Yorks....89 F5
Wilts....25 D7
Aughton Park....86 D2
Auldearn....151 F12
Aulden....49 D6
Auldgirth....114 F2
Auldhame....129 F7
Auldhouse....119 D6
Ault a'chruinn....136 B2
Aultanrynie....156 F6
Aultbea....155 J13
Aultdearg....150 E5
Aultgrishan....155 J12
Aultguish Inn....150 D6
Aultibea....157 G13
Aultiphurst....157 C11
Aultmore....152 C4
Aultnagoire....137 B8
Aultnamain Inn....151 C9
Aultnaslat....136 D4
Aulton....140 B5
Aundorach....139 C5
Aunsby....78 F3
Auquhorthies....141 B7

Aust....36 F2
Austendike....66 B2
Austerfield....89 E7
Austrey....63 D6
Austwick....93 C7
Authorpe....91 F8
Authorpe Row....79 B8
Avebury....25 C6
Aveley....42 F1
Avening....37 E5
Averham....77 D7
Aveton Gifford....6 E4
Avielochan....138 C5
Aviemore....138 C4
Avington Hants....26 F3
W Berks....25 C8
Avoch....151 F10
Avon....14 E2
Avonbridge....120 B2
Avon Dassett....52 E2
Avonmouth....23 B7
Avonwick....6 D5
Awbridge....14 B4
Awhirk....104 D4
Awkley....36 F2
Awliscombe....11 D6
Awre....36 D4
Awsworth....76 E4
Axbridge....23 D6
Axford Hants....26 E4
Wilts....25 B7
Axminster....11 E7
Axmouth....11 E7
Axton....85 F2
Aycliff....31 E7
Aycliffe....101 B7
Aydon....110 C3
Aylburton....36 D3
Ayle....109 E7
Aylesbeare....10 E5
Aylesbury....39 C8
Aylesby....91 D6
Aylesford....29 D8
Aylesham....31 D6
Aylestone....64 D2
Aylmerton....81 D7
Aylsham....81 E7
Aylton....49 F8
Aymestrey....49 C6
Aynho....52 F3
Ayot St Lawrence....40 C4
Ayot St Peter....41 C5
Ayr....112 B3
Aysgarth....101 F5
Ayside....99 F5
Ayston....65 D5
Aythorpe Roding....42 C1
Ayton....122 C5
Aywick....160 E7
Azerley....95 B5

B

Babbacombe....7 C7
Babbinswood....73 F7
Babcary....12 B3
Babel....47 F7
Babell....73 B5
Babraham....55 D6
Babworth....89 F7
Bac....155 C9
Bac....155 C9
Backaland....159 E6
Backaskaill....159 C5
Backbarrow....99 F5
Backe....32 C3
Backfolds....153 C10
Backford....73 B8
Backford Cross....73 B7
Backhill Aberds....153 E7
Aberds....153 E10
Backhill of Clackriach....153 D9
Backhill of Fortree....153 D9
Backhill of Trustach....140 E5
Backies....157 J11
Backlass....158 E4
Back of Keppoch....147 C9
Back Rogerton....113 B5
Backwell....23 C6
Backworth....111 B6
Bacon End....42 C2
Baconsthorpe....81 D7
Bacton Hereford....49 F5
Norf....81 D9
Suff....56 C4
Bacup....87 B6
Badachro....149 A12
Badanloch Lodge....157 F10
Badavanich....150 F4
Badbury....38 F1
Badby....52 D3
Badcall....156 D5
Badcaul....150 B3
Baddeley Green....75 D6
Baddesley Clinton....51 B7
Baddesley Ensor....63 E6
Baddidarroch....156 G3
Badenscoth....153 E7
Badenyon....140 C2
Badger....61 E7
Badger's Mount....29 C5
Badgeworth....37 C6
Badgworth....23 D5
Badicaul....149 F12
Badingham....57 C7
Badlesmere....30 D4
Badlipster....158 F4
Badluarach....150 B2
Badminton....37 F5
Badnaban....156 G3
Badninish....151 B10
Badrallach....150 B3
Badsey....51 E5
Badshot Lea....27 E6
Badsworth....89 C5
Badwell Ash....56 C3
Bae Colwyn
=Colwyn Bay....83 D8
Bagby....102 F2
Bag Enderby....79 B6
Bagendon....37 D7

Bagh a Chaisteil
=Castlebay....148 J1
Baghasdal....148 G2
Bagh Mor....148 C3
Bagh Shiarabhagh....148 H2
Bagillt....73 B6
Baginton....51 B8
Baglan....33 E8
Bagley....60 B4
Bagnall....75 D6
Bagnor....26 C2
Bagshot Sur....27 C7
Wilts....25 C8
Bagthorpe Norf....80 D3
Notts....76 D4
Bagworth....63 D8
Bagwy Llydiart....35 B8
Baildon....94 F4
Baile....154 J4
Baile Ailein....155 E7
Baile a Mhanaich....148 C2
Baile an Truiseil....155 B8
Bailebeag....137 C8
Baile Boidheach....144 F6
Baile Glas....148 C3
Baile Mhartainn....148 A2
Baile Mhic Phail....148 A3
Baile Mor Argyll....146 J5
W Isles....148 B2
Baile na Creige....148 H1
Baile nan Cailleach....148 C2
Baile Raghaill....148 A2
Baileyhead....108 B5
Bailiesward....152 E4
Baillieston....119 C6
Bail'lochdrach....148 C3
Bail Uachdraich....148 B3
Bail'Ur Tholastaidh....155 C10
Bainbridge....100 E4
Bainsford....127 F7
Bainshole....152 E6
Bainton E Yorks....97 D5
Pboro....65 D7
Bairnkine....116 C2
Baker's End....41 C6
Baker Street....42 F2
Bakewell....76 C2
Bala = Y Bala....72 F3
Balachuirn....149 D10
Balavil....138 D3
Balbeg Highld....137 B7
Highld....150 H7
Balbeggie....128 B3
Balbithan....141 C6
Balbithan House....141 C7
Balblair Highld....151 B8
Highld....151 E10
Balby....89 D6
Balchladich....156 F3
Balchraggan Highld....151 G8
Highld....151 H8
Balchrick....156 D4
Balchrystie....129 D6
Balcladaich....137 B5
Balcombe....28 F4
Balcombe Lane....28 F4
Balcomie....129 C8
Balcurvie....128 D5
Baldersby....95 B6
Baldersby St James....95 B6
Balderstone....93 F6
Balderton Ches W....73 C7
Notts....77 D8
Baldhu....3 B6
Baldinnie....129 C6
Baldock....54 F3
Baldovie....134 F4
Baldrine....84 D4
Baldslow....18 D4
Baldwin....84 D3
Baldwinholme....108 D3
Baldwin's Gate....74 E4
Bale....81 D6
Balearn....153 C10
Balemartine....146 G2
Balephuil....146 G2
Balerno....120 C4
Balevullin....146 G2
Balfield....135 C5
Balfour....159 G5
Balfron....126 F4
Balfron Station....126 F4
Balgaveny....153 D6
Balgavies....135 D5
Balgonar....128 E2
Balgove....153 E8
Balgowan....138 E2
Balgown....149 B8
Balgrochan....119 B6
Balgy....149 C13
Balhaldie....127 D7
Balhalgardy....141 B6
Balham....28 B3
Balhary....134 E2
Baliasta....160 C8
Baligill....157 C11
Balintore Angus....134 D2
Highld....151 D11
Balintraid....151 D10
Balk....102 F2
Balkeerie....134 E3
Balkemback....134 F3
Balkholme....89 B8
Balkissock....104 A5
Ball....60 B3
Ballabeg....84 E2
Ballacannell....84 D4
Ballachulish....130 D4
Ballajora....84 C4
Ballaleigh....84 D3
Ballamodha....84 E2
Ballantrae....104 A4
Ballaquine....84 D4
Ballards Gore....43 E5
Ballasalla IoM....84 E2
IoM....84 C3
Ballater....140 E2
Ballaugh....84 C3
Ballaveare....84 E3
Ballcorach....139 B7
Ballechin....133 D6
Balleigh....151 C10
Ballencrieff....121 B7

Ballentoul....133 C5
Ball Haye Green....75 D6
Ball Hill....26 C2
Ballidon....76 D2
Balliemore Argyll....124 C4
Argyll....145 E9
Ballikinrain....126 F4
Ballimeanoch....125 D6
Ballimore Argyll....145 E8
Stirling....126 C4
Ballinaby....142 B3
Ballindean....128 B4
Ballingdon....56 E2
Ballinger Common....40 D2
Ballingham....49 F7
Ballingry....128 E3
Ballinlick....133 E6
Ballinluig....133 D6
Ballintuim....133 D8
Balloch Angus....134 D3
Highld....151 G10
N Lanark....119 B7
W Dunb....126 F2
Ballochan....140 E4
Ballochford....152 E3
Ballochmorrie....112 F2
Balls Cross....16 B3
Balls Green....16 B3
Ballygown....146 G7
Ballygrant....142 B4
Ballyhaugh....146 F4
Balmacara....149 F13
Balmacara Square....149 F13
Balmaclellan....106 B3
Balmacneil....133 D6
Balmacqueen....149 A9
Balmae....106 E3
Balmaha....126 E3
Balmalcolm....128 D5
Balmeanach....149 D10
Balmedie....141 C8
Balmer Heath....73 F8
Balmerino....129 B5
Balmerlawn....14 D4
Balmichael....143 E10
Balmirmer....135 F5
Balmore Highld....149 D7
Highld....150 H6
Highld....151 G11
Highld....151 G11
Perth....133 D6
Balmule....128 F4
Balmullo....129 B6
Balmungie....151 F10
Balnaboth....134 C3
Balnabruaich....151 E10
Balnabruich....158 H3
Balnacoil....157 H11
Balnacra....150 G2
Balnafoich....151 H9
Balnagall....151 C11
Balnaguard....133 D6
Balnahard Argyll....144 D3
Argyll....146 H7
Balnain....150 H7
Balnakeil....156 C6
Balnaknock....149 B9
Balnapaling....151 E10
Balne....89 C6
Balochroy....143 C8
Balone....129 C6
Balornock....119 C6
Balquharn....133 F7
Balquhidder....126 B4
Balsall....51 B7
Balsall Common....51 B7
Balsall Heath....62 F4
Balscott....51 E8
Balsham....55 D6
Baltasound....160 C8
Balterley....74 D4
Baltersan....105 C8
Balthangie....153 C8
Balvaird....151 F8
Balvicar....124 D3
Balvraid Highld....149 G13
Highld....151 H11
Bamber Bridge....86 B3
Bambers Green....42 B1
Bamburgh....123 F7
Bamff....134 D2
Bamford Derbys....88 F3
Gtr Man....87 C6
Bampton Cumb....99 C7
Devon....10 B4
Oxon....38 D3
Bampton Grange....99 C7
Banavie....131 B5
Banbury....52 E2
Bancffosfelen....33 C5
Banchory....141 E5
Banchory-Devenick....141 D8
Bancycapel....33 C5
Bancyfelin....32 C4
Bancyffordd....46 F3
Bandirran....134 F2
Banff....153 B6
Bangor....83 D5
Bangor-is-y-coed
=Bangor-on-Dee....73 E7
Bangor-on-Dee
=Bangor-is-y-coed....73 E7
Banham....68 F3
Bank....14 D3
Bankend....107 C7
Bankfoot....133 F7
Bankglen....113 C6
Bankhead Aberdeen....141 C7
Aberds....141 D5
Banknock....119 B7
Banks Cumb....109 C5
Lancs....85 B4
Bankshill....114 F4
Bank Street....50 C3
Banningham....81 E8
Bannister Green....42 B2
Bannockburn....127 E7
Banstead....28 D3
Bantham....6 E4
Banton....119 B7
Banwell....23 D5
Banyard's Green....57 B6

Bapchild....30 C3
Barabhas....155 C8
Barabhas Iarach....155 C8
Barabhas Uarach....155 B8
Baramore....147 D8
Barassie....118 F3
Baravullin....124 E4
Barbaraville....151 D10
Barber Booth....88 F2
Barbieston....112 C4
Barbon....99 F8
Barbridge....74 D3
Barbrook....21 E6
Barby....52 B3
Barcaldine....130 E3
Barcheston....51 F7
Barcombe....17 C8
Barcombe Cross....17 C8
Barden....101 E6
Bardennoch....113 E5
Barden Scale....94 D3
Bardfield Saling....42 B2
Bardister....160 F5
Bardney....78 C4
Bardon....63 C8
Bardon Mill....109 C7
Bardowie....119 B5
Bardrainney....118 B3
Bardsea....92 B3
Bardsey....95 E6
Bardwell....56 B3
Bare....92 C4
Barfad....145 G7
Barford Norf....68 D4
Warks....51 D7
Barford St John....52 F2
Barford St Martin....25 F5
Barford St Michael....52 F2
Barfrestone....31 D6
Bargod = Bargoed....35 E5
Bargoed = Bargod....35 E5
Bargrennan....105 B7
Barham Cambs....54 B2
Kent....31 D6
Suff....56 D5
Barharrow....106 D3
Barhill....106 C5
Bar Hill....54 C4
Barholm....65 C7
Barkby....64 D3
Barkestone-le-Vale....77 F7
Barkham....27 C5
Barking London....41 F7
Suff....56 D4
Barkingside....41 F7
Barking Tye....56 D4
Barkisland....87 C8
Barkston Lincs....78 E2
N Yorks....95 F7
Barkway....54 F4
Barlaston....75 F5
Barlavington....16 C3
Barlborough....76 B4
Barlby....96 F2
Barlestone....63 D8
Barley Herts....54 F4
Lancs....93 E8
Barley Mow....111 D5
Barleythorpe....64 D5
Barling....43 F5
Barlow Derbys....76 B3
N Yorks....89 B7
T&W....110 C4
Barmby Moor....96 E3
Barmby on the Marsh....89 B7
Barmer....80 D4
Barmoor Castle....123 F5
Barmoor Lane End....123 F6
Barmouth
=Abermaw....58 C3
Barmpton....101 C8
Barmston....97 D7
Barnack....65 D7
Barnacle....63 F7
Barnard Castle....101 C5
Barnard Gate....38 C4
Barnardiston....55 E8
Barnbarroch....106 D5
Barnburgh....89 D5
Barnby....69 F7
Barnby Dun....89 D7
Barnby in the Willows....77 D8
Barnby Moor....89 F7
Barnes Street....29 E7
Barnet....41 E5
Barnetby le Wold....90 D4
Barney....81 D5
Barnham Suff....56 B2
W Sus....16 D3
Barnham Broom....68 D3
Barnhead....135 D6
Barnhill Ches W....73 D8
Dundee....134 F4
Moray....152 C1
Barnhills....104 B3
Barningham Durham....101 C6
Suff....56 B3
Barnoldby le Beck....91 D6
Barnoldswick....93 E8
Barns Green....16 B5
Barnsley Glos....37 D7
S Yorks....88 D4
Barnstaple....20 F4
Barnston Essex....42 C2
Mers....85 F3
Barnstone....77 F7
Barnt Green....50 B5
Barnton Ches W....74 B3
Edin....120 B4
Barnwell All Saints....65 F7
Barnwell St Andrew....65 F7
Barnwood....37 C5
Barochreal....124 C4
Barons Cross....49 D6
Barr....112 E2
Barra Castle....141 B6
Barrachan....105 E7
Barrack....153 D8
Barraglom....154 D6
Barrahormid....144 E6
Barran....124 C4
Barrapol....146 G2
Barras Aberds....141 F7

Barras continued
Cumb.....100 C3
Barrasford.....110 B2
Barravullin.....124 E4
Barregarrow.....84 D3
Barrhead.....118 D4
Barrhill.....112 F2
Barrington Cambs..54 E4
 Som.....11 C8
Barripper.....2 C5
Barmill.....118 D3
Barrock.....158 D4
Barrock House.....158 D4
Barrow Lancs.....93 F7
 Rutland.....65 C5
 Suff.....55 C8
Barroway Drove.....67 D5
Barrowburn.....116 C4
Barrowby.....77 F8
Barrowcliff.....103 F8
Barrowden.....65 D6
Barrowford.....93 F8
Barrow Green.....30 C3
Barrow Gurney.....23 C7
Barrow Haven.....90 B4
Barrow-in-
 Furness.....92 C2
Barrow Island.....92 C1
Barrow Nook.....86 D2
Barrows Green
 Ches E.....74 D3
 Cumb.....99 F7
Barrow's Green.....86 F3
Barrow Street.....24 F3
Barrow upon
 Humber.....90 B4
Barrow upon Soar.64 C2
Barrow upon Trent.63 B7
Barry.....135 F5
 = Y Barri.....22 C3
Barry Island.....22 C3
Barsby.....64 C3
Barsham.....69 F6
Barston.....51 B7
Barthol Chapel.153 E8
Barthomley.....74 D4
Bartley.....10 C2
Bartley Green.....62 F4
Bartlow.....55 E6
Barton Cambs.....54 D5
 Ches W.....73 D8
 Glos.....37 B8
 Lancs.....85 D4
 Lancs.....92 F5
 N Yorks.....101 D7
 Oxon.....39 D5
 Torbay.....7 C6
 Warks.....51 D6
Barton Bendish.....67 D7
Barton Hartshorn.52 F4
Barton in Fabis.....76 F5
Barton in the
 Beans.....63 D7
Barton-le-Clay.....54 F2
Barton-le-Street.96 B3
Barton-le-Willows 96 C3
Barton Mills.....55 B8
Barton on Sea.....14 E3
Barton on the
 Heath.....51 F7
Barton St David.....23 F7
Barton Seagrave.53 B6
Barton Stacey.....26 E2
Barton Turf.....69 B6
Barton-under-
 Needwood.....63 C5
Barton-upon-
 Humber.....90 B4
Barton Waterside.90 B4
Barugh.....88 D4
Barway.....55 B6
Barwell.....63 E8
Barwick Herts.....41 C6
 Som.....12 C3
Barwick in Elmet..95 F6
Baschurch.....60 B4
Bascote.....52 C2
Basford Green.....75 D6
Bashall Eaves.....93 E7
Bashley.....14 E3
Basildon.....42 F3
Basingstoke.....26 D4
Baslow.....76 B2
Bason Bridge.....22 E5
Bassaleg.....35 F6
Bassenthwaite.108 F2
Bassett.....15 C5
Bassingbourn.....54 E4
Bassingfield.....77 F6
Bassingham.....78 C2
Bassingthorpe.....65 B6
Basta.....160 D7
Baston.....65 C8
Bastwick.....69 C7
Baswick Steer.....97 E6
Batchworth Heath.40 E3
Batcombe Dorset..12 D4
 Som.....23 F8
Bate Heath.....74 B3
Batford.....40 C4
Bath.....24 C2
Bathampton.....24 C2
Bathealton.....11 B5
Batheaston.....24 C2
Bathford.....24 C2
Bathgate.....120 C2
Bathley.....77 D7
Bathpool Corn.....5 B7
 Som.....11 B7
Bathville.....120 C2
Batley.....88 B3
Batsford.....51 F6
Battersby.....102 D3
Battersea.....28 B3
Battisborough
 Cross.....6 E3
Battisford.....56 D4
Battisford Tye.....56 D4
Battle E Sus.....18 D4
 Powys.....48 F2
Battledown.....37 B6
Battlefield.....60 C5
Battlesbridge.....42 E3
Battlesden.....40 B2
Battlesea Green...57 B6
Battleton.....10 B4
Battram.....63 D8
Battramsley.....14 E4

Baughton.....50 E3
Baughurst.....26 D3
Baulking.....38 E3
Baumber.....78 B5
Baunton.....37 D7
Baverstock.....24 F5
Bawburgh.....68 D4
Bawdeswell.....81 E6
Bawdrip.....22 F5
Bawdsey.....57 E7
Bawtry.....89 E7
Baxenden.....87 B5
Baxterley.....63 E6
Baybridge.....15 B6
Baycliff.....92 B2
Baydon.....25 B7
Bayford Herts.....41 D6
 Som.....12 B5
Bayles.....109 E7
Baylham.....56 D5
Baynard's Green..39 B5
Bayston Hill.....60 D4
Baythorn End.....55 E8
Bayton.....49 B8
Beach.....130 D1
Beachampton.....53 F5
Beachamwell.....67 D7
Beachans.....151 G13
Beacharr.....143 D7
Beachborough.....19 B8
Beachley.....36 E2
Beacon.....11 D6
Beacon End.....43 B5
Beacon Hill.....27 F6
Beacon's Bottom..39 E7
Beaconsfield.....40 F2
Beacrabhaic.....154 H6
Beadlam.....102 F4
Beadlow.....54 F2
Beadnell.....117 B8
Beaford.....9 C7
Beal Northumb...123 E6
 N Yorks.....89 B6
Beamhurst.....75 F7
Beaminster.....12 D2
Beamish.....110 D5
Beamsley.....94 D3
Bean.....29 B6
Beanacre.....24 C4
Beanley.....117 C6
Beaquoy.....159 F4
Bear Cross.....13 E8
Beardwood.....86 B4
Beare Green.....28 E2
Bearley.....51 C6
Bearnus.....146 G6
Bearpark.....110 E5
Bearsbridge.....109 D7
Bearsden.....118 B5
Bearsted.....29 D8
Bearstone.....74 F4
Bearwood BCP.....13 E8
 Hereford.....49 D5
 W Mid.....62 F4
Beattock.....114 D3
Beauchamp
 Roding.....42 C1
Beauchief.....88 F4
Beaufort.....35 C5
Beaufort Castle.151 G8
Beaulieu.....14 D4
Beauly.....151 G8
Beaumaris.....83 D6
Beaumont Cumb.108 D3
 Essex.....43 B7
Beaumont Hill...101 C7
Beausale.....51 B7
Beauworth.....15 B6
Beaworthy.....9 E6
Beazley End.....42 B3
Bebington.....85 F4
Bebside.....117 F8
Beccles.....69 E7
Becconsall.....86 B2
Beckbury.....61 D7
Beckenham.....28 C4
Beckermet.....98 D2
Beckfoot Cumb....98 D3
 Cumb.....107 E7
Beck Foot.....99 E8
Beckford.....50 F4
Beckhampton.....25 C5
Beck Hole.....103 D6
Beckingham Lincs..77 B8
 Notts.....89 F8
Beckington.....24 D3
Beckley E Sus.....19 C5
 Hants.....14 E3
 Oxon.....39 C5
Beck Row.....55 B7
Beck Side.....98 F4
Beckton.....28 B5
Beckwithshaw.....95 D5
Becontree.....41 F7
Bedale.....101 F7
Bedburn.....110 F4
Bedchester.....13 C6
Beddau.....34 F4
Beddgelert.....71 C6
Beddingham.....17 D8
Beddington.....28 C4
Bedfield.....57 C6
Bedford.....53 D8
Bedham.....16 B4
Bedhampton.....15 D8
Bedingfield.....57 C5
Bedlam.....95 C5
Bedlington.....117 F8
Bedlington
 Station.....117 F8
Bedlinog.....34 D4
Bedminster.....23 B7
Bedmond.....40 D3
Bednall.....62 C3
Bedrule.....116 C2
Bedstone.....49 B5
Bedwas.....35 F5
Bedworth.....63 F7
Bedworth Heath...63 F7
Bed-y-coedwr.....71 E8
Beeby.....64 D3
Beech Hants.....26 F4
 Staffs.....75 F5
Beech Hill Gtr Man..86 D3
 W Berks.....26 C4
Beechingstoke.....25 D5
Beedon.....26 B2
Beeford.....97 D7
Beeley.....76 C2

Beelsby.....91 D6
Beenham.....26 C3
Beeny.....8 E3
Beer.....11 F7
Beercrocombe.....11 B8
Beer Hackett.....12 C3
Beesands.....7 E6
Beesby.....91 F8
Beeson.....7 E6
Beeston C Beds....54 E2
 Ches W.....74 D2
 Norf.....68 C2
 Notts.....76 F5
 W Yorks.....95 F5
Beeston Regis.....81 C7
Beeswing.....107 C5
Beetham.....92 B4
Beetley.....68 C2
Begbroke.....38 C4
Begelly.....32 D2
Beggar's Bush.....48 C4
Beguildy.....48 B3
Beighton Norf.....69 D6
 S Yorks.....88 F5
Beighton Hill.....76 D2
Beith.....118 D3
Bekesbourne.....31 D5
Belaugh.....69 C5
Belbroughton.....50 B4
Belchamp Otten..56 E2
Belchamp St Paul..56 E2
Belchamp Walter..56 E2
Belchford.....79 B5
Belford.....123 F7
Belhaven.....122 B2
Belhelvie.....141 C8
Belhinnie.....140 B3
Bellabeg.....140 C2
Bellamore.....112 F2
Bellanoch.....144 D6
Bellaty.....134 D2
Bell Bar.....41 D5
Bell Busk.....94 D2
Belleau.....79 B7
Bellehiglash.....152 E1
Bell End.....50 B4
Bellerby.....101 E6
Bellever.....6 B4
Belliehill.....135 C5
Bellingdon.....40 D2
Bellingham.....116 F4
Belloch.....143 E7
Bellochantuy.....143 E7
Bell o'th'Hill.....74 E2
Bellsbank.....112 D4
Bellshill N Lanark..119 C7
 Northumb.....123 F7
Bellspool.....120 F4
Bellsquarry.....120 C3
Bells Yew Green...18 B3
Belmaduthy.....151 F9
Belmesthorpe.....65 C7
Belmont Blackburn..86 C4
 London.....28 C3
 S Ayrs.....112 B3
 Shetland.....160 C7
Belnacraig.....140 C2
Belowda.....4 C4
Belper.....76 E3
Belper Lane End..76 E3
Belsay.....110 B4
Belses.....115 B8
Belsford.....7 D5
Belstead.....56 E5
Belston.....112 B3
Belstone.....9 E8
Belthorn.....86 B5
Beltinge.....31 C5
Beltoft.....90 D2
Belton Leics.....63 B8
 Lincs.....78 F2
 N Lincs.....89 D8
 Norf.....69 D7
Belton in Rutland..64 D5
Beltring.....29 E7
Belts of
 Collonach.....141 E5
Belvedere.....29 B5
Belvoir.....77 F8
Bembridge.....15 F7
Bemersyde.....121 F8
Bemerton.....25 F6
Bempton.....97 B7
Benacre.....69 F8
Ben Alder Lodge.132 B2
Ben Armine
 Lodge.....157 H10
Benbuie.....113 E7
Ben Casgro.....155 E9
Benderloch.....124 B5
Bendronaig
 Lodge.....150 H3
Benenden.....18 B5
Benfield.....105 C7
Bengate.....69 B6
Bengeworth.....50 E5
Benhall Green.....57 C7
Benhall Street.....57 C7
Benholm.....135 C8
Beningbrough.....95 D8
Benington Herts...41 B5
 Lincs.....79 E6
Benllech.....82 C5
Benmore Argyll..145 E10
 Stirling.....126 B3
Benmore Lodge..156 H6
Bennacott.....8 E4
Bennan.....143 F10
Benniworth.....91 F6
Benover.....29 E8
Bensham.....110 C5
Benslie.....118 E3
Benson.....39 E6
Bent.....135 B6
Bent Gate.....87 B5
Benthall Northumb..117 B8
 Shrops.....61 D6
Bentham.....37 C6
Benthoul.....141 D7
Bentlawnt.....60 D3
Bentley E Yorks...97 F6
 Hants.....27 E5
 Suff.....56 F5
 S Yorks.....89 D6
 Warks.....63 E6
 Worcs.....50 C4
Bentley Heath.....51 B6
Benton.....21 F5
Bentpath.....115 E6

Bents.....120 C2
Bentworth.....26 E4
Benvie.....134 F3
Benwick.....66 E3
Beoley.....51 C5
Beoraidbeg.....147 B9
Bepton.....16 C2
Berden.....41 B7
Bere Alston.....6 C2
Bere Ferrers.....6 C2
Berepper.....3 D5
Bere Regis.....13 E6
Bergh Apton.....69 D6
Berinsfield.....39 E5
Berkeley.....36 E3
Berkhamsted.....40 D2
Berkley.....24 E3
Berkswell.....51 B7
Bermondsey.....28 B4
Bernera.....149 F13
Bernice.....145 D10
Berrick Salome...39 E6
Berriedale.....158 H3
Berrier.....99 B5
Berriew.....59 D8
Berrington
 Northumb.....123 E6
 Shrops.....60 D5
Berrow.....22 D5
Berrow Green.....50 D2
Berry Down Cross.20 E4
Berryfield.....39 C7
Berry Hill Glos....36 C2
 Pembs.....45 E2
Berryhillock.....152 B5
Berrynarbor.....20 E4
Berry Pomeroy.....7 C6
Bersham.....73 E7
Berstane.....159 G5
Berwick.....18 E2
Berwick Bassett..25 B5
Berwick Hill.....110 B4
Berwick St James.25 F5
Berwick St John...13 B7
Berwick
 St Leonard.....24 F4
Berwick-
 upon-Tweed...123 D5
Bescar.....85 C4
Besford.....50 E4
Bessacarr.....89 D7
Bessels Leigh.....38 D4
Bessingby.....97 C7
Bessingham.....81 D7
Bestbeech Hill....18 B3
Besthorpe Norf....68 E3
 Notts.....77 C8
Bestwood.....77 E5
Bestwood Village..77 E5
Beswick.....97 E6
Betchworth.....28 E3
Bethania Ceredig..46 C4
 Gwyn.....71 C8
 Gwyn.....72 E3
Bethel Anglesey...82 D3
 Gwyn.....82 E5
Bethersden.....30 E3
Bethesda Gwyn...83 E6
 Pembs.....32 C1
Bethlehem.....33 B7
Bethnal Green.....41 F6
Betley.....74 E4
Betsham.....29 B7
Betteshanger.....31 D7
Bettiscombe.....11 E8
Bettisfield.....73 F8
Betton Shrops.....60 D3
 Shrops.....74 F3
Bettws Bridgend...34 F3
 Mon.....35 C6
 Newport.....35 E6
Bettws Cedewain..59 E8
Bettws Gwerfil
 Goch.....72 E4
Bettws Ifan.....46 E2
Bettws Newydd...35 D7
Bettws-y-crwyn...60 F2
Bettyhill.....157 C10
Betws.....33 C7
Betws Bledrws....46 D4
Betws-Garmon....82 F5
Betws-y-coed.....83 F7
Betws-yn-Rhos...72 B3
Beulah Ceredig....45 E4
 Powys.....47 D8
Bevendean.....17 D7
Bevercotes.....77 B6
Beverley.....97 F6
Beverston.....37 E5
Bevington.....36 E3
Bewaldeth.....108 F2
Bewcastle.....109 B5
Bewdley.....50 B2
Bewerley.....94 C4
Bewholme.....97 D7
Bexhill.....18 E4
Bexley.....29 B5
Bexleyheath.....29 B5
Bexwell.....67 D6
Beyton.....56 C3
Bhaltos.....154 D5
Bhatarsaigh.....148 J1
Bibury.....37 D8
Bicester.....39 B5
Bickenhall.....11 C7
Bickenhill.....63 F5
Bicker.....78 F5
Bickershaw.....86 D4
Bickerstaffe.....86 D2
Bickerton Ches E..74 D2
 N Yorks.....95 D7
Bickington Devon...7 B5
 Devon.....20 F4
Bickleigh Devon....6 C3
 Devon.....10 D4
Bickleton.....20 F4
Bickley.....28 C5
Bickley Moss.....74 E2
Bicknacre.....42 D3
Bicknoller.....22 F3
Bicknor.....30 D2
Bicton Shrops.....60 C4
 Shrops.....60 F2
Bidborough.....29 E6
Biddenden.....19 B5
Biddenham.....53 E8

Biddestone.....24 B3
Biddisham.....23 D5
Biddlesden.....52 E4
Biddlestone.....117 D5
Biddulph.....75 D5
Biddulph Moor...75 D6
Bideford.....9 B6
Bidford-on-Avon...51 D6
Bidston.....85 E3
Bielby.....96 E3
Bieldside.....141 D7
Bierley IoW.....15 G6
 W Yorks.....94 F4
Bierton.....39 C8
Big Sand.....149 A12
Bigbury.....6 E4
Bigbury on Sea.....6 F4
Bigby.....90 D4
Biggar Cumb.....92 C1
 S Lanark.....120 F3
Biggin Derbys.....75 D8
 Derbys.....76 E2
 N Yorks.....95 F8
Biggings.....160 G3
Biggin Hill.....28 D5
Biggleswade.....54 E2
Bighouse.....157 C11
Bighton.....26 F4
Bignor.....16 C3
Big Sand.....149 A12
Bigton.....160 L5
Bilberry.....4 C5
Bilborough.....76 E5
Bilbrook.....22 E2
Bilbrough.....95 E8
Bilbster.....158 E4
Bildershaw.....101 B7
Bildeston.....56 E3
Billericay.....42 E2
Billesdon.....64 D4
Billesley.....51 D6
Billingborough...78 F4
Billinge.....86 D3
Billingford.....81 E6
Billingham.....102 B2
Billinghay.....78 D4
Billingley.....88 D5
Billingshurst.....16 B4
Billingsley.....61 F7
Billington C Beds...40 B2
 Lancs.....93 F7
Billockby.....69 C7
Billy Row.....110 F4
Bilsborrow.....92 F5
Bilsby.....79 B7
Bilsham.....16 D3
Bilsington.....19 B7
Bilson Green.....36 C3
Bilsthorpe.....77 D6
Bilsthorpe Moor..77 D6
Bilston Midloth...121 C5
 W Mid.....62 E3
Bilstone.....63 D7
Bilting.....30 E4
Bilton E Yorks.....97 F7
 Northumb.....117 C8
 Warks.....52 B2
Bilton in Ainsty..95 E7
Bimbister.....159 G4
Binbrook.....91 E6
Binchester
 Blocks.....110 F5
Bincombe.....12 F4
Bindal.....151 C12
Binegar.....23 E8
Binfield.....27 B6
Binfield Heath....26 B5
Bingfield.....110 B2
Bingham.....77 F7
Bingley.....94 F4
Bings Heath.....60 C5
Binham.....81 D5
Binley Hants.....26 D2
 W Mid.....51 B8
Binley Woods.....51 B8
Binniehill.....119 B8
Binsoe.....94 B5
Binstead.....15 E6
Binsted.....27 E5
Binton.....51 D6
Bintree.....81 E6
Binweston.....60 D3
Birch Essex.....43 C5
 Gtr Man.....87 D6
Bircham Newton..80 D3
Bircham Tofts.....80 D3
Birchanger.....41 B8
Birchencliffe.....88 C2
Bircher.....49 C6
Birch Green.....43 C5
Birchgrove Cardiff..35 F5
 Swansea.....33 E8
Birch Heath.....74 C2
Birch Hill.....74 B2
Birchington.....31 C6
Birchmoor.....63 D6
Birchover.....76 C2
Birch Vale.....87 F8
Birchwood Lincs...78 C2
 Warr.....86 E4
Bircotes.....89 E7
Birdbrook.....55 E8
Birdforth.....95 B7
Birdham.....16 D2
Birdholme.....76 C3
Birdingbury.....52 C2
Birdlip.....37 C6
Birdsall.....96 C4
Birds Edge.....88 D3
Birdsgreen.....61 F7
Birdsmoor Gate...11 D8
Birdston.....119 B6
Birdwell.....88 D4
Birdwood.....36 C4
Birgham.....122 F3
Birkby.....101 D8
Birkdale.....85 C4
Birkenhead.....85 F4
Birkenhills.....153 D7
Birkenshaw
 N Lanark.....119 C6
 W Yorks.....88 B3
Birkhall.....140 E2
Birkhill Angus.....134 F3
 Borders.....114 C5
Birkholme.....65 B6
Birkin.....89 B6
Birley.....49 D6
Birling Kent.....29 C7
 Northumb.....117 D8

Birling Gap.....18 F2
Birlingham.....50 E4
Birmingham.....62 F4
Birnam.....133 E7
Birse.....140 E4
Birsemore.....140 E4
Birstall Leics.....64 D2
 W Yorks.....88 B3
Birstwith.....94 D5
Birthorpe.....78 F4
Birtley Hereford...49 C5
 Northumb.....109 B8
 T&W.....111 D5
Birts Street.....50 F2
Bisbrooke.....65 E5
Biscathorpe.....91 F6
Biscot.....40 B3
Bisham.....39 F8
Bishampton.....50 D4
Bish Mill.....10 B2
Bishop Auckland.101 B7
Bishopbridge.....90 E4
Bishopbriggs.....119 C6
Bishop Burton....97 F5
Bishop
 Middleham.....111 F6
Bishopmill.....152 B2
Bishop Monkton..95 C6
Bishop Norton....90 E3
Bishopsbourne...31 D5
Bishops Cannings..24 C5
Bishop's Castle...60 F3
Bishop's Caundle..12 C4
Bishop's Cleeve...37 B6
Bishops Frome....49 E8
Bishop's Green....42 C2
Bishop's Hull.....11 B7
Bishop's
 Itchington.....51 D8
Bishops Lydeard..11 B6
Bishops Nympton..10 B2
Bishop's Offley...61 B7
Bishop's Stortford.41 B7
Bishop's Sutton..26 F4
Bishop's
 Tachbrook.....51 C8
Bishops Tawton...20 F4
Bishopsteignton...7 B7
Bishopstoke.....15 C5
Bishopston.....33 F6
Bishopstone
 Bucks.....39 C8
 E Sus.....17 D8
 Hereford.....49 E6
 Swindon.....38 F2
 Wilts.....13 B8
Bishopstrow.....24 E3
Bishop Sutton.....23 D7
Bishop's Waltham..15 C6
Bishopswood.....11 C7
Bishop's Wood....62 D2
Bishopsworth.....23 C7
Bishop Thornton..95 C5
Bishopthorpe.....95 E8
Bishopton Darl...102 B1
 Dumfries.....105 E8
 N Yorks.....95 B6
 Renfs.....118 B4
 Warks.....51 D6
Bishop Wilton.....96 D3
Bishton.....35 F7
Bisley Glos.....37 D6
 Sur.....27 D7
Bispham.....92 E3
Bispham Green...86 C2
Bissoe.....3 B6
Bisterne Close....14 D3
Bitchfield.....65 B6
Bittadon.....20 E4
Bittaford.....6 D4
Bittering.....68 C2
Bitterley.....49 B7
Bitterne.....15 C5
Bitteswell.....64 F2
Bitton.....23 B8
Bix.....39 F7
Bixter.....160 H5
Blaby.....64 E2
Blackacre.....114 E3
Black Crofts.....124 B5
Blackden Heath...74 B4
Blackdog.....141 C8
Black Dog.....10 D3
Blackfell.....111 D5
Blackfield.....14 D5
Blackford Cumb..108 C3
 Perth.....127 D7
 Som.....12 B4
 Som.....23 D6
Blackfordby.....63 C7
Blackgang.....15 G5
Blackhall Colliery 111 F7
Blackhall Mill.....110 D4
Blackhall Rocks...111 F7
Blackham.....29 F5
Blackhaugh.....121 F7
Blackheath Essex..43 B6
 Sur.....27 E8
 W Mid.....62 F3
 W Sus.....27 F8
Black Heddon....110 B3
Blackhill Aberds..153 C10
 Aberds.....153 D10
 Highld.....149 C8
Blackhills.....151 F12
 Moray.....152 C2
Blackhorse.....23 B8
Blackland.....24 C5
Black Lane.....87 D5
Blacklaw.....153 C6
Blackley.....87 D6
Blacklunans.....134 C1

Black Marsh.....60 E3
Blackmill.....34 F3
Blackmoor.....27 F5
Blackmoor Gate...21 E5
Blackmore.....42 D2
Blackmore End
 Essex.....55 F8
 Herts.....40 C4
Black Mount.....131 E6
Blackness.....120 B3
Blacknest.....27 E5
Black Notley.....42 B3
Blacko.....93 E8
Black Pill.....33 E7
Blackpool Blackpool 92 F3
 Devon.....7 E6
 Pembs.....32 C1
Blackpool Gate...108 B5
Blackridge.....119 C8
Blackrock Argyll..142 B4
 Mon.....35 C6
Blackrod.....86 C4
Blackshaw.....107 C7
Blackshaw Head...87 B7
Blacksmith's
 Green.....56 C5
Blackstone.....17 C6
Black Tar.....44 E4
Blackthorn.....39 C6
Blackthorpe.....56 C3
Blacktoft.....90 B2
Blacktop.....141 D7
Black Torrington..9 D6
Blacktown.....35 F6
Blackwall Tunnel..41 F6
Blackwater Corn...3 B6
 Hants.....27 D6
 IoW.....15 F6
Blackwaterfoot..143 F9
Blackwell Darl...101 C7
 Derbys.....75 B8
 Derbys.....76 D4
 Warks.....51 E7
 Worcs.....50 B4
 W Sus.....28 F4
Blackwood.....119 E7
Blackwood
 = Coed Duon...35 E5
Blackwood Hill...75 D6
Blacon.....73 C7
Bladnoch.....105 D8
Bladon.....38 C4
Blaenannerch.....45 E4
Blaenau
 Ffestiniog 71 C8
Blaenavon.....35 D6
Blaencelyn.....46 D2
Blaendyryn.....47 F8
Blaenffos.....45 F3
Blaengarw.....34 E3
Blaengwrach.....34 D2
Blaen-gwynfi.....34 E2
Blaenpennal.....46 C5
Blaenplwyf.....46 B4
Blaenporth.....45 E4
Blaenrhondda.....34 D3
Blaen-waun.....32 B3
Blaen-y-coed.....32 B4
Blaencwm.....34 D3
Blaen-y-Cwm Denb 72 F4
 Gwyn.....71 E8
 Powys.....59 B7
Blagdon N Som...23 D7
 Torbay.....7 C6
Blagdon Hill.....11 C7
Blaguegate.....86 D2
Blaich.....130 B4
Blain.....147 E9
Blaina.....35 D6
Blair Atholl.....133 C5
Blairbeg.....143 E11
Blairdaff.....141 C5
Blair Drummond.127 E6
Blairglas.....126 F2
Blairgowrie.....134 E1
Blairhall.....128 F2
Blairingone.....127 E8
Blairland.....118 E3
Blairlogie.....127 E7
Blairlomond.....125 F7
Blairmore.....145 E10
Blairnamarrow..139 C8
Blairquhosh.....126 F4
Blair's Ferry.....145 G8
Blairskaith.....119 B5
Blaisdon.....36 C4
Blakebrook.....50 B3
Blakedown.....50 B3
Blakelaw.....122 F3
Blakeley.....62 E2
Blakeley Lane.....75 E6
Blakemere.....49 E5
Blakeney Glos.....36 D3
 Norf.....81 C6
Blakenhall Ches E..74 E4
 W Mid.....62 E3
Blakeshall.....50 B3
Blakesley.....52 D4
Blanchland.....110 D2
Blandford Forum..13 D6
Blandford St Mary..13 D6
Bland Hill.....94 D5
Blanefield.....119 B5
Blankney.....78 C3
Blantyre.....119 D6
Blar a'Chaorainn.131 C5
Blaran.....124 D4
Blarghour.....125 D5
Blarmachfoldach.130 C4
Blarnalearoch.....150 B4
Blashford.....14 D2
Blaston.....64 E5
Blatherwycke.....65 E6
Blawith.....98 F4
Blaxhall.....57 D7
Blaxton.....89 D7
Blaydon.....110 C4
Bleadon.....22 D5
Bleak Hey Nook...87 D8
Blean.....30 C5
Bleasby Lincs.....90 F5
 Notts.....77 E7
Bleasdale.....93 E5
Bleatarn.....100 C2
Blebocraigs.....129 C6
Bleddfa.....48 C4
Bledington.....38 B2
Bledlow.....39 D7
Bledlow Ridge.....39 E7

Blegbie.....121 C7
Blencarn.....109 F6
Blencogo.....107 E8
Blendworth.....15 C8
Blenheim Park....80 D4
Blennerhasset...107 E8
Blervie Castle...151 F13
Bletchingdon.....39 C5
Bletchingley.....28 D4
Bletchley M Keynes..53 F6
 Shrops.....74 F3
Bletherston.....32 B1
Bletsoe.....53 D8
Blewbury.....39 F5
Blickling.....81 E7
Blidworth.....77 D5
Blindburn.....116 C4
Blindcrake.....107 F8
Blindley Heath....28 E4
Blisland.....5 B6
Blissford.....14 C2
Bliss Gate.....50 B2
Blisworth.....52 D5
Blithbury.....62 B4
Blitterlees.....107 D8
Blockley.....51 F6
Blofield.....69 D6
Blofield Heath....69 C6
Blo' Norton.....56 B4
Bloomfield.....115 B8
Blore.....75 E7
Blount's Green....75 F7
Blowick.....85 C4
Bloxham.....52 F2
Bloxholm.....78 D3
Bloxwich.....62 D3
Bloxworth.....13 E6
Blubberhouses....94 D4
Blue Anchor Som...22 E2
 Swansea.....33 E6
Blue Row.....43 C6
Blundeston.....69 E8
Blunham.....54 D2
Blunsdon
 St Andrew.....37 F8
Bluntington.....50 B3
Bluntisham.....54 B4
Blunts.....5 C8
Blyborough.....90 E3
Blyford.....57 B8
Blymhill.....62 C2
Blyth Northumb...117 F9
 Notts.....89 F7
Blyth Bridge.....120 E4
Blythburgh.....57 B8
Blythe.....121 E8
Blythe Bridge.....75 E6
Blyton.....90 E2
Boarhills.....129 C7
Boarhunt.....15 D7
Boars Hill.....38 D4
Boarshead.....18 B2
Boars Head.....86 D3
Boarstall.....39 C6
Boasley Cross.....9 E6
Boath.....151 D8
Boat of Garten...138 C5
Bobbing.....30 C2
Bobbington.....62 E2
Bobbingworth.....41 D8
Bocaddon.....5 D6
Bochastle.....126 D5
Bocking.....42 B3
Bocking
 Churchstreet...42 B3
Boddam Aberds..153 D11
 Shetland.....160 M5
Boddington.....37 B5
Bodedern.....82 C3
Bodelwyddan.....72 B4
Bodenham
 Hereford.....49 D7
 Wilts.....14 B2
Bodenham Moor...49 D7
Bodermid.....70 E2
Bodewryd.....82 B3
Bodfari.....72 B4
Bodffordd.....82 D4
Bodham.....81 C7
Bodiam.....18 C4
Bodicote.....52 F2
Bodieve.....4 B4
Bodinnick.....5 D6
Bodle Street
 Green.....18 D3
Bodmin.....5 C5
Bodney.....67 E8
Bodorgan.....82 E3
Bodsham.....30 E5
Boduan.....70 D4
Bodymoor Heath...63 E5
Bogallan.....151 F9
Bogbrae.....153 E10
Bogend Borders..122 E3
 S Ayrs.....118 F3
Boghall.....120 C2
Boghead.....119 E7
Bogmoor.....152 B3
Bogniebrae.....152 D5
Bognor Regis.....16 E3
Bograxie.....141 C6
Bogside.....119 D8
Bogton.....153 C6
Bogue.....113 F6
Bohenie.....137 F5
Bohortha.....3 C7
Bohuntine.....137 F5
Boirseam.....154 J5
Bojewyan.....2 C2
Bolam Durham...101 B6
 Northumb.....117 F6
Bolberry.....6 F4
Bold Heath.....86 F3
Boldon.....111 C6
Boldon Colliery...111 C6
Boldre.....14 E4
Boldron.....101 C5
Bole.....89 F8
Bolehill.....76 D2
Boleside.....121 F7
Bolham.....10 C4
Bolham Water.....11 C6
Bolingey.....4 D2
Bollington.....75 B6
Bollington Cross..75 B6
Bolney.....17 B6
Bolnhurst.....53 D8
Bolshan.....135 D6
Bolsover.....76 B4

Bolsterstone.....88 E3
Bolstone.....49 F7
Boltby.....102 F2
Bolter End.....39 E7
Bolton Cumb.....99 B8
 E Loth.....121 B8
 E Yorks.....96 D3
 Gtr Man.....86 D5
 Northumb.....117 C7
Bolton Abbey.....94 D3
Bolton Bridge.....94 D3
Bolton-by-
 Bowland.....93 E7
Boltonfellend.....108 C4
Boltongate.....108 E2
Bolton-le-Sands..92 C4
Bolton
 Low Houses..108 E2
Bolton-on-Swale 101 E7
Bolton Percy.....95 E8
Bolton Town End..92 C4
Bolton upon
 Dearne.....89 D5
Bolventor.....5 B6
Bomere Heath.....60 C4
Bonar Bridge.....151 B9
Bonawe.....125 B6
Bonby.....90 C4
Boncath.....45 F4
Bonchester
 Bridge.....115 C8
Bonchurch.....15 G6
Bondleigh.....9 D8
Bonehill Devon.....6 B5
 Staffs.....63 D5
Bo'ness.....127 F8
Bonhill.....118 B3
Boningale.....62 D2
Bonjedward.....116 B2
Bonkle.....119 D8
Bonnavoulin.....147 F8
Bonnington Edin..120 C4
 Kent.....19 B7
Bonnybank.....129 D5
Bonnybridge.....127 F7
Bonnykelly.....153 C8
Bonnyrigg and
 Lasswade.....121 C6
Bonnyton Aberds..153 E6
 Angus.....134 F3
 Angus.....135 D6
Bonsall.....76 D2
Bonskeid House..133 C5
Bont.....35 C7
Bontddu.....58 C3
Bont-Dolgadfan..59 D5
Bont-goch.....58 F3
Bonthorpe.....79 B7
Bontnewydd
 Ceredig.....46 C5
 Gwyn.....82 F4
Bont Newydd Gwyn..71 C8
 Gwyn.....71 E8
Bontuchel.....72 D4
Bonvilston.....22 B2
Bon-y-maen.....33 E7
Booker.....39 E8
Boon.....121 E8
Boosbeck.....102 C4
Boot.....98 D3
Booth.....87 B8
Boothby Graffoe..78 D2
Boothby Pagnell..78 F2
Boothen.....75 E5
Boothferry.....89 B8
Boothville.....53 C5
Booth Wood.....87 C8
Bootle Cumb.....98 F3
 Mers.....85 E4
Booton.....81 E7
Boot Street.....57 E6
Boquhan.....126 F4
Boraston.....49 B8
Borden Kent.....30 C2
 W Sus.....16 B2
Bordley.....94 C2
Bordon.....27 F6
Bordon Camp.....27 F5
Boreham Essex....42 D3
 Wilts.....24 E3
Boreham Street...18 D3
Borehamwood.....40 E4
Boreland Dumfries.114 E4
 Stirling.....132 F2
Borgh W Isles.....148 H1
 W Isles.....154 J4
Borghastan.....154 C7
Borgie.....157 D9
Borgue Dumfries..106 E3
 Highld.....158 H3
Borley.....56 E2
Bornais.....148 F2
Bornesketaig.....149 A8
Borness.....106 E3
Boroughbridge....95 C6
Borough Green....29 D7
Borras Head.....73 D7
Borreraig.....148 C6
Borrobol Lodge..157 G11
Borrowash.....76 F4
Borrowby.....102 F2
Borrowdale.....98 C4
Borrowfield.....141 E7
Borth.....58 E3
Borthwickshiels..115 C7
Borth-y-Gest.....71 D6
Borve.....149 D9
Borve Lodge.....154 H5
Borwick.....92 B5
Bosavern.....2 C2
Bosbury.....49 E8
Boscastle.....8 E3
Boscombe BCP....14 E2
 Wilts.....25 F7
Boscoppa.....4 D5
Bosham.....16 D2
Bosherston.....44 F4
Boskenna.....2 D3
Bosley.....75 C6
Bossall.....96 C3
Bossiney.....8 F2
Bossingham.....31 E5
Bossington.....21 E7
Bostock Green....74 C3

Boston....79 E6
Boston Long Hedges....79 E6
Boston Spa....95 E7
Boston West....79 E5
Boswinger....3 B8
Botallack....2 C2
Botany Bay....41 E5
Botcherby....108 D4
Botcheston....63 D8
Botesdale....56 B4
Bothal....117 F8
Bothampstead....77 B6 (Bothamsall....77 B6)
Bothel....107 F8
Bothenhampton....12 E2
Bothwell....119 D7
Botley Bucks....40 D2
  Hants....15 C6
  Oxon....38 D4
Botolph Claydon....39 B7
Botolphs....17 D5
Bottacks....150 E7
Bottesford Leics....77 F8
  N Lincs....90 D2
Bottisham....55 C6
Bottlesford....25 D6
Bottom Boat....88 B4
Bottomcraig....129 B5
Bottom House....75 D7
Bottom of Hutton....86 B2
Bottom o'th'Moor....86 C4
Botusfleming....6 C2
Botwnnog....70 D3
Bough Beech....29 E5
Boughrood....48 F3
Boughspring....36 E2
Boughton Norf....67 D6
  Notts....77 C6
  W Nhants....53 C5
Boughton Aluph....30 E4
Boughton Lees....30 E4
Boughton Malherbe....30 E2
Boughton Monchelsea....29 D8
Boughton Street....30 D4
Boulby....103 C5
Boulden....60 F5
Boulmer....117 C8
Boulston....44 D4
Boultenstone....140 C3
Boultham....78 C2
Bourn....54 D4
Bourne....65 B7
Bourne End Bucks....40 F1
  C Beds....53 E7
  Herts....40 D3
Bournemouth....13 E8
Bournes Green
  Glos....37 D6
  Southend....43 F5
Bournheath....50 B4
Bournmoor....111 D6
Bournville....62 F4
Bourton Dorset....24 F2
  N Som....23 C5
  Oxon....38 F2
  Shrops....61 E5
Bourton on Dunsmore....52 B2
Bourton on the Hill....51 F6
Bourton-on-the-Water....38 B1
Bousd....146 E5
Boustead Hill....108 D2
Bouth....99 F5
Bouthwaite....94 B4
Boveney....27 B7
Boverton....21 C8
Bovey Tracey....7 B6
Bovingdon....40 D3
Bovingdon Green
  Bucks....39 F8
  Herts....40 D3
Bovinger....41 D8
Bovington Camp....13 F6
Bow Borders....121 E7
  Devon....10 D2
  Orkney....159 J4
Bowbank....88 C4
Bow Brickhill....53 F7
Bowburn....111 F6
Bowcombe....15 F5
Bowd....11 E6
Bowden Borders....121 F8
  Devon....7 E6
Bowden Hill....24 C4
Bowderdale....100 D1
Bowdon....87 F5
Bower....116 F3
Bowerchalke....13 B8
Bowerhill....24 C4
Bower Hinton....12 C2
Bowermadden....158 D4
Bowers Gifford....42 F3
Bowershall....128 E2
Bowertower....158 D4
Bowes....100 C4
Bowgreave....92 E4
Bowgreen....87 F5
Bowhill....115 B7
Bowhouse....107 C7
Bowland Bridge....99 F6
Bowley....49 D7
Bowlhead Green....27 F7
Bowling W Dunb....118 B4
  W Yorks....94 F4
Bowling Bank....73 E7
Bowling Green....50 D3
Bowmanstead....99 E5
Bowmore....142 C4
Bowness-on-Solway....108 C2
Bowness-on-Windermere....99 E6
Bow of Fife....128 C5
Bowsden....123 E5
Bowside Lodge....157 C11
Bowston....99 E6
Bow Street....3 B8
Bowthorpe....68 D4
Box Glos....37 D5
  Wilts....24 C3
Boxbush....36 C4
Box End....53 E8

Boxford Suff....56 E3
  W Berks....26 B2
Boxgrove....16 D3
Boxley....29 D8
Boxmoor....40 D3
Boxted Essex....56 F4
  Suff....56 D2
Boxted Cross....56 F4
Boxted Heath....56 F4
Boxworth....54 C4
Boxworth End....54 C4
Boyden Gate....31 C6
Boylestone....75 F8
Boyndie....153 B6
Boynton....97 C7
Boysack....135 E6
Boyton Corn....8 E5
  Suff....57 E7
  Wilts....24 F4
Boyton Cross....42 D2
Boyton End....55 E8
Bozeat....53 D7
Braaid....84 E3
Braal Castle....158 D3
Brabling Green....57 C6
Brabourne....30 E4
Brabourne Lees....30 E4
Brabster....158 D5
Bracadale....149 E8
Bracara....147 B10
Braceborough....65 C7
Braceby....78 C2
Bracewell....93 E8
Brackenfield....76 D3
Brackenthwaite
  Cumb....108 E2
  N Yorks....95 D5
Bracklesham....16 E2
Brackletter....136 F4
Brackley Argyll....143 D8
  W Nhants....52 F3
Brackloch....156 G4
Bracknell....27 C6
Braco....127 D7
Bracobrae....152 C5
Bracon Ash....68 E4
Bracorina....147 B10
Bradbourne....76 D2
Bradbury....101 B8
Bradda....84 F1
Bradden....52 E4
Braddock....5 C6
Bradeley....75 D5
Bradenham Bucks....39 E8
  Norf....68 D2
Bradenstoke....24 B5
Bradfield Essex....56 F5
  Norf....81 D8
  W Berks....26 B4
Bradfield Combust....56 D2
Bradfield Green....74 D3
Bradfield Heath....43 B7
Bradfield St Clare....56 D3
Bradfield St George....56 C3
Bradford Corn....5 B6
  Derbys....76 C2
  Devon....9 D6
  Northumb....123 F7
  W Yorks....94 F4
Bradford Abbas....12 C3
Bradford Leigh....24 C3
Bradford-on-Avon....24 C3
Bradford-on-Tone....11 B6
Bradford Peverell....12 E4
Brading....15 F7
Bradley Derbys....76 E2
  Hants....26 E4
  NE Lincs....91 D6
  Staffs....62 C2
  W Mid....62 E3
  W Yorks....88 B2
Bradley Green....50 C4
Bradley in the Moors....75 E7
Bradley Stoke....36 F3
Bradlow....50 F2
Bradmore Notts....77 F5
  W Mid....62 E2
Bradninch....10 D5
Bradnop....75 D7
Bradpole....12 E2
Bradshaw Gtr Man....86 C5
  W Yorks....87 C8
Bradstone....9 F5
Bradwall Green....74 C4
Bradway....88 F4
Bradwell Derbys....76 E2
  Essex....42 B4
  M Keynes....53 F6
  Norf....69 D8
  Staffs....74 E5
Bradwell Grove....38 D2
Bradwell on Sea....43 D6
Bradwell Waterside....43 D5
Bradworthy....8 C5
Bradworthy Cross....8 C5
Brae Dumfries....107 B5
  Highld....155 J13
  Highld....156 J7
  Shetland....160 G5
Braeantra....151 D8
Braedownie....134 B2
Braefield....150 H7
Braegrum....128 B2
Braehead
  Dumfries....105 D8
  Orkney....159 D5
  Orkney....159 H6
  S Lanark....119 F8
  S Lanark....120 D2
Brae of Achnahaird....156 H3
Brae Roy Lodge....137 E6
Braeside....118 B2

Braes of Enzie....152 C3
Braeswick....159 E7
Braewick....160 H5
Brafferton Darl....101 B7
  N Yorks....95 B7
Brafield-on-the-Green....53 D6
Bragar....155 C7
Bragbury End....41 B5
Bragleenmore....124 C5
Braichmelyn....83 E6
Braid....120 C5
Braides....92 D4
Braidley....101 F5
Braidwood....119 E8
Braigo....142 B3
Brailsford....76 E2
Brainshaugh....117 D8
Braintree....42 B3
Braiseworth....56 B5
Braishfield....14 B4
Braithwaite Cumb....98 B4
  S Yorks....89 C7
  W Yorks....94 E3
Braithwell....89 E6
Bramber....17 C5
Bramcote Notts....76 F5
  Warks....63 F8
Bramdean....15 B7
Bramerton....69 D5
Bramfield Herts....41 C5
  Suff....57 B7
Bramford....56 E5
Bramhall....87 F6
Bramham....95 E7
Bramhope....95 E5
Bramley Hants....26 D4
  Sur....27 E8
  S Yorks....89 E5
  W Yorks....94 F5
Bramling....31 D6
Brampford Speke....10 E4
Brampton Cambs....54 B3
  Cumb....100 B1
  Cumb....108 C5
  Derbys....76 B3
  Hereford....49 F6
  Lincs....77 B8
  Norf....81 E8
  Suff....69 F7
  S Yorks....88 D5
Brampton Abbotts....36 B3
Brampton Ash....64 F4
Brampton Bryan....49 B5
Brampton en le Morthen....89 F5
Bramshall....75 F7
Bramshaw....14 C3
Bramshill....26 C5
Bramshott....27 F6
Branault....147 E8
Brancaster....80 C3
Brancaster Staithe....80 C3
Brancepeth....110 F5
Branderburgh....152 A2
Brandesburton....97 E7
Brandeston....57 C6
Brand End....79 E6
Brand Green....36 B4
Brandhill....49 B6
Brandis Corner....9 D6
Brandiston....81 E7
Brandon Durham....110 F5
  Lincs....78 E2
  Northumb....117 C6
  Suff....67 F7
  Warks....52 B2
Brandon Bank....67 F6
Brandon Creek....67 E6
Brandon Parva....68 D3
Brandsby....95 B8
Brandy Wharf....90 E4
Brane....2 D3
Bran End....42 B2
Branksome....13 E8
Branksome Park....13 E8
Bransby....77 B8
Branscombe....11 F6
Bransford....50 D2
Bransgore....14 E2
Branshill....127 E7
Bransholme....97 F7
Branson's Cross....51 B5
Branston Leics....64 B5
  Lincs....78 C3
  Staffs....63 B6
Branston Booths....78 C3
Branstone....15 F6
Bransty....98 C1
Brant Broughton....78 D2
Brantham....56 F5
Branthwaite Cumb....98 B2
  Cumb....108 F2
Brantingham....90 B3
Branton Northumb....117 C6
  S Yorks....89 D7
Branxholme....115 C7
Branxholm Park....115 C7
Branxton....122 F4
Brassey Green....74 C2
Brassington....76 D2
Brasted....29 D5
Brasted Chart....29 D5
Brathens....141 E5
Bratoft....79 C7
Brattleby....90 F3
Bratton Telford....61 C6
  Wilts....24 D4
Bratton Clovelly....9 E6
Bratton Fleming....20 F5
Bratton Seymour....12 B4
Braughing....41 B6
Braunston....52 C3
Braunston-in-Rutland....64 D5
Braunton....20 F3
Brawby....96 B3
Brawl....157 C11
Brawlbin....158 E2
Bray....27 B7
Braybrooke....64 F4
Braye Ald....16
Brayford....21 F5
Bray Shop....5 B8
Braystones....98 D2
Braythorn....94 E5
Brayton....95 F9

Bray Wick....27 B6
Brazacott....8 E4
Breach....30 C2
Breachacha Castle....146 F4
Breachwood Green....40 B4
Breacleit....154 D6
Breaden Heath....73 F8
Breadsall....76 F3
Breadstone....36 D4
Breage....2 D5
Breakachy....150 G7
Bream....36 D3
Breamore....14 C2
Brean....22 D4
Breanais....154 E4
Brearton....95 C6
Breascleit....154 D7
Breaston....76 F4
Brechfa....46 F4
Brechin....135 C5
Breck of Cruan....159 G4
Breckrey....149 B10
Brecon = Aberhonddu....34 B4
Bredbury....87 E7
Brede....18 D5
Bredenbury....49 D8
Bredfield....57 D6
Bredgar....30 C2
Bredhurst....29 C8
Bredicot....50 D4
Bredon....50 F4
Bredon's Norton....50 F4
Bredwardine....48 E5
Breedon on the Hill....63 B8
Breibhig W Isles....148 J1
  W Isles....155 D9
Breich....120 C2
Breightmet....86 D5
Breighton....96 F3
Breinton....49 F6
Breinton Common....49 E6
Breiwick....160 J6
Bremhill....24 B4
Bremirehoull....160 L6
Brenchley....29 E7
Brendon....21 E6
Brenkley....110 B5
Brent Eleigh....56 E3
Brentford....28 B2
Brentingby....64 C4
Brent Knoll....22 D5
Brent Pelham....54 F5
Brentwood....42 E1
Brenzett....19 C7
Brereton....62 C4
Brereton Green....74 C4
Brereton Heath....74 C5
Bressingham....68 F3
Bretby....63 B6
Bretford....52 B2
Bretforton....51 E5
Bretherdale Head....99 D7
Bretherton....86 B2
Brettabister....160 H6
Brettenham Norf....68 F2
  Suff....56 D3
Bretton Derbys....76 B2
  Flint....73 C7
Brewer Street....28 D4
Brewlands Bridge....134 C1
Brewood....62 D2
Briach....151 F13
Briants Puddle....13 E6
Brick End....42 B1
Brickendon....41 D6
Bricket Wood....40 D4
Brickhampton....50 E4
Bride....84 B4
Bridekirk....107 F8
Bridell....45 E3
Bridestowe....9 F7
Brideswell....152 E5
Bridford....10 F3
Bridfordmills....10 F3
Bridge....31 D5
Bridge End....73 F4
Bridgefoot Angus....134 F3
  Cumb....98 B2
Bridge Green....55 F5
Bridgehampton....12 B3
Bridge Hewick....95 B6
Bridgehill....110 D3
Bridgemary....15 D6
Bridgemont....87 F8
Bridgend Aberds....140 C4
  Aberds....152 E5
  Angus....135 C5
  Argyll....142 B4
  Argyll....143 G8
  Argyll....145 D7
  Cumb....99 C5
  Fife....129 C5
  Moray....152 E3
  N Lanark....119 B6
  Pembs....45 E3
  W Loth....120 B3
Bridgend = Pen-y-Bont Ar Ogwr....21 B8
Bridgend of Lintrathen....134 D2
Bridge of Alford....140 C4
Bridge of Allan....127 E6
Bridge of Avon....152 E1
Bridge of Awe....125 C6
Bridge of Balgie....132 E2
Bridge of Cally....133 D8
Bridge of Canny....141 E5
Bridge of Craigisla....134 D2
Bridge of Dee....106 D4
Bridge of Don....135 C8
Bridge of Dun....135 D6
Bridge of Dye....141 F5
Bridge of Earn....128 C3
Bridge of Ericht....132 D3
Bridge of Feugh....141 E6
Bridge of Forss....157 C13
Bridge of Gairn....140 E2
Bridge of Gaur....132 D2
Bridge of Muchalls....141 E7
Bridge of Oich....137 D6
Bridge of Orchy....125 B8

Bridge of Waith....159 G3
Bridge of Walls....160 H4
Bridge of Weir....118 C3
Bridgerule....8 D4
Bridges....60 E3
Bridge Sollers....49 E6
Bridge Street....56 E2
Bridgeton....119 C6
Bridgetown Corn....8 F5
  Som....21 F8
Bridge Trafford....73 B8
Bridge Yate....23 B8
Bridgham....68 F2
Bridgnorth....61 E7
Bridgtown....62 D3
Bridgwater....22 F5
Bridlington....97 C7
Bridport....12 E2
Bridstow....36 B2
Brierfield....93 F8
Brierley Glos....36 C3
  Hereford....49 D6
  S Yorks....88 C5
Brierley Hill....62 F3
Briery Hill....35 D5
Brigg....90 D4
Briggswath....103 D6
Brigham Cumb....107 F7
  E Yorks....97 D6
Brighouse....88 B2
Brighstone....14 F5
Brightgate....76 D2
Brighthampton....38 D3
Brightling....18 C3
Brightlingsea....43 C6
Brighton Brighton....17 D7
  Corn....4 D4
Brighton Hill....26 E4
Brightons....120 B2
Brightwalton....26 B2
Brightwell....57 E6
Brightwell Baldwin....39 E6
Brightwell cum Sotwell....39 E5
Brignall....101 C5
Brig o'Turk....126 D4
Brigsley....91 D6
Brigsteer....99 F6
Brigstock....65 F6
Brill....39 C6
Brilley....48 E4
Brimaston....44 C4
Brimfield....49 C7
Brimington....76 B4
Brimley....7 B5
Brimpsfield....37 C6
Brimpton....26 C3
Brims....159 K3
Brimscombe....37 D5
Brimstage....85 F4
Brinacory....147 B10
Brind....96 F3
Brindister Shetland....160 H4
  Shetland....160 K6
Brindle....86 B4
Brindley Ford....75 D5
Brineton....62 C2
Bringhurst....64 E5
Brington....53 B8
Brinian....159 F5
Briningham....81 D6
Brinkhill....79 B6
Brinkley....55 D7
Brinklow....52 B2
Brinkworth....37 F7
Brinmore....138 B2
Brinscall....86 B4
Brinsea....23 C6
Brinsley....76 E4
Brinsop....49 E6
Brinsworth....88 F5
Brinton....81 D6
Brisco....108 D4
Brisley....81 E5
Brislington....23 B8
Bristol....23 B7
Briston....81 D6
Britannia....87 B6
Britford....14 B2
Brithdir....58 C4
British Legion Village....29 D8
Briton Ferry....33 E8
Britwell Salome....39 E6
Brixham....7 D7
Brixton Devon....6 D3
  London....28 B4
Brixton Deverill....24 F3
Brixworth....52 B5
Brize Norton....38 D3
Broad Blunsdon....38 E1
Broadbottom....87 E7
Broadbridge....16 D2
Broadbridge Heath....28 F2
Broad Campden....51 F6
Broad Chalke....13 B8
Broadclyst....10 E4
Broadfield Gtr Man....87 C6
  Lancs....86 B3
  Pembs....32 D2
  W Sus....28 F3
Broad Green C Beds....53 E7
  Essex....42 B4
  Worcs....50 D2
Broadhaugh....115 D7
Broadhaven....158 E5
Broad Haven....44 D3
Broadheath....87 F5
Broad Heath....49 C8
Broadhembury....11 D6
Broadhempston....7 C6
Broad Hill....55 B6
Broad Hinton....25 B6
Broadholme Derbys....76 E3
  Lincs....77 B8
Broadland Row....18 D5
Broadlay....32 D4
Broad Laying....26 C2
Broadley Lancs....87 C6
  Moray....152 B3
Broadley Common....41 D7
Broad Marston....51 E6
Broadmayne....12 F5
Broadmeadows....121 F7

Broadmere....26 E4
Broadmoor....32 D1
Broadoak....31 C5
Broad Oak Carms....33 B6
  Cumb....98 E3
  Dorset....12 E2
  Dorset....13 C5
  E Sus....18 C3
  E Sus....18 D5
  Hereford....36 B1
  Mers....86 E3
Broadrashes....152 C4
Broadsea....153 B9
Broadstairs....31 C7
Broadstone BCP....13 E8
  Shrops....60 F5
Broad Street....30 D2
Broad Street Green....42 D4
Broad Town....25 B5
Broadtown Lane....25 B5
Broadwas....50 D2
Broadwater Herts....41 B5
  W Sus....17 D5
Broadway Carms....32 D3
  Pembs....44 D3
  Som....11 C8
  Suff....57 B7
  Worcs....51 F5
Broadwell Glos....36 C2
  Glos....38 B2
  Oxon....38 D2
  Warks....52 C2
Broadwell House....110 D2
Broadwey....12 F4
Broadwindsor....12 D2
Broadwood Kelly....9 D8
Broadwoodwidger....9 F6
Brobury....48 E5
Brochel....149 D10
Brochloch....113 E5
Brochroy....125 B6
Brockamin....50 D2
Brockbridge....15 C7
Brockdam....117 B7
Brockdish....57 B6
Brockenhurst....14 D4
Brocketsbrae....119 F8
Brockford Street....56 C5
Brockhall....52 C4
Brockham....28 E2
Brockhampton Glos....37 B7
  Hereford....49 F7
Brockholes....88 C2
Brockhurst Derbys....76 C3
  Hants....15 D7
Brocklebank....108 E3
Brocklesby....90 C5
Brockley....23 C6
Brockley Green....56 D2
Brockleymoor....108 F4
Brockton Shrops....60 D3
  Shrops....60 F3
  Shrops....61 D7
  Shrops....61 E5
  Telford....61 C7
  V Glam....21 B8
Brockweir....36 D2
Brockwood....15 B7
Brockworth....37 C5
Brocton....62 C3
Brodick....143 E11
Brodsworth....89 D6
Brogaig....149 B9
Brogborough....53 F7
Brokenborough....37 F6
Broken Cross Ches E....75 B5
  Ches W....74 B3
Bromborough....85 F4
Brome....56 B5
Brome Street....57 B5
Bromeswell....57 D7
Bromfield Cumb....107 E8
  Shrops....49 B6
Bromham Bedford....53 D8
  Wilts....24 C4
Bromley London....28 C5
  W Mid....62 F3
Bromley Common....28 C5
Bromley Green....19 B6
Brompton Medway....29 C8
  N Yorks....102 E1
  N Yorks....103 F7
Brompton-on-Swale....101 E7
Brompton Ralph....22 F2
Brompton Regis....21 F8
Bromsash....36 B3
Bromsberrow Heath....50 F2
Bromsgrove....50 B4
Bromyard....49 D8
Bromyard Downs....49 D8
Bronaber....71 D8
Brongest....46 E2
Bronington....73 F8
Bronllys....48 F3
Bronnant....46 C5
Bronwydd Arms....33 B5
Bronydd....48 E4
Brongarth....73 F6
Brook Carms....32 D3
  Hants....14 B4
  Hants....14 C3
  IoW....14 F4
  Kent....30 E4
  Sur....27 E8
  Sur....27 F7
Brooke Norf....69 E5
  Rutland....64 D5
Brookenby....91 E6
Brook End....53 C8
Brookfield....118 C4
Brookhouse....92 C5
Brookhouse Green....74 C5
Brookland....19 C6
Brooklands Dumfries....106 B5
  Gtr Man....87 E5
  Shrops....74 E2
Brookmans Park....41 D5
Brooks....59 E8
Brooks Green....17 B5
Brook Street Kent....19 B6
  Kent....29 E6
  W Sus....17 B7

Brookthorpe....37 C5
Brookville....67 E7
Brookwood....27 D7
Broom C Beds....54 E3
  S Yorks....88 E5
  Warks....51 D5
  Worcs....50 B4
Broome Norf....69 E6
  Shrops....60 F4
Broomedge....86 F5
Broome Park....117 C7
Broomer's Corner....16 B5
Broomfield Aberds....153 E9
  Essex....42 C3
  Kent....30 D2
  Kent....31 C5
  Som....22 F4
Broomfleet....90 B2
Broom Green....81 E5
Broomhall Ches E....74 E3
  Windsor....27 C7
Broomhaugh....110 C3
Broomhill Norf....67 D6
  Northumb....117 D8
  S Yorks....88 D5
Broom Hill....13 D8
Broomholm....81 D9
Broomley....110 C3
Broompark....110 E5
Broom's Green....50 F2
Broomy Lodge....14 C3
Brora....157 J12
Broseley....61 D6
Brotherhouse Bar....66 C2
Brotherstone....122 F2
Brothertoft....79 E5
Brotherton....89 B5
Brotton....102 C4
Broubster....157 C13
Brough Cumb....100 C2
  Derbys....88 F2
  E Yorks....90 B3
  Highld....158 C4
  Notts....77 D8
  Orkney....159 G4
  Shetland....160 F7
  Shetland....160 G7
  Shetland....160 H6
  Shetland....160 J7
Broughall....74 E2
Brough Lodge....160 D7
Brough Sowerby....100 C2
Broughton Borders....120 F4
  Cambs....54 B3
  Flint....73 C7
  Hants....25 F8
  Lancs....92 F5
  M Keynes....53 E6
  N Lincs....90 D3
  N Nhants....53 B6
  N Yorks....94 D2
  N Yorks....96 B5
  Orkney....159 D5
  Oxon....52 F2
  V Glam....21 B8
Broughton Astley....64 E2
Broughton Beck....98 F4
Broughton Common....24 C3
Broughton Gifford....24 C3
Broughton Hackett....50 D4
Broughton in Furness....98 F4
Broughton Mills....98 E4
Broughton Moor....107 F7
Broughton Park....87 D6
Broughton Poggs....38 D2
Broughtown....159 D7
Broughty Ferry....134 F4
Browhouses....108 C2
Browland....160 H4
Brown Candover....26 F3
Brown Edge Lancs....85 C4
  Staffs....75 D6
Brown Heath....73 C8
Brownhill Aberds....153 D8
  Aberds....153 D8
  Blackburn....93 F6
Brownhills Fife....129 C7
  W Mid....62 D4
Brownlow....74 C5
Brownlow Heath....74 C5
Brownmuir....135 B7
Brown's End....50 F2
Brownshill....37 D5
Brownston....6 D4
Brownyside....117 B7
Broxa....103 E7
Broxbourne....41 D6
Broxburn E Loth....122 B2
  W Loth....120 B3
Broxholme....78 B2
Broxted....42 B1
Broxton....73 D8
Broxwood....49 D5
Broyle Side....17 C8
Brù....155 C8
Bruairnis....148 H2
Bruan....158 G5
Bruar Lodge....133 B5
Brucehill....118 B3
Bruckton E Yorks....97 B7
Bruera....73 C8
Bruern Abbey....38 B2
Bruichladdich....142 B3
Bruisyard....57 C7
Brumby....90 D2
Brund....75 C8
Brundall....69 D6
Brundish....57 C6
Brundish Street....57 B6
Brunery....147 D10
Brunshaw....93 F8
Brunswick Village....110 B5
Bruntcliffe....88 B3
Bruntingthorpe....64 E3
Brunton Fife....128 B5
  Northumb....117 B8
  Wilts....25 D7
Brushford Devon....9 D8
  Som....10 B4
Bruton....23 F8
Bryanston....13 D6
Brydekirk....107 B8
Bryher....2 E1

Brymbo....73 D6
Brympton....12 C3
Bryn Carms....33 D6
  Gtr Man....86 D3
  Neath....34 E2
  Shrops....60 F2
Brynamman....33 C8
Brynberian....45 F3
Brynbryddan....34 E1
Brynbuga = Usk....35 D7
Bryncae....34 F3
Bryncethin....34 F3
Bryncir....71 C5
Bryn-coch....33 E8
Bryncroes....70 D3
Bryncrug....58 D3
Bryn Du....82 D3
Bryneglwys....72 E5
Brynford....73 B5
Bryn Gates....86 D3
Bryn-glas....33 E8
Bryn Golau....34 F3
Bryngwran....82 D3
Bryngwyn Ceredig....45 E4
  Mon....35 D7
  Powys....48 E3
Brynhenllan....45 F2
Brynhoffnant....46 D2
Brynithel....35 D6
Bryn-Iwan....46 F2
Brynmawr....35 C5
Bryn-mawr....70 D3
Brynmenyn....34 F3
Brynmill....33 E7
Bryn-nantllech....72 C3
Bryn-penarth....59 D8
Brynrefail Anglesey....82 C4
  Gwyn....83 E5
Bryn Rhyd-yr-Arian....72 C3
Brynsadler....34 F4
Bryn Saith Marchog....72 D4
Brynsiencyn....82 E4
Bryn Sion....59 C5
Brynteg Anglesey....82 C4
  Ceredig....46 E4
Bryn-y-gwenin....35 C7
Bryn-y-maen....83 D8
Bryn-yr-eryr....70 C4
Buaile nam Bodach....148 H2
Bualintur....149 F9
Buarthmeini....72 F2
Bubbenhall....51 B8
Bubwith....96 F3
Buccleuch....115 C6
Buchanan Smithy....126 E4
Buchanhaven....153 D11
Buchanty....127 B8
Buchlyvie....126 E4
Buckabank....108 E3
Buckden Cambs....54 C2
  N Yorks....94 B2
Buckenham....69 D6
Buckerell....11 D6
Buckfast....6 C5
Buckfastleigh....6 C5
Buckhaven....129 E5
Buckholm....121 F7
Buckholt....36 C2
Buckhorn Weston....13 B5
Buckhurst Hill....41 E7
Buckie....152 B4
Buckies....158 D3
Buckingham....52 F4
Buckland Bucks....40 C1
  Devon....6 E4
  Glos....51 F5
  Hants....14 E4
  Herts....54 F4
  Kent....31 E7
  Oxon....38 E3
  Sur....28 D3
Buckland Brewer....9 B6
Buckland Common....40 D2
Buckland Dinham....24 D2
Buckland Filleigh....9 D6
Buckland in the Moor....6 B5
Buckland Monachorum....6 C2
Buckland Newton....12 D4
Buckland St Mary....11 C7
Bucklebury....26 B3
Bucklegate....79 F6
Bucklerheads....134 F4
Bucklers Hard....14 E5
Bucklesham....57 E6
Buckley = Bwcle....73 C6
Bucklow Hill....86 F5
Buckminster....65 B5
Bucknall Lincs....78 C4
  Stoke....75 E6
Bucknell Oxon....39 B5
  Shrops....49 B5
Buckpool....152 B4
Buck's Cross....8 B5
Bucks Green....27 F8
Buckshaw Village....86 B3
Bucks Horn Oak....27 E6
Buckskin....26 D4
Buck's Mills....8 B5
Buckton E Yorks....97 B7
  Hereford....49 B5
  Northumb....123 F6
Buckworth....54 B2
Budbrooke....51 C7
Budby....77 C6
Buddon....135 F5
Budd's Titson....8 D4
Bude....8 D4
Budlake....10 E4
Budle....123 F7
Budleigh Salterton....11 F5
Budock Water....3 C6
Buerton....74 E3
Buffler's Holt....52 F4
Bugbrooke....52 D4
Buglawton....75 C5
Bugle....4 D5
Bugley....24 E3
Bugthorpe....96 D3
Buildwas....61 D6
Builth Road....48 D2
Builth Wells = Llanfair-ym-Muallt....48 D2
Buirgh....154 H5

Bulby....65 B7
Bulcote....77 E6
Buldoo....157 C12
Bulford....25 E6
Bulford Camp....25 E6
Bulkeley....74 D2
Bulkington Warks....63 F7
  Wilts....24 D4
Bulkworthy....9 C5
Bullamoor....102 E1
Bullbridge....76 D3
Bullbrook....27 C6
Bulley....36 C4
Bullgill....107 F7
Bull Hill....14 E4
Bullington Hants....26 E2
  Lincs....78 B3
Bull's Green....41 C5
Bullwood....145 F10
Bulmer Essex....56 E2
  N Yorks....96 C2
Bulmer Tye....56 F2
Bulphan....42 F2
Bulverhythe....18 E4
Bulwark....153 D9
Bulwell....76 E5
Bulwick....65 E6
Bumble's Green....41 D7
Bun Eadarra....154 G6
Bunacaimb....147 C9
Bun a'Mhuillin....148 G2
Bunarkaig....136 F4
Bunbury....74 D2
Bunbury Heath....74 D2
Bunchrew....151 G9
Bundalloch....149 F13
Buness....160 C8
Bunessan....146 J6
Bungay....69 F6
Bunkers Hill....78 D5
Bunker's Hill Lincs....78 B2
  Lincs....79 D5
Bunloit....137 B8
Bun Loyne....136 D5
Bunnahabhain....142 A5
Bunny....64 B2
Buntait....150 H6
Buntingford....41 B6
Bunwell....68 E4
Burbage Derbys....75 B7
  Leics....63 E8
  Wilts....25 C7
Burchett's Green....39 F8
Burcombe....25 F5
Burcot....39 E5
Burcott....40 B1
Burdon....111 D6
Bures....56 F3
Bures Green....56 F3
Burford Ches E....74 D3
  Oxon....38 C2
  Shrops....49 C7
Burg....146 G6
Burgar....159 F4
Burgate Hants....14 C2
  Suff....56 B4
Burgess Hill....17 C7
Burgh....57 D6
Burgh by Sands....108 D3
Burgh Castle....69 D7
Burghclere....26 C2
Burghead....151 E14
Burghfield....26 C4
Burghfield Common....26 C4
Burghfield Hill....26 C4
Burgh Heath....28 D3
Burghill....49 E6
Burgh le Marsh....79 C8
Burgh Muir....141 B6
Burgh next Aylsham....81 E8
Burgh on Bain....91 F6
Burgh St Margaret....69 C7
Burgh St Peter....69 E7
Burghwallis....89 C6
Burham....29 C8
Buriton....15 B8
Burland....74 D3
Burlawn....4 B4
Burleigh....27 C6
Burlescombe....11 C5
Burleston....13 E5
Burley Hants....14 D3
  Rutland....65 C5
  W Yorks....95 F5
Burleydam....74 E3
Burley Gate....49 D7
Burley in Wharfedale....94 E4
Burley Lodge....14 D3
Burley Street....14 D3
Burlingjobb....48 D4
Burlow....18 D2
Burlton....60 B4
Burmarsh....19 B7
Burmington....51 F7
Burn....89 B6
Burnaston....76 F2
Burnbank....119 D7
Burnby....96 E4
Burncross....88 E4
Burneside....99 E7
Burness....159 D7
Burneston....101 F8
Burnett....23 C8
Burnfoot Borders....115 C7
  Borders....115 C8
  E Ayrs....113 C6
  Perth....127 D8
Burnham Bucks....40 F2
  N Lincs....90 C4
Burnham Deepdale....80 C4
Burnham Green....41 C5
Burnham Market....80 C4
Burnham Norton....80 C4
Burnham-on-Crouch....43 E5
Burnham-on-Sea....22 E5
Burnham Overy Staithe....80 C4
Burnham Overy Town....80 C4
Burnham Thorpe....80 C4
Burnhead Dumfries....113 E8
  S Ayrs....112 D2

Burnhervie 141 C6
Burnhill Green 61 D7
Burnhope 110 E4
Burnhouse 118 D3
Burniston 103 E8
Burnlee 88 D2
Burnley 93 F8
Burnley Lane 93 F8
Burnmouth 123 C5
Burn of Cambus . . 127 D6
Burnopfield 110 D4
Burnsall 94 C3
Burnside Angus 135 D5
  E Ayrs 113 C5
  Fife 128 D3
  Shetland 160 F4
  S Lanark 119 C6
  W Loth 120 B3
Burnside of
  Duntrune 134 F4
Burnswark 107 B8
Burntcommon . . . 27 D8
Burnt Heath 76 B2
Burnthouse 3 C6
Burnt Houses . . . 101 B6
Burntisland 128 F4
Burnton 112 D4
Burntwood 62 D4
Burnt Yates 95 C5
Burnwynd 120 C4
Burpham Sur 27 D8
  W Sus 16 D4
Burradon
  Northumb 117 D5
  T&W 111 B5
Burrafirth 160 B8
Burraland Shetland 160 F5
  Shetland 160 J4
Burras 3 D6
Burravoe Shetland 160 F7
  Shetland 160 G5
Burray Village . . . 159 J5
Burrells 100 C1
Burrelton 134 F2
Burridge Devon . . 20 F4
  Hants 15 C6
Burrill 101 F7
Burringham 90 D2
Burrington Devon . . 9 C8
  Hereford 49 B7
  N Som 23 D6
Burrough Green . . . 55 D7
Burrough on
  the Hill 64 C4
Burrow-bridge . . . 11 B8
Burrowhill 27 C7
Burry 33 E5
Burry Green 33 E5
Burry Port
  = Porth Tywyn . . 33 D5
Burscough 86 C2
Burscough Bridge 86 C2
Bursea 96 F4
Burshill 97 E6
Bursledon 15 D5
Burslem 75 E5
Burstall 56 E4
Burstock 12 D2
Burston Norf . . . 68 F4
  Staffs 75 F6
Burstow 28 E4
Burstwick 91 B6
Burtersett 100 F3
Burtle 23 E5
Burton BCP 14 E2
  Ches W 73 B7
  Ches W 74 C2
  Lincs 78 B2
  Northumb 123 F7
  Pembs 44 E4
  Som 22 E3
  Wilts 24 B3
Burton Agnes . . . 97 C7
Burton Bradstock . 12 F2
Burton Dassett . . 51 D8
Burton Fleming . . 97 B6
Burton Green
  W Mid 51 B7
  Wrex 73 D7
Burton Hastings . . 63 E8
Burton-in-Kendal 92 B5
Burton in Lonsdale 93 B6
Burton Joyce 77 E6
Burton Latimer . . 53 B6
Burton Lazars . . . 64 C4
Burton-le-Coggles 65 B6
Burton Leonard . . 95 C6
Burton on the
  Wolds 64 B2
Burton Overy . . . 64 E3
Burton
  Pedwardine . . . 78 E4
Burton Pidsea . . 97 F8
Burton Salmon . . 89 B5
Burton Stather . . 90 C2
Burton upon
  Stather 90 C2
Burton upon Trent 63 B6
Burtonwood 86 E3
Burwardsley 74 D2
Burwarton 61 F6
Burwash 18 C3
Burwash Common . 18 C3
Burwash Weald . . 18 C3
Burwell Cambs . . . 55 C6
  Lincs 79 B6
Burwen 82 B4
Burwick 159 K5
Bury Cambs 66 F2
  Gtr Man 87 C6
  Som 10 B4
  W Sus 16 C4
Bury Green 41 B7
Bury St Edmunds . 56 C2
Burythorpe 96 C3
Busby 119 D5
Buscot 38 E2
Bush Bank 49 D6
Bushbury 62 D3
Bushby 64 D3
Bush Crathie . . . 139 E8
Bushey 40 E4
Bushey Heath . . . 40 E4
Bush Green 93 F6
Bushley 50 F3
Bushton 90 F4
Busta 160 G5
Butcher's Cross . . 18 C2

Butcombe 23 C7
Butetown 22 B3
Butleigh 23 F7
Butleigh Wootton . 23 F7
Butler's Cross . . . 39 D8
Butler's End 63 F6
Butlers Marston . . 51 E8
Butley 57 D7
Butley High
  Corner 57 E7
Butterburn 109 B6
Buttercrambe . . . 96 D3
Butterknowle . . . 101 B6
Butterleigh 10 D4
Buttermere Cumb . 98 C3
  Wilts 25 C8
Buttershaw 88 B2
Butterstone 133 E7
Butterton 75 D7
Butterwick
  Durham 102 B1
  Lincs 79 E6
  N Yorks 96 B3
  N Yorks 97 B5
Butt Green 74 D3
Buttington 60 D2
Buttonoak 50 B2
Buttsash 14 D5
Butt's Green . . . 14 B4
Buxhall 56 D4
Buxhall Fen Street . 56 D4
Buxley 122 C4
Buxted 18 B8
Buxton Derbys . . 75 B7
  Norf 81 E8
Buxworth 87 F8
Bwcle = Buckley . 73 C7
Bwlch 35 B5
Bwlchgwyn 73 D6
Bwlch-Llan 46 D4
Bwlchnewydd . . . 32 B4
Bwlchtocyn 70 E4
Bwlch-y-cibau . . . 59 D8
Bwlchyddar 59 B8
Bwlch-y-fadfa . . 46 E3
Bwlch-y-ffridd . . 59 E7
Bwlchgwroes . . . 45 F4
Bwlch-y-sarnau . . 48 B2
Byermoor 110 D4
Byers Green 110 F5
Byfield 52 D3
Byfleet 27 C8
Byford 49 E5
Bygrave 54 F3
Byker 111 C5
Bylchau 72 C3
Byley 74 C4
Bynea 33 E6
Byrness 116 D3
Bythorn 53 B8
Byton 49 C5
Byworth 16 B3

C

Cabharstadh . . . 155 E8
Cablea 133 F6
Cabourne 90 D5
Cabrach Argyll . . 144 G3
  Moray 140 B2
Cabrich 151 G8
Cabus 92 E4
Cackle Street . . . 18 B8
Cadbury 10 D4
Cadbury Barton . . 9 C8
Cadder 119 B6
Caddington 40 C3
Caddonfoot . . . 121 F7
Cadeby Leics . . . 63 D8
  S Yorks 89 D6
Cadeleigh 10 D4
Cade Street 18 C3
Cadgwith 3 E6
Cadham 128 D4
Cadishead 86 E5
Cadle 33 E7
Cadley Lancs . . . 92 F5
  Wilts 25 C7
  Wilts 25 D7
Cadmore End . . . 39 E7
Cadnam 14 C3
Cadney 90 D4
Cadole 73 C6
Cadoxton 22 C3
Cadoxton-
  Juxta-Neath . . 34 E1
Cadshaw 86 C5
Cadzow 119 D7
Caeathro 82 E4
Caehopkin 34 C2
Caenby 90 F4
Caenby Corner . . 90 F3
Caerau Bridgend . . 34 E2
  Cardiff 22 B3
Caér-bryn 33 C6
Caerdeon 58 C3
Caerddydd = Cardiff . 22 B3
Caerfarchell . . . 44 C2
Caerffili
  = Caerphilly . . 35 F5
Caerfyrddin
  = Carmarthen . . 33 B5
Caergeiliog 82 D3
Caergwrle 73 D7
Caergybi
  = Holyhead . . . 82 C2
Caerleon
  = Caerllion . . 35 E7
Caer Llan 36 D1
Caerllion
  = Caerleon . . 35 E7
Caernarfon 82 E4
Caerphilly
  = Caerffili . . . 35 F5
Caersws 59 E7
Caerwedros . . . 46 D2
Caerwent 36 E1
Caerwych 71 D7
Caerwys 72 B5
Caethle 58 E3
Caim 83 C6
Caio 47 F5
Cairisiadar 154 D5
Cairminis 154 J5
Cairnbaan 145 D7
Cairnbanno
  House 153 D8

Cairnborrow . . . 152 D4
Cairnbrogie . . . 141 B7
Cairnbulg Castle 153 B10
Cairncross Angus . . 134 B4
  Borders 122 C4
Cairndow 125 D7
Cairneyhill 128 F2
Cairnfield House . 152 B4
Cairngaan 104 F5
Cairngarroch . . 104 E4
Cairnhill 153 E6
Cairnie Aberds . . 141 D7
  Aberds 152 D4
Cairnorrie 153 D8
Cairnpark 141 C7
Cairnryan 104 C4
Cairnton 159 H4
Caister 90 D5
Caistor 117 D5
Caistron 117 D5
Caitha Bowland . 121 E7
Calais Street 56 F3
Calanais 154 D7
Calbourne 14 F5
Calceby 79 B6
Calcot Row 26 B4
Calcott 31 C5
Caldback 160 C8
Caldbeck 108 F3
Caldbergh 101 F5
Caldecote Cambs . 54 D4
  Cambs 65 F8
  Herts 54 F3
  N Nhants 53 C7
  Oxon 38 E4
  Rutland 65 E5
Caldecott N Nhants . 53 C7
  Oxon 38 E4
  Rutland 65 E5
Calderbank 119 C7
Calder Bridge . . . 98 D2
Calderbrook . . . 87 C7
Caldercruix 119 C8
Calder Hall 98 D2
Calder Mains . . 158 E2
Caldermill 119 E6
Calder Vale 92 E5
Calderwood . . . 119 D6
Caldhame 134 E4
Caldicot 36 F1
Caldwell Derbys . 63 C6
  N Yorks 101 C6
Caldy 85 F3
Caledrhydiau . . 46 D3
Calfsound 159 E6
Calgary 146 F6
Califer 151 F13
California Falk . . 120 B2
  Norf 69 C8
Calke 63 B7
Callakille 149 C11
Callaly 117 D6
Callander 126 D5
Callaughton . . . 61 E6
Callestick 4 D2
Calligarry 149 H11
Callington 5 C8
Callow 49 F6
Callow End 50 E3
Callow Hill Wilts . 37 F7
  Worcs 50 B2
Callows Grave . . 49 C7
Calmore 14 C4
Calmsden 37 D7
Calne 24 B5
Calow 76 B4
Calshot 15 D5
Calstock 6 C2
Calstone
  Wellington . . . 24 C5
Calthorpe 81 D7
Calthwaite 108 E4
Calton N Yorks . . 94 D2
  Staffs 75 D8
Calveley 74 D2
Calver 76 B2
Calverhall 74 F3
Calver Hill 49 E5
Calverleigh 10 C4
Calverley 94 F5
Calvert 39 B6
Calverton M Keynes . 53 F5
  Notts 77 E6
Calvine 133 C5
Calvo 107 D8
Cam 36 E4
Camas-luinie . . 136 B2
Camasnacroise . . 130 D2
Camastianavaig . 149 E10
Camault Muir . . 151 G8
Camb 160 D7
Camber 19 D6
Camberley 27 C6
Camberwell . . . 28 B4
Camblesforth . . 89 B7
Cambo 117 F6
Cambois 117 F9
Camborne 3 B5
Cambourne 54 D4
Cambridge Cambs . 55 D5
  Glos 36 D4
Cambridge Town . . 43 F5
Cambus 127 E7
Cambusavie
  Farm 151 B10
Cambusbarron . 127 E6
Cambuskenneth . 127 E7
Cambuslang . . . 119 C6
Cambusmore
  Lodge 151 B10
Camden 41 F5
Camelford 8 F3
Camelsdale 27 F6
Camerory 151 H13
Camer's Green . . 50 F2
Camerton Bath . . 23 D8
  Cumb 107 F7
  E Yorks 91 B6
Camghouran . . 132 D2
Cammachmore . 141 E8
Cammeringham . . 90 F3
Camore 151 B10
Campbeltown . . 143 F8
Camperdown . . 111 B5
Camp Hill 63 E7
Campmuir 134 F2
Campsall 89 C6

Campsey Ash . . . 57 D7
Campton 54 F2
Camptown 116 C2
Camrose 44 C4
Camserney 133 E5
Camster 158 F4
Camuschoirk . . 130 C1
Camuscross . . . 149 G11
Camusnagaul
  Highld 130 B4
  Highld 150 C3
Camusrory . . . 147 B11
Camusteel 149 D12
Camusterrach . 149 D12
Camusvrachan . 132 E3
Canada 14 C3
Canadia 18 D4
Canal Side 89 C7
Candacraig
  House 140 C2
Candlesby 79 C7
Candy Mill 120 E3
Cane End 26 B4
Canewdon 42 E4
Canford Bottom . 13 D8
Canford Cliffs . . 13 F8
Canford Magna . 13 E8
Canham's Green . 56 C4
Canholes 75 B7
Canisbay 158 C5
Cann 13 B6
Cannard's Grave . 23 E8
Cann Common . 13 B6
Cannich 150 H6
Cannington 22 F4
Cannock 62 D3
Cannock Wood . 62 C4
Canonbie 108 B3
Canon Bridge . . 49 E6
Canon Frome . . 49 E8
Canon Pyon . . . 49 E6
Canons Ashby . . 52 D3
Canonstown 2 C4
Canterbury 30 D5
Cantley Norf . . . 69 D6
  S Yorks 89 D7
Cantlop 60 D5
Canton 22 B3
Cantraybruich . 151 G10
Cantraydoune . 151 G10
Cantraywood . 151 G10
Cantsfield 93 B6
Canvey Island . . 42 F3
Canwick 78 C2
Canworthy Water . 8 E4
Caol 131 B5
Caolas 146 G3
Caolas Scalpaigh . 154 H7
Caolas Stocinis . 154 H6
Caol Ila 142 A5
Capel 28 E2
Capel Bangor . . 58 F3
Capel Betws
  Lleucu 46 D5
Capel Carmel . . 70 E2
Capel Coch 82 C4
Capel Curig 83 F7
Capel Cynon . . . 46 E2
Capel Dewi Carms . 33 B5
  Ceredig 46 E3
  Ceredig 58 F3
Capel Garmon . . 83 F8
Capel-gwyn . . . 82 D3
Capel Gwyn . . . 33 B5
Capel Gwynfe . . 33 B8
Capel Hendre . . 33 C6
Capel Hermon . . 71 E8
Capel Isaac 33 B6
Capel Iwan 45 F4
Capel le Ferne . . 31 F6
Capel Llanilltern . 34 F4
Capel Mawr . . . 82 D4
Capel St Andrew . 57 E7
Capel St Mary . . 56 F4
Capel Seion . . . 46 B5
Capel Tygwydd . 45 E4
Capel Uchaf . . . 70 C5
Capelulo 83 D7
Capel-y-graig . . 82 E5
Capenhurst 73 B7
Capernwray . . . 92 B5
Capheaton . . . 117 F6
Capplegill 114 D4
Capton 7 D6
Caputh 133 F7
Carbis Bay 2 C4
Carbost Highld . . 149 D9
  Highld 149 E8
Carbrook 88 F4
Carbrooke 68 D2
Carburton 77 B6
Carcant 121 D6
Carcary 135 D6
Carclaze 4 D5
Car Colston 77 E7
Carcroft 89 C6
Cardenden 128 E4
Cardeston 60 C3
Cardiff = Caerdydd . 22 B3
Cardigan = Aberteifi 45 E3
Cardington Bedford 53 E8
  Shrops 60 E5
Cardinham 5 C6
Cardonald 118 C5
Cardow 152 D1
Cardrona 121 F6
Cardross 118 B3
Cardurnock . . . 107 D8
Careby 65 C7
Careston Castle . 135 D5
Carew 32 D1
Carew Cheriton . 32 D1
Carew Newton . 32 D1
Carey 49 F7
Carfrae 121 C8
Cargenbridge . 107 B6
Cargill 134 F1
Cargo 108 D3
Cargreen 6 C2
Carham 122 F4
Carhampton . . . 22 E2
Carharrack 3 B6
Carie Perth . . . 132 D3
  Perth 132 F3
Carines 4 D2
Carisbrooke . . . 15 F5
Cark 92 B3
Carlabhagh . . . 154 C7

Carland Cross . . . 4 D3
Carlby 65 C7
Carlecotes 88 D2
Carlesmoor 94 B4
Carleton Cumb . . 99 B7
  Cumb 108 D4
  Lancs 92 F3
  N Yorks 94 D2
Carleton Forehoe . 68 D3
Carleton Rode . . 68 E4
Carlingcott 23 D8
Carlin How 103 C5
Carlisle 108 D4
Carlops 120 D4
Carlton Bedford . 53 D7
  Cambs 55 D7
  Leics 63 D7
  Notts 77 E6
  N Yorks 89 B7
  N Yorks 101 C6
  N Yorks 101 F5
  N Yorks 102 F4
  Stockton 102 B2
  Suff 57 C7
  S Yorks 88 C4
  W Yorks 88 B4
Carlton Colville . 69 E8
Carlton Curlieu . 64 E3
Carlton
  Husthwaite . . 95 B7
Carlton in
  Cleveland . . . 102 D3
Carlton in Lindrick 89 F6
Carlton le
  Moorland . . . 78 D2
Carlton Miniott . 102 F1
Carlton on Trent . 77 C7
Carlton Scroop . 78 E2
Carluke 119 D8
Carmarthen
  = Caerfyrddin . 33 B5
Carmel Anglesey . 82 C3
  Carms 33 C6
  Flint 73 B5
  Guern 16
  Gwyn 82 F4
Carmont 141 F7
Carmunnock . . 119 D6
Carmyle 119 C6
Carmyllie 135 E5
Carnaby 97 C7
Carnach Highld . 136 B3
  Highld 150 B3
  W Isles 154 H7
Carnachy 157 D10
Càrnais 154 D5
Carnbee 129 D7
Carnbo 128 D2
Carnbrea 3 B5
Carnduff 119 E6
Carnduncan . . 142 B3
Carne 3 C8
Carnforth 92 B4
Carn-gorm . . . 136 B2
Carnhedryn . . . 44 C3
Carnhell Green . . 2 C5
Carnkie Corn . . . 3 C5
  Corn 3 C6
Carno 59 E6
Carnoch Highld . 150 F5
  Highld 150 H6
Carnock 128 F2
Carnon Downs . . 3 B6
Carnousie 153 C6
Carnoustie . . . 135 F5
Carnwath 120 E2
Carperby 101 F5
Carpley Green . 100 F4
Carr 89 E6
Carradale 143 E9
Carragraich . . . 154 H6
Carrbridge . . . 138 B5
Carrefour
  Selous Jersey . . 17
Carreglefn 82 C3
Carreg-wen . . . 45 E4
Carr Hill 111 C5
Carrick Argyll . . 145 E8
  Fife 129 B6
Carrick Castle . 145 D10
Carrick House . 159 E6
Carriden 128 F2
Carrington Gtr Man . 86 E5
  Lincs 79 D6
  Midloth 121 C6
Carrog Conwy . . 71 C8
  Denb 72 E5
Carron Falk . . . 127 F7
  Moray 152 D2
Carronbridge . 113 E8
Carron Bridge . 127 F6
Carronshore . . 127 F7
Carrshield . . . 109 E8
Carrutherstown . 107 B8
Carrville 111 E6
Carsaig Argyll . . 144 E6
  Argyll 147 A8
Carscreugh . . . 105 D6
Carsegowan . . 105 D8
Carse Gray . . . 134 D4
Carse House . . 144 G6
Carseriggan . . 105 C7
Carsethorn . . . 107 D6
Carshalton 28 C3
Carsington 76 D2
Carskiey 143 H7
Carsluith 105 D8
Carsphairn . . . 113 E5
Carstairs 120 E2
Carstairs
  Junction . . . 120 E2
Carswell Marsh . 38 E3
Carter's Clay . . 14 B4
Carterton 38 D2
Carterway Heads . 110 D3
Carthew 4 D5
Carthorpe 101 F8
Cartington . . . 117 D6
Cartland 119 E8
Cartmel 92 B3
Cartmel Fell . . . 99 F6
Carway 33 D5
Cary Fitzpaine . 12 B3
Cascob 48 C4

Casnewydd
  = Newport . . . 35 F7
Cassey Compton . 37 C7
Cassington 38 C4
Cassop 111 F6
Castell 72 C5
Castellau 34 F4
Castell-Howell . 46 E3
Castell-Nedd
  = Neath 33 E8
Castell Newydd Emlyn
  = Newcastle Emlyn 46 E2
Castell-y-bwch . 35 E6
Casterton 93 B6
Castle Acre 67 C8
Castle Ashby . . 53 D6
Castlebay
  = Bagh a Chaisteil 148 J1
Castle Bolton . . 101 E5
Castle Bromwich . 62 F5
Castle Bytham . . 65 C6
Castlebythe . . . 32 B1
Castle Caereinion . 59 D8
Castle Camps . . 55 E7
Castle Carrock . 108 D5
Castlecary 119 B7
Castle Cary . . . 23 F8
Castle Combe . . 24 B3
Castle Donington . 63 B8
Castle Douglas . 106 C4
Castle Eaton . . . 37 E8
Castle Eden . . . 111 F7
Castlefairn . . . 113 F7
Castle Forbes . . 140 C5
Castleford 88 B5
Castle Frome . . 49 E8
Castle Green . . . 27 C7
Castle Gresley . . 63 C6
Castle Heaton . 122 E5
Castle
  Hedingham . . 55 F8
Castlehill Borders . 120 F5
  Highld 158 D3
  W Dunb 118 B3
Castle Hill 29 E7
Castle Huntly . . 128 B5
Castle Kennedy . 104 D5
Castlemaddy . . 113 F5
Castlemartin . . . 44 F4
Castlemilk
  Dumfries . . . 107 B8
  Glasgow . . . 119 D6
Castlemorris . . 44 B4
Castlemorton . . 50 F2
Castle O'er . . . 115 E5
Castle
  Pulverbatch . . 60 D4
Castle Rising . . 67 B6
Castleside 110 E3
Castle Stuart . 151 G10
Castlethorpe . . 53 E6
Castleton Angus . 134 E3
  Argyll 145 E7
  Derbys 88 F2
  Gtr Man 87 C6
  Newport 35 F6
  N Yorks 102 D4
Castletown
  Ches W 73 D8
  Highld 151 G10
  Highld 158 D3
  IoM 84 F2
  T&W 111 D6
Castleweary . . 115 D7
Castley 95 E5
Caston 68 E2
Castor 65 E8
Catacol 143 D10
Catbrain 36 F2
Catbrook 36 D2
Catchall 2 D3
Catchems Corner . 51 B7
Catchgate 110 D4
Catcleugh 116 D3
Catcliffe 88 F5
Catcott 23 F5
Caterham 28 D4
Catfield 69 B6
Catfirth 160 H6
Catford 28 B4
Catforth 92 F4
Cathays 22 B3
Cathcart 119 C5
Cathedine 35 B5
Catherington . . 15 C7
Catherton 49 B8
Catlodge 138 E2
Catlowdy 108 B4
Catmore 38 F4
Caton 92 C5
Caton Green . . 92 C5
Catrine 113 B5
Cat's Ash 35 E7
Catsfield 18 D4
Catshill 50 B4
Cattal 95 D7
Cattawade . . . 56 F5
Catterall 92 E4
Catterick 101 E7
Catterick Bridge . 101 E7
Catterick
  Garrison . . . 101 E6
Catterlen 108 F4
Catterline . . . 135 B8
Catterton 95 E8
Catthorpe 52 B3
Cattistock 12 E3
Catton Northumb . 109 D8
  N Yorks 95 B6
Catwick 97 E7
Catworth 53 B8
Caudlesprings . 68 D2
Caulcott 39 B5
Cauldcots . . . 135 E6
Cauldhame . . 126 E5
Cauldmill . . . 115 C8
Cauldon 75 E7
Caulkerbush . 107 D6
Caulside 115 F7
Caunsall 62 F2
Caunton 77 D7
Causeway-
  head Cumb . . 107 D8
Causewayend . 120 F3
Causeway Foot . 94 F3
Causeway-
  head Perth . . 133 F7
Causewayhead
  Cumb 107 D8
  Stirling 127 E6
Causeyend . . . 141 C8

Causey Park
  Bridge 117 E7
Cautley 100 E1
Cavendish 56 E2
Cavendish Bridge . 63 B8
Cavenham 55 C8
Caversfield . . . 39 B5
Caversham . . . 26 B5
Caverswall . . . 75 E6
Cavil 96 F3
Cawdor 151 F11
Cawkwell 79 B5
Cawood 95 F8
Cawsand 6 D2
Cawston 81 E7
Cawthorne . . . 88 D3
Cawthorpe . . . 65 B7
Cawton 96 B2
Caxton 54 D4
Caynham 49 B7
Caythorpe Lincs . 78 E2
  Notts 77 E6
Cayton 103 F8
Ceann a Bhaigh . 148 B2
Ceann a Deas Loch
  Baghasdail . . 148 G2
Ceann Shiphoirt . 155 F7
Ceann
  Tarabhaigh . . 154 F7
Cearsiadair . . . 155 E8
Ceathramh
  Meadhanach . 148 A3
Cefn Berain . . . 72 C3
Cefn-brith 72 D3
Cefn Canol . . . 73 F6
Cefn-coch 83 E8
Cefn Coch 59 B8
Cefn-coed-y-
  cymmer 34 C4
Cefn Cribwr . . . 34 F2
Cefn Cross . . . 34 F2
Cefn-ddwysarn . 72 F3
Cefn Einion . . . 60 F2
Cefn-gorwydd . 47 E8
Cefn-mawr . . . 73 E6
Cefn-y-bedd . . 73 D7
Cefn-y-pant . . . 32 B2
Cei-bach 46 D3
Ceinewydd
  = New Quay . . 46 D2
Ceint 82 D4
Cellan 46 E5
Cellarhead . . . 75 E6
Cemaes 82 B3
Cemmaes 58 D5
Cemmaes Road . 58 D5
Cenarth 45 E4
Cenin 71 C5
Central 118 B2
Ceos 155 E8
Ceres 129 C6
Cerne Abbas . . 12 D4
Cerney Wick . . 37 E7
Cerrigceinwen . 82 D4
Cerrigydrudion . 72 E3
Cessford 116 B3
Ceunant 82 E5
Chaceley 50 F3
Chacewater 3 B6
Chackmore . . . 52 F4
Chacombe . . . 52 E2
Chadderton . . . 87 D7
Chadderton Fold . 87 D6
Chaddesden . . 76 F3
Chaddesley
  Corbett 50 B3
Chaddington . . 83 B3
Chaddleworth . 38 F4
Chadshunt . . . 51 D8
Chad Valley . . . 62 F4
Chadwell 64 B4
Chadwell St Mary . 29 B7
Chadwick End . . 51 B7
Chadwick Green . 86 E3
Chaffcombe . . . 11 C8
Chagford 10 F2
Chailey 17 C7
Chainbridge . . 66 D4
Chain Bridge . . 79 E6
Chainhurst . . . 29 E8
Chalbury 13 D8
Chalbury
  Common . . . 13 D8
Chaldon 28 D4
Chaldon Herring . 13 F5
Chale 15 G5
Chale Green . . 15 G5
Chalfont Common . 40 E3
Chalfont St Giles . 40 E2
Chalfont St Peter . 40 E3
Chalford 37 D5
Chalgrove 39 E6
Chalk 29 B7
Challacombe . . 21 E5
Challoch 105 C7
Challock 30 D4
Chalton C Beds . 40 B3
  Hants 15 C8
Chalvington . . 18 E2
Chancery 46 B4
Chandler's Ford . 14 B5
Channel Tunnel . 19 B8
Channerwick . 160 L6
Chantry Som . . 24 E2
  Suff 56 E5
Chapel 128 E4
Chapel Allerton
  Som 23 D6
  W Yorks 95 F6
Chapel Amble . . 5 B5
Chapel Brampton . 52 C5
Chapel Chorlton . 74 F5
Chapel End . . . 63 E7
Chapel-en-
  le-Frith 87 F8
Chapelgate . . . 66 B4
Chapel Green
  Warks 52 C2
  Warks 63 F6
Chapel Haddlesey . 89 B6
Chapelhall . . . 119 C7
Chapel Head . . 66 F3
Chapelhill
  Dumfries . . . 114 E3
  Highld 151 D11
  N Ayrs 118 E2
  Perth 128 B4
  Perth 133 F7

Chapel Hill
  Aberds 153 E10
  Lincs 78 D5
  Mon 36 E2
  N Yorks 95 E6
Chapelknowe . 108 B3
Chapel Lawn . . 48 B5
Chapel-le-Dale . 93 B7
Chapel Milton . 87 F8
Chapel of
  Garioch 141 B6
Chapel Row . . . 26 C3
Chapel
  St Leonards . . 79 B8
Chapel Stile . . . 99 D5
Chapelton Angus . 135 E6
  Devon 9 B7
  Highld 138 C5
  S Lanark 119 E6
Chapeltown
  Blackburn . . . 86 C5
  Moray 139 B8
  S Yorks 88 E4
Chapmanslade . 24 E3
Chapmans Well . 9 E5
Chapmore End . 41 C6
Chappel 42 B4
Chard 11 D8
Chardstock . . . 11 D8
Charfield 36 E4
Charford 50 C4
Charing 30 E3
Charing Cross . 14 C2
Charing Heath . 30 E3
Charingworth . 51 F7
Charlbury 38 C3
Charlcombe . . . 24 C2
Charlcote 51 D7
Charles 21 F5
Charlesfield . . 107 C8
Charleston Angus . 134 E3
  Renfs 118 C4
Charlestown
  Aberden 141 D8
  Corn 4 D5
  Derbys 87 E8
  Dorset 12 G4
  Fife 128 F2
  Gtr Man 87 D6
  Highld 149 A13
  Highld 151 G9
  W Yorks 87 B7
Charlestown of
  Aberlour . . . 152 D2
Charles Tye . . . 56 D4
Charlesworth . . 87 E8
Charleton 7 E5
Charlton Hants . 25 E8
  Herts 40 B4
  London 28 B5
  Northumb . . . 116 F4
  Som 23 D8
  Telford 61 C5
  Wilts 13 B7
  Wilts 25 D6
  Wilts 37 F6
  W Nhants 52 F3
  Worcs 50 E5
  W Sus 16 C3
Charlton Abbots . 37 B7
Charlton Adam . 12 B3
Charlton-
  All-Saints . . . 14 B2
Charlton Down . 12 E4
Charlton
  Horethorne . . 12 B4
Charlton Kings . 37 B6
Charlton
  Mackerell . . . 12 B3
Charlton Marshall . 13 D6
Charlton
  Musgrove . . . 12 B5
Charlton on
  Otmoor 39 C5
Charltons 102 C4
Charlwood . . . 28 E3
Charlynch 22 F4
Charminster . . 12 E4
Charmouth . . . 11 E8
Charndon 39 B6
Charney Bassett . 38 E3
Charnock Richard . 86 C3
Charsfield 57 D6
Chart Corner . . 29 D8
Charter Alley . . 26 D3
Charterhouse . . 23 D6
Charterville
  Allotments . . 38 C3
Chartham 30 D5
Chartham Hatch . 30 D5
Chartridge . . . 40 D2
Chart Sutton . . 30 E2
Charvil 27 B5
Charwelton . . . 52 D3
Chasetown . . . 62 D4
Chastleton . . . 38 B2
Chasty 8 D5
Chatburn 93 E7
Chatcull 74 F4
Chatham 29 C8
Chathill 117 B7
Chattenden . . . 29 B8
Chatteris 66 F3
Chattisham . . . 56 E4
Chatto 116 C3
Chatton 117 B6
Chawleigh 9 C8
Chawley 38 D4
Chawston 54 D2
Chawton 26 F5
Cheadle Gtr Man . 87 F6
  Staffs 75 E7
Cheadle Heath . 87 F6
Cheadle Hulme . 87 F6
Cheam 28 C3
Cheapside 27 C8
Chearsley 39 C7
Chebsey 62 B2
Checkendon . . 39 F6
Checkley Ches E . 74 E4
  Hereford 49 F7
  Staffs 75 F7
Chedburgh . . . 55 D8
Cheddar 23 D6
Cheddington . . 40 C2
Cheddleton . . . 75 D6
Cheddon Fitzpaine 11 B7
Chedglow 37 E6
Chedgrave . . . 69 E6

Chedington 12 D2
Chediston 57 B7
Chedworth . . . 37 C7
Chedzoy 22 F5
Cheeklaw . . . 122 D3
Cheeseman's
  Green 19 B7
Cheglinch 20 E4
Cheldon 10 C2
Chelford 74 B5
Chellaston 76 F3
Chell Heath . . . 75 D5
Chellington . . . 53 D7
Chelmarsh 61 F7
Chelmer Village . 42 D3
Chelmondiston . 57 F6
Chelmorton . . . 75 C8
Chelmsford . . . 42 D3
Chelsea 28 B3
Chelsfield 29 C5
Chelsworth . . . 56 E3
Cheltenham . . . 37 B6
Chelveston . . . 53 C7
Chelvey 23 C6
Chelwood 23 C8
Chelwood
  Common . . . 17 B8
Chelwood Gate . 17 B8
Chelworth 37 E6
Chelworth Green . 37 E7
Chemistry 74 E2
Chenies 40 E3
Cheny Longville . 60 F4
Chepstow
  = Cas-gwent . . 36 E2
Chequerfield . . 89 B5
Cherhill 24 B5
Cherington Glos . 37 E6
  Warks 51 F7
Cheriton Devon . 21 E6
  Hants 15 B6
  Kent 19 B8
  Swansea 33 E5
Cheriton Bishop . 10 E2
Cheriton Fitzpaine 10 D3
Cheriton or
  Stackpole Elidor . 44 F4
Cherrington . . . 61 B6
Cherrybank . . 128 B3
Cherry Burton . 97 E5
Cherry Hinton . 55 D5
Cherry Orchard . 50 D3
Cherry Willingham 78 B3
Chertsey 27 C8
Cheselbourne . 13 E5
Chesham 40 D2
Chesham Bois . . 40 E2
Cheshunt 41 D6
Cheslyn Hay . . 62 D3
Chessington . . 28 C2
Chester 73 C8
Chesterblade . . 23 E8
Chesterfield . . 76 B3
Chester-
  le-Street . . . 111 D5
Chester Moor . 111 E5
Chesters Borders . 116 B2
  Borders 116 C2
Chesterton Cambs . 55 C5
  Cambs 65 E8
  Glos 37 D7
  Oxon 39 B5
  Shrops 61 E7
  Staffs 74 E5
  Warks 51 D8
Chesterwood . 109 C8
Chestfield 30 C5
Cheston 6 D4
Cheswardine . . 61 B7
Cheswick 123 E6
Chetnole 12 D4
Chettiscombe . 10 C4
Chettisham . . . 66 F5
Chettle 13 C7
Chetton 61 E6
Chetwode 39 B6
Chetwynd Aston . 61 C7
Cheveley 55 C7
Chevening . . . 29 D5
Chevington . . . 55 D8
Chevithorne . . 10 C4
Chew Magna . . 23 C7
Chew Stoke . . . 23 C7
Chewton
  Keynsham . . . 23 C8
Chewton Mendip . 23 D7
Chicheley 53 E7
Chichester . . . 16 D2
Chickerell 12 F4
Chicklade 24 F4
Chicksgrove . . 24 F4
Chidden 15 C7
Chiddingfold . . 27 F7
Chiddingly . . . 18 D2
Chiddingstone . 29 E5
Chiddingstone
  Causeway . . . 29 E6
Chiddingstone
  Hoath 29 E5
Chideock 12 E2
Chidham 15 D8
Chidswell 88 B3
Chieveley 26 B2
Chignall St James . 42 D2
Chignall Smealy . 42 C2
Chigwell 41 E7
Chigwell Row . . 41 E7
Chilbolton 25 F8
Chilcomb 15 B6
Chilcombe . . . 12 E3
Chilcompton . . 23 D8
Chilcote 63 C6
Childer Thornton . 73 B7
Child Okeford . 13 C6
Childrey 38 F3
Child's Ercall . . 61 B6
Childswickham . 51 F5
Childwall 86 F2
Childwick Green . 40 C4
Chilfrome 12 E3
Chilgrove 16 C2
Chilham 30 D4
Chilhampton . . 25 F5
Chilla 9 D6
Chillaton 9 F6
Chillenden . . . 31 D6

Chillerton 15 F5
Chillesford 57 D7
Chillingham 117 B6
Chillington Devon 7 E5
Som 11 C8
Chilmark 24 F4
Chilson 38 C3
Chilsworthy Corn. 6 B2
Devon 8 D5
Chilthorne Domer . 12 C3
Chiltington 17 C7
Chilton Bucks 39 C6
Durham 101 B7
Oxon 38 F4
Chilton Cantelo . . 12 B3
Chilton Foliat 25 B8
Chilton Lane 111 F6
Chilton Polden . . . 23 F5
Chilton Street 55 E8
Chilton Trinity . . . 22 F4
Chilvers Coton . . . 63 E7
Chilwell 76 F5
Chilworth Hants. . . 14 C5
Sur. 27 E8
Chimney 38 D3
Chineham 26 D4
Chingford 41 E6
Chinley 87 F8
Chinley Head 87 F8
Chinnor 39 D7
Chipnall 74 F4
Chippenhall Green 57 B6
Chippenham Cambs 55 C7
Wilts 24 B4
Chipperfield 40 D3
Chipping Herts. . . . 54 F4
Lancs 93 E6
Chipping Campden 51 F6
Chipping Hill 42 C4
Chipping Norton . 38 B3
Chipping Ongar . . 42 D1
Chipping Sodbury . 36 F4
Chipping Warden . 52 E2
Chipstable 10 B5
Chipstead Kent. . . . 29 D5
Sur. 28 D3
Chirbury 60 E2
Chirk = Y Waun 73 F6
Chirk Bank 73 F6
Chirmorrie 105 B6
Chirnside 122 D4
Chirnsidebridge . . 122 D4
Chirton 25 D5
Chisbury 25 C7
Chiselborough . . . 12 C2
Chiseldon 25 B6
Chiserley 87 B8
Chislehampton . . . 39 E5
Chislehurst 28 B5
Chislet 31 C6
Chiswell Green . . . 40 D4
Chiswick 28 B3
Chiswick End 54 E4
Chisworth 87 E7
Chithurst 16 B2
Chittering 55 B5
Chitterne 24 E4
Chittlehamholt 9 B8
Chittlehampton . . .9 B8
Chittoe 24 C4
Chivenor 20 F4
Chobham 27 C7
Choicelee 122 D3
Cholderton 25 E7
Cholesbury 40 D2
Chollerford 110 B2
Chollerton 110 B2
Cholmondeston . . 74 C3
Cholsey 39 F5
Cholstrey 49 D6
Chop Gate 102 E3
Choppington 117 F8
Chopwell 110 D4
Chorley Ches E . . . 74 D2
Lancs 86 C3
Shrops. 61 F6
Staffs. 62 C4
Chorleywood 40 E3
Chorlton cum
Hardy 87 E6
Chorlton Lane 73 E8
Choulton 60 F3
Chowdene 111 D5
Chowley 73 D8
Chrishall 54 F5
Christchurch BCP . 14 E2
Cambs 66 E4
Glos 36 C2
Newport 35 F7
Christian Malford . 24 B4
Christleton 73 C8
Christmas
Common 39 E7
Christon 23 D5
Christon Bank . . . 117 B8
Christow 10 F3
Chryston 119 B6
Chudleigh 7 B6
Chudleigh Knighton 7 B6
Chulmleigh 9 C8
Chunal 87 E8
Church 86 B5
Churcham 36 C4
Church Aston 61 C7
Churchbank 48 B4
Church Brampton 52 C5
Churchbridge 62 D3
Church Broughton 76 F2
Church Crookham . 27 D6
Churchdown 37 C5
Church Eaton 62 C2
Churchend Essex . . 42 E5
Essex. 43 E6
S Glos. 36 E2
Church End Cambs .66 D3
Cambs. 66 F2
C Beds. 40 B2
C Beds. 53 F7
C Beds. 54 F2
Essex. 42 B3
Essex. 55 E6
E Yorks. 97 D6
Hants. 26 D4
Lincs 78 F5
Warks 63 E6
Warks 63 E6

Church End continued
Wilts 24 B5
Church Enstone . . 38 B3
Church Fenton . . . 95 F8
Churchfield 62 E4
Churchgate Street. 41 C7
Church Green
Devon 11 E6
Norf 68 E3
Church Gresley . . 63 C6
Church
Hanborough 38 C4
Church Hill 74 C3
Church Houses . . . 102 E4
Churchill Devon . . 11 D8
Devon 20 E4
N Som 23 D6
Oxon 38 B2
Worcs 50 B3
Worcs 50 D4
Churchinford 11 C7
Church Knowle . . 13 F7
Church Laneham . 77 B8
Church Langton . . 64 E4
Church Lawford . . 52 B2
Church Lawton . . 74 D5
Church Leigh 75 F7
Church Lench 50 D5
Church Mayfield . 75 E8
Church Minshull . 74 C3
Church Norton . . . 16 E2
Churchover 64 F2
Church Preen 60 E5
Church
Pulverbatch . . . 60 D4
Churchstanton . . . 11 C6
Church Stoke 60 E2
Churchstow 6 E5
Church Stowe 52 D4
Church Street 29 B8
Church Stretton . . 60 E4
Churchtown Derbys 76 C2
IoM 84 C4
Lancs 92 E4
Mers 85 C4
Church Town
N Lincs 89 D8
Sur. 28 D4
Church Village . . . 34 F4
Church Warsop . . 77 C5
Churnsike Lodge . 109 B6
Churston Ferrers . .7 D7
Churt 27 F6
Churton 73 D8
Churwell 88 B3
Chute Standen . . . 25 D8
Chwilog 70 D5
Chyandour 2 C3
Cilan Uchaf 70 E3
Cilcain 73 C5
Cilcennin 46 C4
Cilfor 71 D7
Cilfrew 34 D1
Cilfynydd 34 E4
Cilgerran 45 E3
Cilgwyn Carms . . . 33 B8
Gwyn 82 F4
Pembs 45 F2
Ciliau Aeron 46 D3
Cill Donnain 148 F2
Cille Bhrighde . . . 148 G2
Cille Pheadair . . . 148 G2
Cilmery 48 D2
Cilsan 33 B6
Ciltalgarth 72 E2
Cilwendeg 45 F4
Cilybebyll 33 D8
Cilycwm 47 F6
Cimla 34 E1
Cinderford 36 C3
Cippyn 45 E3
Circebost 154 D6
Cirencester 37 D7
Ciribhig 154 C6
City London 41 F6
City Dulas 82 C4
Clachaig 145 E10
Clachan Argyll. . . 124 D3
Argyll. 125 D7
Argyll. 130 E2
Argyll. 144 H6
Highld 149 E10
W Isles 148 D2
Clachaneasy 105 B7
Clachanmore 104 E4
Clachan na Luib . 148 B3
Clachan of
Campsie 119 B6
Clachan of
Glendaruel 145 E8
Clachan-Seil 124 D3
Clachan Strachur 125 E6
Clachbreck 144 F6
Clachnabrain . . . 134 C3
Clachtoll 156 G3
Clackmannan . . . 127 E8
Clacton-on-Sea . . 43 C7
Cladach
Chireboist 148 B2
Claddach-
knockline 148 B2
Cladich 125 C6
Claggan Highld . . 131 B5
Highld 147 G9
Claigan 148 C7
Claines 50 D3
Clandown 23 D8
Clanfield Hants. . . 15 C7
Oxon 38 D2
Clanville 25 E8
Claonaig 145 H7
Claonel 157 J8
Clapgate Dorset . . 13 D8
Herts. 41 B7
Clapham Bedford . 53 D8
London 28 B3
N Yorks. 93 C7
W Sus 16 D4
Clap Hill 19 B7
Clappers 122 D5
Clappersgate 99 D5
Clapton 12 D2
Clapton-in-
Gordano 23 B6
Clapton-on-
the-Hill 38 C1
Clapworthy 9 B8
Clarach 58 F3

Clara Vale 110 C4
Clarbeston 32 B1
Clarbeston Road . . 32 B1
Clarborough 89 F8
Clardon 158 D3
Clare 55 E8
Clarebrand 106 C4
Clarencefield 107 C7
Clarilaw 115 C8
Clark's Green 28 F2
Clarkston 119 D5
Clashandorran . . 151 G8
Clashcoig 151 B9
Clashindarroch . . 152 E4
Clashmore
Highld 151 C10
Highld 156 F3
Clashnessie 156 F3
Clashnoir 139 B8
Clate 160 G7
Clathy 127 C8
Clatt 140 B4
Clatter 59 E6
Clatterford 15 F5
Clatterin Bridge . 135 B6
Clatworthy 22 F2
Claughton Lancs . 92 E5
Lancs 93 C5
Mers 85 F4
Claverdon 51 C6
Claverham 23 C6
Clavering 55 F5
Claverley 61 E7
Claverton 24 C2
Clawdd-newydd . 72 D4
Clawthorpe 92 B5
Clawton 9 E5
Claxby Lincs. 79 B7
Lincs 90 E5
Claxton Norf 69 D6
N Yorks. 96 C2
Claybokie 139 E6
Claybrooke Magna 63 F8
Claybrooke Parva 63 F8
Clay Common 69 F7
Clay Coton 52 B3
Clay Cross 76 C3
Claydon Oxon . . . 52 D2
Suff 56 D5
Claygate Dumfries 108 B3
Kent. 29 E8
Sur. 28 C2
Claygate Cross . . 29 D7
Clayhanger Devon 10 B5
W Mid 62 D4
Clayhidon 11 C6
Clayhill E Sus. . . . 18 C5
Hants. 14 D4
Clay Hill 26 B3
Clay Lake 66 B2
Clayock 158 E3
Claypole 77 E8
Clayton Staffs . . . 75 E5
S Yorks 89 D5
W Sus 17 C6
W Yorks. 94 F4
Clayton Green . . . 86 B3
Clayton-le-Moors 93 F7
Clayton-le-Woods 86 B3
Clayton West 88 C3
Clayworth 89 F8
Cleadale 146 C7
Cleadon 111 C6
Clearbrook 6 C3
Clearwell 36 D2
Cleasby 101 C7
Cleat 159 K5
Cleatlam 101 C6
Cleator 98 C2
Cleator Moor 98 C2
Clebrig 157 F8
Cleckheaton 88 B2
Cleedownton 61 F5
Cleehill 49 B7
Clee St Margaret . 61 F5
Cleethorpes 91 D7
Cleeton St Mary . 49 B8
Cleeve 23 C6
Cleeve Hill 37 B6
Cleeve Prior 51 E5
Clegyrnant 59 D6
Clehonger 49 F6
Cleish 128 E2
Cleland 119 D8
Clench Common . 25 C6
Clenchwarton . . . 67 B5
Clent 50 B4
Cleobury
Mortimer 49 B8
Cleobury North . . 61 F6
Cleongart 143 E7
Clephanton 151 F11
Clerklands 115 B8
Clestrain 159 H4
Cleuch Head 115 C8
Cleughbrae 107 B7
Clevancy 25 B5
Clevedon 23 B6
Cleveley 38 B3
Cleveleys 92 E3
Cleverton 37 F6
Clevis 21 B7
Clewer 23 D6
Cley next the Sea . 81 C6
Cliaid 148 H1
Cliasmol 154 G5
Cliburn 99 B7
Click Mill 159 F4
Cliddesden 26 E4
Cliffburn 135 E6
Cliffe Medway . . . 29 B8
N Yorks. 96 F2
Cliff End 19 D5
Cliff Woods 29 B8
Clifford Hereford . 48 E4
W Yorks 95 E7
Clifford Chambers 51 D6
Clifford's Mesne . 36 B4
Cliffsend 31 C7
Clifton Bristol 23 B7
C Beds 54 F2
Cumb 99 B7
Derbys 75 E8
Lancs 92 F4
Northum 117 F8
Nottingham 77 F5
N Yorks 94 E4
Oxon 52 F2
Stirling 131 F7

Clifton continued
S Yorks 89 E6
Worcs 50 E3
York 95 D8
Clifton Campville . 63 C6
Cliftoncote 116 B4
Clifton Green 87 D5
Clifton Hampden . 39 E5
Clifton Reynes . . . 53 D7
Clifton upon
Dunsmore 52 B3
Clifton upon Teme . 50 C2
Cliftonville 31 B7
Climaen gwyn . . . 33 D8
Climping 16 D4
Climpy 120 D2
Clink 24 E2
Clint 95 D5
Clint Green 68 C3
Clintmains 122 F2
Cliobh 154 D5
Clippesby 69 C7
Clipsham 65 C6
Clipston 64 F4
Clipstone 77 C5
Clitheroe 93 E7
Cliuthar 154 H6
Clive 60 B5
Clivocast 160 C8
Clixby 90 D5
Clocaenog 72 D4
Clochan 152 B4
Clock Face 86 E3
Clockmill 122 D3
Cloddiau 60 D2
Clodock 35 B7
Clola 153 D10
Clophill 53 F8
Clopton N Nhants . 65 F7
Suff 57 D6
Clopton Corner . . 57 D6
Clopton Green . . . 55 D8
Closeburn 113 E8
Close Clark 84 E2
Closworth 12 C3
Clothall 54 F3
Clotton 74 C2
Clough Foot 87 B7
Cloughton 103 E8
Cloughton
Newlands 103 E8
Clousta 160 H5
Clouston 159 G3
Clova Aberds 140 B3
Angus 134 B3
Clovelly 8 B5
Clove Lodge 100 C4
Clovenfords 121 F7
Clovenstone 141 C6
Clovullin 130 C4
Clow Bridge 87 B6
Clowne 76 B4
Clows Top 50 B2
Cloy 73 E7
Cluanie Inn 136 C3
Cluanie Lodge . . 136 C3
Clun 60 F3
Clunbury 60 F3
Clunderwen 32 C2
Clune 138 B3
Clunes 136 F5
Clungunford 49 B5
Clunie Aberds . . . 153 C6
Perth 133 E8
Clunton 60 F3
Cluny 128 E4
Cluny Castle 138 E2
Clutton Bath 23 D8
Ches W 73 D8
Clwt-grugoer 72 C3
Clwt-y-bont 83 E5
Clydach Mon. 35 C6
Swansea 33 D7
Clydach Vale 34 E3
Clydebank 118 B4
Clydey 45 F4
Clyffe Pypard 25 B5
Clynder 145 E11
Clyne 34 D2
Clynelish 157 J11
Clynnog-fawr 82 F4
Clyro 48 E4
Clyst Honiton 10 E4
Clyst Hydon 10 D5
Clyst St George . . 10 F4
Clyst St Lawrence 10 D5
Clyst St Mary 10 E4
Cnoc Amhlaigh . 155 D10
Cnwch-coch 47 B5
Coachford 152 D4
Coad's Green 5 B7
Coal Aston 76 B3
Coalbrookdale . . . 61 D6
Coalbrookvale . . . 35 D5
Coalburn 119 F8
Coalburns 110 C4
Coalcleugh 109 E8
Coaley 36 D4
Coalhall 112 C4
Coalhill 42 E3
Coalpit Heath 36 F3
Coalport 61 D6
Coalsnaughton . . 127 E8
Coaltown of
Balgonie 128 E4
Coaltown of
Wemyss 128 E5
Coalville 63 C8
Coalway 36 C2
Coat 12 B2
Coatbridge 119 C7
Coatdyke 119 C7
Coate Swindon . . . 37 F8
Wilts 24 C5
Coates Cambs . . . 66 E3
Glos 37 D6
Lancs 93 E8
Notts 90 F2
W Sus 16 C3
N Lincs 90 C2
Coatham 102 B3
Coatham
Mundeville . . . 101 B7
Coatsgate 114 D3
Cobbaton 9 B8
Cobbler's Green . 69 E5
Coberley 37 C6
Cobham Kent 29 C7
Sur. 28 C2
Cobholm Island . . 69 D8

Cobleland 126 E4
Cobnash 49 C6
Coburty 153 B9
Cockayne 102 E4
Cockayne Hatley . 54 E3
Cock Bank 73 E7
Cock Bridge 139 D8
Cockburnspath . . 122 B3
Cock Clarks 42 D4
Cockenzie and
Port Seton 121 B7
Cockerham 92 D4
Cockermouth . . . 107 F8
Cockfield Durham 101 B6
Suff 56 D3
Cockfosters 41 E5
Cocking 16 C2
Cockington 7 C6
Cocklake 23 E6
Cockley Beck 98 D4
Cockley Cley 67 D7
Cockshutt 60 B4
Cockthorpe 81 C5
Cockwood 10 F4
Cockyard 49 F6
Codda 5 B6
Coddenham 56 D5
Coddington
Ches W 73 D8
Hereford 50 E2
Notts 77 D8
Codford St Mary . 24 F4
Codford St Peter . 24 F4
Codicote 41 C5
Codmore Hill 16 B4
Codnor 76 E4
Codrington 24 B2
Codsall 62 D2
Codsall Wood . . . 62 D2
Coed Duon
= Blackwood . . . 35 E5
Coedely 34 F4
Coedkernew 35 F6
Coed Mawr 83 D5
Coed Morgan 35 C7
Coedpoeth 73 D6
Coed-Talon 73 D6
Coedway 60 C3
Coed-y-bryn 46 E2
Coed-y-paen 35 E7
Coed-yr-ynys 35 B5
Coed Ystumgwern 71 E6
Coelbren 34 C2
Coffinswell 7 C6
Cofton Hackett . . . 50 B5
Cogan 22 B3
Cogenhoe 53 C6
Cogges 38 D3
Coggeshall 42 B4
Coggeshall
Hamlet 42 B4
Coggins Mill 18 C2
Coignafearn
Lodge 138 C2
Coig
Peighinnean . . 155 A10
Coig Peighinnean
Bhuirgh 155 B9
Coilacriech 140 E2
Coilantogle 126 D4
Coilleag 148 G2
Coillore 149 E8
Coity 34 F3
Col 155 C9
Colaboll 157 H8
Colan 4 C3
Colaton Raleigh . 11 F5
Colbost 148 D7
Colburn 101 E6
Colby Cumb 100 B1
IoM 84 E2
Norf 81 D8
Colchester 43 B6
Colcot 22 C3
Cold Ash 26 C3
Cold Ashby 52 B4
Cold Ashton 24 B2
Cold Aston 37 C8
Coldbackie 157 D9
Coldbeck 100 D2
Coldblow 29 B6
Cold Blow 32 C2
Cold Brayfield . . . 53 D7
Coldean 17 D7
Coldeast 7 B6
Colden 87 B7
Colden Common . 15 B5
Coldfair Green . . . 57 C8
Coldham 66 D4
Cold Hanworth . . 90 F4
Coldharbour Glos . 36 D2
Kent. 29 D6
Sur. 28 E2
Cold Harbour . . . 78 F2
Cold Hatton 61 B6
Cold Hesledon . . 111 E7
Cold Higham 52 D4
Coldingham 122 C5
Cold Kirby 102 F3
Cold Newton 64 D4
Cold Northcott 8 F4
Cold Norton 42 D4
Cold Overton 64 C5
Coldrain 128 D2
Coldred 31 E6
Coldridge 9 D8
Coldstream Angus. 134 F3
Borders 122 F4
Coldwaltham 16 C4
Coldwells 153 D11
Coldwells Croft . 140 B4
Coldyeld 60 E3
Cole 23 F8
Colebatch 60 F3
Colebrook 10 D5
Colebrooke 10 E2
Coleby Lincs 78 C2
N Lincs 90 C2
Coleford Devon . . 10 D2
Glos 36 C2
Som 23 E8
Cole Green 41 C5
Cole Henley 26 D2
Colehill 13 D8
Coleman's Hatch . 29 F5
Colemere 73 F8
Colemore 26 F5
Coleorton 63 C8

Colerne 24 B3
Colesbourne 37 C6
Colesden 54 D2
Coles Green 56 E4
Cole's Green 57 C6
Coleshill Bucks. . . 40 E2
Oxon 38 E2
Warks 63 F6
Colestocks 11 D5
Colgate 28 F3
Colgrain 126 F2
Colinsburgh 129 D6
Colinton 120 C5
Colintraive 145 F9
Colkirk 80 E5
Collace 134 F2
Collafirth 160 G6
Collaton St Mary . .7 D6
Collessie 128 C4
Collier Row 41 E8
Collier's End 41 B6
Collier's Green . . 18 B4
Collier Street 29 E8
Colliery Row 111 E6
Collieston 141 B9
Collin 107 B7
Collingbourne
Ducis. 25 D7
Collingbourne
Kingston 25 D7
Collingham Notts . 77 C8
W Yorks 95 E6
Collington 49 C8
Collingtree 53 D5
Collins Green 86 E3
Colliston 135 E6
Collycroft 63 F7
Collynie 153 E8
Collyweston 65 D6
Colmonell 104 A5
Colmworth 54 D2
Colnabaichin . . . 139 D8
Colnbrook 27 B8
Colne Cambs 54 B4
Lancs 93 E8
Colne Edge 93 E8
Colne Engaine . . . 56 F2
Colney 68 D4
Colney Heath 41 D5
Colney Street 40 D4
Coln Rogers 37 D7
Coln St Aldwyn's 37 D8
Coln St Dennis . . 37 C7
Colpy 153 E6
Colquhar 121 E6
Colsterdale 101 F6
Colsterworth 65 B6
Colston Bassett . . 77 F6
Coltfield 151 E14
Colthouse 99 E5
Coltishall 69 C5
Coltness 119 D8
Colton Cumb 99 F5
Norf 68 D4
N Yorks. 95 E8
Staffs. 62 B4
W Yorks. 95 F6
Col Uarach 155 D9
Colva 48 D4
Colvend 107 D5
Colvister 160 D7
Colwall Green . . . 50 E2
Colwall Stone . . . 50 E2
Colwell 110 B2
Colwich 62 B4
Colwick 77 E6
Colwinston 21 B8
Colworth 16 D3
Colwyn Bay
= Bae Colwyn . . 83 D8
Colyford 11 E7
Colyton 11 E7
Combe Hereford . 48 C5
Oxon 38 C4
W Berks 25 C8
Combe Common . 27 F7
Combe Down 24 C2
Combe Florey . . . 22 F3
Combe Hay 24 D2
Combeinteignhead .7 B7
Combe Martin . . . 20 E4
Combe Moor 49 C5
Combe Raleigh . . 11 D6
Comberbach 74 B3
Comberton Cambs . 54 D4
Hereford 49 C6
Combe St Nicholas 11 C8
Combpyne 11 E7
Combrook 51 D8
Combs Derbys . . . 75 B7
Suff 56 D4
Combs Ford 56 D4
Combwich 22 E4
Comers 141 D5
Comins Coch 58 F3
Commercial End . 55 C6
Commins Capel
Betws 46 D5
Commins Coch . . 58 D5
Commondale . . . 102 C4
Common Edge . . . 92 F3
Commonmoor 5 C7
Commonside 74 B2
Common Side . . . 76 B3
Compstall 87 E7
Compton Devon . . .7 C6
Hants. 15 B5
Sur. 27 E6
Sur. 27 E7
W Berks 26 B3
Wilts 25 D6
W Sus 15 C8
Compton Abbas . 13 C6
Compton Abdale . 37 C7
Compton Bassett . 24 B5
Compton
Beauchamp . . . 38 F2
Compton Bishop . 23 D5
Compton
Chamberlayne . 13 B8
Compton Dando . 23 C8
Compton Dundon 23 F6
Compton Martin . 23 D7
Compton
Pauncefoot . . . 12 B4
Compton Valence 12 E3
Comrie Fife 128 F2

Comrie continued
Perth 127 B6
Conaglen House . 130 C4
Conchra 145 E9
Concraigie 133 E8
Conder Green 92 D4
Conderton 50 F4
Condicote 38 B1
Condover 60 D4
Coneyhurst 16 B5
Coneysthorpe . . . 96 B3
Coneythorpe 95 D6
Coney Weston . . . 56 B3
Conford 27 F6
Congash 139 B6
Congdon's Shop . .5 B7
Congerstone 63 D7
Congham 80 E3
Congl-y-wal 71 C8
Congresbury 23 C6
Congreve 62 C3
Conicavel 151 F12
Coningsby 78 D5
Conington Cambs . 54 C4
Cambs. 65 F8
Conisbrough 89 E6
Conisby 142 B3
Conisholme 91 E8
Coniston Cumb. . . 99 E5
E Yorks. 97 F7
Coniston Cold . . . 94 D2
Conistone 94 C2
Connah's Quay . . 73 C6
Connel 124 B5
Connel Park 113 C6
Connor Downs 2 C4
Conon Bridge . . . 151 F8
Conon House . . . 151 F8
Cononley 94 E2
Conordan 149 E10
Consall 75 E6
Consett 110 D4
Constable Burton 101 E6
Constantine 3 D6
Constantine Bay . .4 B3
Contin 150 F7
Contlaw 141 D7
Conwy 83 D7
Conyer 30 C3
Conyers Green . . . 56 C2
Cooden 18 E4
Cooil 84 E3
Cookbury 9 D6
Cookham 40 F1
Cookham Dean . . 40 F1
Cookham Rise . . . 40 F1
Cookhill 51 D5
Cookley Suff 57 B7
Worcs 62 F2
Cookley Green . . . 39 E6
Cookney 141 E7
Cookridge 95 E5
Cooksbridge 17 C8
Cooksmill Green . 42 D2
Coolham 16 B5
Cooling 29 B8
Coombe Corn. 4 D4
Corn. 8 C4
Hants. 15 B8
Wilts 25 D6
Coombe Bissett . . 14 B2
Coombe Hill 37 B5
Coombe Keynes . 13 F6
Coombes 17 D5
Coopersale
Common 41 D7
Cootham 16 C4
Copdock 56 E5
Copford Green . . . 43 B5
Copgrove 95 C6
Copister 160 F6
Cople 54 E2
Copley 101 B5
Coplow Dale 75 B8
Copmanthorpe . . 95 E8
Coppathorne 8 D4
Coppenhall 62 C3
Coppenhall Moss 74 D4
Copperhouse 2 C4
Coppingford 65 F8
Copplestone 10 D2
Coppull 86 C3
Coppull Moor . . . 86 C3
Copsale 17 B5
Copster Green . . . 93 F6
Copston Magna . . 63 F8
Copt Heath 51 B6
Copt Hewick 95 B6
Copthorne Shrops . 60 C4
Sur. 28 F4
Copt Oak 63 C8
Copy's Green 80 D5
Copythorne 14 C4
Corbets Tey 42 F1
Corbridge 110 C2
Corby 65 F5
Corby Glen 65 B6
Cordon 143 E11
Coreley 49 B8
Cores End 40 F2
Corfe 11 C7
Corfe Castle 13 F7
Corfe Mullen 13 E7
Corfton 60 F4
Corgarff 139 D8
Corhampton 15 B7
Corlae 113 E6
Corley 63 F7
Corley Ash 63 F6
Corley Moor 63 F6
Cornaa 84 D4
Cornabus 142 D4
Cornel 83 E7
Corner Row 92 F4
Corney 98 E3
Cornforth 111 F6
Cornhill 152 C5
Cornhill-
on-Tweed 122 F4
Cornholme 87 B7
Cornish Hall End . 55 F7
Cornquoy 159 J6
Cornsay 110 E4
Cornsay Colliery . 110 E4
Corntown Highld . 151 F8
V Glam 21 B8
Cornwell 38 B2

Cornwood 6 D4
Cornworthy 7 D6
Corpach 130 B4
Corpusty 81 D7
Corran Highld . . . 130 C4
Highld 149 H13
Corranbuie 145 G7
Corranny 84 D4
Corrany 143 D11
Corrie 143 D11
Corrie Common . 114 F5
Corriecravie 143 F10
Corriemoillie 150 E6
Corriemulzie
Lodge 150 B6
Corrievarkie
Lodge 132 B2
Corrievorrie 138 B3
Corrimony 150 H6
Corringham Lincs . 90 E2
Thurrock 42 F3
Corris 58 D4
Corris Uchaf 58 D4
Corrour Shooting
Lodge 131 C8
Corrow 125 E7
Corry 149 F11
Corrykinloch . . . 156 G6
Corrymuckloch . 133 F5
Corrynachenchy 147 G9
Corry of
Ardnagrask . . . 151 G8
Corsback 158 C4
Corscombe 12 D3
Corse Aberds 152 D6
Glos 36 B4
Corse Lawn 50 F3
Corse of Kinnoir . 152 D5
Corsewall 104 C4
Corsham 24 B3
Corsindae 141 D5
Corsley 24 E3
Corsley Heath . . . 24 E3
Corsock 106 B4
Corston Bath. 23 C8
Wilts 37 F6
Corstorphine 120 B5
Cors-y-Gedol 71 E6
Cortachy 134 D3
Corton Suff 69 E8
Wilts 24 E4
Corton Denham . . 12 B4
Coruanan Lodge . 130 C4
Corunna 148 B3
Corwen 72 E4
Coryton Devon 9 F6
Thurrock 42 F3
Cosby 64 E2
Coseley 62 E3
Cosgrove 53 E5
Cosham 15 D7
Cosheston 32 D1
Coshieville 132 E4
Cossall 76 E4
Cossington Leics . 64 C3
Som 23 E5
Costa 159 F4
Costessey 68 C4
Costock 64 B2
Coston 64 C5
Cote 38 D3
Cotebrook 74 C2
Cotehill 108 D4
Cotes Cumb 99 F6
Leics 64 B2
Staffs. 74 F5
Cotesbach 64 F2
Cotgrave 77 F6
Cotham 77 E7
Cothall 141 C7
Cotham 77 E7
Cothelstone 22 F3
Cotherstone 101 C5
Cothill 38 E4
Cotleigh 11 D7
Cotmanhay 76 E4
Cotmaton 11 F6
Coton Cambs 54 D5
Staffs. 62 B2
Staffs. 75 F6
W Nhants. 52 B4
Coton Clanford . . 62 B2
Coton Hill Shrops . 60 C4
Staffs. 75 F6
Coton in the Elms 63 C6
Cott 7 C5
Cottam E Yorks . . 97 C5
Lancs 92 F5
Notts 77 B8
Cottartown 151 H13
Cottenham 54 C5
Cotterdale 100 E3
Cottered 41 B6
Cotteridge 50 B5
Cotterstock 65 E7
Cottesbrooke 52 B5
Cottesmore 65 C6
Cotteylands 10 C4
Cottingham
E Yorks. 97 F6
N Nhants 64 E5
Cottingley 94 F4
Cottisford 52 F3
Cotton Staffs. 75 E7
Suff 56 C4
Cotton End 53 E8
Cottown Aberds . 140 B4
Aberds 141 C6
Aberds 153 D8
Cotwalton 75 F6
Couch's Mill 5 D6
Coughton Hereford 36 B2
Warks 51 C5
Coulaghailtro . . . 144 G6
Coulags 150 G2
Coulby Newham . 102 C3
Coulderton 98 D1
Coulin 150 F3
Coull Aberds 140 D4
Argyll. 142 B3
Coulport 145 E11
Coulsdon 28 D4
Coulston 24 D4
Coulter 120 F3
Coulton 96 B2
Cound 61 D5
Coundon Durham 101 B7
W Mid 63 F7
Coundon Grange 101 B7
Countersett 100 F4
Countess 25 E6
Countess Wear . . 10 F4

Countesthorpe . . 64 E2
Countisbury 21 E6
County Oak 28 F3
Coupar Angus . . 134 E2
Coup Green 86 B3
Cour 143 D9
Courance 114 E3
Court-at-Street . . 19 B7
Courteenhall 53 D5
Court Henry 33 B6
Courtsend 43 E6
Courtway 22 F4
Cousland 121 C6
Cousley Wood . . . 18 B3
Cove Argyll 145 E11
Borders 122 B3
Devon 10 C4
Hants. 27 D6
Highld 155 H13
Cove Bay 141 D8
Cove Bottom 57 B8
Covehithe 69 F8
Coven 62 D3
Coveney 66 F4
Covenham
St Bartholomew 91 E7
Covenham St Mary 91 E7
Coventry 51 B8
Coverack 3 E6
Coverham 101 F6
Covesea 152 A1
Covington Cambs . 53 B8
S Lanark 120 F2
Cowan Bridge . . . 93 B6
Cow Ark 93 E6
Cowbeech 18 D3
Cowbit 66 C2
Cowbridge Lincs . 79 E6
Som 21 E8
Cowbridge
= Y Bont-Faen . . 21 B8
Cowdale 75 B7
Cowden 29 E5
Cowdenbeath . . . 128 E3
Cowdenburn 120 D5
Cowers Lane 76 E3
Cowes 15 E5
Cowesby 102 F2
Cowfold 17 B6
Cowgill 100 F2
Cowie Aberds . . . 141 F7
Stirling 127 F7
Cowley Devon . . . 10 E4
Glos 37 C6
London 40 F3
Oxon 39 D5
Cowleymoor 10 C4
Cowling Lancs . . . 86 C3
N Yorks. 94 E2
N Yorks. 101 F7
Cowlinge 55 D8
Cowpe 87 B6
Cowpen 117 F8
Cowpen Bewley . 102 B2
Cowplain 15 C7
Cowshill 109 E8
Cowslip Green . . . 23 C6
Cowstrandburn . 128 E2
Cowthorpe 95 D7
Coxbank 74 E3
Coxbench 76 E3
Cox Common 69 F6
Coxford Norf 80 E4
Soton 14 C4
Cox Green 27 B6
Coxheath 29 D8
Coxhill 31 E6
Coxhoe 111 F6
Coxley 23 E7
Cox Moor 76 D5
Coxwold 95 B8
Coychurch 21 B8
Coylton 112 B4
Coylumbridge . . 138 C5
Coynach 140 D3
Coynachie 152 E4
Coytrahen 34 F2
Crabadon 7 D5
Crabbs Cross 50 C5
Crabtree 17 B6
Crackenthorpe . . 100 B1
Crackington Haven .8 E3
Crackley 51 B7
Crackleybank 61 C7
Crackpot 100 E4
Cracoe 94 C2
Craddock 11 C5
Cradhlastadh . . . 154 D5
Cradley 50 E2
Cradley Heath . . . 62 F3
Crafthole 5 D8
Craggan Highld . . 139 B6
Highld 157 H11
Cragg Vale 87 B8
Craghead 110 D5
Crai 34 B2
Craibstone 152 C4
Craichie 135 E5
Craig Dumfries . . 106 B3
Dumfries 106 C3
Highld 150 G3
Craiganor Lodge . 132 D3
Craig Castle 140 B4
Craig-cefn-parc . . 33 D7
Craigdam 153 E8
Craigdarroch
Dumfries 113 E7
Highld 150 F7
Craigdhu 150 G7
Craigearn 141 C6
Craigellachie . . . 152 D2
Craigencross . . . 104 C4
Craigend Perth . . 128 B3
Stirling 127 F6
Craigendive 145 E9
Craigendoran . . . 126 F2
Craigends 118 C4
Craigens Argyll . . 142 B3
E Ayrs. 113 C5
Craighat 126 F3
Craighead 129 D8
Craighlaw Mains 105 C7
Craighouse 144 G4
Craigie Aberds . . 141 C8
Dundee 134 F4
Perth 128 B3
Perth 133 E8

Craigie continued
S Ayrs 118 F4
Craigiefield 159 G5
Craigielaw 121 B7
Craiglockhart 120 B5
Craigmalloch 112 E4
Craigmillar 121 B5
Craigmore 145 G10
Craignant 73 F6
Craigneuk
N Lanark 119 C7
N Lanark 119 D7
Craignure 124 B3
Craigo 135 C6
Craigow 128 D2
Craig Penllyn 21 B8
Craigrothie 129 C5
Craigroy 151 F14
Craigruie 126 B3
Craigston Castle . . 153 C7
Craigton Aberdeen . . 53 B7
Angus 134 D3
Angus 135 F5
Highld 151 B9
Craigtown 157 D11
Craig-y-don 83 C7
Craig-y-nos 34 C2
Craik 115 D6
Crail 129 D8
Crailing 116 B2
Crailinghall 116 B2
Craiselound 89 E8
Crakehill 95 B7
Crakemarsh 75 F7
Crambe 96 C3
Cramlington 111 B5
Cramond 120 B4
Cramond Bridge . . . 120 B4
Cranage 74 C4
Cranberry 74 F5
Cranborne 13 C8
Cranbourne 27 B7
Cranbrook Devon . . . 10 E5
Kent 18 B4
Cranbrook
Common 18 B4
Crane Moor 88 D4
Crane's Corner 68 C2
Cranfield 53 E7
Cranford 28 B2
Cranford
St Andrew 53 B7
Cranford St John . . . 53 B7
Cranham Glos 37 C5
London 42 F1
Crank 86 E3
Crank Wood 86 D4
Cranleigh 27 F8
Cranley 57 B5
Cranmer Green 56 B4
Cranmore 14 F4
Cranna 153 C6
Crannich 147 G8
Crannoch 152 C4
Cranoe 64 E4
Cransford 57 C7
Cranshaws 122 C2
Cranstal 84 B4
Crantock 4 C2
Cranwell 78 E3
Cranwich 67 E7
Cranworth 68 D2
Craobh Haven 124 E3
Crapstone 6 C3
Crarae 125 F5
Crask Inn 157 G8
Craskins 140 D4
Crask of Aigas 150 G7
Craster 117 C8
Craswall 48 F4
Cratfield 57 B7
Crathes 141 E6
Crathie Aberdeen . . 139 E8
Highld 137 E8
Crathorne 102 D2
Craven Arms 60 F4
Crawcrook 110 C4
Crawford Lancs 86 D2
S Lanark 114 B2
Crawfordjohn 113 B8
Crawick 113 C7
Crawley Hants 26 F2
Oxon 38 C3
W Sus 28 F3
Crawley Down 28 F3
Crawleyside 110 E2
Crawshawbooth . . . 87 B6
Crawton 135 B8
Cray N Yorks 94 B2
Perth 133 C8
Crayford 29 B6
Crayke 95 B8
Crays Hill 42 E3
Cray's Pond 39 F6
Creacombe 10 C2
Creagan 130 E3
Creag Ghoraidh . . . 148 D2
Creaguaineach
Lodge 131 C7
Creaksea 43 E5
Creaton 52 B5
Creca 108 B2
Credenhill 49 E6
Crediton 10 D3
Creebridge 105 C8
Creech Heathfield . . 11 B7
Creech St Michael . . 11 B7
Creed 3 B8
Creekmouth 41 F7
Creeting Bottoms . . . 56 D5
Creeting St Mary . . . 56 D4
Creeton 65 B7
Creetown 105 D8
Creggans 125 E6
Cregneash 84 F1
Creg-ny-Baa 84 D3
Cregrina 48 D3
Creich 128 B5
Creigiau 34 F4
Cremyll 6 D2
Creslow 39 C8
Cressage 61 D5
Cressbrook 75 B8
Cresselly 32 D1
Cressing 42 C3
Cresswell
Northumb 117 E8
Staffs 75 F6

Cresswell Quay 32 D1
Cresswell 76 B5
Cretingham 57 C6
Cretshengan 144 G6
Crewe Ches E 74 D4
Ches W 73 D8
Crewgreen 60 C3
Crewkerne 12 D2
Crianlarich 126 B2
Cribyn 46 D4
Criccieth 71 D5
Crich 76 D3
Crichie 153 D9
Crichton 121 C6
Crick Mon 36 E1
W Nhants 52 B3
Crickadarn 48 E2
Cricket Malherbie . . 11 C8
Cricket St Thomas . . 11 D8
Crickheath 60 B2
Crickhowell 35 C6
Cricklade 37 E8
Cricklewood 41 F5
Cridling Stubbs 89 B6
Crieff 127 B7
Criggion 60 C2
Crigglestone 88 C4
Crimble 87 C6
Crimond 153 C10
Crimonmogate 153 C10
Crimplesham 67 D6
Crinan 144 D6
Cringleford 68 D4
Cringles 94 E3
Crinow 32 C2
Cripplesease 2 C4
Cripplestyle 13 C8
Cripp's Corner 18 C4
Croasdale 98 C2
Crockenhill 29 C6
Crockernwell 10 E2
Crockerton 24 E3
Crocketford or
Ninemile Bar 106 B5
Crockey Hill 96 E2
Crockham Hill 28 D5
Crockleford Heath . . 43 B6
Crockness 159 J4
Crock Street 11 C8
Croeserw 34 E2
Croes-goch 44 B3
Croes-lan 46 E2
Croesor 71 C7
Croesyceiliog
Carms 33 C5
Torf 35 E7
Croes-y-mwyalch . . . 35 E7
Croesywaun 82 F5
Croft Leics 64 E2
Lincs 79 C8
Pembs 45 E3
Warr 86 E4
Croftamie 126 F3
Croftmalloch 120 C2
Crofton Wilts 25 C7
W Yorks 88 C4
Croft-on-Tees 101 D7
Crofts of
Benachielt 158 G3
Crofts of Haddo . . . 153 E8
Crofts of
Inverthernie 153 D7
Crofts of Meikle
Ardo 153 D8
Crofty 33 E6
Croggan 124 C3
Croglin 109 E5
Croich 150 B7
Crois Dughaill 148 F2
Cromarty 151 E10
Cromblet 153 E7
Cromdale 139 B6
Cromer Herts 41 B5
Norf 81 C8
Cromford 76 D2
Cromhall 36 E3
Cromhall Common . . 36 F3
Cromor 155 E9
Cromra 137 E8
Cromwell 77 C7
Cronberry 113 B6
Crondall 27 E5
Cronk-y-Voddy 84 D3
Cronton 86 F2
Crook Cumb 99 E6
Durham 110 F4
Crookedholm 118 F4
Crookes 88 F4
Crookham
Northumb 122 F5
W Berks 26 C3
Crookham Village . . 27 D5
Crookhaugh 114 B4
Crookhouse 116 B3
Crooklands 99 F7
Crook of Devon 128 D2
Cropredy 52 E2
Cropston 64 C2
Cropthorne 50 E4
Cropton 103 F5
Cropwell Bishop . . . 77 F6
Cropwell Butler 77 F6
Cros 155 A10
Crosbost 155 E8
Crosby Cumb 107 F7
IoM 84 E3
N Lincs 90 C2
Crosby Garrett 100 D2
Crosby
Ravensworth 99 C8
Crosby Villa 107 F7
Croscombe 23 E7
Cross 23 D6
Crossaig 143 D9
Crossal 149 E9
Crossapol 146 G2
Cross Ash 35 C8
Cross-at-Hand 29 E8
Crossburn 119 B8
Crossbush 16 D4
Crosscanonby 107 F7

Crossgill 93 C5
Cross Green Devon . . . 9 F5
Suff 56 D2
Suff 56 D3
Warks 51 D8
Cross-hands 32 B2
Cross Hands Carms . . 33 C6
Ches W 74 B3
Crosshill E Ayrs . . . 112 B4
Fife 128 E3
S Ayrs 112 D3
Cross Hill 76 E4
Crosshouse 118 F3
Cross Houses 60 D5
Crossings 108 B5
Cross in Hand
E Sus 18 C2
Leics 64 F2
Cross Inn Ceredig . . . 46 C4
Ceredig 46 D2
Rhondda 34 F4
Crosskeys 35 E6
Cross Keys 29 D6
Cross Lane Head . . . 61 D7
Crosslanes 60 C3
Cross Lanes Corn 3 D5
N Yorks 95 C8
Wrex 73 E7
Crossle 118 C4
Crosslee 115 C6
Crossmichael 106 C4
Crossmoor 92 F4
Cross Oak 35 B5
Cross of
Jackston 153 E7
Cross o'th'hands 76 E2
Crossroads Aberds . . 141 E6
E Ayrs 118 F4
Cross Street 57 B5
Crossway Hereford . . 49 F8
Mon 35 C8
Powys 48 D2
Crossway Green 50 C3
Crossways 13 F5
Crosswell 45 F3
Crosswood 47 B5
Crosthwaite 99 E6
Croston 86 C2
Crostwick 69 C5
Crostwight 69 B6
Crothair 154 D6
Crouch 29 D7
Croucheston 13 B8
Crouch Hill 12 C5
Crouch House
Green 28 E5
Croughton 52 F3
Crovie 153 B8
Crow 14 D2
Crowan 2 C5
Crowborough 18 B2
Crowcombe 22 F3
Crowdecote 75 C8
Crowden 87 E8
Crow Edge 88 D2
Crowell 39 E7
Crowfield Suff 56 D5
W Nhants 52 E4
Crow Hill 36 B3
Crowhurst E Sus 18 D4
Sur 28 E4
Crowhurst Lane
End 28 E4
Crowland 66 C2
Crowlas 2 C4
Crowle N Lincs 89 C8
Worcs 50 D4
Crowmarsh
Gifford 39 F6
Crown Corner 57 B6
Crownhill 6 D2
Crownland 56 C4
Crownthorpe 68 D3
Crowntown 2 C5
Crows-an-wra 2 D2
Crowshill 68 D2
Crowsnest 60 D3
Crowthorne 27 C6
Crowton 74 B2
Croxall 63 C5
Croxby 91 E5
Croxdale 111 F5
Croxden 75 F7
Croxley Green 40 E3
Croxton Cambs 54 C3
N Lincs 90 C4
Norf 67 F8
Staffs 74 F4
Croxtonbank 74 F4
Croxton Kerrial 64 B5
Croy Highld 151 G10
N Lanark 119 B7
Croyde 20 F3
Croydon Cambs 54 E4
London 28 C4
Crubenmore
Lodge 138 E2
Cruckmeole 60 D4
Cruckton 60 C4
Cruden Bay 153 E10
Crudgington 61 C6
Crudwell 37 E6
Crug 48 B3
Crugmeer 4 B4
Crugybar 47 F5
Crulabhig 154 D6
Crumlin = Crymlyn . . 35 E6
Denb 72 B4
Crumpsall 87 D6
Crundale Kent 30 E4
Pembs 44 D4
Crux Easton 26 D2
Cruxton 12 E4
Crwbin 33 C5
Crya 159 H4
Cryers Hill 40 E1
Crymlyn = Crymlin . . 83 D6
Crymych 45 F3
Crynant 34 D1
Crynfryn 46 C4
Cuaig 149 C12
Cubbington 51 C8
Cubeck 100 F4
Cubert 4 D2
Cubley 88 D3
Cubley Common 75 F8
Cublington Bucks . . . 39 B8
Hereford 49 F6

Cuckfield 17 B7
Cucklington 13 B5
Cuckney 77 B5
Cuckoo Hill 89 E8
Cuddesdon 39 D6
Cuddington Bucks . . 39 C7
Ches W 74 B3
Cuddington Heath . . 73 E8
Cuddy Hill 92 F4
Cudham 28 D5
Cudliptown 6 B3
Cudworth Som 11 C8
S Yorks 88 D4
Cuffley 41 D6
Cuiashader 155 B10
Cuidhir 148 H1
Cuidhtinis 154 J5
Culbo 151 E9
Culbokie 151 F9
Culburnie 150 G7
Culcabock 151 G9
Culcairn 151 E9
Culcharry 151 F11
Culcheth 86 E4
Culdrain 152 E5
Culduie 149 D12
Culford 56 B2
Culfordheath 56 B2
Culgaith 99 B8
Culham 39 E5
Culkein 156 F3
Culkein Drumbeg . . 156 F4
Culkerton 37 E6
Cullachie 139 B5
Cullen 152 B5
Cullercoats 111 B6
Cullicudden 151 E9
Cullingworth 94 F3
Cullipool 124 D3
Cullivoe 160 C7
Culloch 127 C6
Culloden 151 G10
Cullompton 10 D5
Culmaily 151 B11
Culmazie 105 D7
Culmington 60 F4
Culmstock 11 C6
Culnacraig 156 J3
Culnaknock 149 B10
Culpho 57 E6
Culrain 151 B8
Culross 127 F8
Culroy 112 C3
Culsh Aberds 140 E2
Aberds 153 D8
Culshabbin 105 D7
Culswick 160 J4
Cultercullen 141 B8
Cults Aberdeen 141 D7
Aberds 152 E5
Dumfries 105 E8
Culverstone Green . . 29 C7
Culverthorpe 78 E3
Culworth 52 E3
Culzie Lodge 151 D8
Cumbernauld 119 B7
Cumbernauld
Village 119 B7
Cumberworth 79 B8
Cuminestown 153 C8
Cumlewick 160 L6
Cummersdale 108 D3
Cummertrees 107 C8
Cummingston 152 B1
Cumnock 113 B5
Cumnor 38 D4
Cumrew 108 D5
Cumwhinton 108 D4
Cumwhitton 108 D5
Cundall 95 B7
Cunninghamhead . . 118 E3
Cunnister 160 D7
Cupar 129 C5
Cupar Muir 129 C5
Cupernham 14 B4
Curbar 76 B2
Curbridge Hants 15 C6
Oxon 38 D3
Curdridge 15 C6
Curdworth 63 E5
Curland 11 C7
Curlew Green 57 C7
Currarie 112 E1
Curridge 26 B2
Currie 120 C4
Curry Mallet 11 B8
Curry Rivel 11 B8
Curtisden Green 29 E8
Curtisknowle 6 D5
Cury 3 D5
Cushnie 153 B7
Cushuish 22 F3
Cusop 48 E4
Cutcloy 105 F8
Cutcombe 21 F8
Cutgate 87 C6
Cutiau 58 C3
Cutlers Green 55 F6
Cutnall Green 50 C3
Cutsdean 51 F5
Cutthorpe 76 B3
Cutts 160 K6
Cuxham 39 E6
Cuxton 29 C8
Cuxwold 91 D5
Cwm Bl Gwent 35 D5
Denb 72 B4
Swansea 33 E7
Cwmafan 34 E1
Cwmaman 34 E4
Cwmann 46 E4
Cwmavon 35 D6
Cwmbach Carms . . . 32 B3
Carms 33 D5
Powys 48 D2
Rhondda 34 D4
Cwmbelan 59 F6
Cwmbrân
= Cwmbrân 35 E6
Cwmbrân 35 E6
Cwmbrwyno 58 F4
Cwm-byr 46 F5
Cwmcarn 35 E6
Cwmcarvan 36 D1
Cwm-Cewydd 59 C5
Cwm-cou 46 E2
Cwmcych 45 F4
Cwmdare 34 D3

Cwmderwen 59 D6
Powys 35 B5
Cwmdu Carms 46 F5
Powys 35 B5
Swansea 33 E7
Cwmduad 46 F2
Cwm-Dulais 33 D7
Cwmdwr 47 F6
Cwmfelin Bridgend . . 34 C3
M Tydf 34 D4
Cwmfelin Boeth 32 C2
Cwm-felin-fach 35 E5
Cwmfelin Mynach . . 32 C3
Cwmffrwd 33 C5
Cwm Ffrwd-oer 35 D6
Cwmgiedd 34 C1
Cwmgors 33 C8
Cwmgwili 33 C6
Cwmgwrach 34 D2
Cwm-hesgen 71 E8
Cwmhiraeth 46 F2
Cwm-hwnt 34 D3
Cwmifor 47 F5
Cwm Irfon 47 E7
Cwmisfael 33 C5
Cwm-Llinau 58 D5
Cwmllynfell 33 C8
Cwm-mawr 33 C6
Cwm-morgan 45 F4
Cwm-parc 34 E3
Cwmpengraig 46 F2
Cwm Penmachno . . 71 C8
Cwmrhos 35 B6
Cwmsychpant 46 E3
Cwmtillery 35 D6
Cwm-twrch Isaf 34 C1
Cwm-twrch Uchaf . . 34 C1
Cwmwysg 34 B2
Cwm-y-glo Carms . . . 33 C6
Gwyn 82 E5
Cwmyoy 35 B6
Cwmystwyth 47 B6
Cwrt 58 D3
Cwrt-newydd 46 E3
Cwrt-y-cadno 47 E5
Cwrt-y-gollen 35 C6
Cydweli
= Kidwelly 33 D5
Cyffordd Llandudno
= Llandudno
Junction 83 D7
Cyffylliog 72 D4
Cyfronydd 59 D8
Cymer 34 E2
Cyncoed 35 F5
Cynghordy 47 E7
Cynheidre 33 D5
Cynwyd 72 E4
Cynwyl Elfed 32 B4
Cywarch 59 C5

D

Dacre Cumb 99 B6
N Yorks 94 C4
Dacre Banks 94 C4
Daddry Shield 109 F8
Dadford 52 F4
Dadlington 63 E8
Dafarn Faig 71 C5
Dafen 33 D6
Daffy Green 68 D2
Dagenham 41 F7
Daglingworth 37 D6
Dagnall 40 C2
Dail Beag 154 C7
Dail bho Dheas 155 A9
Dail bho Thuath . . . 155 A9
Daill 142 B4
Dailly 112 D2
Dail Mor 154 C7
Dairsie or
Osnaburgh 129 C6
Daisy Hill 86 D4
Dalabrog 148 F2
Dalavich 125 D5
Dalbeattie 106 C5
Dalblair 113 C6
Dalbog 135 B5
Dalbury 76 F2
Dalby IoM 84 E2
N Yorks 96 B2
Dalchalloch 132 C4
Dalchalm 157 J12
Dalchenna 125 E6
Dalchirach 152 E1
Dalchork 157 H8
Dalchreichart 137 C5
Dalchruin 127 C6
Dalderby 78 C5
Dale 44 E3
Dale Abbey 76 F4
Dale Head 99 C6
Dalelia 147 E10
Dale of Walls 160 H3
Daless 151 H11
Dalfaber 138 C5
Dalgarven 118 E2
Dalgety Bay 128 F3
Dalginross 127 B6
Dalguise 133 E6
Dalhalvaig 157 D11
Dalham 55 C8
Dalinlongart 145 E10
Dalkeith 121 C6
Dallam 86 E3
Dallas 151 F14
Dalleagles 113 C5
Dallinghoo 57 D6
Dallington E Sus . . . 18 D3
W Nhants 52 C5
Dallow 94 B4
Dalmadilly 141 C6
Dalmally 125 C7
Dalmarnock 119 C6
Dalmary 126 E4
Dalmellington 112 D4
Dalmeny 120 B4
Dalmigavie 138 C3
Dalmigavie
Lodge 138 B3
Dalmore 151 E9
Dalmuir 118 B4
Dalnabreck 147 E9
Dalnacardoch
Lodge 132 B4
Dalnacroich 150 F6
Dalnaglar Castle . . 133 C8
Dalnahaitnach 138 B4

Dalnaspidal
Lodge 132 B3
Dalnavaid 133 C7
Dalnavie 151 D9
Dalnawillan
Lodge 157 E13
Dalness 131 D5
Dalnessie 157 H9
Dalqueich 128 D2
Dalreavoch 157 J10
Dalry 118 E2
Dalrymple 112 C3
Dalserf 119 D8
Dalston 108 D3
Dalswinton 114 F2
Dalton Dumfries . . . 107 B8
Lancs 86 D2
Northum 110 B4
N Yorks 101 D6
N Yorks 95 B7
S Yorks 89 E5
Dalton-in-
Furness 92 B2
Dalton-le-Dale 111 E7
Dalton-on-Tees . . . 101 D7
Dalton Piercy 111 F7
Dalveich 126 B5
Dalvina Lodge 157 E9
Dalwood 11 D7
Dalwyne 112 E3
Damerham 14 C2
Damgate 69 D7
Dam Green 68 F3
Damnaglaur 104 F5
Damside 120 E4
Dam Side 92 E4
Danaway 30 C2
Danbury 42 D3
Danby 103 D5
Danby Wiske 101 E8
Dandaleith 152 D2
Danderhall 121 C6
Danebridge 75 C6
Dane End 41 B6
Danehill 17 B8
Danemoor Green . . 68 D3
Danesford 61 E7
Daneshill 26 D4
Dangerous
Corner 86 C3
Danskine 121 C8
Darcy Lever 86 D5
Darenth 29 B6
Daresbury 86 F3
Darfield 88 D5
Darfoulds 77 B5
Dargate 30 C4
Darite 5 C7
Darlaston 62 E3
Darley 94 D5
Darley Bridge 76 C2
Darley Head 94 D4
Darlingscott 51 E7
Darliston 74 F2
Darlton 77 B7
Darnall 88 F4
Darnick 121 F8
Darowen 58 D5
Darra 153 D7
Darracott 20 F3
Darras Hall 110 B4
Darrington 89 B5
Darsham 57 C8
Dartford 29 B6
Dartford Crossing . . 29 B6
Dartington 7 C5
Dartmeet 6 B4
Dartmouth 7 D6
Darton 88 D4
Darvel 119 F5
Darwell Hole 18 D3
Darwen 86 B4
Datchet 27 B7
Datchworth 41 C5
Datchworth Green . . 41 C5
Daubhill 86 D5
Daugh of
Kinermony 152 D2
Dauntsey 37 F6
Dava 151 H13
Davenham 74 B3
Davenport Green . . 74 B5
Daventry 52 C3
Davidson's Mains . . 120 B5
Davidstow 8 F3
David's Well 48 B2
Davington 115 D5
Daviot Aberds 141 B6
Highld 151 H10
Davoch of
Grange 152 C4
Davyhulme 87 E5
Dawley 61 D6
Dawlish 7 B7
Dawlish Warren 7 B7
Dawn 83 D8
Daws Heath 42 F4
Daw's House Corn . . . 8 F5
Corn 8 F5
Dawsmere 79 F7
Dayhills 75 F6
Daylesford 38 B2
Ddôl-Cownwy 59 C7
Ddrydwy 82 D3
Deadwater 116 E2
Deaf Hill 111 F6
Deal 31 D7
Deal Hall 43 E6
Dean Cumb 98 B2
Devon 6 C5
Devon 20 E4
Dorset 13 C7
Hants 15 C6
Som 23 E8
Deanburnhaugh . . . 115 C6
Deane Gtr Man 86 D4
Hants 26 D3
Deanich Lodge 150 C6
Deanland 13 C7
Deans 120 C3
Deanscales 98 B2
Deanshanger 53 F5
Deanston 127 D6
Dearham 107 F7

Debach 57 D6
Debden Essex 41 E7
Essex 55 F6
Debden Cross 55 F6
Debenham 57 C5
Deddington 52 F2
Dedham 56 F4
Dedham Heath 56 F4
Deebank 141 E5
Deene 65 E6
Deenethorpe 65 E6
Deepcar 88 E3
Deepcut 27 D7
Deepdale 100 F2
Deeping Gate 65 D8
Deeping St James . . 65 D8
Deeping
St Nicholas 66 C2
Deerhill 152 C4
Deerhurst 37 B5
Deerness 159 H6
Defford 50 E4
Defynnog 34 B3
Deganwy 83 D7
Deighton N Yorks . . 102 D1
W Yorks 88 C2
York 96 E2
Deiniolen 83 E5
Delabole 8 F2
Delamere 74 C2
Delfrigs 141 B8
Delliefure 151 H13
Dell Lodge 139 C6
Delnabo 139 C7
Delnadamph 139 D8
Delph 87 D7
Delves 110 E4
Delvine 133 E8
Dembleby 78 F3
Denaby Main 89 E5
Denbigh
= Dinbych 72 C4
Denbury 7 C6
Denby 76 E3
Denby Dale 88 D3
Denchworth 38 E3
Dendron 92 B2
Denel End 53 F8
Denend 152 E6
Denford 53 B7
Dengie 43 D5
Denham Bucks 40 F3
Suff 55 C8
Suff 57 B5
Denham Street 57 B5
Denhead Aberds . . . 153 C9
Fife 129 C6
Denhead of
Arbilot 135 E5
Denhead of Gray . . 134 F3
Denholm 115 C8
Denholme 94 F3
Denholme Clough . . 94 F3
Denio 70 D4
Denmead 15 C7
Denmore 141 C8
Denmoss 153 D6
Dennington 57 C6
Denny 127 F7
Dennyloanhead . . . 127 F7
Denny Lodge 14 D4
Denshaw 87 C7
Denside 141 E7
Densole 31 E6
Denston 55 D8
Denstone 75 E8
Dent 100 F2
Denton Cambs 65 F8
Darl 101 C7
E Sus 17 D8
Gtr Man 87 E7
Kent 31 E6
Lincs 77 F8
Norf 69 F5
N Yorks 94 E4
Oxon 39 D5
W Nhants 53 D6
Denton's Green 86 E2
Denver 67 D6
Denwick 117 C8
Deopham 68 D3
Deopham Green . . . 68 E3
Depden 55 D8
Depden Green 55 D8
Deptford London . . 28 B4
Wilts 24 F5
Derby 76 F3
Derbyhaven 84 F2
Dereham 68 C2
Deri 35 D5
Derril 8 D5
Derringstone 31 E6
Derrington 62 B2
Derriton 8 D5
Derry Hill 24 B4
Derrythorpe 90 D2
Dersingham 80 D2
Dervaig 146 F7
Derwen 72 D4
Derwenlas 58 E4
Desborough 64 F5
Desford 63 D8
Detchant 123 F6
Detling 29 D8
Deuddwr 60 C2
Devauden 36 E1
Devil's Bridge 47 B6
Devizes 24 C5
Devol 118 B3
Devonport 6 D2
Devonside 127 E8
Devoran 3 C6
Dewar 121 E6
Dewlish 13 E5
Dewsbury 88 B3
Dewsbury Moor . . . 88 B3
Dewshall Court 49 F6
Dhoon 84 D4
Dhoor 84 C4
Dhowin 84 B4
Dial Post 17 C5
Dibden 14 D5
Dibden Purlieu 14 D5
Dickleburgh 68 F4
Didbrook 51 F5
Didcot 39 F5
Diddington 54 C2

Diddlebury 60 F5
Didley 49 F6
Didling 16 C2
Didmarton 37 F5
Didsbury 87 E6
Didworthy 6 C4
Digby 78 D3
Digg 149 B9
Diggle 87 D8
Digmoor 86 D2
Digswell Park 41 C5
Dihewyd 46 D3
Dilham 69 B6
Dilhorne 75 E6
Dillarburn 119 E8
Dillington 54 C2
Dilston 110 C2
Dilton Marsh 24 E3
Dilwyn 49 D6
Dinas Carms 45 F4
Gwyn 70 D3
Dinas Cross 45 F2
Dinas Dinlle 82 F4
Dinas-Mawddwy . . 59 C5
Dinas Powys 22 B3
Dinbych
= Denbigh 72 C4
Dinbych-y-Pysgod
= Tenby 32 D2
Dinder 23 E7
Dinedor 49 F7
Dingestow 36 C1
Dingle 85 F4
Dingleden 18 B5
Dingley 64 F4
Dingwall 151 F8
Dinlabyre 115 E8
Dinmael 72 E4
Dinnet 140 E3
Dinnington Som . . . 12 C2
S Yorks 89 F6
T&W 110 B5
Dinorwic 83 E5
Dinton Bucks 39 C7
Wilts 24 F5
Dinwoodie
Mains 114 E4
Dinworthy 8 C5
Dippen 143 F11
Dippenhall 27 E6
Dipple Moray 152 C3
S Ayrs 112 D2
Diptford 6 D5
Dipton 110 D4
Dirdhu 139 B6
Dirleton 129 F7
Dirt Pot 109 E8
Discoed 48 C4
Diseworth 63 B8
Dishes 159 F7
Dishforth 95 B6
Disley 87 F7
Diss 56 B5
Disserth 48 D2
Distington 98 B2
Ditchampton 25 F5
Ditcheat 23 F8
Ditchingham 69 E6
Ditchling 17 C7
Ditherington 60 C5
Dittisham 7 D6
Ditton Halton 86 F2
Kent 29 D8
Ditton Green 55 D7
Ditton Priors 61 F6
Divach 137 B7
Divlyn 47 F6
Dixton Glos 50 F4
Mon 36 C2
Dobcross 87 D7
Dobwalls 5 C7
Doccombe 10 F2
Dochfour House . . . 151 H8
Dochgarroch 151 G9
Docking 80 D3
Docklow 49 D7
Dockray 99 B5
Dockroyd 94 F3
Doc Penfro
= Pembroke Dock . . 44 E4
Dodburn 115 D7
Doddinghurst 42 E1
Doddington Cambs . . 66 E3
Kent 30 D3
Lincs 78 B2
Northumb 123 F5
Shrops 49 B8
Doddiscombsleigh . . 10 F3
Dodford W Nhants . . 52 C4
Worcs 50 B4
Dodington 24 A2
Dodleston 73 C7
Dods Leigh 75 F7
Dodworth 88 D4
Doe Green 86 F3
Doe Lea 76 C4
Dogdyke 78 D5
Dogmersfield 27 D5
Dogridge 37 F7
Dogsthorpe 65 D8
Dog Village 10 E4
Dolanog 59 C7
Dolau Powys 48 C3
Rhondda 34 F3
Dolbenmaen 71 C6
Dolfach 59 D6
Dolfor 59 F8
Dol-fôr 58 D5
Dolgarrog 83 E7
Dolgellau 58 C4
Dolgran 46 F3
Dolhendre 72 F2
Doll 157 J11
Dollar 127 E8
Dolley Green 48 C4
Dollwen 58 F3
Dolphin 73 B5
Dolphinholme 92 D5
Dolphinton 120 E4
Dolton 9 C7
Dolwen Conwy 83 D8
Powys 59 D6
Dolwyd 83 D8
Dolwyddelan 83 F7
Dôl-y-Bont 58 F3
Dol-y-cannau 48 E4
Dolyhir 48 D4
Doncaster 89 D6
Dones Green 74 B3

Donhead
St Andrew 13 B7
Donhead St Mary . . 13 B7
Donibristle 128 F3
Donington 78 F5
Donington on Bain . . 91 F6
Donington
South Ing 78 F5
Donington 63 C7
Donkey Town 27 C7
Donnington Glos . . . 38 B1
Hereford 50 F2
Shrops 61 D5
Telford 61 C7
W Berks 26 C2
W Sus 16 D2
Donnington Wood . . 61 C7
Donyatt 11 C8
Doonfoot 112 C3
Dorback Lodge . . . 139 C6
Dorchester Dorset . . 12 E4
Oxon 39 E5
Dordon 63 D6
Dore 88 F4
Dores 151 H8
Dorking 28 E2
Dormansland 28 E5
Dormanstown 102 B3
Dormington 49 E7
Dormston 50 D4
Dornal 105 B6
Dorney 27 B7
Dornie 149 F13
Dornoch 151 C10
Dornock 108 C2
Dorrery 158 E2
Dorridge 51 B6
Dorrington Lincs . . . 78 D3
Shrops 60 D4
Dorsington 51 E6
Dorstone 48 E5
Dorton 39 C6
Dorusduain 136 B2
Dosthill 63 E6
Dottery 12 E2
Doublebois 5 C6
Dougarie 143 E9
Doughton 37 E5
Douglas IoM 84 E3
S Lanark 119 F8
Douglas & Angus . . 134 F4
Douglastown 134 E4
Douglas Water 119 F8
Douglas West 119 F8
Doulting 23 E8
Dounby 159 F3
Doune Highld 156 J7
Stirling 127 D6
Doune Park 153 B7
Douneside 140 D3
Dounie 151 B8
Dounreay 157 C12
Dousland 6 C3
Dovaston 60 B3
Dove Holes 75 B7
Dovenby 107 F7
Dover 31 E7
Dovercourt 57 F6
Doverdale 50 C3
Doveridge 75 F8
Doversgreen 28 E3
Dowally 133 E7
Dowbridge 92 F4
Dowdeswell 37 C6
Dowlais 34 D4
Dowland 9 C7
Dowlish Wake 11 C8
Down Ampney 37 E8
Downcraig
Ferry 145 H10
Downderry 5 D8
Downe 28 C5
Downend IoW 15 F6
S Glos 23 B8
W Berks 26 B2
Downfield 134 F3
Downgate 5 B8
Downham Essex . . . 42 E3
Lancs 93 E7
Northumb 122 F4
Downham Market . . 67 D6
Down Hatherley . . . 37 B5
Downhead 23 E8
Downhill Perth 133 F7
T&W 111 D6
Downholland
Cross 85 D4
Downholme 101 E6
Downies 141 E8
Downley 39 E8
Down St Mary 10 D2
Downside Som 23 E8
Sur 28 D2
Down Thomas 6 D3
Downton Hants 14 E3
Wilts 14 B2
Downton on the
Rock 49 B6
Dowsby 65 B8
Dowsdale 66 C2
Dowthwaitehead . . 99 B5
Doxey 62 B3
Doxford 117 B7
Doxford Park 111 D6
Doynton 24 B2
Draffan 119 E7
Dragonby 90 C3
Drakelow 62 F2
Drakemyre 118 D2
Drake's Broughton . . 50 E4
Drakes Cross 51 B5
Drakewalls 6 B2
Draughton N Yorks . . 94 D3
W Nhants 53 B5
Drax 89 B7
Draycote 52 B2
Draycott Derbys . . . 76 F4
Glos 51 F6
Som 23 D6
Draycott in
the Clay 63 B5
Draycott in the
Moors 75 E6
Drayford 10 C2
Drayton Leics 64 E5
Lincs 78 F5

Drayton *continued*
Norf 68 C4
Oxon 38 E4
Oxon 52 E2
Ptsmth 15 D7
Som 12 B2
Worcs 50 B4
Drayton Bassett 63 D5
Drayton Beauchamp 40 C2
Drayton Parslow 39 B8
Drayton St Leonard 39 E5
Drebley 94 D3
Dreemskerry 84 C4
Dreenhill 44 D4
Drefach Carms 33 C6
Carms 46 F2
Dre-fach Carms 33 C7
Ceredig 46 E4
Drefelin 46 F2
Dreghorn 118 F3
Drellingore 31 E6
Drem 121 B8
Dresden 75 E6
Dreumasdal 148 E2
Drewsteignton 10 E2
Driby 79 B6
Driffield E Yorks 97 D6
Glos 37 E7
Drigg 98 E2
Drighlington 88 B3
Drimnin 147 F8
Drimpton 12 D2
Drimsynie 125 E7
Drinisiadar 154 H6
Drinkstone 56 C3
Drinkstone Green 56 C3
Drishaig 125 D7
Drissaig 124 D5
Drochil 120 E4
Drointon 62 B4
Droitwich Spa 50 C3
Droman 156 D4
Dron 128 C3
Dronfield 76 B3
Dronfield Woodhouse 76 B3
Drongan 112 C4
Dronley 134 F3
Droxford 15 C7
Droylsden 87 E7
Druid 72 E4
Druidston 44 D3
Druimarbin 130 B4
Druimavuic 130 E4
Druimdrishaig 144 F6
Druimindarroch 147 C9
Druimyeon More 143 C7
Drum Argyll 145 F8
Perth 128 D2
Drumbeg 156 F4
Drumblade 152 D5
Drumblair 153 D6
Drumbuie
Dumfries 113 F5
Highld 149 E12
Drumburgh 108 D2
Drumburn 107 C6
Drumchapel 118 B5
Drumchardine 151 G8
Drumchork 155 J13
Drumclog 119 F6
Drumderfit 151 F9
Drumeldrie 129 D6
Drumelzier 120 F4
Drumfearn 149 G11
Drumgask 138 E2
Drumgley 134 D4
Drumguish 138 E3
Drumin 152 E1
Drumlasie 140 D5
Drumlemble 143 G7
Drumligair 141 C8
Drumlithie 141 F6
Drummoddie 105 E7
Drummond 151 E9
Drummore 104 F5
Drummuir 152 D3
Drummuir Castle 152 D3
Drumnadrochit 137 B8
Drumnagorrach 152 C5
Drumoak 141 E6
Drumpark 107 A5
Drumphail 105 C6
Drumrash 106 B3
Drumrunie 156 J4
Drums 141 B8
Drumsallie 130 B3
Drumstinchall 107 D5
Drumsturdy 134 F4
Drumtochty Castle 135 B6
Drumtroddan 105 E7
Drumuie 149 D9
Drumuillie 138 B5
Drumvaich 127 D5
Drumwhindle 153 E9
Drunkendub 135 E6
Drury 73 C6
Drury Square 68 C2
Drybeck 100 C1
Drybridge Moray 152 B4
N Ayrs 118 F3
Drybrook 36 C3
Dryburgh 121 F8
Dry Doddington 77 E8
Dry Drayton 54 C4
Dryhope 115 B5
Drylaw 120 B5
Drym 2 C5
Drymen 126 F3
Drymuir 153 D9
Drynoch 149 E9
Dryslwyn 33 B6
Dryton 61 D5
Dubford 153 B8
Dubton 135 D5
Duchally 156 H6
Duchlage 126 F2
Duck Corner 57 E7
Duckington 73 D8
Ducklington 38 D3
Duckmanton 76 B4
Duck's Cross 54 D2
Duddenhoe End 55 F5
Duddingston 121 B5
Duddington 65 D6
Duddleswell 17 B8
Duddo 122 E5
Duddon 74 C2
Duddon Bridge 98 F4
Dudleston 73 F7
Dudleston Heath 73 F7
Dudley T&W 111 B5
W Mid 62 E3
Dudley Port 62 E3
Duffield 76 E3
Duffryn Neath 34 E2
Newport 35 F6
Dufftown 152 E3
Duffus 152 B1
Dufton 100 B1
Duggleby 96 C4
Duirinish 149 E12
Duisdalemore 149 G12
Duisky 130 B4
Dukestown 35 C5
Dukinfield 87 E7
Dulas 82 C4
Dulcote 23 E7
Dulford 11 D5
Dull 133 E5
Dullatur 119 B7
Dullingham 55 D7
Dulnain Bridge 139 B5
Duloe Bedford 54 C2
Corn 5 D7
Dulsie 151 G12
Dulverton 10 B4
Dulwich 28 B4
Dumbarton 118 B3
Dumbleton 50 F5
Dumcrieff 114 D4
Dumfries 107 B6
Dumgoyne 126 F4
Dummer 26 E3
Dumpford 16 B2
Dumpton 31 C7
Dun 135 D6
Dunain House 151 G9
Dunalastair 132 D4
Dunan 149 F10
Dunans 145 D9
Dunball 22 E5
Dunbar 122 B2
Dunbeath 158 H3
Dunbeg 124 B4
Dunblane 127 D6
Dunbog 128 C4
Duncanston 151 F8
Duncanstone 140 B4
Dun Charlabhaigh 154 C6
Dunchurch 52 B2
Duncote 52 D4
Duncow 114 F2
Duncraggan 126 D4
Duncrievie 128 D3
Duncton 16 C3
Dundas House 159 K5
Dundee 134 F4
Dundeugh 113 F5
Dundon 23 F6
Dundonald 118 F3
Dundonnell 150 C3
Dundonnell Hotel 150 C3
Dundonnell House 150 C4
Dundraw 108 E2
Dundreggan 137 C6
Dundreggan Lodge 137 C6
Dundrennan 106 E4
Dundry 23 C7
Dunecht 141 D6
Dunfermline 128 F2
Dunfield 37 E8
Dunford Bridge 88 D2
Dungworth 88 F3
Dunham 77 B8
Dunham-on-the-Hill 73 B8
Dunhampton 50 C3
Dunham Town 86 F5
Dunholme 78 B3
Dunino 129 C7
Dunipace 127 F7
Dunira 127 B6
Dunkeld 133 E7
Dunkerton 24 D2
Dunkeswell 11 D6
Dunkeswick 95 E6
Dunkirk Kent 30 D4
Norf 81 E8
Dunk's Green 29 D7
Dunlappie 135 C5
Dunley Hants 26 D2
Worcs 50 C2
Dunlichity Lodge 151 H9
Dunlop 118 E4
Dunmaglass Lodge 137 B8
Dunmore Argyll 144 G6
Falk 127 F7
Dunnet 158 C4
Dunnichen 135 E5
Dunninald 135 D7
Dunning 128 C2
Dunnington E Yorks 97 D7
Warks 51 D5
York 96 D2
Dunnockshaw 87 B6
Dunollie 124 B4
Dunoon 145 F10
Dunragit 105 D5
Dunrostan 144 E6
Duns 122 D3
Dunsby 65 B8
Dunscore 113 F8
Dunscroft 89 D7
Dunsdale 102 C4
Dunsden Green 26 B5
Dunsfold 27 F8
Dunsford 10 F3
Dunshalt 128 C4
Dunshillock 153 D9
Dunskey House 104 D4
Dunsley 103 C6
Dunsmore 40 D1
Dunsop Bridge 93 D6
Dunstable 40 B3
Dunstall 63 B5
Dunstall Common 50 E3
Dunstall Green 55 C8
Dunstan 117 C8
Dunstan Steads 117 B8
Dunster 21 E8
Duns Tew 38 B4
Dunston Lincs 78 C3
Norf 68 D5
Staffs 62 C3
T&W 110 C5
Dunsville 89 D7
Dunswell 97 F6
Dunsyre 120 E3
Dunterton 5 B8
Duntisbourne Abbots 37 D6
Duntisbourne Leer 37 D6
Duntisbourne Rouse 37 D6
Duntish 12 D4
Duntocher 118 B4
Dunton Bucks 39 B8
C Beds 54 E3
Norf 80 D4
Dunton Bassett 64 E2
Dunton Green 29 D6
Dunton Wayletts 42 E2
Duntulm 149 A9
Dunure 112 C2
Dunvant 33 E6
Dunvegan 148 D7
Dunwich 57 B8
Dunwood 75 D6
Dupplin Castle 128 C2
Durdar 108 D4
Durgates 18 B3
Durham 111 E5
Durisdeer 113 D8
Durisdeermill 113 D8
Durkar 88 C4
Durleigh 22 F4
Durley Hants 15 C6
Wilts 25 C7
Durnamuck 150 B3
Durness 156 C7
Durno 141 B6
Duror 130 D3
Durran Argyll 125 E5
Highld 158 D3
Durrington Wilts 25 E6
W Sus 16 D5
Dursley 36 E4
Durston 11 B7
Durweston 13 D6
Dury 160 G6
Duston 52 C5
Duthil 138 B5
Dutlas 48 B4
Duton Hill 42 B2
Dutson 8 F5
Dutton 74 B2
Duxford Cambs 55 E5
Oxon 38 E3
Dwygyfylchi 83 D7
Dwyran 82 E4
Dyce 141 C7
Dye House 110 D2
Dyffryn Bridgend 34 E2
Carms 32 B4
Pembs 44 B4
Dyffryn Ardudwy 71 E6
Dyffryn Castell 58 F4
Dyffryn Ceidrych 33 B8
Dyffryn Cellwen 34 D2
Dyke Lincs 65 B8
Moray 151 F12
Dykehead Angus 134 C3
N Lanark 119 D8
Stirling 126 E4
Dykelands 135 C7
Dykends 134 D2
Dykeside 153 D7
Dykesmains 118 E2
Dylife 59 E5
Dymchurch 19 C7
Dymock 50 F2
Dyrham 24 B2
Dysart 128 E5
Dyserth 72 B4

E

Eadar Dha Fhadhail 154 D5
Eagland Hill 92 E4
Eagle 77 C8
Eagle Barnsdale 77 C8
Eagle Moor 77 C8
Eaglescliffe 102 C2
Eaglesfield Cumb 98 B2
Dumfries 108 B2
Eaglesham 119 D5
Eaglethorpe 65 E7
Eairy 84 E2
Eakley Lanes 53 D6
Eakring 77 C6
Ealand 89 C8
Ealing 40 F4
Eals 109 D6
Eamont Bridge 99 B7
Earby 94 E2
Earcroft 86 B4
Eardington 61 E7
Eardisland 49 D6
Eardisley 48 E5
Eardiston Shrops 60 B3
Worcs 49 C8
Earith 54 B4
Earle 117 B5
Earley 27 B5
Earlham 68 D5
Earlish 149 B8
Earls Barton 53 C6
Earls Colne 42 B4
Earl's Croome 50 E3
Earlsdon 51 B8
Earlsferry 129 E6
Earlsfield 78 F2
Earlsford 153 E8
Earl's Green 56 C4
Earlsheaton 88 B3
Earl Shilton 63 E8
Earlsmill 151 F12
Earl Soham 57 C6
Earl Sterndale 75 C7
Earlston Borders 121 F8
E Ayrs 118 F4
Earl Stonham 56 D5
Earlswood Mon 36 E1
Earlswood *continued*
Sur 28 E3
Warks 51 B6
Earnley 16 E2
Earsairidh 148 J2
Earsdon 111 B6
Earsham 69 F6
Earswick 96 D2
Eartham 16 D3
Easby N Yorks 101 D6
N Yorks 102 D3
Easdale 124 D3
Easebourne 16 B2
Easenhall 52 B2
Eashing 27 E7
Easington Bucks 39 C6
Durham 111 E7
E Yorks 91 C7
Northumb 123 F7
Oxon 39 E6
Oxon 52 F2
Redcar 103 C5
Easington Colliery 111 E7
Easington Lane 111 E6
Easingwold 95 C8
Easole Street 31 D6
Eassie 134 E3
East Aberthaw 22 C2
East Adderbury 52 F2
East Allington 7 E5
East Anstey 10 B3
East Appleton 101 E7
East Ardsley 88 B4
East Ashling 16 D2
East Auchronie 141 D7
East Ayton 103 F7
East Bank 35 D6
East Barkwith 91 F5
East Barming 29 D8
East Barnby 103 C6
East Barnet 41 E5
East Barns 122 B3
East Barsham 80 D5
East Beckham 81 D7
East Bedfont 27 B8
East Bergholt 56 F4
East Bilney 68 C2
East Blatchington 17 D8
East Boldre 14 D4
Eastbourne 18 F3
East Brent 22 D5
Eastbridge 57 C8
East Bridgford 77 E6
East Buckland 21 F5
East Budleigh 11 F5
Eastburn 94 E3
East Burrafirth 160 H5
East Burton 13 F6
Eastbury London 40 E3
W Berks 25 B8
East Butsfield 110 E4
East Butterwick 90 D2
Eastby 94 D3
East Cairnbeg 135 B7
East Calder 120 C3
East Carleton 68 D4
East Carlton N Nhants 64 F5
W Yorks 94 E5
East Chaldon 13 F5
East Challow 38 F3
East Chiltington 17 C7
East Chinnock 12 C2
East Chisenbury 25 D6
Eastchurch 30 B3
East Clandon 27 D8
East Claydon 39 B7
East Clyne 157 J12
East Coker 12 C3
Eastcombe 37 D5
East Combe 22 F3
East Common 96 F2
East Compton 23 E8
Eastcote London 40 F4
W Mid 51 B6
W Nhants 52 D4
Eastcott Corn 8 C4
Wilts 24 D5
East Cottingwith 96 E3
Eastcourt Wilts 25 C7
Wilts 37 E6
East Cowes 15 E6
East Cowick 89 B7
East Cowton 101 D8
East Cramlington 111 B5
East Cranmore 23 E8
East Creech 13 F7
East Croachy 138 B2
East Croftmore 139 C5
East Curthwaite 108 E3
East Dean E Sus 18 F2
Hants 14 B3
W Sus 16 C3
East Down 20 E5
East Drayton 77 B7
East Ella 90 B4
East End Dorset 13 E7
E Yorks 91 B6
Hants 14 E4
Hants 15 B7
Hants 26 C2
Herts 41 B7
Kent 18 B5
N Som 23 B6
Oxon 38 C3
Easter Ardross 151 D9
Easter Balmoral 139 E8
Easter Boleskine 137 B8
Easter Compton 36 F2
Easter Cringate 127 F6
Easter Davoch 140 D3
Easter Earshaig 114 D3
Easter Fearn 151 C9
Easter Galcantray 151 G11
Eastergate 16 D3
Easterhouse 119 C6
Easter Howgate 120 C5
Easter Howlaws 122 E3
Easter Kinkell 151 F8
Easter Lednathie 134 C3
Easter Milton 151 F12
Easter Moniack 151 G8
Eastern Green 63 F6
Easter Ord 141 D7
Easter Quarff 160 K6
Easter Rhynd 128 C3
Easter Row 127 E6
Easter Silverford 153 B7
Easter Skeld 160 J5
Easterton 24 D5
Eastertown 22 D5
Eastertown of Auchleuchries 153 E10
Easter Whyntie 152 B6
East Farleigh 29 D8
East Farndon 64 F4
East Ferry 90 E2
Eastfield N Lanark 119 C8
N Yorks 103 F8
Eastfield Hall 117 D8
East Fortune 121 B8
East Garston 25 B8
Eastgate Durham 110 F2
Norf 81 E7
East Ginge 38 F4
East Goscote 64 C3
East Grafton 25 C7
East Grimstead 14 B3
East Grinstead 28 F4
East Guldeford 19 C6
East Haddon 52 C4
East Hagbourne 39 F5
East Halton 90 C5
Eastham 85 F4
East Ham 41 F7
Eastham Ferry 85 F4
Easthampstead 27 C6
East Hanney 38 E4
East Hanningfield 42 D3
East Hardwick 89 C5
East Harling 68 F2
East Harlsey 102 E2
East Harnham 14 B2
East Harptree 23 D7
East Hartford 111 B5
East Harting 15 C8
East Hatley 54 D3
East Hauxwell 101 E6
East Haven 135 F5
Eastheath 27 C6
East Heckington 78 E4
East Hedleyhope 110 E4
East Hendred 38 F4
East Herrington 111 D6
East Heslerton 96 B5
East Hoathly 18 D2
Easthope 61 E5
Easthorpe Essex 43 B5
Leics 77 F8
Notts 77 D7
East Horrington 23 E7
East Horsley 27 D8
East Horton 123 F6
Easthouses 121 C6
East Huntspill 22 E5
East Hyde 40 C4
East Ilkerton 21 E6
East Ilsley 38 F4
Eastington Devon 10 D2
Glos 36 D4
Glos 37 C8
East Keal 79 C6
East Kennett 25 C6
East Keswick 95 E6
East Kilbride 119 D6
East Kirkby 79 C6
East Knapton 96 B4
East Knighton 13 F6
East Knoyle 24 F3
East Kyloe 123 F6
East Lambrook 12 C2
East Lamington 151 D10
East Langdon 31 E7
East Langton 64 E4
East Langwell 157 J10
East Lavant 16 D2
East Lavington 16 C3
East Layton 101 D6
Eastleach Martin 38 D2
Eastleach Turville 38 D1
East Leake 64 B2
East Learmouth 122 F4
Eastleigh Devon 9 B6
Hants 14 C5
East Leigh 9 D8
East Lexham 67 C8
East Lilburn 117 B6
Eastling 30 D3
East Linton 121 B8
East Liss 15 B8
East Looe 5 D7
East Lound 89 E8
East Lulworth 13 F6
East Lutton 96 C5
East Lydford 23 F7
East Mains 141 E5
East Malling 29 D8
East March 134 F4
East Marden 16 C2
East Markham 77 B7
East Marton 94 D2
East Meon 15 B7
East Mere 10 C4
East Mersea 43 C6
East Mey 158 C5
East Molesey 28 C2
Eastmoor Derbys 76 B3
Norf 67 D7
East Morden 13 E7
East Morton 94 E3
East Ness 96 B2
East Newton 97 F8
Eastney 15 E7
Eastnor 50 F2
East Norton 64 D4
East Nynehead 11 B6
East Oakley 26 D3
Eastoft 90 C2
East Ogwell 7 B6
Eastoke 15 E8
Easton Cambs 54 B2
Cumb 108 B4
Cumb 108 D2
Devon 10 F2
Dorset 12 G4
Hants 26 F3
Lincs 65 B6
Norf 68 C4
Som 23 E7
Suff 57 D6
Wilts 24 B3
Easton Grey 37 F5
Easton-in-Gordano 23 B7
Easton Maudit 53 D6
Easton on the Hill 65 D7
Easton Royal 25 C7
East Orchard 13 C6
East Ord 123 D5
East Panson 9 E5
Eastpark 107 C7
East Peckham 29 E7
East Pennard 23 F7
East Perry 54 C2
East Portlemouth 6 F5
East Prawle 7 F5
East Preston 16 D4
East Putford 9 C5
East Quantoxhead 22 E3
East Rainton 111 E6
East Ravendale 91 E6
East Raynham 80 E4
Eastrea 66 E2
East Rhidorroch Lodge 150 B5
Eastriggs 108 C2
East Rigton 95 E6
Eastrington 89 B8
East Rounton 102 D2
East Row 103 C6
East Rudham 80 E4
East Runton 81 C7
East Ruston 69 B6
Eastry 31 D7
East Saltoun 121 C7
East Sleekburn 117 F8
East Somerton 69 C7
East Stockwith 89 E8
East Stoke Dorset 13 F6
Notts 77 E7
East Stour 13 B6
East Stourmouth 31 C6
East Stowford 9 B8
East Stratton 26 F3
East Studdal 31 E7
East Suisnish 149 E10
East Taphouse 5 C6
East-the-Water 9 B6
East Thirston 117 E7
East Tilbury 29 B7
East Tisted 26 F5
East Torrington 90 F5
East Tuddenham 68 C3
East Tytherley 14 B3
East Tytherton 24 B4
East Village 10 D3
Eastville Bristol 23 B8
Lincs 79 D7
East Wall 60 E5
East Walton 67 C7
Eastwell 64 B4
East Wellow 14 B4
East Wemyss 128 E5
East Whitburn 120 C2
Eastwick Herts 41 C7
Shetland 160 F5
East Williamston 32 D1
East Winch 67 C6
East Winterslow 25 F7
East Wittering 15 E8
East Witton 101 F6
Eastwood Notts 76 E4
Southend 42 F4
W Yorks 87 B7
East Woodburn 116 F5
East Woodhay 26 C2
East Worldham 26 F5
East Worlington 10 C2
East Worthing 17 D5
Eathorpe 51 C8
Eaton Ches E 75 C5
Ches W 74 C2
Leics 64 B4
Norf 68 D5
Notts 77 B7
Oxon 38 D4
Shrops 60 F3
Shrops 60 F5
Eaton Bishop 49 F6
Eaton Bray 40 B2
Eaton Constantine 61 D5
Eaton Green 40 B2
Eaton Hastings 38 E2
Eaton on Tern 61 B6
Eaton Socon 54 D2
Eavestone 94 C5
Ebberston 103 F6
Ebbesbourne Wake 13 B7
Ebbw Vale = Glyn Ebwy 35 D5
Ebchester 110 D4
Ebford 10 F4
Ebley 37 D5
Ebnal 73 E8
Ebrington 51 E6
Ecchinswell 26 D2
Ecclaw 122 C3
Ecclefechan 107 B8
Eccles Borders 122 E3
Gtr Man 87 E5
Kent 29 C8
Ecclesall 88 F4
Ecclesfield 88 E4
Ecclesgreig 135 C7
Eccleshall 62 B2
Eccleshill 94 F4
Ecclesmachan 120 B3
Eccles on Sea 69 B7
Eccles Road 68 E3
Eccleston Ches W 73 C8
Lancs 86 C3
Mers 86 E2
Eccleston Park 86 E2
Eccup 95 E5
Echt 141 D6
Eckford 116 B3
Eckington Derbys 76 B4
Worcs 50 E4
Ecton 53 C6
Edale 88 F2
Edburton 17 C6
Edderside 107 E7
Edderton 151 C10
Eddistone 8 B4
Eddleston 120 E5
Edenbridge 28 E5
Edenfield 87 C5
Edenhall 109 F5
Edenham 65 B7
Eden Park 28 C4
Edensor 76 C2
Edentaggart 126 E2
Edenthorpe 89 D7
Edentown 108 D3
Ederline 124 E4
Edern 70 D3
Edgarley 23 F7
Edgbaston 62 F4
Edgcott Bucks 39 B6
Som 21 F7
Edge 60 D3
Edgebolton 61 B5
Edge End 36 C2
Edgefield 81 D6
Edgefield Street 81 D6
Edge Green 73 D8
Edge Hill 85 F4
Edgeside 87 B6
Edgeworth 37 D6
Edgmond 61 C7
Edgmond Marsh 61 B7
Edgton 60 F3
Edgware 40 E4
Edgworth 86 C5
Edinample 126 B4
Edinbane 149 C8
Edinburgh 121 B5
Edingale 63 C6
Edingight House 152 C5
Edingley 77 D6
Edingthorpe 69 A6
Edingthorpe Green 69 A6
Edington Som 23 F5
Wilts 24 D4
Edintore 152 D4
Edithmead 22 E5
Edith Weston 65 D6
Edlesborough 40 C2
Edlingham 117 D7
Edlington 78 B5
Edmondsham 13 C8
Edmondsley 110 E5
Edmondthorpe 65 C5
Edmonstone 159 F6
Edmonton 41 E6
Edmundbyers 110 D3
Ednam 122 F3
Ednaston 76 E2
Edradynate 133 D5
Edrom 122 D4
Edstaston 74 F2
Edstone 51 C6
Edvin Loach 49 D8
Edwalton 77 F5
Edwardstone 56 E3
Edwinsford 46 F5
Edwinstowe 77 C6
Edworth 54 E3
Edwyn Ralph 49 D8
Edzell 135 C5
E Eachwick 110 B4
Efail Isaf 34 F4
Efailnewydd 70 D4
Efailwen 32 B2
Efenechtyd 72 D5
Effingham 28 D2
Effirth 160 H5
Efford 10 D3
Egdon 50 D4
Egerton Gtr Man 86 C5
Kent 30 E3
Egerton Forstal 30 E2
Eggborough 89 B6
Eggbuckland 6 D3
Eggington 40 B2
Egginton 63 B6
Egglescliffe 102 C2
Eggleston 100 B4
Egham 27 B8
Egleton 65 D5
Eglingham 117 C7
Egloshayle 4 B5
Egloskerry 8 F4
Eglwysbach 83 D8
Eglwys-Brewis 22 C2
Eglwys Cross 73 E8
Eglwys Fach 58 E3
Eglwyswen 45 F3
Eglwyswrw 45 F3
Egmanton 77 C7
Egremont Cumb 98 C2
Mers 85 E4
Egton 103 D6
Egton Bridge 103 D6
Eight Ash Green 43 B5
Eignaig 130 E1
Eil 138 C4
Eilanreach 149 G13
Eileanach Lodge 151 E8
Eilean Darach 150 C4
Einacleite 154 E6
Eisgean 155 F8
Eisingrug 71 D7
Elan Village 47 C8
Elberton 36 F3
Elburton 6 D3
Elcho 128 B3
Elcombe 37 F8
Eldernell 66 E3
Eldersfield 50 F3
Elderslie 118 C4
Eldon 101 B7
Eldrick 112 F2
Eldroth 93 C7
Eldwick 94 E4
Elfhowe 99 E6
Elford Northumb 123 F7
Staffs 63 C5
Elgin 152 B2
Elgol 149 G10
Elham 31 E5
Elie 129 D6
Elim 82 C3
Eling 14 C4
Elishader 149 B10
Elishaw 116 E4
Elkesley 77 B6
Elkstone 37 C6
Ellan 138 B4
Elland 88 B2
Ellary 144 F6
Ellastone 75 E8
Ellemford 122 C3
Ellenbrook 84 E3
Ellenhall 62 B2
Ellen's Green 27 F8
Ellerbeck 102 E2
Ellerburn 103 F6
Ellerby 103 C5
Ellerdine Heath 61 B6
Ellerhayes 10 D4
Elleric 130 E4
Ellerker 90 B3
Ellerton E Yorks 96 F3
Shrops 61 B7
Ellesborough 39 D8
Ellesmere 73 F8
Ellesmere Port 73 B8
Ellingham Norf 69 E6
Northumb 117 B7
Ellingstring 101 F6
Ellington Cambs 54 B2
Northumb 117 E8
Elliot 135 F6
Ellisfield 26 E4
Ellistown 63 C8
Ellon 153 E9
Ellonby 108 F4
Ellough 69 F7
Elloughton 90 B3
Ellwood 36 D2
Elm 66 D4
Elmbridge 50 C4
Elmdon Essex 55 F5
W Mid 63 F5
Elmdon Heath 63 F5
Elmers End 28 C4
Elmesthorpe 63 E8
Elmfield 15 E7
Elm Hill 13 B6
Elmhurst 62 C5
Elmley Castle 50 E4
Elmley Lovett 50 C3
Elmore 36 C4
Elmore Back 36 C4
Elm Park 41 F8
Elmscott 8 B4
Elmsett 56 E4
Elmstead Market 43 B6
Elmsted 30 E5
Elmstone 31 C6
Elmstone Hardwicke 37 B6
Elmswell E Yorks 97 D5
Suff 56 C3
Elmton 76 B5
Elphin 156 H5
Elphinstone 121 B6
Elrick 141 D7
Elrig 105 E7
Elsdon 117 E5
Elsecar 88 E4
Elsenham 41 B8
Elsfield 39 C5
Elsham 90 C4
Elsing 68 C3
Elslack 94 E2
Elson 73 F7
Elsrickle 120 E3
Elstead 27 E7
Elsted 16 C2
Elsthorpe 65 B7
Elstob 101 B8
Elston Notts 77 E7
Wilts 25 E5
Elstone 9 C8
Elstow 53 E8
Elstree 40 E4
Elstronwick 97 F8
Elswick 92 F4
Elsworth 54 C4
Elterwater 99 D5
Eltham 28 B5
Eltisley 54 D3
Elton Cambs 65 E7
Ches W 73 B8
Derbys 76 C2
Glos 36 C4
Hereford 49 B6
Notts 77 F7
Stockton 102 C2
Elton Green 73 B8
Elvanfoot 114 C2
Elvaston 76 F4
Elveden 56 B2
Elvingston 121 B7
Elvington Kent 31 D6
York 96 E2
Elwick Hrtlpl 111 F7
Northumb 123 F7
Elworth 74 C4
Elworthy 22 F2
Ely Cambs 66 F5
Cardiff 22 B3
Emberton 53 E6
Embleton Cumb 107 F8
Northumb 117 B8
Embo 151 B11
Emborough 23 D8
Embo Street 151 B11
Embsay 94 D3
Emersons Green 23 B8
Emery Down 14 D3
Emley 88 C3
Emmbrook 27 C5
Emmer Green 26 B5
Emmington 39 D7
Emneth 66 D4
Emneth Hungate 66 D5
Empingham 65 D6
Empshott 27 F5
Emstrey 60 C5
Emsworth 15 D8
Enborne 26 C2
Enchmarsh 60 E5
Enderby 64 E2
Endmoor 99 F7
Endon 75 D6
Endon Bank 75 D6
Enfield 41 E6
Enfield Wash 41 E6
Enford 25 D6
Engamoor 160 H4
Engine Common 36 F3
Englefield 26 B4
Englefield Green 27 B7
Englesea-brook 74 D4
English Bicknor 36 C2
Englishcombe 24 C2
English Frankton 60 B4
Enham Alamein 25 E8
Enmore 22 F4
Ennerdale Bridge 98 C2
Enoch 113 D8
Enochdhu 133 C7
Ensay 146 G6
Ensbury 13 E8
Ensdon 60 C4
Ensis 9 B7
Enstone 38 B3
Enterkinfoot 113 D8
Enterpen 102 D2
Enville 62 F2
Eolaigearraidh 148 H2
Eorabus 146 J6
Eòropaidh 155 A10
Epperstone 77 E6
Epping 41 D7
Epping Green Essex 41 D7
Herts 41 D5
Epping Upland 41 D7
Eppleby 101 C6
Eppleworth 97 F6
Epsom 28 C3
Epwell 51 E8
Epworth 89 D8
Epworth Turbary 89 D8
Erbistock 73 E7
Erbusaig 149 F12
Erchless Castle 150 G7
Erdington 62 E5
Eredine 125 E5
Eriboll 156 D7
Ericstane 114 C3
Eridge Green 18 B2
Erines 145 F7
Eriswell 55 B8
Erith 29 B6
Erlestoke 24 D4
Ermine 78 B2
Ermington 6 D4
Erpingham 81 D7
Errogie 137 B8
Errol 128 B4
Erskine 118 B4
Erskine Bridge 118 B4
Ervie 104 C4
Erwarton 57 F6
Erwood 48 E2
Eryholme 101 D8
Eryrys 73 D6
Escomb 101 B6
Escrick 96 E2
Esgairdawe 46 E5
Esgairgeiliog 58 D4
Esh 110 E4
Esher 28 C2
Esholt 94 E4
Eshott 117 E8
Eshton 94 D2
Esh Winning 110 E4
Eskadale 150 H7
Eskbank 121 C6
Eskdale Green 98 D3
Eskdalemuir 115 E5
Eske 97 E6
Eskham 91 E7
Esk Valley 103 D6
Esprick 92 F4
Essendine 65 C7
Essendon 41 D5
Essich 151 H9
Essington 62 D3
Esslemont 141 B8
Eston 102 C3
Eswick 160 H6
Etal 122 F5
Etchilhampton 24 C5
Etchingham 18 C4
Etchinghill Kent 19 B8
Staffs 62 C4
Ethie Castle 135 E6
Ethie Mains 135 E6
Etling Green 68 C3
Eton 27 B7
Eton Wick 27 B7
Etteridge 138 E2
Ettersgill 100 B3
Ettingshall 62 E3
Ettington 51 E7
Etton E Yorks 97 E5
Pboro 65 D8
Ettrick 115 C5
Ettrickbridge 115 B6
Ettrickhill 115 C5
Etwall 76 F2
Euston 56 B2
Euximoor Drove 66 E4
Euxton 86 C3
Evanstown 34 F3
Evanton 151 E9
Evedon 78 E3
Evelix 151 B10
Evenjobb 48 C4
Evenley 52 F3
Evenlode 38 B2
Evenwood 101 B6
Evenwood Gate 101 B6
Everbay 159 F7
Evercreech 23 F8
Everdon 52 D3
Everingham 96 E4
Everleigh 25 D7
Everley 103 F7
Eversholt 53 F7
Evershot 12 D3
Eversley 27 C5
Eversley Cross 27 C5
Everthorpe 96 F5
Everton C Beds 54 D3
Hants 14 E3
Mers 85 E4
Notts 89 E7
Evertown 108 B3
Evesbatch 49 E8
Evesham 50 E5
Evington 64 D3
Ewden Village 88 E3
Ewell 28 C3
Ewell Minnis 31 E6
Ewelme 39 E6
Ewen 37 E7
Ewenny 21 B8
Ewerby 78 E4
Ewerby Thorpe 78 E4
Ewes 115 E6
Ewesley 117 E6
Ewhurst 27 E8
Ewhurst Green E Sus 18 C4
Sur 27 F8
Ewloe 73 C7
Ewloe Green 73 C6
Ewood 86 B4
Eworthy 9 E6
Ewshot 27 E6
Ewyas Harold 35 B7
Exbourne 9 D8
Exbury 14 E5

Exebridge 10 B4
Exelby 101 F7
Exeter 10 E4
Exford 21 F7
Exhall 51 D6
Exley Head 94 F3
Exminster 10 F4
Exmouth 10 F5
Exnaboe 160 M5
Exning 55 C7
Exton Devon 10 F4
Hants 15 B7
Rutland 65 C6
Som 21 F8
Exwick 10 E4
Eyam 76 B2
Eydon 52 D3
Eye Hereford 49 C6
Pboro 66 D2
Suff 56 B5
Eye Green 66 D2
Eyemouth 122 C5
Eyeworth 54 E3
Eyhorne Street 30 D2
Eyke 57 D7
Eynesbury 54 D2
Eynort 149 F8
Eynsford 29 C6
Eynsham 38 D4
Eype 12 E2
Eyre Highld 149 C9
Highld 149 E10
Eythorne 31 E6
Eyton Hereford 49 C6
Shrops 60 F3
Wrex 73 E7
Eyton upon the Weald Moors 61 C6

F

Faceby 102 D2
Facit 87 C6
Faddiley 74 D2
Fadmoor 102 F4
Faerdre 33 D7
Failand 23 B7
Failford 112 B4
Failsworth 87 D6
Fain 150 D4
Fairbourne 58 C3
Fairburn 89 B5
Fairfield Derbys 75 B7
Stockton 102 C2
Worcs 50 B4
Worcs 50 E5
Fairford 38 D1
Fair Green 67 C6
Fairhaven 85 B4
Fair Hill 108 F5
Fairlie 118 D2
Fairlight 19 D5
Fairlight Cove 19 D5
Fairmile 11 E5
Fairmilehead 120 C5
Fairoak 74 F4
Fair Oak 15 C5
Fair Oak Green 26 C4
Fairseat 29 C7
Fairstead Essex 42 C3
Norf 67 C6
Fairwarp 17 B8
Fairy Cottage 84 D4
Fairy Cross 9 B6
Fakenham 80 E5
Fakenham Magna 56 B3
Fala 121 C7
Fala Dam 121 C7
Falahill 121 D6
Falcon 49 F8
Faldingworth 90 F4
Falfield 36 E3
Falkenham 57 F6
Falkirk 119 B8
Falkland 128 D4
Falla 116 C3
Fallgate 76 C3
Fallin 127 E7
Fallowfield 87 E6
Fallsidehill 122 E2
Falmer 17 D7
Falmouth 3 C7
Falsgrave 103 F8
Falstone 116 F3
Fanagmore 156 E4
Fangdale Beck 102 E3
Fangfoss 96 D3
Fankerton 127 F6
Fanmore 146 G7
Fannich Lodge 150 E5
Fans 122 E2
Far Bank 89 C7
Far Bletchley 53 F6
Farcet 66 E2
Far Cotton 52 D5
Farden 49 B7
Fareham 15 D6
Farewell 62 C4
Far Forest 50 B2
Farforth 79 B6
Faringdon 38 E2
Farington 86 B3
Farlam 109 D5
Farlary 157 J10
Far Laund 76 E3
Farleigh N Som 23 C6
Sur 28 C4
Farleigh Hungerford 24 D3
Farleigh Wallop 26 E4
Farlesthorpe 79 B7
Farleton Cumb 99 F7
Lancs 93 C5
Farley Shrops 60 D3
Staffs 75 E7
Wilts 14 B3
Farley Green 27 E8
Farley Hill Luton 40 B3
Wokingham 26 C5
Farleys End 36 C4
Farlington 96 C2
Farlow 61 F6
Farmborough 23 C8
Farmcote Glos 37 B7
Shrops 61 E7
Farmington 37 C8
Farmoor 38 D4
Farmtown 152 C5
Farnborough Hants 27 D6
London 28 C5
Warks 52 E2
W Berks 38 F4
Farnborough Green 27 D6
Farncombe 27 E7
Farndish 53 C7
Farndon Ches W 73 D8
Notts 77 D7
Farnell 135 D6
Farnham Dorset 13 C7
Essex 41 B7
N Yorks 95 C6
Suff 57 C7
Sur 27 E6
Farnham Common 40 F2
Farnham Green 41 B7
Farnham Royal 40 F2
Farnhill 94 E3
Farningham 29 C6
Farnley N Yorks 94 E5
W Yorks 95 F5
Farnley Tyas 88 C2
Farnsfield 77 D6
Farnworth Gtr Man 86 D5
Halton 86 F3
Farr Highld 138 D4
Highld 151 H9
Highld 157 C10
Farr House 151 H9
Farringdon 10 E5
Farrington Gurney 23 D8
Far Sawrey 99 E5
Farsley 94 F5
Farthinghoe 52 F3
Farthingloe 31 E6
Farthingstone 52 D4
Fartown 88 C2
Farway 11 E6
Fasag 149 C13
Fascadale 147 D8
Faslane Port 145 E11
Fasnacloich 130 E4
Fasnakyle Ho 137 B6
Fassfern 130 B4
Fatfield 111 D6
Fattahead 153 C6
Faugh 108 D5
Fauldhouse 120 C2
Faulkbourne 42 C3
Faulkland 24 D2
Fauls 74 F2
Faversham 30 C4
Favillar 152 E2
Fawdington 95 B7
Fawfieldhead 75 C7
Fawkham Green 29 C6
Fawler 38 C3
Fawley Bucks 39 F7
Hants 15 D5
W Berks 38 F3
Fawley Chapel 36 B2
Faxfleet 90 B2
Faygate 28 F3
Fazakerley 85 E4
Fazeley 63 D6
Fearby 101 F6
Fearn 151 D11
Fearnan 132 E4
Fearnbeg 149 C12
Fearnhead 86 E4
Fearn Lodge 151 C9
Fearnmore 149 B12
Fearn Station 151 D11
Featherstone Staffs 62 D3
W Yorks 88 B5
Featherwood 116 D4
Feckenham 50 C5
Feering 42 B4
Feetham 100 E4
Feizor 93 C7
Felbridge 28 F4
Felbrigg 81 D8
Felcourt 28 E4
Felden 40 D3
Felin-Crai 34 B2
Felindre Carms 33 B6
Carms 33 B8
Carms 46 F2
Carms 47 F5
Ceredig 46 D4
Powys 59 F8
Swansea 33 D7
Felindre Farchog 45 F3
Felinfach Ceredig 46 D4
Powys 48 F2
Felinfoel 33 D6
Felingwmisaf 33 B6
Felingwmuchaf 33 B6
Felinwynt 45 D4
Felixkirk 102 F2
Felixstowe 57 F6
Felixstowe Ferry 57 F7
Felkington 122 E5
Felkirk 88 C4
Felling 111 C5
Fell Side 108 F3
Felmersham 53 D7
Felmingham 81 E8
Felpham 16 E3
Felsham 56 D3
Felsted 42 B2
Feltham 28 B2
Felthorpe 68 C4
Felton Hereford 49 E7
Northumb 117 D7
N Som 23 C7
Felton Butler 60 C3
Feltwell 67 E7
Fenay Bridge 88 C2
Fence 93 F8
Fence Houses 111 D6
Fen Ditton 55 C5
Fen Drayton 54 C4
Fen End 51 B7
Fengate Norf 81 E7
Pboro 66 E2
Fenham 123 E6
Fenhouses 79 E5
Feniscliffe 86 B4
Feniscowles 86 B4
Feniton 11 E6
Fenlake 53 E8
Fenny Bentley 75 D8
Fenny Bridges 11 E6
Fenny Compton 52 D2
Fenny Drayton 63 E7
Fenny Stratford 53 F6
Fenrother 117 E7
Fen Side 79 D6
Fenstanton 54 C4
Fenton Cambs 54 B4
Lincs 77 B8
Lincs 77 D8
Stoke 75 E5
Fenton Barns 129 F7
Fenton Town 123 F5
Fenwick E Ayrs 118 E4
Northumb 110 B3
Northumb 123 E6
S Yorks 89 C6
Feochaig 143 G8
Feock 3 C7
Feolin Ferry 144 G3
Ferindonald 149 H11
Feriniquarrie 148 C6
Ferlochan 130 E3
Fern 134 C4
Ferndale 34 E4
Ferndown 13 D8
Ferness 151 G12
Ferney Green 99 E6
Fernham 38 E2
Fernhill Heath 50 D3
Fernhurst 16 B2
Fernie 128 C5
Ferniegair 119 D7
Fernilea 149 E8
Fernilee 75 B7
Ferrensby 95 C6
Ferring 16 D4
Ferrybridge 89 B5
Ferryden 135 D7
Ferryhill Aberdeen 141 D8
Durham 111 F5
Ferryhill Station 111 F6
Ferry Hill 66 F3
Ferry Point 151 C10
Ferryside 32 C4
Fersfield 68 F3
Fersit 131 B7
Ferwig 45 E3
Feshiebridge 138 D4
Fetcham 28 D2
Fetterangus 153 C9
Fettercairn 135 B6
Fettes 151 F8
Fewcott 39 B5
Fewston 94 D4
F Faccombe 25 D8
Ffairfach 33 B7
Ffair-Rhos 47 C6
Ffaldybrenin 46 E5
Ffarmers 47 E5
Ffawyddog 35 C6
Fforest 33 D6
Fforest-fâch 33 E7
Ffostrasol 46 E2
Ffos-y-ffi 46 C3
Ffridd-Uchaf 83 F5
Ffrith 73 D6
Ffrwd 82 F4
Ffynnon ddrain 33 B5
Ffynnongroyw 85 F2
Ffynnon-oer 46 D4
Fidden 146 J6
Fiddes 141 F7
Fiddington Glos 50 F4
Som 22 E4
Fiddleford 13 C6
Fiddlers Hamlet 41 D7
Field 75 F7
Field Broughton 99 F5
Field Dalling 81 D6
Field Head 63 D8
Fifehead Magdalen 13 B5
Fifehead Neville 13 C5
Fifield Oxon 38 C2
Wilts 25 D6
Windsor 27 B7
Fifield Bavant 13 B8
Figheldean 25 E6
Filands 37 F6
Filby 69 C7
Filey 97 A7
Filgrave 53 E6
Filkins 38 D2
Filleigh Devon 9 B8
Devon 10 C2
Fillingham 90 F3
Fillongley 63 F6
Filton 23 B8
Fimber 96 C4
Finavon 134 D4
Finchairn 124 E5
Fincham 67 D6
Finchampstead 27 C5
Finchdean 15 C8
Finchingfield 55 F7
Finchley 41 E5
Findern 76 F3
Findhorn 151 E13
Findhorn Bridge 138 B4
Findochty 152 B4
Findo Gask 128 B2
Findon Aberds 141 E8
W Sus 16 D5
Findon Mains 151 E9
Findrack House 140 D5
Finedon 53 B7
Fingal Street 57 C6
Fingask 141 B6
Fingerpost 50 B2
Fingest 39 E7
Finghall 101 F6
Fingland Cumb 108 D2
Dumfries 113 C7
Finglesham 31 D7
Fingringhoe 43 B6
Finlarig 132 F2
Finmere 52 F4
Finnart 132 D2
Finningham 56 C4
Finningley 89 E7
Finnygaud 152 C5
Finsbury 41 F6
Finstall 50 C4
Finsthwaite 99 F5
Finstock 38 C3
Finstown 159 G4
Fintry Aberds 153 C7
Dundee 134 F4
Stirling 126 F5
Finzean 140 E5
Fionnphort 146 J6
Fionnsbhagh 154 J5
Firbeck 89 F6
Firby N Yorks 96 C3
N Yorks 101 F7
Firgrove 87 C7
Firsby 79 C7
Firsdown 25 F7
First Coast 150 B2
Fir Tree 110 F4
Fishbourne IoW 15 E6
W Sus 16 D2
Fishburn 111 F6
Fishcross 127 E7
Fisherford 153 E6
Fisher Place 99 C5
Fisher's Pond 15 B5
Fisherstreet 27 F7
Fisherton Highld 151 F10
S Ayrs 112 C2
Fishguard = Abergwaun 44 B4
Fishlake 89 C7
Fishleigh Barton 9 B7
Fishponds 23 B8
Fishpool 36 B3
Fishtoft 79 E6
Fishtoft Drove 79 E6
Fishtown of Usan 135 D7
Fishwick 122 D5
Fiskavaig 149 E8
Fiskerton Lincs 78 B3
Notts 77 D7
Fitling 97 F8
Fittleton 25 E6
Fittleworth 16 C4
Fitton End 66 C4
Fitz 60 C4
Fitzhead 11 B6
Fitzwilliam 88 C5
Fiunary 147 G9
Five Acres 36 C2
Five Ashes 18 C2
Fivecrosses 74 B2
Fivehead 11 B8
Five Oak Green 29 E7
Five Oaks Jersey 17
W Sus 16 B4
Five Roads 33 D5
Flack's Green 42 C3
Flackwell Heath 40 F1
Fladbury 50 E4
Fladdabister 160 K6
Flagg 75 C8
Flamborough 97 B8
Flamstead 40 C3
Flamstead End 41 D6
Flansham 16 D3
Flanshaw 88 B4
Flasby 94 D2
Flash 75 C7
Flashader 149 C8
Flask Inn 103 D7
Flaunden 40 D3
Flawborough 77 E7
Flawith 95 C7
Flax Bourton 23 C7
Flaxby 95 D6
Flaxholme 76 E3
Flaxley 36 C3
Flaxpool 22 F3
Flaxton 96 C2
Fleckney 64 E3
Flecknoe 52 C3
Fledborough 77 B8
Fleet Hants 15 D8
Hants 27 D6
Lincs 66 B3
Fleetham 117 B7
Fleet Hargate 66 B3
Fleetlands 15 D6
Fleetville 40 D4
Fleetwood 92 E3
Flemingston 22 B2
Flemington 119 D6
Flempton 56 C2
Fleoideabhagh 154 J5
Fletchertown 108 E2
Fletching 17 B8
Flexbury 8 D4
Flexford 27 E7
Flimby 107 F7
Flimwell 18 B4
Flint = Y Fflint 73 B6
Flintham 77 E7
Flint Mountain 73 B6
Flinton 97 F8
Flintsham 48 D5
Flitcham 80 E3
Flitton 53 F8
Flitwick 53 F8
Flixborough 90 C2
Flixborough Stather 90 C2
Flixton Gtr Man 86 E5
N Yorks 97 B6
Suff 69 F6
Flockton 88 C3
Flodaigh 148 C3
Flodden 122 F5
Flodigarry 149 A9
Flood's Ferry 66 E3
Flookburgh 92 B3
Florden 68 E4
Flore 52 C4
Flotterton 117 D5
Flowton 56 E4
Flush House 88 D2
Flushing Aberds 153 D10
Corn 3 C7
Flyford Flavell 50 D4
Foals Green 57 B6
Fobbing 42 F3
Fochabers 152 C3
Fochriw 35 D5
Fockerby 90 C2
Fodderletter 139 B7
Fodderty 151 F8
Foel 59 C6
Foel-gastell 33 C6
Foffarty 134 E4
Foggathorpe 96 F3
Fogo 122 E3
Fogorig 122 E3
Foindle 156 E4
Folda 134 C1
Fole 75 F7
Foleshill 63 F7
Folke 12 C4
Folkestone 31 F6
Folkingham 78 F3
Folkington 18 E2
Folksworth 65 F8
Folkton 97 B6
Folla Rule 153 E7
Follifoot 95 D6
Folly Gate 9 E7
Fonthill Bishop 24 F4
Fonthill Gifford 24 F4
Fontmell Magna 13 C6
Fontwell 16 D3
Foolow 75 B8
Foots Cray 29 B5
Forbestown 140 C2
Force Mills 99 E5
Forcett 101 C6
Ford Argyll 124 E4
Bucks 39 D7
Devon 9 B6
Glos 37 B7
Northumb 122 F5
Shrops 60 C4
Staffs 75 D7
Wilts 24 B3
W Sus 16 D3
Fordcombe 29 E6
Fordell 128 F3
Forden 60 D2
Ford End 42 C2
Forder Green 7 C5
Fordham Cambs 55 B7
Essex 43 B5
Norf 67 E6
Fordhouses 62 D3
Fordingbridge 14 C2
Fordon 97 B6
Fordoun 135 B7
Ford's Green 56 C4
Fordstreet 43 B5
Ford Street 11 C6
Fordwells 38 C3
Fordwich 31 D5
Fordyce 152 B5
Forebridge 62 B3
Forest 109 F8
Forest Becks 93 D7
Forestburn Gate 117 E6
Foresterseat 152 C1
Forest Gate 41 F7
Forest Green 28 E2
Forest Hall 99 D7
Forest Head 109 D5
Forest Hill 39 D5
Forest Lane Head 95 D6
Forest Lodge Argyll 131 E6
Highld 139 C6
Perth 133 B6
Forest Mill 127 E8
Forest Row 28 F5
Forestside 15 C8
Forest Town 77 C5
Forfar 134 D4
Forgandenny 128 C2
Forge 58 E4
Forge Side 35 D6
Forgewood 119 D7
Forgie 152 C3
Forglen House 153 C6
Formby 85 D4
Forncett End 68 E4
Forncett St Mary 68 E4
Forncett St Peter 68 E4
Forneth 133 E7
Fornham All Saints 56 C2
Fornham St Martin 56 C2
Forres 151 F13
Forrestfield 119 C8
Forrest Lodge 113 F5
Forsbrook 75 E6
Forse 158 G4
Forse House 158 G4
Forsinain 157 E12
Forsinard 157 E11
Forsinard Station 157 E11
Forston 12 E4
Fort Augustus 137 D6
Forteviot 128 C2
Fort George Guern 16
Highld 151 F10
Forth 120 D2
Forthampton 50 F3
Forth Road Bridge 120 B4
Fortingall 132 E4
Forton Hants 26 E2
Lancs 92 D4
Shrops 60 C4
Som 11 D8
Staffs 61 B7
Forton Heath 60 C4
Fortrie 153 D6
Fortrose 151 F10
Fortuneswell 12 G4
Fort William 131 B5
Forty Green 40 E2
Forty Hill 41 E6
Forward Green 56 D4
Fosbury 25 D8
Fosdyke 79 F6
Foss 132 D4
Foss Cross 37 D7
Fossebridge 37 C7
Fosterhouses 89 C7
Foster Street 41 D7
Foston Derbys 75 F8
Lincs 77 E8
N Yorks 96 C2
Foston on the Wolds 97 D7
Fotherby 91 E7
Fotheringhay 65 E7
Foubister 159 H6
Foulby 88 C4
Foulden Borders 122 D5
Norf 67 E7
Foulis Castle 151 E8
Foul Mile 18 D3
Foulridge 93 E8
Foulsham 81 E6
Fountainhall 121 E7
Four Ashes Staffs 62 F2
Suff 56 B4
Four Crosses Powys 59 D7
Powys 60 C2
Wrex 73 D6
Four Elms 29 E5
Four Forks 22 E4
Four Gotes 66 C4
Fourlane Ends 76 D3
Four Lane Ends 74 C2
Four Lanes 3 C5
Fourlanes End 74 D5
Four Marks 26 F4
Four Mile Bridge 82 D2
Four Oaks E Sus 19 C5
W Mid 62 E5
W Mid 63 F6
Fourpenny 151 B11
Four Roads Carms 33 D5
IoM 84 F2
Fourstones 109 C8
Four Throws 18 C4
Fovant 13 B8
Foveran 141 B8
Fowey 5 D6
Fowley Common 86 E4
Fowlis 134 F3
Fowlis Wester 127 B8
Fowlmere 54 E5
Fownhope 49 F7
Foxbar 118 C4
Foxcombe Hill 38 D4
Fox Corner 27 D7
Foxdale 84 E2
Foxearth 56 E2
Foxfield 98 F4
Foxham 24 B4
Foxhole Corn 4 D4
Swansea 33 E7
Foxholes 97 B6
Foxhunt Green 18 D2
Fox Lane 27 D6
Foxley Norf 81 E6
Wilts 37 F5
Fox Street 43 B6
Foxt 75 E7
Foxton Cambs 54 E5
Durham 102 B1
Leics 64 E4
Foxup 93 B8
Foxwist Green 74 C3
Foxwood 49 B8
Foy 36 B2
Foyers 137 B7
Fraddam 2 C4
Fraddon 4 D4
Fradley 63 C5
Fradswell 75 F6
Fraisthorpe 97 C7
Framfield 17 B8
Framingham Earl 69 D5
Framingham Pigot 69 D5
Framlingham 57 C6
Frampton Dorset 12 E4
Lincs 79 F6
Frampton Cotterell 36 F3
Frampton Mansell 37 D6
Frampton on Severn 36 D4
Frampton West End 79 E5
Framsden 57 D5
Framwellgate Moor 111 E5
Franche 50 B3
Frankby 85 F3
Frankley 62 F3
Frank's Bridge 48 D3
Frankton 52 B2
Frant 18 B2
Fraserburgh 153 B9
Frating Green 43 B6
Fratton 15 E7
Freathy 5 D8
Freckenham 55 B7
Freckleton 86 B2
Freeby 64 B5
Freehay 75 E7
Freeland 38 C4
Freester 160 H6
Freethorpe 69 D7
Freiston 79 E6
Fremington Devon 20 F4
N Yorks 101 E5
Frenchay 23 B8
Frenchbeer 9 F8
Frenich 126 D3
Frensham 27 E6
Fresgoe 157 C12
Freshfield 85 D3
Freshford 24 C2
Freshwater 14 F4
Freshwater Bay 14 F4
Freshwater East 32 E1
Fressingfield 57 B6
Freston 57 F5
Freswick 158 D5
Fretherne 36 D4
Frettenham 68 C5
Freuchie 128 D4
Freuchies 134 C2
Freystrop 44 D4
Friar's Gate 29 F5
Friarton 128 B3
Friday Bridge 66 D4
Friday Street 18 E3
Fridaythorpe 96 D4
Friern Barnet 41 E5
Friesland 146 F4
Friesthorpe 90 F4
Frieston 78 E2
Frieth 39 E7
Frilford 38 E4
Frilsham 26 B3
Frimley 27 D6
Frimley Green 27 D6
Frindsbury 29 B8
Fring 80 D3
Fringford 39 B6
Frinsted 30 D2
Frinton-on-Sea 43 B8
Friockheim 135 E5
Friog 58 C3
Frisby on the Wreake 64 C3
Friskney 79 D7
Friskney Eaudike 79 D7
Friskney Tofts 79 D7
Friston E Sus 18 F2
Suff 57 C8
Fritchley 76 D3
Fritham 14 C3
Frith Bank 79 E6
Frith Common 49 C8
Frithelstock 9 C6
Frithelstock Stone 9 C6
Frithville 79 D6
Frittenden 30 E2
Frittiscombe 7 E6
Fritton Norf 68 E5
Norf 69 D7
Fritwell 39 B5
Frizinghall 94 F4
Frizington 98 C2
Frocester 36 D4
Frodesley 60 D5
Frodingham 90 C2
Frodsham 74 B2
Frogden 116 B3
Froggatt 76 B2
Froghall 75 E7
Frogmore Devon 7 E5
Hants 27 D6
Frognall 65 C8
Frogshail 81 D8
Frolesworth 64 E2
Frome 24 E2
Frome St Quintin 12 D3
Fromes Hill 49 E8
Fron Denb 72 C4
Gwyn 70 D4
Gwyn 82 F5
Powys 48 C2
Powys 59 E8
Powys 60 D2
Froncysyllte 73 E6
Frongoch 72 F3
Frostenden 69 F7
Frosterley 110 F3
Frotoft 159 F5
Froxfield 25 C7
Froxfield Green 15 B8
Froyle 27 E5
Fryerning 42 D2
Fryton 96 B2
Fulbeck 78 D2
Fulbourn 55 D6
Fulbrook 38 C2
Fulford Som 11 B7
Staffs 75 F6
York 96 E2
Fulham 28 B3
Fulking 17 C6
Fullarton Glasgow 119 C6
N Ayrs 118 F3
Fuller's Moor 73 D8
Fuller Street 42 C3
Fullerton 25 F8
Fulletby 79 B5
Full Sutton 96 D3
Fullwood 118 D4
Fulmer 40 F2
Fulmodestone 81 D5
Fulnetby 78 B3
Fulstow 91 E7
Fulwell 111 D6
Fulwood Lancs 92 F5
S Yorks 88 F4
Fundenhall 68 E4
Fundenhall Street 68 E4
Funtington 15 D8
Funtley 15 D6
Funtullich 127 B6
Funzie 160 D8
Furley 11 D7
Furnace Argyll 125 E6
Carms 33 D6
Furnace End 63 E6
Furneaux Pelham 41 B7
Furness Vale 87 F8
Furzehill 21 E6
Furze Platt 40 F1
Fyfett 11 C7
Fyfield Essex 42 D1
Glos 38 D2
Hants 25 E7
Oxon 38 E4
Wilts 25 C6
Fylingthorpe 103 D7
Fyvie 153 E7

G

Gabhsann bho Dheas 155 B9
Gabhsann bho Thuath 155 B9
Gablon 151 B10
Gabroc Hill 118 D4
Gaddesby 64 C3
Gadebridge 40 D3
Gaer 35 B5
Gaerllwyd 35 E8
Gaerwen 82 D4
Gagingwell 38 B4
Gaick Lodge 138 F3
Gailey 62 C3
Gainford 101 C6
Gainsborough Lincs 90 E2
Suff 57 E5
Gainsford End 55 F8
Gairloch 149 A13
Gairlochy 136 F4
Gairney Bank 128 E3
Gairnshiel Lodge 139 D8
Gaisgill 99 D8
Gaitsgill 108 E3
Galashiels 121 F7
Galgate 92 D4
Galhampton 12 B4
Gallaberry 114 F2
Gallachoille 144 E6
Gallanach Argyll 124 C4
Argyll 146 E5
Gallantry Bank 74 D2
Gallatown 128 E4
Galley Common 63 E7
Galleyend 42 D3
Galley Hill 54 C4
Galleywood 42 D3
Gallin 132 E2
Gallowfauld 134 E4
Gallows Green 75 E7
Galltair 149 F13
Galmisdale 146 C7
Galmpton Devon 6 E4
Torbay 7 D6
Galphay 95 B5
Galston 118 F5
Galtrigill 148 C6
Gamblesby 109 F6
Gamesley 87 E8
Gamlingay 54 D3
Gammersgill 101 F5
Gamston 77 B7
Ganarew 36 C2
Ganavan 124 B4
Gang 5 C8
Ganllwyd 71 E8
Gannochy Angus 135 B5
Perth 128 B3
Gansclet 158 F5
Ganstead 97 F7
Ganthorpe 96 B2
Ganton 97 B5
Garbat 150 E7
Garbhallt 125 F6
Garboldisham 68 F3
Garden City 73 C7
Gardenstown 153 B7
Garden Village Wrex 73 D7
W Yorks 95 F7
Garderhouse 160 J5
Gardham 97 E5
Gardin 160 G6
Gare Hill 24 E2
Garelochhead 145 D11
Garford 38 E4
Garforth 95 F7
Gargrave 94 D2
Gargunnock 127 E6
Garlic Street 68 F5
Garlieston 105 E8
Garlinge Green 30 D5
Garlogie 141 D6
Garmond 153 C8
Garmony 147 G9
Garmouth 152 B3
Garnant 33 C7
Garndiffaith 35 D6
Garndolbenmaen 71 C5
Garnedd 83 F7
Garnett Bridge 99 E7
Garnfadryn 70 D3
Garnkirk 119 C6
Garnlydan 35 C5
Garnswllt 33 D7
Garn-yr-erw 35 C6
Garrabost 155 D10
Garraron 124 E4
Garras 3 D6
Garreg 71 C7
Garrick 127 C7
Garrigill 109 E7
Garriston 101 E6
Garroch 113 F5
Garrogie Lodge 137 C8
Garros 149 B9
Garrow 133 E5
Garryhorn 113 E5
Garsdale 100 F2
Garsdale Head 100 E2
Garsdon 37 F6
Garshall Green 75 F6
Garsington 39 D5
Garstang 92 E4
Garston 86 F2
Garswood 86 E3
Gartcosh 119 C6
Garth Bridgend 34 E2
Gwyn 83 D5
Powys 47 E8
Shetland 160 H4
Wrex 73 E6
Garthamlock 119 C6
Garthbrengy 48 F2
Garthdee 141 D8
Gartheli 46 D4
Garthmyl 59 E8
Garthorpe Leics 64 B5
N Lincs 90 C2
Garth Row 99 E7
Gartly 152 E5
Gartmore 126 E4
Gartnagrenach 144 H6
Gartness N Lanark 119 C7
Stirling 126 F4
Gartocharn 126 F3
Garton 97 F8
Garton-on-the-Wolds 97 D5
Gartsherrie 119 C7
Gartymore 157 H13
Garvald 121 B8
Garvamore 137 E8
Garvard 144 D2
Garvault Hotel 157 F10
Garve 150 E6
Garvestone 68 D3
Garvock Aberds 135 B7
Invclyd 118 B2
Garway 36 B1
Garway Hill 35 B8
Gaskan 130 B1
Gastard 24 C3
Gasthorpe 68 F2
Gatcombe 15 F5
Gateacre 86 F2
Gatebeck 99 F7
Gate Burton 90 F2
Gateford 89 F6
Gateforth 89 B6
Gatehead 118 F3
Gate Helmsley 96 D2
Gatehouse 116 F3
Gatehouse of Fleet 106 D3
Gatelawbridge 114 E2
Gateley 81 E5
Gatenby 101 F8
Gateshead 111 C5
Gatesheath 73 C8
Gateside Aberds 140 C5
Angus 134 E4
E Renf 118 D4
Fife 128 D3
N Ayrs 118 D3
Gathurst 86 D3
Gatley 87 F6
Gattonside 121 F8
Gatwick Airport 28 E3
Gaufron 47 C8
Gaulby 64 D3
Gauldry 129 B5
Gaunt's Common 13 D8
Gautby 78 B4
Gavinton 122 D3
Gawber 88 D4
Gawcott 52 F4
Gawsworth 75 C5
Gawthorpe 88 B3
Gawthrop 100 F1
Gawthwaite 98 F4
Gaydon 51 D8
Gayfield 159 C5
Gayhurst 53 E6
Gayle 100 F3
Gayles 101 D6
Gay Street 16 B4
Gayton Mers 85 F3
Norf 67 C7
Staffs 62 B3
W Nhants 52 D5
Gayton le Marsh 91 F8
Gayton le Wold 91 F6
Gayton Thorpe 67 C7
Gaywood 67 B6
Gazeley 55 C8
Geanies House 151 D11
Gearraidh Bhailteas 148 F2
Gearraidh Bhaird 155 E8
Gearraidh na h-Aibhne 154 D7
Gearraidh na Monadh 148 G2
Geary 148 B7
Geddes House 151 F11
Gedding 56 D3
Geddington 65 F5
Gedintailor 149 E10
Gedling 77 E6
Gedney 66 B4
Gedney Broadgate 66 B4
Gedney Drove End 66 B4
Gedney Dyke 66 B4
Gedney Hill 66 C3
Gee Cross 87 E7
Geilston 118 B3
Geirinis 148 D2
Geise 158 D3
Geisiadar 154 D6
Geldeston 69 E6
Gell 83 E8
Gelli Pembs 32 C1
Rhondda 34 E3
Gellideg 34 D4
Gellifor 72 C5
Gelligaer 35 E5
Gellilydan 71 D7
Gellinudd 33 D8
Gellyburn 133 F7
Gellywen 32 B3
Gelston Dumfries 106 D4
Lincs 78 E2
Gembling 97 D7
Gentleshaw 62 C4
Geocrab 154 H6
Georgefield 115 E5
George Green 40 F3
Georgeham 20 F3
George Nympton 10 B2
Georgetown 35 D5
Gerlan 83 E6
Germansweek 9 E6
Germoe 2 D4
Gerrans 3 C7
Gerrards Cross 40 F3
Gestingthorpe 56 F2
Geuffordd 60 C2
Gibbet Hill 64 F2
Gibbshill 106 B4
Gib Hill 74 B3
Gidea Park 41 F8
Gidleigh 9 F8
Giffnock 119 D5
Gifford 121 C8
Giffordland 118 E2
Giffordtown 128 C4
Giggleswick 93 C8
Gilberdyke 90 B2
Gilchriston 121 C7
Gilcrux 107 F8
Gildersome 88 B3
Gildingwells 89 F6
Gileston 22 C2
Gilfach 35 E5
Gilfach Goch 34 F3
Gilfachrheda 46 D3
Gillamoor 102 F4
Gillar's Green 86 E2
Gillen 148 C7
Gilling East 96 B2
Gillingham Dorset 13 B6
Medway 29 C8
Norf 69 E7
Gilling West 101 D6
Gillock 158 E4
Gillow Heath 75 D5
Gills 158 C5
Gill's Green 18 B4
Gilmanscleuch 115 B6
Gilmerton Edin 121 C5
Perth 127 B7
Gilmonby 100 C4
Gilmorton 64 F2
Gilmourton 119 E6
Gilsland 109 C6
Gilsland Spa 109 C6
Gilston Borders 121 D7
Herts 41 C7
Gilwern 35 C6
Gimingham 81 D8
Giosla 154 E6
Gipping 56 C4
Gipsey Bridge 79 E5
Girdle Toll 118 E3
Girlsta 160 H6
Girsby 102 D1
Girtford 54 D2
Girthon 106 D3
Girton Cambs 54 C5
Notts 77 C8
Girvan 112 E1
Gisburn 93 E8
Gisleham 69 F8
Gislingham 56 B4
Gissing 68 F4
Gittisham 11 E6
Gladestry 48 D4
Gladsmuir 121 B7
Glais 33 D8
Glaisdale 103 D5
Glame 149 D10
Glamis 134 E3

Glan Adda 83 D5
Glanaman 33 C7
Glan Conwy Conwy . . 83 D8
Conwy 83 F8
Glandford 81 C6
Glandwr 32 B2
Glan-Dwyfach 71 C5
Glandy Cross 32 B2
Glandyfi 58 E3
Glan Gors 82 D4
Glangrwyney 35 C6
Glanmule 59 E8
Glanrafon 58 F3
Glan-rhyd Gwyn . . 70 D3
Pembs 45 E3
Glan-rhyd 82 F4
Glanton 117 C6
Glanton Pike 117 C6
Glan-traeth 82 D2
Glanvilles
Wootton 12 D4
Glan-y-don 73 B5
Glan-y-nant 59 F6
Glan-yr-afon
Anglesey 83 C6
Gwyn 72 E3
Gwyn 72 E3
Glan-y-wern 71 D7
Glapthorn 65 E7
Glapwell 76 C4
Glas-allt Shiel . . . 139 E8
Glasbury 48 F3
Glaschoil 151 H13
Glascoed Denb 72 B3
Mon 35 D7
Powys 59 C8
Glascorrie 140 E2
Glascote 63 D6
Glascwm 48 D3
Glasdrum 130 E4
Glasfryn 72 D3
Glasgow 119 C5
Glashvin 149 B9
Glasinfryn 83 E5
Glasnacardoch . . 147 B9
Glasnakille 149 G10
Glasphein 148 D6
Glaspwll 58 E4
Glassburn 150 H6
Glasserton 105 F8
Glassford 119 E7
Glasshouse Hill . . . 36 B4
Glasshouses 94 C4
Glasslie 128 D4
Glasson Cumb . . . 108 C2
Lancs 92 D4
Glassonby 109 F5
Glasterlaw 135 D5
Glaston 65 D5
Glastonbury 23 F7
Glatton 65 F8
Glazebrook 86 E4
Glazebury 86 E4
Glazeley 61 F7
Gleadless 88 F4
Gleadsmoss 74 C5
Gleann
Tholàstaidh . . . 155 C10
Gleaston 92 B2
Gleiniant 59 E6
Glemsford 56 E2
Glen Dumfries . . . 106 B5
Dumfries 106 B5
Glenamachrie . . . 124 C5
Glen Auldyn 84 C3
Glenbarr 143 E7
Glenbeg Highld . . 139 B6
Highld 147 E8
Glen Bernisdale . 149 D9
Glenbervie 141 F6
Glenboig 119 C7
Glenborrodale . . . 147 E9
Glenbranter 125 F7
Glenbreck 114 C3
Glenbrein Lodge . 137 C7
Glenbrittle House 149 F9
Glenbuchat
Lodge 140 C2
Glenbuck 113 B7
Glenburn 118 C4
Glencalvie Lodge . 150 C7
Glencanisp
Lodge 156 G4
Glencaple 107 C6
Glencarron
Lodge 150 F3
Glencarse 128 B3
Glencassley
Castle 156 J7
Glenceitlein 131 E5
Glencoe 130 D4
Glencraig 128 E3
Glencripesdale . . . 147 F9
Glencrosh 113 F7
Glendavan House 140 D3
Glendevon 127 D8
Glendoebeg 137 D7
Glendoe Lodge . . . 137 D7
Glendoick 128 B4
Glendoll Lodge . . 134 B2
Glendoune 112 E1
Glenduckie 128 C4
Glendye Lodge . . . 140 F5
Gleneagles
House 127 D8
Glenegedale 142 C4
Glenelg 149 G13
Glenernie 151 G13
Glenfarg 128 C3
Glenfarquhar
Lodge 141 F6
Glenferness
House 151 G12
Glenfeshie Lodge 138 E4
Glenfield 64 D2
Glenfinnan 147 C11
Glenfoot 128 C3
Glenfyne Lodge . . 125 D8
Glengap 106 D3
Glengarnock 118 D3
Glengorm Castle . 146 F7
Glengrasco 149 D9
Glenhead Farm . . 134 C2
Glen Ho 121 F5

Glenhoul 113 F6
Glenhurich 130 C2
Glenkerry 115 C5
Glenkiln 106 B5
Glenkindie 140 C3
Glenlatterach 152 C1
Glenlee 113 F6
Glenlichorn 127 C6
Glenlivet 139 B7
Glenlochsie 133 B7
Glenloig 143 E10
Glenluce 105 D6
Glenmallan 125 F8
Glenmarksie 150 F6
Glenmassan 145 E10
Glenmavis 119 C7
Glenmidge 113 F8
Glen Mona 84 D4
Glenmore Argyll . 124 D4
Highld 149 D9
Glenmore Lodge . 139 D5
Glenmoy 134 C4
Glen Nevis House 131 B5
Glenogil 134 C4
Glen Parva 64 E2
Glenprosen
Lodge 134 C2
Glenprosen
Village 134 C3
Glenquiech 134 C4
Glenreasdell
Mains 145 H7
Glenree 143 F10
Glenridding 99 C5
Glenrossal 156 J7
Glenrothes 128 D4
Glensaugh 135 B6
Glenshero Lodge . 137 E8
Glen Sluain 125 F6
Glenstockadale . . 104 C4
Glenstriven 145 F9
Glentaggart 113 B8
Glen Tanar
House 140 E3
Glentham 90 E4
Glentirranmuir . . 127 E5
Glenton 140 B5
Glentress 121 F5
Glentromie
Lodge 138 E3
Glen Trool Lodge 112 F4
Glentrool Village 105 B7
Glentruan 84 B4
Glentruim House 138 E2
Glentworth 90 F3
Glenuig 147 D9
Glenurquhart . . . 151 E10
Glen Village 119 B8
Glen Vine 84 E3
Glespin 113 B8
Gletness 160 H6
Glewstone 36 B2
Glinton 65 D8
Glooston 64 E4
Glororum 123 F7
Glossop 87 E8
Gloster Hill 117 D8
Gloucester 37 C5
Gloup 160 C7
Glusburn 94 E3
Glutt Lodge 157 F12
Glutton Bridge . . . 75 C7
Glympton 38 B4
Glynarthen 46 E2
Glynbrochan 59 F6
Glyn-Ceiriog 73 F6
Glyncoch 34 E4
Glyncorrwg 34 E2
Glyn-cywarch 71 D7
Glynde 17 D8
Glyndebourne 17 C8
Glyndyfrdwy 72 E5
Glyn Ebwy
= Ebbw Vale . . . 35 D5
Glynedd
= Glynneath . . . 34 D2
Glynedd
= Glynedd 34 D2
Glyn-neath
= Glynneath . . . 34 D2
Glynogwr 34 F3
Glyntaff 34 F4
Glyntawe 34 C2
Gnosall 62 B2
Gnosall Heath 62 B2
Goadby 64 E4
Goadby Marwood . 64 B4
Goatacre 24 B5
Goathill 12 C4
Goathland 103 D6
Goathurst 22 F4
Goat Lees 30 E4
Gobernuisgach
Lodge 156 E7
Gobhaig 154 G5
Gobowen 73 F7
Godalming 27 E7
Godley 87 E7
Godmanchester . . . 54 B3
Godmanstone 12 E4
Godmersham 30 D4
Godney 23 E6
Godolphin Cross . . 2 C5
Godre'r-graig 34 D1
Godshill Hants . . . 14 C2
IoW 15 F6
Godstone 28 D4
Godwinscroft 14 E2
Goetre 35 D7
Goferydd 82 C2
Goff's Oak 41 D6
Gogar 120 B4
Goginan 58 F3
Golan 71 C6
Golant 5 D5
Golberdon 5 B8
Golborne 86 E4
Golcar 88 C2
Goldcliff 35 F7
Golden Cross 18 D2
Golden Green 29 E7
Golden Grove 33 C6
Goldenhill 75 D5
Golden Hill 14 C3
Golden Pot 26 E5
Golden Valley 37 C6
Golders Green 41 F5
Goldhanger 43 D5
Gold Hill 66 E5

Golding 60 D5
Goldington 53 D8
Goldsborough
N Yorks. 95 D6
N Yorks. 103 C6
Goldsithney 2 C4
Goldsworthy 9 B5
Goldthorpe 89 D5
Gollanfield 151 F11
Gollinglith
Foot 101 F6
Golspie 157 J11
Golval 157 C11
Gomeldon 25 F6
Gomersal 88 B3
Gomshall 27 E8
Gonalston 77 E6
Gonfirth 160 G5
Good Easter 42 C2
Gooderstone 67 D7
Goodleigh 20 F5
Goodmanham 96 E4
Goodnestone Kent . 30 C4
Kent 31 D6
Goodrich 36 C2
Goodrington 7 D6
Goodshaw 87 B6
Goodwick = Wdig . 44 B4
Goodworth
Clatford 25 E8
Goole 89 B8
Goonbell 3 B6
Goonhavern 4 D2
Goose Eye 94 E3
Goose Green
Gtr Man 86 D3
Norf 68 F4
W Sus 16 C5
Gooseham 8 C4
Goosey 38 E3
Goosnargh 93 F5
Goostrey 74 B4
Gorcott Hill 51 C5
Gord 160 L6
Gordon 122 E2
Gordonbush 157 J11
Gordonsburgh . . . 152 B1
Gordonstoun 152 B1
Gordonstown
Aberds. 152 C5
Aberds. 153 E7
Gore 31 D7
Gorebridge 121 C6
Gore Cross 24 D5
Gorefield 66 C4
Gore Pit 42 C4
Gorey Jersey 17
Goring 39 F6
Goring-by-Sea . . . 16 D5
Goring Heath 26 B4
Gorleston-on-Sea . 69 D8
Gornalwood 62 E3
Gorrachie 153 C7
Gorran Churchtown .3 B8
Gorran Haven 3 B9
Gorrenberry 115 E7
Gors 46 B5
Gorsedd 73 B5
Gorse Hill 38 F1
Gorseinon 33 E6
Gorseness 159 G5
Gorsgoch 46 D3
Gorslas 33 C6
Gorsley 36 B3
Gorstan 150 E6
Gorstanvorran . . . 130 B2
Gorsteyhill 74 D4
Gorsty Hill 62 B5
Gortantaoid 142 A4
Gorton 87 E6
Gosbeck 57 D5
Gosberton 78 F5
Gosberton Clough . 65 B8
Gosfield 42 B3
Gosford 49 C7
Gosforth Cumb . . . 98 D2
T&W 110 C5
Gosmore 40 B4
Gosport 15 E7
Gossabrough 160 E7
Gossington 36 D4
Goswick 123 E6
Gotham 76 F5
Gotherington 37 B6
Gott 160 J6
Goudhurst 18 B4
Goulceby 79 B5
Gourdas 153 D7
Gourdon 135 B8
Gourock 118 B2
Govan 119 C5
Govanhill 119 C5
Goveton 7 E5
Govilon 35 C6
Gowanhill 153 B10
Gowdall 89 B7
Gowerton 33 E6
Gowkhall 128 F2
Gowthorpe 96 D3
Goxhill E Yorks . . . 97 E7
N Lincs. 90 B5
Goxhill Haven 90 B5
Goytre 34 F1
Grabhair 155 F8
Graby 65 B7
Grade 3 E6
Graffham 16 C3
Grafham Cambs . . 54 C2
Sur 27 E8
Grafton Hereford . 49 F6
N Yorks. 95 C7
Oxon 38 D2
Shrops. 60 C4
Worcs 49 C7
Grafton Flyford . . 50 D4
Grafton Regis 53 E5
Grafton
Underwood 65 F6
Grafty Green 30 E2
Graianrhyd 73 D6
Graig Conwy 83 D8
Denb 72 B4
Graig-fechan 72 D5
Grain 30 B2
Grainsby 91 E6
Grainthorpe 91 E7
Grampound 3 B8
Grampound Road . . 4 D4
Gramsdal 148 C3
Granborough 39 B7

Granby 77 F7
Grandborough . . . 52 C2
Grandtully 133 D6
Grange Cumb 98 C4
E Ayrs. 118 F4
Medway 29 C8
Mers 85 F3
Perth 128 B4
Grange
Crossroads . . . 152 C4
Grange Hall 151 E13
Grange Hill 41 E7
Grangemill 76 D2
Grange Moor 88 C3
Grangemouth . . . 127 F8
Grange of
Lindores 128 C4
Grange-
over-Sands 92 B4
Grangepans 128 F2
Grangetown Cardiff 22 B3
Redcar 102 B3
Grange Villa 110 D5
Granish 138 C5
Gransmoor 97 D7
Granston 44 B3
Grantchester 54 D5
Grantham 78 F2
Grantley 94 C5
Grantlodge 141 C6
Granton Dumfries 114 D3
Edin. 120 B5
Grantown-
on-Spey 139 B6
Grantshouse 122 C4
Grappenhall 86 F4
Grasby 90 D4
Grasmere 99 D5
Grasscroft 87 D7
Grassendale 85 F4
Grassholme 100 B4
Grassington 94 C3
Grassmoor 76 C4
Grassthorpe 77 C7
Grateley 25 E7
Gratwich 75 F7
Graveley Cambs . . 54 C3
Herts. 41 B5
Gravelly Hill 62 E5
Gravels 60 D3
Graven 160 F6
Graveney 30 C4
Gravesend Herts . 41 B7
Kent 29 B7
Grayingham 90 E3
Grayrigg 99 E7
Grays 29 B7
Grayshott 27 F6
Grayswood 27 F7
Graythorp 102 B3
Grazeley 26 C4
Greasbrough 88 E5
Greasby 85 F3
Great Abington . . . 55 E6
Great Addington . . 53 B7
Great Alne 51 D6
Great Altcar 85 D4
Great Amwell 41 C6
Great Asby 100 C1
Great Ashfield 56 C3
Great Ayton 102 C3
Great Baddow 42 D3
Great Bardfield . . . 55 F7
Great Barford 54 D2
Great Barr 62 E4
Great Barrington . . 38 C2
Great Barrow 73 C8
Great Barton 56 C2
Great Barugh 96 B3
Great Bavington . 117 F5
Great Bealings . . . 57 E6
Great Bedwyn 25 C7
Great Bentley 43 B7
Great Billing 53 C6
Great Bircham . . . 80 D3
Great Blakenham . 56 D5
Great Blencow . . . 108 F4
Great Bolas 61 B6
Great Bookham . . 28 D2
Great Bourton . . . 52 E2
Great Bowden 64 F4
Great Bradley 55 D7
Great Braxted 42 C4
Great Bricett 56 D4
Great Brickhill . . . 53 F7
Great Bridge 62 E3
Great Bridgeford . 62 B2
Great Brington . . . 52 C4
Great Bromley . . . 43 B6
Great Broughton
Cumb. 107 F7
N Yorks. 102 D3
Great Budworth . . 74 B3
Great Burdon . . . 101 C8
Great Burgh 28 D3
Great Burstead . . . 42 E2
Great Busby 102 D3
Great Canfield . . . 42 C1
Great Carlton 91 F8
Great Casterton . . 65 D7
Great Chart 30 E3
Great Chatwell . . . 61 C7
Great Chesterford . 55 E6
Great Cheverell . . 24 D4
Great Chishill 54 F5
Great Clacton 43 C7
Great Cliff 88 C4
Great Clifton 98 B2
Great Coates 91 D6
Great Comberton . 50 E4
Great Corby 108 D4
Great Cornard 56 E2
Great Cowden 97 E8
Great Coxwell 38 E2
Great Crakehall . . 101 E7
Great Cransley . . . 53 B6
Great
Cressingham . . . 67 D8
Great Crosby 85 E4
Great Cubley 75 F8
Great Dalby 64 C4
Great Denham 53 E8
Great Doddington . 53 C6
Great Dunham . . . 67 C8
Great Dunmow . . . 42 B2
Great Durnford . . . 25 F6
Great Easton Essex 42 B2
Leics 64 E5
Great Eccleston . . 92 E4

Great Edstone . . . 103 F5
Great Ellingham . . 68 E3
Great Elm 24 E2
Greater Doward . . 36 C2
Great Eversden . . . 54 D4
Great Fencote . . . 101 E7
Great Finborough . 56 D4
Greatford 65 C7
Great Fransham . . 67 C8
Great Gaddesden . 40 C3
Great Gidding 65 F8
Great Givendale . . 96 D4
Great Glemham . . 57 C7
Great Glen 64 E3
Great Gonerby . . . 77 F8
Great Gransden . . 54 D3
Great Green Norf . 69 F5
Suff 56 D3
Great Habton 96 B3
Great Hale 78 E4
Great Hallingbury . 41 C8
Greatham Hants. . 27 F5
Hrtlpl 102 B2
W Sus 16 C4
Great Hampden . . 39 D8
Great Harrowden . 53 B6
Great Harwood . . . 93 F7
Great Haseley 39 D6
Great Hatfield 97 E7
Great Haywood . . . 62 B4
Great Heath 63 F7
Great Heck 89 B6
Great Henny 56 F2
Great Hinton 24 D4
Great Hockham . . . 68 E2
Great Holland 43 C8
Great Horkesley . . 56 F3
Great Hormead . . . 41 B6
Great Horton 94 F4
Great Horwood . . . 53 F5
Great Houghton
S Yorks. 88 D5
W Nhants. 53 D5
Great Hucklow . . . 75 B8
Great Kelk 97 D7
Great Kimble 39 D8
Great Kingshill . . . 40 E1
Great Langton . . . 101 E7
Great Leighs 42 C3
Great Lever 86 D5
Great Limber 90 D5
Great Linford 53 E6
Great Livermere . . 56 B2
Great Longstone . . 76 B2
Great Lumley . . . 111 E5
Great Lyth 60 D4
Great Malvern 50 E2
Great Maplestead . 56 F2
Great Marton 92 F3
Great Massingham . 80 E3
Great Melton 68 D4
Great Milton 39 D6
Great Missenden . 40 D1
Great Mitton 93 F7
Great Mongeham . 31 D7
Great Moulton . . . 68 E4
Great Munden 41 B6
Great Musgrave . 100 C2
Great Ness 60 C3
Great Notley 42 B3
Great Oakley Essex 43 B7
N Nhants. 65 F5
Great Offley 40 B4
Great Ormside . . 100 C2
Great Orton 108 D3
Great Ouseburn . . 95 C7
Great Oxendon . . . 64 F4
Great Oxney
Green 42 D2
Great Palgrave . . . 67 C8
Great Parndon . . . 41 D7
Great Paxton 54 C3
Great Plumpton . . 92 F3
Great Plumstead . 69 C6
Great Ponton 78 F2
Great Preston 88 B5
Great Raveley 66 F2
Great Rissington . . 38 C1
Great Rollright . . . 51 F8
Great Ryburgh . . . 81 E5
Great Ryle 117 C6
Great Ryton 60 D4
Great Saling 42 B3
Great Salkeld 109 F5
Great Sampford . . 55 F7
Great Sankey 86 F3
Great Saxham 55 C8
Great Shefford . . . 25 B8
Great Shelford . . . 54 D5
Great Smeaton . . 101 D8
Great Snoring 81 D5
Great Somerford . 37 F6
Great Stainton . . 101 B8
Great Stambridge . 42 E4
Great Staughton . . 54 C2
Great Steeping . . . 79 C7
Great Stonar 31 D7
Greatstone on Sea 19 C7
Great Strickland . . 99 B7
Great Stukeley . . . 54 B3
Great Sturton 78 B5
Great Sutton
Ches W. 73 B7
Shrops. 60 F5
Great Swinburne . 110 B2
Great Tew 38 B3
Great Tey 42 B4
Great Thurlby 91 F7
Great Thurlow 55 D7
Great Torrington . . 9 C6
Great Tosson 117 D6
Great Totham
Essex 42 C4
Essex 42 C4
Great Tows 91 E6
Great Urswick 92 B2
Great Wakering . . . 43 E5
Great Waldingfield 56 E3
Great Walsingham . 80 D5
Great Waltham . . . 42 C2
Great Warley 42 E1
Great Washbourne . 50 F4
Great Weldon 65 F6
Great Welnetham . 56 D2
Great Wenham . . . 56 F4
Great
Whittington . . . 110 B3
Great Wigborough 43 C5

Great Wilbraham . 55 D6
Great Wishford . . . 25 F5
Great Witcombe . . 37 C5
Great Witley 50 C2
Great Wolford 51 F7
Greatworth 52 E3
Great Wratting . . . 55 E7
Great Wymondley . 41 B5
Great Wyrley 62 D3
Great Wytheford . . 61 C5
Great Yarmouth . . 69 D8
Great Yeldham . . . 55 F8
Greave 87 B6
Greeba 84 D3
Green 72 C4
Greenbank 160 C7
Greenburn 120 C2
Greendikes 117 B6
Green End 54 D2
Greenfield C Beds . 53 F8
Flint 73 B5
Gtr Man 87 D7
Oxon 39 E7
Greenford 40 F4
Greengairs 119 B7
Greenham 26 C2
Greenhaugh 116 F3
Greenhead 109 C6
Greenhill Falk . . . 119 B8
Kent 31 C5
Leics 63 C8
London 40 F4
Greenhills 118 D3
Greenhithe 29 B6
Greenholm 118 F5
Greenholme 99 D7
Greenhow Hill 94 C4
Greenigoe 159 H5
Greenland 158 D4
Greenlands 39 F7
Green Lane 59 E8
Greenlaw Aberds . 153 C6
Borders 122 E3
Greenlea 107 B7
Greenloaning . . . 127 D7
Greenmount 87 C5
Greenmow 160 L6
Greenock 118 B2
Greenock West . . 118 B2
Greenodd 99 F5
Green Ore 23 D7
Greenrow 107 D8
Green St Green . . 29 C5
Greenside 110 C4
Greensidehill . . . 117 C5
Greens Norton . . . 52 E4
Greenstead Green 42 B4
Greensted 41 D8
Green Street 40 E4
Greenway 33 C5
Greenwich 28 B4
Greet 50 F5
Greete 49 B7
Greetham Lincs . . 79 B6
Rutland 65 C6
Greetland 87 B8
Gregg Hall 99 E6
Gregson Lane 86 B3
Greinetobht 148 A3
Greinton 23 F6
Gremista 160 J6
Grenaby 84 E2
Grendon N Nhants . 53 C6
Warks 63 D6
Grendon Common . 63 D6
Grendon Green . . . 49 D7
Grendon
Underwood 39 B6
Grenofen 6 B2
Grenoside 88 E4
Greosabhagh 154 H6
Gresford 73 D7
Gresham 81 D7
Greshornish 149 C8
Gressenhall 68 C2
Gressingham 93 C5
Gresty Green 74 D4
Greta Bridge 101 C5
Gretna 108 C3
Gretna Green 108 C3
Gretton Glos 50 F5
N Nhants. 65 E5
Shrops. 60 E5
Grewelthorpe 94 B5
Greygarth 94 B4
Grey Green 89 D8
Greynor 33 D6
Greysouthen 98 B2
Greystoke 108 F4
Greystone Angus . 135 E5
Dumfries 107 B6
Greywell 26 D5
Griais 155 C9
Grianan 155 D9
Gribthorpe 96 F3
Gribun 146 H7
Gridley Corner 9 E5
Griff 63 F7
Griffithstown 35 E6
Grimbister 159 G4
Grimblethorpe . . . 91 F6
Grimeford Village . 86 C4
Grimethorpe 88 D5
Griminis 148 C2
Grimister 160 D6
Grimley 50 C3
Grimness 159 J5
Grimoldby 91 F7
Grimpo 60 B3
Grimsargh 93 F5
Grimsbury 52 E2
Grimsby 91 C6
Grimscote 52 D4
Grimscott 8 D4
Grimsthorpe 65 B7
Grimston E Yorks . 97 F8
Leics 64 B3
Norf 80 E3
York 96 D2
Grimstone 12 E4
Grinacombe Moor . 9 E6
Grindale 97 B7
Grindigar 159 H6
Grindiscol 160 K6
Grindle 61 D7
Grindleford 76 B2
Grindleton 93 E7
Grindley 62 B4

Grindley Brook . . . 74 E2
Grindlow 75 B8
Grindon Northumb 122 E5
Staffs. 75 D7
Grindonmoor Gate 75 D7
Gringley on the
Hill 89 E8
Grinsdale 108 D3
Grinshill 60 B5
Grinton 101 E5
Griomsidar 155 E8
Grishipoll 146 F4
Grisling Common . 17 B8
Gristhorpe 103 F8
Griston 68 E2
Gritley 159 H6
Grittenham 37 F7
Grittleton 37 F5
Grizebeck 98 F4
Grizedale 99 E5
Grobister 159 F7
Groby 64 D2
Groes Conwy 72 C4
Neath. 34 F1
Groes-faen 34 F4
Groesffordd Marli . 72 B4
Groeslon Gwyn . . 82 E5
Gwyn 82 F4
Groes-lwyd 60 C2
Grogport 143 D9
Gromford 57 D7
Gronant 72 A4
Groombridge 18 B2
Grosmont Mon . . . 35 B8
N Yorks. 103 D6
Groton 56 E3
Groton 56 E3
Grougfoot 120 B3
Grouville Jersey 17
Grove Dorset 12 G5
Kent 31 C6
Notts 77 B7
Oxon 38 E4
Grove Park 28 B5
Grovesend 33 D6
Grove Vale 62 E4
Grudie 150 E6
Gruids 157 J8
Gruinard House . 150 B2
Grula 149 F8
Gruline 147 G8
Grunasound 160 K5
Grundisburgh 57 D6
Grunsagill 93 D7
Grutness 160 N6
Gualachulain . . . 131 E5
Gualin House . . . 156 D6
Guardbridge 129 C6
Guarlford 50 E3
Guay 133 E7
Guestling Green . . 19 D5
Guestling Thorn . . 18 D5
Guestwick 81 E6
Guestwick Green . 81 E6
Guide 86 B5
Guide Post 117 F8
Guilden Morden . . 54 E3
Guilden Sutton . . . 73 C8
Guildford 27 E7
Guildtown 133 F8
Guilsborough 52 B4
Guilsfield 60 C2
Guilton 31 D6
Guineaford 20 F4
Guisborough 102 C4
Guiseley 94 E4
Guist 81 E5
Guith 159 E6
Guiting Power 37 B7
Gulberwick 160 K6
Gullane 129 F6
Gulval 2 C3
Gulworthy 6 B2
Gumfreston 32 D2
Gumley 64 E3
Gummow's Shop . . 4 D3
Gunby E Yorks . . . 96 F3
Lincs 65 B6
Gundleton 26 F4
Gun Hill 18 D2
Gunn 20 F5
Gunnerside 100 E4
Gunnerton 110 B2
Gunness 90 C2
Gunnislake 6 B2
Gunnista 160 J7
Gunthorpe Norf . . 81 D6
Notts 77 E6
Pboro. 65 D8
Gunville 15 F5
Gunwalloe 3 D5
Gurnard 15 E5
Gurney Slade 23 E8
Gurnos 34 D1
Gussage All Saints 13 C8
Gussage
St Michael 13 C7
Guston 31 E7
Gutcher 160 D7
Guthrie 135 D5
Guyhirn 66 D3
Guyhirn Gull 66 D3
Guy's Head 66 B4
Guy's Marsh 13 B6
Guyzance 117 D8
Gwaenysgor 72 A4
Gwalchmai 82 D3
Gwaun-Cae-
Gurwen 33 C8
Gwaun-Leision . . . 33 C8
Gwbert 45 E3
Gweek 3 D5
Gwehelog 35 D7
Gwenddwr 48 E2
Gwennap 3 C6
Gwenter 3 E6
Gwernaffield 73 C6
Gwernesney 35 D8
Gwernogle 46 F4
Gwernymynydd . . . 73 C6
Gwersyllt 73 D7
Gwespyr 73 A6
Gwithian 2 B4
Gwredog 82 C4
Gwyddelwern 72 E4
Gwyddgrug 46 F3
Gwydyr Uchaf 83 E7

Gwystre 48 C2
Gwytherin 83 E8
Gyfelia 73 E7
Gyffin 83 D7
Gyre 159 H4
Gyrn-goch 70 C5

H

Habberley 60 D3
Habergham 93 F8
Habrough 90 C5
Haceby 78 F3
Hacheston 57 D7
Hackbridge 28 C3
Hackenthorpe 88 F5
Hackford 68 D3
Hackforth 101 E7
Hackland 159 F4
Hackleton 53 D6
Hackness N Yorks . 103 E7
Orkney 159 J4
Hackney 41 F6
Hackthorn 90 F3
Hackthorpe 99 B7
Haconby 65 B8
Hacton 41 F8
Hadden 122 F3
Haddenham Bucks 39 D7
Cambs 55 B5
Haddington
E Loth. 121 B8
Lincs 78 C2
Haddiscoe 69 E7
Haddon Cambs . . . 65 E8
Ches E. 74 C6
Hade Edge 88 D2
Hademore 63 D5
Hadfield 87 E8
Hadham Cross . . . 41 C7
Hadham Ford 41 B7
Hadleigh Essex . . 42 F4
Suff 56 E4
Hadley 61 C6
Hadley End 62 B5
Hadlow 29 E7
Hadlow Down 18 C2
Hadnall 60 C5
Hadstock 55 E6
Hady 76 B3
Hadzor 50 C4
Haffenden Quarter 30 E2
Hafod-Dinbych . . . 83 F8
Hafod-lom 83 D8
Haggate 93 F8
Haggbeck 108 B4
Haggerston 123 E6
Haggrister 160 F5
Hagley Hereford . 49 F7
Worcs 62 F3
Hagworthingham . 79 C6
Haigh Gtr Man . . . 86 D4
S Yorks. 88 C3
Haigh Moor 88 B3
Haighton Green . . 93 F5
Hail Weston 54 C2
Hailey Herts 41 C6
Oxon 38 C3
Hailsham 18 E2
Haimer 158 D3
Hainault 41 E7
Hainford 68 C5
Hainton 91 F5
Hairmyres 119 D6
Haisthorpe 97 C7
Hakin 44 E3
Halam 77 D6
Halbeath 128 F3
Halberton 10 C5
Halcro 158 D4
Hale Gtr Man 87 F5
Halton 86 F3
Hants. 14 C2
Hale Bank 86 F2
Halebarns 87 F5
Hales Norf 69 E6
Staffs. 74 F4
Halesfield 61 D7
Halesgate 66 B3
Halesowen 62 F3
Hales Place 30 D5
Hale Street 29 E7
Halesworth 57 B7
Halewood 86 F2
Halford Shrops . . . 60 F4
Warks 51 E7
Halfpenny Furze . . 32 C3
Halfpenny Green . 62 E2
Halfway Carms . . . 46 F5
Carms 47 F7
W Berks 26 C2
Halfway Bridge . . . 16 B3
Halfway House . . . 60 C3
Halfway Houses . . 30 B3
Halifax 87 B8
Halket 118 D4
Halkirk 158 E3
Halkyn 73 B6
Halland 18 D2
Hallaton 64 E4
Hallatrow 23 D8
Hallbankgate . . . 109 D5
Hall Dunnerdale . . 98 E4
Hall Green W Mid . 62 F5
W Yorks. 88 C4
Hall Grove 41 C5
Halliburton 122 E2
Hallin 148 C7
Halling 29 C8
Hallington Lincs . . 91 F7
Northumb 110 B2
Halliwell 86 C5
Hall of
Tankerness . . . 159 H6
Hall of the Forest . 60 F2
Halloughton 77 D6
Hallow 50 D3
Hallrule 115 C8
Halls 122 B2
Hallsands 7 F6
Hall's Green 41 B5
Hallthwaites 98 F3
Hallworthy 8 F3
Hallyburton
House 134 F2

Hallyne 120 E4
Halmer End 74 E4
Halmore 36 D3
Halmyre Mains . . 120 E4
Halnaker 16 D3
Halsall 85 C4
Halse Som 11 B6
Northants 52 E3
Halsetown 2 C4
Halsham 91 B6
Halsinger 20 F4
Halstead Essex . . . 56 F2
Kent 29 C5
Leics 64 D4
Halstock 12 D3
Haltham 78 C5
Haltoft End 79 E6
Halton Bucks 40 C1
Lancs 92 C5
Northumb 110 C2
Wrex 73 F7
W Yorks. 95 F6
Halton East 94 D3
Halton Gill 93 B8
Halton Holegate . . 79 C7
Halton Lea Gate . 109 D6
Halton West 93 D8
Haltwhistle 109 C7
Halvergate 69 D7
Halwell 7 D5
Halwill 9 E6
Halwill Junction . . 9 D6
Ham Devon 11 D7
Glos. 36 E3
Highld 158 C4
Kent 31 D7
London. 28 B2
Shetland 160 K1
Wilts 25 C8
Hambleden 39 F7
Hambledon Hants 15 C7
Sur. 27 F7
Hamble-le-Rice . . 15 D5
Hambleton Lancs . 92 E3
N Yorks. 95 F8
Hambridge 11 B8
Hambrook S Glos . 23 B8
W Sus 15 D8
Ham Common . . . 13 B6
Hameringham . . . 79 C6
Hamerton 54 B2
Hametoun 160 K1
Ham Green
Hereford 50 E2
Kent 19 C5
Kent 30 C2
N Som 23 B7
Worcs 50 C5
Hamilton 119 D7
Hammer 27 F6
Hammerpot 16 D4
Hammersmith 28 B3
Hammerwich 62 D4
Hammerwood 28 F5
Hammond Street . . 41 D6
Hammoon 13 C6
Hamnavoe
Shetland 160 E4
Shetland 160 E6
Shetland 160 F6
Shetland 160 K5
Hampden Park . . . 18 E3
Hamperden End . . 55 F6
Hampnett 37 C7
Hampole 89 C6
Hampreston 13 E8
Hampstead 41 F5
Hampstead
Norreys 26 B3
Hampsthwaite . . . 95 D5
Hampton Phoro . . 65 E8
London. 28 C2
Shrops. 61 F7
Worcs 50 E5
Hampton Bishop . 49 F7
Hampton Heath . . 73 E8
Hampton in Arden 63 F6
Hampton Loade . . 61 F7
Hampton Lovett . . 50 C3
Hampton Lucy . . . 51 D7
Hampton on the
Hill 51 C7
Hampton Poyle . . . 39 C5
Hamrow 80 E5
Hamsey 17 C8
Hamsey Green . . . 28 D4
Hamstall Ridware . 62 C5
Hamstead IoW . . . 14 E5
W Mid 62 E4
Hamstead
Marshall 26 C2
Hamsterley
Durham 110 D4
Durham 110 F4
Hamstreet 19 B7
Ham Street 23 F7
Hamworthy 13 E7
Hanbury Staffs . . 63 B5
Worcs 50 C4
Hanbury Woodend 63 B5
Hanby 78 F3
Hanchurch 74 E5
Handbridge 73 C8
Handcross 17 B6
Handforth 87 F6
Handley 73 D8
Handsacre 62 C4
Handsworth
S Yorks. 88 F5
W Mid 62 E4
Handy Cross 9 B6
Hanford 75 E5
Hanging Langford . 24 F5
Hangleton 16 D4
Hanham 23 B8
Hankelow 74 E3
Hankerton 37 E6
Hankham 18 E3
Hanley 75 E5
Hanley Castle 50 E3
Hanley Child 49 C8
Hanley Swan 50 E3
Hanley William . . . 49 C8
Hanlith 94 C2
Hanmer 73 F8
Hannah 79 B8
Hannington Hants 26 D3
Swindon 38 E1

Hannington *continued*
W Nhants.....53 B6
Hannington Wick...38 E1
Hansel Village....118 F3
Hanslope.....53 E6
Hanthorpe.....65 B7
Hanwell London...40 F4
Oxon.....52 E2
Hanwood.....60 D4
Hanworth London..28 B2
Norf.....81 D7
Happendon....119 F8
Happisburgh....69 A6
Happisburgh
Common.....69 B6
Hapsford.....73 B8
Hapton Lancs....93 F7
Norf.....68 E4
Harberton.....7 D5
Harbertonford.....7 D5
Harbledown.....30 D5
Harborne.....62 F4
Harborough
Magna.....52 B2
Harbottle.....117 D5
Harbury.....51 D8
Harby Leics....77 F7
Notts.....77 B8
Harcombe.....11 E6
Harden W Mid....62 D4
W Yorks.....94 F3
Hardenhuish.....24 B4
Hardgate.....141 D6
Hardham.....16 C4
Hardingham.....68 D3
Hardingstone.....53 D5
Hardington.....24 D2
Hardington
Mandeville.....12 C3
Hardington Marsh.12 D3
Hardley.....14 D5
Hardley Street.....69 D6
Hardmead.....53 E7
Hardrow.....100 E3
Hardstoft.....76 C4
Hardway Hants....15 D7
Som.....24 F2
Hardwick Bucks....39 C8
Cambs.....54 D4
N Nhants.....53 C6
Norf.....67 C6
Norf.....68 F5
Notts.....77 B6
Oxon.....38 D3
Oxon.....39 B5
W Mid.....62 E3
Hardwicke Glos....36 C4
Glos.....37 B6
Hereford.....48 E4
Hardy's Green.....43 B5
Hareby.....79 C6
Hareden.....93 D6
Harefield.....40 E3
Hare Green.....43 B6
Hare Hatch.....27 B6
Harehills.....95 F6
Harehope.....117 B6
Haresceugh.....109 E6
Harescombe.....37 C5
Haresfield.....37 C5
Hareshaw.....119 C8
Hareshaw Head.116 F4
Hare Street.....41 B6
Harewood.....95 E6
Harewood End....36 B2
Harford Carms....46 E5
Devon.....6 D4
Hargate.....68 E4
Hargatewall.....75 B8
Hargrave Ches W..73 C8
N Nhants.....53 B8
Suff.....55 D8
Harker.....108 C3
Harkland.....160 E6
Harkstead.....57 F5
Harlaston.....63 C6
Harlaw House....141 B6
Harlaxton.....77 F8
Harlech.....71 D6
Harlequin.....77 F6
Harlescott.....60 C5
Harlesden.....41 F5
Harleston Devon....7 E5
Norf.....68 F5
Suff.....56 D4
Harlestone.....52 C5
Harle Syke.....93 F8
Harley Shrops....61 D5
S Yorks.....88 E4
Harleyholm.....120 F2
Harlington C Beds..53 F8
London.....27 B8
S Yorks.....89 D5
Harlosh.....149 D7
Harlow.....41 C7
Harlow Hill
Northumb.....110 C3
N Yorks.....95 D5
Harlthorpe.....96 F3
Harlton.....54 D4
Harman's Cross..13 F7
Harmby.....101 F6
Harmer Green....41 C5
Harmer Hill.....60 B4
Harmondsworth...27 B8
Harmston.....78 C2
Harnham.....110 B3
Harnhill.....37 D7
Harold Hill.....41 E8
Haroldswick.....160 B8
Harold Wood.....41 E8
Harome.....102 F4
Harpenden.....40 C4
Harpford.....11 E5
Harpham.....97 C6
Harpley Norf....80 E3
Worcs.....49 C8
Harpole.....52 C4
Harpsdale.....158 E3
Harpsden.....39 F7
Harpswell.....90 F3
Harpurhey.....87 D6
Harpur Hill.....75 C7
Harraby.....108 D4
Harrapool.....149 F11
Harrier.....160 J1
Harrietfield.....127 B8
Harrietsham.....30 D2

Harrington Cumb...98 B1
Lincs.....79 B6
N Nhants.....64 F4
Harringworth....65 E6
Harris.....146 B6
Harrogate.....95 D6
Harrold.....53 D7
Harrow.....40 F4
Harrowbarrow....5 C8
Harrowden.....53 D8
Harrowgate Hill.101 C7
Harrow on the Hill..40 F4
Harrow Street.....56 F3
Harrow Weald....40 E4
Harston Cambs....54 D5
Leics.....77 F8
Harswell.....96 E4
Hart.....111 F7
Hartburn
Northumb.....117 F6
Stockton.....102 C2
Hart Common....86 D4
Hartest.....56 D2
Hartfield.....29 F5
Hartford Cambs....54 B3
Ches W.....74 B3
Hartfordbridge....27 D5
Hartford End.....42 C2
Harthill Ches W...74 D2
N Lanark.....120 C2
S Yorks.....89 F5
Hart Hill.....40 B4
Hartington.....75 C8
Hartland.....8 B4
Hartlebury.....50 B3
Hartlepool.....111 F8
Hartley Cumb....100 D2
Kent.....18 A4
Kent.....29 C7
Northumb.....111 B6
Hartley Westpall..26 D4
Hartley Wintney...27 D5
Hartlip.....30 C2
Hartoft End.....103 E5
Harton N Yorks...96 C3
Shrops.....60 F4
T&W.....111 C6
Hartpury.....36 B4
Hartshead.....88 B2
Hartshill.....63 E7
Hartshorne.....63 B7
Hartsop.....99 C6
Hart Station.....111 F7
Hartwell.....53 D5
Hartwood.....119 D8
Harvieston.....126 F4
Harvington.....51 E5
Harvington Cross..51 E5
Harwell.....38 F4
Harwich.....57 F6
Harwood Durham.109 F8
Gtr Man.....86 C5
Harwood Dale....103 E7
Harworth.....89 E7
Hasbury.....62 F3
Hascombe.....27 E7
Haselbech.....52 B5
Haselbury
Plucknett.....12 C2
Haseley.....51 C7
Haselor.....51 D6
Hasfield.....37 B5
Hasguard.....44 E3
Haskayne.....85 D4
Hasketon.....57 D6
Hasland.....76 C3
Haslemere.....27 F7
Haslingden.....87 B5
Haslingfield.....54 D5
Haslington.....74 D4
Hassall.....74 D4
Hassall Green....74 D4
Hassall Street.....30 E4
Hassendean.....115 B8
Hassingham.....69 D6
Hassocks.....17 C6
Hassop.....76 B2
Hastigrow.....158 D4
Hastingleigh.....30 E4
Hastings.....18 E5
Hastingwood.....41 D7
Hastoe.....40 D2
Haswell.....111 E6
Haswell Plough..111 E6
Hatch C Beds....54 E2
Hants.....26 D4
Wilts.....13 B7
Hatch Beauchamp.11 B8
Hatch End.....40 E4
Hatchet Gate.....14 D4
Hatch Green.....11 C8
Hatching Green...40 C4
Hatchmere.....74 B2
Hatcliffe.....91 D6
Hatfield Hereford..49 D7
Herts.....41 D5
S Yorks.....89 D7
Worcs.....50 D3
Hatfield Broad
Oak.....41 C8
Hatfield Garden
Village.....41 D5
Hatfield Heath....41 C8
Hatfield Hyde....41 C5
Hatfield Peverel...42 C3
Hatfield
Woodhouse.....89 D7
Hatford.....38 E3
Hatherden.....25 D8
Hatherleigh.....9 D7
Hathern.....63 B8
Hatherop.....38 D1
Hathersage.....88 F3
Hathershaw.....87 D7
Hatherton Ches E..74 E3
Staffs.....62 C3
Hatley St George..54 D3
Hatt.....5 C8
Hattingley.....26 F4
Hatton Aberds...153 E10
Derbys.....63 B6
Lincs.....78 B4
Shrops.....60 E4
Warks.....51 C7
Hatton Castle.....153 D7
Hattoncrook.....141 B7
Hatton Heath....73 C8

Hatton of Fintray.141 C7
Haugh E Ayrs....112 B4
Gtr Man.....87 C7
Lincs.....79 B7
Haugham.....91 F7
Haugh Head.....117 B6
Haughley.....56 C4
Haughley Green...56 C4
Haugh of Glass...152 E4
Haugh of Urr....106 C5
Haughs of
Clinterty.....141 C7
Haughton Notts...77 B6
Shrops.....60 B3
Shrops.....60 D3
Shrops.....61 D7
Shrops.....61 E6
Staffs.....62 B2
Haughton Castle.110 B2
Haughton Green...87 E7
Haughton Moss...74 D2
Haultwick.....41 B6
Haunn Argyll....146 G6
W Isles.....148 G2
Haunton.....63 C6
Hauxley.....117 D8
Hauxton.....54 D5
Havant.....15 D8
Haven.....49 D6
Haven Bank.....78 D5
Haven Side.....91 B5
Havenstreet.....15 E6
Havercroft.....88 C4
Haverfordwest
=Hwlffordd.....44 D4
Haverhill.....55 E7
Havering-
atte-Bower.....41 E8
Haveringland.....81 E7
Haversham.....53 E6
Haverthwaite.....99 F5
Haverton Hill.....102 B2
Hawarden
=Penarlâg.....73 C7
Hawcoat.....92 B2
Hawen.....46 E2
Hawes.....100 F3
Hawes' Green....68 E5
Hawes Side.....92 F3
Hawford.....50 C3
Hawkchurch.....11 D8
Hawkedon.....55 D8
Hawkenbury Kent..18 B2
Kent.....30 E2
Hawkeridge.....24 D3
Hawkerland.....11 F5
Hawkesbury S Glos.36 F4
Warks.....63 F7
Hawkesbury Upton 36 F4
Hawkes End.....63 F7
Hawk Green.....87 F7
Hawkhill.....117 C8
Hawkhurst.....18 B4
Hawkinge.....31 F6
Hawkley.....15 B8
Hawkridge.....21 F7
Hawkshead.....99 E5
Hawkshead Hill...99 E5
Hawksland.....119 F8
Hawkswick.....94 B2
Hawksworth Notts..77 E7
W Yorks.....94 E4
W Yorks.....95 F5
Hawkwell.....42 E4
Hawley Hants....27 D6
Kent.....29 B6
Hawling.....37 B7
Hawnby.....102 F3
Haworth.....94 F3
Hawstead.....56 D2
Hawthorn Durham 111 E7
Rhondda.....35 F5
Wilts.....24 C3
Hawthorn Hill
Brack.....27 B6
Lincs.....78 D5
Hawthorpe.....65 B7
Hawton.....77 D7
Haxby.....96 D2
Haxey.....89 D8
Haydock.....86 E3
Haydon.....12 C4
Haydon Bridge...109 C8
Haydon Wick.....37 F8
Haye.....5 C8
Hayes London....28 C5
London.....40 F4
Hayfield Derbys...87 F8
Fife.....128 E4
Hay Green.....66 C5
Hayhill.....112 C4
Hayhillock.....135 E5
Hayle.....2 C4
Hayley Green.....62 F3
Haynes.....53 E8
Haynes Church
End.....53 E8
Hay-on-Wye
=Y Gelli Gandryll..48 E4
Hayscastle.....44 C3
Hayscastle Cross..44 C4
Hayshead.....135 E6
Hay Street.....41 B6
Hayton Aberdeen.141 D8
Cumb.....107 E8
Cumb.....108 D5
E Yorks.....96 E4
Notts.....89 F8
Hayton's Bent....60 F5
Haytor Vale.....7 B5
Haywards Heath...17 B7
Haywood.....89 C6
Haywood Oaks....77 D6
Hazelbank.....119 E8
Hazelbury Bryan..12 D5
Hazeley.....26 D5
Hazel Grove.....87 F7
Hazelhurst.....87 D7
Hazelslade.....62 C4
Hazel Street.....18 B3
Hazelton.....37 C7
Hazelton Walls...128 B5
Hazelwood.....76 E3
Hazlemere.....40 E1
Hazlerigg.....110 B5
Hazlewood.....94 D3
Hazon.....117 D7
Heacham.....80 D2

Headbourne
Worthy.....26 F2
Headbrook.....48 D5
Headcorn.....30 E2
Headingley.....95 F5
Headington.....39 D5
Headlam.....101 C6
Headless Cross...50 C5
Headley Hants....26 C3
Hants.....27 F6
Sur.....28 D3
Head of Muir....127 F7
Headon.....77 B7
Heads.....119 E7
Heads Nook.....108 D4
Heage.....76 D3
Healaugh N Yorks.101 E5
N Yorks.....95 E7
Heald Green.....87 F6
Heale Devon....20 E5
Som.....23 E8
Healey Durham...110 D3
Northumb.....110 D3
N Yorks.....101 F6
Healing.....91 C6
Heamoor.....2 C3
Heanish.....146 G3
Heanor.....76 E4
Heanton
Punchardon.....20 F4
Heapham.....90 F2
Hearthstane.....114 B4
Heasley Mill.....21 F6
Heast.....149 G11
Heath Cardiff....22 B3
Derbys.....76 C4
Heath and Reach..40 B2
Heathcote.....75 C8
Heath End Hants...27 E6
Sur.....27 E6
Warks.....51 C7
Heather.....63 C7
Heatherfield.....149 D9
Heathfield Devon...7 B6
E Sus.....18 C2
Som.....11 B6
Heathhall.....107 B6
Heath Hayes.....62 C4
Heath Hill.....61 C7
Heath House.....23 E6
Heathrow Airport..27 B8
Heathstock.....11 D7
Heathton.....62 E2
Heath Town.....62 E3
Heatley.....86 F5
Heaton Lancs....92 C4
Staffs.....75 C6
T&W.....111 C5
W Yorks.....94 F4
Heaton Moor.....87 E6
Heaverham.....29 D6
Heaviley.....87 F7
Heavitree.....10 E4
Hebburn.....111 C6
Hebden.....94 C3
Hebden Bridge....87 B7
Hebron Anglesey..82 C4
Carms.....32 B2
Northumb.....117 F7
Heck.....114 F3
Heckfield.....26 C5
Heckfield Green...57 B5
Heckfordbridge...43 B5
Heckington.....78 E4
Heckmondwike....88 B3
Heddington.....24 C4
Heddle.....159 G4
Heddon-on-
the-Wall.....110 C4
Hedenham.....69 E6
Hedge End.....15 C5
Hedgerley.....40 F2
Hedging.....11 B8
Hedley on the
Hill.....110 D3
Hednesford.....62 C4
Hedon.....91 B5
Hedsor.....40 F2
Hedworth.....111 C6
Heeley.....88 F4
Heggerscales.....100 C3
Heglibister.....160 H5
Heighington Darl.101 B7
Lincs.....78 C3
Heights of Brae..151 E8
Heights of
Kinlochewe.....150 E3
Heilam.....156 C7
Heiton.....122 F3
Hele Devon....10 D4
Devon.....20 E4
Helensburgh....145 E11
Helford.....3 D6
Helford Passage....3 D6
Helhoughton.....80 E4
Helions
Bumpstead.....55 E7
Hellaby.....89 E6
Helland.....5 B5
Hellandbridge.....5 B5
Hellesdon.....68 C5
Hellidon.....52 D3
Hellifield.....93 D8
Hellingly.....18 D2
Hellington.....69 D6
Hellister.....160 J5
Helm.....117 E7
Helmdon.....52 E3
Helmingham.....57 D5
Helmington Row..110 F4
Helmsdale.....157 H13
Helmshore.....87 B5
Helmsley.....102 F4
Helperby.....95 C7
Helperthorpe.....97 B5
Helpringham.....78 E4
Helpston.....65 D8
Helsby.....73 B8
Helsey.....79 B8
Helston.....3 D5
Helstone.....8 F2
Helton.....99 B7
Helwith Bridge...93 C8
Hemblington.....69 C6
Hemel Hempstead.40 D3
Hemingbrough....96 F2
Hemingby.....78 B5
Hemingford
Abbots.....54 B3
Hemingford Grey..54 B3

Hemingstone.....57 D5
Hemington Leics...63 B8
N Nhants.....65 F7
Som.....24 D2
Hemley.....57 E6
Hemlington.....102 C3
Hemp Green.....57 C7
Hempholme.....97 D6
Hempnall.....68 E5
Hempnall Green...68 E5
Hempriggs
House.....158 F5
Hempstead Essex..55 F7
Medway.....29 C8
Norf.....69 B7
Norf.....81 D7
Hempsted.....37 C5
Hempton Norf....80 E5
Oxon.....52 F2
Hemsby.....69 C7
Hemswell.....90 E3
Hemswell Cliff....90 F3
Hemsworth.....88 C5
Hemyock.....11 C6
Henbury Bristol....23 B7
Ches E.....75 B5
Hendon London...41 F5
T&W.....111 D7
Hendre.....73 C5
Hendre-ddu.....83 E8
Hendreforgan.....34 F3
Hendy.....33 D6
Hen-feddau fawr..45 F4
Henfield.....17 C6
Henford.....9 E5
Henghurst.....19 B6
Hengoed Caerph..35 E5
Powys.....48 D4
Shrops.....73 F6
Hengrave.....56 C2
Henham.....41 B8
Heniarth.....59 D8
Henlade.....11 B7
Henley Shrops....49 B7
Som.....23 F6
Suff.....57 D5
W Sus.....16 B2
Henley-in-Arden..51 C6
Henley-on-
Thames.....39 F7
Henley's Down.....18 D4
Henllan Ceredig..46 E2
Denb.....72 C4
Henllan Amgoed..32 B2
Henllys.....35 E6
Henlow.....54 F2
Hennock.....10 F3
Henny Street.....56 F2
Henryd.....83 D7
Henry's Moat.....32 B1
Hensall.....89 B6
Henshaw.....109 C7
Hensingham.....98 C1
Henstead.....69 F7
Henstridge.....12 C5
Henstridge Ash...12 B5
Henstridge Marsh.12 B5
Henton Oxon....39 D7
Som.....23 E6
Henwood.....5 B7
Heogan.....160 J6
Heol-las.....33 E7
Heol Senni.....34 B3
Heol-y-Cyw.....34 F3
Hepburn.....117 B6
Hepple.....117 D5
Hepscott.....117 F8
Heptonstall.....87 B7
Hepworth Suff....56 B3
W Yorks.....88 D2
Herbrandston.....44 E3
Hereford.....49 E7
Heriot.....121 D6
Hermiston.....120 B4
Hermitage
Borders.....115 E8
Dorset.....12 D4
W Berks.....26 B3
W Sus.....15 D8
Hermon Anglesey..82 E3
Carms.....33 B7
Carms.....46 F2
Pembs.....45 F4
Herne.....31 C5
Herne Bay.....31 C5
Herner.....9 B7
Hernhill.....30 C4
Herodsfoot.....5 C7
Herongate.....42 E2
Heronsford.....104 A5
Herriard.....26 E4
Herringfleet.....69 E7
Herringswell.....55 B8
Hersden.....31 C6
Hersham Corn....8 D4
Sur.....28 C2
Herstmonceux....18 D3
Herston.....159 J5
Hertford.....41 C6
Hertford Heath....41 C6
Hertingfordbury..41 C6
Hesket
Newmarket.....108 F3
Hesketh Bank....86 B2
Hesketh Lane.....93 E6
Heskin Green.....86 C3
Hesleden.....111 F7
Hesledyne.....116 F4
Heslington.....96 D2
Hessay.....95 D8
Hessenford.....5 D8
Hessett.....56 C3
Hessle.....90 B4
Hest Bank.....92 C4
Heston.....28 B2
Hestwall.....159 G3
Heswall.....85 F3
Hethe.....39 B5
Hethersett.....68 D4
Hethersgill.....108 C4
Hethpool.....116 B4
Hett.....111 F5
Hetton.....94 D2
Hetton-le-Hole..111 E6
Hetton Steads...123 F6
Heugh.....110 B3
Heugh-head.....140 C2
Heveningham.....57 B7

Hever.....29 E5
Heversham.....99 F6
Hevingham.....81 E7
Hewas Water.....3 B8
Hewelsfield.....36 D2
Hewish N Som...23 C6
Som.....12 D2
Heworth.....96 D2
Hexham.....110 C2
Hextable.....29 B6
Hexton.....54 F2
Hexworthy.....6 B4
Hey.....93 E8
Heybridge Essex..42 C3
Essex.....42 D4
Heybridge Basin..42 D4
Heybrook Bay.....6 E3
Heydon Cambs....54 E5
Norf.....81 E7
Heydour.....78 F3
Heylipol.....146 G2
Heylor.....160 E4
Heysham.....92 C4
Heyshott.....16 C2
Heyside.....87 D7
Heytesbury.....24 E4
Heythrop.....38 B3
Heywood Gtr Man..87 C6
Wilts.....24 D3
Hibaldstow.....90 D3
Hickleton.....89 D5
Hickling Norf....69 B7
Notts.....64 B3
Hickling Green....69 B7
Hickling Heath....69 B7
Hickstead.....17 B6
Hidcote Boyce....51 E6
High Ackworth....88 C5
Higham Derbys...76 D3
Kent.....29 B8
Lancs.....93 F8
Suff.....55 C8
Suff.....56 F4
Higham Dykes....110 B4
Higham Ferrers...53 C7
Higham Gobion...54 F2
Higham on the Hill 63 E7
Highampton.....9 D6
Higham Wood....29 E6
High Angerton....117 F6
High Bankhill.....109 E5
High Barnes.....111 D6
High Beach.....41 E7
High Bentham....93 C6
High Bickington....9 B8
High Birkwith....93 B7
High Blantyre....119 D6
High
Bonnybridge.....119 B8
High Bradfield....88 E3
High Bray.....21 F5
Highbridge Highld.136 F4
Som.....22 E5
Highbrook.....28 F4
High Brooms.....29 E6
High Bullen.....9 B7
Highbury.....23 E8
High Buston.....117 D8
High Callerton....110 B4
High Catton.....96 D3
Highclere.....26 C2
Highcliffe.....14 E3
High Cogges.....38 D3
High Coniscliffe..101 C7
High Cross Hants..15 B8
Herts.....41 C6
High Easter.....42 C2
High Eggborough.89 B6
High Ellington....101 F6
Higher Ansty.....13 D5
Higher Ashton....10 F3
Higher Ballam....92 F3
Higher Bartle.....92 F5
Higher Boscaswell.2 C2
Higher
Burwardsley.....74 D2
Higher Clovelly.....8 B5
Higher End.....86 D3
Higher Kinnerton..73 C7
Higher
Penwortham.....86 B3
Higher Town.....2 E4
Higher Walreddon..6 B2
Higher Walton
Lancs.....86 B3
Warr.....86 F3
Higher Wheelton..86 B4
Higher Whitley....86 F4
Higher Wincham..74 B3
Higher Wych.....73 E8
High Ercall.....61 C5
High Etherley....101 B6
High Ferry.....79 E6
Highfield E Yorks..96 F3
Gtr Man.....86 D5
N Ayrs.....118 D3
Oxon.....39 B5
S Yorks.....88 F4
T&W.....110 D4
Highfields Cambs..54 D4
Northumb.....123 D5
High Garrett.....42 B3
Highgate.....41 F5
High Grange.....110 F4
High Green Norf...68 D4
S Yorks.....88 E4
Worcs.....50 E3
High Halden.....19 B5
High Halstow.....29 B8
High Ham.....23 F6
High Harrington..98 B2
High Hatton.....61 B6
High Hawsker....103 D7
High Hesket.....108 E4
High Hesleden...111 F7
High Hoyland.....88 C3
High Hunsley.....97 F5
High Hurstwood..17 B8
High Hutton.....96 C3
High Ireby.....108 F2
High Kelling.....81 C7
High Kilburn.....95 B8
High Lands.....101 B6
Highlane Ches E..75 C5
Derbys.....88 F4
High Lane Gtr Man.87 F7
Worcs.....49 C8
High Laver.....41 D8

Highlaws.....107 E8
Highleadon.....36 B4
High Legh.....86 F5
Highleigh.....16 E2
High Leven.....102 C2
Highley.....61 F7
High Littleton....23 D8
High Lorton.....98 B3
High Marishes.....96 B4
High Marnham....77 B8
High Melton.....89 D6
High Mickley.....110 C3
High Mindork....105 D7
Highmoor Cross...39 F7
Highmoor Hill....36 F1
Highnam.....36 C4
Highnam Green...36 B4
High Newton.....99 F6
High Newton-
by-the-Sea....117 B8
High Nibthwaite..98 F4
High Offley.....61 B7
High Ongar.....42 D1
High Onn.....62 C2
High Roding.....42 C2
High Row.....108 F3
High Salvington...16 D5
High Sellafield....98 D2
High Shaw.....100 E3
High Spen.....110 D4
High Stoop.....110 E4
High Street Corn....4 D4
Kent.....18 B4
Suff.....56 E2
Suff.....57 B8
Suff.....57 D8
Highstreet Green..55 F8
High Street Green.56 D4
Hightae.....107 B7
High Throston....111 F7
High Toynton.....79 C5
High Trewhitt....117 D6
High Valleyfield..128 F2
Highway.....24 B5
Highweek.....7 B6
High Westwood..110 D4
Highworth.....38 E2
High Wray.....99 E5
High Wych.....41 C7
High Wycombe....40 E1
Hilborough.....67 D8
Hilcote.....76 D4
Hilcott.....25 D6
Hildenborough....29 E6
Hilden Park.....29 E6
Hildersham.....55 E6
Hilderstone.....75 F6
Hilderthorpe.....97 C7
Hilfield.....12 D4
Hilgay.....67 E6
Hill S Glos....36 E3
W Mid.....62 E5
Hillam.....89 B6
Hillbeck.....100 C2
Hillborough.....31 C6
Hillbrae Aberds...153 E7
Aberds.....152 D6
Hill Brow.....15 B8
Hillbutts.....13 D7
Hillclifflane.....76 E2
Hillcommon.....11 B6
Hill Dale.....86 C2
Hill Dyke.....79 E6
Hilldyke.....79 E6
Hillend.....128 F3
Hill End Durham..110 F3
Fife.....128 E2
N Yorks.....94 D3
Hillerton.....10 D2
Hillesden.....39 B6
Hillesley.....36 F4
Hillfarance.....11 B6
Hillhead Aberds..152 E5
Devon.....7 D7
S Ayrs.....112 C4
Hill Head Hants...15 D6
Northumb.....110 C2
Hillhead of
Auchentumb...153 C9
Hillhead of
Cocklaw.....153 D10
Hillhouse.....121 D8
Hilliclay.....158 D3
Hillingdon.....40 F3
Hillington Glasgow 118 C5
Norf.....80 E3
Hillmorton.....52 B3
Hill Mountain....44 E4
Hillockhead
Aberds.....140 C3
Aberds.....140 D2
Hill of Beath....128 E3
Hill of Fearn.....151 D11
Hill of
Mountblairy...153 C6
Hill Ridware.....62 C4
Hillside Aberds...141 F7
Angus.....135 C7
Mers.....85 C4
Orkney.....159 J5
Shetland.....160 G6
Hillswick.....160 F4
Hill Top Durham..110 B4
Hants.....14 D5
W Mid.....62 E4
W Yorks.....88 C4
Hill View.....13 E7
Hillway.....15 F7
Hillwell.....160 M5
Hilmarton.....24 B5
Hilperton.....24 D3
Hilsea.....15 D7
Hilston.....97 F8
Hilton Aberds...153 E9
Cambs.....54 C3
Cumb.....100 B2
Derbys.....76 F2
Dorset.....13 D5
Durham.....101 B6
Highld.....151 D10
Shrops.....61 E7
Stockton.....102 C2
Hilton of
Cadboll.....151 D11
Himbleton.....50 D4

Himley.....62 E2
Hincaster.....99 F7
Hinckley.....63 E8
Hinderclay.....56 B4
Hinderton.....73 B7
Hinderwell.....103 C5
Hindford.....73 F7
Hindhead.....27 F6
Hindley.....86 D4
Hindley Green....86 D4
Hindlip.....50 D3
Hindolveston.....81 E6
Hindon.....24 F4
Hindringham.....81 D5
Hingham.....68 D3
Hinstock.....61 B6
Hintlesham.....56 E4
Hinton Hants....14 E3
Hereford.....48 F5
S Glos.....24 B2
Shrops.....60 D4
W Nhants.....52 D3
Hinton Ampner....15 B6
Hinton Blewett....23 D7
Hinton
Charterhouse....24 D2
Hinton-in-
the-Hedges....52 F3
Hinton Martell....13 D8
Hinton on the
Green.....50 E5
Hinton Parva.....38 F2
Hinton St George..12 C2
Hinton St Mary...13 C5
Hinton Waldrist...38 E3
Hints Shrops....49 B8
Staffs.....63 D5
Hinwick.....53 C7
Hinxhill.....30 E4
Hinxton.....55 E5
Hinxworth.....54 E3
Hipperholme.....88 B2
Hipswell.....101 E6
Hirael.....83 D5
Hiraeth.....32 B2
Hirn.....141 D6
Hirnant.....59 B7
Hirst N Lanark...119 C8
Northumb.....117 F8
Hirst Courtney....89 B7
Hirwaen.....72 C5
Hirwaun.....34 D3
Hiscott.....9 B7
Histon.....54 C5
Hitcham.....56 D3
Hitchin.....40 B4
Hither Green.....28 B4
Hittisleigh.....10 E2
Hive.....96 F4
Hixon.....62 B4
Hoaden.....31 D6
Hoaldalbert.....35 B7
Hoar Cross.....62 B5
Hoarwithy.....36 B2
Hoath.....31 C6
Hobarris.....48 B5
Hobbister.....159 H4
Hobkirk.....115 C8
Hobson.....110 D4
Hoby.....64 C3
Hockering.....68 C3
Hockerton.....77 D7
Hockley.....42 E4
Hockley Heath....51 B6
Hockliffe.....40 B2
Hockwold cum
Wilton.....67 F7
Hockworthy.....10 C5
Hoddesdon.....41 D6
Hoddlesden.....86 B5
Hoddomcross....107 B8
Hoddom Mains...107 B8
Hodgeston.....32 E1
Hodley.....59 E8
Hodnet.....61 B6
Hodthorpe.....76 B5
Hoe Hants....15 C6
Norf.....68 C2
Hoe Gate.....15 C7
Hoff.....100 C1
Hoggard's Green..56 D2
Hoggeston.....39 B8
Hogha Gearraidh.148 A2
Hoghton.....86 B4
Hognaston.....76 D2
Hog Patch.....27 E6
Hogsthorpe.....79 B8
Holbeach.....66 B3
Holbeach Bank....66 B3
Holbeach Clough..66 B3
Holbeach Drove...66 C3
Holbeach St Johns 66 C3
Holbeach St Marks 79 F6
Holbeach
St Matthew.....79 F7
Holbeck Notts....76 B5
W Yorks.....95 F5
Holbeck
Woodhouse.....76 B5
Holberrow Green..50 D5
Holbeton.....6 D4
Holborn.....41 F6
Holbrook Derbys...76 E3
Suff.....57 F5
S Yorks.....88 F5
Holburn.....123 F6
Holbury.....14 D5
Holcombe Devon...7 B7
Som.....23 E8
Holcombe Rogus..11 C5
Holcot.....53 C5
Holden.....93 E7
Holdenby.....52 C4
Holdenhurst.....14 E2
Holdgate.....61 F5
Holdingham.....78 E3
Holditch.....11 D8
Holefield.....122 F4
Holehouses.....74 B4
Hole-in-the-Wall..36 B3
Holemoor.....9 D6
Holestane.....113 E8
Holford.....22 E3
Holgate.....95 D8
Holker.....92 B3
Holkham.....80 C4
Hollacombe Devon..9 D5
Som.....23 B8

Holland *continued*
Orkney.....159 F7
Holland Fen.....78 E5
Holland-on-Sea....43 C8
Hollandstoun.....159 C8
Hollee.....108 C2
Hollesley.....57 E7
Hollicombe.....7 C6
Hollingbourne....30 D2
Hollington Derbys..76 F2
E Sus.....18 D4
Staffs.....75 F7
Hollingworth
Grove.....76 C4
Hollingworth.....87 E8
Hollins.....87 D6
Hollinsclough.....75 C7
Hollins Green.....86 E4
Hollins Lane.....92 D4
Hollinwood
Gtr Man.....87 D7
Shrops.....74 F2
Hollocombe.....9 C8
Holloway.....76 D3
Hollowell.....52 B4
Hollow Meadows..88 F3
Hollybush Caerph..35 D5
E Ayrs.....112 C3
Worcs.....50 F2
Holly End.....66 D4
Holly Green.....50 E3
Hollym.....91 B7
Hollywood.....51 B5
Holmbridge.....88 D2
Holmbury St Mary 28 E2
Holmbush.....4 D5
Holmcroft.....62 B3
Holme Cambs....65 F8
Cumb.....92 B5
Notts.....77 D8
N Yorks.....102 F1
W Yorks.....88 D2
Holme Chapel....87 B6
Holme Green.....95 E8
Holme Hale.....67 D8
Holme Lacy.....49 F7
Holme Marsh.....48 D5
Holme next the
Sea.....80 C3
Holme-on-
Spalding-Moor..96 F4
Holme on the
Wolds.....97 E5
Holme Pierrepont.77 F6
Holmer.....49 E7
Holmer Green....40 E2
Holme
St Cuthbert.....107 E8
Holmes Chapel...74 C4
Holmesfield.....76 B3
Holmeswood.....86 C2
Holmewood.....76 C4
Holme Wood.....94 F4
Holmfirth.....88 D2
Holmhead
Dumfries.....113 F7
E Ayrs.....113 B5
Holmisdale.....148 D6
Holmpton.....91 B7
Holmrook.....98 E2
Holmsgarth.....160 J6
Holmwrangle.....108 E5
Holne.....6 C5
Holnest.....12 D4
Holsworthy.....8 D5
Holsworthy Beacon.9 D5
Holt Dorset.....13 D8
Norf.....81 D6
Wilts.....24 C3
Worcs.....50 C3
Wrex.....73 D8
Holtby.....96 D2
Holt End Hants...26 F4
Worcs.....51 C5
Holt Fleet.....50 C3
Holt Heath.....50 C3
Holton Oxon....39 D6
Som.....12 B4
Suff.....57 B7
Holton cum
Beckering.....90 F5
Holton Heath.....13 E7
Holton le Clay....91 D6
Holton le Moor....90 E4
Holton St Mary...56 F4
Holt Park.....95 E5
Holwell Dorset....12 C5
Herts.....54 F2
Leics.....64 B4
Oxon.....38 D2
Holwick.....100 B4
Holworth.....13 F5
Holy Cross.....50 B4
Holybourne.....26 E5
Holyhead
=Caergybi.....82 C2
Holy Island.....123 E7
Holymoorside.....76 C3
Holyport.....27 B6
Holystone.....117 D5
Holytown.....119 C7
Holywell Cambs...54 B4
Corn.....4 D2
Dorset.....12 D3
E Sus.....18 F2
Northumb.....111 B6
Holywell
=Treffynnon.....73 B5
Holywell Green....87 C8
Holywell Lake....11 B6
Holywell Row.....55 B8
Holywood.....114 F2
Homer.....61 D6
Homersfield.....69 F5
Hom Green.....36 B2
Homington.....14 B2
Honeyborough....44 E4
Honeybourne.....51 E6
Honeychurch.....9 D8
Honey Hill.....30 C5
Honey Street.....25 C6
Honey Tye.....56 F3
Honiley.....51 B7
Honing.....69 B6
Honingham.....68 C4
Honington Lincs...78 E2
Suff.....56 B3

Honington continued
Warks 51 E7
Honiton 11 D6
Honley 88 C2
Hood Green 88 D4
Hooe E Sus 18 E3
  Plym 6 D3
Hooe Common 18 D3
Hoo Green 86 F5
Hook E Yorks 89 B8
  Hants 26 D5
  London 28 C2
  Pembs 44 D4
  Wilts 37 F7
Hooke 12 E3
Hookgate 74 F4
Hook Green Kent 18 B3
  Kent 29 C7
Hook Norton 51 F8
Hookway 10 E3
Hookwood 28 E3
Hoole 73 C8
Hooley 28 D3
Hoop 36 D2
Hoo St Werburgh 29 B8
Hooton 73 B7
Hooton Levitt 89 E6
Hooton Pagnell 89 D5
Hooton Roberts 89 E5
Hope Derbys 88 F2
  Devon 6 F4
  Highld 156 B7
  Powys 60 D2
  Shrops 60 D3
  Staffs 75 D8
Hope = Yr Hôb 73 D7
Hope Bagot 49 B7
Hope Bowdler 60 E4
Hope End Green 42 B1
Hope Green 87 F7
Hopeman 152 B1
Hope Mansell 36 C3
Hopesay 60 F3
Hope's Green 42 F3
Hope under
  Dinmore 49 D7
Hopley's Green 48 D5
Hopperton 95 D7
Hop Pole 65 C8
Hopstone 61 E7
Hopton Shrops 60 B3
  Shrops 61 B5
  Staffs 62 B3
  Suff 56 B3
Hopton Cangeford 60 F5
Hopton Castle 49 B5
Hoptonheath 49 B5
Hopton on Sea 69 D8
Hopton Wafers 49 B8
Hopwas 63 D5
Hopwood Gtr Man 87 D6
  Worcs 50 B5
Horam 18 D2
Horbling 78 F4
Horbury 88 C3
Horcott 38 D1
Horden 111 E7
Horderley 60 F4
Hordle 14 E3
Hordley 73 F7
Horeb Carms 33 B6
  Carms 33 D5
  Ceredig 46 E2
Horfield 23 B8
Horham 57 B6
Horkesley Heath 43 B5
Horkstow 90 C3
Horley Oxon 52 E2
  Sur. 28 E3
Hornblotton Green 23 F7
Hornby Lancs 93 C5
  N Yorks 101 E7
  N Yorks 102 D1
Horncastle 79 C5
Hornchurch 41 F8
Horncliffe 122 E5
Horndean Borders 122 E4
  Hants 15 C8
Horndon 6 B3
Horndon on the
  Hill 42 F2
Horne 28 E4
Horniehaugh 134 C4
Horning 69 C6
Horninghold 64 E5
Horninglow 63 B6
Horningsea 55 C5
Horningtoft 80 E5
Hornsby 108 D5
Horns Corner 18 C4
Horns Cross Devon 9 B5
  E Sus 18 C5
Hornsea 97 E8
Hornsea Bridge 97 E8
Hornsey 41 F6
Hornton 51 E8
Horrabridge 6 C3
Horringer 56 C2
Horringford 15 F6
Horsebridge Devon 6 B2
  Hants 25 F8
Horse Bridge 75 D6
Horsebrook 62 C2
Horsehay 61 D6
Horseheath 55 E7
Horsehouse 101 F5
Horsell 27 D7
Horseman's Green 73 E8
Horseway 66 F4
Horsey 69 B7
Horsford 68 C4
Horsforth 94 F5
Horsham Worcs 50 D2
  W Sus 28 F2
Horsham St Faith 68 C5
Horsington Lincs 78 C4
  Som 12 B5
Horsley Derbys 76 E3
  Glos 37 E5
  Northumb 110 C3
  Northumb 116 E4
Horsley Cross 43 B7
Horsleycross
  Street 43 B7
Horsleyhill 115 C8

Horsleyhope 110 E3
Horsley
  Woodhouse 76 E3
Horsmonden 29 E7
Horspath 39 D5
Horstead 69 C5
Horsted Keynes 17 B7
Horton Bucks 40 C2
  Dorset 13 D8
  Lancs 93 D8
  S Glos 36 F4
  Shrops 60 B4
  Som 11 C8
  Staffs 75 D6
  Swansea 33 F5
  Wilts 25 C5
  Windsor 27 B8
  W Nhants 53 D6
Horton-cum-
  Studley 39 C5
Horton Green 73 E8
Horton Heath 15 C5
Horton in
  Ribblesdale 93 B8
Horton Kirby 29 C6
Hortonlane 60 C4
Horwich 86 C4
Horwich End 87 F8
Horwood 9 B7
Hose 64 B4
Hoselaw 122 F4
Hoses 98 E4
Hosh 127 B7
Hosta 148 A2
Hoswick 160 L6
Hotham 96 F4
Hothfield 30 E3
Hoton 64 B2
Houbie 160 D8
Houdston 112 E1
Hough Ches E 74 D4
  Ches E 75 B5
Hougham 77 E8
Hough Green 86 F2
Hough-on-
  the-Hill 78 E2
Hougharry 148 A2
Houghton Cambs 54 B3
  Cumb 108 D4
  Hants 25 F8
  Pembs 44 E4
  W Sus 16 C4
Houghton
  Conquest 53 E8
Houghton Green
  E Sus 19 C6
  Warr 86 E4
Houghton-
  le-Side 101 B7
Houghton-
  le-Spring 111 E6
Houghton on the
  Hill 64 D3
Houghton Regis 40 B3
Houghton St Giles 80 D5
Houlland Shetland 160 F7
  Shetland 160 H5
Houlsyke 103 D5
Houlton Warks 52 B3
Hound 15 D5
Hound Green 26 D5
Houndslow 122 E2
Houndwood 122 C4
Hounslow 28 B2
Hounslow Green 42 C2
Housay 160 F8
House of Daviot .151 G10
House of
  Glenmuick 140 E2
Housetter 160 E5
Houss 160 K5
Houston 118 C4
Houstry 158 G3
Houton 159 H4
Hove 17 D6
Hoveringham 77 E6
Hoveton 69 C6
Hovingham 96 B2
How 108 D5
Howbrook 88 E4
How Caple 49 F8
Howden Borders 116 B2
  E Yorks 89 B8
Howden-le-Wear 110 F4
Howe Highld 158 D5
  Norf 69 D5
  N Yorks 101 F8
Howe Bridge 86 D4
Howe Green 42 D3
Howell 78 E4
How End 53 E8
Howe of Teuchar 153 D7
Howe Street Essex 42 C2
  Essex 55 F7
Howey 48 D2
Howgate 120 D5
How Green 29 E5
Howick 117 C8
Howle Durham 101 B5
  Telford 61 B6
Howlett End 55 F6
Howley 11 D7
Hownam 116 C3
Hownam Mains 116 B3
Howpasley 115 D6
Howsham N Lincs 90 D4
  N Yorks 96 C3
Howslack 114 D3
Howtel 122 F4
Howton 35 B8
Howtown 99 C6
Howwood 118 C3
Hoxne 57 B5
Hoy 159 H3
Hoylake 85 F3
Hoyland 88 D3
Hoylandswaine 88 D3
Hubberholme 94 B2
Hubbert's Bridge 79 E5
Huby N Yorks 95 C8
  N Yorks 95 E5
Hucclecote 37 C5
Hucking 30 D2
Hucknall 76 E5
Huddersfield 88 C2
Huddington 50 D4
Hudswell 101 D6
Huggate 96 D4
Hugglescote 63 C8
Hughenden Valley 40 E1

Hughley 61 E5
Hugh Town 2 E4
Huish Devon 9 C7
  Wilts 25 C6
Huish
  Champflower 11 B5
Huish Episcopi 12 B2
Huisinis 154 F4
Hulcott 40 C1
Hulland 76 E2
Hulland Ward 76 E2
Hullavington 37 F5
Hullbridge 42 E4
Hulme 87 E6
Hulme End 75 D8
Hulme Walfield 74 C5
Hulverstone 14 F4
Hulver Street 69 F7
Humber 49 D7
Humber Bridge 90 B4
Humberston 91 D7
Humbie 121 C7
Humbleton E Yorks 97 F8
  Northumb 117 B5
Humby 78 F3
Hume 122 E3
Humshaugh 110 B2
Huna 158 C5
Huncoat 93 F7
Huncote 64 E2
Hundalee 116 C2
Hunderthwaite 100 B4
Hundleby 79 C6
Hundle Houses 79 D5
Hundleton 44 E4
Hundon 55 E8
Hundred Acres 15 C6
Hundred End 86 B2
Hundred House 48 D3
Hungarton 64 D3
Hungerford Hants 14 C2
  W Berks 25 C8
Hungerford
  Newtown 25 B8
Hungerton 65 B5
Hunglader 149 A8
Hunmanby 97 B6
Hunmanby Moor 97 B7
Hunningham 51 C8
Hunny Hill 15 F5
Hunsdon 41 C7
Hunsingore 95 D7
Hunslet 95 F6
Hunsonby 109 F5
Hunspow 158 C4
Hunstanton 80 C2
Hunstanworth 110 E2
Hunsterson 74 E3
Hunston Suff 56 C3
  W Sus 16 D2
Hunstrete 23 C8
Hunt End 50 C5
Hunter's Quay 145 F10
Hunthill Lodge 134 B4
Huntingdon 54 B3
Huntingfield 57 B7
Huntingford 24 F3
Huntington E Loth 121 B7
  Hereford 48 D4
  Staffs 62 C3
  York 96 D2
Huntingtower 128 B2
Huntley 36 C4
Huntly 152 E5
Huntlywood 122 E2
Hunton Kent 29 E8
  N Yorks 101 E6
Hunt's Corner 68 F3
Hunt's Cross 86 F2
Huntsham 10 B5
Huntspill 22 E5
Huntworth 22 F5
Hunwick 110 F4
Hunworth 81 D6
Hurdsfield 75 B6
Hurley Warks 63 E6
  Windsor 39 F8
Hurlford 118 F4
Hurliness 159 K3
Hurn 14 E2
Hurn's End 79 E7
Hursley 14 B5
Hurst N Yorks 101 D5
  Som 12 C2
  Wokingham 27 B5
Hurstbourne
  Priors 26 E2
Hurstbourne
  Tarrant 25 D8
Hurst Green E Sus 18 C4
  Lancs 93 F6
Hurstpierpoint 17 C6
Hurst Wickham 17 C6
Hurstwood 93 F8
Hurtmore 27 E7
Hurworth Place 101 D7
Hury 100 C4
Husabost 148 C7
Husbands
  Bosworth 64 F3
Husborne Crawley 53 F7
Husthwaite 95 B8
Hutchwns 21 B7
Huthwaite 76 D4
Hutoft 79 B8
Hutton Borders 122 D5
  Cumb 99 B6
  Essex 42 E2
  E Yorks 97 D6
  Lancs 86 B2
  N Som 22 D5
Hutton Buscel 103 F7
Hutton Conyers 95 B6
Hutton Cranswick 97 D6
Hutton End 108 F4
Hutton Gate 102 C3
Hutton Henry 111 F7
Hutton-le-Hole 103 E5
Hutton Magna 101 C6
Hutton Roof Cumb 108 F3
  Cumb 93 B5
Hutton Rudby 102 D2
Hutton Sessay 95 B7
Hutton Village 102 C3
Hutton Wandesley 95 D8
Huxley 74 C2
Huxter Shetland 160 G7
  Shetland 160 H5
Huxton 122 C4

Huyton 86 E2
Hwlffordd
  = Haverfordwest 44 D4
Hycemoor 98 F2
Hyde Glos 37 D5
  Gtr Man 87 E7
  Hants 14 C2
Hyde Heath 40 D2
Hyde Park 89 D6
Hydestile 27 E7
Hylton Castle 111 D6
Hyndford Bridge 120 E2
Hynish 146 H2
Hyssington 60 E3
Hythe Hants 14 D5
  Kent 19 B8
Hythe End 27 B8
Hythie 153 C10

I

Ibberton 13 D5
Ible 76 D2
Ibsley 14 D2
Ibstock 63 C8
Ibstone 39 E7
Ibthorpe 25 D8
Ibworth 26 D3
Ichrachan 125 B6
Ickburgh 67 E8
Ickenham 40 F3
Ickford 39 D6
Ickham 31 D6
Ickleford 54 F2
Icklesham 19 D5
Ickleton 55 E5
Icklingham 55 B8
Ickwell Green 54 E2
Icomb 38 B2
Idbury 38 C2
Iddesleigh 9 D7
Ide 10 E3
Ideford 7 B6
Iden 19 C6
Iden Green Kent 18 B4
  Kent 18 B5
Idle 94 F4
Idlicote 51 E7
Idmiston 25 F6
Idole 33 C5
Idridgehay 76 E2
Idrigill 149 B8
Idstone 38 F2
Idvies 135 E5
Iffley 39 D5
Ifield 28 F3
Ifold 27 F8
Iford 17 D8
Ifton Heath 73 F7
Ightfield 74 F2
Ightham 29 D6
Iken 57 D8
Ilam 75 D8
Ilchester 12 B3
Ilderton 117 B6
Ilford 41 F7
Ilfracombe 20 E4
Ilkeston 76 E4
Ilketshall
  St Andrew 69 F6
Ilketshall
  St Lawrence 69 F6
Ilketshall
  St Margaret 69 F6
Ilkley 94 E4
Illey 62 F3
Illingworth 87 B8
Illogan 3 B5
Ilmer 39 D7
Ilmington 51 E7
Ilminster 11 C8
Ilsington 7 B5
Ilston 33 E6
Ilton N Yorks 94 B4
  Som 11 C8
Imachar 143 D9
Imeraval 142 D4
Immingham 91 C5
Impington 54 C5
Ince 73 B8
Ince Blundell 85 D4
Ince in Makerfield 86 D3
Inchbare 135 C6
Inchberry 152 C3
Inchbraoch 135 D7
Incheril 150 E3
Inchgrundle 134 B4
Inchina 150 B2
Inchinnan 118 C4
Inchkinloch 157 E8
Inchlaggan 136 D4
Inchlumpie 151 D8
Inchmore 150 G6
Inchnacardoch
  Hotel 137 C6
Inchnadamph 156 G5
Inch of Arnhall 135 B6
Inchree 130 C4
Inchture 128 B4
Inchyra 128 B3
Indian Queens 4 D4
Inerval 142 D4
Ingatestone 42 E2
Ingbirchworth 88 D3
Ingestre 62 B3
Ingham Lincs 90 F3
  Norf 69 B6
  Suff 56 B2
Ingham Corner 69 B6
Ingleborough 66 C4
Ingleby Derbys 63 B7
  Lincs 77 B8
Ingleby Arncliffe 102 D2
Ingleby Barwick 102 C2
Ingleby
  Greenhow 102 D3
Inglemire 97 F6
Inglesbatch 24 C2
Inglesham 38 E2
Ingleton Durham 101 B6
  N Yorks 93 B6
Inglewhite 92 E5
Ingliston 120 B4
Ingoe 110 B3
Ingol 92 F5
Ingoldisthorpe 80 D2

Ingoldmells 79 C8
Ingoldsby 78 F3
Ingon 51 D7
Ingram 117 C6
Ingrow 94 F3
Ings 99 E6
Ingst 36 F2
Ingworth 81 E7
Inham's End 66 E2
Inkberrow 50 D5
Inkpen 25 C8
Inkstack 158 C4
Inn 99 D6
Innellan 145 F10
Innerleithen 121 F6
Innerleven 129 D5
Innermessan 104 C4
Innerwick E Loth 122 B3
  Perth 132 E2
Innis Chonain 125 C7
Insch 140 B5
Insh 138 D4
Inshore 156 C6
Inskip 92 F4
Instoneville 89 C6
Instow 20 F3
Intake 89 D6
Inver Aberds 139 E8
  Highld 151 C11
  Perth 133 E7
Inverailort 147 C10
Inveraldie 134 F4
Inverallign 149 C13
Inverallochy 153 B10
Inveran 151 B8
Inveraray 125 E6
Inverarish 149 E10
Inverarity 134 E4
Inverarnan 126 C2
Inverasdale 155 J13
Inverbeg 126 E2
Inverbervie 135 B8
Inverboyndie 153 B6
Inverbroom 150 C4
Invercassley 156 J7
Invercauld House .139 E7
Inverchaolain 145 F9
Invercharnan 131 E5
Inverchoran 150 F5
Invercreran 130 E4
Inverdruie 138 C5
Inverebrie 153 E9
Invereck 145 E10
Inverernan
  House 140 C2
Invereshie House .138 D4
Inveresk 121 B6
Inverey 139 F6
Inverfarigaig 137 B8
Invergarry 137 D6
Invergelder 139 E8
Invergeldie 127 B6
Invergordon 151 E10
Invergowrie 134 F3
Inverguseran 149 H12
Inverhadden 132 D3
Inverharroch 152 E3
Inverherive 126 B2
Inverie 147 B10
Inverinan 125 D5
Inverinate 136 B2
Inverkeilor 135 E6
Inverkeithing 128 F3
Inverkeithny 153 D6
Inverkip 118 B2
Inverkirkaig 156 H3
Inverlael 150 C4
Inverlochlarig 126 C3
Inverlochy Argyll 125 C7
  Highld 131 B5
Inverlussa 144 E5
Inver Mallie 136 F4
Invermark Lodge 140 B4
Invermoidart 147 D9
Invermoriston 137 C7
Invernaver 157 C10
Inverneill 145 E7
Inverness 151 G9
Invernettie 153 D11
Invernoaden 125 F7
Inveroran Hotel 131 E6
Inverpolly Lodge 156 H3
Inverquharity 134 D4
Inverquhomery 153 D10
Inverroy 137 F5
Inversanda 130 D3
Invershiel 136 C2
Invershin 151 B8
Inversnaid Hotel .126 D2
Inveruglas 126 D2
Inveruglass 138 D4
Inverurie 141 B6
Invervar 132 E3
Inverythan 153 D7
Inwardleigh 9 E7
Inworth 42 C4
Iochdar 148 D2
Iping 16 B2
Ipplepen 7 C6
Ipsden 39 F6
Ipsley 51 C5
Ipstones 75 E7
Ipswich 57 E5
Irby 85 F3
Irby in the Marsh 79 C7
Irby upon Humber 91 D5
Irchester 53 C7
Ireby Cumb 108 F2
  Lancs 93 B6
Ireland Orkney 159 H4
  Shetland 160 L5
Ireland's Cross 74 E4
Ireleth 92 B2
Ireshopeburn 109 F8
Irlam 86 E5
Irnham 65 B7
Iron Acton 36 F3
Ironbridge 61 D6
Iron Cross 51 D5
Irongray 107 B6
Ironmacannie 106 B3
Ironside 153 D8
Ironville 76 D4
Irstead 69 B6
Irthington 108 C4
Irthlingborough 53 B7
Irton 103 F8
Irvine 118 F3

Isauld 157 C12
Isbister Orkney 159 F3
  Orkney 159 G4
  Shetland 160 D5
  Shetland 160 H5
Isfield 17 C8
Isham 53 B6
Isle Abbotts 11 B8
Isle Brewers 11 B8
Isleham 55 B7
Isle of Whithorn 105 F8
Isleornsay 149 G12
Islesburgh 160 G5
Islesteps 107 B6
Isleworth 28 B2
Isley Walton 63 B8
Islibhig 154 E4
Islington 41 F6
Islip N Nhants 53 B7
  Oxon 39 C5
Istead Rise 29 C7
Isycoed 73 D8
Itchen 14 C5
Itchen Abbas 26 F3
Itchen Stoke 26 F3
Itchingfield 16 B5
Itchington 36 F3
Itteringham 81 D7
Itton 9 E8
Itton Common 36 E1
Ivegill 108 E4
Iver 40 F3
Iver Heath 40 F3
Iveston 110 D4
Ivinghoe 40 C2
Ivinghoe Aston 40 C2
Ivington 49 D6
Ivington Green 49 D6
Ivy Chimneys 41 D7
Ivychurch 19 C7
Ivy Cross 13 B6
Ivy Hatch 29 D6
Iwade 30 C3
Iwerne Courtney
  or Shroton 13 C6
Iwerne Minster 13 C6
Ixworth 56 B3
Ixworth Thorpe 56 B3

J

Jack Hill 94 D5
Jack in the Green 10 E5
Jacksdale 76 D4
Jackstown 153 E7
Jacobstow 8 E3
Jacobstowe 9 D7
Jameston 32 E1
Jamestown
  Dumfries 115 E6
  Highld 150 F7
  W Dunb 126 F2
Jarrow 111 C6
Jarvis Brook 18 C2
Jasper's Green 42 B3
Java 124 B3
Jawcraig 119 B8
Jaywick 43 C7
Jealott's Hill 27 B6
Jedburgh 116 B2
Jeffreyston 32 D1
Jellyhill 119 B6
Jemimaville 151 E10
Jersey Farm 40 D4
Jesmond 111 C5
Jevington 18 E2
Jockey End 40 C3
Johnby 108 F4
John o'Groats 158 C5
John's Cross 18 C4
Johnshaven 135 C7
Johnston E Renfs 118 C4
  Pembs 44 D4
Johnstonebridge .114 E3
Johnstown Carms 33 C5
  Wrex 73 E7
Joppa Edin 121 B6
  S Ayrs 112 C4
Jordans 40 E2
Jordanthorpe 88 F4
Jump 88 D4
Jumpers Green 14 E2
Juniper Green 120 C4
Jurby East 84 C3
Jurby West 84 C3

K

Kaber 100 C2
Kaimend 120 E2
Kaimes 121 C5
Kalemouth 116 B3
Kames Argyll 124 D4
  Argyll 145 F8
  E Ayrs 113 B6
Kea 3 B7
Keadby 90 C2
Keal Cotes 79 C6
Kearsley 87 D5
Kearstwick 99 F8
Kearton 100 E4
Kearvaig 156 B5
Keasden 93 C7
Keckwick 86 F3
Keddington 91 F7
Kedington 55 E8
Kedleston 76 E3
Keelby 91 C5
Keele 74 E5
Keeley Green 53 E8
Keeston 44 D4
Keevil 24 D4
Kegworth 63 B8
Kehelland 2 B5
Keig 140 C5
Keighley 94 E3
Keil 130 D3
Keilarsbrae 127 E7
Keilhill 153 C7
Keillmore 144 E5
Keillor 134 E2
Keillour 127 B8
Keills 142 B5
Keils 144 G4

Keir Mill 113 E8
Keisby 65 B7
Keiss 158 D5
Keith 152 C4
Keith Inch 153 D11
Keithock 135 C6
Kelby 78 E3
Keld Cumb 99 C7
  N Yorks 100 D3
Keldholme 103 F5
Kelfield N Lincs 90 D2
  N Yorks 95 F8
Kelham 77 D7
Kellan 147 G8
Kellas Angus 134 F4
  Moray 152 C1
Kellaton 7 F6
Kelleth 100 D1
Kelleythorpe 97 D5
Kelling 81 C6
Kellingley 89 B6
Kellington 89 B6
Kelloe 111 F6
Kelloholm 113 C7
Kelly 9 F5
Kelly Bray 5 B8
Kelmarsh 52 B5
Kelmscot 38 E2
Kelsale 57 C7
Kelsall 74 C2
Kelsall Hill 74 C2
Kelshall 54 F4
Kelsick 107 D8
Kelso 122 F3
Kelstedge 76 C3
Kelstern 91 E6
Kelston 24 C2
Keltneyburn 132 E4
Kelton 107 B6
Kelty 128 E3
Kelvedon 42 C4
Kelvedon Hatch 42 E1
Kelvin 119 D6
Kelvinside 119 C5
Kelynack 2 C2
Kemback 129 C6
Kemberton 61 D7
Kemble 37 E6
Kemerton 50 F4
Kemeys
  Commander 35 D7
Kemnay 141 C6
Kempley 36 B3
Kempley Green 36 B3
Kempsey 50 E3
Kempsford 38 E1
Kemps Green 51 B6
Kempshott 26 D4
Kempston 53 E8
Kempston
  Hardwick 53 E8
Kempton 60 F3
Kemp Town 17 D7
Kemsing 29 D6
Kemsley 30 C3
Kenardington 19 B6
Kenchester 49 E6
Kencot 38 D2
Kendal 99 E7
Kendoon 113 F6
Kendray 88 D4
Kenfig 34 F2
Kenfig Hill 34 F2
Kenilworth 51 B7
Kenknock 132 F1
Kenley London 28 D4
  Shrops 61 D5
Kenmore Highld .149 C12
  Perth 132 E4
Kenn Devon 10 F4
  N Som 23 C6
Kennacley 154 H6
Kennacraig 145 G7
Kennerleigh 10 D3
Kennet 127 E8
Kennethmont 140 B4
Kennett 55 C7
Kennford 10 F4
Kenninghall 68 F3
Kenninghall Heath 68 F3
Kennington Kent 30 E4
  Oxon 39 D5
Kennoway 129 D5
Kenny Hill 55 B7
Kennythorpe 96 C3
Kenovay 146 G2
Kensaleyre 149 C9
Kensington 28 B3
Kensworth 40 C3
Kensworth
  Common 40 C3
Kentallen 130 D4
Kentchurch 35 B8
Kentford 55 C8
Kentisbeare 11 D5
Kentisbury 20 E5
Kentisbury Ford 20 E5
Kentmere 99 D6
Kenton Devon 10 F4
  Suff 57 C5
  T&W 110 C5
Kenton Bankfoot .110 C5
Kentra 147 E9
Kents Bank 92 B3
Kent's Green 36 B4
Kent's Oak 14 B4
Kent Street E Sus 18 D4
  Kent 29 D7
  W Sus 17 B6
Kenwick 73 F8
Kenwyn 3 B7
Keoldale 156 C6
Keppanach 130 C4
Keppoch 136 B2
Keprigan 143 G7
Kepwick 102 E2
Kerchesters 122 F3
Kerdiston 81 E6
Keresley 63 F7
Kernborough 7 E5
Kerne Bridge 36 C2
Kerris 2 D3
Kerry 59 F8
Kerrycroy 145 G10
Kerry's Gate 49 F5
Kersall 77 C7
Kersey 56 E4
Kershopefoot 115 F7
Kersoe 50 F4

Kerswell 11 D5
Kerswell Green 50 E3
Kesgrave 57 E6
Kessingland 69 F8
Kessingland Beach 69 F8
Kestle 3 B8
Kestle Mill 4 D3
Keston 28 C5
Keswick Cumb 98 B4
  Norf 68 D5
  Norf 81 D8
Ketley 61 C6
Ketley Bank 61 C6
Ketsby 79 B6
Kettering 53 B6
Ketteringham 68 D4
Kettins 134 F2
Kettlebaston 56 D3
Kettlebridge 128 D5
Kettleburgh 57 C6
Kettlehill 128 D5
Kettleholm 107 B8
Kettleness 103 C6
Kettleshume 75 B6
Kettlesing Bottom .94 D5
Kettlesing Head 94 D5
Kettlestone 81 D5
Kettlethorpe 77 B8
Kettletoft 159 E7
Kettlewell 94 B2
Ketton 65 D6
Kew 28 B2
Kew Bridge 28 B2
Kewstoke 22 C5
Kexbrough 88 D4
Kexby Lincs 90 F2
  York 96 D3
Key Green 75 C5
Keyham 64 D3
Keyhaven 14 E4
Keyingham 91 B6
Keymer 17 C7
Keynsham 23 C8
Keysoe 53 C8
Keysoe Row 53 C8
Keyston 53 B8
Keyworth 77 F6
Kibblesworth 110 D5
Kibworth
  Beauchamp 64 E3
Kibworth Harcourt 64 E3
Kidbrooke 28 B5
Kiddemore Green .62 D2
Kidderminster 50 B3
Kiddington 38 B4
Kidlington 38 C4
Kidmore End 26 B4
Kidsgrove 74 D5
Kidstones 100 F4
Kidwelly
  = Cydweli 33 D5
Kiel Crofts 124 B5
Kielder 116 E2
Kierfiold Ho 159 G3
Kilbagie 127 F8
Kilbarchan 118 C4
Kilbeg 149 H11
Kilberry 144 G6
Kilbirnie 118 D3
Kilbride Argyll 124 C5
  Argyll 124 C5
  Highld 149 F10
Kilburn Angus 134 C3
  Derbys 76 E3
  London 41 F5
  N Yorks 95 B8
Kilby 64 E3
Kilchamaig 145 G7
Kilchattan 144 D2
Kilchattan Bay 145 H10
Kilchenzie 143 F7
Kilcheran 124 B4
Kilchiaran 142 B3
Kilchoan Argyll 124 D3
  Highld 146 E7
Kilchoman 142 B3
Kilchrenan 125 C6
Kilconquhar 129 D6
Kilcot 36 B3
Kilcoy 151 F8
Kilcreggan 145 E11
Kildale 102 D4
Kildalloig 143 G8
Kildary 151 D10
Kildermorie
  Lodge 151 D8
Kildonan 143 F11
Kildonan Lodge .157 G12
Kildonnan 146 C7
Kildrummy 140 C3
Kildwick 94 E3
Kilfinan 145 F8
Kilfinnan 137 E5
Kilgetty 32 D2
Kilgwrrwg
  Common 36 E1
Kilham E Yorks 97 C6
  Northumb 122 F4
Kilkenneth 146 G2
Kilkerran 143 G8
Kilkhampton 8 C5
Killamarsh 89 F5
Killay 33 E7
Killbeg 147 G9
Killean 143 D7
Killearn 126 F4
Killen 151 F9
Killerby 101 C6
Killichonan 132 D2
Killiechonate 136 F5
Killiechronan 147 G8
Killiecrankie 133 C6
Killiemor 146 H7
Killiemore House .146 J6
Killilan 150 H2
Killimster 158 E5
Killin 132 F2
Killinallan 142 A4
Killinghall 95 D5
Killington 99 F8
Killingworth 111 B5
Killin Lodge 137 D8
Killmahumaig 144 D6
Killochyett 121 E7
Killocraw 143 E7
Killundine 147 G8
Kilmacolm 118 C3
Kilmaha 124 D5

Kilmahog 126 D5
Kilmalieu 130 D2
Kilmaluag 149 A9
Kilmany 129 B5
Kilmarie 149 G10
Kilmarnock 118 F4
Kilmaron Castle .129 C5
Kilmartin 124 F4
Kilmaurs 118 E4
Kilmelford 124 D4
Kilmeny 142 B4
Kilmersdon 23 D8
Kilmeston 15 B6
Kilmichael 143 F7
Kilmichael
  Glassary 145 D7
Kilmichael of
  Inverlussa 144 E6
Kilmington Devon 11 E7
  Wilts 24 F2
Kilmonivaig 136 F4
Kilmorack 150 G7
Kilmore Argyll 124 C4
  Highld 149 H11
Kilmory Argyll 144 F6
  Highld 147 D8
  Highld 149 H8
  N Ayrs 143 F10
Kilmuir Highld 148 D7
  Highld 149 A8
  Highld 151 D10
  Highld 151 G9
Kilmun Argyll 124 D5
  Argyll 145 E10
Kilncadzow 119 E8
Kilndown 18 B4
Kilnhurst 89 E5
Kilninian 146 G6
Kilninver 124 C4
Kiln Pit Hill 110 D3
Kilnsea 91 C8
Kilnsey 94 C2
Kilnwick 97 E5
Kilnwick Percy 96 D4
Kiloran 144 D2
Kilpatrick 143 F10
Kilpeck 49 F6
Kilphedir 157 H12
Kilpin 89 B8
Kilpin Pike 89 B8
Kilrenny 129 D7
Kilsby 52 B3
Kilspindie 128 B4
Kilsyth 119 B7
Kiltarlity 151 G8
Kilton Notts 77 B5
  Som 22 E3
Kilton Thorpe 102 C4
Kilvaxter 149 B8
Kilve 22 E3
Kilvington 77 E7
Kilwinning 118 E3
Kimberley Norf. 68 D3
  Notts 76 E5
Kimberworth 88 E5
Kimblesworth 111 E5
Kimble Wick 39 D8
Kimbolton Cambs 53 C8
  Hereford 49 C7
Kimcote 64 F2
Kimmeridge 13 G7
Kimmerston 123 F5
Kimpton Hants 25 E7
  Herts 40 C4
Kinbrace 157 F11
Kinbuck 127 D6
Kincape 129 C6
Kincardine Fife 127 F8
  Highld 151 C9
Kincardine
  Bridge 127 F8
Kincardine O'Neil 140 E4
Kinclaven 134 F1
Kincorth 141 D8
Kincorth House .151 E13
Kincraig 138 D4
Kincraigie 133 E6
Kindallachan 133 E6
Kineton Glos. 37 B7
  Warks 51 D8
Kinfauns 128 B3
Kingairloch 130 D2
Kingarth 145 H9
Kingcoed 35 D8
King Edward 153 C7
Kingerby 90 E4
Kingham 38 B2
Kingholm Quay .107 B6
Kinghorn 128 F4
Kingie 136 D4
Kinglassie 128 E4
Kingoodie 128 B5
King's Acre 49 E6
Kingsand 6 D2
Kingsbarns 129 C7
Kingsbridge Devon 6 E5
  Som 21 F8
King's Bromley 62 C5
Kingsburgh 149 C8
Kingsbury London 41 F5
  Warks 63 E6
Kingsbury
  Episcopi 12 B2
King's Caple 36 B2
Kingsclere 26 D3
King's Cliffe 65 E7
Kingscote 37 E5
Kingscott 9 C7
King's Coughton 51 D5
Kingscross 143 F11
Kingsdon 12 B3
Kingsdown 31 E7
Kingseat 128 E3
Kingsey 39 D7
Kingsfold W Sus 28 F2
Kingsford E Ayrs 118 E4
  Worcs 62 F2
Kingsforth 90 C4
Kingsgate 31 B7
Kingsheanton 20 F4
King's Heath 62 F4
Kings Hedges 55 C5
King's Hill 29 D7
Kingshouse
  Hotel 131 D6
Kingside Hill 107 D8
Kingskerswell 7 C6
Kingskettle 128 D5
Kingsland Anglesey .82 C2

Kingsland continued
Hereford 49 C6
Kings Langley . . . 40 D3
Kingsley Ches W . . 74 B2
Hants 27 F5
Staffs 75 E7
Kingsley Green . . 27 F6
Kingsley Holt . . . 75 E7
Kingsley Park . . . 53 C5
King's Lynn . . . 67 B6
King's Meaburn . . 99 B8
King's Mills . . . 7 B1
Kingsmuir Angus . 134 E4
Fife 129 D7
Kings Muir . . . 121 F5
King's Newnham . 52 B2
King's Newton . . 63 B7
Kingsnorth . . . 19 B7
King's Norton Leics . 62 E4
W Mid 51 B5
King's Nympton . . 9 C8
King's Pyon . . . 49 D6
King's Ripton . . 54 B3
King's Somborne . 25 F8
King's Stag . . . 12 C5
King's Stanley . . 37 D5
King's Sutton . . 52 F2
Kingstanding . . . 62 E4
Kingsteignton . . 7 B6
King Sterndale . . 75 B7
King's Thorn . . . 49 F7
Kingsthorpe . . . 53 C5
Kingston Cambs . . 54 D4
Devon 6 E4
Dorset 13 D5
Dorset 13 G7
E Loth 129 F7
Hants 14 D2
IoW 15 F5
Kent 31 D5
Moray 152 B3
Kingston Bagpuize 38 E4
Kingston Blount . . 39 E7
Kingston by Sea . . 17 D4
Kingston Deverill . 24 F3
Kingstone Hereford . 48 E5
Som 11 C8
Staffs 62 B4
Kingston Gorse . . 16 D4
Kingston Lisle . . 38 F3
Kingston
Maurward . . . 12 E5
Kingston near
Lewes 17 D7
Kingston on Soar . 64 B2
Kingston Russell . 12 E3
Kingston St Mary . 11 B7
Kingston Seymour . 23 C6
Kingston upon
Hull 90 B4
Kingston upon
Thames . . . 28 C2
Kingston Vale . . 28 B3
Kingstown . . . 108 D3
King's Walden . . 40 B4
Kingswear . . . 7 D6
Kingswells . . . 141 D7
Kingswinford . . 62 F2
Kingswood Bucks . . 39 C6
Glos 36 E4
Hereford . . . 48 D4
Kent 30 D2
Powys . . . 60 D2
S Glos . . . 23 B8
Sur 28 D3
Warks . . . 51 B6
Kings Worthy . . 26 F2
Kingthorpe . . . 78 B4
Kington Hereford . . 48 D4
Worcs 50 D4
Kington Langley . . 24 B4
Kington Magna . . 13 B5
Kington
St Michael . . 24 B4
Kingussie . . . 138 D3
Kingweston . . . 23 F7
Kininvie House . . 152 D3
Kinkell Bridge . . 127 C8
Kinknockie . . . 153 D10
Kinlet 61 F7
Kinloch Fife 128 C4
Highld 146 B6
Highld 149 G11
Highld 156 F6
Perth 133 E8
Perth 134 E2
Kinlochan . . . 130 C2
Kinlochard . . . 126 D3
Kinlochbeoraid . 147 C11
Kinlochbervie . . 156 D5
Kinlocheil . . . 130 B3
Kinlochewe . . . 150 E3
Kinloch Hourn . . 136 D2
Kinloch Laggan . 137 F8
Kinlochleven . . 131 C5
Kinloch Lodge . . 157 D8
Kinlochmoidart 147 D10
Kinlochmorar . . 147 B11
Kinlochmore . . . 131 C5
Kinloch Rannoch 132 D3
Kinlochspelve . . 124 C2
Kinloid 147 C9
Kinloss 151 E13
Kinmel Bay . . . 72 A3
Kinmuck . . . 141 C7
Kinmundy . . . 141 C7
Kinnadie . . . 153 D9
Kinnaird . . . 128 B4
Kinnaird Castle . . 135 D6
Kinneff 135 B8
Kinnelhead . . . 114 D3
Kinnell 135 D6
Kinnerley . . . 60 B3
Kinnersley Hereford 48 E5
Worcs 50 E3
Kinnerton . . . 48 C4
Kinnesswood . . 128 D3
Kinninvie . . . 101 B5
Kinnordy . . . 134 D3
Kinoulton . . . 74 F2
Kinross . . . 128 D3
Kinrossie . . . 134 F1
Kinsbourne Green . 40 C4
Kinsey Heath . . 74 E3
Kinsham Hereford . 49 C5
Worcs 50 F4
Kinsley 88 C5
Kinson 13 E8
Kintbury . . . 25 C8

Kintessack . . . 151 E12
Kintillo 128 C3
Kintocher . . . 140 D4
Kinton Hereford . . 49 B6
Shrops 60 C3
Kintore . . . 141 C6
Kintour . . . 142 C5
Kintra Argyll . . 142 D4
Argyll . . . 146 J6
Kintraw . . . 124 E4
Kinuachdrachd . 124 F3
Kinveachy . . . 138 C5
Kinver 62 F2
Kippax 95 F7
Kippen 127 E5
Kippford or
Scaur . . . 106 D5
Kirbister Orkney . 159 F7
Orkney . . . 159 H4
Kirbuster . . . 159 F3
Kirby Bedon . . . 69 D5
Kirby Bellars . . 64 C4
Kirby Cane . . . 69 E6
Kirby Cross . . . 43 B8
Kirby Grindalythe . 96 C5
Kirby Hill N Yorks . 95 C6
N Yorks . . . 101 D6
Kirby Knowle . . 102 F2
Kirby-le-Soken . . 43 B8
Kirby Misperton . 96 B3
Kirby Muxloe . . 64 D2
Kirby Row . . . 69 E6
Kirby Sigston . . 102 E2
Kirby Underdale . 96 D4
Kirby Wiske . . . 102 F1
Kirdford . . . 16 B4
Kirk 158 E4
Kirkabister . . 160 K6
Kirkandrews . . 106 E3
Kirkandrews upon
Eden 108 D3
Kirkbampton . . 108 D3
Kirkbean . . . 107 D6
Kirk Bramwith . 89 C7
Kirkbride . . . 108 D2
Kirkbuddo . . . 135 E5
Kirkburn Borders . 121 F5
E Yorks . . . 97 D5
Kirkburton . . . 88 C2
Kirkby Lincs . . . 90 E4
Mers 86 E2
N Yorks . . . 102 D3
Kirkby Fleetham . 101 E7
Kirkby Green . . 78 D3
Kirkby-in-Ashfield 76 D5
Kirkby-in-Furness 98 F4
Kirkby la Thorpe . 78 E3
Kirkby Lonsdale . 93 B6
Kirkby Malham . . 93 C8
Kirkby Mallory . . 63 D8
Kirkby Malzeard . 94 B5
Kirkby Mills . . . 103 F5
Kirkbymoorside . 102 F4
Kirkby on Bain . . 78 C5
Kirkby Overblow . 95 E6
Kirkby Stephen . 100 D2
Kirkby Thore . . 99 B8
Kirkby Underwood 65 B7
Kirkby Wharfe . . 95 E8
Kirkcaldy . . . 128 E4
Kirkcambeck . . 108 C5
Kirkcarswell . . 106 E4
Kirkcolm . . . 104 C4
Kirkconnel . . . 113 C7
Kirkconnell . . . 107 C6
Kirkcowan . . . 105 C7
Kirkcudbright . . 106 D3
Kirkdale . . . 85 E4
Kirk Deighton . . 95 D6
Kirk Ella . . . 90 B4
Kirkfieldbank . . 119 E8
Kirkgunzeon . . 107 C5
Kirk Hallam . . 76 E4
Kirkham Lancs . . 92 F4
N Yorks . . . 96 C3
Kirkhamgate . . 88 B3
Kirk Hammerton . 95 D7
Kirkharle . . . 117 F6
Kirkheaton
Northumb . . . 110 B3
W Yorks . . . 88 C2
Kirkhill Angus . . 135 C6
Highld 151 G8
Midloth . . . 120 C5
Moray 152 E2
Kirkhope . . . 115 B6
Kirkhouse . . . 121 F6
Kirkiboll . . . 157 D8
Kirkibost . . . 149 G10
Kirkinch . . . 134 E3
Kirkinner . . . 105 D8
Kirkintilloch . . 119 B6
Kirk Ireton . . . 76 D2
Kirkland Cumb . . 98 C2
Cumb 109 F6
Dumfries . . . 113 C7
Dumfries . . . 113 E8
Kirk Langley . . 76 F2
Kirkleatham . . . 102 B3
Kirklevington . . 102 D2
Kirkley 69 E8
Kirklington Notts . . 77 D6
N Yorks . . . 101 F8
Kirklinton . . . 108 C4
Kirkliston . . . 120 B4
Kirkmaiden . . . 104 F5
Kirk Merrington . 111 F5
Kirk Michael . . 84 C3
Kirkmichael Perth . 133 D7
S Ayrs 112 D3
Kirk Smeaton . . 89 C6
Kirkstall . . . 95 F5
Kirkstead . . . 78 C4
Kirkstile . . . 152 E5
Kirkstyle . . . 158 C5

Kirkton Aberds . . 140 B5
Aberds 153 D6
Angus 134 E4
Angus 134 F4
Borders . . . 115 C8
Dumfries . . . 114 F2
Fife 129 B5
Highld . . . 149 F13
Highld 150 G2
Highld 151 B10
Highld 151 F10
Perth 127 C8
S Lanark . . . 114 B2
Stirling . . . 126 D4
Kirktonhill . . . 121 D7
Kirkton Manor . . 120 F5
Kirkton of Airlie . 134 D3
Kirkton of
Auchterhouse . 134 F3
Kirkton of
Auchterless . . 153 D7
Kirkton of
Barevan . . . 151 G11
Kirkton of
Bourtie . . . 141 B7
Kirkton of
Collace . . . 134 F1
Kirkton of Craig . 135 D7
Kirkton of
Culsalmond . . 153 E6
Kirkton of Durris 141 E6
Kirkton of
Glenbuchat . . 140 C2
Kirkton of
Glenisla . . . 134 C2
Kirkton of
Kingoldrum . . 134 D3
Kirkton of Largo . 129 D6
Kirkton of
Lethendy . . . 133 E8
Kirkton of Logie
Buchan . . . 141 B8
Kirkton of
Maryculter . . 141 E7
Kirkton of
Menmuir . . . 135 C5
Kirkton of
Monikie . . . 134 F1
Kirkton of Oyne . 141 B5
Kirkton of Rayne . 153 E6
Kirkton of Skene . 141 D7
Kirkton of Tough . 140 C5
Kirktown . . . 153 C10
Kirktown of
Alvah 153 B6
Kirktown of
Deskford . . . 152 B5
Kirktown of
Fetteresso . . 141 F7
Kirktown of
Mortlach . . . 152 E3
Kirktown of
Slains 141 B9
Kirkurd . . . 120 E4
Kirkwall . . . 159 G5
Kirkwhelpington . 117 F5
Kirk Yetholm . . 116 B4
Kirmington . . . 90 C5
Kirmond le Mire . 91 E5
Kirn 145 F10
Kirriemuir . . . 134 D3
Kirstead Green . . 69 E5
Kirtlebridge . . 108 B2
Kirtleton . . . 115 F5
Kirtling . . . 55 D7
Kirtling Green . . 55 D7
Kirtlington . . . 38 C4
Kirtomy . . . 157 C10
Kirton Lincs . . . 79 F6
Notts 77 C6
Suff 57 F6
Kirton End . . . 79 E5
Kirton Holme . . 79 E5
Kirton in Lindsey . 90 E3
Kislingbury . . 52 D4
Kites Hardwick . 52 C2
Kittisford . . . 11 B5
Kittle 33 F6
Kitt's Green . . 63 F5
Kitt's Moss . . . 87 F6
Kittybrewster . . 141 D8
Kitwood . . . 26 F4
Kivernoll . . . 49 F6
Kiveton Park . . 89 F5
Knaith 90 F2
Knaith Park . . 90 F2
Knap Corner . . 13 B6
Knaphill . . . 27 D7
Knapp Perth . . . 134 F2
Som 11 B8
Knapthorpe . . . 77 D7
Knapton Norf . . . 81 D9
York 95 D8
Knapton Green . . 49 D6
Knapwell . . . 54 C4
Knaresborough . 95 D6
Knarsdale . . . 109 D6
Knauchland . . . 152 C5
Knaven . . . 153 D8
Knayton . . . 102 F2
Knebworth . . 41 B5
Knedlington . . . 89 B8
Kneesall . . . 77 C7
Kneesworth . . 54 E4
Kneeton . . . 77 E7
Knelston . . . 33 F5
Knenhall . . . 75 F6
Knettishall . . . 68 F2
Knightacott . . 21 F5
Knightcote . . 51 D8
Knightley Dale . . 62 B2
Knighton Devon . . 6 E3
Leicester . . . 64 D2
Staffs 61 B7
Staffs 74 E4
Knighton
= Tref-y-Clawdd . . 48 B4
Knightswood . . 118 C5
Knightwick . . 50 D2
Knill 48 C4
Knipton . . . 77 F8
Knitsley . . . 110 E4
Kniveton . . . 76 D2
Knock Argyll . . . 124 B2
Cumb 100 B1
Knockally . . . 158 H3
Knockan . . . 156 H5
Knockandhu . . 139 B8

Knockando . . . 152 D1
Knockando
House . . . 152 D2
Knockbain . . . 151 F9
Knockbreck . . 148 B7
Knockbrex . . . 106 E2
Knockdee . . . 158 D3
Knockdolian . . 104 A5
Knockenkelly . . 143 F11
Knockentiber . . 118 F3
Knockespock
House . . . 140 B4
Knockfarrel . . 151 F8
Knockglass . . . 104 D4
Knockholt . . . 29 D5
Knockholt Pound . 29 D5
Knockie Lodge . . 137 C7
Knockin . . . 60 B3
Knockinlaw . . 118 F4
Knocklearn . . . 106 B4
Knocknaha . . . 143 G2
Knocknain . . . 104 C3
Knockrome . . . 144 F4
Knocksharry . . 84 D2
Knodishall . . . 57 C8
Knolls Green . . 74 B5
Knolton . . . 73 F7
Knolton Bryn . . 73 F7
Knook 24 E4
Knossington . . 64 D5
Knott End-on-Sea . 92 E3
Knotting . . . 53 C8
Knotting Green . . 53 C8
Knottingley . . 89 B6
Knotts Cumb . . . 99 B6
Lancs 93 D7
Knotty Ash . . 86 E2
Knotty Green . . 40 E2
Knowbury . . 49 B7
Knowe 105 B7
Knowehead . . . 113 E6
Knowesgate . . 117 F5
Knowes of Elrick . 152 C6
Knoweton . . . 119 D7
Knowhead . . . 153 C9
Knowle Bristol . . 23 B8
Devon 10 D2
Devon 11 F5
Devon 20 F3
Shrops 49 B7
W Mid 51 B6
Knowle Green . . 93 F6
Knowle Park . . 94 E3
Knowl Hill . . . 27 B6
Knowlton Dorset . 13 C8
Kent 31 D6
Knowsley . . . 86 E2
Knowstone . . 10 B3
Knox Bridge . . 29 E8
Knucklas . . . 48 B4
Knuston . . . 53 C7
Knutsford . . . 74 B4
Knutton . . . 74 E5
Knypersley . . . 75 D5
Kuggar . . . 3 E6
Kyleakin . . . 149 F12
Kyle of Lochalsh . 149 F12
Kylerhea . . . 149 F12
Kylesknoydart . 147 B11
Kylesku . . . 156 F5
Kylesmorar . . 147 B11
Kylestrome . . . 156 F5
Kyllachy House . 138 B3
Kynaston . . . 60 B3
Kynnersley . . 61 C6
Kyre Magna . . 49 C8

L

Labost 155 C7
Lacasaigh . . . 155 E8
Lacasdal . . . 155 D9
Laceby 91 D6
Lacey Green . . 39 E8
Lach Dennis . . 74 B4
Lackford . . . 55 B8
Lacock 24 C4
Ladbroke . . . 52 D2
Laddingford . . 29 E7
Lade Bank . . . 79 D6
Ladock . . . 4 D3
Lady 159 D7
Ladybank . . . 128 C5
Ladykirk . . . 122 E4
Ladysford . . . 153 B9
Laga 147 E9
Lagalochan . . 124 D4
Lagavulin . . . 142 D5
Lagg Argyll . . . 144 F4
N Ayrs 143 F10
Laggan Argyll . . 142 C3
Highld 137 E5
Highld 138 E2
Highld 147 D10
S Ayrs 112 F2
Lagganulva . . 146 G7
Laide 155 H13
Laigh Fenwick . 118 F4
Laigh Glengall . 112 C3
Laighmuir . . . 118 F4
Laindon . . . 42 F2
Lair 150 G3
Lairg 157 J8
Lairg Lodge . . 157 J8
Lairg Muir . . . 157 J8
Laisterdyke . . 94 F4
Laithes . . . 108 F4
Lake IoW 15 F6
Wilts 25 F6
Lakenham . . . 68 D5
Lakenheath . . 67 F7
Lakesend . . . 66 E5
Lakeside . . . 99 F5
Laleham . . . 27 C8
Laleston . . . 21 B7
Lamarsh . . . 56 F2
Lamas 81 E8
Lambden . . . 122 E3
Lamberhurst . . 18 B3
Lamberhurst
Quarter . . . 18 B3
Lamberton . . . 123 D5
Lambeth . . . 28 B4
Lambhill . . . 119 C5
Lambley Northumb . 109 D6
Notts 77 E6

Lamborough Hill . . 38 D4
Lambourn . . . 25 B8
Lambourne End . 41 E7
Lambs Green . . 28 F3
Lambston . . . 44 D4
Lambton . . . 111 D5
Lamerton . . . 6 B2
Lamesley . . . 111 D5
Laminess . . . 159 E7
Lamington
Highld . . . 151 D10
S Lanark . . . 120 F2
Lamlash . . . 143 E11
Lamloch . . . 112 E5
Lamonby . . . 108 F4
Lamorna . . . 2 D3
Lamorran . . . 3 B7
Lampardbrook . . 57 C6
Lampeter = Llanbedr
Pont Steffan . 46 E4
Lampeter Velfrey . 32 C2
Lamphey . . . 32 D1
Lamplugh . . . 98 B2
Lamport . . . 53 B5
Lamyatt . . . 23 F8
Lana 8 E5
Lanark . . . 119 E8
Lancaster . . . 92 C4
Lanchester . . . 110 E4
Lancing . . . 17 D5
Landbeach . . . 55 C5
Landcross . . . 9 B6
Landerberry . . 141 D6
Landford . . . 14 C3
Landford Manor . 33 E5
Landimore . . . 33 E5
Landkey . . . 20 F4
Landore . . . 33 E7
Landrake . . . 5 C8
Landscove . . . 7 C5
Landshipping . . 32 C1
Landshipping
Quay 32 C1
Landulph . . . 6 C2
Landwade . . . 55 C7
Lane 4 C3
Laneast . . . 8 F4
Lane End Bucks . . 39 E8
Cumb 98 E3
Dorset . . . 13 C6
Hants . . . 15 B6
IoW 15 F7
Lancs . . . 93 B8
Lancs . . . 93 F7
Laneham . . . 77 B8
Lanehead Durham . 109 E8
Northumb . . 116 F3
Lane Head Derbys . 75 B8
Durham . . . 101 C6
Gtr Man . . . 86 E4
W Yorks . . . 88 D2
Laneshaw Bridge . 94 E2
Lane Side . . . 87 B5
Lanfach . . . 35 E6
Langar . . . 77 F7
Langbank . . . 118 B3
Langbar . . . 94 D3
Langburnshiels . 115 D8
Langcliffe . . . 93 C8
Langdale . . . 157 E9
Langdale End . . 103 E7
Langdon . . . 8 F5
Langdon Beck . . 109 F8
Langdon Hills . . 42 F2
Langdyke . . . 128 D5
Langenhoe . . . 43 C6
Langford C Beds . . 54 E2
Devon . . . 10 D5
Essex . . . 42 D4
Notts . . . 77 D8
Oxon . . . 38 D2
Langford Budville . 11 B6
Langham Essex . . 56 F4
Norf . . . 81 C6
Rutland . . . 64 C5
Suff . . . 56 C3
Langhaugh . . . 120 F5
Langho . . . 93 F7
Langholm . . . 115 F6
Langleeford . . . 117 B5
Langley Ches E . . 75 B6
Hants . . . 14 D5
Herts . . . 41 B5
Kent . . . 30 D2
Northumb . . 109 C8
Slough . . . 27 B8
Warks . . . 51 C6
W Sus . . . 16 B2
Langley Burrell . 24 B4
Langley Common . 76 F2
Langley Heath . . 30 D2
Langley Lower
Green 54 F5
Langley Marsh . . 11 B5
Langley Park . . 110 E5
Langley Street . . 69 D6
Langley Upper
Green 54 F5
Langney . . . 18 E3
Langold . . . 89 F6
Langore . . . 8 F5
Langport . . . 12 B2
Langrick . . . 79 E5
Langridge . . . 24 C2
Langridge Ford . 9 B7
Langrigg . . . 107 E8
Langrish . . . 15 B8
Langsett . . . 88 D3
Langshaw . . . 121 F8
Langside . . . 127 C6
Langskaill . . . 159 D5
Langstone Hants . . 15 D8
Newport . . . 35 E7
Langthorne . . . 101 E7
Langthorpe . . . 95 C6
Langthwaite . . . 101 D5
Langtoft E Yorks . . 97 C6
Lincs . . . 65 C8
Langton Durham . . 101 C6
Lincs . . . 78 C5
Lincs . . . 79 B6
N Yorks . . . 96 C3
Langton by
Wragby . . . 78 B4
Langton Green
Kent . . . 18 B2

Langton Green
continued
Suff 56 B5
Langton Herring . 12 F4
Langton
Matravers . . 13 G8
Langtree . . . 9 C6
Langwathby . . 109 F5
Langwell House . 158 H3
Langwell Lodge . 156 J4
Langwith . . . 76 C5
Langwith Junction 76 C5
Langworth . . . 78 B3
Lanivet . . . 4 C5
Lanlivery . . . 5 D5
Lanner . . . 3 C6
Lanreath . . . 5 D6
Lansallos . . . 5 D6
Lansdown . . . 37 B6
Lanteglos Highway . 5 D6
Lanton Borders . . 116 B2
Northumb . . 122 F5
Lapford . . . 10 D2
Laphroaig . . . 142 D4
La Planque Guern . . 16
Lapley . . . 62 C2
Lapworth . . . 51 B6
Larachbeg . . . 147 G9
Larbert . . . 127 F7
Larden Green . . 74 D2
Largie . . . 152 E6
Largiemore . . 145 E8
Largoward . . . 129 D6
Largs 118 D2
Largybeg . . . 143 F11
Largymore . . . 143 F11
Larkfield . . . 118 B2
Larkhall . . . 119 D7
Larkhill . . . 25 E6
Larling . . . 68 F2
Larriston . . . 115 E8
Lartington . . . 101 C5
Lary 140 D2
Lasham . . . 26 E4
Lashenden . . . 30 E2
Lassington . . . 36 B4
Lassodie . . . 128 E3
Lastingham . . 103 E5
Latcham . . . 23 E6
Latchford Herts . . 41 B6
Warr 86 F4
Latchingdon . . 42 D4
Latchley . . . 6 B2
Lately Common . 86 E4
Lathbury . . . 53 E6
Latheron . . . 158 G3
Latheronwheel . 158 G3
Latheronwheel
House . . . 158 G3
Lathones . . . 129 D6
Latimer . . . 40 E3
Latteridge . . . 36 F3
Lattiford . . . 12 B4
Latton . . . 37 E7
Latton Bush . . 41 D7
Lauchintilly . . . 141 C6
Lauder . . . 121 E8
Laugharne . . . 32 C4
Laughterton . . 77 B8
Laughton E Sus . . 18 D2
Leics 64 F3
Lincs . . . 78 F3
Lincs . . . 90 E2
Laughton Common 89 F6
Laughton en le
Morthen . . . 89 F6
Launcells . . . 8 D4
Launceston . . 8 F5
Launton . . . 39 B6
Laurencekirk . 135 B7
Laurieston
Dumfries . . . 106 C3
Falk 120 B2
Lavendon . . . 53 D7
Lavenham . . . 56 E3
Laverhay . . . 114 E4
Laversdale . . . 108 C4
Laverstock . . 25 F6
Laverstoke . . 26 E2
Laverton Glos . . 51 F5
N Yorks . . . 94 B5
Som 24 D2
Lavister . . . 73 D7
Law 119 D8
Lawers Perth . . . 127 B6
Perth . . . 132 F3
Lawford . . . 56 F4
Lawhitton . . 8 F5
Lawkland . . . 93 C7
Lawley . . . 61 D6
Lawnhead . . . 62 B2
Lawrenny . . . 32 D1
Lawshall . . . 56 D2
Lawton . . . 49 D6
Laxey 84 D4
Laxfield . . . 57 B6
Laxfirth Shetland . . 160 H6
Shetland . . . 160 J6
Laxford Bridge . 156 E5
Laxo 160 G6
Laxobigging . . 160 F6
Laxton E Yorks . . 89 B8
N Nhants . . . 65 E6
Notts . . . 77 C7
Laycock . . . 94 E3
Layer Breton . . 43 C5
Layer de la Haye . 43 C5
Layer Marney . . 43 C5
Layham . . . 56 E4
Laylands Green . 25 C8
Laytham . . . 96 F3
Layton . . . 92 F3
Lazenby . . . 102 B3
Lazonby . . . 108 F5
Lea Derbys . . . 76 D3
Hereford . . . 36 B3
Lincs . . . 90 F2
Shrops . . . 60 D4
Shrops . . . 60 F3
Wilts 37 F6
Leabrooks . . . 76 D4
Leac a Li . . . 154 H6
Leachkin . . . 151 G9
Leadburn . . . 120 D5
Leaden Roding . 42 C1
Leadenham . . . 78 D2
Leadgate Cumb . . 109 E7
Durham . . . 110 D4
T&W 110 D4

Leadhills . . . 113 C8
Leafield . . . 38 C3
Leagrave . . . 40 B3
Leake 102 E2
Leake
Commonside . . 79 D6
Lealholm . . . 103 D5
Lealt Argyll . . . 144 D5
Highld 149 B10
Lea Marston . . 63 E6
Leamington
Hastings . . . 52 C2
Leamonsley . . 62 D5
Leamside . . . 111 E6
Leanaig . . . 151 F8
Leargybreck . . 144 F4
Leasgill . . . 99 F6
Leasingham . . 78 E3
Leasingthorne . 101 B7
Leasowe . . . 85 E3
Leatherhead . . 28 D2
Leatherhead
Common . . . 28 D2
Leathley . . . 94 E5
Leaton . . . 60 C4
Lea Town . . . 92 F4
Leaveland . . . 30 D4
Leavening . . . 96 C3
Leaves Green . . 28 C5
Leazes . . . 110 D4
Lebberston . . 103 F8
Lechlade-on-
Thames . . . 38 E2
Leck 93 B6
Leckford . . . 25 F8
Leckfurin . . . 157 D10
Leckgruinart . . 142 B3
Leckhampstead
Bucks 52 F5
W Berks . . . 26 B2
Leckhampstead
Thicket . . . 26 B2
Leckhampton . . 37 C6
Leckie . . . 150 E3
Leckmelm . . 150 B4
Leckwith . . . 22 B3
Leconfield . . . 97 E6
Ledaig . . . 124 B5
Ledburn . . . 40 B2
Ledbury . . . 50 F2
Ledcharrie . . . 126 B4
Ledgemoor . . 49 D6
Ledicot . . . 49 C6
Ledmore . . . 156 H5
Lednagullin . . 157 C10
Ledsham Ches W . . 73 B7
W Yorks . . . 89 B5
Ledston . . . 88 B5
Ledston Luck . . 95 F7
Ledwell . . . 38 B4
Lee Argyll . . . 146 J7
Devon . . . 20 E3
Hants . . . 14 C4
Lancs . . . 93 D5
Shrops . . . 73 F8
Leeans . . . 160 J5
Leebotten . . . 160 L6
Leebotwood . . 60 E4
Lee Brockhurst . 60 B5
Leece . . . 92 C2
Leechpool . . . 44 D4
Lee Clump . . . 40 D2
Leeds Kent . . . 30 D2
W Yorks . . . 95 F5
Leedstown . . 2 C5
Leek 75 D6
Leekbrook . . . 75 D6
Leek Wootton . . 51 C7
Lee Mill . . . 6 D4
Leeming . . . 101 F7
Leeming Bar . . 101 E7
Lee Moor . . . 6 C3
Lee-on-the-
Solent . . . 15 D6
Lees Derbys . . . 76 F2
Gtr Man . . . 87 D7
W Yorks . . . 94 F3
Leeswood . . . 73 C6
Legbourne . . . 91 F7
Legerwood . . . 121 E8
Legsby . . . 90 F5
Leicester . . . 64 D2
Leicester Forest
East 64 D2
Leigh Dorset . . . 12 D4
Glos 37 B5
Gtr Man . . . 86 D4
Kent 29 E6
Shrops . . . 60 D3
Sur 28 E3
Wilts . . . 37 E7
Worcs . . . 50 D2
Leigh Beck . . . 42 F4
Leigh Common . 12 B5
Leigh Delamere . 24 B3
Leigh Green . . 19 B6
Leigh on Sea . . 42 F4
Leigh Park . . . 15 D8
Leigh Sinton . . 50 D2
Leighswood . . 62 D4
Leighterton . . 37 E5
Leighton N Yorks . . 94 B4
Powys . . . 60 D2
Shrops . . . 61 D6
Som 24 E2
Leighton
Bromswold . . 54 B2
Leighton Buzzard . 40 B2
Leighton upon
Mendip . . . 23 E8
Leigh Woods . . 23 B7
Leinthall Earls . 49 C6
Leinthall Starkes . 49 B6
Leintwardine . . 49 B6
Leire 64 E2
Leirinmore . . 156 C7
Leiston . . . 57 C8
Leith . . . 121 B5
Leitholm . . . 122 E3
Lelant . . . 2 C4
Lelley . . . 97 F8
Lem Hill . . . 50 B2
Lemington . . 110 C4
Lemmington Hall . 117 C7
Lempitlaw . . . 122 F3
Lenchwick . . . 50 E5
Lendalfoot . . 112 F1
Lendrick Lodge . 126 D4
Lenham . . . 30 D2

Lenham Heath . . 30 E3
Lennel . . . 122 E4
Lennoxtown . . 119 B6
Lenton Lincs . . . 78 F3
Nottingham . . 77 F5
Lentran . . . 151 G8
Lenwade . . . 68 C3
Leny House . . 126 D5
Lenzie . . . 119 B6
Leoch . . . 134 F3
Leochel-Cushnie . 140 C4
Leominster . . 49 D6
Leonard Stanley . 37 D5
Leorin . . . 142 D4
Lepe 15 E5
Lephin . . . 148 D6
Lephinchapel . . 145 D8
Lephinmore . . 145 D8
Le Planque Guern . . 16
Leppington . . 96 C3
Lepton . . . 88 C3
Lerryn . . . 5 D6
Lerwick . . . 160 J6
Lesbury . . . 117 C8
Leslie Aberds . . . 140 B4
Fife 128 D4
Lesmahagow . . 119 F8
Lesnewth . . . 8 E3
Lessendrum . . 152 D5
Lessingham . . 69 B6
Lessonhall . . . 108 D2
Leswalt . . . 104 C4
Letchmore Heath . 40 E4
Letchworth Garden
City 54 F3
Letcombe Bassett . 38 F3
Letcombe Regis . 38 F3
Letham Angus . . . 135 E5
Falk 127 F7
Fife 128 C5
Perth . . . 128 B2
Letham Grange . 135 E6
Lethenty . . . 153 D8
Letheringham . . 57 D6
Letheringsett . . 81 D6
Lettaford . . . 10 F2
Lettan . . . 159 D8
Letterewe . . . 150 D2
Letterfearn . . 149 F13
Letterfinlay . . 137 E5
Lettermorar . . 147 C10
Lettermore . . 146 G7
Letters . . . 150 C4
Letterston . . 44 C4
Lettoch Highld . . 139 C6
Highld . . . 151 H13
Letton Hereford . . 48 E5
Hereford . . . 49 B5
Letton Green . . 68 D2
Letty Green . . 41 C5
Letwell . . . 89 F6
Leuchars . . . 129 B6
Leuchars House . 152 B2
Leumrabhagh . . 155 F8
Levan . . . 118 B2
Levanaap . . . 160 G6
Levedale . . . 62 C2
Leven E Yorks . . . 97 E7
Fife 129 D5
Levencorroch . . 143 F11
Levens . . . 99 F6
Levens Green . . 41 B6
Levenshulme . . 87 E6
Levenwick . . . 160 L6
Leverburgh
= An t-Ob . . . 154 J5
Leverington . . 66 C4
Leverton . . . 79 E7
Leverton Highgate 79 E7
Leverton
Lucasgate . . 79 E7
Leverton Outgate . 79 E7
Le Villocq Guern . . 16
Levington . . . 57 F6
Levisham . . . 103 E6
Levishie . . . 137 C7
Lew 38 D3
Lewannick . . 8 F4
Lewdown . . . 9 F6
Lewes . . . 17 C8
Leweston . . . 44 C4
Lewisham . . . 28 B4
Lewiston . . . 137 B8
Lewistown . . . 34 F3
Lewknor . . . 39 E7
Leworthy Devon . . 8 D5
Devon . . . 21 F6
Lewtrenchard . . 9 F6
Lexden . . . 43 B5
Ley Aberds . . . 140 C4
Corn 5 C6
Leybourne . . . 29 D7
Leyburn . . . 101 E6
Leyfields . . . 63 D6
Leyhill . . . 40 D2
Leyland . . . 86 B3
Leylodge . . . 141 C6
Leymoor . . . 88 C2
Leys Aberds . . . 153 C10
Perth . . . 134 F2
Leys Castle . . . 151 G9
Leys of Cossans . 134 E3
Leysdown-on-Sea 30 B4
Leysmill . . . 135 E6
Leys Pole . . . 49 C7
Leyton . . . 41 F6
Leytonstone . . 41 F6
Lezant . . . 5 B8
Leziate . . . 67 C6
Lhanbryde . . . 152 B2
Liatrie . . . 150 H5
Libanus . . . 34 B3
Libberton . . . 120 E2
Liberton . . . 121 C5
Licasto . . . 154 H6
Lichfield . . . 62 D5
Lickey . . . 50 B4
Lickey End . . . 50 B4
Lickfold . . . 16 B3
Liddel . . . 159 K5
Liddesdale . . . 130 C1
Liddington . . 38 F2
Lidgate . . . 55 D8
Lidget . . . 89 D7
Lidget Green . . 94 F4
Lidgett . . . 77 C6
Lidlington . . 53 F7

Lidstone . . . 38 B3
Lieurary . . . 158 D2
Liff 134 F3
Lifton . . . 9 F5
Liftondown . . . 9 F5
Lighthorne . . . 51 D8
Lightwater . . . 27 C7
Lightwood . . . 75 E6
Lightwood Green
Ches E . . . 74 E3
Wrex 73 E7
Lilbourne . . . 52 B3
Lilburn Tower . . 117 B6
Lilleshall . . . 61 C7
Lilley Herts . . . 40 B4
W Berks . . . 26 B2
Lilliesleaf . . . 115 B8
Lillingstone
Dayrell . . . 52 F5
Lillingstone Lovell . 52 E5
Lillington Dorset . . 12 C4
Warks 51 C8
Lilliput . . . 13 E8
Lilstock . . . 22 E3
Lilyhurst . . . 61 C7
Limbury . . . 40 B3
Limebrook . . . 49 C5
Limefield . . . 87 C6
Limekilnburn . . 119 D7
Limekilns . . . 128 F2
Limerigg . . . 119 B8
Limerstone . . 14 F5
Limington . . . 12 B3
Limpenhoe . . . 69 D6
Limpley Stoke . . 24 C2
Limpsfield . . . 28 D5
Limpsfield Chart . 28 D5
Linby 76 D5
Linchmere . . . 27 F6
Lincluden . . . 107 B6
Lincoln . . . 78 B2
Lincomb . . . 50 C3
Lincombe . . . 6 D5
Lindal in Furness . 92 B2
Lindale . . . 99 F6
Lindean . . . 121 F7
Lindfield . . . 17 B7
Lindford . . . 27 F6
Lindifferon . . . 128 C5
Lindley . . . 88 C2
Lindley Green . . 94 E5
Lindores . . . 128 C4
Lindridge . . . 49 C8
Lindsell . . . 42 B2
Lindsey . . . 56 E3
Linford Hants . . . 14 D2
Thurrock . . . 29 B7
Lingague . . . 84 E2
Lingards Wood . 87 C8
Lingbob . . . 94 F3
Lingdale . . . 102 C4
Lingen . . . 49 C5
Lingfield . . . 28 E4
Lingreabhagh . . 154 J5
Lingwood . . . 69 D6
Linicro . . . 149 B8
Linkenholt . . . 25 D8
Linkhill . . . 18 C5
Linkinhorne . . 5 B8
Linklater . . . 159 K5
Linksness . . . 159 H3
Linktown . . . 128 E4
Linley 60 E3
Linley Green . . 49 D8
Linlithgow . . . 120 B3
Linlithgow
Bridge . . . 120 B2
Linshiels . . . 116 D4
Linsiadar . . . 154 D7
Linsidemore . . 151 B8
Linslade . . . 40 B2
Linstead Parva . 57 B7
Linstock . . . 108 D4
Linthwaite . . 88 C2
Lintlaw . . . 122 D4
Lintmill . . . 152 B5
Linton Borders . . 116 B3
Cambs . . . 55 E6
Derbys . . . 63 C6
Hereford . . . 36 B3
Kent 29 E8
Northumb . . 117 E8
N Yorks . . . 94 C2
W Yorks . . . 95 E6
Linton-on-Ouse . 95 C7
Linwood Hants . . 14 D2
Lincs . . . 90 F5
Renfs . . . 118 C4
Lionacleit . . . 148 D2
Lional . . . 155 A10
Liphook . . . 27 F6
Liscard . . . 85 E4
Liscombe . . . 21 F7
Liskeard . . . 5 C7
L'Islet Guern . . . 16
Liss 15 B8
Lissett . . . 97 D7
Liss Forest . . . 15 B8
Lissington . . . 90 F5
Lisvane . . . 35 F5
Liswerry . . . 35 F7
Litcham . . . 67 C8
Litchborough . . 52 D4
Litchfield . . . 26 D2
Litherland . . . 85 E4
Litlington Cambs . . 54 E4
E Sus . . . 18 E2
Little Abington . 55 E6
Little Addington . 53 B7
Little Alne . . . 51 C6
Little Altcar . . 85 D4
Little Asby . . . 100 D1
Little Assynt . . 156 G4
Little Aston . . 62 D4
Little Atherfield . 15 F5
Little Ayre . . . 159 J4
Little-ayre . . . 160 G5
Little Ayton . . 102 C3
Little Baddow . . 42 D3
Little Badminton . 37 F5
Little Ballinluig . 133 D6
Little Bampton . 108 D2
Little Bardfield . 55 F7
Little Barford . . 54 D2
Little Barningham 81 D7
Little Barrington . 38 C2

Little Barrow 73 B8
Little Barugh 96 B3
Little Bavington . . 110 B2
Little Bealings 57 E6
Littlebeck 103 D6
Little Bedwyn 25 C7
Little Bentley 43 B7
Little
  Berkhamsted . . 41 D5
Little Billing 53 C6
Little Birch 49 F7
Little Blakenham . . 56 E5
Little Blencow 108 F4
Little Bollington . . 86 F5
Little Bookham . . . 28 D2
Littleborough
  Gtr Man 87 C7
  Notts 90 F2
Littlebourne 31 D6
Little Bowden 64 F4
Little Bradley 55 D7
Little Brampton . . . 60 F3
Little Brechin 135 C5
Littlebredy 12 F3
Little Brickhill 53 F7
Little Brington 52 C4
Little Bromley 43 B6
Little Broughton . 107 F7
Little Budworth . . . 74 C2
Little Burstead 42 E2
Littlebury 55 F6
Littlebury Green . . 55 F5
Little Bytham 65 C7
Little Carlton Lincs . 91 F7
  Notts 77 D7
Little Casterton . . . 65 D7
Little Cawthorpe . . 91 F7
Little Chalfont 40 E2
Little Chart 30 E3
Little Chesterford . 55 E6
Little Cheverell . . . 24 D4
Little Chishill 54 F5
Little Clacton 43 C7
Little Clifton 98 B2
Little Colp 153 D7
Little Comberton . . 50 E4
Little Common 18 E4
Little Compton . . . 51 F7
Little Cornard 56 F2
Little Cowarne 49 D8
Little Coxwell 38 E2
Little Crakehall . . 101 E7
Little Cressingham 67 D8
Little Crosby 85 D4
Little Dalby 64 C4
Little Dawley 61 D6
Littledean 36 C3
Little Dens 153 D10
Little Dewchurch . . 49 F7
Little Downham . . . 66 F5
Little Driffield 97 D6
Little Dunham 67 C8
Little Dunkeld . . . 133 E7
Little Dunmow 42 B2
Little Easton 42 B2
Little Eaton 76 E3
Little Eccleston . . . 92 E4
Little Ellingham . . . 68 E3
Little End 41 D8
Little Eversden . . . 54 D4
Little Faringdon . . . 38 D2
Little Fencote 101 E7
Little Fenton 95 F8
Littleferry 151 B11
Little Finborough . . 56 D4
Little Fransham . . . 68 C2
Little Gaddesden . . 40 C2
Little Gidding 65 F8
Little Glemham . . . 57 D7
Little Glenshee . . . 133 F6
Little Gransden . . . 54 D3
Little Green 24 E2
Little Grimsby 91 F7
Little Gruinard . . . 150 C2
Little Habton 96 B3
Little Hadham 41 B7
Little Hale 78 E4
Little Hallingbury . 41 C7
Littleham Devon 9 B6
  Devon 10 F5
Little Hampden . . . 40 D1
Littlehampton 16 D4
Little Harrowden . . 53 B6
Little Haseley 39 D6
Little Hatfield 97 E7
Little Hautbois . . . 81 E8
Little Haven 44 D3
Little Hay 62 D5
Little Hayfield 87 F8
Little Haywood . . . 62 B4
Little Heath 63 F7
Littlehempston 7 C6
Little Hereford . . . 49 C7
Little Horkesley . . 56 F3
Little Horsted 17 C8
Little Horton 94 F4
Little Horwood . . . 53 F6
Littlehoughton . . . 117 C8
Little Houghton
  S Yorks 88 D5
  W Nhants 53 D6
Little Hucklow 75 B8
Little Hulton 86 D5
Little Humber 91 B5
Little Hungerford . 26 B3
Little Irchester . . . 53 C7
Little Kimble 39 D8
Little Kineton 51 D8
Little Kingshill 40 E1
Little Langdale . . . 99 D5
Little Langford . . . 25 F5
Little Laver 41 D8
Little Leigh 74 B3
Little Leighs 42 C3
Little Lever 87 D5
Little London Bucks 39 C6
  E Sus 18 D2
  Hants 25 E8
  Hants 26 D4
  Lincs 66 B2
  Lincs 66 B4
  Norf 81 E7
  Powys 59 F7
Little Longstone . . 75 B8
Little Lynturk 140 C4
Little Malvern 50 E2

Little Maplestead . . 56 F2
Little Marcle 49 F8
Little Marlow 40 F1
Little Marsden 93 F8
Little Melton 68 D4
Littlemill Aberds . . 140 E2
  E Ayrs 112 C4
  Highld 151 F12
  Northumb 117 C8
Little Mill 35 D7
Little Milton 39 D6
Little Missenden . . 40 E2
Littlemoor 12 F4
Littlemore 39 D5
Little Musgrave . . 100 C2
Little Ness 60 C4
Little Neston 73 B6
Little Newcastle . . 44 C4
Little Newsham . . 101 C6
Little Oakley Essex . 43 B8
  N Nhants 65 F5
Little Orton 108 D3
Little Ouseburn . . . 95 C7
Littleover 76 F3
Little Paxton 54 C2
Little Petherick 4 B4
Little Pitlurg 152 D4
Little Plumpton . . . 92 F3
Little Plumstead . . 69 C6
Little Ponton 78 F2
Littleport 67 F5
Little Raveley 54 B3
Little Reedness . . . 90 B2
Little Ribston 95 D6
Little Rissington . . 38 C1
Little Ryburgh 81 E5
Little Ryle 117 C6
Little Salkeld 109 F5
Little Sampford . . . 55 F7
Little Sandhurst . . . 27 C6
Little Saxham 55 C8
Little Scatwell . . . 150 F6
Little Sessay 95 B7
Little Shelford 54 D5
Little Singleton . . . 92 F3
Little
  Skillymarno . . . 153 C9
Little Smeaton . . . 89 C6
Little Snoring 81 D5
Little Sodbury 36 F4
Little Somborne . . 25 F8
Little Somerford . . 37 F6
Little Stainforth . . . 93 C8
Little Stainton . . . 101 B8
Little Stanney 73 B8
Little Staughton . . 54 C2
Little Steeping 79 C7
Little Stoke 75 F6
Littlestone on Sea . 19 C7
Little Stonham 56 C5
Little Stretton Leics 64 D3
  Shrops 60 E4
Little Strickland . . . 99 C7
Little Stukeley 54 B3
Little Sutton 73 B7
Little Tew 38 B3
Little Thetford 55 B6
Little Thirkleby . . . 95 B7
Littlethorpe Leics . 64 E2
  N Yorks 95 C6
Little Thurlow 55 D7
Little Thurrock . . . 29 B7
Littleton Ches W . . . 73 C8
  Hants 26 F2
  Perth 134 F2
  Som 23 F6
  Sur 27 C8
  Sur 27 E7
Littleton Drew 37 F5
Littleton-
  on-Severn 36 F2
Littleton Pannell . . 24 D5
Little Torboll 151 B10
Little Torrington . . . 9 C6
Little Totham 42 C4
Little Toux 152 C5
Littletown 111 E6
Little Town Cumb . . 98 C4
  Lancs 93 F6
Little Urswick 92 B2
Little Wakering . . . 43 F5
Little Walden 55 E6
Little Waldingfield . 56 E3
Little Walsingham . 80 D5
Little Waltham 42 C3
Little Warley 42 E2
Little Weighton . . . 97 F5
Little Weldon 65 F6
Little Welnetham . . 56 C2
Little Wenlock 61 D6
Little Whittingham
  Green 57 B6
Littlewick Green . . 27 B6
Little Wilbraham . . 55 D6
Little Wishford . . . 25 F5
Little Witley 50 C2
Little Wittenham . . 39 E5
Little Wolford 51 F7
Littleworth Bedford . 53 E8
  Glos 37 D5
  Oxon 38 E3
  Staffs 62 C4
  Worcs 50 D3
Little Wratting 55 E7
Little Wymington . . 53 C7
Little Wymondley . 41 B5
Little Wyrley 62 D4
Little Yeldham 55 F8
Litton Derbys 75 B8
  N Yorks 94 B2
  Som 23 D7
Litton Cheney 12 E3
Liurbost 155 E9
Liverpool 85 E4
Liverpool Airport . . 86 F2
Liversedge 88 B3
Liverton Devon 7 B6
  Redcar 103 C5
Livingston 120 C3
Livingston
  Village 120 C3
Lixwm 73 B5
Lizard 3 E6
Llaingoch 82 C2
Llaithddu 59 F7
Llan 59 D5
Llanaber 58 C3
Llanaelhaearn 70 C4

Llanafan 47 B5
Llanafan-fawr 47 D8
Llanallgo 82 C4
Llanandras
  =Presteigne . . . 48 C5
Llananno 70 D5
Llanarmon 70 D5
Llanarmon Dyffryn
  Ceiriog 73 F5
Llanarmon-yn-Ial . 73 D5
Llanarth Ceredig . . 46 D3
  Mon 35 C7
Llanarthne 33 B6
Llanasa 85 F2
Llanbabo 82 C3
Llanbadarn
  Fawr 48 B3
Llanbadarn-y-
  Garreg 48 E3
Llanbadoc 35 E7
Llanbadrig 82 B3
Llanbeder 35 E7
Llanbedr Gwyn . . . 71 E6
  Powys 35 B6
  Powys 48 E3
Llanbedr-Dyffryn-
  Clwyd 72 D5
Llanbedrgoch 82 C5
Llanbedrog 70 D4
Llanbedr Pont Steffan
  =Lampeter 46 E4
Llanbedr-y-
  cennin 83 E7
Llanberis 83 E5
Llanbethêry 22 C2
Llanbister 48 B3
Llanblethian 21 B8
Llanboidy 32 B3
Llanbradach 35 E5
Llanbrynmair 59 D5
Llancarfan 22 B2
Llancayo 35 D7
Llancloudy 36 B1
Llancynfelyn 58 E3
Llandaff 22 B3
Llandanwg 71 E6
Llandarcy 33 E8
Llandawke 32 C3
Llanddaniel Fab . . 82 D4
Llanddarog 33 C6
Llanddeiniol 46 B4
Llanddeiniolen . . . 82 E5
Llandderfel 72 F3
Llanddeusant
  Anglesey 82 C3
  Carms 34 B1
Llanddew 48 F2
Llanddewi 33 F5
Llanddewi-Brefi . . 47 D5
Llanddewi'r Cwm . 48 E2
Llanddewi
  Rhydderch 35 C7
Llanddewi Velfrey . 32 C2
Llanddoged 83 E8
Llanddona 83 D5
Llanddowror 32 C3
Llanddulas 72 B3
Llanddwywe 71 E6
Llanddyfnan 82 D5
Llandefaelog Fach 48 F2
Llandefaelog-
  tre'rgraig 35 B5
Llandefalle 48 F3
Llandegai 83 D5
Llandegfan 83 D5
Llandegla 73 D5
Llandegley 48 C3
Llandegveth 35 E7
Llandegwning 70 D3
Llandeilo 33 B7
Llandeilo Graban . 48 E2
Llandeilo'r Fan . . . 47 F7
Llandeloy 44 C3
Llandenny 35 D8
Llandevenny 35 F8
Llandewednock 3 E6
Llandewi
  Ystradenny . . . 48 C3
Llandinabo 36 B2
Llandinam 59 F7
Llandissilio 32 B2
Llandogo 36 D2
Llandough V Glam . 21 B8
  V Glam 22 B3
Llandovery
  =Llanymddyfri . 47 F6
Llandow 21 B8
Llandre Carms 47 E5
  Ceredig 58 F3
Llandrillo 72 F4
Llandrillo-yn-
  Rhos 83 C8
Llandrindod 48 C2
Llandrindod Wells
  =Llandrindod . . 48 C2
Llandrinio 60 C2
Llandudno 83 C7
Llandudno Junction
  =Cyffordd Llandudno 83 D7
Llandwrog 82 F4
Llandybie 33 C7
Llandyfaelog 33 C5
Llandyfan 33 C7
Llandyfriog 46 E2
Llandyfrydog 82 C4
Llandygwydd 45 E4
Llandynan 73 E5
Llandyrnog 72 C5
Llandysilio 60 C2
Llandyssil 59 E8
Llandysul 46 E3
Llanedeyrn 35 F6
Llanedi 33 D6
Llaneglwys 48 F2
Llanegryn 58 D2
Llanegwad 33 B6
Llaneilian 82 B4
Llanelian-yn-Rhos 83 D8
Llanelidan 72 D5
Llanelieu 48 F3
Llanellen 35 C7
Llanelli 33 E6
Llanelltyd 58 C4
Llanelly 35 C6
Llanelly Hill 35 C6
Llanelwedd 48 D2
Llanenddwyn 71 E6
Llanengan 70 E3
Llanerchymedd . . . 82 C4
Llanerfyl 59 D7
Llanfachraeth 82 C3
Llanfachreth 71 E8
Llanfaelog 82 D3
Llanfaelrhys 70 E3
Llanfaenor 35 C8
Llanfaes Anglesey . 83 D6
  Powys 35 B5
Llanfaethlu 82 C3
Llanfaglan 82 E4
Llanfair 71 E6
Llanfair-Dyffryn
  Clwyd 72 D5
Llanfairfechan . . . 83 D6
Llanfair
  Kilgheddin 35 D7
Llanfair-Nant-
  Gwyn 45 F3
Llanfairpwllgwyngyll
  . . . . 82 D5
Llanfair Talhaiarn . 72 B3
Llanfair Waterdine 48 B4
Llanfair-ym-Muallt
  =Builth Wells . . 48 D2
Llanfairyneubwll . 82 D3
Llanfairynghornwy 82 B3
Llanfallteg 32 C2
Llanfaredd 48 D2
Llanfarian 46 B4
Llanfechain 59 B8
Llanfechan 47 D8
Llanfechell 82 B3
Llanfendigaid 58 D2
Llanferres 73 C5
Llan Ffestiniog . . . 71 C8
Llanfflewyn 82 C3
Llanfihangel-
  ararth 46 F3
Llanfihangel-
  Crucorney 35 B7
Llanfihangel Glyn
  Myfyr 72 E3
Llanfihangel Nant
  Bran 47 F8
Llanfihangel-nant-
  Melan 48 D3
Llanfihangel
  Rhydithon 48 C3
Llanfihangel
  Rogiet 35 F8
Llanfihangel Tal-y-
  llyn 35 B5
Llanfihangel-uwch-
  Gwili 33 B5
Llanfihangel-y-
  Creuddyn 47 B5
Llanfihangel-yn-
  Ngwynfa 59 C7
Llanfihangel yn
  Nhowyn 82 D3
Llanfihangel-
  ypennant
  Gwyn 58 D3
  Gwyn 71 C6
Llanfihangel-
  ytraethau 71 D6
Llanfilo 48 F3
Llanfoist 35 C6
Llanfor 72 F3
Llanfrechfa 35 E7
Llanfrothen 71 C7
Llanfrynach 34 B4
Llanfwrog Anglesey 82 C3
  Denb 72 D5
Llanfyllin 59 C8
Llanfynydd Carms . 33 B6
  Flint 73 D6
Llanfyrnach 45 F4
Llangadfan 59 C7
Llangadog 33 B8
Llangadwaladr
  Anglesey 82 E3
  Powys 73 F5
Llangaffo 82 E4
Llangain 32 C4
Llangammarch
  Wells 47 E8
Llangan 21 B8
Llangarron 36 B2
Llangasty Talyllyn . 35 B5
Llangathen 33 B6
Llangattock 35 C6
Llangattock
  Lingoed 35 B7
Llangattock nigh
  Usk 35 D7
Llangattock-Vibon-
  Avel 36 C1
Llangedwyn 59 B8
Llangefni 82 D4
Llangeinor 34 F3
Llangeitho 46 D5
Llangeler 46 F2
Llangelynin 58 D2
Llangendeirne 33 C5
Llangennech 33 D6
Llangennith 33 E5
Llangenny 35 C6
Llangernyw 83 E8
Llangian 70 E3
Llanglydwen 32 B2
Llangoed 83 D6
Llangoedmor 45 E3
Llangollen 73 E6
Llangolman 32 B2
Llangors 35 B5
Llangovan 36 D1
Llangower 72 F3
Llangranog 46 D2
Llangristiolus 82 D4
Llangrove 36 C2
Llangua 35 B7
Llangunllo 48 B4
Llangunnor 33 C5
Llangurig 47 B8
Llangwm Conwy . . 72 E3
  Mon 35 D8
  Pembs 44 E4
Llangwnnadl 70 D3
Llangwyfan 72 C5
Llangwyfan-isaf . . 82 E3
Llangwyllog 82 D4

Llangwyryfon 46 B4
Llangybi Ceredig . . 46 D5
  Gwyn 70 C5
  Mon 35 E7
Llangyfelach 33 E7
Llangynhafal 72 C5
Llangynidr 35 C5
Llangynin 32 C3
Llangynog Carms . . 32 C4
  Powys 59 B7
Llangynwyd 34 F2
Llanhamlach 34 B4
Llanharan 34 F4
Llanharry 34 F4
Llanhennock 35 E7
Llanhiledd
  =Llanhilleth . . . 35 D6
Llanhilleth 35 D6
Llanidloes 59 F6
Llaniestyn 70 D3
Llanifyny 59 F5
Llanigon 48 F4
Llanilar 46 B5
Llanilid 34 F3
Llanilltud Fawr
  =Llantwit Major . 21 C8
Llanishen Cardiff . . 35 F5
  Mon 36 D1
Llanllawddog 33 B5
Llanllechid 83 E6
Llanllowell 35 E7
Llanllugan 59 D7
Llanllwch 32 C4
Llanllwchaiarn . . . 59 E8
Llanllwni 46 F3
Llanllyfni 82 F4
Llanmadoc 33 E5
Llanmaes 21 C8
Llanmartin 35 F7
Llanmihangel 21 B8
Llanmorlais 33 E6
Llannefydd 72 B3
Llannon 33 D6
Llannor 70 D4
Llanon 46 C4
Llanover 35 D7
Llanpumsaint 33 B5
Llanreithan 44 C3
Llanrhaeadr 72 C4
Llanrhaeadr-ym-
  Mochnant 59 B8
Llanrhian 44 B3
Llanrhidian 33 E5
Llanrhos 83 C7
Llanrhyddlad 82 C3
Llanrhystud 46 C4
Llanrosser 48 F4
Llanrothal 36 C1
Llanrug 82 E5
Llanrumney 35 F6
Llanrwst 83 E8
Llansadurnen 32 C3
Llansadwrn
  Anglesey 83 D5
  Carms 47 F5
Llansaint 32 D4
Llansamlet 33 E7
Llansanffraid-
  ym-Mechain . . . 60 B2
Llansannan 72 C3
Llansannor 21 B8
Llansantffraed
  Ceredig 46 C4
  Powys 35 B5
Llansantffraed
  Cwmdeuddwr . . 47 C8
Llansantffraed-
  in-Elvel 48 D2
Llansawel 46 F5
Llansilin 60 B2
Llansoy 35 D8
Llanspyddid 34 B4
Llanstadwell 44 E4
Llansteffan 32 C4
Llanstephan 48 E3
Llantarnam 35 E7
Llanteg 32 C2
Llanthony 35 B6
Llantilio
  Crossenny 35 C7
Llantilio
  Pertholey 35 C7
Llantood 45 E3
Llantrisant Anglesey 82 C3
  Mon 35 E7
  Rhondda 34 F4
Llantrithyd 22 B2
Llantwit Fardre . . . 34 F4
Llantwit Major
  =Llanilltud Fawr . 21 C8
Llanuwchllyn 72 F2
Llanvaches 35 E8
Llanvair Discoed . . 35 E8
Llanvapley 35 C7
Llanvetherine 35 C7
Llanveynoe 48 F5
Llanvihangel
  Gobion 35 D7
Llanvihangel-Ystern-
  Llewern 35 C8
Llanwarne 36 B2
Llanwddyn 59 C7
Llanwenog 46 E3
Llanwern 35 F7
Llanwinio 32 B3
Llanwnda Gwyn . . 82 F4
  Pembs 44 B4
Llanwnnen 46 E4
Llanwnog 59 E7
Llanwrda 47 F6
Llanwrin 58 D4
Llanwrthwl 47 C8
Llanwrtud
  =Llanwrtyd Wells 47 E7
Llanwrtyd 47 E7
Llanwrtyd Wells
  =Llanwrtud . . . 47 E7
Llanwyddelan 59 D7
Llanyblodwel 60 B2
Llanybri 32 C4
Llanybydder 46 E4
Llanycefn 32 B1
Llanychaer 44 B4
Llanycil 72 F3
Llanycrwys 46 E5
Llanymawddwy . . . 59 C6
Llanymddyfri
  =Llandovery . . . 47 F6
Llanymynech 60 B2
Llanynghenedl . . . 82 C3
Llanynys 72 C5
Llan-y-pwll 73 D7
Llanyre 48 C2
Llanystumdwy 71 D5
Llanywern 35 B5
Llawhaden 32 C1
Llawnt 73 F6
Llawr Dref 70 E3
Llawryglyn 59 E6
Llay 73 D7
Llechcynfarwy . . . 82 C3
Llecheiddior 71 C5
Llechfaen 34 B4
Llechryd Caerph . . 35 D5
  Ceredig 45 E4
Llechrydau 73 F6
Lledrod 46 B5
Llenmerewig 59 E8
Llethrid 33 E6
Llidiad Nenog 46 F4
Llidiardau 72 F2
Llidiart-y-parc . . . 72 E5
Llithfaen 70 C4
Llong 73 C6
Llowes 48 E3
Llundain-fach 46 D4
Llwydcoed 34 D3
Llwyn 60 F2
Llwyncelyn 46 D3
Llwyndafydd 46 D2
Llwynderw 60 D2
Llwyn-du 35 C6
Llwyndyrys 70 C4
Llwyngwril 58 D2
Llwyn-hendy 33 E6
Llwynmawr 73 F6
Llwyn-têg 33 D6
Llwyn-y-brain 32 C2
Llwyn-y-groes 46 D4
Llwynypia 34 E3
Llynclys 60 B2
Llynfaes 82 D4
Llysfaen 83 D8
Llyswen 48 F3
Llysworney 21 B8
Llys-y-frân 32 B1
Llywel 47 F7
Loan 120 B2
Loanend 122 D5
Loanhead 121 C5
Loans 118 F3
Loans of Tullich . . 151 D11
Lobb 20 F3
Loch a Charnain . 148 D3
Loch a'
  Ghainmhich . . 155 E7
Lochailort 147 C10
Lochaline 147 G9
Lochanhully 138 B5
Lochans 104 D4
Locharbriggs 114 F2
Lochassynt
  Lodge 156 G4
Lochavich House . 124 D5
Lochawe 125 C7
Loch Baghasdail
  =Lochboisdale . 148 G2
Lochboisdale =
  Loch Baghasdail 148 G2
Lochbuie 124 C2
Lochcarron 149 E13
Loch Choire
  Lodge 157 F9
Lochdhu 157 E13
Lochdochart
  House 126 B3
Lochdon 124 B3
Lochdrum 150 D5
Lochearnhead . . . 126 B4
Lochee 134 F3
Lochend Highld . . 151 H8
  Highld 158 D4
Locherben 114 E2
Loch Euphoirt . . . 148 B3
Lochfoot 107 B5
Lochgair 145 D8
Lochgarthside . . . 137 C8
Lochgelly 128 E3
Lochgilphead . . . 145 E7
Lochgoilhead . . . 125 E8
Loch Head 105 E7
Lochhill 152 B2
Lochindorb
  Lodge 151 H12
Lochinver 156 G3
Lochlane 127 B7
Loch Loyal Lodge . 157 E8
Lochluichart 150 E6
Lochmaben 114 F3
Lochmaddy =
  Loch nam Madadh 148 B4
Lochmore
  Cottage 158 F2
Lochmore Lodge . 156 F5
Loch nam Madadh
  =Lochmaddy . . 148 B4
Lochore 128 E3
Lochportain 148 A4
Lochranza 143 C10
Loch Sgioport . . . 148 E3
Lochside Aberds . 151 F11
  Highld 151 F11
  Highld 156 D7
  Highld 157 F11
Lochslin 151 C11
Lochstack Lodge . 156 E5
Lochton 141 E6
Lochty Angus 135 C5
  Fife 129 D7
  Perth 128 B2
Lochuisge 130 D1
Lochurr 113 F7
Lochwinnoch 118 D3
Lochwood 114 E3
Lochyside 131 B5
Lockengate 4 C5
Lockerbie 114 F4
Lockeridge 25 C6
Lockerley 14 B3
Locking 23 D5
Lockinge 38 F4
Lockington E Yorks 97 E5
  Leics 63 B8
Lockleywood 61 B6
Locks Heath 15 D6

Lockton 103 E6
Lockwood 88 C2
Loddington Leics . . 64 D4
  N Nhants 53 B6
Loddiswell 6 E5
Loddon 69 E6
Lode 55 C6
Loders 12 E2
Lodsworth 16 B3
Lofthouse N Yorks . 94 B4
  W Yorks 88 B4
Loftus 103 C5
Logan 113 B5
Loganlea 120 C2
Logan Mains 104 E4
Loggerheads 74 F4
Logie Angus 135 C6
  Fife 129 B6
  Moray 151 F13
Logiealmond
  Lodge 133 F6
Logie Coldstone . 140 D3
Logie Hill 151 D10
Logie Newton . . . 153 E6
Logie Pert 135 C6
Logierait 133 D6
Login 32 B2
Lolworth 54 C4
Lonbain 149 C11
Londesborough . . . 96 E4
London Colney . . . 40 D4
Londonderry 101 F8
Londonthorpe 78 F2
Londubh 155 J13
Lonemore 151 C10
Long Ashton 23 B7
Longbar 118 D3
Long Bennington . 77 E8
Longbenton 111 C5
Longborough 38 B1
Long Bredy 12 E3
Longbridge Warks . 51 C7
  W Mid 50 B5
Longbridge
  Deverill 24 E3
Long Buckby 52 C4
Longburton 12 C4
Long Clawson 64 B4
Longcliffe 76 D2
Long Common . . . 15 C6
Long Compton
  Staffs 62 B2
  Warks 51 F7
Longcot 38 E2
Long Crendon 39 D6
Long Crichel 13 C7
Longcroft 119 B7
Long Ditton 28 C2
Longdon Staffs . . . 62 C4
  Worcs 50 F3
Long Drax 89 B7
Longdon Green . . . 62 C4
Longdon on Tern . 61 C6
Longdown 10 E3
Longdowns 3 C6
Long Duckmanton 76 B4
Long Eaton 76 F4
Longfield Kent . . . 29 C7
  Shetland 160 M5
Longford Derbys . . 76 F2
  Glos 37 B5
  London 27 B8
  Shrops 74 F3
  Telford 61 C7
  W Mid 63 F7
Longfordlane 76 F2
Longforgan 128 B5
Longformacus . . . 122 D2
Longframlington . 117 D7
Long Green 50 F3
Longham Dorset . . 13 E8
  Norf 68 C2
Long Hanborough . 38 C4
Longhaven 153 E11
Longhill 153 C9
Longhirst 117 F8
Longhope Glos . . . 36 C3
  Orkney 159 J4
Longhorsley 117 E7
Longhoughton . . . 117 C8
Long Itchington . . 52 C2
Longlane Derbys . . 76 F2
  W Berks 26 B2
Long Lawford 52 B2
Longlevens 37 B5
Longley 88 D2
Longley Green . . . 50 D2
Long Load 12 B2
Longmanhill 153 B7
Long Marston
  Herts 40 C1
  N Yorks 95 D8
  Warks 51 E6
Long Marton 100 B1
Long Melford 56 E2
Longmoor Camp . . 27 F5
Longmorn 152 C2
Long Newnton . . . 37 E6
Longnewton
  Borders 115 B8
  Stockton 102 C1
Long Newton . . . 121 C8
Longney 36 C4
Longniddry 121 B7
Longnor Shrops . . 60 D4
  Staffs 75 C7
Longparish 26 E2
Longport 75 E5
Long Preston 93 D8
Longridge Lancs . . 93 F6
  Staffs 62 C3
  W Loth 120 C2
Longriggend 119 B8
Long Riston 97 E7
Longsdon 75 D6
Long Sight 87 D7
Longstanton 54 C4
Longstock 25 F8
Longstone 32 D2
Longstowe 54 D4
Long Stratton 68 E4
Long Street 53 E5
Long Sutton Hants . 26 E5
  Lincs 66 B4
  Som 12 B2
Longthorpe 65 E8

Long Thurlow 56 C4
Longthwaite 99 B6
Longton Lancs . . . 86 B2
  Stoke 75 E6
Longtown Cumb . . 108 C3
  Hereford 35 B7
Longville in the
  Dale 60 E5
Long Whatton . . . 63 B8
Long Wittenham . . 39 E5
Longwitton 117 F6
Longwood 61 D6
Longworth 38 E3
Longyester 121 C8
Lonmay 153 C10
Lonmore 148 D7
Looe 5 D7
Loose 29 D8
Loosley Row 39 D8
Lopcombe Corner . 25 F7
Lopen 12 C2
Loppington 60 B4
Lopwell 6 C2
Lorbottle 117 D6
Lorbottle Hall . . . 117 D6
Lornty 134 E1
Loscoe 76 E4
Losgaintir 154 H5
Lossiemouth 152 A2
Lossit 142 C2
Lostford 74 F3
Lostock Gralam . . 74 B3
Lostock Green . . . 74 B3
Lostock Hall 86 B3
Lostock Junction . 86 D4
Lostwithiel 5 D6
Loth 159 E7
Lothbeg 157 H12
Lothersdale 94 E2
Lothmore 157 H12
Loudwater 40 E2
Loughborough . . . 64 C2
Loughor 33 E6
Loughton Essex . . 41 E7
  M Keynes 53 F6
  Shrops 61 F6
Lound Lincs 65 C7
  Notts 89 F7
  Suff 69 E8
Lount 63 C7
Louth 91 F7
Love Clough 87 B6
Lovedean 15 C7
Lover 14 B3
Loversall 89 E6
Loves Green 42 D2
Lovesome Hill . . . 102 E1
Loveston 32 D1
Lovington 23 F7
Low Ackworth . . . 89 C5
Low Barlings 78 B3
Low Bentham 93 C6
Low Bradfield 88 E3
Low Bradley 94 E3
Low Braithwaite . 108 E4
Low Brunton 110 B2
Low Burnham 89 D8
Low Burton 101 F7
Low Buston 117 D8
Low Catton 96 D3
Low Clanyard 104 F5
Low Coniscliffe . . 101 C7
Low Crosby 108 D4
Low Dalby 103 F6
Low Dinsdale 101 C8
Lowe 74 F2
Lowe Hill 75 D6
Low Ellington . . . 101 F7
Lower Aisholt 22 F4
Lower Ashton 10 F3
Lower Assendon . . 39 F7
Lower Badcall . . . 156 E4
Lower Bartle 92 F4
Lower Basildon . . 26 B4
Lower Beeding . . . 17 B6
Lower Benefield . . 65 F6
Lower Boddington 52 D2
Lower Brailes 51 F8
Lower Breakish . 149 F11
Lower Broadheath . 50 D3
Lower Bullingham 49 F7
Lower Cam 36 D4
Lower Chapel 48 F2
Lower Chute 25 D8
Lower Cragabus . 142 D4
Lower Crossings . . 87 F8
Lower
  Cumberworth . . 88 D3
Lower Darwen . . . 86 B4
Lower Dean 53 C8
Lower Diabaig . . 149 B12
Lower Dicker 18 D2
Lower Down 60 F3
Lower Drift 2 D3
Lower Dunsforth . 95 C7
Lower Egleton . . . 49 E8
Lower Elkstone . . 75 D7
Lower End 40 B2
Lower Everleigh . . 25 D6
Lower Farringdon . 26 F5
Lower Foxdale . . . 84 E2
Lower Frankton . . 73 F7
Lower Froyle 27 E5
Lower Gledfield . . 151 B8
Lower Green 81 D5
Lower Hacheston . 57 D7
Lower Halistra . . . 148 C7
Lower Halstow . . . 30 C2
Lower Hardres . . . 31 D5
Lower Hawthwaite 98 F4
Lower Heath 75 C5
Lower
  Hempriggs . . . 151 E14
Lower Hergest . . . 48 D4
Lower Heyford . . . 38 B4
Lower Higham . . . 29 B8
Lower Holbrook . . 57 F5
Lower Hordley . . . 60 B3
Lower
  Horsebridge . . . 18 D2
Lower Killeyan . . 142 D3
Lower Kingswood . 28 D3

Lower Kinnerton . 73 C7
Lower Langford . . 23 C6
Lower Largo 129 D6
Lower Leigh 75 F7
Lower Lemington . 51 F7
Lower Lenie 137 B8
Lower Lydbrook . . 36 C2
Lower Lye 49 C6
Lower Machen . . . 35 F6
Lower Maes-coed . 48 F5
Lower Mayland . . . 43 D5
Lower Midway . . . 63 B7
Lower Milovaig . . 148 C6
Lower Moor 50 E4
Lower Nazeing . . . 41 D6
Lower Netchwood . 61 E6
Lower Ollach . . . 149 E10
Lower Penarth . . . 22 B3
Lower Penn 62 E2
Lower Pennington . 14 E4
Lower Peover 74 B4
Lower Pexhill 75 B5
Lower Place 87 C7
Lower Quinton . . . 51 E6
Lower Rochford . . 49 C8
Lower Seagry 37 F6
Lower Shelton . . . 53 E7
Lower Shiplake . . 27 B5
Lower
  Shuckburgh . . . 52 C2
Lower Slaughter . 38 B1
Lower Stanton
  St Quintin 37 F6
Lower Stoke 30 B2
Lower Stondon . . . 54 F2
Lower Stow Bedon 68 E2
Lower Street Norf . 69 E6
  Norf 81 D8
Lower Strensham . 50 E4
Lower Stretton . . . 86 F4
Lower Sundon . . . 40 B3
Lower Swanwick . 15 D5
Lower Swell 38 B1
Lower Tean 75 F7
Lower Thurlton . . 69 E7
Lower Tote 149 B10
Lower Town 44 B4
Lower Tysoe 51 E8
Lower Upham 15 C6
Lower Vexford . . . 22 F3
Lower Weare 23 D6
Lower Welson 48 D4
Lower Whitley . . . 74 B3
Lower Wield 26 E4
Lower
  Winchendon . . . 39 C7
Lower Withington . 74 C5
Lower Woodend . . 39 F8
Lower Woodford . 25 F6
Lower Wyche 50 E2
Lowesby 64 D4
Lowestoft 69 E8
Loweswater 98 B3
Low Etherley 101 B6
Low Fell 111 D5
Lowford 15 C5
Low Fulney 66 B2
Low Garth 103 D5
Lowgill Cumb 99 E8
  Lancs 93 C6
Low Grantley 94 B5
Low Habberley . . . 50 B3
Low Ham 12 B2
Low Hesket 108 E4
Low Hesleyhurst . 117 E6
Low Hutton 96 C3
Lowick N Nhants . . 65 F6
  Northumb 123 F6
Lowick Bridge . . . 98 F4
Lowick Green 98 F4
Low Laithe 94 C4
Lowlands 35 E6
Low Leighton 87 F8
Low Lorton 98 B3
Low Marishes 96 B4
Low Marnham . . . 77 C8
Low Mill 102 E4
Low Moor Lancs . . 93 E7
  W Yorks 88 B2
Low Moorsley . . . 111 E6
Low Newton 99 F6
Low Newton-
  by-the-Sea . . . 117 B8
Low Row Cumb . . 108 F3
  Cumb 109 C5
  N Yorks 100 E4
Low Salchrie 104 C4
Low Smerby 143 F8
Lowsonford 51 C6
Lowther 99 B7
Lowthorpe 97 C6
Lowton 86 E4
Lowton Common . 86 E4
Low Torry 128 F2
Low Worsall 102 D1
Low Wray 99 D5
Loxbeare 10 C4
Loxhill 27 F8
Loxhore 20 F5
Loxley 51 D7
Loxton 23 D5
Loxwood 27 F8
Lubcroy 156 J6
Lubenham 64 F4
Luccombe 21 E8
Luccombe Village . . 15 G6
Lucker 123 F7
Luckett 5 B8
Luckington 37 F5
Lucklawhill 129 B6
Luckwell Bridge . . 21 F8
Lucton 49 C6
Ludag 148 G2
Ludborough 91 E6
Ludchurch 32 C2
Luddenden 87 B8
Luddenden Foot . . 87 B8
Luddesdown 29 C7
Luddington N Lincs 90 C2
  Warks 51 D6
Luddington in
  the Brook 65 F8
Lude House 133 C5
Ludford Lincs 91 F6
  Shrops 49 B7
Ludgershall Bucks . 39 C6

Ludgershall *continued*
Wilts 25 D7
Ludgvan 2 C4
Ludham 69 C6
Ludlow 49 B7
Ludwell 13 B7
Ludworth 111 E6
Luffincott 8 E5
Lugar 113 B5
Luggate Burn 122 B2
Lugg Green 49 C6
Luggiebank 119 B7
Lugton 118 D4
Lugwardine 49 E7
Luib 149 F10
Lulham 49 E6
Lullenden 28 E5
Lullington Derbys 63 C6
Som 24 D2
Lulsgate Bottom 23 C7
Lulsley 50 D2
Lumb 87 B8
Lumby 95 F7
Lumloch 119 C6
Lumphanan 140 D4
Lumphinnans 128 E3
Lumsdaine 122 C4
Lumsden 140 B3
Lunan 135 D6
Lunanhead 134 D4
Luncarty 128 B2
Lund E Yorks 97 E5
N Yorks 96 F2
Shetland 160 C7
Lunderton 153 D11
Lundie Angus 134 F2
Highld 136 C4
Lundin Links 129 D6
Lunga 124 E3
Lunna 160 G6
Lunning 160 G7
Lunnon 33 F6
Lunsford's Cross 18 D4
Lunt 85 D4
Luntley 49 D5
Luppitt 11 D6
Lupset 88 C4
Lupton 99 F7
Lurgashall 16 B3
Lusby 79 C6
Luson 6 E4
Luss 126 E2
Lussagiven 144 E5
Lusta 149 C7
Lustleigh 10 F2
Luston 49 C6
Luthermuir 135 C6
Luthrie 128 C5
Luton Devon 7 B7
Luton 40 B3
Medway 29 C8
Lutterworth 64 F2
Lutton Devon 6 D3
Lincs 66 B4
N Nhants 65 F8
Lutworthy 10 C2
Luxborough 21 F8
Luxulyan 5 D5
Lybster 158 G4
Lydbury North 60 F3
Lydcott 21 F5
Lydd 19 C7
Lydden 31 E6
Lyddington 65 E5
Lydd on Sea 19 C7
Lydeard St Lawrence 22 F3
Lyde Green 26 D5
Lydford 9 F7
Lydford-on-Fosse 23 F7
Lydgate 87 B7
Lydham 60 E3
Lydiard Green 37 F7
Lydiard Millicent 37 F7
Lydiate 85 D4
Lydlinch 12 C5
Lydney 36 D3
Lydstep 32 E1
Lye 62 F3
Lye Green Bucks 40 D2
E Sus 18 B2
Lyford 38 E3
Lymbridge Green 30 E5
Lyme Regis 11 E8
Lyminge 31 E5
Lymington 14 E4
Lyminster 16 D4
Lymm 86 F4
Lymore 14 E3
Lympne 19 B8
Lympsham 22 D5
Lympstone 10 F4
Lynchat 138 D3
Lyndale House 149 C8
Lyndhurst 14 D4
Lyndon 65 D6
Lyne 27 C8
Lyneal 73 F8
Lyne Down 49 F8
Lyneham Oxon 38 B2
Wilts 24 B5
Lynemore 139 B6
Lynemouth 117 E8
Lyne of Gorthleck 137 B8
Lyne of Skene 141 C6
Lyness 159 J4
Lyng Norf 68 C3
Som 11 B8
Lynmouth 21 E6
Lynsted 30 C3
Lynton 21 E6
Lyon's Gate 12 D4
Lyonshall 48 D5
Lytchett Matravers 13 E7
Lytchett Minster 13 E7
Lyth 158 D4
Lytham 85 B4
Lytham St Anne's 85 B4
Lythe 103 C6
Lythes 159 K5

M

Mabe Burnthouse 3 C6
Mabie 107 B6
Mablethorpe 91 F9
Macclesfield 75 B6
Macclesfield Forest 75 B6
Macduff 153 B7
Mace Green 56 E5
Machariock 143 H8
Machen 35 F6
Machrihanish 143 F7
Machynlleth 58 D4
Machynys 33 E6
Mackerel's Common 16 B4
Mackworth 76 F3
Macmerry 121 B7
Madderty 127 B8
Maddiston 120 B2
Madehurst 16 C3
Madeley Staffs 74 E4
Telford 61 D6
Madeley Heath 74 E4
Madeley Park 74 E4
Madingley 54 C4
Madley 49 F6
Madresfield 50 E3
Madron 2 C3
Maenaddwyn 82 C4
Maenclochog 32 B1
Maendy 22 B2
Maentwrog 71 C7
Maen-y-groes 46 D2
Maer 74 F4
Maerdy Conwy 72 E4
Rhondda 34 E3
Maesbrook 60 B2
Maesbury 60 B3
Maesbury Marsh 60 B3
Maesgwyn-Isaf 59 C8
Maesgwynne 32 B3
Maeshafn 73 C6
Maesllyn 46 E2
Maesmynis 48 E2
Maesteg 34 E2
Maestir 46 E4
Maes-Treylow 48 C4
Maesybont 33 C6
Maesycrugiau 46 E3
Maesy cwmmer 35 E5
Maesymeillion 46 E3
Magdalen Laver 41 D8
Maggieknockater 152 D3
Magham Down 18 D3
Maghull 85 D4
Magor 35 F8
Magpie Green 56 B4
Maiden Bradley 24 F3
Maidencombe 7 C7
Maidenhall 57 E5
Maidenhead 40 F1
Maiden Law 110 E4
Maiden Newton 12 E3
Maidens 112 D2
Maidensgrave 57 E6
Maiden's Green 27 B6
Maidenwell Corn 5 B6
Lincs 79 B6
Maiden Wells 44 F4
Maidford 52 D4
Maids Moreton 52 F5
Maidstone 29 D8
Maidwell 52 B5
Mail 160 L6
Main 59 C8
Maindee 35 F7
Mainsforth 111 F6
Mains of Airies 104 C3
Mains of Allardice 135 B8
Mains of Annochie 153 D9
Mains of Ardestie 135 F5
Mains of Balhall 135 C5
Mains of Ballindarg 134 D4
Mains of Balnakettle 135 B6
Mains of Birness 153 E9
Mains of Burgie 151 F13
Mains of Clunas 151 G11
Mains of Crichie 153 D9
Mains of Dalvey 151 H14
Mains of Dellavaird 141 F6
Mains of Drum 141 E7
Mains of Edingight 152 C5
Mains of Fedderate 153 D8
Mains of Inkhorn 153 E9
Mains of Mayen 152 D5
Mains of Melgund 135 D5
Mains of Thornton 135 B6
Mains of Watten 158 E4
Mainsriddle 107 D6
Mainstone 60 F2
Maisemore 37 B5
Malacleit 148 A2
Malborough 6 F5
Malcoff 87 F8
Maldon 42 D4
Malham 94 C2
Maligar 149 B9
Mallaig 147 B9
Malleny Mills 120 C4
Malling 126 D4
Malltraeth 82 E4
Mallwyd 59 C5
Malmesbury 37 F6
Malmsmead 21 E6
Malpas Ches W 73 E8
Corn 3 B7
Newport 35 E7
Malswick 36 B4
Maltby Stockton 102 C2
S Yorks 89 E6
Maltby le Marsh 91 F8
Malting Green 43 B5
Maltman's Hill 30 E3
Malton 96 B3
Malvern Link 50 E2
Malvern Wells 50 E2
Mamble 49 B8
Manaccan 3 D6
Manafon 59 D8
Manais 154 J6
Manar House 141 B6
Manaton 10 F2
Manby 91 F7
Mancetter 63 E7
Manchester 87 E6
Manchester Airport 87 F6
Mancot 73 C7
Mandally 137 D5
Manea 66 F4
Manfield 101 C7
Mangaster 160 F5
Mangotsfield 23 B8
Mangurstadh 154 D5
Mankinholes 87 B7
Manley 74 B2
Manmoel 35 D5
Mannal 146 G2
Mannerston 120 B3
Manningford Bohune 25 D6
Manningford Bruce 25 D6
Manningham 94 F4
Mannings Heath 17 B6
Mannington 13 D8
Manningtree 56 F4
Mannofield 141 D8
Manor 41 F7
Manorbier 32 E1
Manordeilo 33 B7
Manor Estate 88 F4
Manorhill 122 F2
Manorowen 44 B4
Manselfield 33 F6
Mansel Lacy 49 E6
Mansell Gamage 49 E5
Mansergh 99 F8
Mansfield E Ayrs 113 C6
Notts 76 C5
Mansfield Woodhouse 76 C5
Mansriggs 98 F4
Manston Dorset 13 C6
Kent 31 C7
W Yorks 95 F6
Manswood 13 D7
Manthorpe Lincs 65 C7
Lincs 78 F2
Manton N Lincs 90 D3
Notts 77 B5
Rutland 65 D5
Wilts 25 C6
Manuden 41 B7
Maperton 12 B4
Maplebeck 77 C7
Maple Cross 40 E3
Mapledurham 26 B4
Mapledurwell 26 D4
Maplehurst 17 B5
Maplescombe 29 C6
Mapleton 75 E8
Mapperley 76 E4
Mapperley Park 77 E5
Mapperton 12 E3
Mappleborough Green 51 C5
Mappleton 97 E8
Mappowder 12 D5
Maraig 154 G6
Marazanvose 4 D3
Marazion 2 C4
Marbhig 155 F9
Marbury 74 E2
March Cambs 66 E4
S Lanark 114 C2
Marcham 38 E4
Marchamley 61 B5
Marchington 75 F8
Marchington Woodlands 62 B5
Marchroes 70 E4
Marchwiel 73 E7
Marchwood 14 C4
Marcross 21 C8
Marden Hereford 49 E7
Kent 29 E8
T&W 111 B6
Wilts 25 D5
Marden Beech 29 E8
Marden Thorn 29 E8
Mardy 35 C7
Marefield 64 D4
Mareham le Fen 79 C5
Mareham on the Hill 79 C5
Marehay 76 E3
Marehill 16 C4
Maresfield 17 B8
Marfleet 90 B5
Marford 73 D7
Margam 34 F1
Margaret Marsh 13 C6
Margaret Roding 42 C1
Margaretting 42 D2
Margate 31 B7
Margnaheglish 143 E11
Margrove Park 102 C4
Marham 67 C7
Marhamchurch 8 D4
Marholm 65 D8
Mariandyrys 83 C6
Marianglas 82 C5
Mariansleigh 10 B2
Marionburgh 141 D6
Marishader 149 B9
Marjoriebanks 114 F3
Mark Dumfries 104 D5
S Ayrs 104 B4
Som 23 E5
Markbeech 29 E5
Markby 79 B7
Mark Causeway 23 E5
Mark Cross E Sus 17 C8
E Sus 18 B2
Market Bosworth 63 D8
Market Deeping 65 D8
Market Drayton 74 F3
Market Harborough 64 F4
Markethill 134 F2
Market Lavington 24 D5
Market Overton 65 C5
Market Rasen 90 F5
Market Stainton 78 B5
Market Warsop 77 C5
Market Weighton 96 E4
Market Weston 56 B3
Markfield 63 C8
Markham 35 D5
Markham Moor 77 B7
Markinch 128 D4
Markington 95 C5
Marksbury 23 C8
Marks Tey 43 B5
Markyate 40 C3
Marland 87 C6
Marlborough 25 C6
Marlbrook Hereford 49 D7
Worcs 50 B4
Marlcliff 51 D5
Marldon 7 C6
Marlesford 57 D7
Marley Green 74 E2
Marley Hill 110 D5
Marley Mount 14 E3
Marlingford 68 D4
Mar Lodge 139 E6
Marloes 44 E2
Marlow Bucks 39 F8
Hereford 49 B6
Marlow Bottom 40 F1
Marlpit Hill 28 E5
Marlpool 76 E4
Marnhull 13 C5
Marnoch 152 C5
Marnock 119 C7
Marple 87 F7
Marple Bridge 87 F7
Marr 89 D6
Marrel 157 H13
Marrick 101 E5
Marrister 160 G7
Marros 32 D3
Marsden T&W 111 C6
W Yorks 87 C8
Marsett 100 F4
Marsh Devon 11 C7
W Yorks 94 F3
Marshall's Heath 40 C4
Marshalsea 11 D8
Marshalswick 40 D4
Marsham 81 E7
Marshaw 93 D5
Marsh Baldon 39 E5
Marshborough 31 D7
Marshbrook 60 F4
Marshchapel 91 E7
Marshfield Newport 35 F6
S Glos 24 B2
Marshgate 8 E3
Marsh Gibbon 39 B6
Marsh Green Devon 10 E5
Kent 28 E5
Staffs 75 D5
Marshland St James 66 D5
Marsh Lane 76 B4
Marshside 85 C4
Marsh Street 21 E8
Marshwood 11 E8
Marske 101 D6
Marske-by-the-Sea 102 B4
Marston Ches W 74 B3
Hereford 49 D5
Lincs 77 E8
Oxon 39 D5
Staffs 62 B3
Staffs 62 C2
Warks 63 E6
Wilts 24 D4
Marston Doles 52 D2
Marston Green 63 F5
Marston Magna 12 B3
Marston Meysey 37 E8
Marston Montgomery 75 F8
Marston Moretaine 53 E7
Marston on Dove 63 B6
Marston St Lawrence 52 E3
Marston Stannett 49 D7
Marston Trussell 64 F3
Marstow 36 C2
Marsworth 40 C2
Marten 25 D7
Marthall 74 B5
Martham 69 C7
Martin Hants 13 C8
Kent 31 E7
Lincs 78 C5
Lincs 78 D4
Martin Dales 78 C4
Martin Drove End 13 B8
Martinhoe 21 E5
Martinhoe Cross 21 E5
Martin Hussingtree 50 C3
Martin Mill 31 E7
Martinscroft 86 F4
Martinstown 12 F4
Martlesham 57 E6
Martlesham Heath 57 E6
Martletwy 32 C1
Martley 50 D2
Martock 12 C2
Marton Ches E 75 C5
E Yorks 97 F7
Lincs 90 F2
Mbro 102 C3
N Yorks 95 C7
N Yorks 103 F5
Shrops 60 B4
Shrops 60 D2
Warks 52 C2
Marton-le-Moor 95 B6
Martyr's Green 27 D8
Martyr Worthy 26 F3
Marwick 159 F3
Marwood 20 F4
Marybank 150 F7
Maryburgh 151 F8
Maryhill 119 C5
Marykirk 135 C6
Marylebone 86 D3
Marypark 152 E1
Maryport Cumb 107 F7
Dumfries 104 F5
Mary Tavy 6 B3
Maryton 135 D6
Marywell Aberds 140 E4
Aberds 141 E8
Angus 135 E6
Masham 101 F7
Mashbury 42 C2
Masongill 93 B6
Masonhill 112 B3
Mastin Moor 76 B4
Mastrick 141 D7
Matching 41 C8
Matching Green 41 C8
Matching Tye 41 C8
Matfen 110 B3
Matfield 29 E7
Mathern 36 E2
Mathon 50 E2
Mathry 44 B3
Matlaske 81 D7
Matlock 76 C2
Matlock Bath 76 D2
Matson 37 C5
Matterdale End 99 B5
Mattersey 89 F7
Mattersey Thorpe 89 F7
Mattingley 26 D5
Mattishall 68 C3
Mattishall Burgh 68 C3
Mauchline 112 B4
Maud 153 D9
Maugersbury 38 B2
Maughold 84 C4
Mauld 150 H7
Maulden 53 F8
Maulds Meaburn 99 C8
Maunby 102 F1
Maund Bryan 49 D7
Maundown 11 B5
Mautby 69 C7
Mavis Enderby 79 C6
Mawbray 107 E7
Mawdesley 86 C2
Mawdlam 34 F2
Mawgan 3 D6
Maw Green 74 D4
Mawla 3 B6
Mawnan 3 D6
Mawnan Smith 3 D6
Mawsley 53 B6
Maxey 65 D8
Maxstoke 63 F6
Maxton Borders 122 F2
Kent 31 E7
Maxwellheugh 122 F3
Maxwelltown 107 B6
Maxworthy 8 E4
Mayals 33 E7
May Bank 75 E5
Maybole 112 D3
Mayfield E Sus 18 C2
Midloth 121 C6
Staffs 75 E8
W Loth 120 C2
Mayford 27 D7
Mayland 43 D5
Maynard's Green 18 D2
Maypole Mon 36 C1
Scilly 2 E4
Maypole Green Essex 43 B5
Norf 69 E7
Suff 57 C6
Maywick 160 L5
Meadle 39 D8
Meadowtown 60 D3
Meaford 75 F5
Mealabost 155 D9
Mealabost Bhuirgh 155 B9
Meal Bank 99 E7
Mealsgate 108 E2
Meanwood 95 F5
Mearbeck 93 C8
Meare 23 E6
Meare Green 11 B8
Mears Ashby 53 C6
Measham 63 C7
Meath Green 28 E3
Meathop 99 F6
Meaux 97 F6
Meavy 6 C3
Medbourne 64 E4
Medburn 110 B4
Meddon 8 C4
Meden Vale 77 C5
Medlam 79 D6
Medmenham 39 F8
Medomsley 110 D4
Medstead 26 F4
Meerbrook 75 C6
Meer End 51 B7
Meers Bridge 91 F8
Meesden 54 F5
Meeth 9 D7
Meggethead 114 B4
Meidrim 32 B3
Meifod Denb 72 D4
Powys 59 C8
Meigle N Ayrs 118 C1
Perth 134 E2
Meikle Earnock 119 D7
Meikle Ferry 151 C10
Meikle Forter 134 C1
Meikle Gluich 151 C9
Meikleour 134 F1
Meikle Pinkerton 122 B3
Meikle Strath 135 B6
Meikle Tarty 141 B8
Meikle Wartle 153 E7
Meinciau 33 C5
Meir 75 E6
Meir Heath 75 E6
Melbourn 54 E4
Melbourne Derbys 63 B7
E Yorks 96 E3
S Lanark 120 E3
Melbury Abbas 13 B6
Melbury Bubb 12 D3
Melbury Osmond 12 D3
Melbury Sampford 12 D3
Melby 160 H3
Melchbourne 53 C8
Melcombe Bingham 13 D5
Melcombe Regis 12 F4
Meldon Devon 9 E7
Northumb 117 F7
Meldreth 54 E4
Meldrum House 141 B7
Melfort 124 D4
Melgarve 137 E7
Meliden 72 A4
Melinbyrhedyn 58 E5
Melincourt 34 D2
Melin-y-coed 83 E8
Melin-y-ddôl 59 D7
Melin-y-grug 59 D7
Melin-y-Wig 72 E4
Melkinthorpe 99 B7
Melkridge 109 C7
Melksham 24 C4
Melldalloch 145 F8
Melling Lancs 93 B5
Mers 85 D4
Melling Mount 86 D2
Mellis 56 B5
Mellon Charles 155 H13
Mellon Udrigle 155 H13
Mellor Gtr Man 87 F7
Lancs 93 F6
Mellor Brook 93 F6
Mells 24 E2
Melmerby Cumb 109 F6
N Yorks 95 B6
N Yorks 101 F5
Melplash 12 E2
Melrose 121 F8
Melsetter 159 K3
Melsonby 101 D6
Meltham 88 C2
Melton 57 D6
Meltonby 96 D3
Melton Constable 81 D6
Melton Mowbray 64 C4
Melton Ross 90 C4
Melvaig 155 J12
Melverley 60 C3
Melverley Green 60 C3
Melvich 157 C11
Membury 11 D7
Memsie 153 B9
Memus 134 D4
Menabilly 5 D5
Menai Bridge = *Porthaethwy* 83 D5
Mendham 69 F5
Mendlesham 56 C5
Mendlesham Green 56 C4
Menheniot 5 C7
Mennock 113 D8
Menston 94 E4
Menstrie 127 E7
Menthorpe 96 F2
Mentmore 40 C2
Meoble 147 C10
Meole Brace 60 C4
Meols 85 E3
Meonstoke 15 C7
Meopham 29 C7
Meopham Station 29 C7
Mepal 66 F4
Meppershall 54 F2
Merbach 48 E5
Mere Ches E 86 F5
Wilts 24 F3
Mere Brow 86 C2
Mereclough 93 F8
Mere Green 62 E5
Mereside 92 F3
Mereworth 29 D7
Mergie 141 F6
Meriden 63 F6
Merkadale 149 E8
Merkland Dumfries 106 B4
S Ayrs 112 E2
Merkland Lodge 156 G7
Merley 13 E8
Merlin's Bridge 44 D4
Merrington 60 B4
Merrion 44 F4
Merriott 12 C2
Merrivale 6 B3
Merrow 27 D8
Merrymeet 5 C7
Mersham 19 B7
Merstham 28 D3
Merston 16 D2
Merstone 15 F6
Merther 3 B7
Merthyr 32 B4
Merthyr Cynog 47 F8
Merthyr-Dyfan 22 C3
Merthyr Mawr 21 B7
Merthyr Tudful = *Merthyr Tydfil* 34 D4
Merthyr Tydfil = *Merthyr Tudful* 34 D4
Merthyr Vale 34 E4
Merton Devon 9 C7
London 28 B3
Norf 68 E2
Oxon 39 C5
Mervinslaw 116 C2
Meshaw 10 C2
Messing 42 C4
Messingham 90 D2
Metfield 69 F5
Metheringham 78 C3
Methil 129 E5
Methlem 70 D2
Methley 88 B4
Methlick 153 E8
Methven 128 B2
Methwold 67 E7
Methwold Hythe 67 E7
Mettingham 69 F6
Mevagissey 3 B9
Mewith Head 93 C7
Mexborough 89 D5
Mey 158 C4
Meysey Hampton 37 E8
Miabhag W Isles 154 G5
W Isles 154 H6
Miabhig 154 D5
Michaelchurch 36 B2
Michaelchurch Escley 48 F5
Michaelchurch on Arrow 48 D4
Michaelston-le-Pit 22 B3
Michaelston-y-Fedw 35 F6
Michaelstow 5 B5
Michealston-super-Ely 22 B3
Micheldever 26 F3
Michelmersh 14 B4
Mickfield 56 C5
Micklebring 89 E6
Mickleby 103 C6
Mickleham 28 D2
Mickleover 76 F3
Micklethwaite 94 E4
Mickleton Durham 100 B4
Glos 51 E6
Mickletown 88 B4
Mickle Trafford 73 C8
Mickley 95 B5
Mickley Square 110 C3
Mid Ardlaw 153 B9
Mid Auchinleck 118 B3
Midbea 159 D5
Mid Beltie 140 D5
Mid Calder 120 C3
Mid Cloch Forbie 153 C7
Mid Clyth 158 G4
Middle Assendon 39 F7
Middle Aston 38 B4
Middle Barton 38 B4
Middlebie 108 B2
Middle Cairncake 153 D8
Middle Claydon 39 B7
Middle Drums 135 D5
Middleforth Green 86 B3
Middleham 101 F6
Middle Handley 76 B4
Middlehope 60 F4
Middle Littleton 51 E5
Middle Maes-coed 48 F5
Middlemarsh 12 D4
Middle Mill 44 C3
Middlemuir 141 B8
Middle Rasen 90 F4
Middle Rigg 128 D2
Middlesbrough 102 B2
Middleshaw Cumb 99 F7
Dumfries 107 B8
Middlesmoor 94 B3
Middlestone 111 F5
Middlestone Moor 110 F5
Middlestown 88 C3
Middlethird 122 E2
Middleton Aberds 141 C7
Argyll 146 G2
Cumb 99 F8
Derbys 75 C8
Derbys 76 D2
Essex 56 F2
Gtr Man 87 D6
Hants 26 E2
Hereford 49 C7
Lancs 92 D4
Midloth 121 D6
N Nhants 64 F5
Norf 67 C6
Northumb 117 F6
Northumb 123 F7
N Yorks 94 E4
N Yorks 103 F5
Perth 128 D3
Perth 133 E8
Shrops 49 B7
Shrops 60 B3
Shrops 60 E2
Suff 57 C8
Swansea 33 F5
Warks 63 E5
W Yorks 88 B3
Middleton Cheney 52 E2
Middleton Green 75 F6
Middleton Hall 117 B5
Middleton-in-Teesdale 100 B4
Middleton Moor 57 C8
Middleton One Row 102 C1
Middleton-on-Leven 102 D2
Middleton-on-Sea 16 D3
Middleton on the Hill 49 C7
Middleton-on-the-Wolds 96 E5
Middleton Priors 61 E6
Middleton Quernham 95 B6
Middleton St George 101 C8
Middleton Scriven 61 F6
Middleton Stoney 39 B5
Middleton Tyas 101 D7
Middletown Cumb 98 D1
Powys 60 C3
Middle Tysoe 51 E8
Middle Wallop 25 F7
Middlewich 74 C3
Middle Winterslow 25 F7
Middle Woodford 25 F6
Middlewood Green 56 C4
Middlezoy 23 F5
Middridge 101 B7
Midfield 157 C8
Midge Hall 86 B3
Midgeholme 109 D6
Midgham 26 C3
Midgley W Yorks 87 B8
W Yorks 88 C3
Midhopestones 88 E3
Midhurst 16 B2
Mid Lavant 16 D2
Midlem 115 B8
Mid Main 150 H7
Midmar 141 D5
Midsomer Norton 23 D8
Midton 118 B2
Midtown Highld 155 J13
Highld 157 C8
Midtown of Buchromb 152 D3
Mid Urchany 151 G11
Midville 79 D6
Mid Walls 160 H4
Midway 87 F7
Mid Yell 160 D7
Migdale 151 B9
Migvie 140 D3
Milarrochy 126 E3
Milborne Port 12 C4
Milborne St Andrew 13 E6
Milborne Wick 12 B4
Milbourne 110 B4
Milburn 100 B1
Milbury Heath 36 E3
Milcombe 52 F2
Milden 56 E3
Mildenhall Suff 55 B8
Wilts 25 C7
Milebrook 48 B5
Milebush 29 E8
Mile Cross 68 C5
Mile Elm 24 C4
Mile End Essex 43 B5
Glos 36 C2
Mileham 68 C2
Mile Oak 17 D6
Milesmark 128 F2
Milfield 122 F5
Milford Derbys 76 E3
Devon 8 B4
Powys 59 E7
Staffs 62 B3
Sur 27 E7
Wilts 14 B2
Milford Haven = *Aberdaugleddau* 44 E4
Milford on Sea 14 E3
Milkwall 36 D2
Milkwell 13 B7
Milland 16 B2
Millarston 118 C4
Millbank Aberds 153 D11
Highld 158 D3
Mill Bank 87 B8
Millbeck 98 B4
Millbounds 159 E6
Millbreck 153 D10
Millbridge 27 E6
Millbrook C Beds 53 F8
Corn 6 D2
Soton 14 C4
Millburn 112 B4
Millcombe 7 E6
Mill Common 69 F7
Millcorner 18 C5
Milldale 75 D8
Millden Lodge 135 B5
Milldens 135 D5
Mill End Bucks 39 F7
Herts 54 F4
Millerhill 121 C6
Miller's Dale 75 B8
Miller's Green 76 D2
Millgreen 61 B6
Mill Green Essex 42 D2
Norf 68 F4
Suff 56 E3
Millhalf 48 E4
Millhayes 11 D7
Millhead 92 B4
Millheugh 119 D7
Mill Hill 41 E5
Millholme 99 E7
Millhouse Argyll 145 F8
Cumb 108 F3
Millhousebridge 114 F4
Millhouse Green 88 D3
Millhouses 88 F4
Millikenpark 118 C4
Millin Cross 44 D4
Millington 96 D4
Mill Lane 27 D5
Millmeece 74 F5
Mill of Kingoodie 141 B7
Mill of Muiresk 153 D6
Mill of Sterin 140 E2
Mill of Uras 141 F7
Millom 98 F3
Millook 8 E3
Mill Place 90 D3
Millpool 5 B6
Millport 145 H10
Millquarter 113 F6
Mill Side 99 F6
Mill Street 68 C3
Millthorpe 78 F4
Millthrop 100 E1
Milltimber 141 D7
Milltown Corn 5 D6
Derbys 76 C3
Devon 20 F4
Dumfries 108 B3
Milltown of Aberdalgie 128 B2
Milltown of Auchindoun 152 D3
Milltown of Craigston 153 C7
Milltown of Edinvillie 152 D2
Milltown of Kildrummy 140 C3
Milltown of Rothiemay 152 D5
Milltown of Towie 140 C3
Milnathort 128 D3
Milner's Heath 73 C8
Milngavie 119 B5
Milnrow 87 C7
Milnshaw 87 B5
Milnthorpe 99 F6
Milo 33 C6
Milson 49 B8
Milstead 30 D3
Milston 25 E6
Milton Angus 134 E3
Cambs 55 C5
Cumb 109 C5
Derbys 63 B7
Dumfries 105 D6
Dumfries 106 B5
Dumfries 113 F8
Highld 150 F6
Highld 150 H7
Highld 151 D10
Highld 151 G8
Highld 158 E5
Moray 152 B5
Notts 77 B7
N Som 22 C5
Oxon 38 E4
Oxon 52 F2
Pembs 32 D1
Perth 127 C8
Ptsmth 15 E7
Stirling 126 D4
Stoke 75 D6
W Dunb 118 B4
Milton Abbas 13 D6
Milton Abbot 6 B2
Milton Bridge 120 C5
Milton Bryan 53 F7
Milton Clevedon 23 F8
Milton Coldwells 153 E9
Milton Combe 6 C2
Milton Damerel 9 C5
Miltonduff 152 B1
Milton End 37 D8
Milton Ernest 53 D8
Milton Green 73 D8
Miltonhill 151 E13
Milton Hill 38 E4
Miltonise 105 B5
Milton Keynes 53 F6
Milton Keynes Village 53 F6
Milton Lilbourne 25 C6
Milton Malsor 52 D5
Milton Morenish 132 F3
Milton of Auchinhove 140 D4
Milton of Balgonie 128 D5
Milton of Buchanan 126 E3
Milton of Campfield 140 D5
Milton of Campsie 119 B6
Milton of Corsindae 141 D5
Milton of Cushnie 140 C4
Milton of Dalcapon 133 D6
Milton of Edradour 133 D6
Milton of Gollanfield 151 F10
Milton of Lesmore 140 B3
Milton of Logie 140 D3
Milton of Murtle 141 D7
Milton of Noth 140 B4
Milton of Tullich 140 E2
Milton on Stour 13 B5
Milton Regis 30 C3
Milton under Wychwood 38 C2
Milverton Som 11 B6
Warks 51 C8
Milwich 75 F6
Minard 125 F5
Minchinhampton 37 D5
Mindrum 122 F4
Minehead 21 E8
Minera 73 D6
Minety 37 E7
Minffordd Gwyn 58 C4
Gwyn 71 D6
Gwyn 83 D5
Miningsby 79 C6
Minions 5 B7
Minishant 112 C3
Minllyn 59 C5
Minnes 141 B8
Minngearraidh 148 F2
Minnigaff 105 C8
Minnonie 153 B7
Minskip 95 C6
Minstead 14 C3
Minsted 16 B2
Minster Kent 30 B3
Kent 31 C7
Minsterley 60 D3
Minster Lovell 38 C3
Minsterworth 36 C4
Minterne Magna 12 D4
Minting 78 B4
Mintlaw 153 D9
Minto 115 B8
Minton 60 E4
Minwear 32 C1
Minworth 63 E5
Mirbister 159 F4
Mirehouse 98 C1
Mireland 158 D5
Mirfield 88 C3
Miserden 37 D6
Miskin 34 F4
Misson 89 E7
Misterton Leics 64 F2
Notts 89 E8
Som 12 D2
Mistley 56 F5
Mitcham 28 C3
Mitcheldean 36 C3
Mitchell 4 D3
Mitchel Troy 36 C1
Mitcheltroy Common 36 D1
Mitford 117 F7
Mithian 4 D2
Mitton 62 C2
Mixbury 52 F4
Moat 108 B4
Moats Tye 56 D4
Mobberley Ches E 74 B4
Staffs 75 E7
Moccas 49 E5
Mochdre Conwy 83 D8
Powys 59 F7
Mochrum 105 E7
Mockbeggar 14 D2
Mockerkin 98 B2
Modbury 6 D4
Moddershall 75 F6
Moelfre Anglesey 82 C5
Powys 59 B8
Moffat 114 D3
Moggerhanger 54 E2
Moira 63 C7
Molash 30 D4
Mol-chlach 149 G9
Mold = *Yr Wyddgrug* 73 C6
Moldgreen 88 C2
Molehill Green 42 B1
Molescroft 97 E6
Molesden 117 F7
Molesworth 53 B8
Moll 149 E10
Molland 10 B3
Mollington Ches W 73 B7
Oxon 52 E2
Mollinsburn 119 B7
Monachty 46 C4
Monachylemore 126 C3
Monar Lodge 150 G5
Monaughty 48 C4
Monboddo House 135 B7
Mondynes 135 B7
Monevechadan 125 E7
Monewden 57 D6
Moneydie 128 B2

Moniaive........113 E7
Monifieth......134 F4
Monikie........135 F4
Monimail.......128 C4
Monington......45 E3
Monk Bretton....88 D4
Monken Hadley...41 E5
Monk Fryston....89 B6
Monkhopton......51 B6
Monkland........49 D6
Monkleigh........9 B6
Monknash........21 B8
Monkokehampton...9 D7
Monkseaton.....111 B6
Monks Eleigh....56 E3
Monk's Gate.....17 B6
Monks Heath.....74 B5
Monk Sherborne..26 D4
Monkshill......153 D7
Monksilver......22 F2
Monks Kirby.....63 F8
Monk Soham......57 C6
Monkspath.......51 B6
Monks Risborough 39 D8
Monk Street.....42 B2
Monkswood.......35 D7
Monkton Devon...11 D6
  Kent..........31 C6
  Pembs.........44 E4
  S Ayrs.......112 B3
Monkton Combe...24 C2
Monkton Deverill.24 F3
Monkton Farleigh.24 C3
Monkton
  Heathfield....11 B7
Monkton Up
  Wimborne......13 C8
Monkwearmouth.111 D6
Monkwood.......26 F4
Monmouth
  = Trefynwy....36 C2
Monmouth Cap....35 B7
Monnington on
  Wye...........49 E5
Monreith......105 E7
Monreith Mains.105 E7
Montacute......12 C2
Montcoffer
  House........153 B6
Montford Argyll.145 G10
  Shrops........60 C4
Montford Bridge..60 C4
Montgarrie.....140 C4
Montgomery
  = Trefaldwyn..60 E2
Montrave.......129 D5
Montrose.......135 D7
Mont Saint Guern..16
Montsale........43 E6
Monxton.........25 E8
Monyash.........75 C8
Monymusk.......141 C5
Monzie.........127 B7
Monzie Castle..127 B7
Moodiesburn....119 B6
Moonzie........128 C5
Moor Allerton...95 F5
Moorby..........79 C5
Moor Crichel....13 D7
Moordown........13 E8
Moore...........86 F3
Moorend.........36 D4
Moor End E Yorks.96 F4
  York..........96 D2
Moorends........89 C7
Moorgate........88 E4
Moorgreen.......76 E4
Moorhall........75 C8
Moorhampton....49 E5
Moorhead........94 F4
Moorhouse Cumb.108 D3
  Notts.........77 C7
Moorlinch.......23 F5
Moor Monkton....95 D8
Moor of Granary.151 F13
Moor of
  Ravenstone..105 E7
Moor Row........98 C2
Moorsholm.....102 C4
Moorside........87 D7
Moor Street.....30 C2
Moorthorpe......89 C5
Moortown Hants..14 D2
  IoW...........14 F5
  Lincs.........90 E4
Morangie......151 C10
Morar..........147 B9
Morborne........65 E8
Morchard Bishop.10 D2
Morcombelake....12 E2
Morcott.........65 D6
Morda...........60 B2
Morden Dorset...13 E7
  London........28 C3
Mordiford.......49 F7
Mordon........101 B8
More............60 E3
Morebath........10 B4
Morebattle....116 B3
Morecambe.......92 C4
Morefield.....150 B4
Moreleigh........7 D5
Morenish......132 F2
Moresby.........98 B1
Moresby Parks...98 C1
Morestead.......15 B6
Moreton Dorset..13 F6
  Essex.........41 D8
  Mers..........85 E3
  Oxon..........39 D6
  Staffs........61 C7
Moreton Corbet..61 B5
Moretonhampstead
  ....10 F2
Moreton-in-Marsh 51 F7
Moreton Jeffries.49 E8
Moreton Morrell.51 D8
Moreton Pinkney.52 E3
Moreton Say.....74 F3
Moreton Valence.50 E3
Morfa Carms.....33 C6
  Carms.........33 E6
Morfa Bach......32 C4
Morfa Bychan....71 D6
Morfa Dinlle....82 F4

Morfa Glas......34 D2
Morfa Nefyn.....70 C3
Morfydd.........72 E5
Morgan's Vale...14 B2
Moriah..........46 B5
Morland.........99 B7
Morley Derbys...76 E3
  Durham.......101 B6
  W Yorks.......88 B3
Morley Green....87 F6
Morley St Botolph.68 E3
Morningside Edin.120 B5
  N Lanark.....119 D8
Morningthorpe...68 E5
Morpeth........117 F8
Morphie.......135 C7
Morrey..........62 C5
Morris Green....55 F8
Morriston.......33 E7
Morston.........81 C6
Mortehoe........20 E3
Morthen.........89 F5
Mortimer........26 C4
Mortimer's Cross.49 C6
Mortimer West
  End...........26 C4
Mortlake........28 B3
Morton Cumb....108 D3
  Derbys........76 C4
  Lincs.........65 B7
  Lincs.........77 C8
  Lincs.........90 E2
  Norf..........68 C4
  Notts.........77 D7
  S Glos........36 E3
  Shrops........60 B2
Morton Bagot....51 C6
Morton-
  on-Swale....101 E8
Morvah...........2 C3
Morval...........5 D7
Morvich Highld.136 B2
  Highld......157 J10
Morville........61 E6
Morville Heath..61 E6
Morwenstow......8 C4
Mosborough......88 F5
Moscow........118 E4
Mosedale......108 F3
Moseley W Mid...62 E3
  W Mid.........62 F4
  Worcs.........50 D3
Moss Argyll....146 G2
  Highld.......147 E9
  S Yorks.......89 C6
  Wrex..........73 D7
Mossat........140 C3
Mossbank......160 F6
Moss Bank.......86 E3
Mossbay.........98 B1
Mossblown.....112 B4
Mossbrow........86 F5
Mossburnford..116 C2
Mossdale......106 B3
Moss Edge.......92 E4
Moss End........27 B6
Mossend.......119 C7
Mossfield.....151 D9
Mossgiel......112 B4
Mosside.......134 D4
Mossley Ches E..75 C7
  Gtr Man.......87 D7
Mossley Hill....85 F4
Moss of
  Barmuckity..152 B2
Moss Pit........62 B3
Moss-side.....151 F11
Moss Side.......92 F3
Mosstodloch...152 B3
Mosston.......135 E5
Mossy Lea.......86 C3
Mosterton......12 D2
Moston Gtr Man..87 D6
  Shrops........61 B5
Moston Green....74 C4
Mostyn..........85 F2
Mostyn Quay.....85 F2
Motcombe........13 B6
Mothecombe......6 E4
Motherby........99 B6
Motherwell....119 D7
Mottingham......28 B5
Mottisfont......14 B4
Mottistone......14 F5
Mottram in
  Longdendale..87 E7
Mottram
  St Andrew.....75 B5
Mouilpied Guern..16
Mouldsworth.....74 B2
Moulin.........133 D6
Moulsecoomb....17 D7
Moulsford.......39 F5
Moulsoe.........53 E7
Moulton Ches W..74 C3
  Lincs.........66 B3
  N Yorks......101 D7
  Suff..........55 C7
  V Glam........22 B2
  W Nhants......53 C5
Moulton Chapel..66 C2
Moulton Eaugate.66 C3
Moulton St Mary.69 D6
Moulton Seas End.66 B3
Mounie Castle..141 B6
Mount Corn......4 D2
  Corn...........5 C6
  Highld......151 G12
Mountain........94 F3
Mountain Ash
  = Aberpennar..34 E4
Mountain Cross.120 E4
Mountain Water..44 C4
Mountbenger...115 B6
Mount Bures.....56 F3
Mount Canisp..151 D10
Mountfield......18 C4
Mountgerald...151 E8
Mount Hawke......3 B6
Mountjoy.........4 C3
Mountnessing....42 E2
Mounton.........36 E2
Mount Pleasant
  Ches E........74 D5
  Derbys........63 C6
  Derbys........76 E3
  Flint.........73 B6
  Hants.........14 E3
  W Yorks.......88 B3

Mountsorrel.....64 C2
Mount Sorrel....13 B8
Mount Tabor.....87 B8
Mousehole........2 D3
Mousen.........123 F7
Mouswald......107 B7
Mow Cop.........75 D5
Mowhaugh......116 B4
Mowsley.........64 F3
Moxley..........62 E3
Moy Highld.....137 F7
Moy Hall......151 H10
Moy House.....151 E13
Moyles Court....14 D2
Moylgrove.......45 E3
Moy Lodge.....137 F7
Muasdale......143 D7
Muchalls......141 E8
Much Birch......49 F7
Much Cowarne....49 E8
Much Dewchurch..49 F6
Muchelney.......12 B2
Much Hadham.....41 C7
Much Hoole......86 B2
Muchlarnick......5 D7
Much Marcle.....49 F8
Muchrachd.....150 H5
Much Wenlock....61 D6
Muckernich....151 F8
Mucking.........42 F2
Muckleford......12 E4
Mucklestone.....74 F4
Muckleton......61 B5
Muckletown....140 B4
Muckley Corner..62 D4
Muckton.........91 F7
Mudale........157 F8
Muddiford.......20 F4
Mudeford.......14 E2
Mudford.........12 C3
Mudgley........23 E6
Mugdock.......119 B5
Mugeary.......149 E9
Mugginton......76 E2
Muggleswick...110 E3
Muie..........157 J9
Muir..........139 F6
Muirden.......153 C7
Muirdrum......135 F5
Muirhead Angus.134 F3
  Fife.........128 D4
  N Lanark.....119 C6
  S Ayrs.......118 F3
Muirhouselaw..116 B2
Muirhouses....128 F2
Muirkirk......113 B6
Muirmill......127 F6
Muir of Fairburn.150 F7
Muir of Fowlis.140 C4
Muir of Ord....151 F8
Muir of Pert...134 F4
Muirshearlich.136 F4
Muirskie......141 E7
Muirtack......153 E9
Muirton Highld.151 E10
  Perth........127 C8
  Perth........128 B3
Muirton Mains..150 F7
Muirton of
  Ardblair....134 E1
Muirton of
  Ballochy....135 C6
Muiryfold.....153 C7
Muker.........100 E4
Mulbarton......68 D4
Mulben........152 C3
Mulindry......142 C4
Mullardoch
  House........150 H5
Mullion..........3 E5
Mullion Cove.....3 E5
Mumby..........79 B8
Munderfield Row.49 D8
Munderfield
  Stocks.......49 D8
Mundesley......81 D9
Mundford.......67 E8
Mundham........69 E6
Mundon.........42 D4
Mundurno......141 C8
Munerigie......137 D5
Muness........160 C8
Mungasdale....150 B2
Mungrisdale...108 F3
Munlochy......151 F9
Munsley........49 E8
Munslow........60 F5
Murchington.....9 F8
Murcott........39 C5
Murkle........158 D3
Murlaggan Highld.136 E3
  Highld.......137 F6
Murra.........159 H3
Murrayfield...120 B5
Murrow.........66 D3
Mursley........39 B8
Murthill......134 D4
Murthly.......133 F7
Murton Cumb...100 B2
  Durham.......111 E6
  Northum......123 E5
  York..........96 D2
Musbury........11 E7
Muscoates.....102 F4
Musdale.......124 C5
Musselburgh...121 B6
Muston Leics...77 F8
  N Yorks.......97 B6
Mustow Green....50 B3
Mutehill......106 E3
Mutford........69 F7
Muthill.......127 C7
Mutterton......10 D5
Muxton.........61 C7
Mybster.......158 E3
Myddfai........34 B1
Myddle.........60 B4
Mydroilyn......46 D3
Myerscough.....92 F4
Mylor Bridge....3 C7
Mynachlog-ddu..45 F3
Myndtown.......60 F3
Mynydd Bach....47 B6
Mynydd-bach....36 E1
Mynydd Bodafon.82 C4
Mynydd Isa.....73 C6
Mynyddygarreg..33 D5
Mynytho........70 D4

Myrebird......141 E6
Myrelandhorn..158 E4
Myreside......128 B4
Myrtle Hill....47 F6
Mytchett.......27 D6
Mytholm........87 B7
Mytholmroyd....87 B8
Myton-on-Swale.95 C7
Mytton.........60 C4

N

Naast.........155 J13
Naburn.........95 E8
Nackington.....31 D5
Nacton.........57 E6
Nafferton......97 D6
Na Gearrannan.154 C6
Nailbridge.....36 C3
Nailsbourne....11 B7
Nailsea.........23 B6
Nailstone......63 D8
Nailsworth.....37 E5
Nairn.........151 F11
Nalderswood....28 E3
Nancegollan.....2 C5
Nancledra.......2 C3
Nanhoron.......70 D3
Nannau.........71 E8
Nannerch.......73 C5
Nanpantan......64 C2
Nanpean.........4 D4
Nanstallon......4 C5
Nant-ddu........34 C4
Nanternis......46 D2
Nantgaredig....33 B5
Nantgarw.......35 F5
Nant-glas......47 C8
Nantglyn.......72 C4
Nantgwyn.......47 B8
Nantlle........82 F5
Nantmawr.......60 B2
Nantmel........48 C2
Nantmor........71 C7
Nant Peris.....83 F6
Nant Uchaf.....72 D4
Nantwich.......74 D3
Nant-y-Bai.....47 E6
Nant-y-cafn....34 D2
Nantycaws......33 C5
Nant-y-derry...35 D7
Nant-y-ffin....46 F4
Nantyffyllon...34 E2
Nantyglo.......35 C5
Nant-y-moel....34 E3
Nant-y-pandy...83 D6
Naphill........39 E8
Nappa..........93 D8
Napton on the Hill.52 C2
Narberth
  = Arberth....32 C2
Narborough Leics.64 E2
  Norf..........67 C7
Nasareth.......82 F4
Naseby.........52 B4
Nash Bucks.....53 F5
  Hereford......48 C5
  Newport.......35 F7
  Shrops........49 B8
Nash Lee.......39 D8
Nassington.....65 E7
Nasty..........41 B6
Nateby Cumb...100 D2
  Lancs.........92 E4
Natland........99 F7
Naughton.......56 E4
Naunton Glos...37 B8
  Worcs.........50 F3
Naunton
  Beauchamp...50 D4
Navenby........78 D2
Navestock Heath.41 E8
Navestock Side..42 E1
Navidale......157 H13
Nawton........102 F4
Nayland........56 F3
Nazeing........41 D7
Neacroft.......14 E2
Neal's Green...63 F7
Neap..........160 H7
Near Sawrey....99 E5
Neasham.......101 C8
Neath
  = Castell-Nedd.33 E8
Neath Abbey....33 E8
Neatishead.....69 B6
Nebo Anglesey..82 B4
  Ceredig.......46 C4
  Conwy.........83 F8
  Gwyn..........82 F4
Necton.........67 D8
Nedd..........156 F4
Nedderton.....117 F8
Nedging Tye....56 E4
Needham........68 F5
Needham Market.56 D4
Needingworth...54 B4
Needwood.......63 B5
Neen Savage....49 B8
Neen Sollars...49 B8
Neenton........61 F6
Nefyn..........70 C4
Neilston......118 D4
Neinthirion....59 D6
Neithrop.......52 E2
Nelly Andrews
  Green........60 D2
Nelson Caerph..35 E5
  Lancs.........93 F8
Nelson Village.111 B5
Nemphlett.....119 E8
Nempnett
  Thrubwell....23 C7
Nene Terrace...66 D2
Nenthall......109 E7
Nenthead......109 E7
Nenthorn......122 F2
Nerabus.......142 C3
Nercwys........73 C6
Nerston.......119 D6
Nesbit........123 F5
Ness...........73 B7
Nesscliffe.....60 C3
Neston Ches W..73 B6
  Wilts.........24 C3
Nether Alderley.74 B5
Netheravon.....25 E6
Nether Blainslie.121 E8

Nether Booth...88 F2
Netherbrae....153 C7
Netherbrough..159 G4
Nether Broughton.64 B3
Netherburn....119 E8
Nether Burrow..93 B6
Netherbury.....12 E2
Netherby Cumb.108 B3
  N Yorks.......95 E6
Nether Cerne...12 E4
Nether Compton.12 C3
Nethercote.....52 C3
Nethercott.....20 F3
Nether
  Howecleuch..114 C3
Nether Kellet..92 C5
Nether
  Kinmundy...153 D10
Nether Langwith.76 B5
Netherlaw.....106 C4
Nether Leask..153 E10
Nether Lenshie.153 D7
Netherley Aberds.141 E7
  Mers..........86 F2
Nethermill....114 F3
Nether Monynut.122 C3
Nethermuir....153 D9
Nether Padley..76 B2
Nether Park...153 C10
Netherplace...118 D5
Nether Poppleton.95 D8
Netherseal.....63 C6
Nether Silton.102 E2
Nether Stowey..22 F3
Netherthird...113 C5
Netherthong...88 D2
Netherthorpe...89 F5
Netherton Angus.135 D5
  Devon..........7 B6
  Hants.........25 C8
  Mers..........85 D4
  Northum......117 D5
  Oxon..........38 E4
  Perth........133 D8
  Stirling.....119 B5
  W Mid.........62 F3
  Worcs.........50 E4
  W Yorks.......88 B3
  W Yorks.......88 C2
Nethertown Cumb.98 D1
  Highld.......158 C5
Nether Urquhart.128 D3
Nether Wallop..25 F8
Nether Wasdale.98 D3
Nether Whitacre.63 E6
Netherwitton..117 E7
Netherwood....113 B6
Nether Worton..52 F2
Nethy Bridge..139 B6
Netley.........15 D5
Netley Marsh...14 C4
Netteswell.....41 C7
Nettlebed......39 F7
Nettlebridge...23 E8
Nettlecombe....12 E3
Nettleden......40 C3
Nettleham......78 B3
Nettlestead....29 D7
Nettlestead Green.29 D7
Nettlestone....15 E7
Nettlesworth..111 E5
Nettleton Lincs.90 D5
  Wilts.........24 B3
Neuadd.........33 B7
Nevendon.......42 E3
Nevern.........45 E2
New Abbey.....107 C6
New Aberdour..153 B8
New Addington..28 C4
Newall.........94 E4
New Alresford..26 F3
New Alyth.....134 E2
Newark Orkney.159 D8
  Pboro.........66 D2
Newark-on-Trent.77 D7
New Arley......63 F6
Newarthill....119 D7
New Ash Green..29 C7
New Barn.......29 C7
New Barnetby...90 C4
Newbarns.......92 B2
New Barton.....53 C6
Newbattle.....121 C6
New Bewick....117 B6
Newbiggin Cumb.98 B2
  Cumb..........99 B8
  Cumb..........99 E8
  Cumb........109 E5
  Durham.......100 B4
  N Yorks......100 E4
  N Yorks......100 F4
Newbiggin-by-
  the-Sea.....117 F9
Newbigging Angus.134 E3
  Angus........134 F4
  S Lanark.....120 E3
Newbiggin-
  on-Lune.....100 D2
New Bilton.....52 B2
Newbold Derbys..76 B3
  Leics.........63 C8
Newbold on Avon.52 B2
Newbold on Stour.51 E7
Newbold Pacey..51 D7
Newbold Verdon.63 D8
New Bolingbroke.79 D6
Newborough
  Anglesey......82 E4
  Pboro.........66 D2
  Staffs........62 B5
Newbottle T&W.111 D6
  W Nhants......52 F3
New Boultham...78 B2
Newbourne......57 E6

New Bradwell...53 E6
New Brancepeth.110 E5
Newbridge Caerph.35 E6
  Ceredig.......46 D4
  Corn...........2 C3
  Corn...........5 C8
  Dumfries....107 B6
  Edin.........120 B4
  Hants.........14 C3
  IoW...........14 F5
  Pembs.........44 B4
New Bridge.....23 B7
Newbridge Green.50 F3
Newbridge-
  on-Usk.......35 E7
Newbridge
  on Wye.......48 D2
New Brighton Flint.73 C6
  Mers..........85 E4
New Brinsley...76 D4
Newbrough.....109 C8
New Broughton..73 D7
New Buckenham..68 E3
Newbuildings...10 D2
Newburgh Aberds.141 B8
  Aberds.......153 C9
  Borders......115 C6
  Fife.........128 C4
  Lancs.........86 C2
Newburn.......110 C4
Newbury........26 C2
Newbury Park...41 F7
Newby Cumb.....99 B7
  Lancs.........93 E8
  N Yorks.......93 B7
  N Yorks......102 C3
  N Yorks......103 E8
Newby Bridge...99 F5
Newby East....108 D4
New Byth......153 C8
Newby West....108 D3
Newby Wiske...102 F1
Newcastle Mon..35 C8
Newcastle Emlyn
  = Castell Newydd
  Emlyn........46 E2
Newcastleton or
  Copshaw Holm.115 F7
Newcastle-
  under-Lyme...74 E5
Newcastle
  upon Tyne...110 C5
New Catton.....68 C5
Newchapel Pembs.45 F4
  Powys.........59 F6
  Staffs........75 D5
  Sur...........28 E4
New Cheriton...15 B6
Newchurch Carms.32 B4
  IoW...........15 F6
  Kent..........19 B7
  Lancs.........93 F8
  Mon...........36 E1
  Powys.........48 D4
  Staffs........62 B5
New Costessey..68 C4
Newcott........11 D7
New Cowper....107 E8
Newcraighall..121 B6
New Cross Ceredig.46 B5
  London........28 B4
New Cumnock...113 C6
New Deer......153 D8
New Delaval...111 B5
Newdigate......28 E2
New Duston.....52 C5
New Earswick...96 D2
New Edlington..89 E6
New Elgin.....152 B2
New Ellerby....97 F7
Newell Green...27 B6
New Eltham.....28 B5
New End........51 D5
Newenden.......18 C5
Newent.........36 B4
Newerne........36 D3
New Farnley....94 F5
New Ferry......85 F4
Newfield Durham.110 F5
  Highld......151 D10
Newford.........2 E4
Newfound.......26 D3
New Fryston....89 B5
Newgale........44 C3
New Galloway..106 B3
Newgate........81 C6
Newgate Street.41 D6
New Gilston...129 D6
New Grimsby.....2 E3
New Hainford...68 C5
Newhall Ches E..74 E3
  Derbys........63 B6
Newhall House.151 E9
Newhall Point.151 E10
Newham........117 B7
Newham Hall...117 B7
New Hartley...111 B6
Newhaven Derbys.75 D8
  Edin.........121 B5
  E Sus.........17 D8
New Haw........27 C8
New Hedges.....32 D2
New Herrington.111 D6
Newhey.........87 C7
New Hinksey....39 D5
New Holkham....80 D4
New Holland....90 B4
Newholm......103 C6
New Houghton
  Derbys........76 C4
  Norf..........80 E3
Newhouse......119 C7
New Houses.....93 B8
New Humberstone 64 D3
New Hutton.....99 E7
New Hythe......29 D8
Newick.........17 B8
Newingreen.....19 B8
Newington Kent..19 B7
  Kent..........30 C2
  Kent..........31 C7
  Notts.........89 E7
  Oxon..........39 E6
  Shrops........60 F4
Newington
  Bagpath......37 E5
New Inn Carms...46 F3
  Mon...........36 D1
  Pembs.........45 F2
  Torf..........35 E7

New Invention
  Shrops........48 B4
  W Mid.........62 D3
New Kelso.....150 G2
New Kingston...64 B2
New Lanark....119 E8
Newland Glos...36 D2
  Hull..........97 F6
  N Yorks.......89 B7
  Worcs.........50 E2
Newlandrig....121 C6
Newlands Borders.115 E8
  Highld......151 G10
  Moray........152 C3
  Northum......110 D3
Newland's Corner.27 E8
Newlandsmuir..119 D6
Newlands of
  Geise........158 D2
Newlands of
  Tynet........152 B3
Newlands Park..82 C2
New Lane.......86 C2
New Lane End...86 E4
New Leake......79 D7
New Leeds.....153 C9
New Longton....86 B3
Newlot........159 G6
New Luce......105 C5
Newlyn..........2 D3
Newmachar.....141 C7
Newmains......119 D8
New Malden.....28 C3
Newmarket Suff..55 C7
  W Isles......155 D9
New Marske....102 B4
New Marton.....73 F7
New Micklefield.95 F7
New Mill Aberds.141 F6
  Herts.........40 C2
  Wilts.........25 C6
  W Yorks.......88 D2
Newmill Borders.115 C7
  Corn...........2 C3
  Moray........152 C4
Newmill of
  Inshewan....134 C4
New Mills Ches E.87 F5
  Corn...........4 D3
  Derbys........87 F7
  Powys.........59 D7
Newmills of
  Boyne........152 C5
Newmiln.......133 F8
Newmilns......118 F5
New Milton.....14 E3
New Moat.......32 B1
Newnham Cambs..54 D5
  Glos..........36 C3
  Hants.........26 D5
  Herts.........54 F3
  Kent..........30 D3
  W Nhants......52 D3
Newnham Bridge..49 C8
New Ollerton...77 C6
New Oscott.....62 E4
New Park.......95 D5
New Pitsligo..153 C8
New Polzeath....4 B4
Newport Devon..20 F4
  Essex.........55 F6
  E Yorks.......96 F4
  Highld.......158 H3
  IoW...........15 F6
  Norf..........69 C8
  Telford.......61 C7
Newport
  = Casnewydd..35 F7
Newport
  = Trefdraeth..45 F2
Newport-on-Tay.129 B6
Newport Pagnell.53 E6
Newpound
  Common.......16 B4
Newquay.........4 C3
New Quay
  = Ceinewydd..46 D2
New Rackheath..69 C5
New Radnor.....48 C4
New Rent......108 F4
New Ridley....110 D3
New Road Side..94 E2
New Romney.....19 C7
New Rossington.89 E7
New Row Ceredig.46 B5
  Lancs.........93 F6
  N Yorks......102 C4
New Sarum......25 F6
Newsbank.......74 C5
Newseat Aberds.153 D10
  Aberds.......153 E7
Newsham
  Northum......111 B6
  N Yorks......101 C6
  N Yorks......102 F1
Newsholme
  E Yorks.......89 B8
  Lancs.........93 D8
New Silksworth.111 D6
Newsome........88 C2
Newstead Borders.121 F8
  Northum......117 B7
  Notts.........76 D5
New Stevenston.119 D7
New Street.....75 D7
New Street Lane.74 F3
New Swanage....13 F8
Newthorpe......76 E4
Newton Argyll.125 F6
  Borders......116 B2
  Bridgend......21 B7
  Cambs.........54 E5
  Cambs.........66 C4
  Cardiff.......35 F6
  Ches W........73 C8
  Ches W........74 B2
  Ches W........74 D2
  Cumb..........92 B2
  Derbys........76 D4
  Dorset........13 C5
  Dumfries....108 B2
  Dumfries....114 E4
  Gtr Man.......87 E7
  Hereford......48 F5
  Hereford......49 E7
  Highld......151 E10
  Highld......151 G10
  Highld......156 F5

Newton *continued*
  Highld.......158 F5
  Lancs.........92 F4
  Lancs.........93 B5
  Lancs.........93 D6
  Lincs.........78 F3
  Moray........152 B1
  N Hants.......65 F5
  Norf..........67 C8
  Northum......110 C3
  Notts.........77 E6
  Perth........133 F5
  S Lanark.....119 C6
  S Lanark.....120 F2
  Staffs........62 B4
  Suff..........56 E3
  Swansea.......33 F7
  S Yorks.......89 D6
  Warks.........52 B3
  Wilts.........13 B7
  W Loth.......120 B3
Newton Abbot....7 B6
Newtonairds...113 F8
Newton Arlosh.107 D8
Newton Aycliffe.101 B7
Newton Bewley.102 B2
Newton
  Blossomville.53 D7
Newton
  Bromswold...53 C7
Newton
  Burgoland...63 D7
Newton by Toft..90 F4
Newton Ferrers..6 E3
Newton Flotman.68 E5
Newtongrange..121 C6
Newton Hall...110 C3
Newton Harcourt.64 E3
Newton Heath...87 D6
Newtonhill Aberds.141 E8
  Highld......151 G8
Newton House..141 B5
Newton Kyme....95 E7
Newton-le-Willows
  Mers..........86 E3
  N Yorks......101 F7
Newton Longville.53 F6
Newton Mearns.118 D5
Newtonmill....135 C6
Newtonmore....138 E3
Newton Morrell.101 D7
Newton
  Mulgrave....103 C5
Newton of
  Ardtoe.......147 D9
Newton of
  Balcanquhal.128 C3
Newton of
  Falkland....128 D4
Newton on Ayr.112 B3
Newton on Ouse.95 D8
Newton-on-
  Rawcliffe...103 E6
Newton-on-the-
  Moor........117 D7
Newton on Trent.77 B8
Newton Park...145 G10
Newton
  Poppleford...11 E5
Newton Purcell.52 F4
Newton Regis...63 D6
Newton Reigny.108 F4
Newton St Cyres.10 E3
Newton St Faith.68 C5
Newton St Loe..24 C2
Newton St Petrock.9 C6
Newton Solney..63 B6
Newton Stacey..26 E2
Newton Stewart.105 C8
Newton Tony....25 E7
Newton Tracey...9 B7
Newton under
  Roseberry...102 C3
Newton upon
  Derwent......96 E3
Newton Valence.26 F5
New Totley.....76 B3
Newtown Argyll.125 E6
  BCP...........13 E8
  Ches W........74 B2
  Corn...........3 D6
  Cumb.........107 E7
  Cumb.........108 C5
  Derbys........87 F7
  Devon.........10 B2
  Glos..........36 D3
  Glos..........50 F4
  Hants.........14 B4
  Hants.........14 C3
  Hants.........15 C7
  Hereford......49 E8
  Highld.......137 F6
  IoM...........84 E3
  IoW...........14 E5
  Northumb.....117 B6
  Northumb.....117 C6
  Northumb.....123 F5
  Shrops........73 F8
  Staffs........75 C6
  Staffs........75 D6
  Wilts.........13 B7
New Town......121 B7
Newtown
  = Y Drenewydd.59 E8
Newtown Linford.64 D2
Newtown
  St Boswells.121 F8
Newtown Unthank.63 D8
New Tredegar
  = Tredegar Newydd.35 D5
New Trows.....119 F8
New Ulva......144 E6
New Walsoken...66 D4
New Waltham....91 D6
New Whittington.76 B3
New Wimpole....54 E4
New Winton....121 B7
New Yatt.......38 C3
New York Lincs..78 D5
  N Yorks.......94 C4
Neyland........44 E4
Niarbyl........84 E2
Nibley.........36 F3
Nibley Green...36 E4
Nibon.........160 F5

Nicholashayne..11 C6
Nicholaston....33 F6
Nidd...........95 C6
Nigg Aberdeen.141 D8
  Highld......151 D11
Nigg Ferry....151 E10
Nightcott......10 B3
Nilig..........72 D4
Nine Ashes.....42 D1
Ninebanks....109 D7
Nine Mile Burn.120 D4
Nine Wells.....44 C2
Ninfield.......18 D4
Ningwood.......14 F4
Nisbet........116 B2
Nisthouse Orkney.159 G4
  Shetland.....160 G7
Niton..........15 G6
Nitshill......118 C5
Noak Hill......41 E8
Nobelthorpe....88 D3
Nobottle.......52 C4
Nocton.........78 C3
Noke...........39 C5
Nolton.........44 D3
Nolton Haven...44 D3
No Man's Heath
  Ches W........74 E2
  Warks.........63 D6
Nomansland Devon.10 C3
  Wilts.........14 C3
Noneley........60 B4
Nonikiln......151 D9
Nonington......31 D6
Noonsbrough...160 H4
Norbreck.......92 E3
Norbridge......50 E2
Norbury Ches E..74 E2
  Derbys........75 E8
  Shrops........60 E3
  Staffs........61 B7
Nordelph.......67 D5
Norden.........87 C6
Norden Heath...13 F7
Nordley........61 E6
Norham.......122 E5
Norley.........74 B2
Norleywood.....14 E4
Normanby N Lincs.90 C2
  N Yorks......103 F5
  Redcar.......102 C3
Normanby-
  by-Spital....90 F4
Normanby by Stow 90 F2
Normanby le Wold.90 E5
Norman Cross...65 E8
Normandy.......27 D7
Norman's Bay...18 E3
Norman's Green.11 D5
Normanstone....69 E8
Normanton Derby.76 F3
  Leics.........77 E8
  Lincs.........78 E2
  Notts.........77 D7
  Rutland.......65 D6
  W Yorks.......88 B4
Normanton
  le Heath.....63 C7
Normanton
  on Soar......64 B2
Normanton-on-
  the-Wolds....77 F6
Normanton
  on Trent.....77 C7
Normoss........92 F3
Norney.........27 E7
Norrington
  Common.......24 C3
Norris Green...85 E4
Norris Hill....63 C7
Northacre......68 E2
Northallerton.102 E1
Northam Devon...9 B6
  Soton.........14 C5
Northampton...53 C5
North Anston...89 F6
North Aston....38 B4
Northaw........41 D5
North Baddesley.14 C4
North
  Ballachulish.130 C4
North Barrow...12 B4
North Barsham..80 D5
Northbeck......78 E3
North Benfleet.42 F3
North Bersted..16 D3
North Berwick.129 F7
North Boarhunt.15 C7
Northborough...65 D8
Northbourne....31 D7
North Bovey....10 F2
North Bradley..24 D3
North Brentor...9 F6
North Brewham..24 F2
Northbridge
  Street.......18 C4
North Buckland.20 E3
North Burlingham 69 C6
North Cadbury..12 B4
North Cairn...104 B3
North Carlton..78 B2
North Carrine.143 H7
North Cave.....96 F4
North Cerney...37 D7
Northchapel....16 B3
North Charford.14 C2
North Charlton.117 B7
North Cheriton.12 B4
Northchurch....40 D2
North Cliff....97 E8
North Cliffe....96 F4
North Clifton..77 B8
North
  Cockerington.91 E7
North Coker....12 C3
North Collafirth.160 E5
North Common...17 B7
North Connel..124 B5
North Cornelly.34 F2
North Cotes....91 D7
Northcott.......8 E5
North Cove.....69 F7
North Cowton..101 D7
North Crawley..53 E7
North Cray.....29 B5
North Creake...80 D4
North Curry....11 B8
North Dalton...96 D5
North Dawn...159 H5

North Deighton....95 D6
Northdown....31 B7
North Duffield....96 F2
Northdyke....159 F3
North Elkington....91 E6
North Elmham....81 E5
North Elmshall....89 C5
Northend Bath....24 C2
Bucks.....39 E7
Warks.....51 B8
North End Bucks...39 B8
Essex.....42 C2
E Yorks.....97 F8
Hants.....26 C2
Lincs.....78 E5
N Som.....23 C6
Ptsmth.....15 D7
Som.....11 B7
W Sus.....16 D5
Northenden....87 E6
North Erradale....155 J12
North Fearns....149 E10
North Featherstone....88 B5
North Ferriby....90 B3
Northfield
Aberdeen....141 D8
Borders....122 C5
E Yorks.....90 B4
W Mid.....50 B5
Northfields....65 D7
Northfleet....29 B7
North Frodingham....97 D7
Northgate.....65 B8
North Gluss....160 F5
North Gorley.....14 C2
North Green Norf...65 F5
Suff.....57 C7
North Greetwell....78 B3
North Grimston....96 C4
North Halley....159 H6
North Halling....29 C8
North Hayling....15 D8
North Hazelrigg....123 F6
North Heasley.....21 F6
North Heath....16 B4
North Hill Cambs....55 B5
Corn.....5 B7
North Hinksey....26 C2
North Holmwood....28 E2
Northhouse....115 D7
North Howden....96 F3
North Huish....6 E5
North Hykeham....78 C2
Northiam....18 C5
Northill.....54 E2
Northington....26 F3
North Johnston....44 D4
North Kelsey....90 D4
North Kelsey Moor....90 D4
North Kessock....151 G9
North Killingholme....90 C5
North Kilvington....102 F2
North Kilworth....64 F3
North Kiscadale....143 F11
North Kyme....78 D4
Northlands.....79 D6
Northlea.....111 D7
Northleach....37 C8
North Lee....39 D8
Northleigh.....11 E6
North Leigh....38 C3
North Leverton with Habblesthorpe....89 F8
Northlew....11 E5
North Littleton....51 E5
North Lopham....68 F3
North Luffenham....65 D6
North Marden....16 C2
North Marston....39 B7
North Middleton
Midloth....121 D6
Northumb....117 B6
North Molton....21 F6
Northmoor....38 D4
Northmoor Green or Moorland....22 F5
North Moreton....39 F5
Northmuir....134 D3
North Mundham....16 D2
North Muskham....77 D7
North Newbald.....96 F5
North Newington....52 F2
North Newton....22 F4
Northney.....15 D8
North Nibley....36 E4
North Oakley....26 D3
North Ockendon....42 F1
Northolt.....40 F4
Northop.....73 C6
Northop Hall....73 C6
North Ormesby....102 B3
North Ormsby....91 E6
Northorpe Lincs....65 C7
Lincs.....78 F5
Lincs.....90 E2
North Otterington....102 F1
North Otterington....102 F1
Northover Som...12 B3
Som.....23 F6
North Owersby....90 E4
Northowram.....88 B2
North Perrott....12 D2
North Petherton....22 F4
North Petherwin....8 F4
North Pickenham....67 D8
North Piddle.....50 D4
North Poorton....12 E3
North Port....125 C6
Northpunds....160 L6
North Queensferry....128 F3
North Radworth....21 F6
North Rauceby....78 D3
Northrepps.....81 D8
North Reston....91 F7
North Rigton....95 E5
North Rode....15 C6
North Roe.....160 E5
North Runcton....67 C6
North Sandwick....160 D7
North Scale....92 C1
North Scarle....77 C8

North Seaton....117 F8
North Shian....130 E3
North Shields....111 C6
North Shoebury....43 F5
North Shore.....92 F3
North Side Cumb....66 E2
Pboro.....66 E2
North Skelton....102 C4
North Somercotes....91 E8
North Stainley.....95 B5
North Stainmore....100 C3
North Stifford.....42 F2
North Stoke Bath....24 C2
Oxon.....39 F6
W Sus.....16 C4
Northstowe.....54 C5
North Street Hants....26 F4
Kent.....30 D4
Medway.....30 B2
W Berks.....26 B4
North Sunderland....123 F8
North Tamerton....8 E5
North Tawton....9 D8
North Thoresby....91 E6
North Tidworth....25 E7
North Togston....117 D8
Northtown....159 J5
North Tuddenham....68 C3
North Walbottle....110 C4
North Walsham....81 D8
North Waltham....26 E3
North Warnborough....26 D5
North Water Bridge....135 C6
North Watten....158 E4
Northway.....50 F4
North Weald Bassett....41 D7
North Wheatley....89 F8
North Whilborough....7 C6
Northwich.....74 B3
Northwick.....36 F2
North Wick....23 C7
North Willingham....90 F5
North Wingfield....76 C4
North Witham....65 B6
Northwold.....67 E7
Northwood Derbys....76 C2
IoW.....15 E5
Kent.....31 C7
London....40 E3
Shrops.....73 F8
Northwood Green....36 C4
North Woolwich....28 B5
North Wootton Dorset....12 C4
Norf.....67 B6
Som.....23 E7
North Wraxall....24 B3
North Wroughton....38 F1
Norton E Sus...17 D8
Glos.....37 B5
Halton.....86 F3
Herts.....54 F3
IoW.....14 F4
Mon.....35 C8
Notts.....77 B5
Powys.....48 C5
Shrops.....60 F4
Shrops.....61 D5
Shrops.....61 D7
Stockton....102 B2
Suff.....56 C3
S Yorks.....89 C6
Wilts.....37 F5
W Nhants....52 C4
Worcs.....50 D3
Worcs.....50 E5
W Sus.....16 D3
W Sus.....16 E2
Norton Bavant....24 E4
Norton Bridge....75 F5
Norton Canes....49 E5
Norton Canon....49 E5
Norton Corner....81 E6
Norton Disney....77 D8
Norton East....62 D4
Norton Ferris....24 E2
Norton Fitzwarren....11 B6
Norton Green....14 F4
Norton Hawkfield....23 C7
Norton Heath....42 D2
Norton in Hales....74 F4
Norton-in-the-Moors....75 D6
Norton-Juxta-Twycross....63 D7
Norton-le-Clay....95 B7
Norton Lindsey....51 C7
Norton Malreward....23 C8
Norton Mandeville....42 D1
Norton-on-Derwent....96 B3
Norton St Philip....24 D2
Norton sub Hamdon....12 C2
Norton Woodseats....88 F4
Norwell.....77 C7
Norwell Woodhouse....77 C7
Norwich....68 D5
Norwick....160 B8
Norwood.....89 F5
Norwood Hill....28 E3
Norwoodside....66 E4
Noseley.....64 E4
Noss....160 M5
Noss Mayo....6 E3
Nosterfield....101 F7
Nostie....149 F13
Notgrove.....37 B8
Nottage.....21 B7
Nottingham....77 F5
Nottington....12 F4
Notton Wilts....24 C4
W Yorks.....88 C4
Nounsley.....42 C3
Noutard's Green....50 C2
Novar House....151 E9
Nox....60 C4
Nuffield.....39 F6
Nunburnholme....96 E4
Nuncargate....76 D5
Nuneaton....63 E7
Nuneham Courtenay....39 E5
Nun Hills....87 B6

Nun Monkton....95 D8
Nunney.....24 E2
Nunnington....96 B2
Nunnykirk....117 E6
Nunsthorpe....91 D6
Nunthorpe Mbro....102 C3
York.....96 D2
Nunton....14 B2
Nunwick.....95 B6
Nupend.....36 D4
Nursling....14 C4
Nursted....15 B8
Nutbourne W Sus...15 D8
W Sus.....16 C4
Nutfield.....28 D4
Nuthall.....76 E5
Nuthampstead....54 F5
Nuthurst.....17 B5
Nutley E Sus....17 B8
Hants.....26 E4
Nutwell.....89 D7
Nybster....158 D5
Nyetimber....16 E2
Nyewood....16 B2
Nymet Rowland....10 D2
Nymet Tracey....10 D2
Nympsfield....37 D5
Nynehead....11 B6
Nyton.....16 D3

O

Oadby.....64 D3
Oad Street....30 C2
Oakamoor....75 E7
Oakbank....120 C3
Oak Cross.....9 E7
Oakdale.....35 E5
Oake.....11 B6
Oaken.....62 D2
Oakenclough....92 E5
Oakengates....61 C7
Oakenholt....73 B6
Oakenshaw Durham....110 F5
W Yorks.....88 B2
Oakerthorpe....76 D3
Oakes.....88 C2
Oakfield.....35 E7
Oakford Ceredig....46 D3
Devon.....10 B4
Oakfordbridge....10 B4
Oakgrove....75 C6
Oakham....65 D5
Oakhanger.....27 F5
Oakhill.....23 E8
Oakhurst.....29 D6
Oaklands Herts....41 C5
Powys.....48 D2
Oak Street....36 C4
Oakthorpe....63 C7
Oakwoodhill....28 F2
Oakworth....94 F3
Oape....156 J7
Oare Kent....30 C4
Som.....21 E7
W Berks.....26 B3
Wilts.....25 C6
Oasby.....78 F3
Oathlaw.....134 D4
Oatlands....95 D6
Oban Argyll....124 C4
Highld....147 C11
Oborne.....12 C4
Obthorpe....65 C7
Occlestone Green....74 C3
Occold.....57 B5
Ochiltree....112 B5
Ochtermuthill....127 C7
Ochtertyre....127 B7
Ockbrook....76 F4
Ockham.....27 D8
Ockle.....147 D8
Ockley.....28 F2
Ocle Pychard....49 E7
Octon.....97 C6
Octon Cross Roads....97 C6
Odcombe....12 C3
Odd Down....24 C2
Oddendale....99 C7
Odder.....78 B2
Oddingley....50 D4
Oddington Glos....38 B2
Oxon.....39 C5
Odell.....53 D7
Odie.....159 F7
Odiham.....26 D5
Odstock....14 B2
Odstone....63 D7
Offchurch....51 C8
Offenham....51 E5
Offham E Sus....17 C7
Kent.....29 D7
W Sus.....16 D4
Offord Cluny....54 C3
Offord Darcy....54 C3
Offton.....56 E4
Offwell.....11 E6
Ogbourne Maizey....25 B6
Ogbourne St Andrew....25 B6
Ogbourne St George....25 B7
Ogil.....134 C4
Ogle.....110 B4
Ogmore.....21 B7
Ogmore-by-Sea....21 B7
Ogmore Vale....34 E3
Okeford Fitzpaine....13 C6
Okehampton....9 E7
Okehampton Camp....9 E7

Okraquoy....160 K6
Old.....53 B5
Old Aberdeen....141 D8
Old Alresford....26 F3
Oldany.....156 F4
Old Arley....63 E6
Old Basford....76 E5
Old Basing....26 D4
Oldberrow....51 C6
Old Bewick....117 B6
Old Bolingbroke....79 C6
Oldborough....10 D2
Old Bramhope....94 E5
Old Brampton....76 C3
Old Bridge of Tilt....133 C5
Old Bridge of Urr....106 C4
Old Buckenham....68 E3
Old Burghclere....26 D2
Oldbury Shrops...61 E7
Warks.....63 E7
W Mid.....62 F3
Oldbury-on-Severn....36 E3
Oldbury on the Hill....37 F5
Old Byland....102 F3
Old Cassop....111 F6
Oldcastle Bridgend....21 B8
Mon.....35 B7
Old Castleton....115 E8
Old Catton....68 C5
Old Clee.....91 D6
Old Cleeve.....22 E2
Old Clipstone....77 C6
Old Colwyn....83 D8
Oldcotes....89 F6
Old Coulsdon....28 D4
Old Crombie....152 C5
Old Dailly....112 E2
Old Dalby....64 B3
Old Deer.....153 D9
Old Denaby....89 E5
Old Edlington....89 E6
Old Eldon....101 B7
Old Ellerby....97 F7
Oldfallow....62 C3
Old Felixstowe....57 F7
Oldfield.....50 C3
Old Fletton....65 E8
Oldford.....24 D2
Old Glossop....87 F8
Old Goole....89 B8
Old Hall.....59 F6
Oldham.....87 D7
Oldhamstocks....122 B3
Old Heath....43 B6
Old Heathfield....18 C2
Old Hill.....62 F3
Old Hunstanton....80 C2
Old Hurst....54 B3
Old Hutton....99 F7
Old Kea.....3 B7
Old Kilpatrick....118 B4
Old Kinnernie....141 D6
Old Knebworth....41 B5
Oldland....23 B8
Old Langho....93 F7
Old Laxey....84 D4
Old Leake....79 D7
Old Malton....96 B3
Oldmeldrum....141 B7
Old Micklefield....95 F7
Old Milton....14 E3
Old Milverton....51 C7
Old Monkland....119 C7
Old Netley....15 D5
Old Philpstoun....120 B3
Old Quarrington....111 F6
Old Radnor....48 D4
Old Rattray....153 C10
Old Rayne....141 B5
Old Romney....19 C7
Oldshore Beg....156 D4
Oldshoremore....156 D5
Old Sodbury....36 F4
Old Somerby....78 F2
Oldstead....102 F3
Old Stratford....53 E5
Old Thirsk....102 F2
Oldtown....140 B4
Old Town Cumb....99 F7
Cumb.....108 E4
Northumb....116 E4
Scilly.....2 E4
Oldtown of Ord....152 C6
Old Trafford....87 E6
Old Tupton....76 C3
Old Warden....54 E2
Oldway.....33 F6
Oldways End....10 B3
Old Weston....53 B8
Oldwhat....153 C8
Old Whittington....76 B3
Old Wick....158 E5
Old Windsor....27 B8
Old Wives Lees....30 D4
Old Woking....27 D8
Old Woodhall....78 C5
Olgrinmore....158 E2
Oliver's Battery....15 B5
Ollaberry....160 E5
Ollerton Ches E....74 B4
Notts.....77 C6
Shrops.....61 B6
Olmarch.....46 D5
Olney.....53 D6
Olrig House....158 D3
Olton.....36 F3
Olveston....36 F3
Olwen.....46 E4
Ombersley....50 C3
Ompton.....77 C6
Onchan.....84 E3
Onecote....75 D7
Onen.....35 C8
Ongar Hill....67 B5
Ongar Street....49 C5
Onibury....49 B6
Onich.....130 C4
Onllwyn....34 C2
Onneley.....74 E4
Onslow Village....27 E7
Onthank....118 E4
Openwoodgate....76 E3
Opinan Highld....149 A12
Highld....155 H13
Orange Lane....122 E3
Orange Row....66 B5
Orasaigh....155 F8
Orbliston....152 C3

Orbost....148 D7
Orby.....79 C7
Orchard Hill.....9 B6
Orchard Portman....11 B7
Orcheston....25 E5
Orcop.....36 B1
Orcop Hill....36 B1
Ord....149 G11
Ordhead....141 C5
Ordie....140 D3
Ordiequish....152 C3
Ordsall.....89 F7
Ore.....18 D5
Oreton.....61 F6
Orford Suff....57 E8
Warr.....86 E4
Orgreave....63 C5
Orlestone....19 B6
Orleton Hereford....49 C6
Worcs.....49 C8
Orlingbury....53 B6
Ormesby....102 C3
Ormesby St Margaret....69 C7
Ormesby St Michael....69 C7
Ormiclate Castle....148 E2
Ormiscaig....155 H13
Ormiston....121 C7
Ormsaigbeg....146 E7
Ormsaigmore....146 E7
Ormsary....144 F6
Ormsgill....92 B1
Ormskirk....86 D2
Orpington....29 C5
Orrell Gtr Man...86 D3
Mers.....85 E4
Orrisdale....84 C3
Orroland....106 E4
Orsett.....42 F2
Orslow.....62 C2
Orston.....77 E7
Orthwaite....108 F2
Ortner.....92 D5
Orton Cumb....99 D8
N Hants.....53 B6
Orton Longueville....65 E8
Orton-on-the-Hill....63 D7
Orton Waterville....65 E8
Orwell.....54 D4
Osbaldeston....93 F6
Osbaldwick....96 D2
Osbaston....60 B3
Osbournby....78 F3
Oscroft.....74 C2
Ose.....149 D8
Osgathorpe....63 C8
Osgodby Lincs...90 E4
N Yorks.....96 F2
N Yorks.....103 F8
Oskaig....149 E10
Oskamull....146 G2
Osmaston Derby....76 F3
Derbys.....76 E2
Osmington....12 F5
Osmington Mills....12 F5
Osmotherley....102 E2
Ospisdale....151 C10
Ospringe....30 C4
Ossett.....88 B3
Ossington....77 C7
Ostend.....43 E5
Oswaldkirk....96 B2
Oswaldtwistle....86 B5
Oswestry....60 B2
Otford.....29 D6
Otham.....29 D8
Othery.....23 F5
Otley Suff....57 D6
W Yorks.....94 E5
Otterburn Northumb....116 E4
N Yorks.....93 D8
Otterburn Camp....116 E4
Otter Ferry....145 E8
Otterham....8 E3
Otterhampton....22 E4
Ottershaw....27 C8
Otterswick....160 E7
Otterton....11 F5
Ottery St Mary....11 E6
Ottinge.....31 E5
Ottringham....91 B6
Oughterby....108 D2
Oughtershaw....100 F3
Oughterside....107 E8
Oughtibridge....88 E4
Oughtrington....86 F4
Oulston....95 B8
Oulton Cumb....108 D2
Norf.....81 E7
Staffs.....75 F6
Suff.....69 E8
W Yorks.....88 B4
Oulton Broad....69 E8
Oulton Street....81 E7
Oundle.....65 F7
Ousby.....109 F6
Ousdale....158 H2
Ousden.....55 D8
Ousefleet....90 B2
Ouston Durham....111 D5
Northumb....110 B3
Outertown....159 G3
Outgate.....99 E5
Outhgill....100 D2
Outlane.....87 C8
Out Newton....91 B7
Out Rawcliffe....92 E4
Outwell.....66 D4
Outwick....14 C2
Outwood Sur....28 E4
W Yorks.....88 B4
Outwoods....63 C7
Ovenden....87 B8
Ovenscloss....121 F7
Over Cambs...54 B4
Ches W.....74 C3
S Glos.....36 F2
Overbister....159 D7
Overbury....50 F4
Overcombe....12 F4
Over Compton....12 C3
Over Green....63 E5
Over Haddon....76 C2
Over Hulton....86 D4
Over Kellet....92 B5

Over Kiddington....38 B4
Over Knutsford....74 B4
Overleigh....23 F6
Overley Green....51 D5
Over Monnow....36 C2
Over Norton....38 B3
Over Peover....74 B4
Overpool....73 B7
Overscaig Hotel....156 G7
Overseal....63 C6
Over Silton....102 E2
Oversland....30 D4
Overstone....53 C6
Over Stowey....22 F3
Overstrand....81 C8
Over Stratton....12 C2
Over Tabley....86 F5
Overthorpe....52 E2
Overton Aberdeen....141 C7
Ches W.....74 B2
Hants.....26 E3
Lancs.....92 D4
N Yorks.....95 D8
Shrops.....49 B7
Swansea.....33 F5
Overton = Owrtyn....73 E7
Overton Bridge....73 E7
Overtown....119 D8
Over Wallop....25 F7
Over Whitacre....63 E6
Over Worton....38 B4
Oving Bucks...39 B7
W Sus.....16 D3
Ovingdean....17 D7
Ovingham....110 C3
Ovington Durham....101 C6
Essex.....55 E8
Hants.....26 F3
Norf.....68 D2
Northumb....110 C3
Ower.....14 C4
Owermoigne....13 F5
Owlbury.....60 E3
Owler Bar....76 B2
Owlerton....88 F4
Owl's Green....57 C6
Owlswick....39 D7
Ownby.....90 D4
Owmby-by-Spital....90 F4
Owrtyn = Overton...73 E7
Owslebury....15 B6
Owston Leics....64 D4
S Yorks.....89 C6
Owston Ferry....90 D2
Owstwick....97 F8
Owthorne....91 B7
Owthorpe....77 F6
Oxborough....67 D7
Oxcombe....79 B6
Oxen End....55 F7
Oxenholme....99 F7
Oxenhope....94 F3
Oxen Park....99 F5
Oxenton....50 F4
Oxenwood....25 D8
Oxford.....39 D5
Oxhey.....40 E4
Oxhill.....51 E8
Oxley.....62 D3
Oxley Green....43 C5
Oxley's Green....18 C3
Oxnam.....116 C2
Oxshott....28 C2
Oxspring....88 D3
Oxted.....28 D4
Oxton Borders...121 D7
Notts.....77 D6
Oxwich....33 F5
Oxwick.....80 E5
Oykel Bridge....156 J6
Oyne.....141 B5

P

Pabail Iarach....155 D10
Pabail Uarach....155 D10
Pace Gate....94 D4
Packington....63 C7
Padanaram....134 D4
Padbury.....52 F5
Paddington....41 F5
Paddlesworth....19 B8
Paddockhaugh....152 C2
Paddockhole....115 F5
Paddock Wood....29 E7
Padfield.....87 E8
Padiham.....93 F7
Padog.....83 F8
Padside.....94 D4
Padstow.....4 B4
Padworth....26 C4
Page Bank....110 F5
Pagham.....16 E2
Paglesham Eastend....43 E5
Paglesham Churchend....43 E5
Paibeil.....148 B2
Paible.....154 H5
Paignton....7 C6
Pailton.....63 F8
Painscastle....48 E3
Painshawfield....110 C3
Painsthorpe....96 D4
Painswick....37 D5
Pairc Shiaboist....154 C7
Paisley.....118 C4
Pakefield.....69 E8
Pakenham....56 C3
Pale.....72 F3
Palestine....25 E7
Paley Street....27 B6
Palfrey.....62 E4
Palgowan....112 F3
Palgrave.....56 B5
Pallion.....111 D6
Palmarsh....19 B8
Palnackie....106 D5
Palnure.....105 C8
Palterton....76 C4
Pamber End....26 D4
Pamber Green....26 D4
Pamber Heath....26 C4
Pamphill....13 D7
Pampisford....55 E5
Pan.....159 J4
Panbride.....135 F5

Pancrasweek....8 D4
Pandy Gwyn...58 D3
Mon.....35 B7
Powys.....59 D6
Wrex.....73 F5
Pandy Tudur....83 E8
Panfield.....42 B3
Pangbourne....26 B4
Pannal.....95 D6
Panshanger....41 C5
Pant.....60 B2
Pant-glas Carms...33 C7
Gwyn.....71 C5
Pant-glas.....73 F6
Pantgwyn Carms...33 C6
Ceredig.....45 E4
Pant-lasau....33 E7
Pant Mawr....59 F5
Panton.....78 B4
Pantperthog....58 D4
Pant-teg.....33 B5
Pant-y-Caws....32 B2
Pant-y-dwr....47 B8
Pant-y-ffridd....59 D8
Pantyffynnon....33 C7
Pantymwyn....73 C5
Pant-yr-awel....34 F3
Pant-y-Wacco....72 B5
Panxworth....69 C6
Papcastle....107 F8
Papigoe....158 E5
Papil.....160 K5
Papley.....159 J5
Papple.....121 B8
Papplewick....76 D5
Papworth Everard....54 C3
Papworth St Agnes....54 C3
Par.....4 D5
Parbold.....86 C2
Parbrook Som...23 F7
W Sus.....16 B4
Parc.....72 F2
Parcllyn.....45 D4
Parc-Seymour....35 E8
Parc-y-rhôs....46 E4
Pardshaw....98 B2
Parham.....57 C7
Park.....114 C2
Park Corner Oxon...39 F6
Windsor.....27 B6
Parkend.....36 D3
Park End Mbro...102 C3
Northumb....109 B8
Parkeston....57 F6
Parkgate Ches W...73 B6
Dumfries.....114 F3
Kent.....19 B5
Sur.....28 E3
Park Gate....15 D6
Parkham.....9 B5
Parkham Ash.....9 B5
Park Hill Notts...77 D6
N Yorks.....95 D6
Parkhill House....141 C7
Parkhouse....36 D1
Parkhouse Green....76 C4
Parkhurst....15 E5
Parkmill....33 F6
Parkneuk....135 B7
Parkstone....13 E8
Park Street....28 E2
Parley Cross....13 E8
Parracombe....21 E5
Parrog.....45 F2
Parsley Hay....75 C8
Parsonage Green....42 D3
Parsonby....107 F8
Parson Cross....88 E4
Parson Drove....66 D3
Parson's Heath....43 B6
Partick.....119 C5
Partington....86 E5
Partney.....79 C7
Parton Cumb...98 B1
Dumfries.....106 B3
Glos.....37 B5
Partridge Green....17 C5
Parwich.....75 D8
Passenham....53 F5
Paston.....81 D9
Patchacott....9 E6
Patcham.....17 D7
Patching....16 D4
Patchole.....20 E5
Pateley Bridge....94 C4
Paternoster Heath....43 C5
Pathe.....23 F5
Pathhead Aberds...135 C7
E Ayrs.....113 C6
Fife.....128 E4
Midloth.....121 C6
Path of Condie....128 C2
Pathstruie....128 C2
Patna.....112 C4
Patney.....25 D5
Patrick.....84 D2
Patrick Brompton....101 E7
Patrington....91 B7
Patrixbourne....31 D5
Patterdale....99 C5
Pattingham....62 E2
Pattishall....52 D4
Pattiswick Green....42 B4
Patton Bridge....99 E7
Paul.....2 D3
Paulerspury....52 E5
Paull.....91 B5
Paulton.....23 D8
Pavenham....53 D7
Pawlett.....22 E5
Pawston....122 F4
Paxford.....51 F6
Paxton.....122 D5
Payhembury....11 D5
Paythorne....93 D8
Peacehaven....17 D8
Peak Dale....75 B7
Peak Forest....75 B8
Peakirk.....65 D8
Pearsie.....134 D3
Peasedown St John....24 D2
Peasemore....26 B2
Peasenhall....57 C7
Pease Pottage....28 F3
Peaslake.....27 E8

Peasley Cross....86 E3
Peasmarsh....19 C5
Peaston.....121 C7
Peastonbank....121 C7
Peathill.....153 B9
Peat Inn.....129 D6
Peatling Magna....64 E2
Peatling Parva....64 F2
Peaton.....60 F5
Pebmarsh....56 F2
Pebworth....51 E6
Pecket Well....87 B7
Peckforton....74 D2
Peckham.....28 B4
Peckleton....63 D8
Pedlinge.....19 B8
Pedmore.....62 F3
Pedwell.....23 F6
Peebles.....121 E5
Peel.....84 D2
Peel Common....15 D6
Peel Park....119 D6
Peening Quarter....19 C5
Pegsdon.....54 F2
Pegswood....117 F8
Pegwell.....31 C7
Peinchorran....149 E10
Peinlich....149 C9
Pelaw.....111 C5
Pelcomb Bridge....44 D4
Pelcomb Cross....44 D4
Peldon.....43 C5
Pellon.....87 B8
Pelsall.....62 D4
Pelton.....111 D5
Pelutho.....107 E8
Pelynt.....5 D7
Pemberton....86 D3
Pembrey.....33 D5
Pembridge....49 D5
Pembroke = Penfro....44 E4
Pembroke Dock = Doc Penfro....44 E4
Pembury....29 E7
Penallt.....36 C2
Penally.....32 E2
Penalt.....36 B2
Penare.....3 B8
Penarlâg = Hawarden....73 C7
Penarth.....22 B3
Penbryn.....45 D4
Pencader....46 F3
Pencaenewydd....70 C5
Pencaitland....121 C7
Pencarnisiog....82 D3
Pencarreg....46 E4
Pencelli.....34 B4
Pen-clawdd....33 E6
Pencoed.....34 F3
Pencombe....49 D7
Pencoyd.....36 B2
Pencraig Hereford...36 B2
Powys.....59 B7
Pendeen.....2 C2
Penderyn....34 D3
Pendine.....32 D3
Pendlebury....87 D5
Pendleton....93 F7
Pendock.....50 F2
Pendoggett....4 B5
Pendomer....12 C3
Pendoylan....22 B2
Pendre.....34 F3
Penegoes....58 D4
Pen-ffordd....32 B1
Penfro = Pembroke....44 E4
Pengam.....35 E5
Penge.....28 B4
Pengenffordd....48 F3
Pengorffwysfa....82 B4
Pengover Green....5 C7
Pen-groes-oped....35 D7
Penhale Corn...3 D5
Corn.....4 D4
Penhalvaen....3 C6
Penhill.....38 F1
Penhow.....35 E8
Penhurst....18 D3
Peniarth.....58 D3
Penicuik....120 C5
Peniel Carms....33 B5
Denb.....72 C4
Penifiler....149 D9
Peninver....143 F8
Penisarwaun....83 E5
Penistone....88 D3
Penjerrick....3 C6
Penketh.....86 F3
Penkill.....112 E2
Penkridge....62 C3
Penley.....73 F8
Penllergaer....33 E7
Penllyn.....21 B8
Pen-llyn.....82 C3
Pen-lon.....82 E4
Penmachno....83 F7
Penmaen.....33 F6
Penmaenan....83 D7
Penmaenmawr....83 D7
Penmaenpool....58 C3
Penmark....22 C2
Penmarth....3 C6
Penmon.....83 C6
Penmore Mill....146 F7
Penmorfa Ceredig...45 D4
Gwyn.....71 C6
Penmynydd....82 D5

Penny Bridge....99 F5
Pennycross....147 J8
Pennygate....69 B6
Pennygown....147 G8
Pennymoor....10 C3
Pennywell....111 D6
Penparc Ceredig...45 E4
Pembs.....44 B3
Penparcau....58 F2
Penperlleni....35 D7
Penpillick....5 D5
Penpol.....3 C7
Penpoll.....5 D6
Penpont Dumfries...113 E8
Powys.....34 B3
Penrherber....45 F4
Penrhiwceiber....34 E4
Penrhiw goch....33 C6
Penrhiw-llan....46 E2
Penrhiw-pâl....46 E2
Penrhos.....70 D4
Penrhôs.....35 C8
Penrhos.....34 C1
Penrhosfeilw....82 C2
Penrhyn Bay....83 C8
Penrhyn-coch....58 F3
Penrhyndeudraeth....71 D7
Penrhynside....83 C8
Penrice.....33 F5
Penrith.....108 F5
Penrose.....4 B3
Penruddock....99 B6
Penryn.....3 C6
Pensarn Carms...33 C5
Conwy.....72 B3
Pen-sarn Gwyn...70 C5
Gwyn.....71 E6
Pensax.....50 C2
Pensby.....85 F3
Penselwood....24 F2
Pensford....23 C8
Penshaw....111 D6
Penshurst....29 E6
Pensilva.....5 C7
Penston.....121 B7
Pentewan....3 B9
Pentir.....83 E5
Pentire.....4 C2
Pentlow.....56 E2
Pentney.....67 C7
Penton Mewsey....25 E8
Pentraeth....82 D5
Pentre Carms...33 C6
Powys.....59 F7
Powys.....60 E2
Rhondda.....34 E3
Shrops.....60 C3
Wrex.....72 F5
Wrex.....73 E6
Pentrebach M Tydf...34 D4
Swansea.....33 D7
Pentre-bâch....46 E4
Pentre-bach....47 F8
Pentrebeirdd....59 C8
Pentre Berw....82 D4
Pentre-bont....83 F7
Pentrecagal....46 E2
Pentre-celyn Denb....72 D5
Powys.....59 D5
Pentre-chwyth....33 E7
Pentre-cwrt....46 F2
Pentre Dolau-Honddu....47 E8
Pentredwr....73 E5
Pentre-dwr....33 E7
Pentrefelin Carms...33 B6
Ceredig.....46 E5
Conwy.....83 D8
Gwyn.....71 D6
Pentrefoelas....83 F8
Pentre-galar....45 F3
Pentregat....46 D2
Pentre Gwenlais....33 C7
Pentre Gwynfryn....71 E6
Pentre Halkyn....73 B6
Pentreheyling....60 E2
Pentre-Isaf....83 E8
Pentre Llanrhaeadr....72 C4
Pentre-llwyn-llwyd....47 D8
Pentre-llyn....46 B5
Pentre-llyn cymmer....72 D3
Pentre Meyrick....21 B8
Pentre-poeth....35 F6
Pentre'r Felin....83 E8
Pentre'r-felin....47 F5
Pentre-rhew....47 D5
Pentre-tafarn-yfedw....83 E8
Pentre-ty-gwyn....47 F7
Pentrich.....76 D3
Pentridge....13 C8
Pen-twyn....36 D2
Pentyrch....35 F5
Penuchadre....21 B7
Penuwch....46 C4
Penwithick....4 D5
Penwyllt....34 C2
Penybanc....33 C7
Pen-y-banc....33 B7
Penybont....48 C3
Pen-y-bont Carms...32 B4
Gwyn.....58 D4
Gwyn.....71 E7
Powys.....60 B2
Pen-y-Bont Ar Ogwr = Bridgend....21 B8
Penybontfawr....59 B7
Pen-y-bryn Gwyn...58 C3
Pen-y-bryn....45 F3
Penycae....73 E6
Pen-y-cae....34 C2
Pen-y-cae-mawr....35 E8
Pen-y-cefn....72 B5
Pen-y-clawdd....36 D1
Pen-y-coedcae....34 F4
Penycwm....44 C3
Pen-y-fai....34 F2
Penyffordd....73 C7
Penyffridd....82 E5
Pen-y-garn Carms...46 F4
Ceredig.....58 F3
Pen-y-garnedd....59 B8
Pen-y-garnedd....82 D5

Pen-y-gop ... 72 E3
Penygraig ... 34 E3
Pen-y-graig ... 70 D2
Penygroes Gwyn ... 82 F4
  Pembs ... 45 F3
Pen-y-groes ... 33 C6
Pen-y-groeslon ... 70 D3
Pen-y-Gwryd
  Hotel ... 83 F6
Penyrheol ... 35 F5
Pen-y-heol ... 35 C8
Pen-yr-
  Heolgerrig ... 34 D4
Penysarn ... 82 B4
Pen-y-stryt ... 73 D5
Penywaun ... 34 D3
Penzance ... 2 C3
Peopleton ... 50 D4
Peover Heath ... 74 B4
Peper Harow ... 27 E7
Perceton ... 118 E3
Percie ... 140 E4
Percyhorner ... 153 B9
Periton ... 21 E8
Perivale ... 40 F4
Perkinsville ... 111 D5
Perlethorpe ... 77 B6
Perranarworthal ... 3 C6
Perranporth ... 4 D2
Perranuthnoe ... 2 D4
Perranzabuloe ... 4 D2
Perry Barr ... 62 E4
Perryfoot ... 88 F2
Perry Green Herts ... 41 C7
  Wilts ... 37 F6
Perry Street ... 29 B7
Pershall ... 74 F5
Pershore ... 50 E4
Pert ... 135 C6
Pertenhall ... 53 C8
Perth ... 128 B3
Perthy ... 73 F7
Perton ... 62 E2
Pertwood ... 24 F3
Peterborough ... 65 E8
Peterburn ... 155 J12
Peterchurch ... 48 F7
Peterculter ... 141 D7
Peterhead ... 153 D11
Peterlee ... 111 E7
Petersfield ... 15 B8
Peter's Green ... 40 C4
Peters Marland ... 9 C6
Peterstone
  Wentlooge ... 35 F6
Peterston-
  super-Ely ... 22 B2
Peterstow ... 36 B2
Peter Tavy ... 6 B3
Petertown ... 159 H4
Petham ... 30 D5
Petrockstow ... 9 D7
Pett ... 19 D5
Pettaugh ... 57 D5
Petteridge ... 29 E7
Pettinain ... 120 E2
Pettistree ... 57 D6
Petton Devon ... 10 B5
  Shrops ... 60 B4
Petts Wood ... 28 C5
Petty ... 153 E7
Pettycur ... 128 F4
Pettymuick ... 141 B8
Petworth ... 16 B3
Pevensey ... 18 E3
Pevensey Bay ... 18 E3
Pewsey ... 25 C6
Philham ... 8 B4
Philiphaugh ... 115 B7
Phillack ... 2 C4
Philleigh ... 3 C7
Philpstoun ... 120 B3
Phocle Green ... 36 B3
Phoenix Green ... 27 D5
Pica ... 98 B2
Piccotts End ... 40 D3
Pickering ... 103 F5
Picket Piece ... 25 E8
Picket Post ... 14 D2
Pickhill ... 101 F8
Picklescott ... 60 E4
Pickletillem ... 129 B6
Pickmere ... 74 B3
Pickney ... 11 B6
Pickstock ... 61 B7
Pickwell Devon ... 20 E3
  Leics ... 64 C4
Pickworth Lincs ... 78 F3
  Rutland ... 65 C6
Picton Ches W ... 73 B8
  Flint ... 85 F2
  N Yorks ... 102 D2
Piddinghoe ... 17 D8
Piddington Oxon ... 39 C6
  W Nhants ... 53 D6
Piddlehinton ... 12 E5
Piddletrenthide ... 12 E5
Pidley ... 54 B4
Piercebridge ... 101 C7
Pierowall ... 159 D5
Pigdon ... 117 F7
Pikehall ... 75 D8
Pilgrims Hatch ... 42 E1
Pilham ... 90 E2
Pill ... 23 B7
Pillaton ... 5 C8
Pillerton Hersey ... 51 E8
Pillerton Priors ... 51 E7
Pilleth ... 48 C4
Pilley Hants ... 14 E4
  S Yorks ... 88 D4
Pilling ... 92 E4
Pilling Lane ... 92 E3
Pillowell ... 36 D3
Pillwell ... 13 C5
Pilning ... 36 F2
Pilsbury ... 75 C8
Pilsdon ... 12 E2
Pilsgate ... 65 D7
Pilsley Derbys ... 76 B2
  Derbys ... 76 C4
Pilton Devon ... 20 F4
  N Nhants ... 65 F7
  Rutland ... 65 D6
  Som ... 23 E7
Pilton Green ... 33 F5

Pimperne ... 13 D7
Pinchbeck ... 66 B2
Pinchbeck Bars ... 65 B8
Pinchbeck West ... 66 B2
Pincheon Green ... 89 C7
Pinehurst ... 38 F1
Pinfold ... 85 C4
Pinged ... 33 D5
Pinhoe ... 10 E4
Pinkneys Green ... 40 F1
Pinley ... 51 B8
Pin Mill ... 57 F6
Pinminnoch ... 112 E1
Pinmore ... 112 E2
Pinmore Mains ... 112 E2
Pinner ... 40 F4
Pinvin ... 50 E4
Pinwherry ... 112 F1
Pinxton ... 76 D4
Pipe and Lyde ... 49 E7
Pipe Gate ... 74 E4
Piperhill ... 151 F11
Piper's Pool ... 8 F4
Pipewell ... 64 F5
Pippacott ... 20 F4
Pipton ... 48 F3
Pirbright ... 27 D7
Pirnmill ... 143 D9
Pirton Herts ... 54 F2
  Worcs ... 50 E3
Pisgah Ceredig ... 47 B5
  Stirling ... 127 D6
Pishill ... 39 F7
Pistyll ... 70 C4
Pitagowan ... 133 C5
Pitblae ... 153 B9
Pitcairngreen ... 128 B2
Pitcalnie ... 151 D11
Pitcaple ... 141 B6
Pitchcombe ... 37 D5
Pitchcott ... 39 B7
Pitchford ... 60 D5
Pitch Green ... 39 D7
Pitch Place ... 27 D7
Pitcombe ... 23 F8
Pitcorthie ... 129 D7
Pitcox ... 122 B2
Pitcur ... 134 F2
Pitfichie ... 141 C5
Pitforthie ... 135 B8
Pitgrudy ... 151 B10
Pitkennedy ... 135 D5
Pitkevy ... 128 D4
Pitkierie ... 129 D7
Pitlessie ... 128 D5
Pitlochry ... 133 D6
Pitmachie ... 141 B5
Pitmain ... 138 D3
Pitmedden ... 141 B7
Pitminster ... 11 C7
Pitmuies ... 135 E5
Pitmunie ... 141 C5
Pitney ... 12 B2
Pitscottie ... 129 C6
Pitsea ... 42 F3
Pitsford ... 53 C5
Pitsmoor ... 88 F4
Pitstone ... 40 C2
Pitstone Green ... 40 C2
Pittendreich ... 152 B1
Pittentrail ... 157 J10
Pittenweem ... 129 D7
Pittington ... 111 E6
Pittodrie ... 141 B5
Pitton ... 25 F7
Pittswood ... 29 E7
Pittulie ... 153 B9
Pityme ... 4 B4
Pity Me ... 111 E5
Pityoulish ... 138 C5
Pixey Green ... 57 B6
Pixham ... 28 D2
Pixley ... 49 F8
Place Newton ... 96 B4
Plaidy ... 153 C7
Plains ... 119 C7
Plaish ... 60 E5
Plaistow ... 27 F8
Plaitford ... 14 C3
Plank Lane ... 86 E4
Plas-canol ... 58 C2
Plas Gogerddan ... 58 F3
Plas Llwyngwern ... 58 D4
Plas Nantyr ... 73 F5
Plastow Green ... 26 C3
Plas-yn-Cefn ... 72 B4
Platt ... 29 D7
Platt Bridge ... 86 D4
Platts Common ... 88 D4
Plawsworth ... 111 E5
Plaxtol ... 29 D7
Playden ... 19 C6
Playford ... 57 E6
Play Hatch ... 26 B5
Playing Place ... 3 B7
Playley Green ... 50 F2
Plealey ... 60 D4
Plean ... 127 F7
Pleasington ... 86 B4
Pleasley ... 76 C5
Pleckgate ... 93 F6
Plenmeller ... 109 C7
Pleshey ... 42 C2
Plockton ... 149 E13
Plocrapol ... 154 H6
Ploughfield ... 49 E5
Plowden ... 60 F3
Ploxgreen ... 60 D3
Pluckley ... 30 E3
Pluckley Thorne ... 30 E3
Plumbland ... 107 F8
Plumley ... 74 B4
Plumpton Cumb ... 108 F4
  E Sus ... 17 C7
Plumpton Green ... 17 C7
Plumpton Head ... 108 F5
Plumstead London ... 29 B5
  Norf ... 81 D7
Plumtree ... 77 F6
Plungar ... 77 F7
Plush ... 12 D5
Plwmp ... 46 D2
Plymouth ... 6 D2
Plympton ... 6 D3
Plymstock ... 6 D3
Plymtree ... 11 D5
Pockley ... 102 F4
Pocklington ... 96 E4
Pode Hole ... 66 B2

Podimore ... 12 B3
Podington ... 53 C7
Podmore ... 74 F4
Point Clear ... 43 C6
Pointon ... 78 F4
Pokesdown ... 14 E2
Pol a Charra ... 148 G2
Polbae ... 105 B6
Polbain ... 156 H2
Polbathic ... 5 D8
Polbeth ... 120 C3
Polchar ... 138 D4
Polebrook ... 65 F7
Pole Elm ... 50 E3
Polegate ... 18 E2
Poles ... 151 B10
Polesworth ... 63 D6
Polgigga ... 2 D2
Polglass ... 156 J3
Polgooth ... 4 D4
Poling ... 16 D4
Polkerris ... 5 D5
Polla ... 156 D6
Pollington ... 89 C7
Polloch ... 130 C1
Pollok ... 118 C5
Pollokshields ... 119 C5
Polmassick ... 3 B8
Polmont ... 120 B2
Polnessan ... 112 C4
Polnish ... 147 C10
Polperro ... 5 D7
Polruan ... 5 D6
Polsham ... 23 E7
Polstead ... 56 F3
Poltalloch ... 124 F4
Poltimore ... 10 E4
Polton ... 121 C5
Polwarth ... 122 D3
Polyphant ... 8 F4
Polzeath ... 4 B4
Ponders End ... 41 E6
Pondtail ... 27 D6
Ponsanooth ... 3 C6
Ponsonby ... 98 D2
Ponsworthy ... 6 B5
Pont Aber ... 33 B8
Pont Aber-Geirw ... 71 E8
Pontamman ... 33 C7
Pontantwn ... 33 C5
Pontardawe ... 33 D8
Pontarddulais ... 33 D6
Pont-ar-gothi ... 33 B6
Pont ar Hydfer ... 34 B2
Pont-ar-llechau ... 33 B8
Pontarsais ... 33 B5
Pontblyddyn ... 73 C6
Pontbren Araeth ... 33 B7
Pontbren Llwyd ... 34 D3
Pont Cwm Pydew ... 72 F4
Pont Cyfyng ... 83 F7
Pont Cysyllte ... 73 E6
Pont Dolydd
  Prysor ... 71 D8
Pontefract ... 89 B5
Ponteland ... 110 B4
Ponterwyd ... 58 F4
Pontesbury ... 60 D3
Pontfadog ... 73 F6
Pontfaen ... 45 F2
Pont-faen ... 47 F8
Pont Fronwydd ... 58 B5
Pont-garreg ... 45 E3
Pontgarreg ... 46 D2
Pont-Henri ... 33 D5
Ponthir ... 35 E7
Ponthirwaun ... 45 E4
Pontllanfraith ... 35 E5
Pontlliw ... 33 D7
Pont-Llogel ... 59 C7
Pontllyfni ... 82 F4
Pontlottyn ... 35 D5
Pontneddfechan ... 34 D3
Pontnewydd ... 35 E6
Pont Pen-y-
  benglog ... 83 E6
Pontrhydfendigaid ... 47 C6
Pont Rhyd-goch ... 83 E6
Pont-Rhyd-sarn ... 59 B5
Pont Rhyd-y-cyff ... 34 F2
Pontrhydyfen ... 34 E1
Pont-rhyd-
  y-groes ... 47 B6
Pontrilas ... 35 B7
Pontrobert ... 59 C8
Pont-rug ... 82 E5
Pont Senni
  =Sennybridge ... 34 B3
Ponts Green ... 18 D3
Pontshill ... 36 B3
Pont-siân ... 46 E3
Pontsticill ... 34 C4
Pontwgan ... 83 D7
Pontyates ... 33 D5
Pontyberem ... 33 C6
Pontyclun ... 34 F4
Pontycymer ... 34 E3
Pontyglasier ... 45 F3
Pont-y-gwaith ... 34 E4
Pont-y-pant ... 83 F7
Pont y Pennant ... 59 B6
Pontypool ... 35 D6
Pontypridd ... 34 F4
Pont-y-pŵl
  =Pontypool ... 35 D6
Pont-yr-hafod ... 44 C4
Pontywaun ... 35 E6
Pooksgreen ... 14 C4
Pool Corn ... 3 B5
  W Yorks ... 94 E5
Poole ... 13 E8
Poole Keynes ... 37 E6
Poolend ... 75 D6
Poolewe ... 155 J13
Pooley Bridge ... 99 B6
Poolfold ... 75 D5
Poolhill ... 36 B4
Pool o'Muckhart ... 128 D2
Pool Quay ... 60 C2
Poolsbrook ... 76 B4
Pootings ... 29 E5
Pope Hill ... 44 D4
Popeswood ... 27 C6
Popham ... 26 E3
Poplar ... 41 F6
Popley ... 26 D4
Porchester ... 77 D5

Porchfield ... 14 E5
Porin ... 150 F6
Poringland ... 69 D5
Porkellis ... 3 C5
Porlock ... 21 E7
Porlock Weir ... 21 E7
Portachoillan ... 144 H6
Port Ann ... 145 E8
Port Appin ... 130 E3
Port Arthur ... 160 K5
Port Askaig ... 142 B5
Portavadie ... 145 G8
Port Bannatyne ... 145 G9
Portbury ... 23 B7
Port Carlisle ... 108 C2
Port Charlotte ... 142 C3
Portchester ... 15 D7
Portclair ... 137 C7
Port Clarence ... 102 B2
Port Driseach ... 145 F8
Port Ellen ... 142 D4
Port Elphinstone ... 141 C6
Portencalzie ... 104 B4
Portencross ... 118 E1
Port Erin ... 84 F1
Port Erroll ... 153 E10
Portesham ... 12 F4
Portessie ... 152 B4
Port e Vullen ... 84 C4
Port-Eynon ... 33 F5
Portfield Gate ... 44 D4
Portgate ... 9 F6
Port Gaverne ... 8 F2
Port Glasgow ... 118 B3
Portgordon ... 152 B3
Portgower ... 157 H13
Porth Corn ... 4 C3
  Rhondda ... 34 E4
Porthaethwy
  =Menai Bridge ... 83 D5
Porthallow Corn ... 3 D6
  Corn ... 5 D7
Porthcawl ... 21 B7
Porthcothan ... 4 B3
Porthcurno ... 2 D2
Port Henderson ... 149 A12
Porthgain ... 44 B3
Porthill ... 60 C4
Porthkerry ... 22 C2
Porthleven ... 2 D5
Porthllechog ... 82 B4
Porthmadog ... 71 D6
Porthmeor ... 2 C3
Porth Navas ... 3 D6
Portholland ... 3 B8
Porthoustock ... 3 D7
Porthpean ... 4 D5
Porthtowan ... 3 B5
Porth Tywyn
  =Burry Port ... 33 D5
Porthyrhyd Carms ... 33 C6
  Carms ... 47 F6
Porth-y-waen ... 60 B2
Portincaple ... 145 D11
Portington ... 96 F3
Portinnisherrich ... 125 D5
Portinscale ... 98 B4
Port Isaac ... 4 A4
Portishead ... 23 B6
Portkil ... 145 E11
Portknockie ... 152 B4
Port Lamont ... 145 F9
Portlethen ... 141 E8
Portling ... 107 D5
Port Lion ... 44 E4
Portloe ... 3 C8
Port Logan ... 104 E4
Portmahomack ... 151 C12
Portmeirion ... 71 D6
Portmellon ... 3 B9
Port Mholair ... 155 D10
Port Mor ... 146 D7
Portmore ... 14 E4
Port Mulgrave ... 103 C5
Portnacroish ... 130 E3
Portnahaven ... 142 C2
Portnalong ... 149 E8
Portnaluchaig ... 147 C9
Portnancon ... 156 C7
Port Nan
  Giùran ... 155 D10
Port nan Long ... 148 A3
Portnellan ... 126 B3
Port Nis ... 155 A10
Portobello ... 121 B6
Port of Menteith ... 126 D5
Porton ... 25 F6
Portpatrick ... 104 D4
Port Quin ... 4 A4
Port Ramsay ... 130 E2
Portreath ... 3 B5
Portree ... 149 D9
Port St Mary ... 84 F2
Portscatho ... 3 C7
Portsea ... 15 D7
Portskerra ... 157 C11
Portskewett ... 36 F2
Portslade ... 17 D6
Portslade-by-Sea ... 17 D6
Portsmouth Ptsmth ... 15 D7
  W Yorks ... 87 B7
Portsonachan ... 125 C6
Portsoy ... 152 B5
Port Sunlight ... 85 F4
Portswood ... 14 C5
Port Talbot ... 34 E1
Porttanachy ... 152 B3
Port Tennant ... 33 E7
Portuairk ... 146 E7
Portway Hereford ... 49 F6
  Worcs ... 51 B5
Port Wemyss ... 142 C2
Port William ... 105 E7
Portwrinkle ... 5 D8
Posenhall ... 61 D6
Poslingford ... 55 E8
Postbridge ... 6 B4
Postcombe ... 39 E7
Postling ... 19 B8
Postwick ... 69 D5
Potsgrove ... 40 B2
Potten End ... 40 D3
Potter Brompton ... 97 B5
Potterhanworth ... 78 C3
Potterhanworth
  Booths ... 78 C3
Potter Heigham ... 69 C7
Potterne ... 24 D4
Potterne Wick ... 24 D5

Potternewton ... 95 F6
Potters Bar ... 41 D5
Potter's Cross ... 62 F2
Potterspury ... 53 E5
Potter Street ... 41 D7
Potterton Aberds ... 141 C8
  W Yorks ... 95 F7
Potto ... 102 D2
Potton ... 54 E3
Pott Row ... 80 E3
Pott Shrigley ... 75 B6
Poughill Corn ... 8 D4
  Devon ... 10 D3
Poulshot ... 24 D4
Poulton Glos ... 37 D8
  Mers ... 85 E4
Poulton-le-Fylde ... 92 F3
Pound Bank ... 50 B2
Poundbury ... 12 E4
Poundfield ... 18 B2
Pound Green
  E Sus ... 18 C2
  IoW ... 14 F4
  Worcs ... 50 B2
Pound Hill ... 28 F3
Poundland ... 112 F1
Poundon ... 39 B6
Poundsgate ... 6 B5
Poundstock ... 8 E4
Powburn ... 117 C6
Powderham ... 10 F4
Powerstock ... 12 E3
Powfoot ... 107 C8
Powick ... 50 D3
Powmill ... 128 E2
Poxwell ... 12 F5
Poyle ... 27 B8
Poynings ... 17 C6
Poyntington ... 12 C4
Poynton ... 87 F7
Poynton Green ... 61 C5
Poystreet Green ... 56 D3
Praa Sands ... 2 D4
Pratt's Bottom ... 29 C5
Praze ... 2 C4
Praze-an-Beeble ... 2 C5
Prednannack Wollas ... 3 E5
Prees ... 74 F2
Preesall ... 92 E3
Prees Green ... 74 F2
Preesgweene ... 73 F6
Prees Heath ... 74 F2
Prees Higher
  Heath ... 74 F2
Prees Lower Heath ... 74 F2
Prendergast ... 122 D5
Prendwick ... 117 C6
Prengwyn ... 46 E3
Prenteg ... 71 C6
Prenton ... 85 F4
Prescot ... 86 E2
Prescott ... 60 B4
Pressen ... 122 F4
Prestatyn ... 72 A4
Prestbury Ches E ... 75 B6
  Glos ... 37 B6
Presteigne
  =Llanandras ... 48 C5
Presthope ... 61 E5
Prestleigh ... 23 E8
Preston Borders ... 122 D3
  Brighton ... 17 D7
  Devon ... 7 B6
  Dorset ... 12 F5
  E Loth ... 121 B8
  E Yorks ... 97 F7
  Glos ... 37 D7
  Glos ... 49 F8
  Herts ... 40 B4
  Kent ... 30 C4
  Kent ... 31 C6
  Lancs ... 86 B3
  Northum ... 117 B7
  Rutland ... 65 D5
  Shrops ... 60 C5
  Wilts ... 24 B5
  Wilts ... 25 B7
Preston Bagot ... 51 C6
Preston Bissett ... 39 B6
Preston Bowyer ... 11 B6
Preston
  Brockhurst ... 60 B5
Preston Brook ... 86 F3
Preston Candover ... 26 E4
Preston Capes ... 52 D3
Preston
  Crowmarsh ... 39 E6
Preston Gubbals ... 60 C4
Prestonmill ... 107 D6
Preston on Stour ... 51 E7
Preston on the Hill ... 86 F3
Preston on Wye ... 49 E5
Prestonpans ... 121 B6
Preston Plucknett ... 12 C3
Preston St Mary ... 56 D3
Preston-
  under-Scar ... 101 E5
Preston upon the
  Weald Moors ... 61 C6
Preston Wynne ... 49 E7
Prestwich ... 87 D6
Prestwick
  Northumb ... 110 B4
  S Ayrs ... 112 B3
Prestwood ... 40 D1
Price Town ... 34 E3
Prickwillow ... 67 F5
Priddy ... 23 D7
Priesthaugh ... 115 D7
Priest Hutton ... 92 B5
Priest Weston ... 60 E2
Primethorpe ... 64 E2
Primrose Green ... 68 C3
Primrosehill ... 40 D3
Primrose Valley ... 97 B7
Princes Gate ... 32 C2
Princes
  Risborough ... 39 D8
Princethorpe ... 52 B2
Princetown Caerph ... 35 C5
  Devon ... 6 B4
Prion ... 72 C4
Prior Muir ... 129 C7
Prior Park ... 123 D5
Priors Frome ... 49 F7
Priors Hardwick ... 52 D2
Priorslee ... 61 C7
Priors Marston ... 52 D2
Priory Wood ... 48 E4

Priston ... 23 C8
Pristow Green ... 68 F4
Prittlewell ... 42 F4
Privett ... 15 B7
Prixford ... 20 F4
Probus ... 3 B7
Proncy ... 151 B10
Prospect ... 107 E8
Prudhoe ... 110 C3
Ptarmigan Lodge ... 126 D2
Pubil ... 132 E1
Puckeridge ... 41 B6
Puckington ... 11 C8
Pucklechurch ... 23 B8
Pucknall ... 14 B4
Puckrup ... 50 F3
Puddinglake ... 74 C4
Puddington
  Ches W ... 73 B7
  Devon ... 10 C3
Puddledock ... 68 E3
Puddletown ... 13 E5
Pudleston ... 49 D7
Pudsey ... 94 F5
Pulborough ... 16 C4
Puleston ... 61 B7
Pulford ... 73 D7
Pulham ... 12 D5
Pulham Market ... 68 F5
Pulham St Mary ... 68 F5
Pulloxhill ... 53 F8
Pumpherston ... 120 C3
Pumsaint ... 47 E5
Puncheston ... 32 B1
Puncknowle ... 12 F3
Punnett's Town ... 18 C3
Purbrook ... 15 D7
Purewell ... 14 E2
Purfleet ... 29 B6
Puriton ... 22 E5
Purleigh ... 42 D4
Purley London ... 28 C4
  W Berks ... 26 B4
Purlogue ... 48 B4
Purls Bridge ... 66 F4
Purse Caundle ... 12 C4
Purslow ... 60 F3
Purston Jaglin ... 88 C5
Purton Glos ... 36 D3
  Glos ... 36 D3
  Wilts ... 37 F7
Purton Stoke ... 37 E7
Pury End ... 52 E5
Pusey ... 38 E3
Putley ... 49 F8
Putney ... 28 B3
Putsborough ... 20 E3
Puttenham Herts ... 40 C1
  Sur ... 27 E7
Puxton ... 23 C6
Pwll ... 33 D5
Pwllcrochan ... 44 E4
Pwll-glas ... 72 D5
Pwllgloyw ... 48 F2
Pwllheli ... 70 D4
Pwllmeyric ... 36 E2
Pwll-trap ... 32 C3
Pwll-y-glaw ... 34 E1
Pyecombe ... 17 C6
Pye Corner ... 35 F7
Pye Green ... 62 C3
Pyewipe ... 91 C6
Pyle ... 15 G5
Pyle = Y Pîl ... 34 F2
Pylle ... 23 F8
Pymoor ... 66 F4
Pyrford ... 27 D8
Pyrton ... 39 E6
Pytchley ... 53 B6
Pyworthy ... 8 D5

Q
Quabbs ... 60 F2
Quadring ... 78 F5
Quainton ... 39 C7
Quarley ... 25 E7
Quarndon ... 76 E3
Quarrier's
  Homes ... 118 C3
Quarrington ... 78 E3
Quarrington Hill ... 111 F6
Quarry Bank ... 62 F3
Quarryford ... 121 C8
Quarryhill ... 151 C10
Quarrywood ... 152 B1
Quarter ... 119 D7
Quatford ... 61 E7
Quatt ... 61 F7
Quebec ... 110 E4
Quedgeley ... 37 C5
Queen Adelaide ... 67 F5
Queenborough ... 30 B3
Queen Camel ... 12 B3
Queen Charlton ... 23 C8
Queenhill ... 50 F3
Queen Oak ... 24 F2
Queensbury ... 94 F4
Queensferry Edin ... 120 B4
  Flint ... 73 C7
Queensferry
  Crossing ... 120 B4
Queen's Head ... 60 B3
Queen's Park
  Bedford ... 53 E8
  W Nhants ... 53 C5
Queenstown ... 92 F3
Queen Street Kent ... 29 E7
  Wilts ... 37 F7
Queenzieburn ... 119 B6
Quemerford ... 24 C5
Quendale ... 160 M5
Quendon ... 55 F6
Queniborough ... 64 C3
Quenington ... 37 D8
Quernmore ... 92 D5
Quethiock ... 5 C8
Quholm ... 159 G3
Quicks Green ... 26 B3
Quidenham ... 68 F3
Quidhampton
  Hants ... 26 D3
  Wilts ... 25 F6
Quilquox ... 153 E9
Quina Brook ... 74 F2
Quindry ... 159 J5
Quinton W Mid ... 62 F3

Quinton continued
  W Nhants ... 53 D5
Quintrell Downs ... 4 C3
Quixhill ... 75 E8
Quoditch ... 9 E6
Quoig ... 127 B7
Quothquan ... 120 F2
Quoyloo ... 159 F3
Quoyness ... 159 H3
Quoys Shetland ... 160 B8
  Shetland ... 160 G6

R
Raasay House ... 149 E10
Rabbit's Cross ... 29 E8
Raby ... 73 B7
Rachan Mill ... 120 F4
Rachub ... 83 E6
Rackenford ... 10 C3
Rackham ... 16 C4
Rackheath ... 69 C5
Racks ... 107 B7
Rackwick Orkney ... 159 D5
  Orkney ... 159 J3
Radbourne ... 76 F2
Radcliffe Gtr Man ... 87 D5
  Northumb ... 117 D8
Radcliffe on Trent ... 77 F6
Radclive ... 52 F4
Radcot ... 38 E2
Raddery ... 151 F10
Radernie ... 129 D6
Radford Semele ... 51 C8
Radipole ... 12 F4
Radlett ... 40 E4
Radley ... 39 E5
Radmanthwaite ... 76 C5
Radmoor ... 61 B6
Radmore Green ... 74 D2
Radnage ... 39 E7
Radstock ... 23 D8
Radstone ... 52 E3
Radway ... 51 E8
Radway Green ... 74 D4
Radwell Bedford ... 53 D8
  Herts ... 54 F3
Radwinter ... 55 F7
Radyr ... 35 F5
Rafford ... 151 F13
Ragdale ... 64 C3
Raglan ... 35 D8
Ragnall ... 77 B8
Rahane ... 145 E11
Rainford ... 86 D2
Rainford Junction ... 86 D2
Rainham London ... 41 F8
  Medway ... 30 C2
Rainhill ... 86 E2
Rainhill Stoops ... 86 E3
Rainow ... 75 B6
Rainton ... 95 B6
Rainworth ... 77 D5
Raisbeck ... 99 D8
Raise ... 109 E7
Rait ... 128 B4
Raithby Lincs ... 79 C6
  Lincs ... 91 F7
Rake ... 16 B2
Rakewood ... 87 C7
Ram ... 46 E4
Ramasaig ... 148 D6
Rameldry Mill
  Bank ... 128 D5
Ram Lane ... 30 E3
Ramnageo ... 160 C8
Rampisham ... 12 D3
Rampside ... 92 C2
Rampton Cambs ... 54 C5
  Notts ... 77 B7
Ramsbottom ... 87 C5
Ramsbury ... 25 B7
Ramscraigs ... 158 H3
Ramsdean ... 15 B8
Ramsdell ... 26 D3
Ramsden ... 38 C3
Ramsden
  Bellhouse ... 42 E3
Ramsden Heath ... 42 E3
Ramsey Cambs ... 66 F2
  Essex ... 57 F6
  IoM ... 84 C4
Ramseycleuch ... 115 C5
Ramsey Forty Foot ... 66 F3
Ramsey Heights ... 66 F2
Ramsey Island ... 43 D5
Ramsey Mereside ... 66 F2
Ramsey St Mary's ... 66 F2
Ramsgate ... 31 C7
Ramsgill ... 94 B4
Ramshorn ... 75 E7
Ramsnest
  Common ... 27 F7
Ranais ... 155 E9
Ranby Lincs ... 78 B5
  Notts ... 89 F7
Rand ... 78 B4
Randwick ... 37 D5
Ranfurly ... 118 C3
Rangag ... 158 F3
Rangemore ... 63 B5
Rangeworthy ... 36 F3
Rankinston ... 112 C4
Ranmoor ... 88 F4
Ranmore Common ... 28 D2
Rannerdale ... 98 C3
Rannoch Station ... 131 D8
Ranochan ... 147 C11
Ranskill ... 89 F7
Ranton ... 62 B2
Ranworth ... 69 C6
Raploch ... 127 E6
Rapness ... 159 D6
Rascal Moor ... 96 F4
Rascarrel ... 106 E4
Rashiereive ... 141 B8
Raskelf ... 95 B7
Rassau ... 35 C5
Rastrick ... 88 B2
Ratagan ... 136 C2
Ratby ... 64 D2
Ratcliffe Culey ... 63 E7
Ratcliffe on Soar ... 63 B8
Ratcliffe on the
  Wreake ... 64 C3

Rathen ... 153 B10
Rathillet ... 129 B5
Rathmell ... 93 D8
Ratho ... 120 B4
Ratho Station ... 120 B4
Rathven ... 152 B4
Ratley ... 51 E8
Ratlinghope ... 60 E4
Rattar ... 158 C4
Ratten Row ... 92 E4
Rattery ... 6 C5
Rattlesden ... 56 D3
Rattray ... 134 E1
Raughton Head ... 108 E3
Raunds ... 53 B7
Ravenfield ... 89 E5
Ravenglass ... 98 E2
Raveningham ... 69 E6
Ravenscar ... 103 D7
Ravenscraig ... 118 B2
Ravensdale ... 84 C3
Ravensden ... 53 D8
Ravenseat ... 100 D3
Ravenshead ... 77 D5
Ravensmoor ... 74 D3
Ravensthorpe
  W Nhants ... 52 B4
  W Yorks ... 88 B3
Ravenstone Leics ... 63 C8
  M Keynes ... 53 D6
Ravenstonedale ... 100 D2
Ravenstown ... 92 B3
Ravenstruther ... 120 E2
Ravensworth ... 101 D6
Raw ... 103 D7
Rawcliffe E Yorks ... 89 B7
  York ... 95 D8
Rawcliffe Bridge ... 89 B7
Rawdon ... 94 F5
Rawmarsh ... 88 E5
Rawreth ... 42 E3
Rawridge ... 11 D7
Rawtenstall ... 87 B6
Raxton ... 153 E8
Raydon ... 56 F4
Raylees ... 117 E5
Rayleigh ... 42 E4
Rayne ... 42 B3
Rayners Lane ... 40 F4
Raynes Park ... 28 C3
Reach ... 55 C6
Read ... 93 F7
Reading ... 26 B5
Reading Street ... 19 B6
Reagill ... 99 C8
Rearquhar ... 151 B10
Rearsby ... 64 C3
Reaster ... 158 D4
Reawick ... 160 J5
Reay ... 157 C12
Rechullin ... 149 C13
Reculver ... 31 C6
Redberth ... 32 D1
Redbourn ... 40 C4
Redbourne ... 90 E3
Redbrook Mon ... 36 C2
  Wrex ... 74 E2
Redburn Highld ... 151 E8
  Highld ... 151 G12
  Northumb ... 109 C7
Redcar ... 102 B4
Redcastle Angus ... 135 D6
  Highld ... 151 G8
Redcliff Bay ... 23 B6
Red Dial ... 108 E2
Redding ... 120 B2
Reddingmuirhead
  ... 120 B2
Reddish ... 87 E6
Redditch ... 50 C5
Rede ... 56 D2
Redenhall ... 69 F5
Redesdale Camp ... 116 E4
Redesmouth ... 116 F4
Redford Aberds ... 135 B7
  Angus ... 135 E5
  Durham ... 110 F3
Redfordgreen ... 115 C6
Redgorton ... 128 B2
Redgrave ... 56 B4
Redhill Aberds ... 141 D6
  N Som ... 23 C7
  Sur ... 28 D3
Red Hill ... 50 D3
Redhouse ... 145 G7
Redhouses ... 142 B4
Redisham ... 69 F7
Redland Bristol ... 23 B7
  Orkney ... 159 F4
Redlingfield ... 57 B5
Red Lodge ... 55 B7
Redlynch Som ... 23 F9
  Wilts ... 14 B3
Redmarley
  D'Abitot ... 50 F2
Redmarshall ... 102 B1
Redmile ... 77 F7
Redmire ... 101 E5
Redmoor ... 5 C5
Rednal ... 60 B3
Redpath ... 121 F8
Redpoint ... 149 B12
Red Rail ... 36 B2
Red Rock ... 86 D3
Red Roses ... 32 C3
Red Row ... 117 E8
Redruth ... 3 B5
Red Street ... 74 D5
Redvales ... 87 D6
Red Wharf Bay ... 82 C5
Redworth ... 101 B7
Reed ... 54 F4
Reedham ... 69 D7
Reedness ... 89 B8
Reeds Beck ... 78 C5
Reepham Lincs ... 78 B3
  Norf ... 81 E6
Reeth ... 101 E5
Regaby ... 84 C4
Regoul ... 151 F11
Reiff ... 156 H2
Reigate ... 28 D3
Reighton ... 97 B7
Reighton Gap ... 97 B7
Reinigeadal ... 154 G7

Reiss ... 158 E5
Rejerrah ... 4 D2
Releath ... 3 C5
Relubbus ... 2 C4
Relugas ... 151 G12
Remenham ... 39 F7
Remenham Hill ... 39 F7
Remony ... 132 E4
Rempstone ... 64 B2
Rendcomb ... 37 D7
Rendham ... 57 C7
Rendlesham ... 57 D7
Renfrew ... 118 C5
Renhold ... 53 D8
Renishaw ... 76 B4
Rennington ... 117 C8
Renton ... 118 B3
Renwick ... 109 E5
Repps ... 69 C7
Repton ... 63 B7
Reraig ... 149 F13
Rescobie ... 135 D5
Resipole ... 147 E10
Resolfen ... 34 D2
Resolis ... 151 E9
Resolven ... 34 D2
Reston ... 122 C4
Reswallie ... 135 D5
Retew ... 4 D4
Retford ... 89 F8
Rettendon ... 42 E3
Rettendon Place ... 42 E3
Revesby ... 79 C5
Revesby Bridge ... 79 C6
Rewe ... 10 E4
Rew Street ... 15 E5
Reydon ... 57 B8
Reydon Smear ... 57 B8
Reymerston ... 68 D3
Reynalton ... 32 D1
Reynoldston ... 33 E5
Rezare ... 5 B8
Rhaeadr Gwy
  =Rhayader ... 47 C8
Rhandirmwyn ... 47 E6
Rhayader
  =Rhaeadr Gwy ... 47 C8
Rhedyn ... 70 D3
Rhemore ... 147 F8
Rhencullen ... 84 C3
Rhes-y-cae ... 73 B5
Rhewl Denb ... 72 C5
  Denb ... 73 E5
Rhian ... 157 H9
Rhicarn ... 156 G3
Rhiconich ... 156 D5
Rhicullen ... 151 D9
Rhidorroch
  House ... 150 B4
Rhifail ... 157 E10
Rhigos ... 34 D3
Rhilochan ... 157 J10
Rhiroy ... 150 C4
Rhisga = Risca ... 35 E6
Rhiw ... 70 E3
Rhiwabon
  =Ruabon ... 73 E7
Rhiwbina ... 35 F5
Rhiwbryfdir ... 71 C7
Rhiwderin ... 35 F6
Rhiwlas Gwyn ... 72 F3
  Gwyn ... 83 E5
  Powys ... 73 F5
Rhodes ... 87 D6
Rhodesia ... 77 B5
Rhodes Minnis ... 31 E5
Rhodiad ... 44 C2
Rhondda ... 34 E3
Rhonehouse or
  Kelton Hill ... 106 D4
Rhoose = Y Rhws ... 22 C2
Rhôs Carms ... 46 F2
  Neath ... 33 D8
Rhosaman ... 33 C8
Rhosbeirio ... 82 B3
Rhoscefnhir ... 82 D5
Rhoscolyn ... 82 D2
Rhoscrowther ... 44 E4
Rhosesmor ... 73 C6
Rhos-fawr ... 70 D4
Rhosgadfan ... 82 E5
Rhosgoch ... 82 C4
Rhos-goch ... 48 E3
Rhos-hill ... 45 E3
Rhoshirwaun ... 70 E2
Rhoslan ... 71 C5
Rhoslefain ... 58 D2
Rhosllanerchrugog
  ... 73 E6
Rhosmaen ... 33 B7
Rhosmeirch ... 82 D4
Rhosneigr ... 82 D3
Rhosnesni ... 73 D7
Rhôs-on-Sea ... 83 C8
Rhosrobin ... 73 D7
Rhossili ... 33 F5
Rhosson ... 44 C2
Rhostryfan ... 82 F4
Rhostyllen ... 73 E7
Rhosybol ... 82 C4
Rhos-y-brithdir ... 59 B8
Rhos-y-garth ... 46 B5
Rhos-y-gwaliau ... 72 F3
Rhos-y-llan ... 70 D3
Rhos-y-Madoc ... 73 E7
Rhos-y-meirch ... 48 C4
Rhu Argyll ... 145 E11
  Argyll ... 145 G7
Rhuallt ... 72 B4
Rhuddall Heath ... 74 C2
Rhuddlan Ceredig ... 46 E3
  Denb ... 72 B4
Rhue ... 150 B3
Rhulen ... 48 E3
Rhunahaorine ... 143 D8
Rhuthun = Ruthin ... 72 D5
Rhyd Gwyn ... 71 C7
  Powys ... 59 D6
Rhydaman
  =Ammanford ... 33 C7
Rhydargaeau ... 33 B5
Rhydcymerau ... 46 F4
Rhydd ... 50 E3
Rhydding ... 33 E8
Rhydfudr ... 46 C4
Rhydlewis ... 46 E2
Rhydlios ... 70 D2
Rhydlydan ... 83 F8
Rhyd-moel-ddu ... 48 B2

Rhydness ... 48 E3
Rhydowen ... 46 E3
Rhyd-Rosser ... 46 C4
Rhydspence ... 48 E4
Rhydtalog ... 73 D6
Rhyd-uchaf ... 72 C3
Rhyd-wen ... 58 C4
Rhydwyn ... 82 C3
Rhydycroesau ... 73 F6
Rhyd-y-clafdy ... 70 D4
Rhyd-y-foel ... 72 B3
Rhyd-y-fro ... 33 D7
Rhydymain ... 58 B5
Rhyd-y-meirch ... 35 D7
Rhyd-y-meudwy ... 72 D5
Rhydymwyn ... 73 C6
Rhyd-y-pandy ... 33 D7
Rhyd-yr-onen ... 58 D3
Rhyd-y-sarn ... 71 C7
Rhyl = Y Rhyl ... 72 A4
Rhymney = Rhymni ... 35 D5
Rhymni = Rhymney ... 35 D5
Rhynd Fife ... 129 B6
  Perth ... 128 B3
Rhynie Aberds. ... 140 B3
  Highld ... 151 D11
Ribbesford ... 50 B2
Ribblehead ... 93 B7
Ribbleton ... 93 F5
Ribchester ... 93 F6
Ribigill ... 157 D8
Riby ... 91 D5
Riby Cross Roads ... 91 D5
Riccall ... 96 F2
Riccarton ... 118 F4
Richards Castle ... 49 C6
Richings Park ... 27 B8
Richmond London ... 28 B2
  N Yorks. ... 101 D6
Rickarton ... 141 F7
Rickinghall ... 56 B4
Rickleton ... 111 D5
Rickling ... 55 F5
Rickmansworth ... 40 E3
Riddings Cumb. ... 108 B4
  Derbys. ... 76 D4
Riddlecombe ... 9 C8
Riddlesden ... 94 E3
Riddrie ... 119 C6
Ridge Dorset ... 13 F7
  Hants. ... 14 C4
  Wilts ... 24 F4
Ridgebourne ... 48 C2
Ridge Green ... 28 E4
Ridgehill ... 23 C7
Ridge Lane ... 63 E6
Ridgeway Cross ... 50 E2
Ridgewell ... 55 E8
Ridgewood ... 17 C8
Ridgmont ... 53 F7
Riding Mill ... 110 C3
Ridleywood ... 73 D8
Ridlington Norf ... 69 A6
  Rutland ... 64 D5
Ridsdale ... 116 F5
Riechip ... 133 E7
Riemore ... 133 E7
Rienachait ... 156 F3
Rievaulx ... 102 F3
Rift House ... 111 F7
Rigg ... 108 C2
Riggend ... 119 B7
Rigsby ... 79 B7
Rigside ... 119 F8
Riley Green ... 86 B4
Rileyhill ... 62 C5
Rilla Mill ... 5 B7
Rillington ... 96 B4
Rimington ... 93 E8
Rimpton ... 12 B4
Rimswell ... 91 B7
Rinaston ... 44 C4
Ringasta ... 160 M5
Ringford ... 106 D3
Ringinglow ... 88 F3
Ringland ... 68 C4
Ringles Cross ... 17 C8
Ringmer ... 17 C8
Ringmore ... 6 E4
Ringorm ... 152 D2
Ring's End ... 66 D3
Ringsfield ... 69 F7
Ringsfield Corner ... 69 F7
Ringshall Herts ... 40 C2
  Suff ... 56 D4
Ringshall Stocks ... 56 D4
Ringstead N Hants ... 53 B7
  Norf ... 80 C3
Ringwood ... 14 D2
Ringwould ... 31 E7
Rinmore ... 140 C3
Rinnigill ... 159 J4
Rinsey ... 2 D4
Riof ... 154 D6
Ripe ... 18 D2
Ripley Derbys ... 76 D3
  Hants. ... 14 E2
  N Yorks. ... 95 C5
  Sur. ... 27 D8
Riplingham ... 97 F5
Ripon ... 95 B6
Rippingale ... 65 B8
Ripple Kent ... 31 E7
  Worcs ... 50 F3
Ripponden ... 87 C8
Rireavach ... 150 B3
Risabus ... 142 D4
Risbury ... 49 D7
Risby ... 55 C8
Risca = Rhisga ... 35 E6
Rise ... 97 E7
Riseden ... 18 B3
Risegate ... 66 B2
Riseholme ... 78 B2
Riseley Bedford. ... 53 C8
  Wokingham ... 26 C5
Rishangles ... 57 C5
Rishton ... 93 F7
Rishworth ... 87 C8
Rising Bridge ... 87 B5
Risley Derbys. ... 76 F4
  Warr. ... 86 E4
Risplith ... 94 C5
Rispond ... 156 C7

Rivar ... 25 C8
Rivenhall End ... 42 C4
River Bank ... 55 C6
Riverhead. ... 29 D6
Rivington ... 86 C4
Roachill ... 10 B3
Roade ... 53 D5
Road Green ... 69 E5
Roadhead. ... 108 B5
Roadmeetings ... 119 E8
Roadside ... 158 D3
Roadside of Catterline ... 135 B8
Roadside of Kinneff ... 135 B8
Roadwater ... 22 F2
Roag. ... 149 D7
Roa Island ... 92 C2
Roath ... 22 B3
Roberton Borders ... 115 C7
  S Lanark. ... 114 B2
Robertsbridge ... 18 C4
Roberttown ... 88 B2
Robeston Cross ... 44 E3
Robeston Wathen ... 32 C1
Robin Hood ... 88 B4
Robin Hood's Bay. ... 103 D7
Roborough Devon ... 6 C3
  Devon ... 9 C7
Roby. ... 86 E2
Roby Mill ... 86 D3
Rocester ... 75 F8
Roch. ... 44 C3
Rochdale ... 87 C6
Roche ... 4 C4
Rochester Medway ... 29 C8
  Northumb ... 116 E4
Rochford ... 42 E4
Rock Corn ... 4 B4
  Northumb ... 117 B8
  Worcs ... 50 B2
  W Sus ... 16 C5
Rockbeare ... 10 E5
Rockbourne. ... 14 C2
Rockcliffe Cumb. ... 108 C3
  Dumfries. ... 107 D5
Rock Ferry ... 85 F4
Rockfield Highld. ... 151 C12
  Mon ... 36 C1
Rockford. ... 14 D2
Rockhampton ... 36 E3
Rockingham ... 65 E5
Rockland All Saints ... 68 E2
Rockland St Mary ... 69 D6
Rockland St Peter ... 68 E2
Rockley ... 25 B6
Rockwell End ... 39 F7
Rockwell Green ... 11 B6
Rodborough ... 37 D5
Rodbourne Swindon 37 F8
  Wilts ... 37 F6
Rodbourne Cheney 37 F8
Rodd ... 48 C5
Roddam ... 117 B6
Rodden ... 12 F4
Rode ... 24 D3
Rodeheath ... 75 C5
Rode Heath ... 74 D5
Roden ... 61 C5
Rodhuish ... 22 F2
Rodington ... 61 C5
Rodley Glos. ... 36 C4
  W Yorks. ... 94 F5
Rodmarton. ... 37 E6
Rodmell ... 17 D8
Rodmersham ... 30 C3
Rodney Stoke ... 23 D6
Rodsley ... 76 E2
Rodway ... 22 F4
Rodwell ... 12 G4
Roecliffe ... 95 C6
Roe Green ... 54 F4
Roehampton ... 28 B3
Roesound ... 160 G5
Roffey ... 28 F2
Rogart ... 157 J10
Rogart Station ... 157 J10
Rogate. ... 16 B2
Rogerstone ... 35 F6
Roghadal ... 154 J5
Rogiet ... 36 F1
Rogue's Alley ... 66 D3
Roke. ... 39 E6
Roker ... 111 D7
Rollesby ... 69 C7
Rolleston Leics. ... 64 D4
  Notts ... 77 D7
Rolleston-on-Dove. ... 63 B6
Rolston ... 97 E8
Rolvenden ... 18 B5
Rolvenden Layne ... 19 B5
Romaldkirk ... 100 B4
Romanby ... 102 E1
Romannobridge. ... 120 E4
Romansleigh. ... 10 B2
Romford ... 41 F8
Romiley. ... 87 E7
Romsey ... 14 B4
Romsey Town ... 55 D5
Romsley Shrops ... 61 F7
  Worcs ... 50 B4
Ronague ... 84 E2
Rookhope. ... 110 E2
Rookley ... 15 F6
Rooks Bridge ... 23 D5
Roos. ... 97 F8
Roosebeck ... 92 C2
Rootham's Green ... 54 D2
Rootpark ... 120 D2
Ropley ... 26 F4
Ropley Dean ... 26 F4
Ropsley ... 78 F2
Rora ... 153 C10
Rorandle ... 141 C5
Rorrington ... 60 D3
Roscroggan ... 3 B5
Rose. ... 4 D2
Roseacre Kent ... 29 D8
  Lancs. ... 92 F4
Rose Ash. ... 10 B2
Rosebank ... 119 E8
Rosebrough. ... 117 B7
Rosebush ... 32 B1
Rosecare. ... 8 E3
Rosedale Abbey ... 103 E6

Roseden ... 117 B6
Rosefield ... 151 F1
Rose Green ... 16 E3
Rose Grove. ... 93 F8
Rosehall ... 156 J7
Rosehaugh Mains ... 151 F9
Rosehearty ... 153 B9
Rosehill ... 74 F3
Rose Hill E Sus ... 17 C8
  Lancs. ... 93 F8
  Suff ... 57 E5
Roseisle ... 152 B1
Roselands ... 18 E3
Rosemarket. ... 44 E4
Rosemarkie ... 151 F10
Rosemary Lane ... 11 C6
Rosemount ... 134 E1
Rosenannon ... 4 C4
Rosewell ... 121 C5
Roseworth ... 102 B2
Roseworthy ... 2 C5
Rosgill ... 99 C7
Roshven ... 147 D10
Roskhill ... 149 D7
Roskill House ... 151 F9
Rosley ... 108 E3
Roslin ... 121 C5
Rosliston ... 63 C6
Rosneath ... 145 E11
Ross Dumfries ... 106 E3
  Northumb ... 123 F7
  Perth ... 127 B6
Rossett ... 73 D7
Rossett Green ... 95 D6
Rossie Ochill ... 128 C2
Rossie Priory ... 134 F2
Rossington ... 89 E7
Rosskeen ... 151 E9
Rossland ... 118 B4
Rosster ... 158 G4
Rostherne ... 86 F5
Rosthwaite. ... 98 C4
Roston ... 75 E8
Rosyth ... 128 F3
Rothbury ... 117 D6
Rotherby. ... 64 C3
Rotherfield ... 18 C2
Rotherfield Greys. ... 39 F7
Rotherfield Peppard. ... 39 F7
Rotherham. ... 88 E5
Rothersthorpe ... 52 D5
Rotherwick ... 26 D5
Rothes. ... 152 D2
Rothesay ... 145 G9
Rothiebrisbane ... 153 E7
Rothienorman ... 153 E7
Rothiesholm ... 159 F7
Rothley Leics. ... 64 C2
  Northumb ... 117 F6
Rothley Shield East ... 117 E6
Rothmaise ... 153 E6
Rothwell Lincs. ... 91 E5
  N Nhants ... 64 F5
  W Yorks. ... 88 B4
Rothwell Haigh... 88 B4
Rotsea ... 97 D6
Rottal ... 134 C3
Rotten End ... 57 C7
Rottingdean ... 17 D7
Rottington ... 98 C1
Roud ... 15 F6
Rough Close ... 75 F6
Rough Common ... 30 D5
Roughlee ... 93 E8
Roughley ... 62 E5
Roughsike ... 108 B5
Roughton Lincs. ... 78 C5
  Norf ... 81 D8
Roughton Moor ... 78 C5
Roundbush ... 42 D4
Roundhay. ... 95 F6
Roundstreet Common ... 16 B4
Roundway ... 24 C5
Rousdon ... 11 E7
Rous Lench ... 50 D5
Routenburn ... 118 C1
Routh. ... 97 E6
Row Corn ... 5 B5
  Cumb. ... 99 F6
Rowanburn ... 108 B4
Rowardennan ... 126 E2
Rowen. ... 24 C4
Rowen ... 83 D7
Rowfoot ... 109 C6
Row Heath ... 43 C7
Rowhedge ... 43 B6
Rowhook ... 28 F2
Rowington ... 51 C7
Rowland ... 76 B2
Rowlands Castle ... 15 C8
Rowlands Gill ... 110 D4
Rowledge ... 27 E6
Rowlestone ... 35 B7
Rowley E Yorks ... 97 F5
  Shrops ... 60 D3
Rowley Hill ... 88 C2
Rowley Regis ... 62 F3
Rowly. ... 27 E8
Rowney Green ... 50 B5
Rownhams ... 14 C4
Rowrah ... 98 C2
Rowsham ... 39 C8
Rowsley ... 76 C2
Rowstock ... 38 F4
Rowston ... 78 D3
Rowton Ches W ... 73 C8
  Shrops. ... 60 C3
  Telford ... 61 C6
Roxburgh ... 122 F3
Roxby N Lincs. ... 90 C3
  N Yorks. ... 103 C5
Roxton ... 54 D2
Roxwell ... 42 D2
Royal Leamington Spa ... 51 C8
Royal Oak Darl ... 101 B7
  Lancs. ... 86 D2
Royal Tunbridge Wells. ... 18 B2

Royal Wootton Bassett. ... 37 F7
Roybridge ... 137 F5
Roydhouse. ... 88 C3
Roydon Essex ... 41 D7
  Norf. ... 68 F3
  Norf ... 80 E3
Roydon Hamlet... 41 D7
Royston Herts. ... 54 E4
  S Yorks ... 88 C4
Royton. ... 87 D7
Rozel Jersey ... 17
Ruabon = Rhiwabon ... 73 E7
Ruaig. ... 146 G3
Ruan Lanihorne ... 3 B7
Ruan Minor ... 3 E6
Ruarach ... 136 B2
Ruardean ... 36 C3
Ruardean Woodside ... 36 C3
Rubery. ... 50 B4
Ruckcroft. ... 108 E5
Ruckhall ... 49 F6
Ruckinge ... 19 B7
Ruckland ... 79 B6
Ruckley ... 60 D5
Rudbaxton ... 44 C4
Rudby ... 102 D2
Ruddington ... 77 F5
Rudford. ... 36 B4
Rudge Shrops. ... 62 E2
  Som ... 24 D3
Rudgeway ... 36 F3
Rudgwick ... 27 F8
Rudhall ... 36 B3
Rudheath ... 74 B3
Rudley Green ... 42 D4
Rudry. ... 35 F5
Rudston ... 97 C6
Rudyard ... 75 D6
Rufford ... 86 C2
Rufforth ... 95 D8
Rugby ... 52 B3
Rugeley. ... 62 C4
Ruglen. ... 112 D2
Ruilick. ... 151 G8
Ruishton ... 11 B7
Ruisigearraidh ... 154 J4
Ruislip ... 40 F3
Ruislip Common ... 40 F3
Rumbling Bridge 128 E2
Rumburgh ... 69 F6
Rumford ... 4 B3
Rumney ... 22 B4
Runcorn ... 86 F3
Runcton ... 16 D2
Runcton Holme ... 67 D6
Rundlestone ... 6 B3
Runfold ... 27 E6
Runhall ... 68 D3
Runham Norf ... 69 C7
  Norf ... 69 D8
Runnington ... 11 B6
Runsell Green ... 42 D3
Runswick Bay ... 103 C6
Runwell ... 42 E3
Ruscombe ... 27 B5
Rush-head. ... 153 D8
Rushall Hereford ... 49 F8
  Norf. ... 68 F4
  Wilts ... 25 D6
  W Mid ... 62 D4
Rushbrooke ... 56 C2
Rushbury ... 60 E5
Rushden Herts ... 54 F4
  N Nhants ... 53 C7
Rushenden ... 30 B3
Rushford. ... 68 F2
Rush Green ... 41 F8
Rush-head. ... 153 D8
Rushlake Green ... 18 D3
Rushmere ... 69 F7
Rushmere St Andrew ... 57 E6
Rushmoor ... 27 E6
Rushock ... 50 B3
Rusholme ... 87 E6
Rushton ChesW ... 74 C2
  N Nhants ... 64 F5
  Shrops. ... 61 D6
Rushton Spencer ... 75 C6
Rushwick ... 50 D3
Rushyford. ... 101 B7
Ruskie ... 126 D5
Ruskington ... 78 D3
Rusland ... 99 F5
Rusper ... 28 F3
Ruspidge ... 36 C3
Russell's Water. ... 39 F7
Russel's Green ... 57 B6
Rusthall. ... 18 B2
Rustington. ... 16 D4
Ruston ... 103 F7
Ruston Parva. ... 97 C6
Ruswarp ... 103 D6
Rutherford ... 122 F2
Rutherglen ... 119 C6
Ruthernbridge ... 4 C5
Ruthin = Rhuthun ... 72 D5
Ruthrieston ... 141 D8
Ruthven Aberds ... 152 D5
  Angus ... 134 E2
  Highld ... 138 E3
  Highld ... 151 H11
Ruthven House ... 134 E3
Ruthvoes ... 4 C4
Ruthwell ... 107 C7
Ruyton-XI-Towns ... 60 B3
Ryal ... 110 B3
Ryal Fold. ... 86 B4
Ryall ... 12 E2
Ryarsh ... 29 D7
Rydal ... 99 D5
Ryde ... 15 E6
Rye ... 19 C6
Ryecroft Gate ... 75 C6
Rye Foreign ... 19 C5
Rye Harbour ... 19 D6
Ryehill ... 91 B6
Rye Park ... 41 C6
Rye Street. ... 50 F2
Ryhall ... 65 C7
Ryhill ... 88 C4
Ryhope ... 111 D7
Rylstone ... 94 D2
Ryme Intrinseca. ... 12 C3
Ryther ... 95 F8
Ryton Glos. ... 50 F2
  N Yorks. ... 96 B3

Ryton continued
  Shrops. ... 61 D7
  T&W ... 110 C4
Ryton-on-Dunsmore ... 51 B8

S

Sabden ... 93 F7
Sacombe ... 41 C6
Sacriston ... 110 E5
Sadberge ... 101 C8
Saddell ... 143 E8
Saddington ... 64 E3
Saddle Bow ... 67 C6
Saddlescombe ... 17 C6
Sadgill. ... 99 D6
Saffron Walden ... 55 F6
Sageston ... 32 D1
Saham Hills ... 68 D2
Saham Toney ... 68 D2
Saighdinis ... 148 B3
Saighton ... 73 C8
St Abbs ... 122 C5
St Abb's Haven ... 122 C5
St Agnes Corn. ... 4 D2
  Scilly ... 2 F3
St Albans ... 40 D4
St Allen ... 4 D3
St Andrews. ... 129 C7
St Andrew's Major ... 22 B3
St Anne Ald ... 16
St Annes ... 85 B4
St Ann's ... 114 E3
St Ann's Chapel Corn. ... 6 B2
  Devon ... 6 E4
St Anthony-in-Meneage ... 3 D6
St Anthony's Hill ... 18 E3
St Arvans ... 36 E2
St Asaph = Llanelwy ... 72 B4
St Athan ... 22 C2
St Aubin Jersey ... 17
St Austell ... 4 D5
St Bees ... 98 C1
St Blazey ... 5 D5
St Boswells ... 121 F8
St Brelade Jersey ... 17
St Breock ... 4 B4
St Breward ... 5 B5
St Briavels ... 36 D2
St Bride's ... 44 D3
St Brides Major. ... 21 B7
St Bride's Netherwent ... 35 F8
St Brides-super-Ely. ... 22 B2
St Brides Wentlooge. ... 35 F6
St Budeaux. ... 6 D2
Saintbury ... 51 F6
St Buryan ... 2 D3
St Catherine ... 24 B2
St Catherine's ... 125 E7
St Clears = Sanclêr . 32 C3
St Cleer ... 5 C7
St Clement ... 3 B7
St Clements Jersey ... 17
St Clether ... 8 F4
St Colmac ... 145 G9
St Columb Major ... 4 C4
St Columb Minor ... 4 C3
St Columb Road ... 4 D4
St Combs ... 153 B10
St Cross South Elmham ... 69 F5
St Cyrus ... 135 C7
St David's ... 127 B8
St David's = Tyddewi ... 44 C2
St Day ... 3 B6
St Dennis ... 4 D4
St Devereux ... 49 F6
St Dogmaels ... 45 E3
St Dogwells ... 44 C4
St Dominick ... 6 C2
St Donat's ... 21 C8
St Edith's ... 24 C4
St Endellion ... 4 B4
St Enoder ... 4 D3
St Erme ... 4 D3
St Erney ... 5 D8
St Erth ... 2 C4
St Ervan ... 4 B3
St Eval ... 4 C3
St Ewe ... 3 B8
St Fagans ... 22 B3
St Fergus ... 153 C10
St Fillans ... 127 B5
St Florence ... 32 D1
St Genny's ... 8 E3
St George ... 72 B3
St George's ... 22 B2
St Germans ... 5 D8
St Giles ... 78 B2
St Giles in the Wood ... 9 C7
St Giles on the Heath ... 9 E5
St Harmon ... 47 B8
St Helen Auckland ... 101 B6
St Helens IoW ... 15 F7
  Mers ... 86 E3
St Helen's ... 18 E5
St Helier Jersey ... 17
  London. ... 28 C3
St Hilary Corn ... 2 C4
  V Glam ... 22 B2
St Illtyd ... 35 D6
St Ippollytts ... 40 B4
St Ishmael's ... 44 E3
St Issey ... 4 B4
St Ive ... 5 C8
St Ives Cambs ... 54 B4
  Corn. ... 2 B4
  Dorset ... 14 D2
St James South Elmham ... 69 F6
St Jidgey ... 4 C4
St John ... 6 D2
St John's IoM ... 84 D2
  Jersey ... 17

St John's continued
  Sur. ... 27 D7
  Worcs ... 50 D3
St John's Chapel ... 109 F8
St John's Fen End ... 66 C5
St John's Highway. 66 C5
St John's Town of Dalry ... 113 F6
St Judes ... 84 C3
St Just ... 2 C2
St Just in Roseland . 3 C7
St Katherine's ... 153 E7
St Keverne ... 3 D6
St Kew ... 4 B5
St Kew Highway ... 4 B5
St Keyne ... 5 C7
St Lawrence Corn. ... 4 C5
  Essex ... 43 D5
  IoW ... 15 G6
St Leonards Dorset ... 14 D2
  E Sus. ... 18 E4
  S Lanark. ... 119 D6
St Leonard's ... 40 D2
St Levan ... 2 D2
St Lythans. ... 22 B3
St Mabyn. ... 4 B5
St Madoes ... 128 B3
St Margarets ... 41 C6
St Margaret's ... 49 F5
St Margaret's at Cliffe ... 31 E7
St Margaret's Hope ... 159 J5
St Margaret South Elmham ... 69 F6
St Mark's ... 84 E2
St Martin ... 5 D7
St Martins Corn ... 3 C7
  Perth ... 134 F1
St Martin's Jersey ... 17
  Shrops. ... 73 F7
St Mary Bourne ... 26 D2
St Mary Church. ... 22 B2
St Mary Cray ... 29 C5
St Mary Hill ... 21 B8
St Mary Hoo. ... 30 B2
St Mary in the Marsh ... 19 C7
St Mary's Jersey. ... 17
  Orkney. ... 159 H5
St Mary's Bay. ... 19 C7
St Maughans ... 36 C1
St Mawes ... 3 C7
St Mawgan ... 4 C3
St Mellion ... 6 C2
St Mellons ... 35 F6
St Merryn ... 4 B3
St Mewan ... 4 D4
St Michael Caerhays ... 3 B8
St Michael Penkevil 3 B7
St Michaels ... 49 C7
St Michael's ... 19 B5
St Michael's on Wyre ... 92 E4
St Michael South Elmham ... 69 F6
St Minver ... 4 B4
St Monans ... 129 D7
St Neot ... 5 C6
St Neots ... 54 C2
St Newlyn East ... 4 D3
St Nicholas Pembs. ... 44 B3
  V Glam ... 22 B2
St Nicholas at Wade. ... 31 C6
St Ninians ... 127 E6
St Osyth. ... 43 C7
St Osyth Heath ... 43 C7
St Ouens Jersey ... 17
St Owens Cross ... 36 B2
St Paul's Cray ... 29 C5
St Paul's Walden ... 40 B4
St Peter Port Guern. ... 16
St Peter's Jersey ... 17
  Kent. ... 31 C7
St Petrox ... 44 F4
St Pinnock ... 5 C7
St Quivox ... 112 B3
St Ruan ... 3 E6
St Sampson Guern. ... 16
St Stephen ... 4 D4
St Stephens Corn. ... 6 D2
  Herts ... 40 D4
St Stephen's ... 8 F5
St Teath ... 8 F2
St Thomas ... 10 E4
St Tudy ... 5 B5
St Twynnells ... 44 F4
St Veep. ... 5 D6
St Vigeans ... 135 E6
St Wenn ... 4 C4
St Weonards ... 36 B1
Salcombe. ... 6 F5
Salcombe Regis ... 11 F6
Salcott ... 43 C5
Sale ... 87 E5
Saleby ... 79 B7
Sale Green ... 50 D4
Salehurst ... 18 C4
Salem Carms ... 33 B7
  Ceredig ... 58 F3
Salen Argyll ... 147 G8
  Highld ... 147 E9
Salesbury ... 93 F6
Salford CBeds. ... 53 F7
  Gtr Man ... 87 E6
  Oxon ... 38 B2
Salford Priors ... 51 D5
Salfords ... 28 E3
Salhouse ... 69 C6
Saline ... 128 E2
Salisbury ... 14 B2
Sallachan ... 130 C3
Sallachy Highld. ... 150 H2
  Highld ... 157 J8
Salle. ... 81 E7
Salmonby ... 79 B6
Salmond's Muir . 135 F5
Salperton ... 37 B7
Salph End ... 53 D8
Salsburgh ... 119 C8
Salt. ... 62 B3
Saltaire ... 94 F4
Saltash ... 6 D2
Saltburn ... 151 E10
Saltburn-by-the-Sea ... 102 B4
Saltby ... 65 B5

Saltcoats Cumb. ... 98 E2
  N Ayrs ... 118 E2
Saltdean ... 17 D7
Salt End. ... 91 B5
Salter. ... 93 C6
Salterforth ... 93 E8
Saltfleet ... 91 E8
Saltfleetby All Saints ... 91 E8
Saltfleetby St Clements ... 91 E8
Saltfleetby St Peter ... 91 F8
Saltford ... 23 C8
Salthouse ... 81 C6
Saltmarshe ... 89 B8
Saltness ... 160 J4
Saltney ... 73 C7
Salton ... 96 B3
Saltwick ... 110 B4
Saltwood ... 19 B8
Salum ... 146 G3
Salvington ... 16 D5
Salwarpe ... 50 C3
Salwayash ... 12 E2
Sambourne ... 51 C5
Sambrook ... 61 B7
Samhla ... 148 B2
Samlesbury ... 93 F5
Samlesbury Bottoms ... 86 B4
Sampford Arundel. 11 C6
Sampford Brett. ... 22 E2
Sampford Courtenay ... 9 D8
Sampford Peverell 10 C5
Sampford Spiney ... 6 B3
Sampool Bridge. ... 99 F6
Samuelston ... 121 B7
Sanachan. ... 149 D13
Sanaigmore ... 142 A3
Sanclêr = St Clears. 32 C3
Sancreed ... 2 D3
Sancton ... 96 F5
Sand Highld ... 150 B2
  Shetland ... 160 J5
Sandaig. ... 149 H12
Sandale. ... 108 E2
Sandbach ... 74 C4
Sandbank ... 145 E10
Sandbanks ... 13 F8
Sandend ... 152 B5
Sanderstead ... 28 C4
Sandfields ... 37 B6
Sandford Cumb. ... 100 C2
  Devon ... 10 D3
  Dorset ... 13 F7
  IoW ... 15 F6
  N Som ... 23 D6
  Shrops. ... 74 F2
  Shrops. ... 61 B6
  S Lanark. ... 119 E7
Sandfordhill ... 153 D11
Sandford on Thames ... 39 D5
Sandford Orcas. ... 12 B4
Sandford St Martin 38 B4
Sandgate ... 19 B8
Sandgreen ... 106 D2
Sandhaven ... 153 B9
Sandhead ... 104 E4
Sandhills ... 27 F7
Sand Hole ... 96 F4
Sandholme EYorks ... 96 F4
  Lincs ... 79 F6
Sandhurst Brack. ... 27 C6
  Glos. ... 37 B5
  Kent. ... 18 C4
Sandhutton ... 102 F1
Sand Hutton ... 96 D2
Sandiacre ... 76 F4
Sandilands Lincs ... 91 F9
  S Lanark. ... 119 F8
Sandiway ... 74 B3
Sandleheath ... 14 C2
Sandling. ... 29 D8
Sandlow Green ... 74 C4
Sandness ... 160 H3
Sandon Essex ... 42 D3
  Herts ... 54 F4
  Staffs. ... 75 F6
Sandown ... 15 F6
Sandplace ... 5 D7
Sandridge Herts ... 40 C4
  Wilts ... 24 C4
Sandringham ... 67 B6
Sandsend ... 103 C6
Sandside House ... 157 C12
Sandsound ... 160 J5
Sandtoft ... 89 D8
Sandway ... 30 D2
Sandwell ... 62 F4
Sandwich ... 31 D7
Sandwick Cumb ... 99 C6
  Orkney. ... 159 K5
  Shetland ... 160 L6
Sandwith ... 98 C1
Sandy Carms ... 33 D5
  C Beds. ... 54 E2
Sandy Bank ... 79 D5
Sandycroft ... 73 C7
Sandyford Dumfries. ... 114 E5
  Stoke ... 75 D5
Sandygate ... 84 C3
Sandyhills ... 107 D5
Sandylands ... 92 C4
Sandy Lane Wilts ... 24 C4
  Wrex ... 73 E7
Sandypark ... 10 F2
Sangobeg ... 156 C7
Sangomore ... 156 C7
Sanna ... 146 E7
Sandbabhaig W Isles ... 148 D3
Sannox ... 143 D11
Sanquhar ... 113 D7
Santon ... 90 C3
Santon Bridge. ... 98 D3
Santon Downham ... 67 F8
Sapcote ... 63 E8
Sapey Common ... 50 C2

Sapiston ... 56 B3
Sapley ... 54 B3
Sapperton Glos. ... 37 D6
  Lincs ... 78 F3
Saracen's Head ... 66 B3
Sarclet. ... 158 F5
Sardis ... 33 D6
Sarn Bridgend ... 34 F3
  Powys ... 60 E2
Sarnau Carms ... 32 B4
  Ceredig ... 46 D2
  Gwyn. ... 72 F3
  Powys ... 48 F2
  Powys ... 60 C2
Sarn Bach ... 70 E4
Sarnesfield ... 49 D5
Sarn Meyllteyrn ... 70 D3
Saron Carms ... 33 C7
  Carms ... 46 F2
  Denb ... 72 C4
  Gwyn. ... 82 E5
  Gwyn. ... 82 E4
Sarratt ... 40 E3
Sarre ... 31 C6
Sarsden ... 38 B2
Sarsgrum ... 156 C6
Satley ... 110 E4
Satron ... 100 E4
Satterleigh. ... 9 B8
Satterthwaite ... 99 E5
Satwell ... 39 F7
Sauchen ... 141 C5
Saucher ... 134 F1
Sauchie ... 127 E7
Sauchieburn ... 135 C6
Saughall ... 73 B7
Saughtree ... 115 E8
Saul ... 36 D4
Saundby ... 89 F8
Saundersfoot ... 32 D2
Saunderton ... 39 D7
Saunton ... 20 F3
Sausthorpe ... 79 C6
Saval ... 157 J8
Savary ... 147 G9
Savile Park. ... 87 B8
Sawbridge ... 52 C3
Sawbridgeworth ... 41 C7
Sawdon. ... 103 F7
Sawley Derbys ... 76 F4
  Lancs. ... 93 E7
  N Yorks. ... 94 C5
Sawston ... 55 E5
Sawtry. ... 65 F8
Saxby Leics. ... 64 C5
  Lincs ... 90 F4
Saxby All Saints ... 90 C3
Saxelby ... 64 B3
Saxham Street ... 56 C4
Saxilby. ... 77 B8
Saxlingham ... 81 D6
Saxlingham Green. 68 E5
Saxlingham Nethergate ... 68 E5
Saxlingham Thorpe ... 68 E5
Saxmundham ... 57 C7
Saxondale ... 77 F6
Saxon Street ... 55 D7
Saxtead ... 57 C6
Saxtead Green ... 57 C6
Saxthorpe ... 81 D7
Saxton ... 95 F7
Sayers Common ... 17 C6
Scackleton ... 96 B2
Scadabhagh ... 154 H6
Scaftworth. ... 89 E7
Scagglethorpe ... 96 B4
Scalasaig ... 144 D2
Scalby E Yorks ... 90 B2
  N Yorks. ... 103 E8
Scaldwell ... 53 B5
Scale Houses. ... 108 E5
Scales Cumb ... 92 B2
  Cumb. ... 99 B5
  Lancs. ... 92 F4
Scalford ... 64 B4
Scaling ... 103 C5
Scallastle ... 124 B2
Scalloway ... 160 K6
Scalpay ... 154 H7
Scalpay House ... 149 F11
Scalpsie ... 145 H9
Scamadale ... 147 B10
Scamblesby ... 79 B5
Scamodale ... 130 B2
Scampston ... 96 B4
Scampton ... 78 B2
Scapa. ... 159 H5
Scapegoat Hill ... 87 C8
Scar ... 159 D7
Scarborough ... 103 F8
Scarcliffe ... 76 C4
Scarcroft ... 95 E6
Scarcroft Hill ... 95 E6
Scardroy. ... 150 F5
Scarff. ... 160 E4
Scarfskerry ... 158 C4
Scargill ... 101 C5
Scarinish ... 146 G3
Scarisbrick ... 85 C4
Scarning ... 68 C2
Scarrington ... 77 E7
Scartho ... 91 D6
Scarwell ... 159 F3
Scatness ... 160 M5
Scatraig ... 151 H10
Scawby ... 90 D3
Scawsby ... 89 D6
Scawton ... 102 F3
Scayne's Hill ... 17 B7
Scethrog ... 35 B5
Scholar Green ... 74 D5
Scholes W Yorks ... 88 B2
  W Yorks ... 88 D2
  W Yorks ... 95 F6
School Green ... 74 C3
Scleddau ... 44 B4
Scofton ... 89 F7
Scole ... 56 B5
Scolpaig ... 148 A2
Scone ... 128 B3
Sconser ... 149 E10
Scoonie ... 129 D5
Scoor ... 146 K7
Scopwick ... 78 D3

Scoraig ... 150 B3
Scorborough. ... 97 E6
Scorrier ... 3 B6
Scorton Lancs. ... 92 E5
  N Yorks. ... 101 D7
Sco Ruston ... 81 E8
Scotbheinn ... 148 C3
Scotby. ... 108 D4
Scotch Corner ... 101 D7
Scotforth ... 92 D4
Scothern. ... 78 B3
Scotland Gate ... 117 F8
Scotlandwell ... 128 D3
Scotsburn. ... 151 D10
Scotscalder Station ... 158 E2
Scotscraig ... 129 B6
Scot's Gap ... 117 F6
Scotston Aberds. ... 135 B7
  Perth ... 133 E6
Scotstoun. ... 118 C5
Scotstown ... 130 C2
Scotswood ... 110 C4
Scottas ... 149 H12
Scotter ... 90 D2
Scotterthorpe. ... 90 D2
Scottlethorpe ... 65 B7
Scotton Lincs ... 90 E2
  N Yorks. ... 95 D6
  N Yorks. ... 101 E6
Scottow ... 81 E8
Scoughall ... 129 F8
Scoulag ... 145 H10
Scoulton ... 68 D2
Scourie ... 156 E4
Scourie More ... 156 E4
Scousburgh ... 160 M5
Scrabster ... 158 C2
Scrafield. ... 79 C6
Scrainwood ... 117 D5
Scrane End ... 79 E6
Scraptoft ... 64 D3
Scratby ... 69 C8
Scrayingham ... 96 C3
Scredington ... 78 E3
Scremby ... 79 C7
Scremerston ... 123 E6
Screveton ... 77 E7
Scrivelsby. ... 79 C5
Scriven ... 95 D6
Scrooby ... 89 E7
Scropton ... 75 F8
Scrub Hill ... 78 D5
Scruton ... 101 E7
Sculcoates ... 97 F6
Sculthorpe. ... 80 D4
Scunthorpe ... 90 C2
Scurlage ... 33 F5
Seaborough ... 12 D2
Seacombe ... 85 E4
Seacroft Lincs. ... 79 C8
  W Yorks. ... 95 F6
Seadyke ... 79 F6
Seafield S Ayrs ... 112 B3
  W Loth ... 120 C3
Seaford ... 17 E8
Seaforth ... 85 E4
Seagrave ... 64 C3
Seaham. ... 111 E7
Seahouses ... 123 F8
Seal ... 29 D6
Sealand ... 73 C7
Seale ... 27 E6
Seamer NYorks. ... 102 C2
  N Yorks. ... 103 F8
Sea Palling ... 69 B7
Searby ... 90 D4
Seasalter ... 30 C4
Seascale ... 98 D2
Seathorne ... 79 C8
Seathwaite Cumb. ... 98 C4
  Cumb. ... 98 E4
Seatoller ... 98 C4
Seaton Corn ... 5 D8
  Cumb. ... 107 F7
  Devon ... 11 F7
  Durham ... 111 D6
  E Yorks. ... 97 E7
  Northumb ... 111 B6
  Rutland ... 65 E6
Seaton Burn ... 110 B5
Seaton Carew ... 102 B3
Seaton Delaval ... 111 B6
Seaton Ross ... 96 E3
Seaton Sluice ... 111 B6
Seatown Aberds. ... 152 B5
  Dorset ... 12 E2
Seave Green ... 102 D3
Seaview ... 15 E7
Seaville ... 107 D8
Seavington St Mary ... 12 C2
Seavington St Michael ... 12 C2
Sebergham ... 108 E3
Seckington ... 63 D6
Second Coast ... 150 B2
Sedbergh ... 100 E1
Sedbury ... 36 E2
Sedbusk ... 100 E3
Seddington ... 54 E2
Sedgeberrow ... 50 F5
Sedgebrook ... 77 F8
Sedgefield ... 102 B1
Sedgeford ... 80 D3
Sedgehill ... 13 B6
Sedgley ... 62 E3
Sedgwick ... 99 F7
Sedlescombe ... 18 D4
Sedlescombe Street ... 18 D4
Seend ... 24 C4
Seend Cleeve ... 24 C4
Seer Green ... 40 E2
Seething ... 69 E6
Sefton ... 85 D4
Seghill ... 111 B5
Seifton ... 60 F4
Seighford ... 62 B2
Seilebost ... 154 H5
Seion ... 82 E5
Seisdon ... 62 E2
Seisiadar ... 155 D10
Selattyn ... 73 F6
Selborne. ... 26 F5
Selby ... 96 F2

Selham 16 B3
Selhurst 28 C4
Selkirk 115 B7
Sellack 36 B2
Sellafirth 160 D7
Sellindge 19 F7
Sellindge Lees 19 B8
Selling 30 D4
Sells Green 24 C4
Selly Oak 62 F4
Selmeston 18 E2
Selsdon 28 C4
Selsey 16 E2
Selsfield Common 28 F4
Selsted 31 E6
Selston 76 D4
Selworthy 21 E8
Semblister 160 H5
Semer 56 E3
Semington 24 C3
Semley 13 B6
Send 27 D8
Send Marsh 27 D8
Senghenydd 35 E5
Sennen 2 D2
Sennen Cove 2 D2
Sennybridge = *Pont Senni* 34 B3
Serlby 89 F7
Sessay 95 B7
Setchey 67 C6
Setley 14 D4
Setter *Shetland* 160 E6
Setter *Shetland* 160 H5
Setter *Shetland* 160 J7
Settiscarth 159 G4
Settle 93 C8
Settrington 96 B4
Sevenhampton 37 B7
Seven Kings 41 F7
Sevenoaks 29 D6
Sevenoaks Weald 29 D6
Seven Sisters 34 D2
Severn Beach 36 F2
Severnhampton 38 E2
Severn Stoke 50 E3
Sevington 30 E4
Sewards End 55 F6
Sewardstone 41 E6
Sewardstonebury 41 E6
Sewerby 97 C7
Seworgan 3 C6
Sewstern 65 B5
Sezincote 51 F6
Sgarasta Mhor 154 H5
Sgiogarstaigh 155 A10
Shabbington 39 D6
Shackerstone 63 D7
Shackleford 27 E7
Shade 87 B7
Shadforth 111 E6
Shadingfield 69 F7
Shadoxhurst 19 B6
Shadsworth 86 B5
Shadwell *Norf* 68 F2
Shadwell *W Yorks* 95 F6
Shaftesbury 13 B6
Shafton 88 C4
Shalbourne 25 C8
Shalcombe 14 F4
Shalden 26 E4
Shaldon 7 B7
Shalfleet 14 F5
Shalford *Essex* 42 B3
Shalford *Sur* 27 E8
Shalford Green 42 B3
Shallowford 21 E6
Shalmsford Street 30 D4
Shalstone 52 F4
Shamley Green 27 E8
Shandon 145 E11
Shandwick 151 D11
Shangton 64 E4
Shankhouse 111 B5
Shanklin 15 F6
Shanquhar 152 E5
Shanzie 134 D2
Shap 99 C7
Shapwick *Dorset* 13 D7
Shapwick *Som* 23 F6
Shardlow 76 F4
Shareshill 62 D3
Sharlston 88 C4
Sharlston Common 88 C4
Sharnbrook 53 D7
Sharnford 63 E8
Sharoe Green 92 F5
Sharow 95 B6
Sharpenhoe 53 F8
Sharperton 117 D5
Sharpness 36 D3
Sharp Street 69 B6
Sharpthorne 28 F4
Sharrington 81 D6
Shatterford 61 F7
Shaugh Prior 6 C3
Shavington 74 D4
Shaw *Gtr Man* 87 D7
Shaw *W Berks* 26 C2
Shaw *Wilts* 24 C3
Shawbury 61 B5
Shawdon Hall 117 C6
Shawell 64 F2
Shawford 15 B5
Shawforth 87 B6
Shaw Green 86 C3
Shawhead 107 B5
Shawhill 108 C2
Shaw Mills 95 C5
Shawton 119 E6
Shawtonhill 119 E6
Shear Cross 24 E3
Shearington 107 C7
Shearsby 64 E3
Shebbear 9 D6
Shebdon 61 B7
Shebster 157 C13
Sheddens 119 D5
Shedfield 15 C6
Sheen 75 C8
Sheepscar 95 F6
Sheepscombe 37 C5
Sheepstor 6 C3
Sheepwash 9 D6

Sheepway 23 B6
Sheepy Magna 63 D7
Sheepy Parva 63 D7
Sheering 41 C8
Sheerness 30 B3
Sheet 15 B8
Sheffield 88 F4
Sheffield Bottom 26 C4
Sheffield Green 17 B8
Shefford 54 F2
Shefford Woodlands 25 B8
Sheigra 156 C4
Sheinton 61 D6
Shelderton 49 B6
Sheldon *Derbys* 75 C8
Sheldon *Devon* 11 D6
Sheldon *W Mid* 63 F5
Sheldwich 30 D4
Shelf 88 B2
Shelfanger 68 F4
Shelfield *Warks* 51 C6
Shelfield *W Mid* 62 D4
Shelford 77 E6
Shellacres 122 E4
Shelley *Essex* 42 D1
Shelley *Suff* 56 F4
Shelley *W Yorks* 88 C3
Shellingford 38 E3
Shellow Bowells 42 D2
Shelsley Beauchamp 50 C2
Shelsley Walsh 50 C2
Shelthorpe 64 C2
Shelton *Bedford* 53 C8
Shelton *Norf* 68 E5
Shelton *Notts* 77 E7
Shelton *Shrops* 60 C4
Shelton Green 68 E5
Shelve 60 E3
Shelwick 49 E7
Shenfield 42 E2
Shenington 51 E8
Shenley 40 D4
Shenley Brook End 53 F6
Shenleybury 40 D4
Shenley Church End 53 F6
Shenmore 49 F5
Shennanton 105 C7
Shenstone *Staffs* 62 D5
Shenstone *Worcs* 50 B3
Shenton 63 D7
Shenval *Highld* 137 B7
Shenval *Moray* 139 B8
Shepeau Stow 66 C3
Shephall 41 B5
Shepherd's Green 39 F7
Shepherd's Port 80 D2
Shepherdswell 31 E6
Shepley 88 D2
Shepperdine 36 E3
Shepperton 27 C8
Shepreth 54 E4
Shepshed 63 C8
Shepton Beauchamp 12 C2
Shepton Mallet 23 E8
Shepton Montague 23 F8
Shepway 29 D8
Sheraton 111 F7
Sherborne *Dorset* 12 C4
Sherborne *Glos* 38 C1
Sherborne St John 26 D4
Sherbourne 51 C7
Sherburn *Durham* 111 E6
Sherburn *N Yorks* 97 B5
Sherburn Hill 111 E6
Sherburn in Elmet 95 F7
Shere 27 E8
Shereford 80 E4
Sherfield English 14 B3
Sherfield on Loddon 26 D4
Sherford 7 E5
Sheriffhales 61 C7
Sheriff Hutton 96 C2
Sheringham 81 C7
Sherington 53 E6
Shernal Green 50 C4
Shernborne 80 D3
Sherrington 24 F4
Sherston 37 F5
Sherwood Green 9 B7
Shettleston 119 C6
Shevington 86 D3
Shevington Moor 86 C3
Shevington Vale 86 D3
Sheviock 5 D8
Shide 15 F5
Shiel Bridge 136 C2
Shieldaig *Highld* 149 A13
Shieldaig *Highld* 149 C13
Shieldhill *Dumfries* 114 F3
Shieldhill *Falk* 119 B8
Shieldhill *S Lanark* 120 E3
Shielfoot 147 F9
Shielhill *Angus* 134 D4
Shielhill *Invclyd* 118 B2
Shifford 38 D3
Shifnal 61 D7
Shilbottle 117 D7
Shildon 101 B7
Shillingford *Devon* 10 B4
Shillingford *Oxon* 39 E5
Shillingford St George 10 F4
Shillingstone 13 C6
Shillington 54 F2
Shillmoor 116 D4
Shilton *Oxon* 38 D2
Shilton *Warks* 63 F8
Shilvington 117 F7
Shimpling *Norf* 68 F4
Shimpling *Suff* 56 D2
Shimpling Street 56 D2
Shincliffe 111 E5
Shiney Row 111 D6
Shinfield 26 C5
Shingham 67 D7
Shingle Street 57 E7
Shinner's Bridge 7 C5
Shinness 157 H8
Shipbourne 29 D6
Shipdham 68 D2
Shipham 23 D6
Shiphay 7 C6
Shiplake 27 B5

Shipley *Derbys* 76 E4
Shipley *Northumb* 117 C7
Shipley *Shrops* 62 E2
Shipley *W Sus* 16 B5
Shipley *W Yorks* 94 F4
Shipley Shiels 116 E3
Shipmeadow 69 F6
Shippea Hill Station 67 F6
Shippon 38 E4
Shipston-on-Stour 51 E7
Shipton *Glos* 37 C7
Shipton *N Yorks* 95 D8
Shipton *Shrops* 61 E5
Shipton Bellinger 25 E7
Shipton Gorge 12 E2
Shipton Green 16 D2
Shipton Moyne 37 F5
Shipton on Cherwell 38 C4
Shipton Solers 37 C7
Shiptonthorpe 96 E4
Shipton-under-Wychwood 38 C2
Shirburn 39 E6
Shirdley Hill 85 C4
Shirebrook 76 C5
Shiregreen 88 E4
Shirehampton 23 B7
Shiremoor 111 B6
Shirenewton 36 E1
Shireoaks 89 F6
Shirkoak 19 B6
Shirland 76 D3
Shirley *Derbys* 76 E2
Shirley *London* 28 C4
Shirley *Soton* 14 C5
Shirley *W Mid* 51 B6
Shirl Heath 49 D6
Shirrell Heath 15 C6
Shirwell 20 F4
Shirwell Cross 20 F4
Shiskine 143 F10
Shobdon 49 C6
Shobnall 63 B6
Shobrooke 10 D3
Shoby 64 C3
Shocklach 73 E8
Shoeburyness 43 F5
Sholden 31 D7
Sholing 14 C5
Shoot Hill 60 C4
Shop *Corn* 4 B3
Shop *Corn* 8 C4
Shop Corner 57 F6
Shoreditch 41 F6
Shoresdean 123 E5
Shoreswood 122 E5
Shoreton 151 E9
Shorncote 37 E7
Shorne 29 B7
Shortacombe 9 F7
Shortgate 17 C8
Short Heath 62 D3
Shortlanesend 3 B7
Shortlees 118 F4
Shortstown 53 E8
Shorwell 15 F5
Shoscombe 24 D2
Shotatton 60 B3
Shotesham 69 E5
Shotgate 42 E3
Shotley 57 F6
Shotley Bridge 110 D3
Shotleyfield 110 D3
Shotley Gate 57 F6
Shottenden 30 D4
Shottermill 27 F6
Shottery 51 D6
Shotteswell 52 E2
Shottisham 57 E7
Shottle 76 E3
Shottlegate 76 E3
Shotton *Durham* 111 F7
Shotton *Flint* 73 C7
Shotton *Northumb* 122 F4
Shotton Colliery 111 E6
Shotts 119 C8
Shotwick 73 B7
Shouldham 67 D6
Shouldham Thorpe 67 D6
Shoulton 50 D3
Shoulton 50 D3
Shover's Green 18 B3
Shrawardine 60 C4
Shrawley 50 C3
Shrewley Common 51 C7
Shrewsbury 60 C4
Shrewton 25 E5
Shripney 16 D3
Shrivenham 38 F2
Shropham 68 E2
Shrub End 43 B5
Shucknall 49 E7
Shudy Camps 55 E7
Shulishadermor 149 D9
Shurdington 37 C6
Shurlock Row 27 B6
Shurrery 157 D13
Shurrery Lodge 157 D13
Shurton 22 E4
Shustoke 63 E6
Shute *Devon* 10 D3
Shute *Devon* 11 E7
Shutford 51 E8
Shuthonger 50 F3
Shutlanger 52 D5
Shuttington 63 D6
Shuttlewood 76 B4

Sibbertoft 64 F3
Sibdon Carwood 60 F4
Sibford Ferris 51 F8
Sibford Gower 51 F8
Sible Hedingham 55 F8
Sibsey 79 D6
Sibson *Cambs* 65 E7
Sibson *Leics* 63 D7
Sibthorpe 77 E7
Sibton 57 C7
Sibton Green 57 B7
Sicklesmere 56 C2
Sicklinghall 95 E6
Sid 11 F6
Sidbury *Devon* 11 E6
Sidbury *Shrops* 61 F6
Sidcot 23 D6
Sidcup 29 B5
Siddick 107 F7
Siddington *Ches E* 74 B5
Siddington *Glos* 37 E7
Sidemoor 50 B4
Sidestrand 81 D8
Sidford 11 E6
Sidlesham 16 E2
Sidley 18 E4
Sidlow 28 E3
Sidmouth 11 F6
Sigford 7 B5
Sigglesthorne 97 E7
Sighthill 120 B4
Sigingstone 21 B8
Signet 38 C2
Silchester 26 C4
Sildinis 155 F7
Sileby 64 C2
Silecroft 98 F3
Silfield 68 E4
Silian 46 D4
Silkstone 88 D3
Silkstone Common 88 D3
Silk Willoughby 78 E3
Silloth 107 D8
Sills 116 D4
Sillyearn 152 C5
Siloh 47 F6
Silpho 103 E7
Silsden 94 E3
Silsoe 53 F8
Silverburn 120 C5
Silverdale *Lancs* 92 B4
Silverdale *Staffs* 74 E5
Silver End 42 C4
Silvergate 81 E7
Silverhill 18 D4
Silverley's Green 57 B6
Silverstone 52 E4
Silverton 10 D4
Silvington 49 B8
Silwick 160 J4
Simmondley 87 E8
Simonburn 109 B8
Simonsbath 21 F6
Simonstone 93 F7
Simprim 122 E4
Simpson 53 F6
Simpson Cross 44 D3
Sinclair's Hill 122 D4
Sinclairston 112 C4
Sinderby 101 F8
Sinderhope 109 D8
Sindlesham 27 C5
Singdean 115 D8
Singleborough 53 F5
Singleton *Lancs* 92 F3
Singleton *W Sus* 16 C2
Singlewell 29 B7
Sinkhurst Green 30 E2
Sinnahard 140 C3
Sinnington 103 F5
Sinton Green 50 C3
Sipson 27 B8
Sirhowy 35 C5
Sisland 69 E6
Sissinghurst 18 B4
Sisterpath 122 E3
Siston 23 B8
Sithney 2 D5
Sittingbourne 30 C2
Six Ashes 61 F7
Sixhills 91 F5
Six Hills 64 B3
Six Mile Bottom 55 D6
Sixpenny Handley 13 C7
Sizewell 57 C8
Skail 157 E10
Skaill *Orkney* 159 E5
Skaill *Orkney* 159 G3
Skaill *Orkney* 159 H6
Skares 113 C5
Skateraw 122 B3
Skaw 160 G7
Skeabost 149 D9
Skeabrae 159 F3
Skeeby 101 D7
Skeffington 64 D4
Skeffling 91 C7
Skegby 76 C4
Skegness 79 C8
Skelberry 160 M5
Skelbo 151 B10
Skelbrooke 89 C6
Skeldyke 79 F6
Skellingthorpe 78 B2
Skellister 160 H6
Skellow 89 C6
Skelmanthorpe 88 C3
Skelmersdale 86 D2
Skelmonae 153 E8
Skelmorlie 118 C1
Skelmuir 153 D9
Skelpick 157 D10
Skelton *Cumb* 108 F4
Skelton *E Yorks* 89 B8
Skelton *N Yorks* 101 D5
Skelton *Redcar* 102 C4
Skelton *York* 95 D8
Skelton-on-Ure 95 C6
Skelwick 159 D5
Skelwith Bridge 99 D5
Skendleby 79 C7
Skene House 141 D6
Skenfrith 36 B1
Skerne 97 D6
Skeroblingarry 143 F8
Skerray 157 C9
Skerton 92 C4
Sketchley 63 E8
Sketty 33 E7
Skewen 33 E8
Skewsby 96 B2
Skeyton 81 E8
Skiag Bridge 156 G5
Skibo Castle 151 C10
Skidbrooke 91 E8

Skidbrooke North End 91 E8
Skidby 97 F6
Skilgate 10 B4
Skillington 65 B5
Skinburness 107 D8
Skinflats 127 F8
Skinidin 148 D7
Skinnet 157 C8
Skinningrove 103 B5
Skipness 145 H7
Skippool 92 E3
Skipsea 97 D7
Skipsea Brough 97 D7
Skipton 94 D2
Skipton-on-Swale 95 B6
Skipwith 96 F2
Skirbeck 79 E6
Skirbeck Quarter 79 E6
Skirlaugh 97 F7
Skirling 120 F3
Skirmett 39 F7
Skirpenbeck 96 D3
Skirwith 109 F6
Skirza 158 D5
Skulamus 149 F11
Skullomie 157 C9
Skyborry Green 48 B4
Skye of Curr 139 B5
Skyreholme 94 C3
Slackhall 87 F8
Slackhead 152 B4
Slad 37 D5
Slade *Devon* 20 E4
Slade *Pembs* 44 D4
Slade Green 29 B6
Slaggyford 109 D6
Slaidburn 93 D7
Slaithwaite 87 C8
Slaley 110 D2
Slamannan 119 B8
Slapton *Bucks* 40 B2
Slapton *Devon* 7 E6
Slapton *Northants* 52 E4
Slatepit Dale 76 C3
Slattocks 87 D6
Slaugham 17 B6
Slaughterford 24 B3
Slawston 64 E4
Sleaford *Hants* 27 F6
Sleaford *Lincs* 78 E3
Sleagill 99 C7
Sleapford 61 C6
Sledge Green 50 F3
Sledmere 96 C5
Sleightholme 100 C4
Sleights 103 D6
Slepe 13 E7
Slickly 158 D4
Sliddery 143 F10
Sligachan Hotel 149 F9
Slimbridge 36 D4
Slindon *Staffs* 74 F5
Slindon *W Sus* 16 D3
Slinfold 28 F2
Sling 83 E6
Slingsby 96 B2
Slioch 152 E5
Slip End *C Beds* 40 C3
Slip End *Herts* 54 F3
Slipton 53 B7
Slitting Mill 62 C4
Slochd 138 B4
Slockavullin 124 F4
Sloley 81 E8
Sloothby 79 B7
Slough 27 B7
Slough Green 17 B6
Sluggan 138 B4
Slumbay 149 E13
Slyfield 27 D7
Slyne 92 C4
Smailholm 122 F2
Small Dole 17 C6
Smalley 76 E4
Smallfield 28 E4
Small Hythe 19 B5
Smallridge 11 D8
Smannell 25 E8
Smardale 100 D2
Smarden 30 E2
Smarden Bell 30 E2
Smeatharpe 11 C6
Smeeth 19 B7
Smeeton Westerby 64 E3
Smercleit 148 G2
Smerral 158 G3
Smethwick 62 F4
Smirisary 147 D9
Smisby 63 C7
Smith Green 92 D4
Smithincott 11 C5
Smith's Green 42 B1
Smithston 151 G10
Smithstown 149 A12
Smithton 151 G10
Smithy Green 74 B4
Smockington 63 F8
Smoogro 159 H4
Smythe's Green 43 C5
Snaigow House 133 E7
Snailbeach 60 D3
Snailwell 55 C7
Snainton 103 F7
Snaith 89 B7
Snape *N Yorks* 101 F7
Snape *Suff* 57 D7
Snape Green 85 C4
Snarestone 63 D7
Snarford 90 F4
Snargate 19 C6
Snave 19 C7
Snead 60 E3
Sneath Common 68 F4
Sneaton 103 D6
Sneatonthorpe 103 D7
Snelland 90 F4
Snelston 75 E8
Snettisham 80 D2
Snibston 63 C8
Sniseabhal 148 E2
Snitter 117 D6
Snitterby 90 E3
Snitterfield 51 D7
Snitton 49 B7

Snodhill 48 E5
Snodland 29 C7
Snowden Hill 88 D3
Snowdown 31 D6
Snowshill 51 F5
Snydale 88 C5
Soar *Anglesey* 82 D3
Soar *Carms* 33 B7
Soar *Devon* 6 F5
Soar-y-Mynydd 47 D6
Soberton 15 C7
Soberton Heath 15 C7
Sockbridge 99 B7
Sockburn 101 D8
Soham 55 B6
Soham Cotes 55 B6
Solas 148 A3
Soldon Cross 8 C5
Soldridge 26 F4
Sole Street *Kent* 29 C7
Sole Street *Kent* 30 E4
Solihull 51 B6
Sollers Dilwyn 49 D6
Sollers Hope 49 F8
Sollom 86 C2
Solva 44 C2
Somerby *Leics* 64 C4
Somerby *Lincs* 90 D4
Somercotes 76 D4
Somerford 14 E2
Somerford Keynes 37 E7
Somerley 16 E2
Somerleyton 69 E7
Somersal Herbert 75 F8
Somersby 79 B6
Somersham *Cambs* 54 B4
Somersham *Suff* 56 E4
Somerton *Oxon* 38 B4
Somerton *Som* 12 B2
Sompting 17 D5
Sonning 27 B5
Sonning Common 39 F7
Sonning Eye 27 B5
Sontley 73 E7
Sopley 14 E2
Sopwell 40 D4
Sopworth 37 F5
Sorbie 105 E8
Sordale 158 D3
Sorisdale 146 E5
Sorn 113 B5
Sornhill 118 F5
Sortat 158 D4
Sotby 78 B5
Sots Hole 78 C4
Sotterley 69 F7
Soudley 61 B7
Soughton 73 C6
Soulbury 40 B1
Soulby 100 C2
Souldern 52 F3
Souldrop 53 C7
Sound *Ches E* 74 E3
Sound *Shetland* 160 H5
Sound *Shetland* 160 J6
Sound Heath 74 E3
Soundwell 23 B8
Sourhope 116 B4
Sourin 159 E5
Sourton 9 E7
Soutergate 98 F4
South Acre 67 C8
Southall 40 F4
South Allington 7 F5
South Alloa 127 E7
Southam *Glos* 37 B6
Southam *Warks* 52 C2
South Ambersham 16 B3
Southampton 14 C5
South Anston 89 F6
South Ascot 27 C7
South Ballachulish 130 D4
South Balloch 112 E3
South Bank 102 B3
South Barrow 12 B4
South Beach 70 D4
South Benfleet 42 F3
Southborough 29 E6
Southbourne *BCP* 14 E2
Southbourne *W Sus* 15 D8
South Brent 6 C4
South Brewham 24 F2
South Broomhill 117 E8
Southburgh 68 D2
South Burlingham 69 D6
Southburn 97 D5
South Cadbury 12 B4
South Cairn 104 C3
South Carlton 78 B2
South Cave 96 F5
South Cerney 37 E7
South Chard 11 D8
South Charlton 117 B7
South Cheriton 12 B4
Southchurch 43 F5
South Cliffe 96 F4
South Clifton 77 B8
South Cockerington 91 F7
South Cornelly 34 F2
Southcott 25 D6
Southcourt 39 C8
South Cove 69 F7
South Creagan 130 E3
South Creake 80 D4
South Croxton 64 C3
South Croydon 28 C4
South Dalton 97 E5
South Darenth 29 C6
Southdean 116 D2
Southease 17 D8
South Elkington 91 F6
South Elmsall 89 C5
South End *Bucks* 40 B1
South End *N Lincs* 90 B5
Southend *Argyll* 143 H7
Southend *W Berks* 26 B3
Southend *Wilts* 25 B6
Southend-on-Sea 42 F4
Southernden 30 E2
Southerndown 21 B7
Southerness 107 D6
South Erradale 149 A12
Southery 67 E6

South Fambridge 42 E4
South Fawley 38 F3
South Ferriby 90 B3
Southfleet 29 B7
South Garth 160 D7
South Garvan 130 B3
Southgate *Ceredig* 46 B4
Southgate *London* 41 E5
Southgate *Norf* 81 E7
Southgate *Swansea* 33 F6
South Glendale 148 G2
South Godstone 28 E4
South Gorley 14 C2
South Green *Essex* 42 E2
South Green *Kent* 30 C2
South Hanningfield 42 E3
South Harting 15 C8
South Hatfield 41 D5
South Hayling 15 E8
South Hazelrigg 123 F6
South Heath 40 D2
South Heighton 17 D8
South Hetton 111 E6
South Hiendley 88 C4
South Hill 5 B8
South Hinksey 39 D5
South Holme 96 B2
South Holmwood 28 E2
South Hornchurch 41 F8
South Hykeham 78 C2
South Hylton 111 D6
South Kelsey 90 E4
South Kessock 151 G9
South Killingholme 91 C5
South Kilvington 102 F1
South Kilworth 64 F3
South Kirkby 89 C5
South Kirkton 141 D6
South Kiscadale 143 F11
South Kyme 78 E4
South Lancing 17 D5
South Leverton 89 F8
South Littleton 51 E5
South Lopham 68 F3
South Luffenham 65 D6
South Malling 17 C8
South Marston 38 F1
South Middleton 117 B5
South Milford 95 F7
South Millbrex 153 D8
South Milton 6 E5
South Mimms 41 D5
Southminster 43 E5
South Molton 10 B2
Southmoor 38 E3
South Moreton 39 F5
South Mundham 16 D2
South Muskham 77 D7
South Newbald 96 F5
South Newington 52 F2
South Newton 25 F5
South Normanton 76 D4
South Norwood 28 C4
South Nutfield 28 E4
South Ockendon 42 F1
Southoe 54 C2
Southolt 57 C5
South Ormsby 79 B6
Southorpe 65 D7
South Otterington 102 F1
South Owersby 90 E4
Southowram 88 B2
South Oxhey 40 E4
South Perrott 12 D2
South Petherton 12 C2
South Petherwin 8 F5
South Pickenham 67 D8
South Pool 7 E5
Southport 85 C4
South Port 125 C6
Southpunds 160 L6
South Radworthy 21 F6
South Rauceby 78 E3
South Raynham 80 E4
Southrepps 81 D8
South Reston 91 F8
Southrey 78 C4
Southrop 38 D1
Southrope 26 E4
South Runcton 67 D6
South Scarle 77 C8
Southsea 15 E7
South Shian 130 E3
South Shields 111 C6
South Shore 92 F3
South Somercotes 91 E8
South Stainley 95 C6
South Stainmore 100 C3
South Stifford 29 B7
South Stoke *Oxon* 39 F5
South Stoke *W Sus* 16 D4
South Street *E Sus* 17 C7
South Street *Kent* 30 C5
South Street *Kent* 30 D5
South Street *London* 28 D5
South Tawton 9 E8
South Thoresby 79 B7
South Tidworth 25 E7
Southtown *Norf* 69 D8
Southtown *Orkney* 159 J5
South Town 26 F4
South View 26 D4
Southwaite 108 E4
South Walsham 69 C6
Southwark 28 B4
South Warnborough 26 E5
Southwater 17 B5
Southwater Street 17 B5
Southway 23 E7
Southwell *Dorset* 12 G4
Southwell *Notts* 77 D7
South Weston 39 E7
South Wheatley *Corn* 8 E4
South Wheatley *Notts* 89 F8
Southwick *Hants* 15 D7
Southwick *N Hants* 65 E7
Southwick *T&W* 111 D6
Southwick *Wilts* 24 D3
Southwick *W Sus* 17 D6
South Widcombe 23 D7
South Wigston 64 E2
South Willingham 91 F5
South Wingfield 76 D3
South Witham 65 C6
Southwold 57 B9
South Wonston 26 F2
Southwood *Norf* 69 D6
Southwood *Som* 23 F7
South Woodham Ferrers 42 E4
South Wootton 67 B6
South Wraxall 24 C3
South Zeal 9 E8
Soval Lodge 155 E8
Sowber Gate 102 F1
Sowerby *N Yorks* 102 F2
Sowerby *W Yorks* 87 B8
Sowerby Bridge 88 B3
Sowerby Row 108 F3
Sowood 87 C8
Sowton 10 E4
Soyal 151 B8
Spacey Houses 95 D6
Spadeadam Farm 109 B5
Spalding 66 B2
Spaldington 96 F3
Spaldwick 54 B2
Spalford 77 C8
Spanby 78 F3
Sparham 68 C3
Spark Bridge 99 F5
Sparkford 12 B4
Sparkhill 62 F4
Sparkwell 6 D3
Sparrow Green 68 C2
Sparrowpit 87 F8
Sparsholt *Hants* 26 F2
Sparsholt *Oxon* 38 F3
Spartylea 109 E8
Spaunton 103 F5
Spaxton 22 F4
Spean Bridge 136 F5
Spear Hill 16 C5
Speen *Bucks* 39 E8
Speen *W Berks* 26 C2
Speeton 97 B7
Speke 86 F2
Speldhurst 29 E6
Spellbrook 41 C7
Spelsbury 38 B3
Spelter 34 E2
Spencers Wood 26 C5
Spennithorne 101 F6
Spennymoor 111 F5
Spetchley 50 D3
Spetisbury 13 D7
Spexhall 69 F6
Spey Bay 152 B3
Speybridge 139 B6
Speyview 152 D2
Spilsby 79 C7
Spindlestone 123 F7
Spinkhill 76 B4
Spinningdale 151 C9
Spirthill 24 B4
Spital Hill 89 E7
Spital in the Street 90 F3
Spithurst 17 C8
Spittal *Dumfries* 105 D7
Spittal *E Loth* 121 B7
Spittal *Highld* 158 E3
Spittal *Northumb* 123 D6
Spittal *Pembs* 44 C4
Spittal *Stirling* 126 F4
Spittalfield 133 E8
Spittal of Glenmuick 140 F2
Spittal of Glenshee 133 B8
Spixworth 68 C5
Splayne's Green 17 B8
Spofforth 95 D6
Spondon 76 F4
Spon End 51 B8
Spon Green 73 C6
Spooner Row 68 E3
Sporle 67 C8
Spott 122 B2
Spratton 52 B5
Spreakley 27 E6
Spreyton 9 E8
Spridlington 90 F4
Springburn 119 C6
Springfield *Dumfries* 108 C3
Springfield *Essex* 42 D3
Springfield *Fife* 128 C5
Springfield *Moray* 151 F13
Springfield *W Mid* 62 F4
Springhill 62 D3
Springholm 106 C5
Springkell 108 B2
Springside 118 F3
Springthorpe 90 F2
Spring Vale 88 D3
Spring Valley 84 E3
Springwell 111 D5
Sproatley 97 F7
Sproston Green 74 C4
Sprotbrough 89 D6
Sproughton 56 E5
Sprouston 122 F3
Sprowston 68 C5
Sproxton *Leics* 65 B5
Sproxton *N Yorks* 102 F4
Spurstow 74 D2
Spynie 152 B2
Squires Gate 92 F3
Sranda 154 J5
Sronphadruig Lodge 132 B4
Stableford *Shrops* 61 E7
Stableford *Staffs* 74 F5
Stacey Bank 88 E3
Stackhouse 93 C8
Stackpole 44 F4
Staddiscombe 6 D3
Staddlethorpe 90 B2
Stadhampton 39 E6
Stadhlaigearraidh 148 E2
Staffi 149 B9

Staffield 108 E5
Stafford 62 B3
Stagsden 53 E7
Stainburn *Cumb* 98 B2
Stainburn *N Yorks* 94 E5
Stainby 65 B6
Staincross 88 C4
Staindrop 101 B6
Staines-upon-Thames 27 B8
Stainfield *Lincs* 65 B7
Stainfield *Lincs* 78 B4
Stainforth *N Yorks* 93 C8
Stainforth *S Yorks* 89 C7
Staining 92 F3
Stainland 87 C8
Stainsacre 103 D7
Stainsby 76 C4
Stainton *Cumb* 99 B6
Stainton *Cumb* 99 F7
Stainton *Durham* 101 C5
Stainton *Mbro* 102 C2
Stainton *N Yorks* 101 E6
Stainton *S Yorks* 89 E6
Stainton by Langworth 78 B3
Staintondale 103 E7
Stainton le Vale 91 E5
Stainton with Adgarley 92 B2
Stair *Cumb* 98 B4
Stair *E Ayrs* 112 B4
Stairhaven 105 D6
Staithes 103 C5
Stakeford 117 F8
Stake Pool 92 E4
Stalbridge 12 C5
Stalbridge Weston 12 C5
Stalham 69 B6
Stalham Green 69 B6
Stalisfield Green 30 D3
Stallingborough 91 C5
Stalling Busk 100 F4
Stalmine 92 E3
Stalybridge 87 E7
Stambourne 55 F8
Stambourne Green 55 F8
Stamford 65 D7
Stamford Bridge *Ches W* 73 C8
Stamford Bridge *E Yorks* 96 D3
Stamfordham 110 B3
Stanah 99 C5
Stanborough 41 C5
Stanbridge *C Beds* 40 B2
Stanbridge *Dorset* 13 D8
Stanbrook 50 E3
Stanbury 94 F3
Stand *Gtr Man* 87 D5
Standburn 120 B2
Standeford 62 D3
Standen 30 E2
Standford 27 F6
Standingstone 107 F7
Standish 86 C3
Standlake 38 D3
Standon *Hants* 14 B5
Standon *Herts* 41 B6
Standon *Staffs* 74 F5
Stane 119 D8
Stanfield 80 E5
Stanford *C Beds* 54 E2
Stanford *Kent* 19 B8
Stanford Bishop 49 D8
Stanford Bridge 50 C2
Stanford Dingley 26 B3
Stanford in the Vale 38 E3
Stanford-le-Hope 42 F2
Stanford on Avon 52 B3
Stanford on Soar 64 B2
Stanford on Teme 50 C2
Stanford Rivers 41 D2
Stanfree 76 B4
Stanghow 102 C4
Stanground 66 E2
Stanhoe 80 D4
Stanhope *Borders* 114 B4
Stanhope *Durham* 110 F2
Stanion 65 F6
Stanley *Derbys* 76 E4
Stanley *Durham* 110 D4
Stanley *Lancs* 86 D2
Stanley *Perth* 133 F8
Stanley *Staffs* 75 D6
Stanley *W Yorks* 88 B4
Stanley Common 76 E4
Stanley Gate 86 D2
Stanley Hill 49 E8
Stanlow 73 B8
Stanmer 17 D7
Stanmore *Hants* 15 B5
Stanmore *London* 40 E4
Stanmore *W Berks* 26 B2
Stannergate 134 F4
Stanningley 94 F5
Stannington *Northumb* 110 B5
Stannington *S Yorks* 88 F4
Stansbatch 48 C5
Stansfield 55 D8
Stanstead 56 D2
Stanstead Abbotts 41 C6
Stansted 29 C7
Stansted Airport 42 B1
Stansted Mountfitchet 41 B8
Stanton *Glos* 51 F5
Stanton *Mon* 35 B7
Stanton *Northumb* 117 F7
Stanton *Staffs* 75 E8
Stanton *Suff* 56 B3
Stanton by Bridge 63 B7
Stanton-by-Dale 76 F4
Stanton Drew 23 C7
Stanton Fitzwarren 38 E1
Stanton Harcourt 38 D4
Stanton Hill 76 C4
Stanton in Peak 76 C2
Stanton Lacy 49 B6
Stanton Long 61 E5
Stanton-on-the-Wolds 77 F6
Stanton Prior 23 C8
Stanton St Bernard 25 C5
Stanton St John 39 D5

Stanton St Quintin. 24 B4
Stanton Street 56 C3
Stanton under Bardon... 63 C8
Stanton upon Hine Heath 61 B5
Stanton Wick... 23 C8
Stanwardine in the Fields.... 60 B4
Stanwardine in the Wood 60 B4
Stanway Essex ... 43 B5
Glos............51 F5
Stanway Green .. 57 B6
Stanwell 27 B8
Stanwell Moor .. 27 B8
Stanwick...... 53 B7
Stanwick-St-John......101 C6
Stanwix 108 D4
Stanydale 160 H4
Stape 103 E5
Stapehill 13 D8
Stapeley 74 E3
Stapenhill 63 B6
Staple Kent 31 D6
Som..........22 E3
Staple Cross ... 18 C4
Staplefield 17 B6
Staple Fitzpaine. 11 C7
Stapleford Cambs .. 55 D5
Herts......... 41 C6
Leics........ 64 C5
Lincs........ 77 D8
Notts........76 F4
Wilts........ 25 F5
Stapleford Abbotts 41 E8
Stapleford Tawney. 41 E8
Staplegrove 11 B7
Staplehay 11 B7
Staplehurst 29 E8
Staplers 15 F6
Stapleton Bristol .. 23 B8
Cumb........108 B5
Hereford 48 C5
Leics........ 63 E8
N Yorks.......101 C7
Shrops....... 60 D4
Som.........12 B2
Stapley 11 C6
Staploe 54 C2
Staplow....... 49 E8
Star Fife 128 D5
Pembs........45 F4
Som......... 23 D6
Stara 159 F3
Starbeck 95 D6
Starbotton 94 B2
Starcross 10 F4
Stareton 51 B8
Starkholmes ... 76 D3
Starlings Green .. 55 F5
Starston 68 F5
Startforth 101 C5
Startley 37 F6
Stathe 11 B8
Stathern 77 F7
Station Town ... 111 F7
Staughton Green . 54 C2
Staughton Highway.......54 C2
Staunton Glos.... 36 B4
Glos......... 36 C2
Staunton in the Vale 77 E8
Staunton on Arrow 49 C5
Staunton on Wye . 49 E5
Staveley Cumb ... 99 E6
Cumb.........99 F5
Derbys.......76 B4
N Yorks.......95 C6
Staverton Devon .. 7 C5
Glos......... 37 B5
Wilts........ 24 C3
W Nhants...... 52 C3
Staverton Bridge . 37 B5
Stawell 23 F5
Staxigoe 158 E5
Staxton 97 B6
Staylittle 59 E5
Staynall 92 E3
Staythorpe 77 D7
Stean 94 B3
Stearsby 96 B2
Steart........ 22 E4
Stebbing 42 B2
Stebbing Green .. 42 B2
Stedham 16 B2
Steele Road 115 E8
Steen's Bridge .. 49 D7
Steep........ 15 B8
Steeple Dorset ... 13 F7
Essex......... 43 D5
Steeple Ashton .. 24 D4
Steeple Aston .. 38 B4
Steeple Barton .. 38 B4
Steeple Bumpstead ... 55 E7
Steeple Claydon.. 39 B6
Steeple Gidding . 65 F8
Steeple Langford . 24 F5
Steeple Morden.. 54 E3
Steep Marsh ... 15 B8
Steeton 94 E3
Stein 148 C7
Steinmanhill .153 D7
Stelling Minnis .. 30 E5
Stemster.....158 D3
Stemster House . 158 D3
Stenalees 4 D5
Stenhousemuir .127 F7
Stenigot 91 F6
Stenness 160 F4
Stenscholl 149 B9
Stenso........159 F4
Stenson...... 63 B7
Stenton E Loth.. 122 B2
Fife.........128 E4
Stenwith 77 F8
Stepaside..... 32 D2
Stepping Hill ... 87 F7
Steppingley ... 53 F8
Stepps 119 C6
Sterndale Moor .. 75 C8
Sternfield 57 C7
Sterridge 20 E4
Stert......... 24 D5

Stetchworth 55 D7
Stevenage 41 B5
Stevenston 118 E2
Steventon Hants .. 26 E3
Oxon.........38 E4
Stevington 53 D7
Stewartby 53 E8
Stewarton Argyll .143 G2
E Ayrs........118 E4
Stewkley 40 B1
Stewton 91 F7
Steyne Cross ... 15 F7
Steynton 44 E4
Stibb 8 C4
Stibbard 81 E5
Stibb Cross 9 C6
Stibb Green ... 25 C7
Stibbington ... 65 E7
Stichill 122 F3
Sticker........ 4 D4
Stickford 79 D6
Sticklepath 9 E8
Stickney 79 D6
Stiffkey 81 C5
Stifford's Bridge . 50 E2
Stillingfleet ... 95 E8
Stillington N Yorks .. 95 C8
Stockton.......102 B1
Stilton 65 F8
Stinchcombe ... 36 E4
Stinsford 12 E5
Stirchley 61 D7
Stirkoke House ..158 E5
Stirling Aberds ..153 D11
Stirling.......127 E6
Stisted 42 B3
Stithians 3 C6
Stittenham 151 D9
Stivichall 51 B8
Stixwould 78 C4
Stoak 73 B8
Stobieside 119 F6
Stobo........120 F4
Stoborough ... 13 F7
Stoborough Green .13 F7
Stobshiel 121 C7
Stobswood 117 E8
Stock 42 E2
Stockbridge ... 25 F8
Stockbury 30 C2
Stockcross ... 26 C2
Stockdalewath .108 E3
Stockerston ... 64 E5
Stock Green ... 50 D4
Stockheath ... 15 D8
Stockiemuir ... 126 F4
Stockingford .. 63 E7
Stocking Pelham . 41 B7
Stockland.... 11 D7
Stockland Bristol .. 22 E4
Stockleigh English 10 D3
Stockleigh Pomeroy 10 D3
Stockley 24 C5
Stocklinch ... 11 C8
Stockport 87 E6
Stocksbridge .. 88 E3
Stocksfield ...110 C3
Stockton Hereford .. 49 C7
Norf..........69 E6
Shrops........60 D2
Shrops.......61 E7
Warks........52 C2
Wilts........ 24 F4
Stockton Heath .. 86 F4
Stockton-on-Tees.......102 C2
Stockton on Teme . 50 C2
Stockton on the Forest........96 D2
Stock Wood ... 50 D5
Stodmarsh ... 31 C6
Stody........ 81 D6
Stoer 156 G3
Stoford Som ... 12 C3
Wilts........ 25 F5
Stogumber 22 F2
Stogursey 22 E4
Stoke Devon 8 B4
Hants......... 15 D8
Hants......... 26 D2
Medway....... 30 B2
Suff..........57 C5
Stoke Abbott ... 12 D2
Stoke Albany ... 64 F5
Stoke Ash 56 B5
Stoke Bardolph .. 77 E6
Stoke Bliss 49 C8
Stoke Bruerne .. 52 E5
Stoke by Clare .. 55 E8
Stoke-by-Nayland 56 F3
Stoke Canon ... 10 E4
Stoke Charity .. 26 F2
Stoke Climsland .. 5 B8
Stoke D'Abernon . 28 D2
Stoke Doyle ... 65 F7
Stoke Dry..... 65 E5
Stoke Farthing .. 13 B8
Stoke Ferry ... 67 E7
Stoke Fleming ... 7 E6
Stokeford 13 F6
Stoke Gabriel ... 7 D6
Stoke Gifford .. 23 B8
Stoke Golding .. 63 E7
Stoke Goldington 53 E6
Stoke Green ... 40 F2
Stokeham 77 B7
Stoke Hammond . 40 B1
Stoke Heath ... 61 B6
Stoke Holy Cross . 68 D5
Stokeinteignhead . 7 B7
Stoke Lacy 49 E8
Stoke Lyne 39 B5
Stoke Mandeville . 39 C7
Stokenchurch .. 39 E7
Stoke Newington 41 F6
Stokenham 7 E6
Stoke-on-Tern .. 61 B6
Stoke-on-Trent .. 75 E5
Stoke Orchard .. 37 B6
Stoke Poges ... 40 F2
Stoke Prior Hereford 49 D7
Worcs........ 50 C4
Stoke Rivers ... 20 F5
Stoke Rochford . 65 B6
Stoke Row 39 F6
Stoke St Gregory . 11 B8

Stoke St Mary 11 B7
Stoke St Michael . 23 E8
Stoke St Milborough .. 61 F5
Stokesay 60 F4
Stokesby 69 C7
Stokesley 102 D3
Stoke sub Hamdon 12 C2
Stoke Talmage .. 39 E6
Stoke Trister .. 12 B5
Stoke Wake ... 13 D5
Stolford 22 E4
Stondon Massey .. 42 D1
Stone Bucks..... 39 C7
Glos..........36 E3
Kent..........19 C6
Kent..........29 B6
Staffs........75 F6
S Yorks........89 F6
Worcs........50 B3
Stone Allerton .. 23 D6
Ston Easton ... 23 D8
Stone Bridge Corner 66 D2
Stonebroom ... 76 D4
Stone Chair ... 88 B2
Stone Cross E Sus .. 18 E3
Kent..........31 D7
Stone-edge Batch. 23 B6
Stoneferry 97 F7
Stonefield 119 D6
Stonegate E Sus .. 18 C3
N Yorks.......103 D5
Stonegrave ... 96 B2
Stonehaugh ...109 B7
Stonehaven 141 F7
Stonehouse Glos .. 37 D5
Northumb ... 109 D6
S Lanark.......119 E7
Stone House ...100 F2
Stoneleigh ... 51 B8
Stonely 54 C2
Stoner Hill ... 15 B8
Stonesby..... 64 B5
Stonesfield ... 38 C3
Stone's Green .. 43 B7
Stone Street Kent .. 29 D6
Suff..........56 F3
Suff..........69 F6
Stonethwaite .. 98 C4
Stoneybreck ...160 N8
Stoneyburn 120 C2
Stoney Cross .. 14 C3
Stoney Middleton .76 B2
Stoney Stanton .. 63 E8
Stoney Stoke ... 24 F2
Stoney Stratton . 23 F8
Stoney Stretton . 60 D3
Stoneywood Aberdeen 141 C7
Falk..........127 F6
Stonganess 160 C7
Stonham Aspal .. 56 D5
Stonnall 62 D4
Stonor........ 39 F7
Stonton Wyville . 64 E4
Stony Cross ... 50 E2
Stonyfield 151 D9
Stony Stratford . 53 E5
Stoodleigh ... 10 C4
Stopes....... 88 F3
Stopham 16 C4
Stopsley 40 B4
Stores Corner .. 57 E7
Storeton 85 F4
Stornoway 155 D9
Storridge 50 E2
Storrington .. 16 C4
Storrs 99 E5
Storth........ 99 F6
Storwood 96 E3
Stotfield 152 A2
Stotfold 54 F3
Stottesdon ... 61 F6
Stoughton Leics .. 64 D3
Sur...........28 D2
W Sus.........16 C2
Stoul 147 B10
Stoulton 50 E4
Stourbridge .. 62 F3
Stourpaine ... 13 D6
Stourport on Severn........50 B3
Stour Provost .. 13 B5
Stour Row 13 B6
Stourton Staffs.. 62 F2
Warks........51 F7
Wilts........ 24 F2
Stourton Caundle .12 C5
Stove Orkney 159 E7
Shetland 160 L6
Stoven 69 F7
Stow Borders 121 E7
Lincs..........78 F3
Lincs.........90 F2
Stow Bardolph .. 67 D6
Stow Bedon ... 68 E2
Stowbridge ... 67 D6
Stow cum Quy .. 55 C6
Stowe 48 B5
Stowe-by-Chartley 62 B4
Stowe Green ... 36 D2
Stowell 12 B4
Stowford...... 9 F6
Stowlangtoft .. 56 C3
Stow Longa ... 54 B2
Stow Maries .. 42 E4
Stowmarket... 56 D4
Stow-on-the-Wold 38 B1
Stowting 30 E5
Stowupland ... 56 D4
Straad 145 G9
Strachan 141 E5
Stradbroke.... 57 B6
Stradishall ... 55 D8
Stradsett..... 67 D6
Stragglethorpe .. 78 D2
Straid 112 E1
Straith 113 F8
Straiton Edin ...121 C5
S Ayrs........112 D3

Straloch Aberds .141 B7
Perth.........133 C7
Stramshall 75 F7
Strang 84 E3
Stranraer 104 C4
Stratfield Mortimer 26 C4
Stratfield Saye .. 26 C4
Stratfield Turgis .. 26 D4
Stratford 41 F6
Stratford St Andrew 57 C7
Stratford St Mary . 56 F4
Stratford Sub Castle 25 F6
Stratford Tony .. 13 B8
Stratford-upon-Avon ... 51 D6
Strath Highld ...149 A12
Highld........158 H4
Strathan Highld .. 136 E2
Highld........156 G3
Highld........157 C8
Strathaven 119 E7
Strathblane ...119 B5
Strathcanaird ..156 J4
Strathcarron ..150 G2
Strathcoil 124 B2
Strathdon 140 C2
Strathellie 153 B10
Strathkinness ..129 C6
Strathmashie House 137 E8
Strathmiglo ...128 C4
Strathmore Lodge........158 F3
Strathpeffer ...150 F7
Strathrannoch ..150 D6
Strathtay 133 D6
Strathvaich Lodge........150 D6
Strathwhillan ..143 E11
Strathy 157 C11
Strathyre 126 C4
Stratton Corn 8 D4
Dorset........12 E4
Glos..........37 D7
Stratton Audley .. 39 B6
Stratton on the Fosse........ 23 D8
Stratton St Margaret .. 38 F1
Stratton St Michael 68 E5
Stratton Strawless 81 E8
Stravithie 129 C7
Streat........ 17 C7
Streatham 28 B4
Streatley C Beds .. 40 B3
W Berks.......39 F5
Street Lancs ... 92 D5
N Yorks.......103 D5
Som..........23 F6
Street Dinas .. 73 F7
Street End Kent .. 30 D5
W Sus.........16 E2
Street Gate 110 D5
Streethay 62 C5
Streetlam 101 E8
Streetly 62 E4
Street Lydan .. 73 F8
Streetly End .. 55 E7
Strefford 60 F4
Strelley 76 E5
Strensall 96 C2
Stretcholt 22 E4
Strete........ 7 E6
Stretford 87 E6
Strethall 55 F6
Stretham 55 B6
Strettington .. 16 D2
Stretton Ches W .. 73 D8
Derbys........76 C3
Rutland 65 C6
Staffs........61 B7
Staffs........63 B6
Warr..........86 F4
Stretton Grandison 49 E8
Stretton-on-Dunsmore 52 B2
Stretton-on-Fosse 51 F7
Stretton Sugwas . 49 E6
Stretton under Fosse........ 63 F8
Stretton Westwood 61 E5
Strichen 153 C9
Strines........ 87 F7
Stringston ... 22 E3
Strixton 53 C7
Stroat........ 36 E2
Stromeferry ...149 E13
Stromemore ...149 E13
Stromness 159 H3
Stronaba 137 F5
Stronachlachar ..126 C3
Stronchreggan .. 138 B4
Stronchrubie ..156 H5
Strone Argyll ...145 E10
Highld........137 B8
Highld........137 B8
Invclyd.......118 B2
Stronmilchan ..125 C7
Strontian 138 C3
Strood 29 C8
Strood Green Sur .. 28 E3
W Sus.........16 B4
W Sus.........28 F2
Stroud Glos.... 37 D5
Hants......... 15 B8
Stroud Green .. 42 E4
Stroxton 78 F2
Struan Highld ...149 E8
Perth.........133 C5
Strubby 91 F8
Strumpshaw ... 69 D6
Strutherhill ...119 E7
Struy 150 H6
Stryd-issa 72 D3
Stuartfield ...153 D9
Stubbington ... 15 D6
Stubbins 87 C5
Stubbs Cross .. 19 B6
Stubbs Green .. 69 E6
Stubb's Green .. 69 E6
Stubhampton .. 13 C7
Stubton 77 E8
Stuckgowan ...126 D2
Stuckton 14 C2
Stud Green ... 27 B6
Studham 40 C3
Studland 13 F8
Studley Warks... 51 C5
Wilts......... 24 B4
Studley Roger .. 95 B5
Stump Cross .. 55 E6
Stuntney..... 55 B6
Sturbridge ... 74 F5
Sturmer 55 E7
Sturminster Marshall...... 13 D7
Sturminster Newton....... 13 C5
Sturry 31 C5
Sturton 90 D3
Sturton by Stow .. 90 F2
Sturton le Steeple 89 F8
Stuston 56 B5
Stutton N Yorks... 95 E7
Suff..........57 F5
Styal 87 F6
Styrrup 89 E7
Suainebost 155 A10
Suardail 155 D9
Succoth Aberds ..152 E4
Argyll........125 E8
Suckley 50 D2
Suckquoy 159 K5
Sudborough ... 65 F6
Sudbourne ... 57 D8
Sudbrook Lincs ... 78 E2
Mon..........36 F2
Sudbrooke ... 78 B3
Sudbury Derbys .. 75 F8
London........28 B2
Suff..........56 E2
Suddie 151 F9
Sudgrove..... 37 D6
Suffield Norf ... 81 D8
N Yorks.......103 E7
Sugnall 74 F4
Sugwas Pool .. 49 E6
Suladale 149 C8
Sulaisiadar ...155 D10
Sulby 84 C3
Sulgrave..... 52 E3
Sulham 26 B4
Sulhamstead .. 26 C4
Sulland 159 D6
Sullington ... 16 C4
Sullom 160 F5
Sullom Voe Oil Terminal ..160 F5
Sully......... 22 C3
Sumburgh 160 N6
Summer Bridge .. 94 C5
Summercourt .. 4 D3
Summerfield .. 80 D3
Summergangs .. 97 F7
Summer-house ..101 C7
Summerleaze .. 35 F9
Summersdale .. 16 D2
Summerseat ... 87 C5
Summertown .. 39 D5
Summit 87 D7
Sunbury-on-Thames 28 C2
Sundaywell ...113 F8
Sunderland Argyll .142 B3
Cumb.........107 F8
Sunderland Bridge........111 F5
Sundhope 115 B6
Sundon Park .. 40 B3
Sundridge ... 29 D5
Sunipol 146 F6
Sunk Island .. 91 C6
Sunningdale .. 27 C7
Sunninghill .. 27 C7
Sunningwell .. 38 D4
Sunniside Durham .110 F4
T&W..........110 D5
Sunnyhurst ... 86 B4
Sunnylaw 127 E6
Sunnyside ... 28 F4
Sunton 25 D7
Surbiton 28 C2
Surby 84 E2
Surfleet 66 B2
Surfleet Seas End . 66 B2
Surlingham ... 69 D6
Sustead 81 D7
Susworth 90 D2
Sutcombe 8 C5
Suton 68 E3
Sutors of Cromarty 151 E11
Sutterby 79 B6
Sutterton ... 79 F5
Sutton Cambs ... 54 B5
C Beds........54 E3
Kent..........31 E7
London........28 C3
Mers..........86 E3
Norf..........69 B6
Notts.........77 F7
N Yorks.......89 B5
Oxon..........38 D4
Pboro.........65 E8
Shrops........61 F7
Shrops........74 F3
Som..........23 F8
Staffs........61 B7
Suff..........57 E7
Sur...........27 D8
S Yorks........89 C6
W Sus.........16 C3
Sutton at Hone .. 29 B6
Sutton Bassett .. 64 E4
Sutton Benger .. 24 B4
Sutton Bonington 64 B2
Sutton Bridge .. 66 B4
Sutton Cheney .. 63 E8
Sutton Coldfield .. 62 E5
Sutton Courtenay 39 E5
Sutton Crosses .. 66 B4
Sutton Grange .. 95 B5
Sutton Green .. 27 D8
Sutton Howgrave . 95 B6
Sutton in Ashfield 76 D4
Sutton-in-Craven. 94 E3
Sutton Ings ... 97 F7
Sutton in the Elms. 64 E2
Sutton Lane Ends . 75 B6
Sutton Leach .. 86 E3

Sutton Maddock . 61 D7
Sutton Mallet .. 23 F5
Sutton Mandeville. 13 B7
Sutton Manor .. 86 E3
Sutton Montis .. 12 B4
Sutton on Hull .. 97 F7
Sutton on Sea .. 91 F9
Sutton-on-the-Forest ... 95 C8
Sutton on the Hill . 76 F2
Sutton on Trent .. 77 C7
Sutton St Edmund .66 C3
Sutton St James .. 66 C3
Sutton St Nicholas. 49 E7
Sutton Scarsdale .76 C4
Sutton Scotney . 26 F2
Sutton under Braile 51 F8
Sutton-under-Whitestonecliffe 102 F2
Sutton upon Derwent....... 96 E3
Sutton Valence . 30 E2
Sutton Veny ... 24 E3
Sutton Waldron . 13 C6
Sutton Weaver .. 74 B2
Sutton Wick ... 23 D7
Swaby 79 B6
Swadlincote ... 63 C7
Swaffham 67 D8
Swaffham Bulbeck 55 C6
Swaffham Prior .. 55 C6
Swafield 81 D8
Swainby 102 D2
Swainshill 49 E6
Swainsthorpe .. 68 D5
Swainswick ... 24 C2
Swalcliffe 51 F8
Swalecliffe ... 30 C5
Swallow 91 D5
Swallowcliffe .. 13 B7
Swallowfield .. 26 C5
Swallownest .. 89 F5
Swallows Cross . 42 E2
Swanage 13 G8
Swanbister ... 159 H4
Swanbourne .. 39 B8
Swan Green Ches W........74 B4
Suff..........57 B6
Swanland 90 B3
Swanley 29 C6
Swanley Village . 29 C6
Swanmore ... 15 C6
Swannington Leics .63 C8
Norf..........68 C4
Swanscombe .. 29 B7
Swansea = Abertawe .. 33 E7
Swanton Abbott . 81 E8
Swanton Morley .. 68 C3
Swanton Novers .. 81 D6
Swanton Street . 30 D2
Swanwick Derbys .. 76 D4
Hants......... 15 D6
Swarby 78 E3
Swardeston .. 68 D5
Swarister 160 E7
Swarkestone .. 63 B7
Swarland 117 D7
Swarland Estate .117 D7
Swarthmoor ... 92 B2
Swathwick 76 C3
Swaton 78 F4
Swavesey 54 C4
Sway 14 E3
Swayfield 65 B6
Swaythling ... 14 C5
Sweet Green .. 49 C8
Sweetham 10 E3
Sweethouse 5 C5
Sweffling 57 C7
Swepstone ... 63 C7
Swerford 51 F8
Swettenham .. 74 C5
Swetton 94 B4
Swffryd 35 E6
Swiftsden ... 18 C4
Swilland 57 D5
Swillington .. 95 F6
Swimbridge 9 B8
Swimbridge Newland...... 20 F5
Swinbrook ... 38 C2
Swinderby ... 77 C8
Swindon Glos .. 37 B6
Staffs........62 E2
Swindon......38 F1
Swine 97 F7
Swinefleet 89 B8
Swineshead Bedford 53 C8
Lincs..........78 E5
Swineshead Bridge........78 E5
Swiney 158 G4
Swinford Leics .. 52 B3
Oxon..........38 D4
Swingate 76 E5
Swingfield Minnis .31 E6
Swingfield Street. 31 E6
Swinhoe......117 B8
Swinhope 91 E6
Swining 160 G6
Swinithwaite ..101 F5
Swinnow Moor .. 94 F5
Swinscoe 75 E8
Swinside Hall ..116 C3
Swinstead ... 65 B7
Swinton Borders .122 E4
Gtr Man........87 D5
N Yorks........94 B5
N Yorks........96 B3
S Yorks........88 E5
Swintonmill ...122 E4
Swithland ... 64 C2
Swordale 151 E8
Swordland ...147 B10
Swordly......157 C10
Sworton Heath .. 86 F4
Swydd-ffynnon. 47 C5
Swynnerton .. 75 F5
Swyre 12 F3
Sychtyn 59 D6
Syde 37 C6
Sydenham London. 28 B4
Oxon..........39 D7
Sydenham Damerel.6 B2

Syderstone 80 D4
Sydling St Nicholas ... 12 E4
Sydmonton ... 26 D2
Syerston 77 E7
Syke 87 C6
Sykehouse ... 89 C7
Sykes 93 D6
Syleham 57 B6
Sylen 33 D6
Symbister 160 G7
Symington S Ayrs .. 118 F3
S Lanark.......120 F2
Symondsbury .. 12 E2
Symonds Yat .. 36 C2
Synod Inn 46 D3
Syre 157 E9
Syreford 37 B7
Syresham 52 E4
Syston Leics ... 64 C3
Lincs..........78 E2
Sytchampton .. 50 C3
Sywell 53 C6

T

Taagan 150 E3
Tàbost 155 A10
Tabost 155 F8
Tackley 38 B4
Tacleit......154 D6
Tacolneston .. 68 E4
Tadcaster ... 95 E7
Taddington .. 75 B8
Taddiport 9 C6
Tadley 26 C4
Tadlow 54 E3
Tadmarton ... 51 F8
Tadworth 28 D3
Tafarnau-bach .. 35 C5
Tafarn-y-gelyn .. 73 C5
Taff's Well 35 F5
Tafolwern 59 D5
Tai 83 E7
Taibach 34 F1
Tai-bach..... 59 B8
Taigh a Ghearraidh ..148 A2
Tai-mawr 72 E3
Tain Highld 151 C10
Highld........158 D4
Tainant 73 E6
Tainlon 82 F4
Tairbeart = Tarbert 154 G6
Tai'r-Bull 34 B3
Tairgwaith ... 33 C8
Tai-Ucha 72 D4
Takeley 42 B1
Takeley Street .. 41 B8
Talachddu ... 48 F2
Talacre 85 F2
Talardd 59 B5
Talaton 11 E5
Talbenny 44 D3
Talbot Green .. 34 F4
Talbot Village .. 13 E8
Tale 11 D5
Talerddig 59 D6
Talgarreg 46 D3
Talgarth 48 F3
Taliesin 58 E3
Talisker 149 E8
Talke 74 D5
Talkin 109 D5
Talladale 150 D2
Talla Linnfoots .114 B4
Tallarn Green .. 73 E8
Tallentire 107 F8
Talley 46 F5
Tallington ... 65 D7
Talmine 157 C8
Talog 32 B4
Talsarn 34 B1
Talsarnau 71 D7
Talskiddy 4 C4
Talwrn Anglesey .. 82 D5
Wrex..........73 E6
Tal-y-bont Ceredig. 58 F3
Conwy........83 E7
Gwyn..........71 E6
Gwyn..........83 D6
Talybont-on-Usk . 35 B5
Tal-y-cafn 83 D7
Talygarn 34 F4
Talyllyn 35 B5
Tal-y-llyn 58 D4
Talysarn 82 F4
Tal-y-wern ... 58 D5
Tame Bridge ..102 D3
Tamerton Foliot . 6 C2
Tamworth 63 D6
Tandem 88 C2
Tanden 19 B6
Tandridge ... 28 D4
Tanerdy 33 B5
Tanfield 110 D4
Tanfield Lea .. 110 D4
Tangiers 44 D4
Tangley 25 D8
Tanglwst 46 F2
Tangmere 16 D3
Tangwick 160 F4
Tan Hinon ... 59 F5
Tankersley ... 88 D4
Tankerton ... 30 C5
Tan-lan Conwy .. 83 E7
Gwyn..........71 C7
Tannach 158 F5
Tannachie ...141 F6
Tannadice ...134 D4
Tannington .. 57 C6
Tansley 76 D3
Tansley Knoll .. 76 C3
Tansor 65 E7
Tantobie 110 D4
Tanton 102 D3
Tanworth-in-Arden 51 B6
Tan-y-bwlch .. 71 C7
Tan-y-fron ... 72 C3
Tan-y-graig Anglesey 82 D5
Gwyn..........70 D4
Tanygrisiau .. 71 C7
Tan-y-groes .. 45 E4

Tan-y-pistyll 59 B7
Tan-yr-allt 82 F4
Tanyrhydiau ...47 C6
Taobh a Chaolais .148 G2
Taobh a'Ghlinne.. 155 F8
Taobh a Thuath Loch Aineort . 148 F2
Taobh a Tuath Loch Baghasdail ..148 F2
Taobh Tuath ..154 J4
Taplow 40 F2
Tapton 76 B3
Tarbat House ..151 D10
Tarbert Argyll ...143 C7
Argyll........144 E5
Argyll........145 G7
Tarbert = Tairbeart ...154 G6
Tarbet Argyll ...126 D2
Highld........147 B10
Highld........156 F5
Tarbock Green .. 86 F2
Tarbolton 112 B4
Tarbrax 120 D3
Tardebigge ... 50 C5
Tarfside 134 B4
Tarland 140 D3
Tarleton 86 B2
Tarlogie 151 C10
Tarlscough ... 86 C2
Tarlton 37 E6
Tarnbrook ... 93 D5
Tarporley 74 C2
Tarr 22 F3
Tarrant Crawford. 13 D7
Tarrant Gunville . 13 C7
Tarrant Hinton .. 13 C7
Tarrant Keyneston . 13 D7
Tarrant Launceston .. 13 D7
Tarrant Monkton. 13 D7
Tarrant Rawston. 13 D7
Tarrant Rushton . 13 D7
Tarrel 151 C11
Tarring Neville .. 17 D8
Tarrington ... 49 E8
Tarsappie 128 B3
Tarskavaig ...149 H10
Tarves 153 E8
Tarvie Highld ...150 F7
Perth.........133 C7
Tarvin 73 C8
Tasburgh 68 E5
Tasley 61 E6
Taston 38 B3
Tatenhill 63 B6
Tathall End .. 53 E6
Tatham...... 93 C6
Tathwell 91 F7
Tatling End .. 40 F3
Tatsfield 28 D5
Tattenhall ... 73 D8
Tattenhoe ... 53 F6
Tatterford ... 80 E4
Tattersett ... 80 D4
Tattershall .. 78 D5
Tattershall Bridge .78 D5
Tattershall Thorpe. 78 D5
Tattingstone .. 56 F5
Tatworth 11 D8
Taunton 11 B7
Taverham 68 C4
Tavernspite .. 32 C2
Tavistock 6 B2
Taw Green 9 E8
Tawstock 9 B7
Taxal 75 B7
Tay Bridge ...129 B6
Tayinloan 143 D7
Taymouth Castle .132 E4
Taynish 144 E6
Taynton Glos... 36 B4
Oxon..........38 C2
Taynuilt 125 C6
Tayport 129 B6
Tayvallich ...144 E6
Tealby 91 E5
Tealing 134 F4
Teangue 149 H11
Teanna Mhachair .148 B2
Tebay 99 D8
Tebworth 40 B2
Tedburn St Mary . 10 E3
Teddington Glos.. 50 F4
London........28 B2
Tedstone Delamere.49 D8
Tedstone Wafre .. 49 D8
Teeton 52 B4
Teffont Evias .. 24 F4
Teffont Magna .. 24 F4
Tegryn 45 F4
Teigh 65 C5
Teigncombe 9 F8
Teigngrace 7 B6
Teignmouth 7 B7
Telford 61 D6
Telham 18 D4
Tellisford 24 D3
Telscombe ... 17 D8
Telscombe Cliffs . 17 D7
Templand 114 F3
Temple Corn 5 B6
Glasgow.......118 C5
Midloth.......121 D6
Temple Balsall . 51 B7
Temple Bar Carms .33 C6
Ceredig.......46 D4
Temple Cloud .. 23 D8
Temple Combe .. 12 B5
Temple Ewell .. 31 E6
Temple Grafton . 51 D6
Temple Guiting . 37 B7
Templehall ...128 E4
Temple Herdewyke ... 51 D8
Temple Hirst .. 89 B7
Temple Normanton .. 76 C4
Temple Sowerby . 99 B8
Templeton Devon. 10 C3
Pembs........32 C2
Templeton Bridge. 10 C3
Templetown ...110 D4
Tempsford 54 D2
Tenbury Wells .. 49 C7
Tenby = Dinbych-y-Pysgod.32 D2
Tendring 43 B7

Tendring Green .. 43 B7
Ten Mile Bank .. 67 E6
Tenston 159 G3
Tenterden ... 19 B5
Terling 42 C3
Ternhill 74 F3
Terregles Banks .107 B6
Terrick 39 D8
Terrington ... 96 B2
Terrington St Clement ... 66 C5
Terrington St John 66 C5
Teston 29 D8
Testwood 14 C4
Tetbury 37 E5
Tetbury Upton .. 37 E5
Tetcott 73 F7
Tetchill 8 E5
Tetford 79 B6
Tetney 91 D7
Tetney Lock .. 91 D7
Tetsworth ... 39 D6
Tettenhall ... 62 E2
Teuchan 153 E10
Teversal 76 C4
Teversham ... 55 D5
Teviothead ...115 D7
Tewel 141 F7
Tewin 41 C5
Tewkesbury .. 50 F3
Teynham 30 C3
Thackthwaite .. 98 B3
Thainston ...135 B6
Thakeham ... 16 C5
Thame 39 D7
Thames Ditton .. 28 C2
Thames Haven .. 42 F3
Thamesmead .. 41 F7
Thanington ... 30 D5
Thankerton ..120 F2
Tharston 68 E4
Thatcham 26 C3
Thatto Heath .. 86 E3
Thaxted 55 F7
The Aird 149 C9
Theakston ...101 F8
Thealby 90 C2
Theale Som 23 E6
W Berks.......26 B4
The Arms 67 E8
Thearne 97 F6
The Bage 48 E4
The Balloch ..127 C7
The Barony ...159 F3
Theberton ... 57 C8
The Bog 60 E3
The Bourne .. 27 E6
The Braes 149 E10
The Broad 49 C6
The Butts 24 E2
The Camp Glos.. 37 D6
Herts.........40 D4
The Chequer .. 73 E8
The City 39 E7
The Common .. 25 F7
The Craigs ...150 B7
The Cronk 84 C3
Theddingworth . 64 F3
Theddlethorpe All Saints 91 F8
Theddlethorpe St Helen 91 F8
The Dell 69 E7
The Den 118 D3
The Eals 116 F3
The Eaves 36 D3
The Flatt 109 B5
The Four Alls .. 74 F3
The Garths ...160 B8
The Green Cumb .. 98 F3
Wilts.........24 F3
The Grove ...107 B6
The Hall 160 D8
The Haven ... 27 F8
The Heath Norf. 81 E7
Suff..........56 F5
The Hill 98 F3
The Howe Cumb .. 99 F6
IoM..........84 F1
The Hundred .. 49 C7
Thelbridge Barton. 10 C2
The Lee 40 D2
The Lhen 84 B3
Thelnetham .. 56 B4
Thelveton ... 68 F4
Thelwall 86 F4
The Marsh Powys .. 60 E3
Wilts.........37 F7
Themelthorpe .. 81 E6
The Middles ..110 D5
The Moor 18 C4
The Mumbles = Y Mwmbwls... 33 F7
The Murray ...119 D6
The Neuk 141 E6
Thenford 52 E3
The Oval 24 C2
The Pole of Itlaw .153 C6
The Quarry .. 36 E4
Therfield 54 F4
The Rhos 32 C1
The Rock 61 D6
The Ryde 41 D5
The Sands ... 27 E6
The Stocks ... 19 C6
Thetford Lincs .. 65 C8
Norf..........67 F8
The Throat ... 27 C6
The Vauld 49 E7
The Wyke 61 D7
Theydon Bois .. 41 E7
Thickwood ... 24 B3
Thimbleby Lincs. 78 C5
N Yorks.......102 E2
Thingwall 85 F3
Thirdpart 118 E1
Thirlby 102 F2
Thirlestane ..121 E8
Thirn 101 F7
Thirsk 102 F2
Thirtleby 97 F7
Thistleton Lancs .. 92 F4
Rutland 65 C6
Thistley Green . 55 B7
Thixendale ... 96 C4

Thockrington 110 B2
Tholomas Drove 66 D3
Tholthorpe 95 C7
Thomas Chapel 32 D2
Thomas Close 108 E4
Thomastown 152 E5
Thompson 68 E2
Thomshill 152 C2
Thong 29 B7
Thongsbridge 88 D2
Thoralby 101 F5
Thoresway 91 E5
Thorganby Lincs 91 E6
NYorks 96 E2
Thorgill 103 E5
Thorington 57 B8
Thorington Street 56 F4
Thorlby 94 D2
Thorley 41 C7
Thorley Street
Herts 41 C7
IoW 14 F4
Thormanby 95 B7
Thornaby-on-Tees 102 C2
Thornage 81 D6
Thornborough
Bucks 52 F5
NYorks 95 B5
Thornbury Devon 9 D6
Hereford 49 D8
S Glos 36 E3
W Yorks 94 F4
Thornby 52 B4
Thorncliffe 75 D7
Thorncombe
Dorset 11 D8
Dorset 13 D6
Thorncombe Street 27 E8
Thorncote Green 54 E2
Thorncross 14 F5
Thorndon 56 C5
Thorndon Cross 9 E7
Thorne 89 C7
Thorner 95 E6
Thorne St Margaret 11 B5
Thorney Notts 77 B8
Pboro 66 D2
Thorney Crofts 91 B6
Thorney Green 56 C4
Thorney Hill 14 E2
Thorney Toll 66 D3
Thornfalcon 11 B7
Thornford 12 C4
Thorngumbald 91 B6
Thornham 80 C3
Thornham Magna 56 B5
Thornham Parva 56 B5
Thornhaugh 65 D7
Thornhill Cardiff 35 F5
Cumb 98 D2
Derbys 88 F2
Dumfries 113 E8
Soton 15 C5
Stirling 127 E5
W Yorks 88 C3
Thornhill Edge 88 C3
Thornhill Lees 88 C3
Thornholme 97 C7
Thornley Durham 110 F4
Durham 111 F6
Thornliebank 118 D5
Thorns 55 D8
Thornsett 87 F8
Thorns Green 87 F5
Thornthwaite
Cumb 98 B4
NYorks 94 D4
Thornton Angus 134 E3
Bucks 53 F5
E Yorks 96 E3
Fife 128 E4
Lancs 92 E3
Leics 63 D8
Lincs 78 C5
Mbro 102 C2
Mers 85 D4
Northumb 123 E5
Pembs 44 E4
W Yorks 94 F4
Thornton Curtis 90 C4
Thorntonhall 119 D5
Thornton Heath 28 C4
Thornton Hough 85 F4
Thornton in Craven 94 E2
Thornton-le-Beans 102 E1
Thornton-le-Clay 96 C2
Thornton-le-Dale 103 F6
Thornton le Moor 90 E4
Thornton-le-Moor 102 F1
Thornton-le-Moors 73 B8
Thornton-le-Street 102 F2
Thorntonloch 122 B3
Thorntonpark 122 E5
Thornton Rust 100 F4
Thornton Steward 101 F6
Thornton Watlass 101 F7
Thornwood Common 41 D7
Thornydykes 122 E2
Thoroton 77 E7
Thorp Arch 95 E7
Thorpe Derbys 75 D8
E Yorks 97 E5
Lincs 91 F8
Norf 69 E7
Notts 77 E7
NYorks 94 C3
Sur 27 C8
Thorpe Abbotts 57 B5
Thorpe Acre 64 B2
Thorpe Arnold 64 B4
Thorpe Audlin 89 C5
Thorpe Bassett 96 B4
Thorpe Bay 43 F5
Thorpe by Water 65 E5
Thorpe Common 57 F6
Thorpe Constantine 63 D6
Thorpe Culvert 79 C7
Thorpe End 69 C5
Thorpe Fendykes 79 C7
Thorpe Green
Essex 43 B7
Suff 56 D3
Thorpe Hesley 88 E4
Thorpe in Balne 89 C6
Thorpe in the Fallows 90 F3
Thorpe Langton 64 E4
Thorpe Larches 102 B1
Thorpe-le-Soken 43 B7
Thorpe le Street 96 E4
Thorpe Malsor 53 B6
Thorpe Mandeville 52 E3
Thorpe Market 81 D8
Thorpe Marriot 68 C4
Thorpe Morieux 56 D3
Thorpeness 57 D8
Thorpe on the Hill 78 C2
Thorpe St Andrew 69 D5
Thorpe St Peter 79 C7
Thorpe Salvin 89 F6
Thorpe Satchville 64 C4
Thorpe Thewles 102 B2
Thorpe Tilney 78 D4
Thorpe Underwood 95 D7
Thorpe Waterville 65 F7
Thorpe Willoughby 95 F8
Thorrington 43 C6
Thorverton 10 D4
Thrandeston 56 B5
Thrapston 53 B7
Thrashbush 119 C7
Threapland Cumb 107 F8
NYorks 94 C2
Threapwood
Ches W 73 E8
Staffs 75 E7
Three Ashes 36 B2
Three Bridges 28 F3
Three Burrows 3 B6
Three Chimneys 18 B5
Three Cocks 48 F3
Three Crosses 33 E6
Three Cups Corner 18 C3
Threehammer Common 69 C6
Three Holes 66 D5
Threekingham 78 F3
Three Leg Cross 18 B3
Three Legged Cross 13 D8
Threemile Cross 26 C5
Threemilestone 3 B6
Threemiletown 120 B3
Three Oaks 18 D5
Threlkeld 99 B5
Threshfield 94 C2
Thrigby 69 C7
Thringarth 100 B4
Thringstone 63 C8
Thrintoft 101 E8
Thriplow 54 E5
Throckenholt 66 D3
Throcking 54 F4
Throckley 110 C4
Throckmorton 50 E4
Throphill 117 F7
Thropton 117 D6
Throsk 127 E7
Throwleigh 9 E8
Throwley 30 D3
Thrumpton 76 F5
Thrumster 158 F5
Thrunton 117 C6
Thrupp Glos 37 D5
Oxon 38 C4
Thrushelton 9 F6
Thrussington 64 C3
Thruxton Hants 25 E7
Hereford 49 F6
Thrybergh 89 E5
Thulston 76 F4
Thundergay 143 D9
Thundersley 42 F3
Thundridge 41 C6
Thurcaston 64 C2
Thurcroft 89 F5
Thurgarton Norf 81 D7
Notts 77 E6
Thurgoland 88 D3
Thurlaston Leics 64 E2
Warks 52 B2
Thurlbear 11 B7
Thurlby Lincs 65 C8
Lincs 78 C2
Thurleigh 53 D8
Thurlestone 6 E4
Thurloxton 22 F4
Thurlstone 88 D3
Thurlton 69 E7
Thurlwood 74 D5
Thurmaston 64 D3
Thurnby 64 D3
Thurne 69 C7
Thurnham Kent 30 D2
Lancs 92 D4
Thurning N Nhants 65 F7
Norf 81 E6
Thurnscoe 89 D5
Thurnscoe East 89 D5
Thursby 108 D3
Thursford 81 D5
Thursley 27 F7
Thurso 158 D3
Thurso East 158 D3
Thurstaston 85 F3
Thurston 56 C3
Thurstonfield 108 D3
Thurstonland 88 C2
Thurton 69 D6
Thurvaston 76 F2
Thuxton 68 D3
Thwaite N Yorks 100 E3
Suff 56 C5
Thwaites 94 E3
Thwaite St Mary 69 E6
Thwaites Brow 94 E3
Thwing 97 B6
Tibbermore 128 B2
Tibberton Glos 36 B4
Telford 61 B6
Worcs 50 D4
Tibenham 68 F4
Tibshelf 76 C4
Tibthorpe 97 D5
Ticehurst 18 B3
Tichborne 26 F3
Tickencote 65 D6
Tickenham 23 B6
Tickhill 89 E6
Ticklerton 60 E4
Ticknall 63 B7
Tickton 97 E6
Tidcombe 25 D7
Tiddington Oxon 39 D6
Warks 51 D7
Tidebrook 18 C3
Tideford 5 D8
Tideford Cross 5 C8
Tidenham 36 E2
Tideswell 75 B8
Tidmarsh 26 B4
Tidmington 51 F7
Tidpit 13 C8
Tidworth 25 E7
Tiers Cross 44 D4
Tiffield 52 D4
Tifty 153 D7
Tigerton 135 C5
Tigh-na-Blair 127 C6
Tighnabruaich 145 F8
Tighnafiline 155 J13
Tigley 7 C5
Tilbrook 53 C8
Tilbury 29 B7
Tilbury Juxta Clare 55 E8
Tile Cross 63 F5
Tile Hill 51 B7
Tilehurst 26 B4
Tilford 27 E6
Tilgate 28 F3
Tilgate Forest Row 28 F3
Tillathrowie 152 E4
Tilley 60 B5
Tillicoultry 127 E8
Tillingham 43 D5
Tillington Hereford 49 E6
W Sus 16 B3
Tillington Common 49 E6
Tillyarblet 135 C5
Tillybirloch 141 D5
Tillycorthie 141 B8
Tillydrine 140 E5
Tillyfour 140 C4
Tillyfourie 140 C5
Tillygarmond 140 E5
Tillygreig 141 B7
Tillykerrie 141 B7
Tilmanstone 31 D7
Tilney All Saints 67 C5
Tilney High End 67 C5
Tilney St Lawrence 66 C5
Tilshead 24 E5
Tilstock 74 F2
Tilston 73 D8
Tilstone Fearnall 74 C2
Tilsworth 40 B2
Tilton on the Hill 64 D4
Timberland 78 D4
Timbersbrook 75 C5
Timberscombe 21 E8
Timble 94 D4
Timperley 87 F5
Timsbury Bath 23 D8
Hants 14 B4
Timsgearraidh 154 D5
Timworth Green 56 C2
Tincleton 13 E5
Tindale 109 D6
Tingewick 52 F4
Tingley 88 B3
Tingrith 53 F8
Tingwall 159 F4
Tinhay 9 F5
Tinshill 95 F5
Tinsley 88 E5
Tintagel 8 F2
Tintern Parva 36 D2
Tintinhull 12 C3
Tintwistle 87 E8
Tinwald 114 F3
Tinwell 65 D7
Tipperty 141 B8
Tipsend 66 E5
Tipton 62 E3
Tipton St John 11 E5
Tiptree 42 C4
Tirabad 47 E7
Tiraghoil 146 J6
Tirley 37 B5
Tirphil 35 D5
Tirril 99 B7
Tir-y-dail 33 C7
Tisbury 13 B7
Tisman's Common 27 F8
Tissington 75 D8
Titchberry 8 B4
Titchfield 15 D6
Titchmarsh 53 B8
Titchwell 80 C3
Tithby 77 F6
Titley 48 C5
Titlington 117 C7
Titsey 28 D5
Tittensor 75 F5
Tittleshall 80 E4
Tiverton Ches W 74 C2
Devon 10 C4
Tivetshall St Margaret 68 F4
Tivetshall St Mary 68 F4
Tividale 62 E3
Tivy Dale 88 D3
Tixall 62 B3
Tixover 65 D6
Toab Orkney 159 H6
Shetland 160 M5
Toadmoor 76 D3
Tobermory 147 F8
Toberonochy 124 E3
Tobha Mor 148 E2
Tobhtarol 154 D6
Tobson 154 D6
Tocher 153 E6
Tockenham 24 B5
Tockenham Wick 37 F7
Tockholes 86 B4
Tockington 36 F3
Tockwith 95 D7
Todber 13 B6
Todding 49 B6
Toddington C Beds 40 B3
Glos 50 F5
Todenham 51 F7
Todhills 108 C3
Todlachie 141 C5
Todmorden 87 B7
Todrig 115 C7
Todwick 89 F5
Toft Cambs 54 D4
Lincs 65 C7
Toft Hill Durham 101 B6
Lincs 78 C5
Toft Monks 69 E7
Toft next Newton 90 F4
Toftrees 80 E4
Tofts 158 D5
Toftwood 68 C2
Togston 117 D8
Tokavaig 149 G11
Tokers Green 26 B5
Tolastadh a Chaolais 154 D6
Tolastadh bho Thuath 155 C10
Tolland 22 F3
Tollard Royal 13 C7
Toll Bar 89 D6
Tollbar End 51 B8
Toll End 62 E3
Toller Fratrum 12 E3
Toller Porcorum 12 E3
Tollerton Notts 77 F6
N Yorks 95 C8
Tollesbury 43 C5
Tolleshunt D'Arcy 43 C5
Tolleshunt Major 43 C5
Toll of Birness 153 E10
Tolm 155 D9
Tolpuddle 13 E5
Tolvah 138 E4
Tolworth 28 C2
Tomatin 138 B4
Tombreck 151 H9
Tomchrasky 137 C5
Tomdoun 136 D4
Tomich Highld 137 B6
Highld 151 D9
Tomich House 151 G8
Tomintoul Aberds 139 E7
Moray 139 C7
Tomnaven 152 E4
Tomnavoulin 139 B8
Tonbridge 29 E6
Tondu 34 F2
Tonfanau 58 D2
Tong Shrops 61 D7
W Yorks 94 F5
Tonge 63 B8
Tongham 27 E6
Tongland 106 D3
Tong Norton 61 D7
Tongue 157 D8
Tongue End 65 C8
Tongwynlais 35 F5
Tonna 34 E1
Ton-Pentre 34 E3
Tonwell 41 C6
Tonypandy 34 E3
Tonyrefail 34 F4
Toot Baldon 39 D5
Toothill 14 C4
Toot Hill 41 D8
Topcliffe 95 B7
Topcroft 69 E5
Topcroft Street 69 E5
Top of Hebers 87 D6
Toppesfield 55 F8
Toppings 86 C5
Topsham 10 F4
Torbay 7 D7
Torbeg 143 F10
Torboll Farm 151 B10
Torbrex 127 E6
Torbryan 7 C6
Torcross 7 E6
Tore 151 F9
Torinturk 145 G7
Torksey 77 B8
Torlum 148 C2
Torlundy 131 B5
Tormarton 24 B2
Tormisdale 142 C2
Tormitchell 112 E2
Tormore 143 E9
Tornagrain 151 G10
Tornahaish 139 D8
Tornaveen 140 D5
Torness 137 B8
Toronto 110 F4
Torpenhow 108 F2
Torphichen 120 B2
Torphins 140 D5
Torpoint 6 D2
Torquay 7 C7
Torquhan 121 E7
Torran Argyll 124 E4
Highld 149 D10
Highld 151 D10
Torrance 119 B6
Torrans 146 J7
Torranyard 118 E3
Torre 7 C7
Torridon 150 F2
Torridon House 149 C13
Torrin 149 F10
Torrisdale 157 C9
Torrisdale-Square 143 E8
Torrish 157 H12
Torrisholme 92 C4
Torroble 157 J8
Torry Aberdeen 141 D8
Aberds 152 E4
Torryburn 128 F2
Torterston 153 D10
Torthorwald 107 B7
Tortington 16 D4
Tortworth 36 E4
Torvaig 149 D9
Torver 98 E4
Torwood 127 F7
Torworth 89 F7
Tosberry 8 B4
Toscaig 149 E12
Toseland 54 C3
Tosside 93 D7
Tostock 56 C3
Totaig Highld 148 C7
Highld 149 F13
Tote 149 D9
Totegan 157 C11
Tothill 91 F8
Totland 14 F4
Totnes 7 C6
Toton 76 F5
Totronald 146 F4
Totscore 149 B8
Tottenham 41 E6
Tottenhill 67 C6
Tottenhill Row 67 C6
Totteridge 41 E5
Totternhoe 40 B2
Tottington 87 C5
Totton 14 C4
Touchen End 27 B6
Tournaig 155 J13
Toux 153 C9
Tovil 29 D8
Toward 145 G10
Towcester 52 E4
Towednack 2 C3
Tower End 67 C6
Towersey 39 D7
Towie Aberds 140 C3
Aberds 153 B8
Towiemore 152 D3
Tow Law 110 F4
Townend 118 B4
Town End Cambs 66 E4
Cumb 99 F6
Towngate 65 C8
Townhead Cumb 108 F5
Dumfries 106 E3
S Ayrs 112 D2
S Yorks 88 D2
Townhead of Greenlaw 106 C4
Townhill 128 F3
Town Row 18 B2
Townsend Bucks 39 D7
Herts 40 D4
Townshend 2 C4
Town Yetholm 116 B4
Towthorpe 96 D2
Towton 95 F7
Towyn 72 B3
Toxteth 85 F4
Toynton All Saints 79 C6
Toynton Fen Side 79 C6
Toynton St Peter 79 C7
Toy's Hill 29 D5
Trabboch 112 B4
Traboe 3 D6
Tradespark
Highld 151 F11
Orkney 159 H5
Trafford Park 87 E5
Trallong 34 B3
Tranent 121 B7
Tranmere 85 F4
Trantlebeg 157 D11
Trantlemore 157 D11
Tranwell 117 F7
Trapp 33 C7
Traprain 121 B8
Traquair 121 F6
Trawden 94 F2
Trawsfynydd 71 D8
Trealaw 34 E4
Treales 92 F4
Trearddur 82 D2
Treaslane 149 C8
Trebanog 34 E4
Trebanos 33 D8
Trebartha 5 B7
Trebarwith 8 F2
Trebetherick 4 B4
Treborough 22 F2
Trebudannon 4 C3
Trebullett 5 B8
Treburley 5 B8
Trebyan 5 C5
Trecastle 34 B2
Trecenydd 35 F5
Trecwn 44 B4
Trecynon 34 D3
Tredavoe 2 D3
Treddiog 44 C3
Tredegar 35 D5
Tredegar = Newydd New Tredegar 35 D5
Tredington Glos 37 B6
Warks 51 E7
Tredinnick 4 B4
Tredomen 48 F3
Tredunnock 35 E7
Tredustan 48 F3
Treen 2 D2
Treeton 88 F5
Trefaldwyn = Montgomery 60 E2
Trefasser 44 B3
Trefdraeth 82 D4
Trefdraeth = Newport 45 F2
Trefecca 48 F3
Trefechan 58 F2
Trefeglwys 59 E6
Trefenter 46 C5
Treffgarne 44 C4
Treffynnon 44 C3
Treffynnon = Holywell 73 B5
Trefgarn Owen 44 C3
Trefi 44 B3
Trefil 35 C5
Trefilan 46 D4
Trefin 44 B3
Treflach 60 B2
Trefnanney 60 C2
Trefnant 72 B4
Trefonen 60 B2
Trefor Anglesey 82 C3
Gwyn 70 C4
Treforest 34 F4
Trefriw 83 E7
Tref-y-Clawdd = Knighton 48 B4
Trefynwy = Monmouth 36 C2
Tregadillett 8 F4
Tregaian 82 D4
Tregare 35 C8
Tregaron 47 D5
Tregarth 83 E6
Tregeare 8 F4
Tregeiriog 73 F5
Tregele 82 B3
Tre-Gibbon 34 D3
Tregidden 3 D6
Treglemais 44 C3
Tregole 8 E3
Tregonetha 4 C4
Tregony 3 B8
Tregoss 4 C4
Tregoyd 48 F4
Tregroes 46 E3
Tregurrian 4 C3
Tregynon 59 E7
Trehafod 34 E4
Treharris 34 E4
Treherbert 34 E3
Trekenner 5 B8
Treknow 8 F2
Trelan 3 E6
Trelash 8 E3
Trelassick 4 D3
Trelawnyd 72 B4
Trelech 45 F4
Treleddyd-fawr 44 C2
Trelewis 35 E5
Treligga 8 F2
Trelights 4 B4
Trelill 4 B5
Trelissick 3 C7
Trellech 36 D2
Trelleck Grange 36 D1
Trelogan 85 F2
Trelystan 60 D2
Tremadog 71 C6
Tremail 8 F3
Tremain 45 E4
Tremaine 8 F4
Tremar 5 C7
Trematon 5 D8
Tremeirchion 72 B4
Trenance 4 C3
Trenarren 3 B9
Trench 61 C6
Treneglos 8 F4
Trenewan 5 D6
Trent 12 C3
Trentham 75 E5
Trentishoe 20 E5
Trent Vale 75 E5
Treoes 21 B8
Treorchy = Treorci 34 E3
Treorci = Treorchy 34 E3
Tre'r-ddôl 58 E3
Trerulefoot 5 D8
Tresaith 45 D4
Tresawle 3 B7
Trescott 62 E2
Trescowe 2 C4
Tresham 36 E4
Tresillian 3 B7
Tresinwen 44 A4
Treskinnick Cross 8 E4
Tresmeer 8 F4
Tresparrett 8 E3
Tresparrett Posts 8 E3
Tressait 133 C5
Tresta Shetland 160 D8
Shetland 160 H5
Treswell 77 B7
Tre-Taliesin 58 E3
Trethosa 4 D4
Trethurgy 4 D5
Tretio 44 C2
Tretire 36 B2
Tretower 35 B5
Treuddyn 73 D6
Trevalga 8 F2
Trevalyn 73 D7
Trevanson 4 B4
Trevarren 4 C4
Trevarrian 4 C3
Trevarrick 3 B8
Trevaughan 32 C2
Tre-vaughan 32 B4
Treveighan 5 B5
Trevellas 4 D2
Treverva 3 C6
Trevethin 35 D6
Trevigro 5 C8
Treviscoe 4 D4
Trevone 4 B3
Trewarmett 8 F2
Trewassa 8 F3
Trewellard 2 C2
Trewen 8 F4
Trewennack 3 D5
Trewern 60 C2
Trewethern 4 B5
Trewidland 5 D7
Trewint Corn 8 E3
Corn 8 F4
Trewithian 3 C7
Trewoofe 2 D3
Trewoon 4 D4
Treworga 3 B7
Treworlas 3 C7
Tre-wyn 35 B7
Treyarnon 4 B3
Treyford 16 C2
Trezaise 4 D4
Triangle 87 B8
Trickett's Cross 13 D8
Triffleton 44 C4
Trimdon 111 F6
Trimdon Colliery 111 F6
Trimdon Grange 111 F6
Trimingham 81 D8
Trimley Lower Street 57 F6
Trimley St Martin 57 F6
Trimley St Mary 57 F6
Trimpley 50 B2
Trimsaran 33 D5
Trimstone 20 E3
Trinafour 132 C4
Trinant 35 D6
Tring 40 C2
Tring Wharf 40 C2
Trinity Angus 135 C6
Jersey 17
Trisant 47 B6
Trislaig 130 B4
Trispen 4 D3
Tritlington 117 E8
Trochry 133 E6
Trodigal 143 F7
Troed-rhiwdalar 47 D8
Troedyraur 46 E2
Troedyrhiw 34 D4
Tromode 84 E3
Trondavoe 160 F5
Troon Corn 3 C5
S Ayrs 118 F3
Trosaraidh 148 G2
Trossachs Hotel 126 D4
Troston 56 B2
Trottiscliffe 29 C7
Trotton 16 B2
Troutbeck Cumb 99 B5
Cumb 99 D6
Troutbeck Bridge 99 D6
Trowbridge 24 D3
Trowell 76 F4
Trow Green 36 D2
Trowle Common 24 D3
Trowley Bottom 40 C3
Trows 122 F2
Trowse Newton 68 D5
Trudoxhill 24 E2
Trull 11 B7
Trumaisgearraidh 148 A3
Trumpan 148 B7
Trumpet 49 F8
Trumpington 54 D5
Trunch 81 D8
Trunnah 92 E3
Truro 3 B7
Trusham 10 F3
Trusley 76 F2
Trusthorpe 91 F9
Trysull 62 E2
Tubney 38 E4
Tuckenhay 7 D6
Tuckhill 61 F7
Tuckingmill 3 B5
Tuddenham 55 B8
Tuddenham St Martin 57 E5
Tudeley 29 E7
Tudhoe 111 F5
Tudorville 36 B2
Tudweiliog 70 D3
Tuesley 27 E7
Tuffley 37 C5
Tufton Hants 26 E2
Pembs 32 B1
Tugby 64 D4
Tugford 61 F5
Tullibardine 127 C8
Tullibody 127 E7
Tullich Argyll 125 D6
Highld 138 B2
Tullich Muir 151 D10
Tulliemet 133 D6
Tulloch Aberds 135 B7
Aberds 153 E8
Perth 128 B2
Tulloch Castle 151 E8
Tullochgorm 125 F5
Tulloes 135 E5
Tullybannocher 127 B6
Tullybelton 133 F7
Tullyfergus 134 E2
Tullymurdoch 134 D1
Tullynessle 140 C4
Tumble 33 C6
Tumby Woodside 79 D5
Tummel Bridge 132 D4
Tunga 155 D9
Tunstall E Yorks 97 F9
Kent 30 C2
Lancs 93 B6
Norf 69 D7
N Yorks 101 E7
Stoke 75 D5
Suff 57 D7
T&W 111 D6
Tunstead Derbys 75 B8
Gtr Man 87 D8
Norf 81 E8
Tunworth 26 E4
Tupsley 49 E7
Tupton 76 C3
Turgis Green 26 D4
Turin 135 D5
Turkdean 37 C8
Tur Langton 64 E4
Turleigh 24 C3
Turn 87 C6
Turnastone 49 F5
Turnberry 112 D2
Turnditch 76 E2
Turners Hill 28 F4
Turners Puddle 13 E6
Turnford 41 D6
Turnhouse 120 B4
Turnworth 13 D6
Turriff 153 C7
Turton Bottoms 86 C5
Turves 66 E3
Turvey 53 D7
Turville 39 E7
Turville Heath 39 E7
Turweston 52 F4
Tushielaw 115 C6
Tutbury 63 B6
Tutnall 50 B4
Tutshill 36 E2
Tuttington 81 E8
Tutts Clump 26 B3
Tuxford 77 B7
Twatt Orkney 159 F3
Shetland 160 H5
Twechar 119 B7
Tweedmouth 123 D5
Tweedsmuir 114 B3
Twelve Heads 3 B6
Twemlow Green 74 C4
Twenty 65 B8
Twerton 24 C2
Twickenham 28 B2
Twigworth 37 B5
Twineham 17 C6
Twinhoe 24 D2
Twinstead 56 F2
Twinstead Green 56 F2
Twiss Green 86 E4
Twiston 93 E8
Twitchen Devon 21 F6
Shrops 49 B5
Two Bridges 6 B4
Two Dales 76 C2
Two Mills 73 B7
Twycross 63 D7
Twyford Bucks 39 B6
Derbys 63 B7
Hants 15 B5
Leics 64 C4
Twyford *continued*
Lincs 65 B6
Norf 81 E6
Wokingham 27 B5
Twyford Common 49 F7
Twynholm 106 D3
Twyning 50 F3
Twyning Green 50 F4
Twynllanan 34 B1
Twynmynydd 33 C7
Twyn-y-Sheriff 35 D8
Twywell 53 B7
Tyberton 49 F5
Tyburn 62 E5
Tycroes 33 C7
Tycrwyn 59 C8
Tyddewi = St David's 44 C2
Tydd Gote 66 C4
Tydd St Giles 66 C4
Tydd St Mary 66 C4
Tyddyn-mawr 71 C6
Ty-draw 83 F8
Tye Green Essex 41 D7
Essex 42 B3
Essex 55 F6
Ty-hen Carms 32 B4
Gwyn 70 D2
Tyldesley 86 D4
Tyler Hill 30 C5
Tylers Green 40 E2
Tylorstown 34 E4
Tylwch 59 F6
Ty-mawr 82 C4
Ty Mawr 46 E4
Ty Mawr Cwm 72 E3
Ty-nant Conwy 72 E3
Gwyn 59 B6
Tyncelyn 46 C5
Tyndrum 131 F7
Tyneham 13 F6
Tynehead 121 D6
Tynemouth 111 C6
Tyne Tunnel 111 C6
Tynewydd 34 E3
Tyninghame 122 B2
Tynron 113 E8
Tyn-y-celyn 73 F5
Tyn-y-coed 60 B2
Tyn-y-fedwen 72 F5
Tyn-y-ffridd 72 F5
Tynygongl 82 C5
Tynygraig 47 C5
Tyn-y-graig 48 D2
Ty'n-y-groes 83 D7
Ty'n-y-maes 83 E6
Tyn-y-pwll 82 C4
Ty'n-yr-eithin 47 C5
Ty'r-felin-isaf 83 E8
Tyrie 153 B9
Tyringham 53 E6
Tythecott 9 C6
Tythegston 21 B7
Tytherington
Ches E 75 B6
S Glos 36 F3
Som 24 E2
Wilts 24 E4
Tytherleigh 11 D8
Ty-uchaf 59 B7
Tywardreath 5 D5
Tywyn Conwy 83 D7
Gwyn 58 D2

U

Uachdar 148 C2
Uags 149 E12
Ubbeston Green 57 B7
Ubley 23 D7
Uckerby 101 D7
Uckfield 17 B8
Uckington 37 B6
Uddingston 119 C6
Uddington 119 F8
Udimore 19 D5
Udny Green 141 B7
Udny Station 141 B8
Udston 119 D6
Udstonhead 119 E7
Uffcott 25 B6
Uffculme 11 C5
Uffington Lincs 65 D7
Oxon 38 F3
Shrops 60 C5
Ufford Pboro 65 D7
Suff 57 D6
Ufton 51 C8
Ufton Nervet 26 C4
Ugadale 143 F8
Ugborough 6 D4
Uggeshall 69 F7
Ugglebarnby 103 D6
Ughill 88 E3
Ugley 41 B8
Ugley Green 41 B8
Ugthorpe 103 C5
Uidh 148 J1
Uig Argyll 145 E10
Highld 148 C6
Highld 149 B8
Uigen 154 D5
Uigshader 149 D9
Uisken 146 K6
Ulbster 158 F5
Ulceby Lincs 79 B7
N Lincs 90 C5
Ulceby Skitter 90 C5
Ulcombe 30 E2
Uldale 108 F2
Uley 36 E4
Ulgham 117 E8
Ullapool 150 B4
Ullenhall 51 C6
Ullenwood 37 C6
Ulleskelf 95 E8
Ullesthorpe 64 F2
Ulley 89 F5
Ullingswick 49 E7
Ullinish 149 E8
Ullock 98 B2
Ulnes Walton 86 C3
Ulpha 98 E3
Ulrome 97 D7
Ulsta 160 E6
Ulva House 146 H7
Ulverston 92 B2
Ulwell 13 F8
Umberleigh 9 B8
Unapool 156 F5
Unasary 148 F2
Underbarrow 99 E6
Undercliffe 94 F4
Underhoull 160 C7
Underriver 29 D6
Underwood 76 D4
Undy 35 F8
Unifirth 160 H4
Union Cottage 141 E7
Union Mills 84 E3
Union Street 18 B4
Unstone 76 B3
Unstone Green 76 B3
Unthank Cumb 108 F4
Cumb 109 E6
Unthank End 108 F4
Upavon 25 D6
Up Cerne 12 D4
Upchurch 30 C2
Upcott 48 D5
Upend 55 D7
Up Exe 10 D4
Upgate 68 C4
Uphall 120 B3
Uphall Station 120 B3
Upham Devon 10 D3
Hants 15 B6
Uphampton 50 C3
Up Hatherley 37 B6
Uphill 22 D5
Up Holland 86 D3
Uplawmoor 118 D4
Upleadon 36 B4
Upleatham 102 C4
Uplees 30 C3
Uploders 12 E3
Uplowman 10 C5
Uplyme 11 E8
Up Marden 15 C8
Upminster 42 F1
Up Nately 26 D4
Upnor 29 B8
Upottery 11 D7
Upper Affcot 60 F4
Upper Ardchronie 151 C9
Upper Arley 61 F7
Upper Arncott 39 C6
Upper Astrop 52 F3
Upper Badcall 156 E4
Upper Basildon 26 B3
Upper Beeding 17 C5
Upper Benefield 65 F6
Upper Bighouse 157 D11
Upper Boddington 52 D2
Upper Borth 58 F3
Upper Boyndlie 153 B9
Upper Brailes 51 F8
Upper Breakish 149 F11
Upper Breinton 49 E6
Upper Broadheath 50 D3
Upper Broughton 64 B3
Upper Bucklebury 26 C3
Upper Burnhaugh 141 E7
Upperby 108 D4
Upper Caldecote 54 E2
Upper Catesby 52 D3
Upper Chapel 48 E2
Upper Church Village 34 F4
Upper Chute 25 D7
Upper Clatford 25 E8
Upper Clynnog 71 C5
Upper Cumberworth 88 D3
Upper Cwmbran 35 E6
Upper Dallachy 152 B3
Upper Dean 53 C8
Upper Denby 88 D3
Upper Denton 109 C6
Upper Derraid 151 H13
Upper Dicker 18 E2
Upper Dovercourt 57 F6
Upper Druimfin 147 F8
Upper Dunsforth 95 C7
Upper Eathie 151 E10
Upper Elkstone 75 D7
Upper End 75 B7
Upper Farringdon 26 F5
Upper Framilode 36 C4
Upper Glenfintaig 137 F5
Upper Gornal 62 E3
Upper Gravenhurst 54 F2
Upper Green Mon 35 C7
W Berks 25 C8
Upper Grove Common 36 B2
Upper Hackney 76 C2
Upper Hale 27 E6
Upper Halistra 148 C7
Upper Halling 29 C7
Upper Hambleton 65 D6
Upper Hardres Court 31 D5
Upper Hartfield 29 F5
Upper Haugh 88 E5
Upper Heath 61 F5
Upper Hellesdon 68 C5
Upper Helmsley 96 D2
Upper Hergest 48 D4
Upper Heyford Oxon 38 B4
W Nhants 52 D4
Upper Hill 49 D6
Upper Hopton 88 C2
Upper Horsebridge 18 D2
Upper Hulme 75 C7
Upper Inglesham 38 E2
Upper Inverbrough 151 H11
Upper Killay 33 E6
Upper Knockando 152 D1
Upper Lambourn 38 F3
Upper Leigh 75 F7
Upper Lenie 137 B8
Upper Lochton 141 E5
Upper Longdon 62 C4
Upper Lybster 158 G4
Upper Lydbrook 36 C3
Upper Maes-coed 48 F5
Upper Midway 63 B6

Uppermill 87 D7
Upper Milovaig . . 148 D6
Upper Minety . . . 37 E7
Upper Mitton . . . 50 B3
Upper North Dean . 39 E8
Upper Obney . . . 133 F7
Upper Ollach . . . 149 E10
Upper Padley . . . 76 B2
Upper Poppleton . 95 D8
Upper Pollicott . . 39 C7
Upper Quinton . . 51 E6
Upper Ratley . . . 14 B4
Upper Rissington . 38 C2
Upper Rochford . . 49 C8
Upper Sandaig . . 149 G12
Upper Sanday . . 159 H6
Upper Sapey . . . 49 C8
Upper Saxondale . 77 F6
Upper Seagry . . . 37 F6
Upper Shelton . . . 53 E7
Upper Sheringham 81 C7
Upper Skelmorlie . . 118 C2
Upper Slaughter . 38 B1
Upper Soudley . . 36 C3
Uppersound . . . 160 J6
Upper Stondon . . 54 F2
Upper Stowe . . . 52 D4
Upper Stratton . . 38 F1
Upper Street Hants . 14 C2
  Norf . . . 69 C6
  Norf . . . 69 C6
  Suff . . . 56 F5
Upper Strensham . 50 F4
Upper Sundon . . 40 B3
Upper Swell . . . 38 B1
Upper Tean . . . 75 F7
Upperthong . . . 88 D2
Upperthorpe . . . 89 D8
Upper Tillyrie . . 128 D3
Upperton . . . 16 B3
Upper Tooting . . 28 B3
Upper Tote . . 149 C10
Uppertown Derbys . 76 C3
  Highld . . . 158 C5
  Orkney . . . 159 J5
Upper Town . . . 23 C7
Upper Treverward . 48 B4
Upper Tysoe . . . 51 E8
Upper Upham . . . 25 B7
Upper Wardington . 52 E2
Upper Weald . . . 53 F5
Upper Weedon . . 52 D4
Upper Wield . . . 26 F4
Upper Winchendon . 39 C7
Upper Witton . . . 62 E4
Upper Woodend . 141 C5
Upper Woodford . 25 F6
Upper Wootton . . 26 D3
Upper Wyche . . . 50 E2
Uppingham . . . 65 E5
Uppington . . . 61 D6
Upsall . . . 102 F2
Upshire . . . 41 D7
Up Somborne . . 25 F8
Upstreet . . . 31 C6
Up Sydling . . . 12 D4
Upthorpe . . . 56 B3
Upton Ches W . . 73 C8
  Corn. . . . 8 D4
  Dorset. . . . 12 F5
  Dorset. . . . 13 E7
  Hants. . . . 14 C4
  Hants. . . . 25 D8
  Leics. . . . 63 E7
  Lincs . . . 90 F2
  Mers . . . 85 F3
  Norf . . . 69 C6
  Notts. . . . 77 B7
  Oxon . . . 39 F5
  Pboro. . . . 65 D8
  Slough . . . 27 B7
  Som . . . 10 B4
  W Nhants. . . . 52 C5
  W Yorks . . . 89 C5
Upton Bishop . . 36 B3
Upton Cheyney . 23 C8
Upton Cressett . 61 E6
Upton Cross . . 5 B7
Upton Grey . . . 26 E4
Upton Hellions . 10 D3
Upton Lovell . . 24 E4
Upton Magna . . 61 C5
Upton Noble . . 24 F2
Upton Pyne . . 10 E4
Upton St Leonard's . 37 C5
Upton Scudamore . 24 E3
Upton Snodsbury . 50 D4
Upton upon Severn . . 50 E3
Upton Warren . . 50 C4
Upwaltham . . 16 C3
Upware . . 55 B6
Upwell . . 66 D4
Upwey . . 12 F4
Upwood . . 66 F2
Uradale . . 160 K6
Urafirth . . 160 F5
Urchfont . . 24 D5
Urdimarsh . . 49 E7
Ure . . 160 F4
Ure Bank . . 95 B6
Urgha . . 154 H6
Urishay Common . . 48 F5
Urlay Nook . . 102 C1
Urmston . . 87 E5
Urpeth . . 110 D5
Urquhart Highld . 151 F12
  Moray . . . 152 B2
Urra . . 102 D3
Urray . . 151 F8
Ushaw Moor . . 110 E5
Usk = Brynbuga . . 35 D7
Usselby . . 90 E4
Usworth . . 111 D6
Utkinton . . 74 C2
Utley . . 94 E3
Uton . . 10 E3
Utterby . . 91 E2
Uttoxeter . . 75 F7
Uwchmynydd . . 70 E2
Uxbridge . . 40 F3
Uyeasound . . 160 C7
Uzmaston . . 44 D4

V

Valley . . 82 D2
Valleyfield . . 106 D3
Valley Truckle . . 8 F2
Valsgarth . . 160 B8
Valtos . . 149 B10
Van . . 59 F6
Vange . . 42 F3
Varteg . . 35 D6
Vatten . . 149 D7
Vaul . . 146 G3
Vaynor . . 34 C4
Veensgarth . . 160 J6
Velindre . . 48 F3
Vellow . . 22 F2
Veness . . 159 F6
Venn Green . . 9 C5
Vennington . . 60 D3
Venn Ottery . . 11 E5
Venny Tedburn . . 10 E3
Ventnor . . 15 G6
Vernham Dean . . 25 D8
Vernham Street . 25 D8
Vernolds Common. 60 F4
Verwood . . 13 D8
Veryan . . 3 C8
Vicarage . . 11 F7
Vickerstown . . 92 C1
Victoria Corn. . . 4 C4
  S Yorks. . . . 88 D2
Vidlin . . 160 G6
Viewpark . . 119 C7
Vigo Village . . 29 C7
Vinehall Street . . 18 C4
Vine's Cross . . 18 D2
Viney Hill . . 36 D3
Virginia Water . . 27 C8
Virginstow . . 9 E5
Vobster . . 24 E2
Voe Shetland . . 160 E5
  Shetland . . . 160 G6
Vowchurch . . 49 F5
Voxter . . 160 F5
Voy . . 159 G3

W

Wackerfield . . 101 B6
Wacton . . 68 E4
Wadbister . . 160 J6
Wadborough . . 50 E4
Waddesdon . . 39 C7
Waddingham . . 90 E3
Waddington Lancs . 93 E7
  Lincs . . . 78 C2
Wadebridge . . 4 B4
Wadeford . . 11 C8
Wadenhoe . . 65 F7
Wadesmill . . 41 C6
Wadhurst . . 18 B3
Wadshelf . . 76 B3
Wadsley . . 88 E4
Wadsley Bridge . . 88 E4
Wadworth . . 89 E6
Waen Denb . . 72 C3
  Denb . . . 72 C5
Waen Fach . . 60 C2
Waen Goleugoed . . 72 B4
Wag . . 157 G13
Wainfleet All Saints . . 79 D7
Wainfleet Bank . . 79 D7
Wainfleet St Mary . 79 D8
Wainfleet Tofts . . 79 D7
Wainhouse Corner . . 8 E3
Wainscott . . 29 B8
Wainstalls . . 87 B8
Waitby . . 100 D2
Waithe . . 91 D6
Wakefield . . 88 B4
Wake Lady Green . 102 E4
Wakerley . . 65 E6
Wakes Colne . . 42 B4
Walberswick . . 57 B8
Walberton . . 16 D3
Walbottle . . 110 C4
Walcot Lincs . . 78 F3
  N Lincs . . . 90 B2
  Shrops. . . . 60 F3
  Swindon . . . 38 F1
  Telford. . . . 61 C5
Walcote Leics . . 64 F2
  Warks . . . 51 D6
Walcott Lincs . . 78 D4
  Norf . . . 69 A6
Walden . . 101 F5
Walden Head . . 100 F4
Walden Stubbs . . 89 C6
Waldersey . . 66 D4
Walderslade . . 29 C8
Walderton . . 15 C8
Walditch . . 12 E2
Waldley . . 75 F8
Waldridge . . 111 D5
Waldringfield . . 57 E6
Waldringfield Heath . . 57 E6
Waldron . . 18 D2
Wales . . 89 F5
Walesby Lincs . . 90 E5
  Notts. . . . 77 B6
Walford Hereford . . 36 B2
  Hereford . . . 49 B5
  Shrops. . . . 60 B4
Walford Heath . . 60 C4
Walgherton . . 74 E3
Walgrave . . 53 B6
Walhampton . . 14 E4
Walkden . . 86 D5
Walker . . 111 C5
Walker Barn . . 75 B6
Walkerburn . . 121 F6
Walker Fold . . 93 E6
Walkeringham . . 89 E8
Walkerith . . 89 E8
Walkern . . 41 B5
Walker's Green . . 49 E7
Walkerville . . 101 E7
Walkford . . 14 E3
Walkhampton . . 6 C3
Walkington . . 97 F5
Walkley . . 88 F4
Walk Mill . . 93 F8
Wall Northumb . . 110 C2
  Staffs. . . . 62 D5

Wallaceton . . 113 F8
Wallacetown
  S Ayrs. . . . 112 B3
  S Ayrs. . . . 112 D2
Wallands Park . . 17 C8
Wallasey . . 85 E4
Wall Bank . . 60 E5
Wallcrouch . . 18 B3
Wall Heath . . 62 F2
Wallingford . . 39 F6
Wallington Hants. 15 D6
  Herts. . . . 54 F3
  London. . . . 28 C3
Wallis . . 32 B1
Walliswood . . 28 F2
Walls . . 160 J4
Wallsend . . 111 C5
Wallston . . 22 B3
Wallyford . . 121 B6
Walmer . . 31 D7
Walmer Bridge . . 86 B2
Walmersley . . 87 C6
Walmley . . 62 E5
Walpole . . 57 B7
Walpole Cross Keys. 66 C5
Walpole Highway. 66 C5
Walpole Marsh . . 66 C4
Walpole St Andrew . 66 C5
Walpole St Peter . 66 C5
Walsall . . 62 E4
Walsall Wood . . 62 D4
Walsden . . 87 B7
Walsgrave on Sowe . . 63 F7
Walsham le Willows . . 56 B3
Walshaw . . 87 C5
Walshford . . 95 D7
Walsoken . . 66 C4
Walston . . 120 E3
Walsworth . . 54 F3
Walters Ash . . 39 E8
Walterston . . 22 B2
Walterstone . . 35 B7
Waltham Kent . . 30 E5
  NE Lincs . . . 91 D6
Waltham Abbey . . 41 D6
Waltham Chase . . 15 C6
Waltham Cross . . 41 D6
Waltham on the Wolds . . 64 B5
Waltham St Lawrence . 27 B6
Walthamstow . . 41 F6
Walton Cumb. . . 108 C5
  Derbys. . . . 76 C3
  Leics. . . . 64 F2
  Mers . . . 85 E4
  M Keynes. . . . 53 F6
  Pboro. . . . 65 D8
  Powys . . . 48 D4
  Som . . . 23 F6
  Staffs. . . . 75 F5
  Suff . . . 57 F6
  Telford. . . . 61 C5
  Warks . . . 51 D7
  W Yorks . . . 88 C4
  W Yorks . . . 95 E7
Walton Cardiff . . 50 F4
Walton East . . 32 B1
Walton-in-Gordano . . 23 B6
Walton-le-Dale . . 86 B3
Walton-on-Thames. 28 C2
Walton on the Hill
  Staffs. . . . 62 B3
  Sur. . . . 28 D3
Walton-on-the-Naze . . 43 B8
Walton on the Wolds . . 64 C2
Walton-on-Trent . 63 C6
Walton West . . 44 D3
Walwen . . 73 B6
Walwick . . 110 B2
Walworth . . 101 C7
Walworth Gate . 101 B7
Walwyn's Castle . . 44 D3
Wambrook . . 11 D7
Wanborough Sur. . . 27 E7
  Swindon . . . 38 F2
Wandsworth . . 28 B3
Wangford . . 57 B8
Wanlockhead . . 113 C8
Wansford E Yorks . . 97 D6
  Pboro. . . . 65 E7
Wanstead . . 41 F7
Wanstrow . . 24 E2
Wanswell . . 36 D3
Wantage . . 38 F3
Wapley . . 23 B8
Wappenbury . . 51 C8
Wappenham . . 52 E4
Warbleton . . 18 D3
Warblington . . 15 D8
Warborough . . 39 E5
Warboys . . 66 F3
Warbreck . . 92 F3
Warbstow . . 8 E4
Warburton . . 86 F5
Warcop . . 100 C2
Warden Kent . . 30 B4
  Northumb . . . 110 C2
Ward End . . 62 F5
Ward Green . . 56 C4
Wardhill . . 159 F7
Wardington . . 52 E2
Wardlaw . . 115 C5
Wardle Ches E . . 74 D3
  Gtr Man . . . 87 C7
Wardley . . 64 D5
Wardlow . . 75 B8
Wardy Hill . . 66 F4
Ware Herts . . 41 C6
  Kent. . . . 31 C6
Wareham . . 13 F7
Warehorne . . 19 B6
Warenford . . 117 B7
Waren Mill . . 123 F7
Warenton . . 123 F7
Wareside . . 41 C6
Waresley Cambs. . . 54 D3
  Worcs. . . . 50 B3
Warfield . . 27 B6

Warfleet . . 7 D6
Wargrave . . 27 B5
Warham . . 80 C5
Warhill . . 87 E7
Wark Northumb . . 109 B8
  Northumb . . . 122 F4
Warkleigh . . 9 B8
Warkton . . 53 B6
Warkworth Northumb . 117 D8
  W Nhants. . . . 52 E2
Warlaby . . 101 E8
Warland . . 87 B7
Warleggan . . 5 C6
Warlingham . . 28 D4
Warmfield . . 88 B4
Warmingham . . 74 C4
Warmington N Nhants. . . 65 E7
  Warks . . . 52 E2
Warminster . . 24 E3
Warmlake . . 30 D2
Warmley . . 23 B8
Warmley Tower . . 23 B8
Warmonds Hill . . 53 C7
Warmsworth . . 89 D6
Warmwell . . 13 F5
Warndon . . 50 D3
Warnford . . 15 B7
Warnham . . 28 F2
Warninglid . . 17 B6
Warren Ches E . . 75 B5
  Pembs . . . 44 F4
Warren Heath . . 57 E6
Warren Row . . 39 F8
Warren Street . . 30 D3
Warrington M Keynes . . 53 D6
  Warr. . . . 86 F4
Warsash . . 15 D5
Warslow . . 75 D7
Warter . . 96 D4
Warthermarske . . 94 B5
Warthill . . 96 D2
Wartling . . 18 E3
Wartnaby . . 64 B4
Warton Lancs . . 86 B2
  Lancs. . . . 92 B4
  Northumb . . . 117 D6
  Warks . . . 63 D6
Warwick . . 51 C7
Warwick Bridge . 108 D4
Warwick on Eden . 108 D4
Wasbister . . 159 E4
Wasdale Head . . 98 D3
Washaway . . 4 C5
Washbourne . . 7 D5
Wash Common . . 26 C2
Washfield . . 10 C4
Washfold . . 101 D5
Washford . . 22 E2
Washford Pyne . . 10 C3
Washingborough . 78 B3
Washington T&W . 111 D6
  W Sus . . . 16 C4
Wasing . . 26 C3
Waskerley . . 110 E3
Wasperton . . 51 D7
Wasps Nest . . 78 C3
Wass . . 95 B8
Watchet . . 22 E2
Watchfield Oxon . . 38 E2
  Som . . . 22 E5
Watchgate . . 99 E7
Watchhill . . 107 E8
Watcombe . . 7 C7
Watendlath . . 98 C4
Water Devon . . 10 F2
  Lancs. . . . 87 B6
Waterbeach . . 55 C5
Waterbeck . . 108 B2
Waterden . . 80 D4
Water End E Yorks . . 96 F3
  Herts. . . . 40 C3
  Herts. . . . 41 D5
Waterfall . . 75 D7
Waterfoot E Renf . 119 D5
  Lancs. . . . 87 B6
Waterford Hants . . 14 E4
  Herts. . . . 41 C6
Waterhead Cumb. . . 99 D5
  Dumfries . . . 114 E4
Waterheads . . 120 D5
Waterhouses Durham . . 110 E4
  Staffs. . . . 75 D7
Wateringbury . . 29 D7
Waterloo BCP . . 13 E8
  Gtr Man . . . 87 D7
Waterloo Highld . 149 F11
  Mers . . . 85 E4
  N Lanark . . . 119 D8
  Norf . . . 68 C5
  Perth . . . 133 F7
  Shrops. . . . 74 F2
Waterloo Port . . 82 E4
Waterlooville . . 15 D7
Watermeetings . . 114 C2
Watermillock . . 99 B6
Water Newton . . 65 E8
Water Orton . . 63 E5
Waterperry . . 39 D6
Waterrow . . 11 B5
Watersfield . . 16 C4
Waterside Aberds . . 141 B9
  Blackburn. . . . 86 B5
  Cumb. . . . 108 E2
  E Ayrs. . . . 112 D4
  E Ayrs. . . . 118 E4
  E Dunb . . . 119 B6
  E Renf . . . 118 D5
Water's Nook . . 86 D4
Waterstock . . 39 D6
Waterston . . 44 E4
Water Stratford . 52 F4
Waters Upton . . 61 C6
Water Yeat . . 98 F4
Watford Herts. . . 40 E4
  W Nhants. . . . 52 C4
Watford Gap . . 62 D5
Wath N Yorks . . 94 C4
  N Yorks. . . . 95 B6
  N Yorks. . . . 96 B2
Wath Brow . . 98 C2
Wath upon Dearne . . 88 D5
Watlington Norf . . 67 C6
  Oxon . . . 39 E6
Watnall . . 76 E5

Watten . . 158 E4
Wattisfield . . 56 B4
Wattisham . . 56 D4
Wattlesborough Heath . . 60 C3
Watton E Yorks . . 97 D6
  Norf . . . 68 D2
Watton at Stone . . 41 C6
Wattston . . 119 B7
Wattstown . . 34 E4
Wauchan . . 136 F2
Waulkmill Lodge . 159 H4
Waun . . 59 D5
Waunarlwydd . . 33 E7
Waunclunda . . 47 F5
Waunfawr . . 82 F5
Waungron . . 33 D6
Waunlwyd . . 35 D5
Waun-y-clyn . . 33 D5
Wavendon . . 53 F7
Waverbridge . . 108 E2
Waverley S Yorks . . 88 F5
Waverton Ches W . . 73 C8
  Cumb . . . 108 E2
Wavertree . . 85 F4
Wawne . . 97 F6
Waxham . . 69 B7
Waxholme . . 91 B7
Way . . 31 C7
Wayfield . . 29 C8
Wayford . . 12 D2
Waymills . . 74 E2
Wayne Green . . 35 C8
Way Village . . 10 C3
Wdig =Goodwick . . 44 B4
Weachyharn . . 153 C6
Weald . . 38 D3
Wealdstone . . 40 F4
Weardley . . 95 E5
Weare . . 23 D6
Weare Giffard . . 9 B6
Wearhead . . 109 F8
Weasdale . . 100 D1
Weasenham All Saints . . 80 E4
Weasenham St Peter . . 80 E4
Weatherhill . . 28 E4
Weaverham . . 74 B3
Weaverthorpe . . 97 B5
Webheath . . 50 C5
Wedderlairs . . 153 E8
Wedderlie . . 122 D2
Weddington . . 63 E7
Wedhampton . . 25 D5
Wedmore . . 23 E6
Wednesbury . . 62 E3
Wednesfield . . 62 D3
Weedon . . 39 C8
Weedon Bec . . 52 D4
Weedon Lois . . 52 E4
Weeford . . 62 D5
Week . . 10 C2
Weeke . . 26 F2
Weekley . . 65 F5
Week St Mary . . 8 E4
Weel . . 97 F6
Weeley . . 43 B7
Weeley Heath . . 43 B7
Weem . . 133 E5
Weeping Cross . . 62 B3
Weethley Gate . . 51 D5
Weeting . . 67 F7
Weeton E Yorks . . 91 B7
  Lancs. . . . 92 F3
  N Yorks. . . . 95 E5
Weetwood Hall . 117 H13
Weir . . 87 B6
Weir Quay . . 6 C2
Welborne . . 68 D3
Welbourn . . 78 D2
Welburn N Yorks . . 96 C3
  N Yorks. . . . 102 F4
Welbury . . 102 D1
Welby . . 78 F2
Welches Dam . . 66 F4
Welcombe . . 8 C4
Weld Bank . . 86 C3
Weldon . . 117 E7
Welford W Berks. . . 26 B2
  W Nhants. . . . 64 F3
Welford-on-Avon . 51 D6
Welham Leics . . 64 E4
  Notts. . . . 89 F8
Welham Green . . 41 D5
Well Hants . . 27 E5
  Lincs . . . 79 B7
  N Yorks. . . . 101 F7
Welland . . 50 E2
Wellbank . . 134 F4
Welldale . . 107 C8
Well End . . 40 F1
Wellesbourne . . 51 D7
Well Heads . . 94 F3
Well Hill . . 29 C5
Welling . . 29 B5
Wellingborough . . 53 C6
Wellingham . . 80 E4
Wellingore . . 78 D2
Wellington Cumb. . . 98 D2
  Hereford . . . 49 E6
  Som . . . 11 B6
  Telford. . . . 61 C6
Wellington Heath. 50 E2
Wellington Hill . . 95 F6
Wellow Bath . . 24 D2
  IoW . . . 14 F4
  Notts. . . . 77 C6
Wellpond Green . . 41 B7
Wells . . 23 E7
Wellsborough . . 63 D7
Wells Green . . 74 D3
Wells-next-the-Sea . . 80 C5
Wellswood . . 7 C7
Well Town . . 10 D4
Wellwood . . 128 F2
Welney . . 66 E5
Welshampton . . 73 F8
Welsh Bicknor . . 36 C2
Welsh End . . 74 F2
Welsh Frankton . . 73 F7
Welsh Hook . . 44 C4
Welsh Newton . . 36 C1
Welshpool = Y Trallwng . . 60 D2
Welsh St Donats . . 22 B2
Welton Cumb. . . 108 E3
  E Yorks . . . 90 B3

Welton continued
  Lincs . . . 78 B3
  W Nhants. . . . 52 C3
Welton Hill . . 90 F4
Welton le Marsh . 79 C7
Welton le Wold . . 91 F6
Welwick . . 91 B7
Welwyn . . 41 C5
Welwyn Garden City . . 41 C5
Wem . . 60 B5
Wembdon . . 22 F4
Wembley . . 40 F4
Wembury . . 6 E3
Wembworthy . . 9 D8
Wenallt Ceredig . . 47 B5
  Gwyn . . . 72 E3
Wendens Ambo . . 55 F6
Wendlebury . . 39 C5
Wendling . . 68 C2
Wendover . . 40 D1
Wendron . . 3 C5
Wendy . . 54 E4
Wenfordbridge . . 5 B5
Wenhaston . . 57 B8
Wennington Cambs. 54 B3
  Lancs. . . . 93 B6
  London. . . . 41 F8
Wensley Derbys . . 76 C2
  N Yorks. . . . 101 F5
Wentbridge . . 89 C5
Wentnor . . 60 E3
Wentworth Cambs. 55 B5
  S Yorks. . . . 88 E4
Wenvoe . . 22 B3
Weobley . . 49 D6
Weobley Marsh . . 49 D6
Wereham . . 67 D6
Wergs . . 62 D2
Wern Powys . . 59 C6
  Powys . . . 60 C2
Wernffrwd . . 33 E6
Wernyrheolydd. . 35 C7
Werrington Corn. . . 8 F5
  Pboro. . . . 65 D8
  Staffs. . . . 75 E6
Wervin . . 73 B8
Wesham . . 92 F4
Wessington . . 76 D3
Westacott . . 20 F4
West Acre . . 67 C7
West Adderley . . 52 F2
West Allerdean . 123 E5
West Alvington . . 6 E5
West Amesbury . . 25 E6
West Anstey . . 10 B3
West Ashby . . 79 B5
West Ashling . . 16 D2
West Ashton . . 24 D3
West Auckland . 101 B6
West Ayton . . 103 F7
West Bagborough . 22 F3
West Barkwith . . 91 F5
West Barnby . . 103 C6
West Barns . . 122 B2
West Barsham . . 80 D5
West Bay . . 12 E2
West Beckham . . 81 D7
West Bedfont . . 27 B8
West Benhar . . 119 C8
West Bergholt . . 43 B5
West Bexington . . 12 F3
West Bilney . . 67 C7
West Blatchington . 17 D6
West Bowling . . 94 F4
West Bradford . . 93 E7
West Bradley . . 23 F7
West Bretton . . 88 C3
West Bridgford . . 77 F5
West Bromwich . . 62 E4
Westbrook . . 26 B2
West Buckland
  Devon . . . 21 F5
  Som . . . 11 B6
West Burrafirth . 160 H4
West Burton
  N Yorks. . . . 101 F5
  W Sus . . . 16 C3
Westbury Bucks . . 52 F4
  Shrops. . . . 60 D3
  Wilts . . . 24 D3
Westbury Leigh . . 24 D3
Westbury-on-Severn . . 36 C4
Westbury on Trym . 23 B7
Westbury-sub-Mendip . . 23 E7
West Butterwick . . 90 D2
West Byfleet . . 27 C8
West Caister . . 69 C8
West Calder . . 120 C3
West Camel . . 12 B3
West Challow . . 38 F3
West Chelborough 12 D3
West Chevington . 117 E8
West Chiltington . . 16 C4
West Chiltington Common . . 16 C4
West Chinnock . . 12 C2
West Chisenbury . . 25 D6
West Clandon . . 27 D8
West Cliffe . . 31 E7
Westcliff-on-Sea . 42 F4
West Clyne . . 157 J11
West Clyth . . 158 G4
West Coker . . 12 C3
West Compton
  Dorset. . . . 12 E3
  Som . . . 23 E7
Westcote . . 38 B2
Westcott Bucks. . . 39 C7
  Devon . . . 10 D5
  Sur. . . . 28 E2
Westcott Barton . . 38 B4
West Cowick . . 89 B7
West Cranmore . . 23 E8
West Cross . . 33 F7
West Cullery . . 141 D6
West Curry . . 8 E4
West Curthwaite . 108 E3
West Darlochan . 143 F7

West Dean . . 14 B3
  W Sus . . . 16 C2
Westdean . . 18 F2
West Deeping . . 17 D6
West Derby . . 85 E4
West Dereham . . 67 D6
West Didsbury . . 87 E6
West Ditchburn . 117 B7
West Down . . 20 E4
West Drayton London. . . 27 B8
  Notts. . . . 77 B7
West Ella . . 90 B4
West End Bedford. . . 53 D7
  E Yorks . . . 96 F5
  E Yorks . . . 97 F7
  Hants. . . . 15 C5
  Lancs. . . . 86 B5
  Norf . . . 69 C8
  N Som . . . 23 C6
  Oxon . . . 38 D4
  S Lanark . . . 120 E2
  Suff . . . 69 F7
  Sur. . . . 27 C7
  S Yorks. . . . 89 D7
  Wilts . . . 13 B7
  Wilts . . . 24 B4
West End Green . . 26 C4
Wester Aberchalder . 137 B8
Wester Balgedie. 128 D3
Wester Culbeuchly . 153 B6
Wester Dechmont . 120 B3
Wester Denoon . 134 E3
Westerdale Highld . . 158 E3
  N Yorks. . . . 102 D4
Wester Fintray . 141 C7
Westergate . . 16 D3
Wester Gruinards 151 B8
Westerham . . 28 D5
Westerhope . . 110 C4
Wester Lealty . . 151 D9
Westerleigh . . 23 B9
Wester Milton . . 151 F12
Wester Newburn . 129 D6
Wester Quarff . . 160 K6
Wester Skeld . . 160 J4
Westerton Angus . 135 D6
  Durham . . . 110 F5
  W Sus . . . 16 D2
Westerwick . . 160 J4
West Farleigh . . 29 D8
West Felton . . 60 B3
West Fenton . . 129 F6
West Ferry . . 134 F4
Westfield Cumb . . 98 B1
  E Sus . . . 18 D5
  Hereford . . . 50 E2
  Highld . . . 158 D2
  N Lanark . . . 119 B7
  Norf . . . 68 D2
  W Loth . . . 120 B2
Westfields . . 12 D5
Westfields of Rattray . . 134 E1
Westgate Durham . 110 F2
  N Lincs . . . 89 D8
  Norf . . . 80 C4
Westgate on Sea . 31 B7
West Ginge . . 38 F4
West Grafton . . 25 C7
West Green . . 26 D5
West Greenskares 153 B7
West Grimstead . . 14 B3
West Grinstead . . 17 B5
West Haddlesey . . 89 B6
West Haddon . . 52 B4
West Hagbourne . 39 F5
West Hagley . . 62 F3
Westhall Aberds . . 141 B5
  Suff . . . 69 F7
West Hall . . 109 C5
West Hallam . . 76 E4
West Halton . . 90 B3
Westham Dorset. . . 12 G4
  E Sus . . . 18 E3
  Som . . . 23 E6
West Ham . . 41 F7
Westhampnett . . 16 D2
West Handley . . 76 B3
West Hanney . . 38 E4
West Hanningfield 42 E3
West Hardwick . . 88 C5
West Harnham . . 14 B2
West Harptree . . 23 D7
West Hatch . . 11 B7
Westhay . . 23 E6
West Head . . 67 D5
Westhead . . 86 D2
West Heath Ches E . . 74 C5
  Hants. . . . 26 D3
  Hants. . . . 27 D6
West Helmsdale . 157 H13
West Hendred . . 38 F4
West Heslerton . . 96 B5
Westhide . . 49 E7
Westhill Aberds . . 141 D7
  Highld . . . 151 G10
West Hill Devon . . 11 E5
  E Yorks . . . 97 F7
West Hoathly . . 17 B7
West Holme . . 13 F6
Westhope Hereford . . 49 D6
  Shrops. . . . 60 F4
West Horndon . . 42 F2
Westhorpe Lincs . . 78 F5
  Suff . . . 56 C4
West Horrington . . 23 E7
West Horsley . . 27 D8
West Horton . . 123 F6
West Hougham . . 31 E6
Westhoughton . . 86 D4
West Houlland . . 160 H4
Westhouse . . 93 B6
Westhouses . . 76 D4
West Huntington . 96 D2
West Hythe . . 19 B8
West Ilsley . . 38 F4
Westing . . 160 C7
West Itchenor . . 15 D8
West Keal . . 79 C6
West Kennett . . 25 C6
West Kilbride . . 118 E2
West Kingsdown . 29 C6
West Kinharrachie 153 E9
West Kirby . . 85 F3
West Knapton . . 96 B4
West Knighton . . 12 F5
West Knoyle . . 24 F3
West Kyloe . . 123 E6
Westlake . . 6 D4
West Lambrook . . 12 C2
West Langdon . . 31 E7
West Langwell . 157 J9
West Lavington
  Wilts . . . 24 D5
  W Sus . . . 16 B2
West Layton . . 101 D6
West Lea . . 111 E7
West Leake . . 64 B2
West Learmouth . 122 F4
West Leigh . . 9 D8
Westleigh Devon . . 9 B6
  Devon . . . 11 C5
  Gtr Man . . . 86 D4
Westleton . . 57 C8
West Lexham . . 67 C8
Westley Shrops . . 60 D3
  Suff . . . 56 C2
Westley Waterless 55 D7
West Lilling . . 96 C2
Westlington . . 39 C7
West Linton . . 120 D4
West Liss . . 15 B8
West Littleton . . 24 B2
West Looe . . 5 D7
West Luccombe . . 21 E7
West Lulworth . . 13 F6
West Lutton . . 96 C5
West Lydford . . 23 F7
West Lyng . . 11 B8
West Lynn . . 67 B6
West Malling . . 29 D7
West Malvern . . 50 E2
West Marden . . 15 C8
West Marina . . 18 E4
West Markham . . 77 B7
Westmarsh . . 31 C6
West Marsh . . 91 C6
West Marton . . 93 D8
West Meon . . 15 B7
West Mersea . . 43 C6
Westmeston . . 17 C7
Westmill . . 41 B6
West Milton . . 12 E3
Westminster . . 28 B4
West Minster . . 30 B3
West Molesey . . 28 C2
West Monkton . . 11 B7
West Moors . . 13 D8
West Morriston . . 122 E2
Westmuir . . 134 D3
West Muir . . 135 C5
Westness . . 159 F4
West Ness . . 96 B2
West Newham . . 110 B3
Westnewton Cumb 107 E8
  Northumb . . . 122 F5
West Newton
  E Yorks . . . 97 F7
  Norf . . . 67 B6
  N Som . . . 23 C6
Westoe . . 111 C6
West Ogwell . . 7 B6
Weston Bath . . 24 C2
  Ches E . . . 74 D4
  Devon . . . 11 F6
  Dorset. . . . 12 G4
  Halton . . . 86 F3
  Hants. . . . 15 B8
  Herts. . . . 54 F3
  Lincs . . . 66 B2
  Notts. . . . 77 C7
  N Yorks. . . . 94 E4
  Shrops. . . . 61 B5
  Shrops. . . . 61 B6
  Staffs. . . . 62 B3
  W Berks. . . . 25 B8
  W Nhants. . . . 52 E3
Weston Beggard . . 49 E7
Westonbirt . . 37 F5
Weston by Welland . . 64 E4
Weston Colville . . 55 D7
Westoncommon . . 60 B4
Weston Coyney . . 75 E6
Weston Favell . . 53 C5
Weston Green
  Cambs. . . . 55 D7
  Norf . . . 68 C4
Weston Heath . . 61 C7
Weston Hills . . 66 B2
Westoning . . 53 F8
Weston-in-Gordano . . 23 B6
Weston Jones . . 61 B7
Weston Longville . 68 C4
Weston Lullingfields . . 60 B4
Weston-on-the-Green . . 39 C5
Weston-on-Trent . 63 B8
Weston Patrick . . 26 E4
Weston Rhyn . . 73 F6
Weston-sub-Edge 51 E6
Weston-super-Mare . . 22 C5
Weston Turville . . 40 C1
Weston under Lizard . . 62 C2
Weston under Penyard . . 36 B3
Weston under Wetherley . . 51 C8
Weston Underwood
  Derbys. . . . 76 E2
  M Keynes. . . . 53 D6
Westonzoyland . . 23 F5
West Orchard . . 13 C6
West Overton . . 25 C6

West Park . . 111 F7
West Parley . . 13 E8
West Peckham . . 29 D7
West Pelton . . 110 D5
West Pennard . . 23 F7
West Pentire . . 4 C2
West Perry . . 54 C2
Westport Argyll. . . 143 F7
  Som . . . 11 C8
West Putford . . 9 C5
West Quantoxhead 22 E3
West Rainton . . 111 E6
West Rasen . . 90 F4
West Raynham . . 80 E4
West Retford . . 89 F7
West Rounton . . 102 D2
West Row . . 55 B7
West Rudham . . 80 E4
West Runton . . 81 C7
Westruther . . 122 E2
Westry . . 66 E3
West Saltoun . . 121 C7
West Sandwick . . 160 E6
West Scrafton . . 101 F5
West Sleekburn . 117 F8
West Somerton . . 69 C7
West Stafford . . 12 F5
West Stockwith . . 89 E8
West Stoke . . 16 D2
West Stonesdale . 100 D3
West Stoughton . . 23 E6
West Stour . . 13 B5
West Stourmouth . 31 C6
West Stow . . 56 B2
West Stowell . . 25 C6
West Strathan . 157 C8
West Stratton . . 26 E3
West Street . . 30 D3
West Tanfield . . 95 B5
West Taphouse . . 5 C6
West Tarbert . 145 G7
West Thirston . 117 E7
West Thorney . . 15 D8
West Thurrock . . 29 B6
West Tilbury . . 29 B7
West Tofts Norf . . 67 E8
  Perth . . . 133 F8
West Torrington . . 90 F5
West Town Hants . . 15 E8
  N Som . . . 23 C6
West Tytherley . . 14 B3
West Tytherton . . 24 B4
Westville . . 76 E5
West Walton . . 66 C4
West Walton Highway. 66 C4
Westward . . 108 E2
Westward Ho! . . 9 B6
Westwell Kent . . 30 E3
  Oxon . . . 38 D2
Westwell Leacon . 30 E3
West Wellow . . 14 C3
West Wemyss . . 128 E5
West Wick Cambs . . 54 C5
  Durham . . . 101 C5
  Norf . . . 81 E8
West Wick . . 23 C5
West Wickham
  Cambs. . . . 55 E7
  London. . . . 28 C4
West Williamston . 32 D1
West Willoughby . 78 E2
West Winch . . 67 C6
West Winterslow . . 25 F7
West Wittering . . 15 E8
West Witton . . 101 F5
Westwood Devon . . 10 E5
  Wilts . . . 24 D3
West Woodburn . 116 F4
West Woodhay . . 25 C8
West Woodlands . . 24 E2
Westwoodside . . 89 E8
West Worldham . . 26 F5
West Worlington . 10 C2
West Worthing . . 16 D5
West Wratting . . 55 D7
West Wycombe . . 39 E8
West Wylam . . 110 C4
West Yell . . 160 E6
Wetheral . . 108 D4
Wetherby . . 95 E7
Wetherden . . 56 C4
Wetheringsett . . 56 C5
Wethersfield . . 55 F8
Wethersta . . 160 G5
Wetherup Street . . 56 C5
Wetley Rocks . . 75 E6
Wettenhall . . 74 C3
Wetton . . 75 D8
Wetwang . . 96 D5
Wetwood . . 74 F4
Wexcombe . . 25 D7
Wexham Street . . 40 F2
Weybourne Norf . . 81 C7
  Sur. . . . 27 E6
Weybread . . 68 F5
Weybridge . . 27 C8
Weycroft . . 11 E8
Weydale . . 158 D3
Weyhill . . 25 E8
Weymouth . . 12 G4
Whaddon Bucks . . 53 F6
  Cambs. . . . 54 E4
  Glos. . . . 37 C5
  Wilts . . . 14 B2
Whale . . 99 B7
Whaley . . 76 B5
Whaley Bridge . . 87 F8
Whaley Thorns . . 76 B5
Whaligoe . . 158 F5
Whalley . . 93 F7
Whalton . . 117 F7
Wham . . 93 C7
Whaplode . . 66 B3
Whaplode Drove . 66 C3
Whaplode St Catherine . . 66 B3
Wharfe . . 93 C7
Wharles . . 92 F4
Wharncliffe Side . 88 E3
Wharram le Street. 96 C4
Wharton . . 74 C3
Wharton Green . . 74 C3
Whashton . . 101 D6
Whatcombe . . 13 D6

Whatcote 51 E8
Whatfield 56 E4
Whatley Som. . . . . . 11 B
Som 24 E2
Whatlington 18 D4
Whatstandwell 76 D3
Whatton 77 F7
Whauphill 105 E8
Whaw 100 D4
Wheatacre 69 E7
Wheatcroft 76 D3
Wheathampstead . . 40 C4
Wheathill 61 F6
Wheatley Devon . . . 10 E4
Hants 27 E5
Oxon 39 D5
S Yorks 89 D6
W Yorks 87 B8
Wheatley Hill 111 F6
Wheaton Aston . . . 62 C2
Wheddon Cross . . . 21 F8
Wheelock 74 D4
Wheelock Heath . . . 74 D4
Wheelton 86 B4
Wheen 134 B3
Wheldrake 96 E2
Whelford 38 E1
Whelpley Hill 40 D2
Whempstead 41 B6
Whenby 96 C2
Whepstead 56 D2
Wherstead 57 E5
Wherwell 25 E8
Wheston 75 B8
Whetsted 29 E7
Whetstone 64 E2
Whicham 98 F3
Whichford 51 F8
Whickham 110 C5
Whiddon Down 9 E8
Whigstreet 134 E4
Whilton 52 C4
Whimble 9 D5
Whim Farm 120 D5
Whimple 10 E5
Whimpwell Green . . 69 B6
Whinburgh 68 D3
Whinnieliggate . . . 106 D4
Whinnyfold 153 E10
Whippingham 15 E6
Whipsnade 40 C3
Whipton 10 E4
Whirlow 88 F4
Whisby 78 C2
Whissendine 64 C5
Whissonsett 80 E5
Whistlefield
Argyll 145 D10
Argyll 145 D11
Whistley Green 27 B5
Whiston Mers 86 E2
Staffs 62 C2
Staffs 75 E7
S Yorks 88 F5
W Nhants 53 C6
Whitbeck 98 F3
Whitbourne 50 D2
Whitburn T&W . . . 111 C7
W Loth 120 C2
Whitburn
Colliery 111 C7
Whitby Ches W 85
N Yorks 103 C6
Whitbyheath 73 B7
Whitchurch Bath . . 23 C8
Bucks 39 B7
Cardiff 35 F5
Devon 6 B2
Hants 26 E2
Hereford 36 C2
Oxon 26 B4
Pembs 44 C2
Shrops 74 E2
Whitchurch
Canonicorum . . . 11 E8
Whitchurch Hill . . . 26 B4
Whitcombe 12 F5
Whitcott Keysett . . . 60 F2
Whiteacen 152 D2
Whiteacre Heath . . . 63 E6
Whitebridge 137 C7
Whitebrook 36 D2
Whiteburn 122 D2
Whitecairn 105 D6
Whitecairns 141 C8
Whitecastle 120 E3
Whitechapel 93 E5
Whitecleat 159 H6
White Coppice 86 C4
Whitecraig 121 B6
Whitecroft 36 D3
Whitecross Corn 4 B4
Falk 120 B2
Staffs 62 B2
Whiteface 151 C10
Whitefarland 143 D9
Whitefaulds 112 D2
Whitefield Gtr Man . 87 D6
Perth 134 F1
Whiteford 141 B6
Whitegate 74 C3
Whitehall Blackburn 86 B4
W Sus 16 B5
Whitehall Village . 159 F7
Whitehaven 98 C1
Whitehill 27 F5
Whitehills Aberds . 153 B6
S Lanark 119 D6
Whitehough 87 F8
Whitehouse
Aberds 140 C5
Argyll 145 G7
Whiteinch 118 C5
Whitekirk 129 F7
White Ladies
Aston 50 D4
Whitelaw 119 E6
Whiteleas 111 C6
Whiteley Bank 15 F6
Whiteley Green 75 B6
Whiteley Village . . . 27 C8
White Lund 92 C4
Whitemans Green . . 17 B7

White Mill 33 B5
Whitemire 151 F12
Whitemoor 4 D4
Whitemore 75 C5
Whitenap 14 B4
White Ness 160 J5
White Notley 42 C3
Whiteoak Green . . . 38 C3
Whiteparish 14 B3
White Pit 79 B6
White Post 77 D6
Whiterashes 141 B7
White Rocks 35 B8
White Roding 42 C1
Whiterow 158 F5
Whiteshill 37 D5
Whiteside
Northumb 109 C7
W Loth 120 C2
Whitesmith 18 D2
Whitestaunton 11 C7
Whitestone Devon . . 10 E3
Devon 20 E3
Warks 63 F7
Whitestones 153 D8
Whitestreet Green . . 56 F3
Whitewall Corner . . 96 B3
Whiteway Glos 37 C6
Glos 37 E5
Whitewell Aberds . 153 B9
Lancs 93 E6
Whitewell Bottom . . 87 B6
Whiteworks 6 B4
Whitfield Kent 31 E7
Northumb 109 D7
S Glos 36 E3
W Nhants 52 F4
Whitford Devon . . . 11 E7
Flint 72 B5
Whitgift 90 B2
Whitgreave 62 B2
Whithorn 105 E8
Whiting Bay 143 F11
Whitkirk 95 F6
Whitland 32 C2
Whitletts 112 B3
Whitley N Yorks . . . 89 B6
Reading 26 B5
Wilts 24 C3
Whitley Bay 111 B6
Whitley Chapel . . . 110 D2
Whitley Lower 88 C3
Whitley Row 29 E5
Whitlock's End 51 B6
Whitminster 36 D4
Whitmore 74 E5
Whitnage 10 C5
Whitnash 51 C8
Whitney-on-Wye . . . 48 E4
Whitrigg Cumb . . . 108 D2
Cumb 108 F2
Whitsbury 14 C2
Whitsome 122 D4
Whitson 35 F7
Whitstable 30 C5
Whitstone 8 E4
Whittingham 117 C6
Whittingslow 60 F4
Whittington Glos . . 37 B7
Lancs 93 B6
Norf 67 E7
Shrops 73 F7
Staffs 62 F2
Staffs 63 D5
Worcs 50 D3
Whittlebury 52 E4
Whittle-le-Woods . . 86 B3
Whittlesey 66 E2
Whittlesford 55 E5
Whittlestone Head . . 86 C5
Whitton Borders . . 116 B3
Ches W 73 B7
N Lincs 90 B3
Northumb 117 D6
Powys 48 C4
Shrops 49 B7
Stockton 102 B1
Suff 56 E5
Whittonditch 25 B7
Whittonstall 110 D3
Whitway 26 D2
Whitwell Derbys . . . 76 B5
Herts 40 B4
IoW 15 G6
N Yorks 101 E7
Rutland 65 D6
Whitwell-on-the-
Hill 96 C3
Whitwell Street . . . 81 E7
Whitwick 63 C8
Whitwood 88 B5
Whitworth 87 C6
Whixall 74 F2
Whixley 95 D7
Whoberley 51 B8
Whorlton Durham . 101 C6
N Yorks 102 D2
Whygate 109 B7
Whyle 49 C7
Whyteleafe 28 D4
Wibdon 36 E2
Wibsey 88 A2
Wibtoft 63 F8
Wichenford 50 C2
Wichling 30 D3
Wick BCP 14 E2
Devon 11 D6
Highld 158 E5
S Glos 24 B2
Shetland 160 K6
V Glam 21 B8
Wilts 14 B2
Worcs 50 E4
W Sus 16 D4
Wicken Cambs 55 B6
W Nhants 52 F5
Wicken Bonhunt . . 55 F5
Wickenby 90 F4
Wicken Green
Village 80 D4
Wickersley 89 E5
Wickford 42 E3
Wickham Hants . . . 15 C6
W Berks 25 B8
Wickham Bishops . . 42 C4
Wickhambreaux . . . 31 D6
Wickhambrook 55 D8
Wickhamford 51 E5
Wickham Market . . 57 D7

Wickhampton 69 D7
Wickham St Paul . . 56 F2
Wickham Skeith . . . 56 C4
Wickham Street
Suff 55 D8
Suff 56 C4
Wick Hill 27 C5
Wicklewood 68 D3
Wickmere 81 D7
Wick St Lawrence . 23 C5
Wickwar 36 F4
Widdington 55 F6
Widdrington 117 E8
Widdrington
Station 117 E8
Widecombe in the
Moor 6 B5
Widegates 5 D7
Widemouth Bay 8 D4
Wide Open 110 B5
Widewall 159 J5
Widford Essex 42 D2
Herts 41 C7
Widham 37 F7
Widmer End 40 E1
Widmerpool 64 B3
Widnes 86 F3
Wigan 86 D3
Wiggaton 11 E6
Wiggenhall
St Germans 67 C5
Wiggenhall St Mary
Magdalen 67 C5
Wiggenhall St Mary
the Virgin 67 C5
Wigginton Herts . . 40 C2
Oxon 51 F8
Staffs 63 D6
York 95 D8
Wigglesworth 93 D8
Wiggonby 108 D2
Wiggonholt 16 C4
Wighill 95 E7
Wighton 80 D5
Wigley 14 C4
Wigmore Hereford . 49 C6
Medway 30 C2
Wigsley 77 B8
Wigsthorpe 65 F7
Wigston 64 E3
Wigthorpe 89 F6
Wigtoft 79 F5
Wigton 108 E2
Wigtown 105 D8
Wigtwizzle 88 E3
Wike 95 E6
Wike Well End 89 C7
Wilbarston 64 F5
Wilberfoss 96 D3
Wilberlee 87 C8
Wilburton 55 B5
Wilby N Nhants . . . 53 C6
Norf 68 F3
Suff 57 B6
Wilcot 25 C6
Wilcott 60 C3
Wilcrick 35 F8
Wilday Green 76 B3
Wildboarclough . . . 75 C6
Wilden Bedford . . . 53 D8
Worcs 50 B3
Wildhern 25 D8
Wildhill 41 D5
Wildmoor 50 B4
Wildsworth 90 E2
Wilford 77 F5
Wilkesley 74 E3
Wilkhaven 151 C12
Wilkieston 120 C4
Willand 10 C5
Willaston Ches E . . 74 D3
Ches W 73 B7
Willen 53 E6
Willenhall W Mid . . 51 B8
W Mid 62 E3
Willerby E Yorks . . 97 F6
N Yorks 97 B6
Willersey 51 F6
Willersley 48 E5
Willesborough 30 E4
Willesborough
Lees 30 E4
Willesden 41 F5
Willett 22 F3
Willey Shrops 61 E6
Warks 63 F8
Willey Green 27 D7
Williamscott 52 E2
Willian 54 F3
Willingale 42 D1
Willingdon 18 E2
Willingham 54 B5
Willingham by
Stow 90 F2
Willington Bedford . 54 E2
Derbys 63 B6
Durham 110 F4
T&W 111 C6
Warks 51 F7
Willington Corner . 74 C2
Willisham Tye 56 D4
Willitoft 96 F3
Williton 22 E2
Willoughbridge . . . 74 E4
Willoughby Lincs . . 79 B7
Warks 52 C3
Willoughby-on-
the-Wolds 64 B3
Willoughby
Waterleys 64 E2
Willoughton 90 E3
Willows Green 42 C3
Willsbridge 23 B8
Willsworthy 9 F7
Wilmcote 51 D6
Wilmington Devon . 11 E7
E Sus 18 E2
Kent 29 B6
Wilminstone 6 B2
Wilmslow 87 F6
Wilnecote 63 D6
Wilpshire 93 F6
Wilsden 94 F3
Wilsford Lincs 78 E3
Wilts 25 C6
Wilts 25 F6
Wilsill 94 C4
Wilsley Pound 18 B4
Wilson 26 F5

Wilson 63 B8
Wilsontown 120 D2
Wilstead 53 E8
Wilsthorpe 65 C7
Wilstone 40 C2
Wilton Borders . . . 115 C7
Cumb 98 C2
N Yorks 103 F6
Redcar 102 C3
Wilts 25 C7
Wilts 25 F5
Wimbish 55 F6
Wimbish Green . . . 55 F7
Wimblebury 62 C4
Wimbledon 28 B3
Wimblington 66 E4
Wimborne Minster 13 E8
Wimborne
St Giles 13 C8
Wimbotsham 67 D6
Wimpson 14 C4
Wimpstone 51 E7
Wincanton 12 B5
Wincham 74 B3
Winchburgh 120 B3
Winchcombe 37 B7
Winchelsea 19 D6
Winchelsea Beach . 19 D6
Winchester 15 B5
Winchet Hill 29 E8
Winchfield 27 D5
Winchmore Hill
Bucks 40 E2
London 41 E6
Wincle 75 C6
Wincobank 88 E4
Windermere 99 E6
Winderton 51 E8
Windhill 151 G8
Windhouse 160 D6
Windlehurst 87 F7
Windlesham 27 C7
Windley 76 E3
Windmill Hill
E Sus 18 D3
Som 11 C8
Windrush 38 C1
Windsor N Lincs . . . 89 C7
Windsor 27 B7
Windsoredge 37 D5
Windygates 128 D5
Windyknowe 120 C2
Windywalls 122 F3
Wineham 17 C6
Winestead 91 B6
Winewall 94 E2
Winfarthing 68 F4
Winford IoW 15 F6
N Som 23 C7
Winforton 48 E4
Winfrith
Newburgh 13 F6
Wing Bucks 40 B1
Rutland 65 D5
Wingate 111 F7
Wingates Gtr Man . 86 D4
Northumb 117 E7
Wingerworth 76 C3
Wingfield C Beds . . 40 B2
Suff 57 B6
Wilts 24 D3
Wingham 31 D6
Wingmore 31 E5
Wingrave 40 C1
Winkburn 77 D7
Winkfield 27 B7
Winkfield Row 27 B6
Winkhill 75 D7
Winklebury 26 D4
Winkleigh 9 D8
Winksley 95 B5
Winlaton 110 C4
Winless 158 E5
Winmarleigh 92 E4
Winnal 49 F6
Winnall 15 B5
Winnersh 27 B5
Winscales 98 B2
Winscombe 23 D6
Winsford Ches W . . 74 C3
Som 21 F8
Winsham 11 D8
Winshill 63 B6
Winskill 109 F5
Winslade 26 E4
Winsley 24 C3
Winslow 39 B7
Winson 37 D7
Winson Green 62 F4
Winsor 14 C4
Winster Cumb 99 E6
Derbys 76 C2
Winston Durham . 101 C6
Suff 57 C5
Winstone 37 D6
Winston Green 57 C5
Winswell 9 C6
Winter Gardens . . . 42 F3
Winteringham 90 B3
Winterley 74 D4
Wintersett 88 C4
Wintershill 15 C6
Winterton 90 C3
Winterton-on-Sea 69 C7
Winthorpe Lincs . . . 79 C8
Notts 77 D8
Winton BCP 13 E8
Cumb 100 C2
N Yorks 102 E2
Wintringham 96 B4
Winwick Cambs . . . 65 F8
Warr 86 E4
N Sus 52 B4
Wirksworth 76 D2
Wirksworth Moor . 76 D3
Wirswall 74 E2
Wisbech 66 D4
Wisbech St Mary . . 66 D4
Wisborough Green 16 B4
Wiseton 89 F8
Wishaw N Lanark . 119 D7
Warks 63 E5
Wisley 27 D8
Wispington 78 B5
Wissenden 30 E3
Wissett 57 B7
Wistanstow 60 F4
Wistanswick 61 B6
Wistaston 74 D3
Wistaston Green . . 74 D3
Wiston Pembs 32 C1
S Lanark 120 F2
W Sus 16 C5
Wistow Cambs 66 F2
N Yorks 95 F8
Wiswell 93 F7
Witcham 66 F4
Witchampton 13 D7
Witchford 55 B6
Witham 42 C4
Witham Friary 24 E2
Witham on the Hill 65 C7
Withcall 91 F6
Withdean 17 D7
Witherenden Hill . . 18 C3
Witheridge 10 C3
Withern 91 F8
Withernsea 91 B7
Withernwick 97 E7
Withersdale Street 69 F5
Withersfield 55 E7
Witherslack 99 F6
Withiel 4 C4
Withiel Florey 21 F8
Withington Glos . . . 37 C7
Gtr Man 87 E6
Hereford 49 E7
Shrops 61 C5
Staffs 75 F7
Withington Green . 74 B5
Withleigh 10 C4
Withnell 86 B4
Withybrook 63 F8
Withycombe 22 E2
Withycombe
Raleigh 10 F5
Withyham 29 F5
Withypool 21 F7
Witley 27 F7
Witnesham 57 D5
Witney 38 C3
Wittering 65 D7
Wittersham 19 C5
Witton Angus 135 B5
Worcs 50 C3
Witton Bridge 69 A6
Witton Gilbert 110 E5
Witton-le-Wear . . 110 F4
Witton Park 110 F4
Wiveliscombe 11 B5
Wivelrod 26 F4
Wivelsfield 17 B7
Wivelsfield Green . 17 B7
Wivenhoe 43 B6
Wivenhoe Cross . . 43 B6
Wiveton 81 C6
Wix 43 B7
Wixford 51 D5
Wixhill 61 B5
Wixoe 55 E8
Woburn 53 F7
Woburn Sands 53 F7
Wokefield Park . . . 26 C4
Woking 27 D8
Wokingham 27 C6
Wolborough 7 B6
Woldingham 28 D4
Wold Newton
E Yorks 97 B6
NE Lincs 91 E6
Wolfclyde 120 F3
Wolferton 67 B6
Wolfhill 134 F1
Wolf's Castle 44 C4
Wolfsdale 44 C4
Woll 115 B7
Wollaston
N Nhants 53 C7
Shrops 60 C3
Wollaton 76 F5
Wollerton 74 F3
Wollescote 62 F3
Wolsingham 110 F3
Wolstanton 75 E5
Wolston 52 B2
Wolvercote 38 D4
Wolverhampton . . 62 E3
Wolverley Shrops . . 73 F8
Worcs 50 B3
Wolverton Hants . . 26 D3
M Keynes 53 E6
Warks 51 C7
Wolverton
Common 26 D3
Wolvesnewton . . . 36 E1
Wolvey 63 F8
Wolviston 102 B2
Wombleton 102 F4
Wombourne 62 E2

Wombwell 88 D4
Womenswold 31 D6
Womersley 89 C6
Wonastow 36 C1
Wonersh 27 E8
Wonson 9 F8
Wooburn 40 F2
Wooburn Green . . . 40 F2
Woodacott 9 D5
Woodale 94 B3
Woodbank 143 G7
Woodbastwick 69 C6
Woodbeck 77 B7
Woodborough
Notts 77 E6
Wilts 25 D6
Woodbridge Dorset 13 D5
Suff 57 E6
Woodbury 10 F5
Woodbury
Salterton 10 F5
Woodchester 37 D5
Woodchurch Kent . 19 B6
Mers 85 F3
Woodcombe 21 E8
Woodcote 39 F6
Woodcott 26 D2
Woodcroft 36 E2
Woodcutts 13 C7
Wood Dalling 81 E6
Woodditton 55 D7
Woodeaton 39 C5
Woodend Cumb . . . 98 E3
W Nhants 52 E4
W Sus 16 D2
Wood End Herts . . 41 B6
Warks 51 B6
Warks 63 E6
Wood Enderby 79 C5
Woodend Green . . . 52 E4
Woodfalls 14 B2
Woodfield Oxon . . . 39 B5
S Ayrs 112 B3
Wood Field 28 D2
Woodford Corn 8 C4
Devon 7 D5
Glos 36 E3
Gtr Man 87 F6
London 41 E7
N Nhants 53 B7
Woodford Bridge . . 41 E7
Woodford Halse . . . 52 D3
Woodgate Norf . . . 68 C3
W Mid 62 F3
Worcs 50 C4
W Sus 16 D3
Woodgreen 14 C2
Wood Green 41 E6
Woodhall Herts . . . 41 C5
Inclyd 118 B3
N Yorks 100 E4
Woodhall Spa 78 C4
Woodham 27 C8
Woodham Ferrers . 42 E3
Woodham
Mortimer 42 D4
Woodham Walter . . 42 D4
Woodhaven 129 B6
Wood Hayes 62 D3
Woodhead 153 E7
Woodhey 87 C5
Woodhill 61 F7
Woodhorn 117 F8
Woodhouse Leics . . 64 C2
N Lincs 89 D7
S Yorks 88 F5
W Yorks 88 B4
Woodhouse Eaves 64 C2
Woodhouselee . . . 120 C5
Woodhouselees . . 108 B3
Woodhouse Park . . 87 F6
Woodhouses 63 C5
Woodhurst 54 B4
Woodingdean 17 D7
Woodkirk 88 B3
Woodland Devon . . . 7 C5
Durham 101 B5
Woodlands Aberds 141 E6
Dorset 13 D8
Hants 14 C4
Highld 151 E8
N Yorks 95 D6
S Yorks 89 D6
Woodlands Park . . 27 B6
Woodlands
St Mary 25 B8
Woodlane 62 B5
Wood Lanes 87 F7
Woodleigh 6 E5
Woodlesford 88 B4
Woodley Gtr Man . 87 E7
Wokingham 27 B5
Woodmancote Glos 36 E4
Glos 37 B6
Glos 37 D7
W Sus 15 D8
W Sus 17 C6
Woodmancott 26 E3
Woodmansey 97 F6
Woodmansterne . . 28 D3
Woodminton 13 B8
Woodnesborough . 31 D7
Woodnewton 65 E7
Wood Norton 81 E6
Woodplumpton . . . 92 F5
Woodrising 68 D2
Woodseaves Shrops 74 F3
Staffs 61 B7
Woodsend 25 B7
Woodsetts 89 F6
Woodsford 13 E5
Wood's Green 18 B3
Woodside
Aberdeen 141 D8
Aberds 153 D10
Brack 27 B7
Fife 129 D6
Hants 14 E4
Herts 41 D5
Perth 134 F2
Woodside of
Arbeadie 141 E6
Woodstock Oxon . . 38 C4
Pembs 32 C1
Wood Street Norf . 69 B6
Sur 27 D7
Woodthorpe Derbys 76 B4

Woodthorpe continued
Leics 64 C2
Lincs 91 F8
York 95 D8
Woodton 69 E5
Woodtown Devon . . . 9 B6
Devon 9 B6
Woodvale 85 C4
Woodville 63 C7
Wood Walton 66 F2
Woodyates 13 C8
Woofferton 49 C7
Wookey 23 E7
Wookey Hole 23 E7
Wool 13 F6
Woolacombe 20 E3
Woolage Green . . . 31 E6
Woolaston 36 E2
Woolavington 22 E5
Woolbeding 16 B2
Wooldale 88 D2
Wooler 117 B5
Woolfardisworthy
Devon 8 B5
Devon 10 D3
Woolfords
Cottages 120 D3
Woolhampton 26 C3
Woolhope 49 F8
Woolhope
Cockshoot 49 F8
Woolland 13 D5
Woollaton 9 C6
Woolley Bath 24 C2
Cambs 54 B2
Corn 8 C4
Derbys 76 C3
W Yorks 88 C4
Woolmer Green . . . 41 C5
Woolmere Green . . 50 C4
Woolpit 56 C3
Woolscott 52 C2
Woolsington 110 C4
Woolstanwood . . . 74 D3
Woolstaston 60 E4
Woolsthorpe Lincs . 65 B6
Lincs 77 F8
Woolston Devon 6 E5
Shrops 60 B3
Shrops 60 F4
Soton 14 C5
Warr 86 F4
Woolstone
M Keynes 53 F6
Oxon 38 F2
Woolton 86 F2
Woolton Hill 26 C2
Woolverstone 57 F5
Woolverton 24 D2
Woolwich 28 B5
Woolwich Ferry . . 28 B5
Woonton 49 D5
Wooperton 117 B6
Woore 74 E4
Wootten Green . . . 57 B6
Wootton Bedford . . 53 E8
Hants 14 E3
Hereford 48 D5
Kent 31 E6
N Lincs 90 C4
Oxon 38 C4
Oxon 38 D4
Shrops 49 B7
Shrops 60 B3
Staffs 62 B2
Staffs 75 E8
Wootton Bridge . . 15 E6
Wootton Common . 15 E6
Wootton
Courtenay 21 E8
Wootton Fitzpaine 11 E8
Wootton Rivers . . . 25 C6
Wootton
St Lawrence . . . 26 D3
Wootton Wawen . . 51 C6
Worcester 50 D3
Worcester Park . . . 28 C3
Wordsley 62 F2
Worfield 61 E7
Work 159 G5
Workington 98 B1
Worksop 77 B5
Worlaby 90 C4
World's End 26 B2
Worle 23 C5
Worleston 74 D3
Worlingham 69 F7
Worlington 55 B7
Worlingworth 57 C6
Wormald Green . . . 95 C6
Wormbridge 49 F6
Wormegay 67 C6
Wormelow Tump . . 49 F6
Wormhill 75 B8
Wormingford 56 F3
Worminghall 39 D6
Wormington 50 F5
Worminster 23 E7
Wormit 129 B5
Wormleighton 52 D2
Wormley Herts . . . 41 D6
Sur 27 F7
Wormley West
End 41 D6
Wormshill 30 D2
Wormsley 49 E6
Worplesdon 27 D7
Worrall 88 E4
Worsbrough 88 D4
Worsbrough
Common 88 D4
Worsley 86 D5
Worstead 69 B6
Worsthorne 93 F8
Worston 93 E7
Worswell 6 E3
Worth Kent 31 D7
W Sus 28 F4
Wortham 56 B4
Worthen 60 D3
Worthenbury 73 E8
Worthing Norf . . . 68 C2
W Sus 16 D5
Worthington 63 B8
Worth Matravers . 13 G7
Worting 26 D4
Wortley S Yorks . . 88 E4
W Yorks 95 F5

Worton N Yorks . . 100 E4
Wilts 24 D4
Wortwell 69 F5
Wotherton 60 D2
Wotter 6 C3
Wotton 28 E2
Wotton-
under-Edge . . . 36 E4
Wotton
Underwood . . . 39 C6
Woughton on
the Green 53 F6
Wouldham 29 C8
Wrabness 57 F6
Wrafton 20 F3
Wragby Lincs 78 B4
W Yorks 88 C5
Wragholme 91 E7
Wramplingham . . . 68 D4
Wrangbrook 89 C5
Wrangham 153 E6
Wrangle 79 D7
Wrangle Bank 79 D7
Wrangle Lowgate . 79 D7
Wrangway 11 C6
Wrantage 11 B8
Wrawby 90 D4
Wraxall Dorset . . . 12 D3
N Som 23 B6
Som 23 F8
Wray 93 C6
Wraysbury 27 B8
Wrayton 93 B6
Wrea Green 92 F3
Wreay Cumb 99 B6
Cumb 108 E4
Wrecclesham 27 E6
Wrecsam
= Wrexham . . . 73 D7
Wrekenton 111 D5
Wrelton 103 F5
Wrenbury 74 E2
Wrench Green . . . 103 F7
Wreningham 68 E4
Wrentham 69 F7
Wrenthorpe 88 B4
Wrentnall 60 D4
Wressle E Yorks . . . 96 F3
N Lincs 90 D3
Wrestlingworth . . . 54 E3
Wretham 68 F2
Wretton 67 E6
Wrexham
= Wrecsam . . . 73 D7
Wrexham
Industrial Estate 73 E7
Wribbenhall 50 B2
Wrightington Bar . 86 C3
Wrinehill 74 E4
Wrington 23 C6
Writhlington 24 D2
Writtle 42 D2
Wrockwardine 61 C6
Wroot 89 D8
Wrotham 29 D7
Wrotham Heath . . 29 D7
Wroughton 37 F8
Wroxall IoW 15 G6
Warks 51 B7
Wroxeter 61 D5
Wroxham 69 C6
Wroxton 52 E2
Wyaston 75 E8
Wyberton 79 E6
Wyboston 54 D2
Wybunbury 74 E4
Wychbold 50 C4
Wych Cross 28 F5
Wyck 27 F5
Wyck Rissington . . 38 B1
Wycoller 94 F2
Wycomb 64 B4
Wycombe Marsh . . 40 E1
Wyddial 54 F4
Wye 30 E4
Wyesham 36 C2
Wyfordby 64 C4
Wyke Dorset 13 B5
Shrops 61 D6
Sur 27 D7
W Yorks 88 B2
Wykeham N Yorks . 96 B4
N Yorks 103 F7
Wyken 63 F7
Wyke Regis 12 G4
Wykey 60 B3
Wylam 110 C4
Wylde Green 62 E5
Wyllie 35 E5
Wylye 24 F5
Wymering 15 D7
Wymeswold 64 B3
Wymington 53 C7
Wymondham Leics . 65 C5
Norf 68 D4
Wyndham 34 E3
Wynford Eagle . . . 12 E3
Wyng 159 J4
Wynyard Village . 102 B2
Wyre Piddle 50 E4
Wysall 64 B3
Wythall 51 B5
Wytham 38 D4
Wythburn 99 C5
Wythenshawe 87 F6
Wythop Mill 98 B3
Wyton 54 B3
Wyverstone 56 C4
Wyverstone Street . 56 C4
Wyville 65 B5
Wyvis Lodge 150 D7

Y

Yaddlethorpe 90 D2
Yafford 14 F5
Yafforth 101 E8
Yalding 29 E8
Yanworth 37 C7
Yapham 96 D3
Yapton 16 D3
Yarburgh 91 E7
Yarcombe 11 D7
Yard 22 F2
Yardley 62 F5
Yardley Gobion . . . 52 E5
Yardley Hastings . . 53 D6
Yardro 48 D4

Yarkhill 49 E8
Yarlet 62 B3
Yarlington 12 B4
Yarlside 92 C2
Yarm 102 C2
Yarmouth 14 F4
Yarnbrook 24 D3
Yarnfield 75 F5
Yarnscombe 9 B7
Yarnton 38 C4
Yarpole 49 C6
Yarrow 115 B6
Yarrow Feus 115 B6
Yarwell 65 E7
Yate 36 F4
Yateley 27 C6
Yatesbury 25 B5
Yattendon 26 B3
Yatton Hereford . . . 49 C6
N Som 23 C6
Yatton Keynell . . . 24 B3
Yaverland 15 F7
Yaxham 68 C3
Yaxley Cambs 65 E8
Suff 56 B5
Yazor 49 E6
Y Bala = Bala . . . 72 F3
Y Barri = Barry . . 22 C3
Y Bont-Faen
= Cowbridge . . 21 B8
Y Drenewydd
= Newtown . . . 59 E8
Yeading 40 F4
Yeadon 94 E5
Yealand Conyers . . 92 B5
Yealand
Redmayne 92 B5
Yealmpton 6 D3
Yearby 102 B4
Yearsley 95 B8
Yeaton 60 C4
Yeaveley 75 E8
Yedingham 96 B4
Yeldon 53 C8
Yelford 38 D3
Yelland 20 F3
Yelling 54 C3
Yelvertoft 52 B3
Yelverton Devon . . . 6 C3
Norf 69 D5
Yenston 12 B5
Yeoford 10 E2
Yeolmbridge 8 F5
Yeo Mill 10 B3
Yeovil 12 C3
Yeovil Marsh 12 C3
Yeovilton 12 B3
Yerbeston 32 D1
Yesnaby 159 G3
Yetlington 117 D6
Yetminster 12 C3
Yettington 11 F5
Yetts o'Muckhart . 128 D2
Y Felinheli 82 E5
Y Fenni
= Abergavenny . 35 C6
Y Fflint = Flint . . . 73 B6
Y Ffôr 70 D4
Y-Ffrith 72 A4
Y Gelli Gandryll
= Hay-on-Wye . . 48 E4
Yieldshields 119 D8
Yiewsley 40 F3
Y Mwmbwls
= The Mumbles . 33 F7
Ynysboeth 34 E4
Ynysddu 35 E5
Ynysgyfflog 58 C3
Ynyshir 34 E4
Ynyslas 58 E3
Ynys-meudwy 33 D7
Ynystawe 33 D7
Ynysybwl 34 E4
Yockenthwaite . . . 94 B2
Yockleton 60 C3
Yokefleet 90 B2
Yoker 118 C5
Yonder Bognie . . . 152 D6
York 95 D8
Yorkletts 30 C4
Yorkley 36 D3
York Town 27 C6
Yorton 60 B5
Youlgreave 76 C2
Youlstone 8 C4
Youlthorpe 96 D3
Youlton 95 C7
Young's End 42 C3
Young Wood 78 B4
Yoxall 62 C5
Yoxford 57 C7
Y Pîl = Pyle 34 F2
Yr Hôb = Hope . . 73 D7
Y Rhws = Rhoose . 22 C2
Y Rhyl = Rhyl . . . 72 A4
Yr Wyddgrug
= Mold 73 C6
Ysbyty-Cynfyn . . . 47 B6
Ysbyty Ifan 72 E2
Ysbyty Ystwyth . . 47 B6
Ysceifiog 73 B5
Yspitty 33 E6
Ystalyfera 34 D1
Ystrad 34 E3
Ystrad Aeron 46 D4
Ystradfellte 34 C3
Ystradffîn 47 E6
Ystradgynlais 34 C1
Ystradmeurig 47 C6
Ystrad-mynach . . . 35 E5
Ystradowen Carms . 33 C8
V Glam 22 B2
Ystumtuen 47 B6
Ythanbank 153 E9
Ythanwells 153 E6
Ythsie 153 E8

Y Trallwng
= Welshpool . . . 60 D2
Y Waun = Chirk . . 73 F6

Z

Zeal Monachorum . 10 D2
Zeals 24 F2
Zelah 4 D3
Zennor 2 C3